PHILIP'S

Motoring Atlas

EUROPE

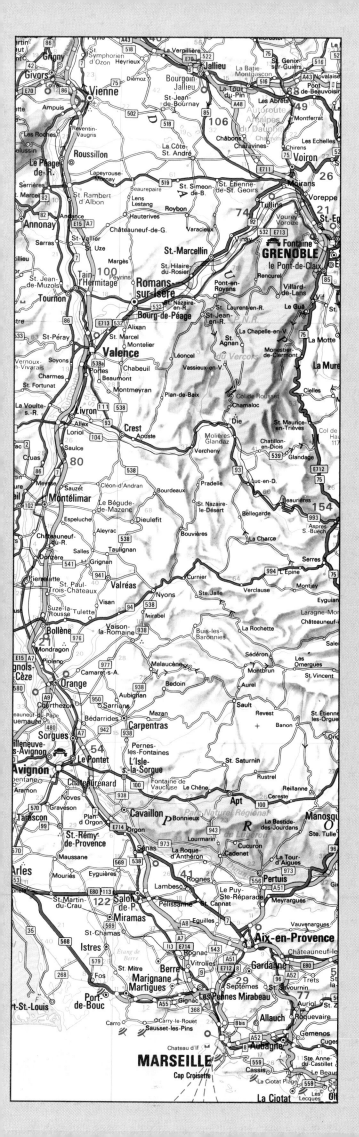

Motoring Atlas

EUROPE

Contents

Map symbols

Motorways	European road numbers
Principal trunk highways	Other road numbers
Other main highways	Distances: Major
Other important roads	Distances: Minor (in kilometres)
Other roads	Car ferries: River Sea Rail
Unsurfaced roads	
Motorways under construction	International airports
Roads under construction	Castles
Railways	Monasteries and cathedrals
Funiculars, Ski Lifts	Ancient monuments
Toll roads	Caves
Steep hills	Other points of interest
Passes	National Parks
International boundaries	Beaches
	Ski Resorts

Country index

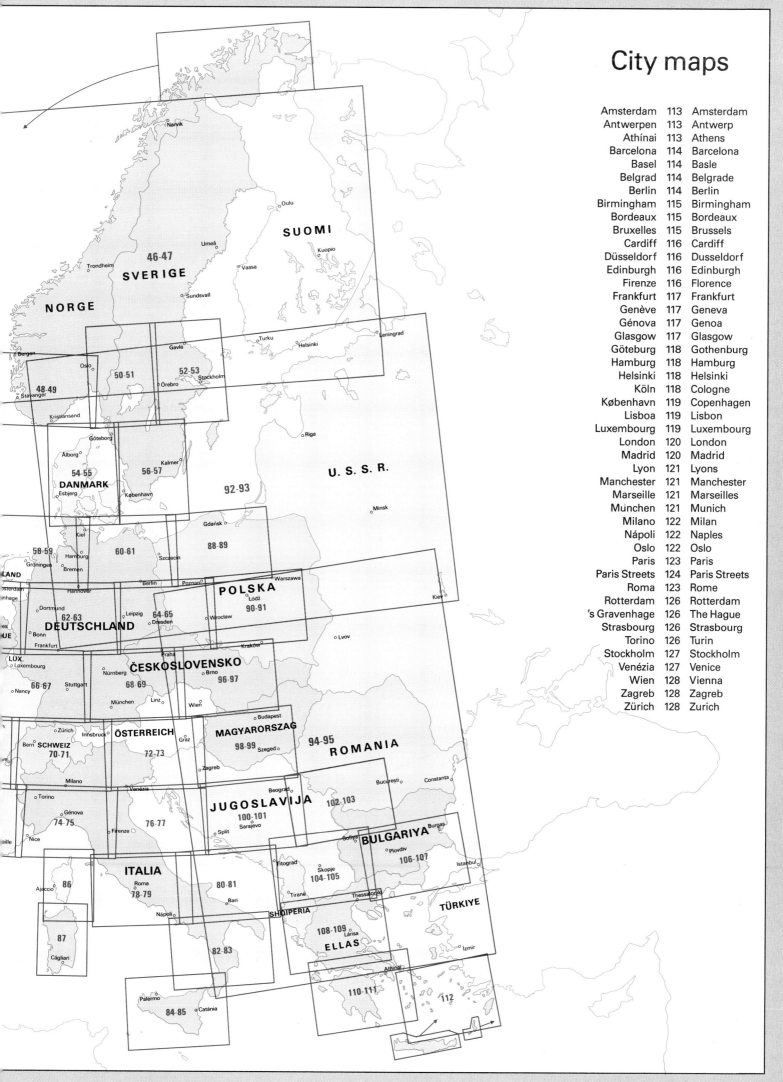

City maps

IV DISTANCE TABLE

* By ferry

Kilometres

	Amsterdam	Athínai	Barcelona	Basel	Beograd	Berlin	Bordeaux	Brindisi	Bruxelles	Bucuresti	Budapest	Calais	Cherbourg	Dover	Edinburgh	Frankfurt	Genève	Genova	Gibraltar	Hamburg	Helsinki	Istanbul	København
Amsterdam		1840	940	457	1130	406	686	1305	123	1403	887	229	465	229*	683*	275	565	769	1571	279	975*	1722	473
Athínai	2945		1995	1561	710	1507	2019	132*	1809	761	956	1937	2036	1937*	2391*	1561	1572	1431	2734	1699	1574*	714	1738*
Barcelona	1505	3192		649	1285	1164	375	1225	812	1641	1241	788	775	788*	1238*	815	468	559	734	1105	1451*	1856	1297*
Basel	732	2499	1039		855	538	574	848	334	1181	665	449	531	449*	903*	206	163	311	1387	509	829*	1447	715*
Beograd	1809	1136	2056	1369		797	1310	362*	1099	388	246	1227	1327	1227*	1681*	854	862	712	2015	989	871*	591	1028*
Berlin	650	2412	1863	861	1276		1018	1218	477	1066	551	587	819	587*	1060*	343	695	753	1903	178	295*	1389	231*
Bordeaux	1099	3231	601	919	2095	1630		1283	564	1698	1275	518	405	518*	966*	726	440	639	879	909	1307*	1889	1102*
Brindisi	2089	542*	1990	1357	580*	1950	2053		1176	1415	1008	1289	1365	1289*	1740*	1047	839	676	1958	1317	1353*	679*	1510*
Bruxelles	197	2895	1308	535	1759	764	902	1894		1354	843	133	339	133*	584*	237	441	643	1439	349	769*	1680	542*
Bucuresti	2245	1219	2644	1890	622	1707	2717	2280	2181		512	1489	1645	1489*	1940*	1120	1243	1103	2388	1250	1139*	428	1289*
Budapest	1420	1530	1999	1065	394	882	2041	1624	1358	852		976	1132	976*	1427*	608	832	693	1968	738	626*	832	777*
Calais	367	3100	1269	719	1964	956	830	2076	215	2398	1573		280	*	450*	357	491	736	1394	471	888*	1807	664*
Cherbourg	744	3259	1249	850	2122	1311	648	2199	547	2649	1824	452		142*	447*	577	529	774	1281	690	1380*	1905	881*
Dover	367*	3150*	1269*	719*	1964*	956*	830*	2076*	215*	2398*	1573*	*	228*		450	357*	491*	736*	1394*	471*	888*	1807*	664*
Edinburgh	1093*	3826*	1995*	1445*	2690*	1696*	1556*	2802*	941*	3124*	2299*	726*	720*	726		732	942*	1187*	1845*	922*	767*	2270*	1115*
Frankfurt	441	2499	1313	330	1367	550	1170	1687	383	1804	979	575	930	575*	1301*		372	514	1550	301	992*	1436	493*
Genève	905	2516	754	262	1380	1123	709	1352	710	2002	1340	791	852	791*	1517*	599		245	1202	642	1333*	1437	834*
Genova	1231	2291	901	499	1140	1206	1030	1089	1036	1777	1116	1186	1247	1186*	1912*	829	395		1294	785	1476*	1301	977*
Gibraltar	2515	4375	1183	2220	3224	3046	1416	3153	2318	3846	3170	2246	2064	2246*	2972*	2496	1937	2084		1788	2480*	2590	1981*
Hamburg	447	2719	1780	815	1583	286	1465	2122	563	2014	1189	760	1120	760*	1486	485	1034	1264	2880		691*	1571	192*
Helsinki	1560*	2539*	2338*	1336*	1403*	475*	2105*	2180*	1239*	1834*	1009*	1431*	2223*	1431*	1236*	1598*	2147*	2377*	3994*	1113*		1459*	498*
Istanbul	2756	1145	2990	2316	947	2223	3042	1094*	2706	690	1341	2911	3069	2911*	3657*	2314	2315	2095	4171	2530	2350*		1610*
København	757*	2782*	2090*	1145*	1646*	370*	1775*	2432*	873*	2077*	1252*	1070*	1420*	1070*	479*	795*	1344*	1574*	3191*	310*	803*	2593*	
Köln	256	2684	1376	512	1553	566	1070	1872	198	1983	1158	390	745*	390*	1116*	180	696	1014	2493	404	1517*	2499	714*
Lisboa	2331	4460	1268	2158	3295	2869	1239	3213	3141	3917	3222	2069	1887	2069*	2795*	2400	2022	2169	659	2700	3817*	4342	3014*
London	480*	3200*	1387*	837*	2064*	1074*	948*	2194*	333*	2591*	1766*	118*	112*	118	608	693*	909*	1304*	2364*	878*	1991*	3107*	1188*
Luxembourg	406	2661	1190	326	1525	749	930	1683	209	2052	1227	424	693	424*	1150*	240	510	825	2349	590	1703*	2472	900*
Madrid	1790	3809	617	1617	2640	2364	698	2601	1600	3262	2622	1528	1346	1528*	2254*	1930	1371	1518	718	2160	3276*	3589	2473*
Marseille	1210	2683	509	680	1532	1541	652	1481	1030	2154	1505	1063	1124	1063*	1789*	1023	423	392	1692	1412	2525*	2479	1722*
Milano	1085	2182	1038	353	1046	1060	1049	1004	890	1668	992	1072	1195	1072*	1798*	683	348	146	2230	1118	1535*	1993	1428*
München	839	2106	1340	393	970	594	1295	1370	789	1497	672	994	1152	994*	1720*	398	586	589	2523	765	1069*	1907	969*
Napoli	1908	930*	1602	1176	1503*	1719	1720	388	1715	2125*	1470	1887	1948	1887*	2613*	1506	1096	701	2785	1941	2194*	2451*	2200*
Narvik	2827*	4852*	4160*	3215*	3716*	2440*	3845*	4502*	2943*	4147*	3322*	3140*	3550*	3140*	2178*	2866*	3414*	3644*	5261*	2360*	1289	4569*	2070*
Nürnberg	670	2270	1471	432	1134	429	1324	1525	616	1565	740	810	1123	810*	1412*	233	694	735	2631	600	904*	2081	799*
Oslo	1347*	3372*	2680*	1735*	2236*	960*	2365*	3022*	1463*	2667*	1842*	1660*	2070*	1660*	729*	1385*	1934*	2164*	3781*	900*	697*	3089*	590*
Paris	510	2917	988	504	1780	1051	582	1850	320	2307	1482	281	342	281*	1007*	591	510	905	1998	899	2012*	2727	1209*
Porto	2120	4384	1192	1947	3052	2661	1028	3027	1927	3674	3034	1858	1676	1858*	2584*	2201	1737	1938	979	2490	3603*	3990	2800*
Praha	950	2067	1750	712	931	345	1604	1708	888	1362	537	1097	1403	1090*	1816*	512	974	977	2911	652	770*	1878	715*
Roma	1691	1140*	1385	959	1290*	1502	1513	590	1520	1904	1263	1678	1731	1678*	2404*	1289	879	484	2564	1683	1977*	2237*	1993*
Sevilla	2347	4223	1031	2060	3087	2894	1248	2995	2150	3709	3010	2078	1896	2078*	2804*	2344	1785	1932	258	2713	3826*	4034	3023*
Sofiya	2206	828	2453	1766	397	1673	2492	2047	2156	391	790	2361	2519	2361*	3087*	1764	1775	1537	3621	1980	1800*	550	2043*
Stockholm	1393*	3418*	2726*	1780*	2282*	1006*	2411*	2960*	1509*	2713*	1888*	1673*	2056*	1706*	1069*	1431*	1980*	2210*	3827*	946*	167*	3185*	498*
Strasbourg	631	2461	1130	134	1325	768	998	1523	434	1858	1027	639	798	639*	1365*	219	394	665	2313	704	1817*	2276	1014*
Thessaloniki	2410	509	2683	1996	677	1903	2722	458*	2386	710	1021	2591	2749	2591*	3317*	1994	2007	1782	3851	2210	2030*	636	2273*
Valencia	1851	3545	353	1392	2390	2216	824	2313	1661	3012	2360	1654	1472	1645*	2380*	1666	1107	1254	830	2133	2691*	3337	2443*
Venezia	1324	1914	1258	621	778	1079	1316	890	1158	1400	739	1340	1468	1340*	2066*	883	616	377	2460	1250	1253*	1725	1449*
Warszawa	1256	2128	2366	1328	1042	606	2220	2140	1350	1473	648	1542	1969	1542*	2268*	1136	1590	1593	3527	886	361*	1989	956*
Wien	1168	1772	1856	823	633	640	1733	1472	1114	1067	242	1308	1582	1308*	2034*	731	1016	965	3042	947	1088*	1583	1010*

Distances in these tables are based upon Main Routes as far as possible
and are not necessarily the shortest distances between any two towns.

Miles

London	Luxembourg	Madrid	Marseille	Milano	München	Napoli	Narvik	Nürnberg	Oslo	Paris	Porto	Praha	Roma	Sevilla	Sofiya	Stockholm	Strasbourg	Thessaloniki	Valencia	Venezia	Warszawa	Wien	
298*	252	1111	751	673	521	1184	1755*	416	836	316	1316	590	1050	1457	1370	865*	391	1496	1149	822	780	725	Amsterdam
1987*	1652	2365	1666	1355	1307	577	3013*	1409	2094*	1811	2722	1283	707*	2622	514	2122*	1528	316	2201	1188	1352	1100	Athínai
861*	739	383	316	644	832	994	2583*	913	1664*	613	740	1086	860	640	1523	1692*	701	1666	219	781	1469	1152	Barcelona
519*	202	1004	422	219	244	730	1996*	268	1077*	313	1209	442	595	1279	1096	1105*	83	1239	864	385	824	511	Basel
1281*	947	1639	951	649	602	939*	2307*	704	1388*	1105	1895	578	628*	1917	246	1417*	822	389	1484	483	647	395	Beograd
667*	465	1468	957	658	369	1067	1515*	267	596*	653	1652	214	932	1797	1038	624*	477	1181	1376	670	376	397	Berlin
588*	577	434	405	651	804	1075	2387*	822	1468*	361	638	996	939	775	1547	1497*	620	1690	511	817	1378	1076	Bordeaux
1362*	1045	1615	919	623	850	240	2795*	970	1876*	1148	1879	1058	366	1859	1271	1838*	945	284*	1436	552	1328	914	Brindisi
206*	129	993	639	552	490	1086	1827*	382	908*	198	1195	551	943	1335	1339	937*	269	1481	1031	719	838	691	Bruxelles
1609*	1274	2025	1337	1035	929	1319	2575*	971	1656*	1432	2281	845	1182	2303	243	1684*	1150	440	1870	869	914	662	Bucuresti
1096*	763	1628	934	616	417	912	2062*	459	1143*	920	1884	333	784	1869	490	1172*	637	634	1465	459	402	150	Budapest
73*	263	948	660	665	617	1171	1949*	503	1030*	174	1153	676	1042	1290	1466	1059*	396	1609	1027	832	957	812	Calais
69*	430	835	698	742	715	1209	2204*	697	1285*	212	1040	871	1080	1177	1564	1276*	495	1707	914	911	1222	988	Cherbourg
73	263*	948*	660*	665*	617*	1171*	1949*	503*	1030*	174*	1153*	676*	1042*	1290*	1466	1059*	396*	1609*	1027*	832*	957*	812*	Dover
377	714*	1399*	1110*	1116*	1068*	1622*	1134*	876*	452*	625*	1604*	1127*	1492*	1741*	1917*	663*	847*	2059*	1478*	1282*	1408*	1271*	Edinburgh
430*	149	1198	635	424	247	935	1779*	144	860*	367	1366	317	800	1455	1095	888*	136	1238	1034	548	705	454	Frankfurt
564*	316	851	263	216	364	680	2120*	431	1201*	316	1078	605	542	1108	1102	1229*	244	1246	687	382	987	631	Genève
809*	512	942	243	91	366	435	2262*	456	1343*	562	1203	606	300	1199	954	1372*	413	1106	778	234	989	599	Genova
1468*	1458	445	1050	1384	1566	1729	3257*	1633	2348*	1240	607	1807	1604	160	2248	2376*	1438	2391	515	1517	2190	1889	Gibraltar
545*	366	1341	876	694	475	1205	1477*	372	558*	558	1546	404	1045	1684	1229	587*	437	1372	1324	776	550	588	Hamburg
1236*	1037*	2034*	1570*	953*	663*	1362*	800	561*	432*	1249*	2237*	478*	1277*	2375*	1117*	103*	1128*	1260*	1682*	778*	224*	675*	Helsinki
1929*	1535	2228	1539	1237	1190	1522	2837*	1292	1918*	1693	2477	1166	1389*	2505	341	1975*	1413	395	2072	1071	1235	983	Istanbul
737*	558*	1535*	1069*	886*	601*	1366*	1285*	496*	366*	750*	1738*	444*	1237*	1877*	1268*	366*	629*	1411*	1517*	899*	598*	627*	København
315*	115	1116	624	539	360	1050	1728*	257	809*	307	1307	428	915	1439	1210	838*	234	1353	1068	661	715	568	Köln
1358*	1341	404	1103	1437	1580	1782	3157*	1608	2238*	1130	199	1782	1647	249	2301	2266*	1389	2431	622	1551	2161	1935	Lisboa
	336*	1022*	734*	739*	679*	1250*	2023*	575*	1104*	247*	1227*	748*	1115*	1363*	1528	1132*	470*	1671*	1104*	905*	1043*	946*	London
542*		1010	510	421	344	925	1844*	294	925*	218	1215	467	798	1352	1193	953*	139	1336	958	588	835	616	Luxembourg
1646*	1628		699	1028	1248	1378	2821*	1272	1902*	794	357	1446	1243	341	1885	1930*	1084	2028	218	1176	1838	1535	Madrid
1182*	822	1126		334	627	678	2354*	690	1435*	485	968	868	544	956	1197	1464*	499	1328	535	477	1251	840	Marseille
1190*	679	1655	538		293	511	2172*	391	1253*	532	1294	529	376	1290	896	1281*	322	1038	869	166	912	507	Milano
1094*	555	2010	1011	473		698	1877*	103	968*	503	1452	241	570	1472	848	993*	220	991	1051	301	618	267	München
2013*	1490	2219	1093	823	1125		2652*	807	1732*	997	1638	934	135	1653	1179	1761*	820	530	1214	460	1317	822	Napoli
3258*	2970*	4543*	3792*	3498*	3039*	4270*		1850*	919	2036*	3024*	1729*	2523*	2553*	2553*	916	1915*	2697*	2802*	2185*	1879*	1853*	Narvik
926*	473	2049	1112	630	165	1300	2980*		931	485	1460	174	673	1552	950	878*	202	1093	1132	403	556	309	Nürnberg
1778*	1490	3063*	2312*	2018*	1559*	2790*	1480	1500*		1117*	2105*	810*	1604*	2243*	1634*	329*	996*	1777*	1883*	1351*	980*	1000*	Oslo
399*	351	1280	782	857	810	1606	3279*	781	1799*		999	658	862	1136	1351	1145*	283	1494	832	695	1041	770	Paris
1976*	1958	575	1560	2084	2340	2639	4870*	2352	3390*	1610		1634	1504	447	2141	2133*	1259	2284	575	1425	2017	1720	Porto
1205*	753	2329	1399	853	388	1505	2785*	280	1305*	1061	2632		812	1727	824	838*	376	967	1306	506	382	183	Praha
1796*	1285	2002	876	606	918	217	4063	1083	2583*	1389	2422	1309		1518	1047	1632*	678	1190	1079	325	1150	699	Roma
2196*	2178	550	1540	2078	2371	2663	5093*	2500*	3613*	1830	721	2781	2446		2163	2272*	1340	2306	421	1421	2109	1785	Sevilla
2461*	1922	3037	1929	1443	1367	1900	4112*	1531	2632*	2177	3449	1328	1687	3484		1663*	1069	198	1717	711	893	641	Sofiya
1824*	1536*	3109*	2358*	2064*	1600*	2836*	1476	1415*	530	1845*	3436*	1351*	2629*	3659*	2679		1024*	1806*	1912*	1294*	1001*	1028*	Stockholm
757*	225	1747	805	519	355	1322	3084*	326	1604*	455	2026	606	1093	2158	1722	1650*		1246	912	487	758	487	Strasbourg
2691*	2152	3267	2139	1673	1597	840*	4343*	1761	2863	2407	3679	1558	1917	3714	319	2909*	1952		1873	872	1012	784	Thessaloniki
1772*	1543	351	862	1400	1693	1955	4513*	1824	3033*	1341	926	2104	1738	678	2765	3079*	1470	3017		1012	1689	1374	Valencia
1458*	947	1895	769	268	485	741	3519*	650	2039*	1120	2295	815	524	2289	1146	2085*	785	1405	1631		776	373	Venezia
1680*	1345	2960	2015	1469	996	2121	3026*	896	1506*	1677	3248	616	1853	3397	1439	1612	1222	1669	2720	1250		451	Warszawa
1524*	993	2473	1353	818	430	1325	2985*	498	1600*	1240	2770	295	1126	2876	1033	1646*	785	1263	2213	602	727		Wien

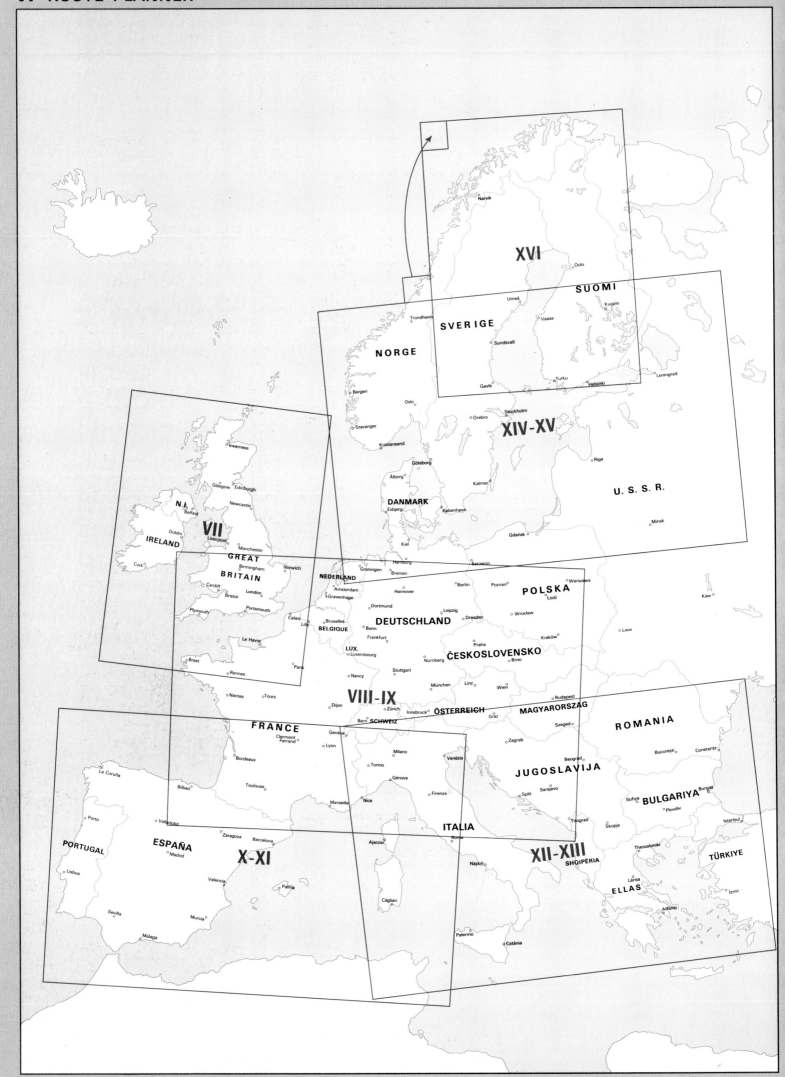

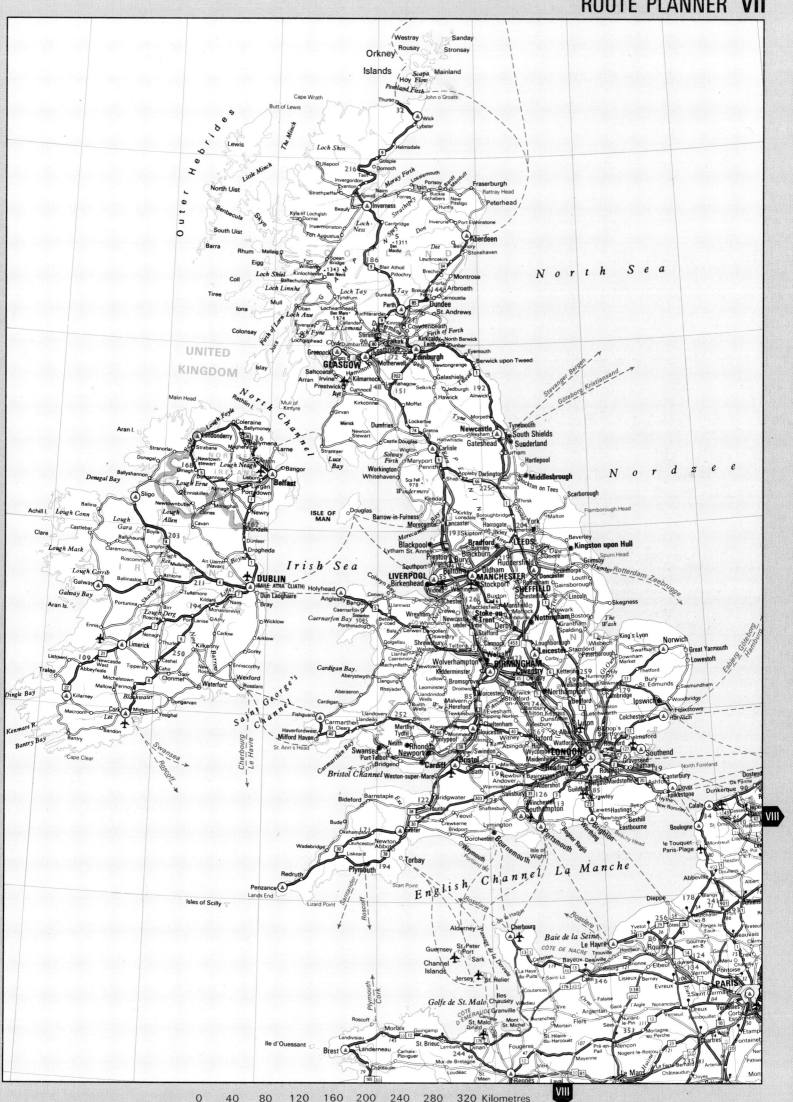

0   40   80   120   160   200   240   280   320 Kilometres

English Channel La Manche

Golfe de St. Malo

Baie de la Seine

Golfo de Vizcaya

Golfe du Lion

0 20 40 60 80 100 120 140 160 180 200 Miles

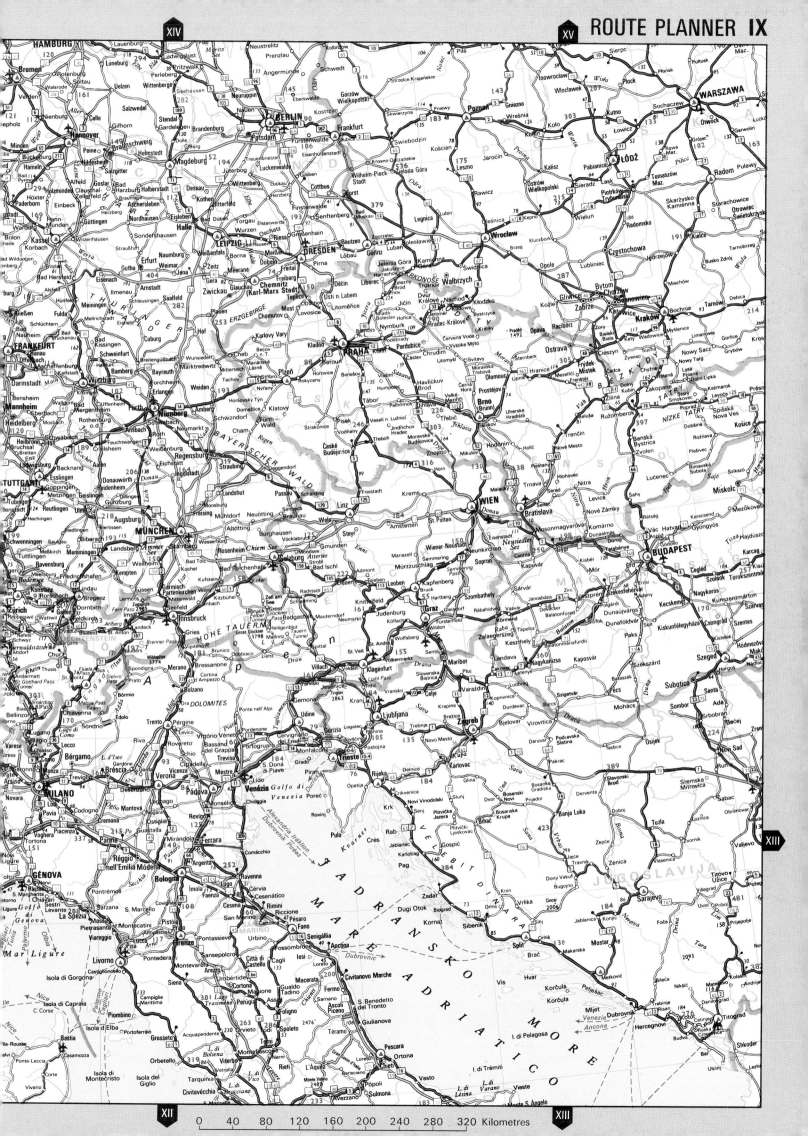

0 20 40 60 80 100 120 140 160 180 200 Miles

0 20 40 60 80 100 120 140 160 180 200 Miles

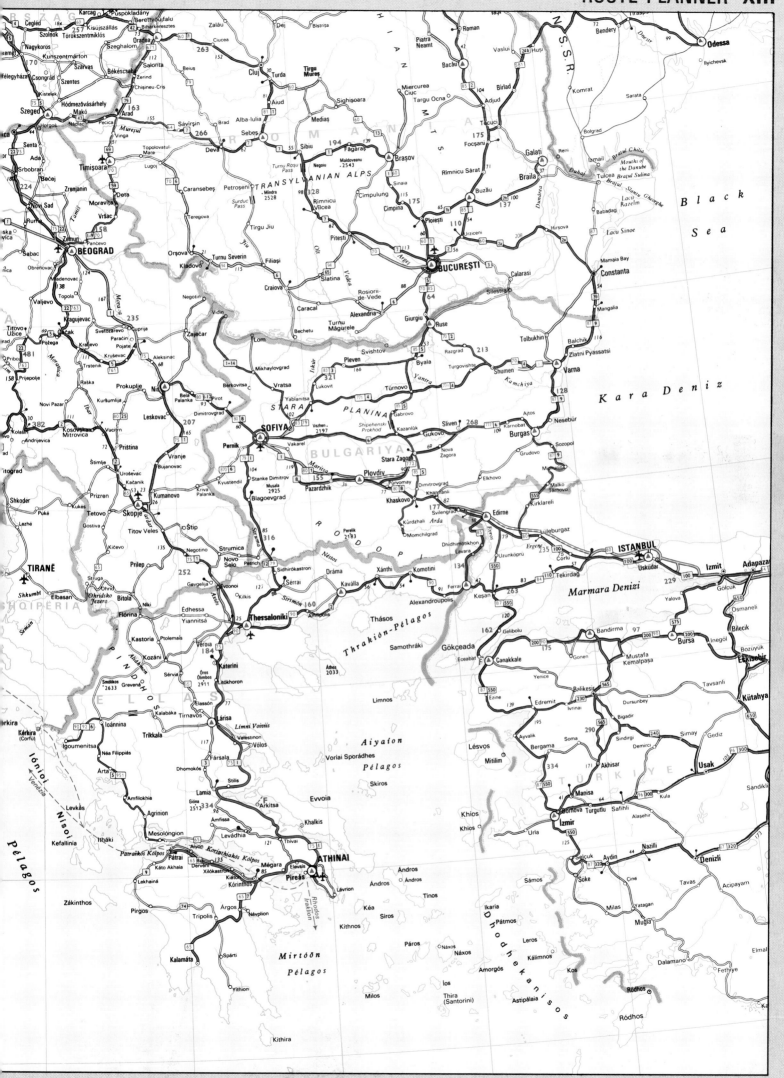

0   40   80   120   160   200   240   280   320 Kilometres

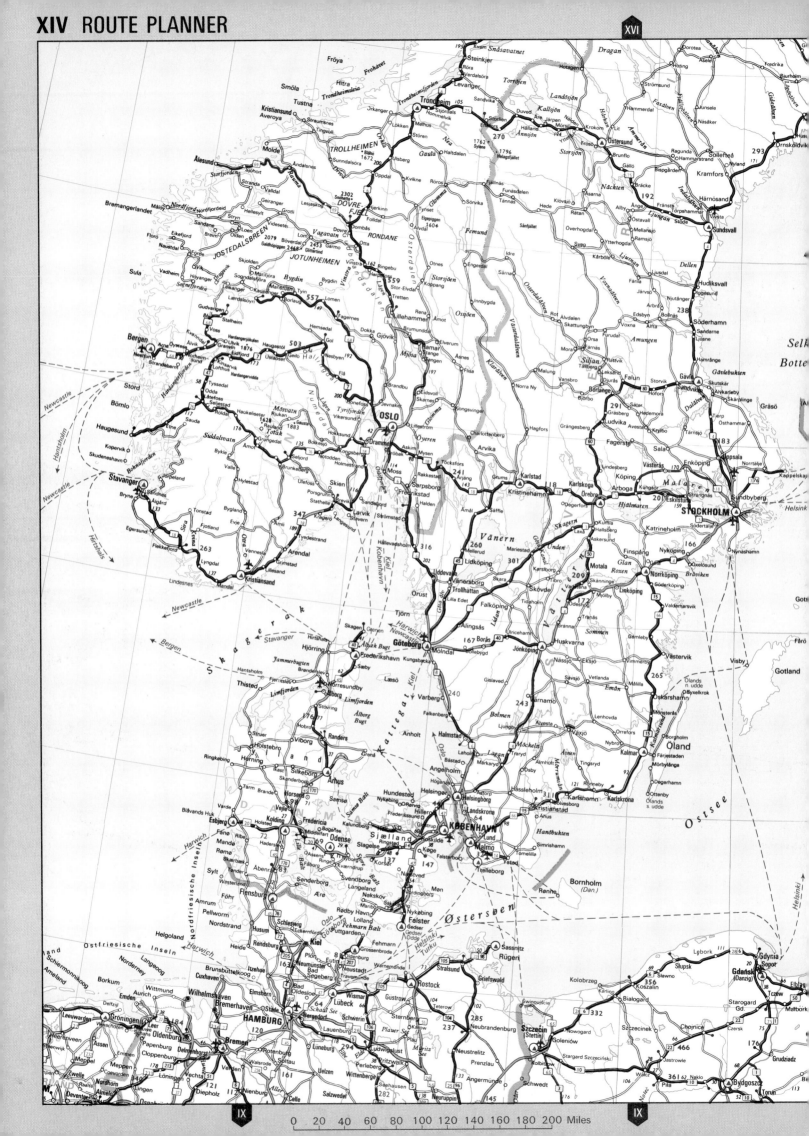

0 20 40 60 80 100 120 140 160 180 200 Miles

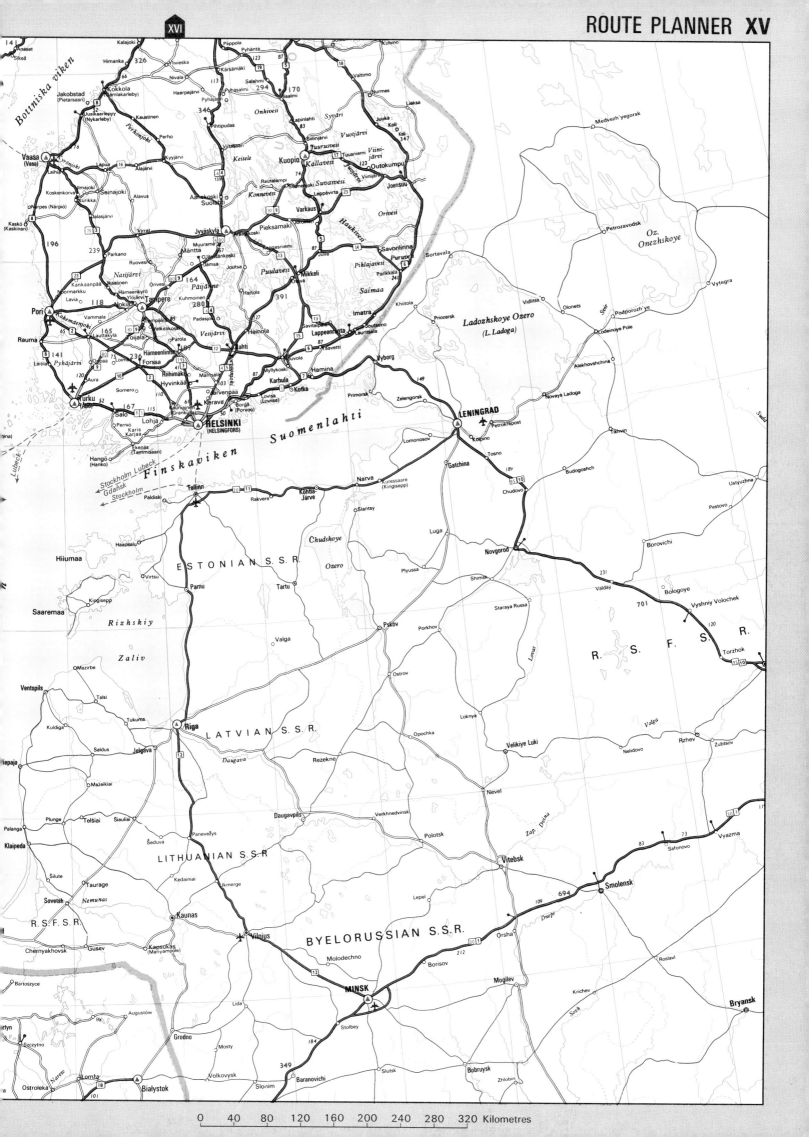

141 Anäset
Sikeå
Bottniska viken
Jakobstad (Pietarsaari)
Kokkola (Gamlakarleby)
Kalajoki
Himanka 326
Ylivieska
Nivala
Haapajärvi
Pyhäjärvi
Pihtipudas
Kärsämäki
Salahmi
Pyhäntä
Pöppölä
Valtimo
Kuhmo
Nurmes
Lieksa
Koli
Kali 347
Juuka
Outokumpu
Medvezh'yegorsk

Vaasa (Vasa)
Laihia
Koskenkorva
Ilmajoki
Kurikka
Närpes (Närpiö)
Kaskö (Kaskinen)
Seinäjoki
Alavus
Alajärvi
Kyyjärvi
Keitele
Suolahti
Äänekoski
Rautalampi
Konnevesi
Kuopio
Kallavesi
Siilinjärvi
Lapinlahti
Iisalmi
Juurusvesi
Vuotjärvi
Tuusniemi
Viinijärvi
Joensuu
Petrozavodsk
Oz. Onezhskoye

196
239
Parkano
Ruovesi
Nasijärvi
Ikaalinen
Kankaanpää
Noormarkku
Lavia
Pori
Nokia
Tampere
Hämeenkyrö
Ylöjärvi
Orivesi
Mänttä
Jämsänkoski
Jämsä
Padasjoki
Päijänne
Puulavesi
Mikkeli
Otava
Savonlinna
Pihlajavesi
Puruvesi
Parikkala
Sortavala
Vidlitsa
Vytegra
Jyväskylä
Muurame
Äänekoski
Pieksämäki
Varkaus
Orivesi
Haukivesi
Juva
Saimaa
Khiitola
Ladozhskoye Ozero (L. Ladoga)
Priozersk
Olonets
Podporozh'ye
Lodeynoye Pole

Rauma
Laitila
Pyhäjärvi
Uusikaupunki
Aura
Turku (Åbo)
Salo
Lohja
Somero
Forssa
Hämeenlinna
Riihimäki
Hyvinkää
Järvenpää
Kerava
Heinola
Lahti
Kuhmoinen
Vesijärvi
Heinola
Kouvola
Myllykoski
Karhula
Kotka
Hamina
Imatra
Lappeenranta
Lauritsala
Joutseno
Vyborg
Primorsk
Zelengorsk
Novaya Ladoga
Alekhovshchina
Tikhvin

Pernio
Karis
Karjaa
Ekenäs (Tammisaari)
Salo
Raisio
Naantali
Borgå (Porvoo)
Lovisa (Loviise)
HELSINKI (HELSINGFORS)
Suomenlahti
Kotka
Leningrad
Petrokrepost
Lomonosov
Kolpino
Tosno
Gatchina
Budogoshch
Ustyuzhna

Hangö (Hanko)
Stockholm Lubeck Gdansk
Stockholm
Paldiski
Tallinn
Rakvere
Kohtla-Järve
Narva
Kuressaare (Kingisepp)
Slantsy
Chudovo
Pestovo
Finskaviken
Lubeck

Haapsalu
Hiiumaa
Virtsu
Pärnu
Tartu
Chudskoye Ozero
Plyussa
Luga
Shimsk
Novgorod
Borovichi
Bologoye
Valday
Vyshniy Volochek

ESTONIAN S.S.R.
Kingisepp
Saaremaa
Rizhskiy
Zaliv
Valga
Valga
Pskov
Porkhov
Staraya Russa
701
120
Torzhok
R. S. F. S. R.

Ventspils
Mazirbe
Talsi
Kuldiga
Tukums
Riga
LATVIAN S.S.R.
Saldus
Jelgava
Daugava
Rezekne
Ostrov
Opochka
Loknya
Velikiye Luki
Nelidovo
Rzhev
Zubtsov
Volga
Zap. Dvina

iepaja
Plunge
Telsiai
Siauliai
Seduta
Panevezys
Daugavpils
Verkhnedvinsk
Nevel
Nelidovo

Palanga
Klaipeda
Silute
Taurage
Kedainiai
Ukmerge
LITHUANIAN S.S.R.
Polotsk
Vitebsk
Vyazma
Safonovo

Sovetsk
Nemunas
R.S.F.S.R.
Kaunas
Vilnius
BYELORUSSIAN S.S.R.
Lepel
Orsha
Smolensk
694
109
83
73

Chernyakhovsk
Gusev
Kapsukas (Mariyampole)
Molodechno
Borisov
Mogilev
Krichev
Roslavl

Bartoszyce
Augustów
Lida
MINSK
Stolbey
184
Bryansk

Szczytno
Narew
Lomza
Bialystok
Grodno
Mosty
349
Volkovysk
Baranovichi
Slonim
Slutsk
Bobruysk
Zhlobin
Ostroleka

0   40   80   120   160   200   240   280   320   Kilometres

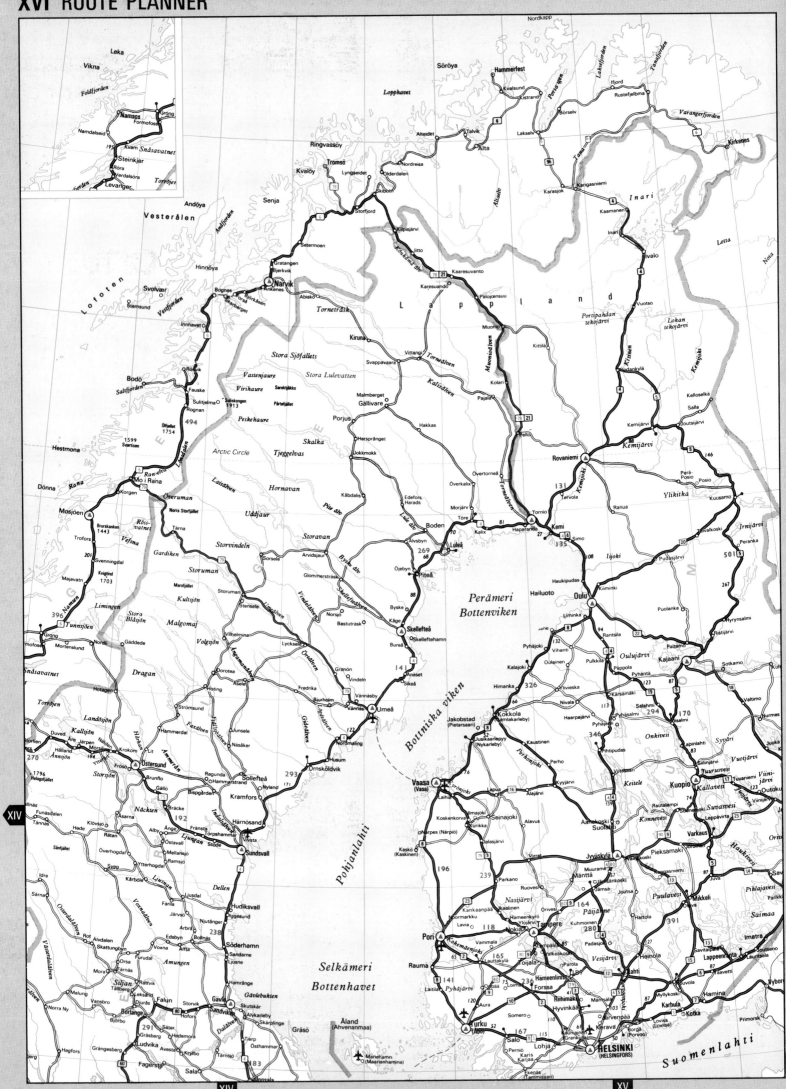

0 20 40 60 80 100 120 140 160 180 200 Miles

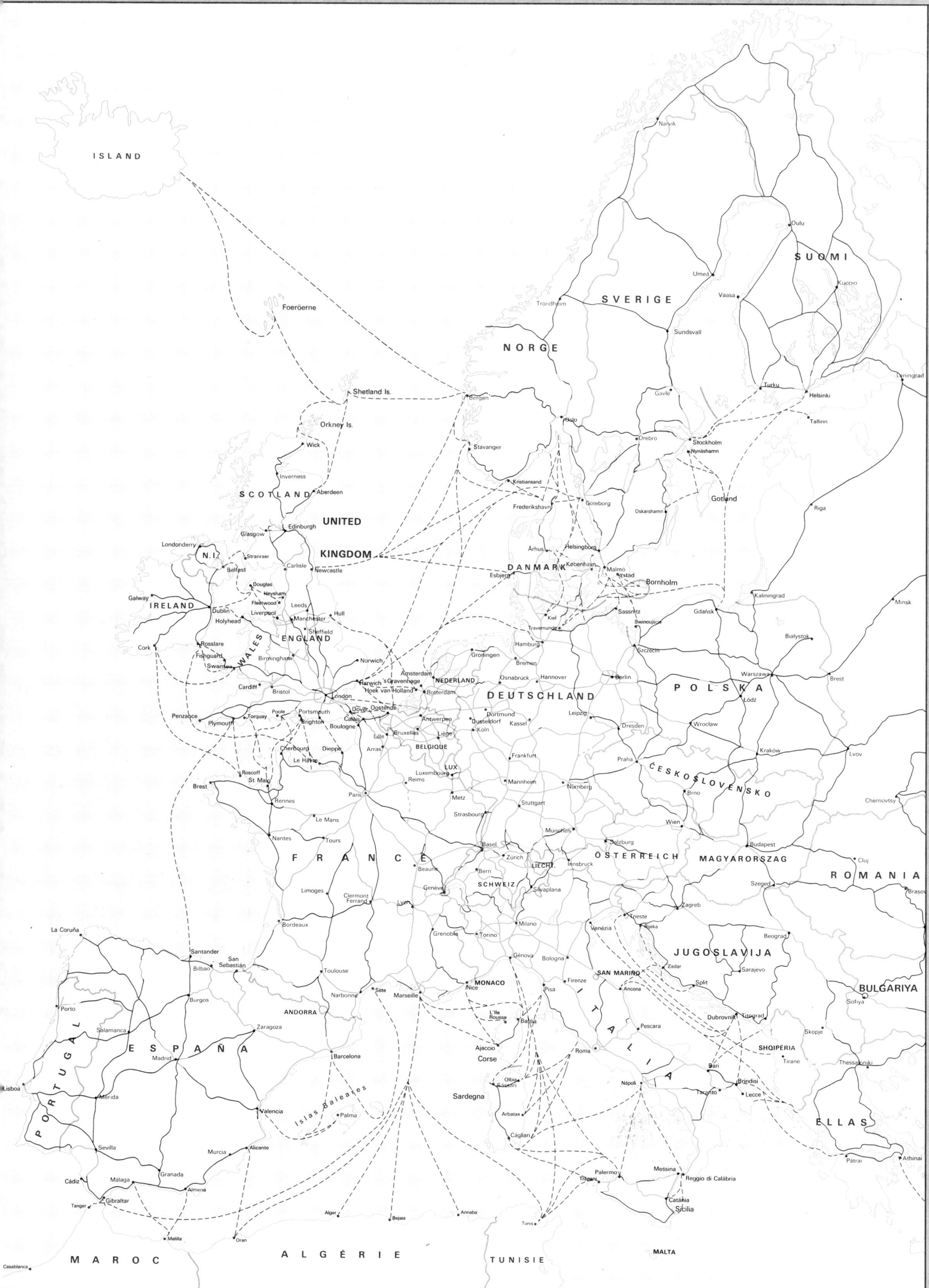

ISLAND

Foeröerne

Shetland Is.

Orkney Is.

Wick

Inverness

SCOTLAND

Aberdeen

UNITED

Edinburgh

Glasgow

Londonderry

N.I.

KINGDOM

Stranraer

Belfast

Carlisle

Newcastle

Galway

Douglas

Heysham

IRELAND

Fleetwood

Leeds

Hull

Dublin

Liverpool

Manchester

Holyhead

Sheffield

Rosslare

ENGLAND

Fishguard

WALES

Birmingham

Swansea

Cork

Norwich

Cardiff

Bristol

's Gravenhage

Amsterdam

Harwich

London

Hoek van Holland

Rotterdam

NEDERLAND

Penzance

Torquay

Poole

Portsmouth

Dover

Oostende

Antwerpen

Dortmund

DEUTSCHLAND

Plymouth

Brighton

Calais

Boulogne

Bruxelles

Liège

Düsseldorf

Köln

Kassel

Cherbourg

Dieppe

Lille

Arras

BELGIQUE

Roscoff

Le Havre

LUX

Luxembourg

Frankfurt

St. Malo

Paris

Reims

Mannheim

Brest

Rennes

Metz

Nürnberg

Le Mans

Strasbourg

Stuttgart

Nantes

Tours

FRANCE

München

Salzburg

Limoges

Clermont

Ferrand

Lyon

Basel

Zürich

LIECHT.

Innsbruck

ÖSTERREICH

Beaune

Bern

SCHWEIZ

Silvaplana

Bordeaux

Genève

Grenoble

Torino

Milano

Venézia

Trieste

Rijeka

La Coruña

Santander

Bilbao

San Sebastián

Toulouse

Narbonne

Génova

Bologna

SAN MARINO

Santiago

Porto

Burgos

Zaragoza

ANDORRA

Sète

Marseille

MONACO

Nice

Pisa

Firenze

Ancona

Salamanca

ESPAÑA

Madrid

Barcelona

L'Ile

Rousse

Bastia

Roma

Pescara

Lisboa

PORTUGAL

Mérida

Valencia

Islas Baleares

Palma

Ajaccio

Corse

Olbia

Sassari

Nápoli

Bari

Sevilla

Murcia

Alicante

Sardegna

Arbatax

Cágliari

Málaga

Granada

Almería

Palermo

Messina

Reggio di Calábria

Cádiz

Gibraltar

Tanger

Trapani

Catánia

Sicília

Melilla

Oran

MAROC

ALGÉRIE

Alger

Bejaia

Annaba

TUNISIE

Tunis

MALTA

Casablanca

NORGE

SVERIGE

SUOMI

Narvik

Oulu

Umeå

Vaasa

Kuopio

Trondheim

Sundsvall

Bergen

Gävle

Turku

Helsinki

Leningrad

Stavanger

Örebro

Stockholm

Tallinn

Kristiansand

Oslo

Nynäshamn

Frederikshavn

Göteborg

Oskarshamn

Gotland

Riga

Århus

Helsingborg

DANMARK

København

Malmö

Minsk

Esbjerg

Ystad

Bornholm

Kaliningrad

Kiel

Sassnitz

Gdańsk

Travemünde

Swinoujscie

Białystok

Hamburg

Szczecin

Groningen

Bremen

POLSKA

Warszawa

Osnabrück

Hannover

Berlin

Brest

Leipzig

Łódź

Wrocław

Dresden

Praha

ČESKOSLOVENSKO

Kraków

Lvov

Brno

Chernovtsy

Wien

MAGYARORSZAG

Budapest

Cluj

ROMANIA

Zagreb

Szeged

Brasov

JUGOSLAVIJA

Beograd

Zadar

Sarajevo

BULGARIYA

Split

Sofiya

ITALIA

Dubrovnik

Titograd

Skopje

SHQIPÉRIA

Tirane

Thessaloniki

Brindisi

Lecce

Taranto

ELLAS

Pátrai

Athinai

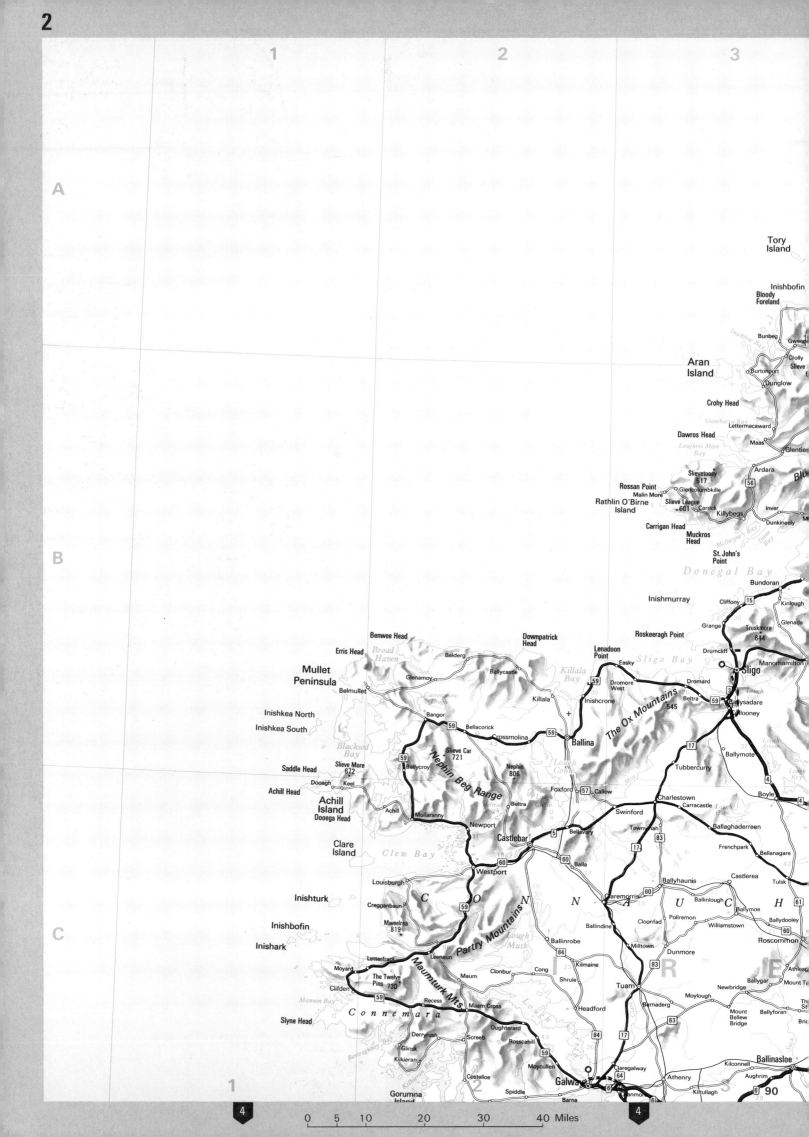

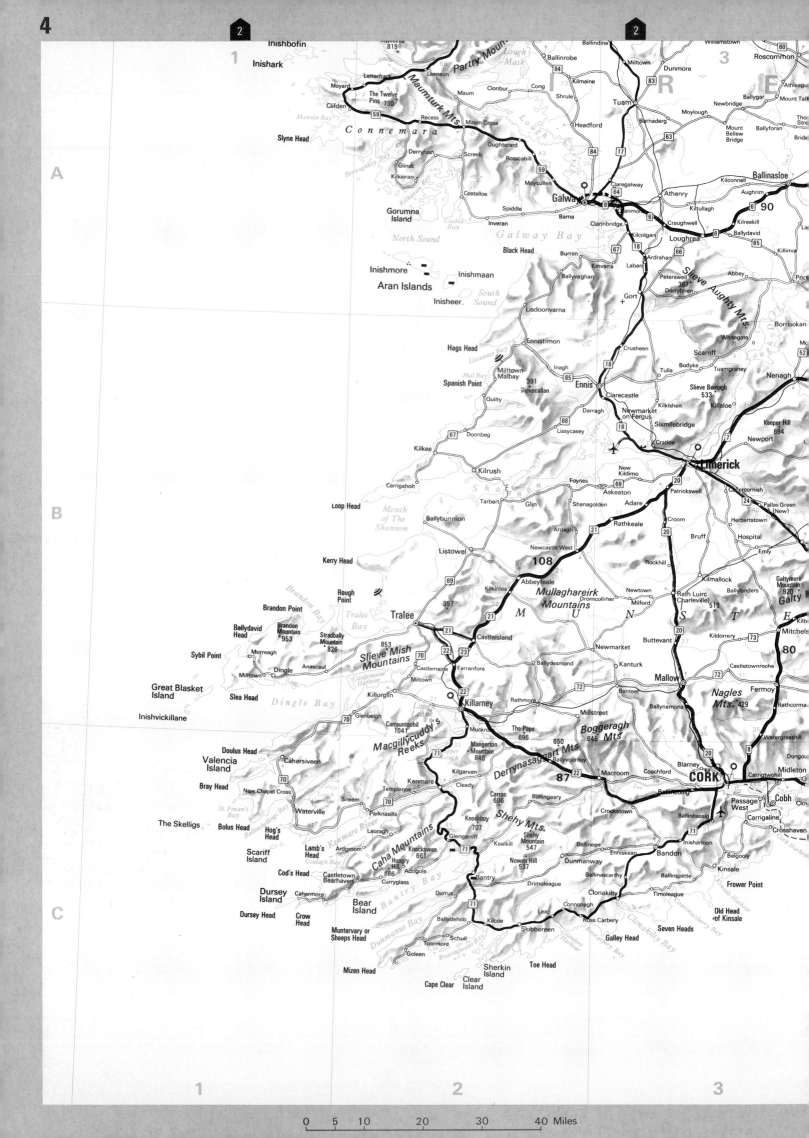

7

Fair Isle

North Ronaldsay
Mull Head
Hollandstoun
Papa Westray
Noup Head Pierowall
Burness
Northwaa
Westray Langskaill Start Point
Rapness Overbister
Sacquoy Head Millbounds Sanday
Wasbister Backaland
Brough Head Rousay Eday Braeswick
Brinyan Egilsay Whitehall
Wyre Aith
Gairsay Stronsay
ORKNEY
Twatt Redland Balfour Shapinsay Auskerry
986 Dounby Sandgarth
Lerwick ISLANDS
Mainland 966
Voy 965 Finstown Mull Head
Stromness Kirkwall
Graemsay Hobbister 964 961 960
Orphir St. Mary's Gritley
Orgill Rose Ness
Rora Head Ward Hill
477 Fara St. Margaret's Hope
Hoy Little South
Ayre Flotta Ronaldsay
Melsetter Wateringhouse
Aberdeen South Burwick
Walls Brough Ness
Swona Stroma
Dunnet Head Pentland
John o' Groats Skerries
House Hotel
Holborn Duncansby Head
Head Scrabster 836 Mey John o' Groats
Whiten Bridge of Forss Dunnet Freswick
Head Strathy Point 882 Castletown Nybster
Portskerra Buldoo Sordale Keiss
Melvich Reay Hastigrow Reiss Noss Head
Bettyhill Craigtown Halkirk Olgrinmore Watten
Tongue Dalhalvaig 882 Wick
Ben Hope Forsinain Mybster
927 Skail Hotel 895 Thrumster
Loch Loyal Forsinard 27
Lodge Syre Station Achavanich Ulbster
Altnaharra Badanloch Latheron Lybster
Ben Klibreck Kinbrace Dunbeath
961 Morven Borgue
Crask Inn 705 Kildonan Berriedale
Overscaig Torrish Ousdale
Hotel Shinness Helmsdale
Dalmichy Lothmore Portgower
Lairg Brora
Torroboll Golspie
Inveran
Bonar Bridge Clashmore Dornoch
Easter Fearn Tarbat Ness
836 Tain Portmahomack
Kilmuir Fearn
Balintore
Ben Wyvis Alness Kinnairds Troup Rosehearty Fraserburgh
1045 Invergordon Head Head Inverallochy
Cromarty Burghead Lossiemouth Findochty Portknockie St. Combs
Dingwall Hopeman Cullen Banff Macduff New Aberdour Rathen
Rosemarkie Garmouth 98 Portsoy New Byth Rattray Head
Fortrose Findhorn Elgin Buckie Plaidy Strichen Crimond
Contin 835 Campbelltown Nairn Forres Fochabers 95 981 92 St. Fergus
Muir of Ord 832 (Ardersier) Auldearn 941 Aberchirder New Cuminestown 952 Peterhead
832 Cawdor Kellas Keith Turriff Pitsligo New Deer Mintlaw Boddam
Inverness Dalcross Littlemill Rothes 95 Bogniebrae Fortrie Maud Old Deer Longside Buchan Ness
862 939 Archiestown Craigellachie 96 Kirktown of Methlick 948 Clola Port Erroll
Daviot 940 Ferness Dufftown 920 Auchterless Fyvie Birness 952
Moy Charlestown Huntly Ellon Newburgh
of Aberdour Culdrain Colpy Oldmeldrum
Tomatin Grantown-on-Spey 95 Laggan Ardwell Insch Pitcaple Stromness
Farr Dulnain Bridge Lettoch Rhynie Tarves Lerwick
Dores Tomnavoulin Cabrach 941 Mossat Inverurie Balmedie
Carrbridge Boat of Garten Càrn Mòr Bridge of Newmachar
Errogie 95 939 Tomintoul 803 Alford Kemnay Kintore Dyce
Whitebridge Aviemore Ladder Hills Ordhead 944 Bridge of Don
Coylumbridge Crossroad Inn Bucksburn ABERDEEN
82 Cock Cults Girdle Ness

0 10 20 30 40 50 60 Kilometres

A

B

C

D

Map labels

Cairngorm Mountains
Cairn Gorm 1245
Braeriach 1295
Ben Macdui 1311
Boat of Garten
Coylumbridge
Aviemore
Tomintoul
Càrn Mor 803
Mossat
Alford
Kemnay
Kintore
Newmachar
Balmedie
Dyce
Bridge of Don
Bucksburn
ABERDEEN
Girdle Ness
Cults
Peterculter
Banchory
Cammachmore
Skateraw
Stonehaven
Candy
Mowtie
Inverbervie
Gourdon
Johnshaven
St. Cyrus
Montrose
Lunan Bay
Inchcape or Bell Rock
Arbroath
Carnoustie
Buddon Ness
Tayport
Newport on Tay
Wormit
Leuchars
St. Andrews
Kingsbarns
Crail
Fife Ness
Anstruther Wester
Pittenweem
Isle of May
Bass Rock
North Berwick
Whitekirk
Dunbar
Skateraw
St. Abb's Head
St. Abb's
Coldingham
Eyemouth
Burnmouth
Berwick-upon-Tweed
Holy Island
Farne Islands
Bamburgh
Seahouses
Embleton
Longhoughton
Alnwick
Lesbury
Alnmouth
Warkworth
Amble
Broomhill
Widdrington
Ashington
Newbiggin-by-the-Sea
Bedlington
Blyth
Seaton Delaval
Whitley Bay
Tynemouth
SOUTH SHIELDS
SUNDERLAND
Seaham
Murton
Easington Colliery
Peterlee
Hartlepool
NEWCASTLE UPON TYNE
GATESHEAD
Durham
Consett
Chester le Street
Houghton le Spring
Carlisle
Dumfries
Lockerbie
Annan
Gretna
Brampton
Haltwhistle
Hexham
EDINBURGH
Musselburgh
Dalkeith
Haddington
Tranent
Prestonpans
Lammermuir Hills
Galashiels
Selkirk
Hawick
Jedburgh
Kelso
Coldstream
Cheviot Hills
The Cheviot 816
Southern Uplands
Moffat
Langholm
Peebles
DUNDEE
Perth
Forfar
Brechin
Blairgowrie
Crieff
Dunfermline
Kirkcaldy
Glenrothes
Cowdenbeath
Falkirk
Motherwell
Lanark

Scale

0 10 20 30 40 50 60 Kilometres

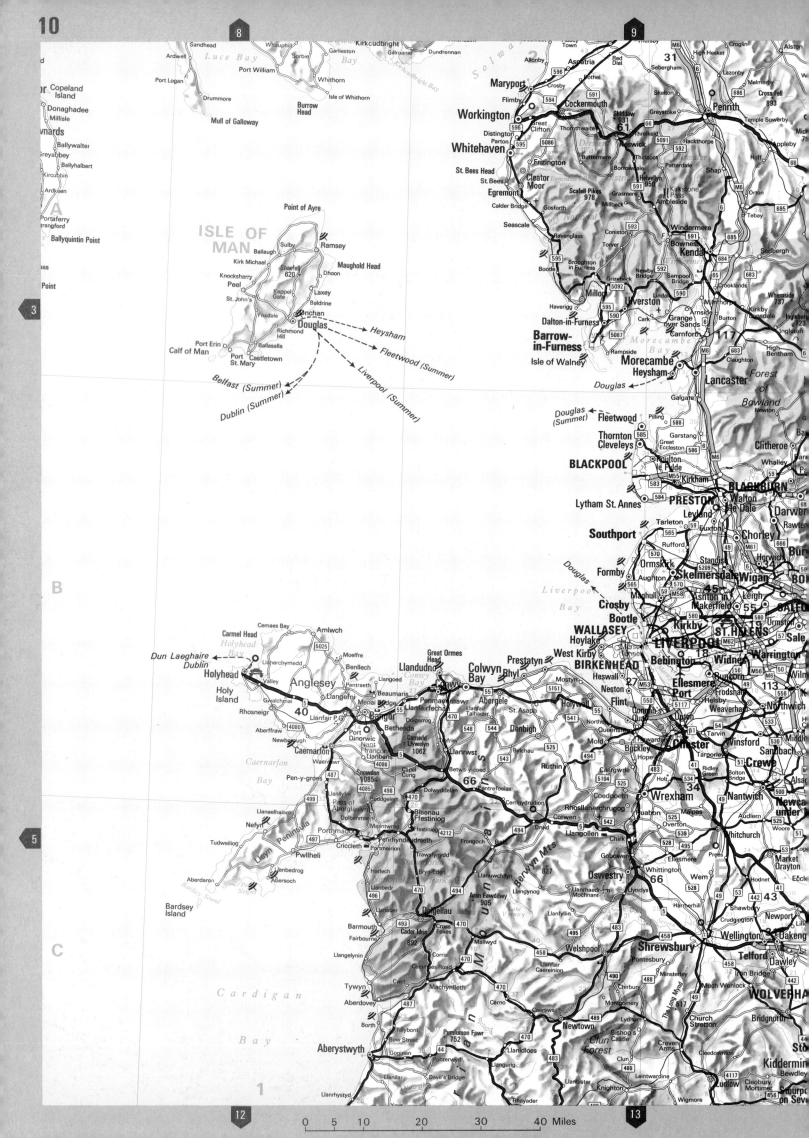

9

5 6

A

Castleside Lanchester le Street Murton
Durham 691 Hetton le Hole Easington Colliery
Tow Law 68 Brandon Willington Peterlee
Wolsingham Crook Spennymoor Ferryhill Trimdon Hartlepool
Bishop Auckland West Auckland Shildon Sedgefield Greatham Redcar
Staindrop Newton Aycliffe Wolviston Billingham Marske by the Sea
Barnard Castle Gainford Stockton on Tees Saltburn by the Sea
Bowes Darlington Middlesbrough Guisborough Loftus Hinderwell Whitby
Richmond Scotch Corner Thornaby on Tees High Hawsker
Reeth Catterick Catterick Camp Stokesley Great Ayton Cleveland Hills Robin Hood's Bay
Aysgarth Middleham Northallerton Cleveland Tontine Sleights
Leyburn Bedale Laskill Eller Beck Bridge
Great Whernside Ripon Leeming Bar Thirsk Saltergate Cloughton
Kettlewell Masham Kirkby Moorside Scalby Scarborough
Grassington Boroughbridge Helmsley Pickering Thornton-le-Dale Seamer Filey
Threshfield Summer Bridge Pateley Bridge Easingwold Sowerby Hovingham Snainton Sherburn Hunmanby Reighton
Skipton Knaresborough Strensall Malton Norton Rillington Foxholes Flamborough
Harrogate Stillington Haxby Sledmere Rudston Flamborough Head
Ilkley Burley in Wharfedale Wetherby Fridaythorpe Burton Agnes Bridlington
Silsden Bingley Collingham Green Hammerton York Stamford Bridge Nafferton Lissett Bridlington Bay
Keighley Shipley Otley Harewood Barmby Moor Driffield Skipsea
BRADFORD Pudsey LEEDS Tadcaster Pocklington Middleton on the Wolds Hornsea
Hebden Bridge Halifax Rothwell Riccall Market Weighton Leven Beverley Aldbrough
Brighouse Dewsbury Castleford Sherburn in Elmet Selby Holme upon Spalding Moor South Cave KINGSTON UPON HULL Withernsea
Littleborough Wakefield Pontefract Snaith Goole Howden Cottingham Preston Roos
Huddersfield Hemsworth Thorne North Ferriby Hessle Hedon Keyingham Patrington
Holmfirth South Kirkby Adwick le Street Crowle Winterton Barton upon Humber Barrow upon Humber Immingham Dock Easington
Ashton under Lyne Darton Barnsley Bentley Hatfield Scunthorpe Immingham Grimsby Spurn Head
Penistone Goldthorpe Mexborough Doncaster Belton Broughton Barnetby le Wold Healing Cleethorpes
Stocksbridge Grenoside Conisbrough New Rossington Epworth Messingham Brigg Laceby Humberston Rotterdam Zeebrugge
MANCHESTER Stocksbridge Rotherham Bawtry Misterton Hibaldstow Caistor Grainthorpe North Somercotes Saltfleet
STOCKPORT New Mills SHEFFIELD Maltby Tickhill Kirton in Lindsey Binbrook Ludborough Ludford Magna Saltfleetby St. Clement
Hazel Grove Whaley Bridge Hathersage Bolsover Blyth Beckingham Gainsborough Caenby Corner Market Rasen Mablethorpe
Macclesfield Dronfield Worksop East Retford Lea Faldingworth Louth Sutton-on-Sea
Chapel en le Frith Chesterfield Eckington Whitwell East Markham Saxilby Nettleham Scamblesby Withern Tothill
Buxton Staveley Warsop Tuxford North Hykeham Wragby Ulceby Cross Alford Hogsthorpe
Bakewell Ollerton Lincoln Bardney Horncastle Burgh le Marsh
Youlgreave Clay Cross Mansfield Mansfield Woodhouse Bracebridge Heath Woodhall Spa Spilsby Skegness
Matlock Sutton in Ashfield Waddington Metheringham Mareham le Fen Wainfleet All Saints
Leek Cromford Alfreton Newark Navenby Martin Coningsby Sibsey
Wirksworth Ripley Southwell Leadenham Ruskington Billinghay Wrangle Wells next the Sea
Ashbourne Belper Hucknall Balderton Caythorpe Sleaford Heckington Benington Boston Hunstanton Brancaster
Mayfield Eastwood Arnold Sheaf Heckington Swineshead Kirton Heacham Burnham Market Little Walsingham
Heanor Ilkeston Carlton Long Bennington Honington Swaffham Snettisham Docking
Upper Tean Stapleford Nottingham Bottesford Grantham Donington Gosberton Fosdyke Dersingham
Uttoxeter Rocester Beeston West Bridgford Denton Folkingham Pinchbeck Weston Holbeach Sutton Bridge King's Lynn
Sudbury Long Eaton Castle Donington Waltham on the Wolds Colsterworth Corby Glen Spalding Long Sutton Terrington St. Clement Gayton Castle Acre
DERBY Melbourne Kegworth Bourne Deeping St. Nicholas Tydd St. Giles Middleton Litcham
Abbot's Bromley Tutbury Shepshed Barrow upon Soar Market Deeping Crowland Wisbech Swaffham
Burton upon Trent Swadlincote Loughborough Melton Mowbray Twenty Thorney Outwell
Rugeley Ashby de la Zouch Mountsorrel Syston Cottesmore Baston Peterborough March Downham Market
Cannock Measham Ibstock Thurmaston Oakham Ketton Stamford Eye Whittlesey Wimblington Methwold
Lichfield Markfield Anstey Leicester Ketton Duddington Wansford Yaxley Peterborough Hilgay Stoke Ferry
Tamworth Earl Shilton Oadby Wigston Uppington Thorney Crowland Whittlesey March Feltwell Brandland
Nuneaton Hinckley Blaby Kibworth Beauchamp Market Harborough Corby Wansford Norman Cross Dundle Stamford Ramsey Chatteris Downham Littleport Thetford
BIRMINGHAM Bedworth Lutterworth Husbands Bosworth Naseby Desborough Rothwell Kettering Brigstock Sawtry Warboys Somersham Ely Lakenheath Mildenhall
SOLIHULL COVENTRY Rugby Crick Broughton Burton Latimer Finedon Aconbury Hill Huntingdon St. Ives Godmanchester Soham Fordham
Kenilworth Welford Long Buckby Pushden Brampton Earith Mildenhall Lackford

0 10 20 30 40 50 60 Kilometres

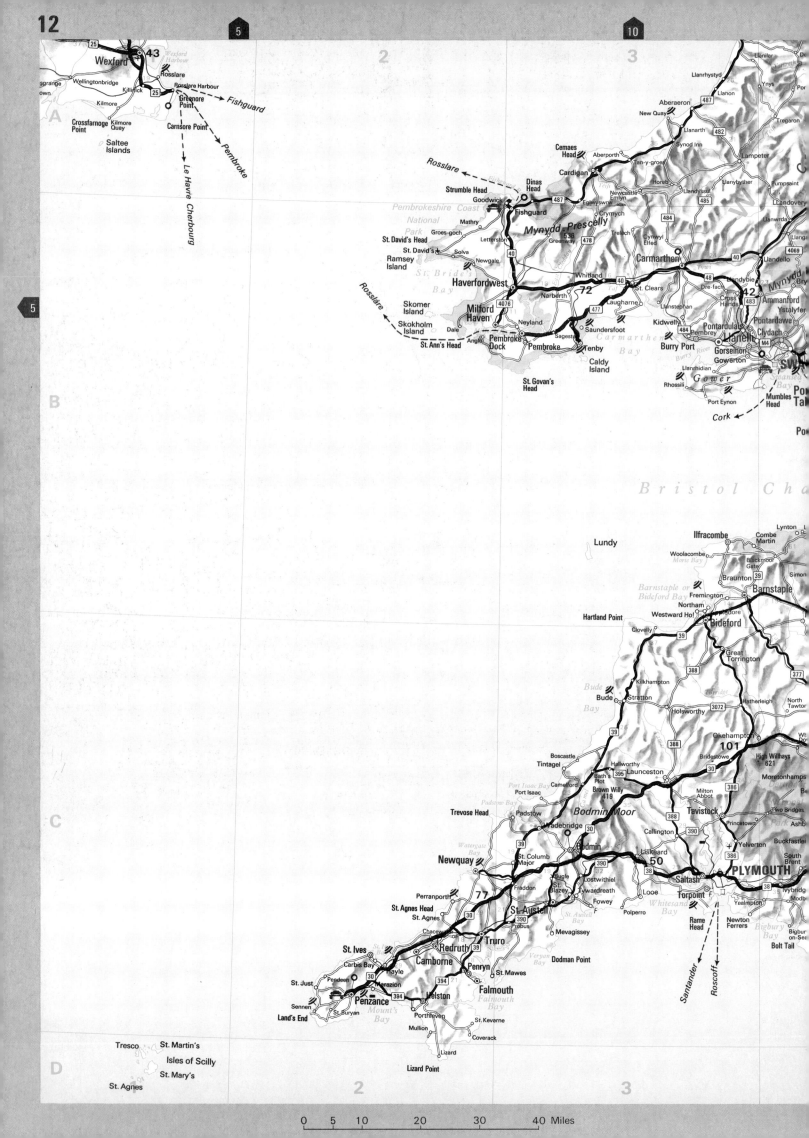

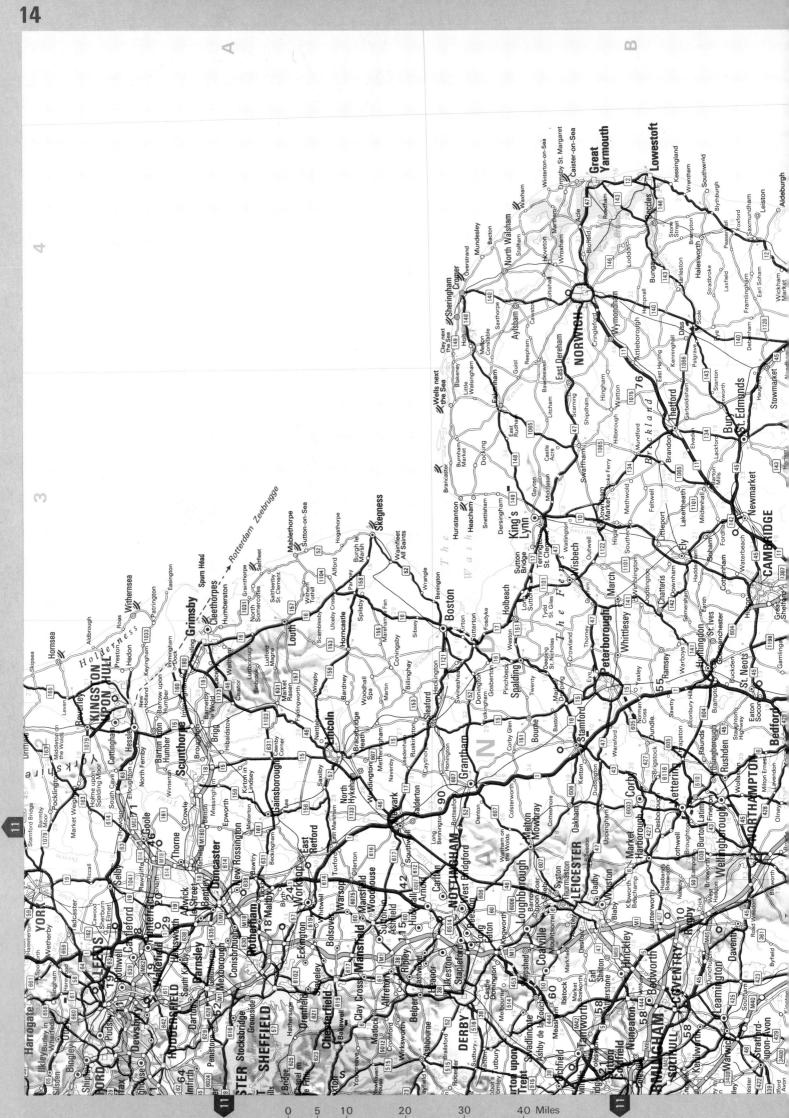

LUTON Stevenage Hitchin Harlow Bishop's Stortford Braintree Colchester Halstead Harwich Felixstowe Clacton-on-Sea Brightlingsea Walton-on-the-Naze Frinton

Welwyn Garden City St. Albans Hatfield Potters Bar Barnet Enfield Waltham Forest Chelmsford Maldon Burnham-on-Crouch Rayleigh SOUTHEND-ON-SEA Canvey Rochford

Hemel Hempstead Chesham Watford Bushey Harrow BARKING BASILDON Brentwood Billericay Wickford Benfleet Sheerness Minster Margate Broadstairs Ramsgate Deal

Aylesbury Amersham Beaconsfield Slough HILLINGDON LONDON BROMLEY CROYDON MERTON BEXLEY Gravesend Northfleet Rochester Chatham Gillingham Maidstone Whitstable Herne Bay Canterbury Sandwich Dover Folkestone Hythe

High Wycombe Marlow Maidenhead Windsor Staines RICHMOND KINGSTON Sutton Purley Sevenoaks Tonbridge Tunbridge Wells Ashford New Romney Dymchurch

Oxford Henley on Thames READING Bracknell Egham Chertsey Woking Leatherhead Dorking Reigate Redhill Oxted East Grinstead Crawley Haywards Heath Uckfield Hastings Bexhill Eastbourne

Bicester Wallingford Wokingham Camberley Farnborough Aldershot Guildford Godalming Cranleigh Horsham Billingshurst Lewes Newhaven Seaford BRIGHTON Hove Worthing

Abingdon Newbury Basingstoke Alton Farnham Petersfield Midhurst Chichester Bognor Regis Littlehampton Arundel

Swindon Hungerford Andover Winchester Eastleigh SOUTHAMPTON Havant PORTSMOUTH Gosport Fareham Selsey Bill West Wittering

Salisbury Romsey Totton Lymington Cowes Newport Isle of Wight Sandown Shanklin Ventnor The Needles St. Catherine's Point

Calais Gravelines Marck Guines Ardres St. Omer Desvres Samer Boulogne-sur-Mer le Portel Hardelot Plage le Touquet-Paris-Plage Étaples Berck-Plage Montreuil Hesdin Crécy-en-Ponthieu St. Valéry-sur-Somme Cayeux-s.-Mer le Crotoy

Cap Gris-Nez Wissant Wimereux Wimille Marquise

Zeebrugge Hook of Holland Vlissingen Ostende Dieppe Le Havre Caen Cherbourg St. Malo Guernsey

2 3

1075
Attleborough
11
East Harling
Hempnall
Loddon
143
Beccles
16
Thetford
140
Bungay
146
12
Lowestoft
Garboldisham
1066
Diss
143
Stone Street
Kessingland
Palgrave
Harleston
Brampton
Wrentham
Edmunds
Scole
Stradbroke
Blythburgh
Southwold
Haughley
Debenham
Framlingham
Yoxford
Laxfield
Peasenhall
Stowmarket
45
Earl Soham
Saxmundham
19
Needham Market
1120
Wickham Market
Leiston
Claydon
12
Melton
Aldeburgh
Monks Eleigh
Bramford
Woodbridge
Orford
Hadleigh
IPSWICH
Orford Ness
29
Nayland
Chelmondiston
Trimley
Esbjerg
Gothenburg
Hamburg
134
12
Felixstowe
Zeebrugge
Manningtree
Shotley Gate
120
120
Harwich
Hook of Holland
15
31
Thorpe-le-Soken
The Naze
Wivenhoe
Walton-on-the-Naze
Brightlingsea
Little Clacton
Frinton
West Mersea
Mersea Island
Clacton-on-Sea
Tollesbury
Bradwell on Sea
Tillingham
Southminster
Burnham-on-Crouch

B

Harwich

Haamstede
Brouw
Domburg
Westkapelle
Walcheren
Middelburg
Oost-en West-Souburg
Sheerness
Vlissingen
Zuid
Breskens
Felixstowe
Hull
Knokke
Heist
Blankenberge
Oostburg
Schoondijke
N61
Zeebrugge
Dover
Bredene
Uitkerke
N251
Oostende
Brugge
St.
St. Kruis
Maldegem
Middelkerke
Moerkerke
Eeklo
Nieuwpoort
Stene
St. Andries
St. Michiels
Oedelem
Knesselare
Evergem
Koksijde
Oudenburg
Gistel
Oostkamp
Beernem
Zomergem
GENT
De Panne
Bray Dunes
Koekelare
Torhout
Wingene
Lovendegem
Drongen
Adinkerke
Veurne
Koelkelare
Ruiselede
Nevele
Deinze
Malo-les-Bains
51
Diksmuide
Lichtervelde
Zwevezele
St. Pol-sur-Mer
Woumen
Zarren
Ardooie
Tielt
Petegem
Dunkerque
Staden
Meulebeke
Waregem
Loone-Plage
Roeselare
Izegem
Oostrozebeke
Bergues
Hondschoote
Passendale
Ingelmunster
Kruishoutem
Gravelines
Bourbourg
Merkem
Moorslede
Harelbeke
Poperinge
Vlamertinge
Kortrijk
Oudenaarde
Steenvoorde
Ieper
Dadizele
Menen
Nederbrakel
Watten
Wormhoudt
Cassel
Werik
Lauwe
Geraardsbergen
Ronse
Mouscron
Marquise
Steenvoorde
Bailleul
Comines
Avelgem
Berchem
Escoeuilles
Ploegsteert
Tourcoing
Herseaux
St. Omer
Arques
Hazebrouck
Armentières
ROUBAIX
Lumbres
Wizernes
LILLE
TOURNAI
Desvres
Aire-sur-la-Lys
Merville
Estaires
Haubourdin
Leuze
Thérouanne
St. Venant
Seclin
Cysoing
Antoing
Samer
Estrée Blanche
Béthune
Beuvry
La Bassée
Carvin
Orchies
St. Amand-les-Eaux
Condé-sur-l'Escaut
Bruay-en-Artois
Noeux-les-Mines
Bully
Vendin-le-Vieil
Anvin
Houdain
Liévin
Lens
Douai
Aniche
Denain
Valenciennes
St. Pol-sur-Ternoise
Hénin-Beaumont
Somain
Dechy
Bouchain
Hesdin
le Parcq
Aubigny
Arras
Cambrai
Caudry
le Cateau
Abbeville
Doullens
Bapaume
Solesmes

20 21

0 5 10 20 30 40 Miles

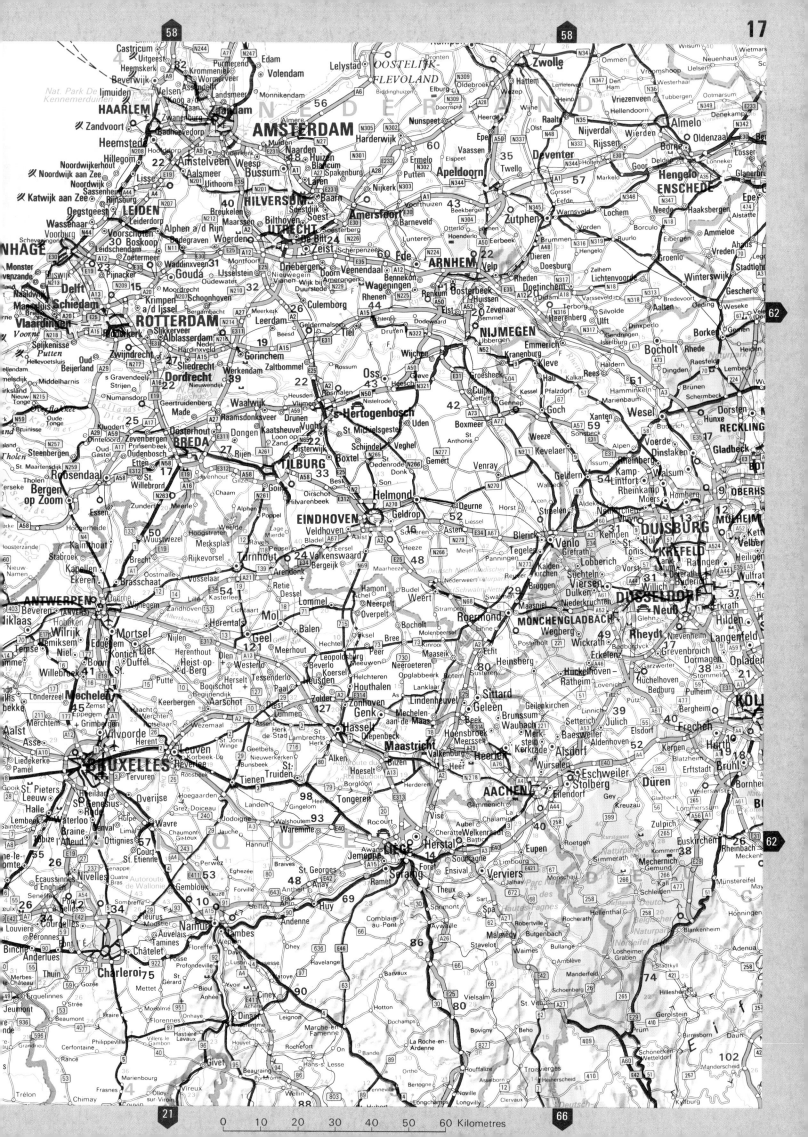

0 5 10   20   30   40 Miles

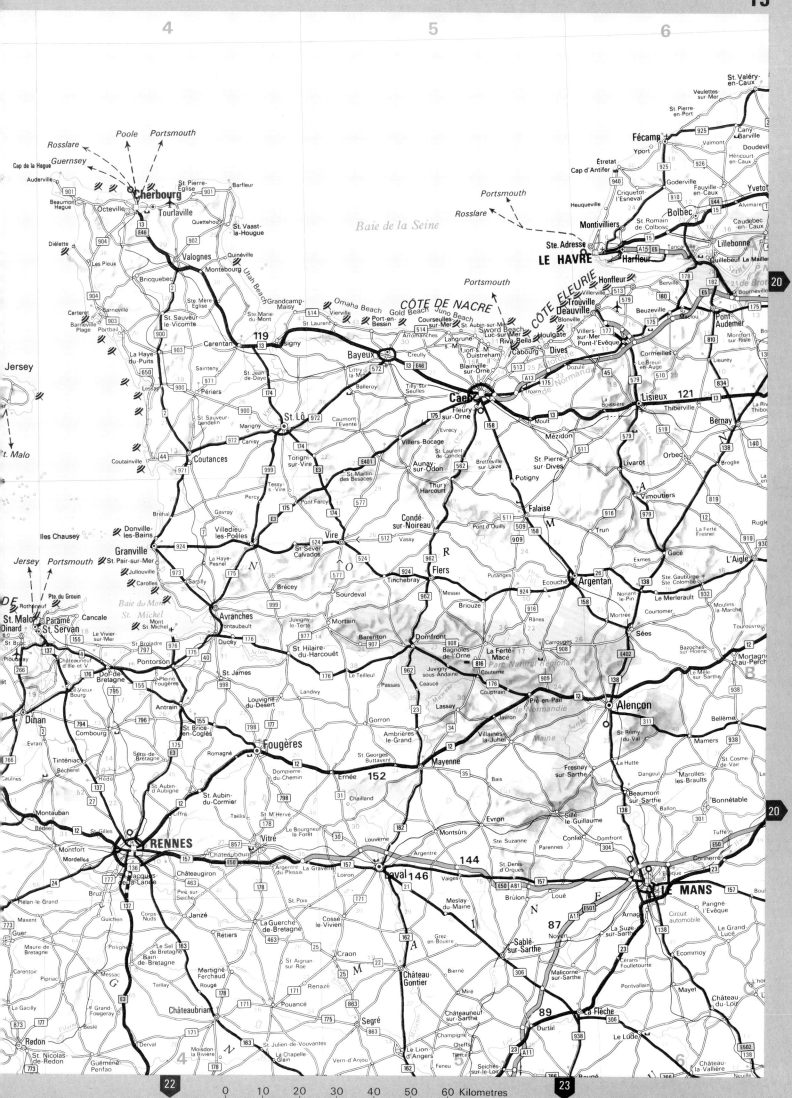

0   10   20   30   40   50   60 Kilometres

1

A

B

3

Newhaven

Cayeux-s.-Mer
St-Valéry-sur-Somme
Noyelle
Doullens
Abbeville
St-Riquier
Beauval
Acheux-en-Amienois
Albe
Villers-Bocage
Corbie
AMIENS
Albert-Bretonne
Moreuil
Longueau
Boves
St-Sauflieu
Essertaux
Ailly-sur-Somme
Picquigny
Flixecourt
Pont-Remy
Mers-les-Bains
Le Tréport
Criel-Plage
Criel-sur-Mer
Eu
Biville
Fressenville
Gamaches
Le Translay
Bouttencourt
Oisemont
Senarpont
Blangy
Aumale
47
99
45
28
112
44
Poix
Quevauvillers
Conty
Grandvilliers
Formerie
Forges-les-Eaux
Marseille-en-Beauvaisis
Songeons
Gournay-en-Bray
Beauvais
77
Clermont
Mouy
Noailles
Liancourt
Nogent-sur-Oise
Creil
Chantilly
Senlis
Chambly
Persan
Beaumont-sur-Oise
L'Isle-Adam
Luzarches
Pontoise
Taverny
Conflans
MONTMORENCY
ARGENTEUIL
ST-DENIS
NANTERRE
BOBIGNY
PARIS
NOGENT-s.-M

Dieppe
Neuville
St-Valéry-en-Caux
Quiberville
Offranville
Varengeville
Veules-les-Roses
Veulettes-sur-Mer
St-Pierre-en-Port
Envermeu
Arques-la-Bataille
Bacqueville
Londinières
Torcy-le-Petit
Les Grandes-Ventes
Fécamp
Yport
Étretat
Cap d'Antifer
925
926
Valmont
Cany-Barville
Doudeville
Yvetot
St-Laurent-en-Caux
Yerville
Limésy
Tôtes
St-Saëns
Les Hayons
Neufchâtel-en-Bray
Gaillefontaine
St-Samson-la-Poterie
Criquetot-l'Esneval
Goderville
Fauville-en-Caux
Bolbec
Barentin
Clères
Quincampoix
Buchy
Argueil
La Feuillie
Crillon
Songeons
Heuqueville
Montivilliers
Ste. Adresse
LE HAVRE
Harfleur
Tancarville
Lillebonne
Caudebec-en-Caux
Duclair
Malaunay
Mt.-St-Aignan
Bois-Guillaume
ROUEN
Darnétal
Maromme
Pavilly
Jumièges
P.N.R. de Brotonne
Quillebeuf
La Mailleraye
120
Pt. Couronne
Grd. Couronne
Otteville
Elbeuf
Boos
Lyons-la-Forêt
Gournay-en-Bray
916
915
E46
Beauvais
Auneuil
Bresles
Sérifontaine
Étrépagny
Gisors
Chaumont-en-Vexin
Ste. Geneviève
Méru
Neuilly-en-Thelle
124
Les Andelys
Gaillon
Vesly
Magny-en-Vexin
Marines
Persan
Chambly
Boran
Honfleur
Trouville
Deauville
CÔTE FLEURIE
Villerville
Blonville
Houlgate
Villers-sur-Mer
Pont-l'Évêque
Dives
Cabourg
Beuzeville
Cormeilles
Le Breuil-en-Auge
Pont-Audemer
Montfort-sur-Risle
Bourg-Achard
Bourgtheroulde
Brionne
Lieurey
Dozulé
Autoroute Normandie
Moult
Mézidon
St-Pierre-sur-Dives
Livarot
Orbec
Lisieux
121
Thiberville
Bernay
La Rivière-Thibouville
Beaumont-le-Roger
Le Neubourg
Acquigny
Louviers
133
Autheuil
63
Conches-en-Ouche
Évreux
28
Pacy-sur-Eure
Vernon
Gasny
La Roche-Guyon
Bonnières
Mantes-la-Jolie
Mantes-la-Ville
Limay
Les Mureaux
Meulan
Poissy
70
Maule
Triel
ST-GERMAIN
VERSAILLES
Falaise
158
Vimoutiers
Trun
Gacé
Argentan
138
Exmes
Sées
La Ferté-Fresnel
L'Aigle
Rugles
Breteuil
Verneuil-sur-Avre
Nonancourt
188
Dreux
Damville
St-André-de-l'Eure
Ivry-la-Bataille
Anet
Houdan
Montfort-l'Amaury
Septeuil
Rambouillet
90
Trappes
PALAISEAU
ANTONY
Orsay
JUVISY-s.-O.
RIS-Orangis
ÉVRY
Montlhéry
Arpajon
48
Brétigny-sur-Orge
88
Ballancourt
Ecouché
Carrouges
908
Alençon
St-Rémy-du-Val
Mamers
938
Nogent-le-Rotrou
120
122
Bellême
La Ferté-Bernard
La Loupe
Courville
Chartres
35
Gallardon
Épernon
Ablis
Dourdan
Étrechy
Étampes
Maisse
Milly-la-Forêt
Malesherbes
Puiseaux
Fresnay-sur-Sarthe
La Hutte
Beaumont-sur-Sarthe
Sillé-le-Guillaume
Conlie
Domfront
Pré-en-Pail
Mortagne-au-Perche
Le Mêle-sur-Sarthe
Bazoches-sur-Hoëne
Tourouvre
Longny-au-Perche
Senonches
Digny
Dangeau
Illiers-Combray
Thiron
Angerville
73
116
Sermaises
Monnerville
Méréville
Pithiviers
Beaumont-du-Gâtinais
LE MANS
87
Arnage
La Suze-sur-Sarthe
Parigné-l'Évêque
Circuit automobile
Le Grand-Lucé
St-Calais
143
Vibraye
Montmirail
Brou
Bonneval
Châteaudun
Cloyes
Patay
Arthenay
Chilleurs-aux-Bois
Neuville-aux-Bois
Bazoches-les-Gallerandes
Ascoux
Bonnétable
Authon-du-Perche
La Bazoche-Gouet
Chapelle-Royale
Courtalain
Droué
La Ferté-Villeneuil
Morée
Ouzouer-le-Marché
Meung-sur-Loire
ORLÉANS
5
St-Jean-de-la-R.
Olivet
Loué
Malicorne-sur-Sarthe
La Flèche
Mayet
Château-du-Loir
La Chartre-sur-le-Loir
Montoire-sur-le-Loir
Vendôme
Villeromain
Pontijou
Beaugency
Tavers
Cléry
Baule
Messas
Jargeau
Sandillon
Sully

0 5 10 20 30 40 Miles

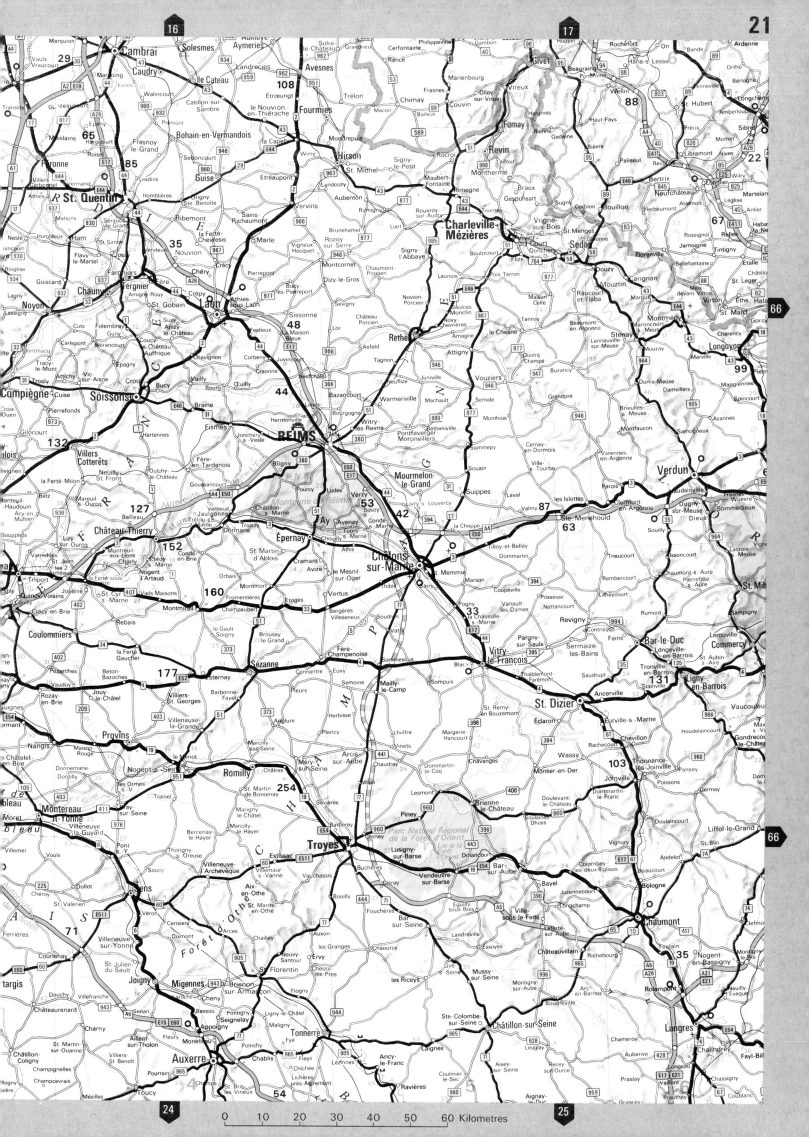

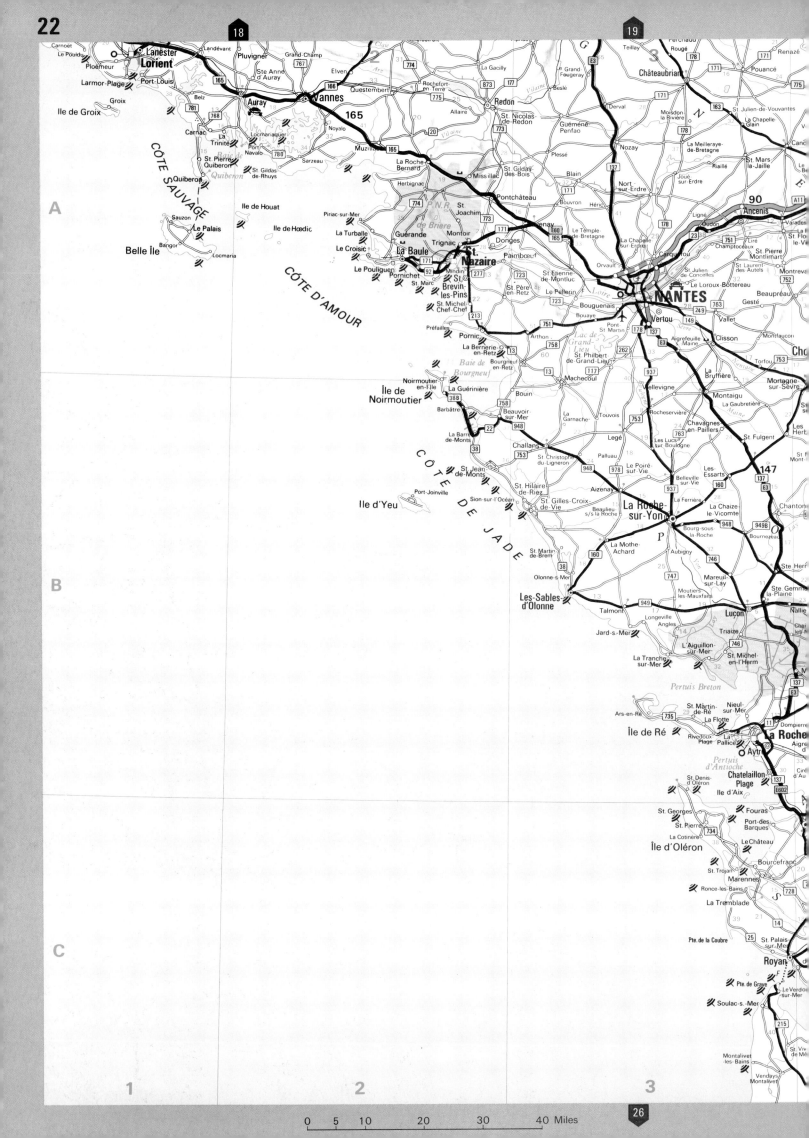

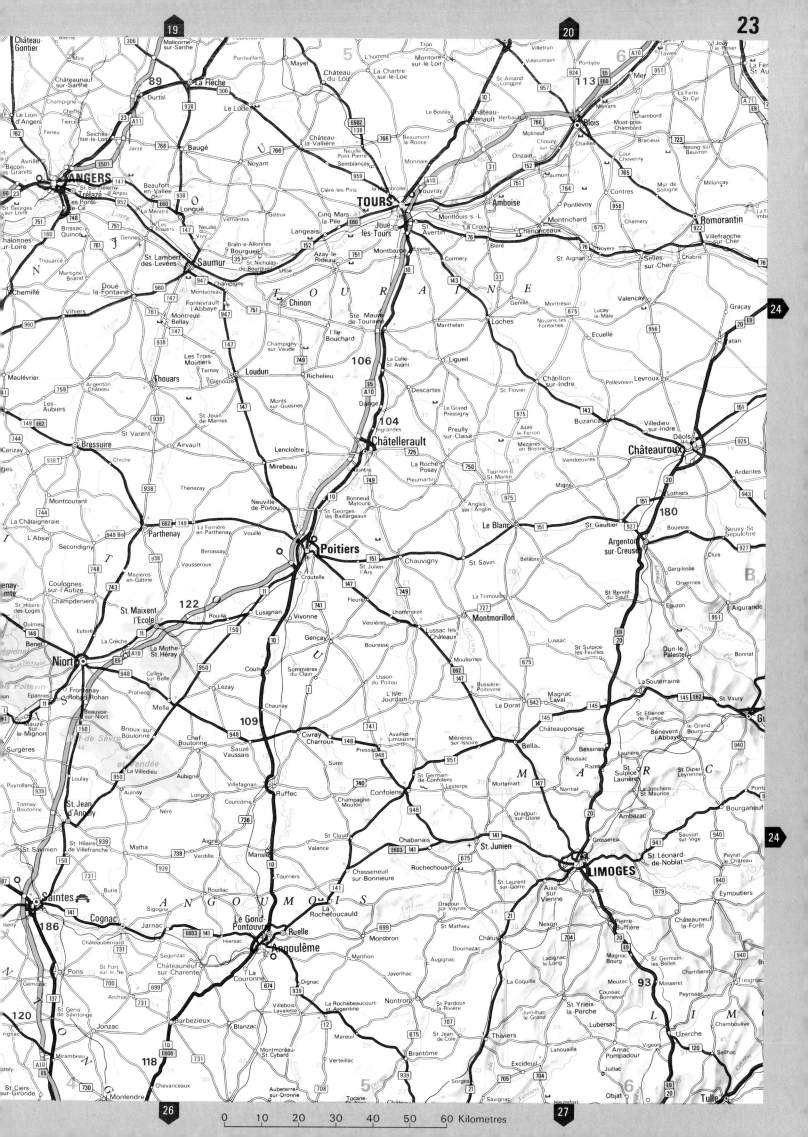

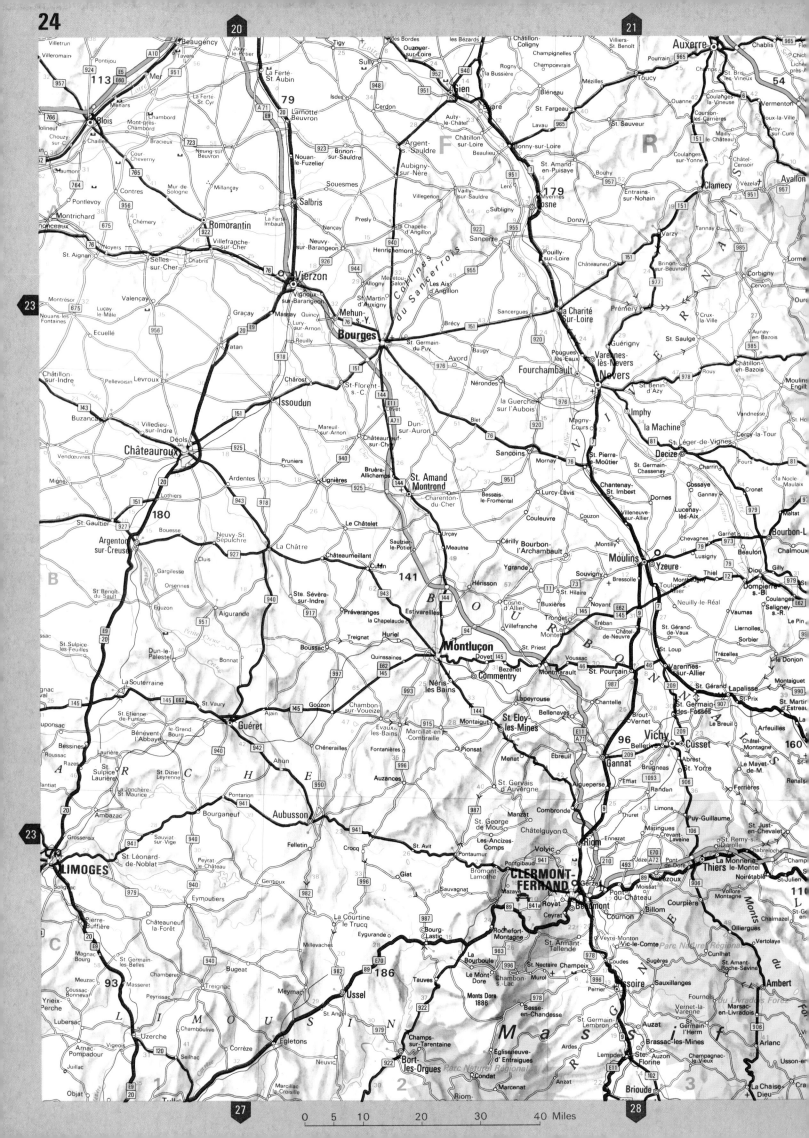

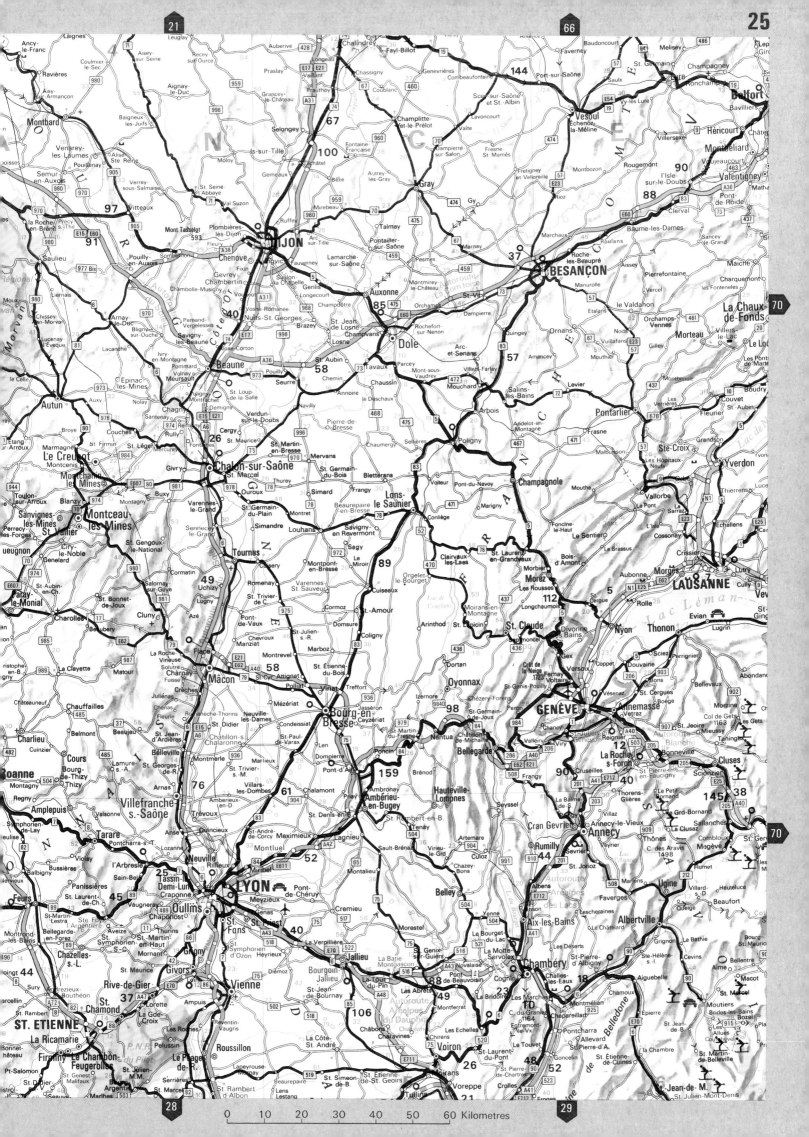

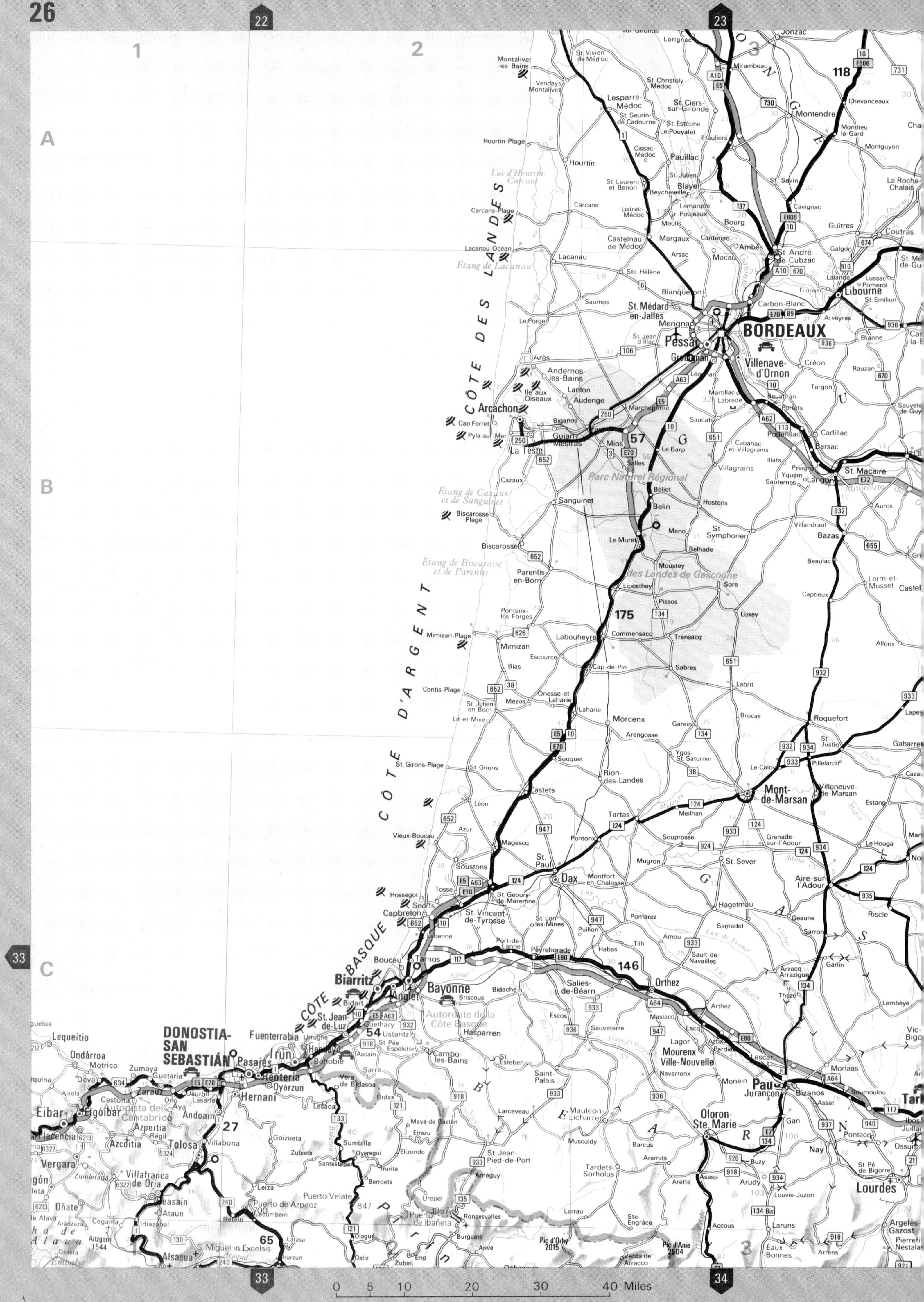

1 2 3

A

B

C

BORDEAUX

Pessac · Gruaudan · Villenave-d'Ornon

Arcachon · Cap Ferret · Pyla-sur-Mer · La Teste

CÔTE DES LANDES

CÔTE D'ARGENT

Parc Naturel Régional des Landes de Gascogne

Libourne · St Émilion · St André-de-Cubzac · Montendre

118

Mont-de-Marsan · Villeneuve-de-Marsan · Roquefort

Dax · Tartas · St Sever · Aire-sur-l'Adour

Biarritz · Anglet · Bayonne · St Jean-de-Luz · Hendaye

CÔTE BASQUE · Autoroute de la Côte Basque

146

Orthez · Salies-de-Béarn · Sauveterre · Mourenx Ville-Nouvelle

Pau · Jurançon · Bizanos · Oloron-Ste Marie · Lourdes

DONOSTIA-SAN SEBASTIÁN · Irún · Renteria · Hernani · Andoain · Tolosa

Eibar · Elgóibar · Vergara · Oñate · Villafranca de Oria

57 175 54 27 65 33 34

PIRINEOS · Pic d'Orhy 2015 · Pic d'Anie 2504

0 5 10 20 30 40 Miles

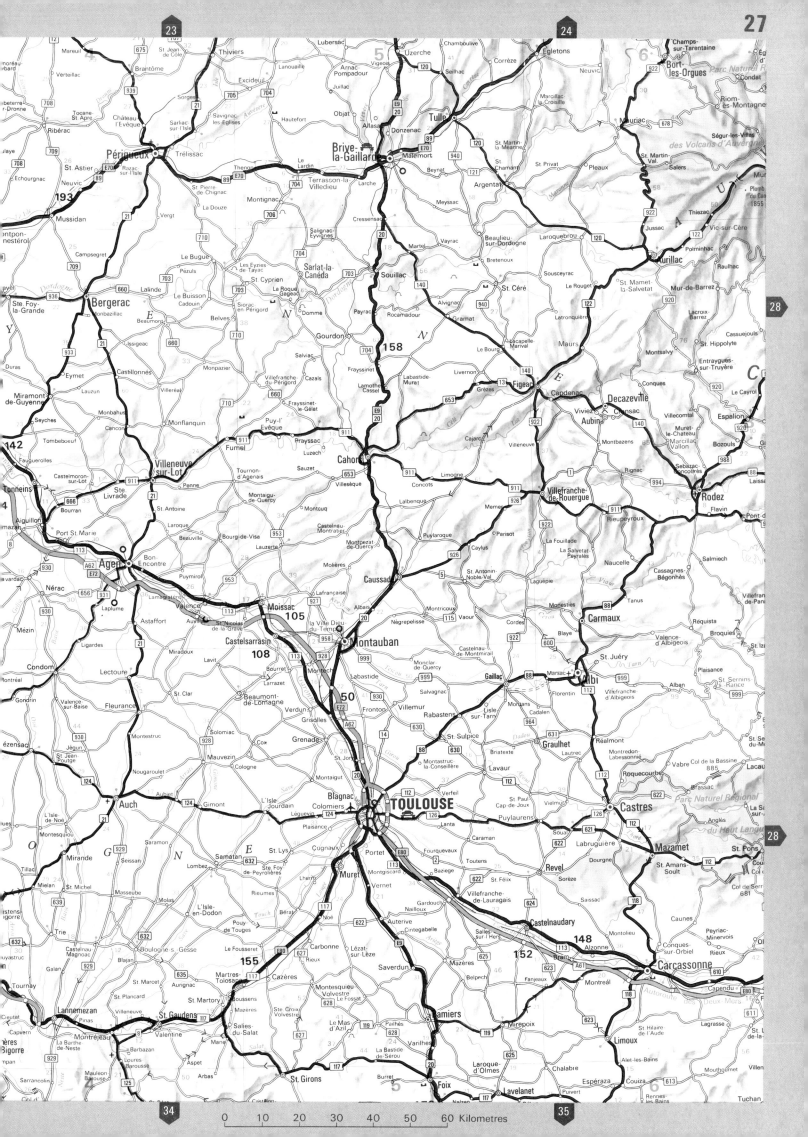

MASSIF

ST. ETIENNE
La Ricamarie

Egletons
Corrèze
St Chamant
St Privat
St Martin-la-Meanne
Argentat
Beaulieu-sur-Dordogne
Bretenoux
St Céré
Laroquebrou
Mauriac
Bort-les-Orgues
Champs-sur-Tarentaine
Riom-ès-Montagnes
Ségur-les-Villas
Murat
Thiezac
Plomb du Cantal 1855
Vic-sur-Cère
Polminhac
Aurillac
Le Rouget
St Mamet-la-Salvetat
Maurs
Figeac
Capdenac
Decazeville
Viviez
Aubin
Villecomtal
Espalion
St Côme-d'Olt
Bozouls
Gabriac
St Geniez-d'Olt
Rodez
Flavin
Laissac
Pont-de-Salars
Vézins
Villefranche-de-Rouergue
Rieupeyroux
Naucelle
Carmaux
Cordes
Albi
St Juéry
Graulhet
Réalmont
Castres
Mazamet
Revel
Castelnaudary
Carcassonne
Limoux

Brioude
Massiac
Langeac
Le Puy
Espaly-St-Marcel
Polignac
St Chély-d'Apcher
Aumont-Aubrac
Marvejols
Mende
Sévérac-le-Château
Millau
St Affrique
Lodève
Bédarieux
Béziers
Agde
Sète
Mèze
Pézenas
MONTPELLIER
Lunel
NÎMES
Alès
La Grand-Combe
Bessèges
Aubenas
Villefort
Langogne
Yssingeaux

Causse
Larzac
Méjean
Parc National des Cévennes
Monts d'Aubrac
Central

Côte d'Améthyste
Narbonne
Port-la-Nouvelle
Gruissan

0 5 10 20 30 40 Miles

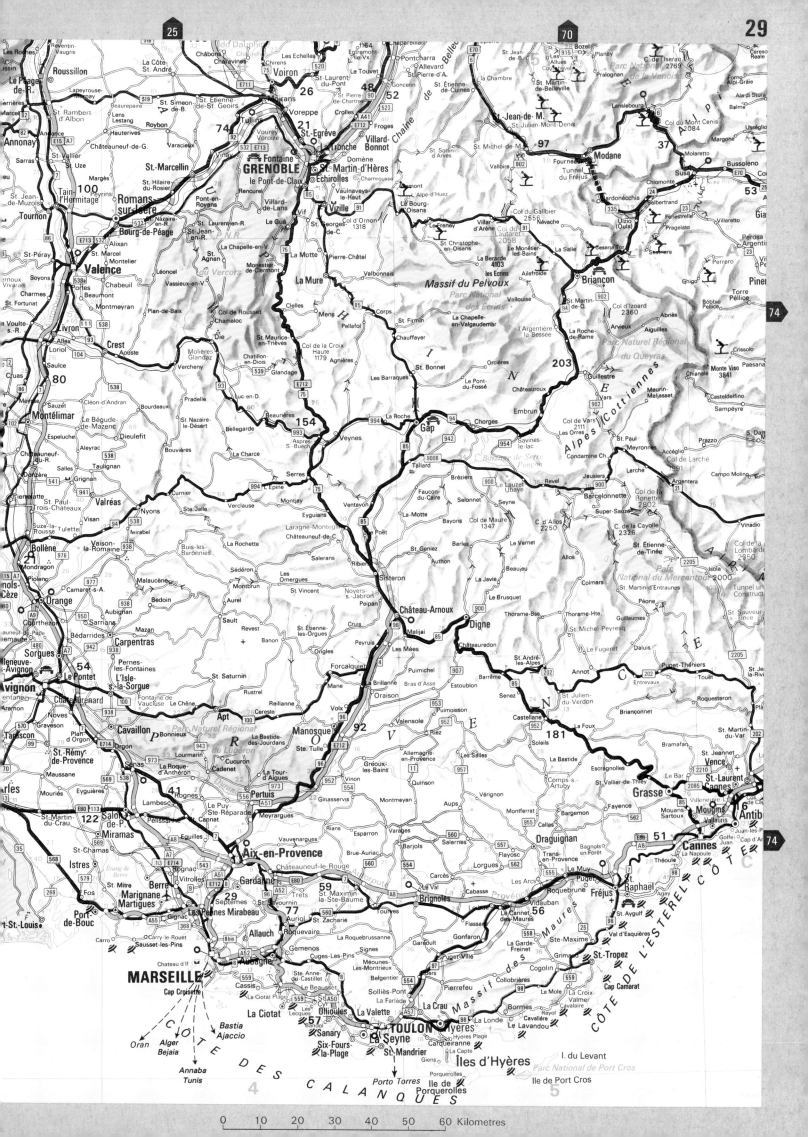

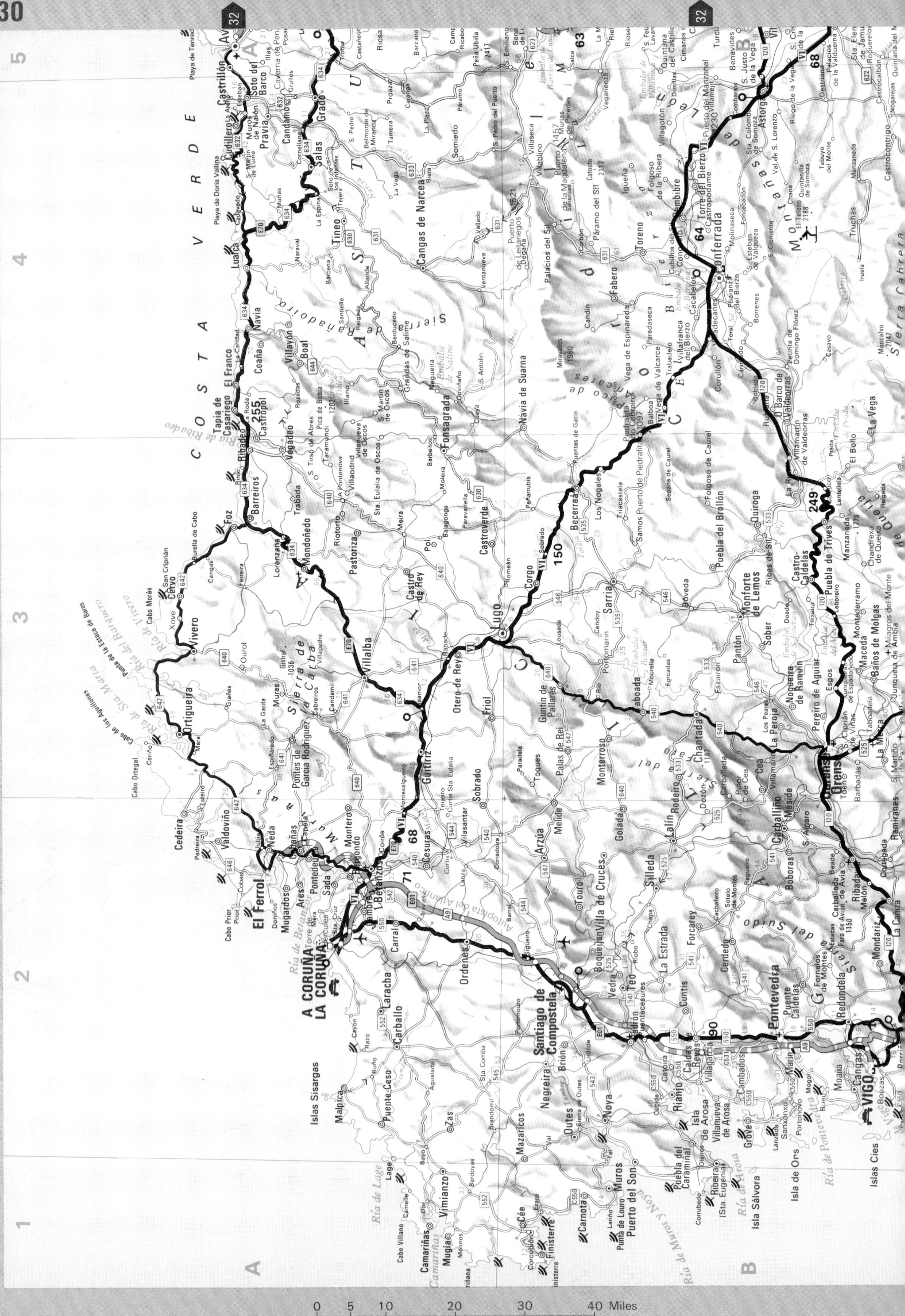

COSTA VERDE

A S T U R

Sierra de Rañadoira

Sierra de la Carba

M o n t e s d e L e ó n

Montañas

Montes del Bierzo

A CORUÑA / LA CORUÑA

El Ferrol

Santiago de Compostela

Lugo

Ponferrada

Astorga

Orense / Ourense

Pontevedra

VIGO

Villaviciosa

Castrillón · Cudillero · Pravia · Grado · Salas · Tineo · Cangas de Narcea · Villayón · Boal · Navia · Coaña · El Franco · Tapia de Casariego · Castropol · Ribadeo · Vegadeo · Barreiros · Foz · Mondoñedo · Lorenzana · Pastoriza · Riotorto · Meira · Castroverde · Fonsagrada · Navia de Suarna · Becerreá · Los Nogales · Sarria · Puebla del Brollón · Quiroga · Monforte de Lemos · Castro Caldelas · Puebla de Trives

Foz · Burela de Cabo · San Ciprián · Cervo · Xove · Vivero · Ortigueira · Cedeira · Valdoviño · Neda · Betanzos · Sada · Ares · Mugardos · Pontedeume · Puentes de García Rodríguez · Villalba · Guitiriz · Otero de Rey · Friol · Guntín de Pallarés · Palas de Rei · Monterroso · Chantada · Taboada · Carballedo

Cabo Ortegal · Cabo Ortegal · Cabo Prior · Islas Sisargas · Malpica · Carballo · Laracha · Ordenes · Arzúa · Melide · Sobrado · Curtis · Cesuras · Golada · Lalín · Silleda · Villa de Cruces · Forcarey · La Estrada · Vedra · Teo · Padrón

Camariñas · Mugía · Camariñas · Cée · Finisterre · Corcubión · Carnota · Muros · Puerto del Son · Noya · Outes · Mazaricos · Negreira · Brión · Puebla del Caramiñal · Ribeira · Isla de Arosa · Villanueva de Arosa · Villagarcía · Cambados · Grove · Sangenjo · Marín · Bueu · Cangas · Moaña · Redondela · Puente Caldelas · Mondariz · La Cañiza · Carballino · Ribadavia · Melón · Boboras · Maside · Cea · Villamarín

Ría de Ribadeo · Ría del Barquero · Ría de Sta. Marta · Ría de Betanzos · Ría de Lage · Ría de Muros y Noya · Ría de Arosa · Ría de Pontevedra · Ría de Vigo

Embalse de Salime · Embalse de Barrios de Luna

32 · **32** · **63** · **64** · **68**

255 · **249** · **150** · **68** · **71** · **190**

Autopista del Atlántico · A9 · E01 · E70

| 0 | 5 | 10 | 20 | 30 | 40 Miles |

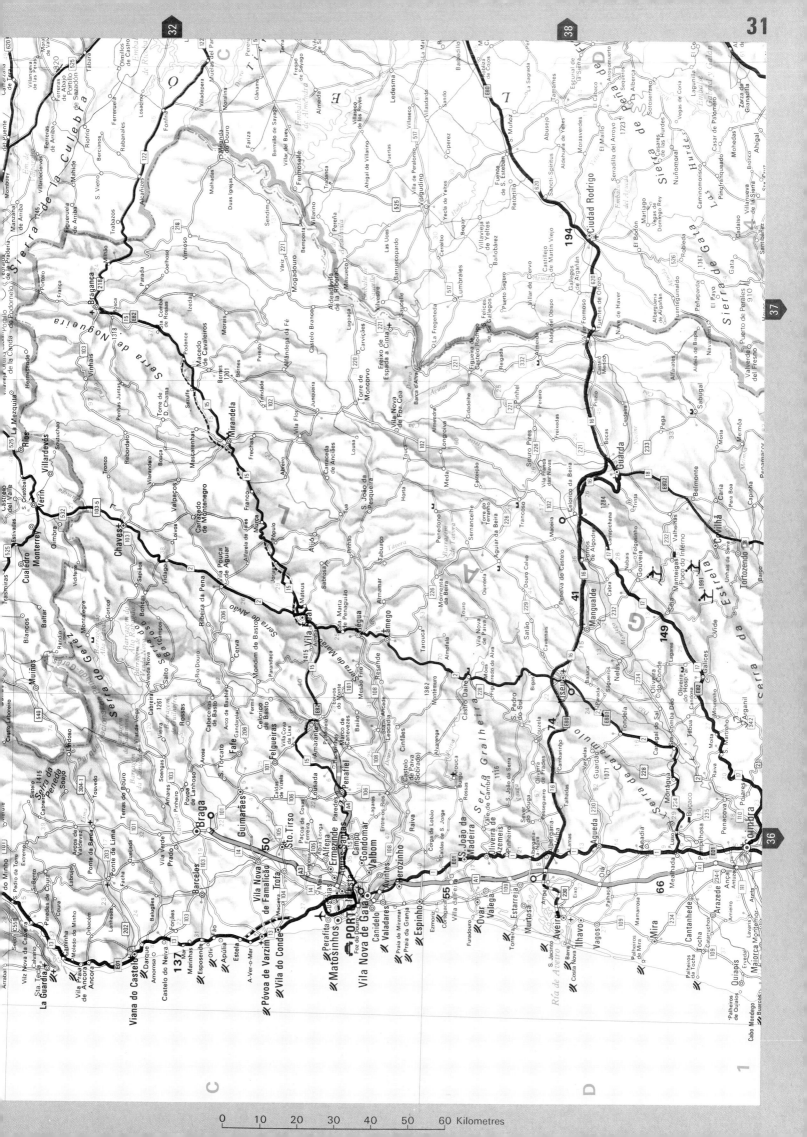

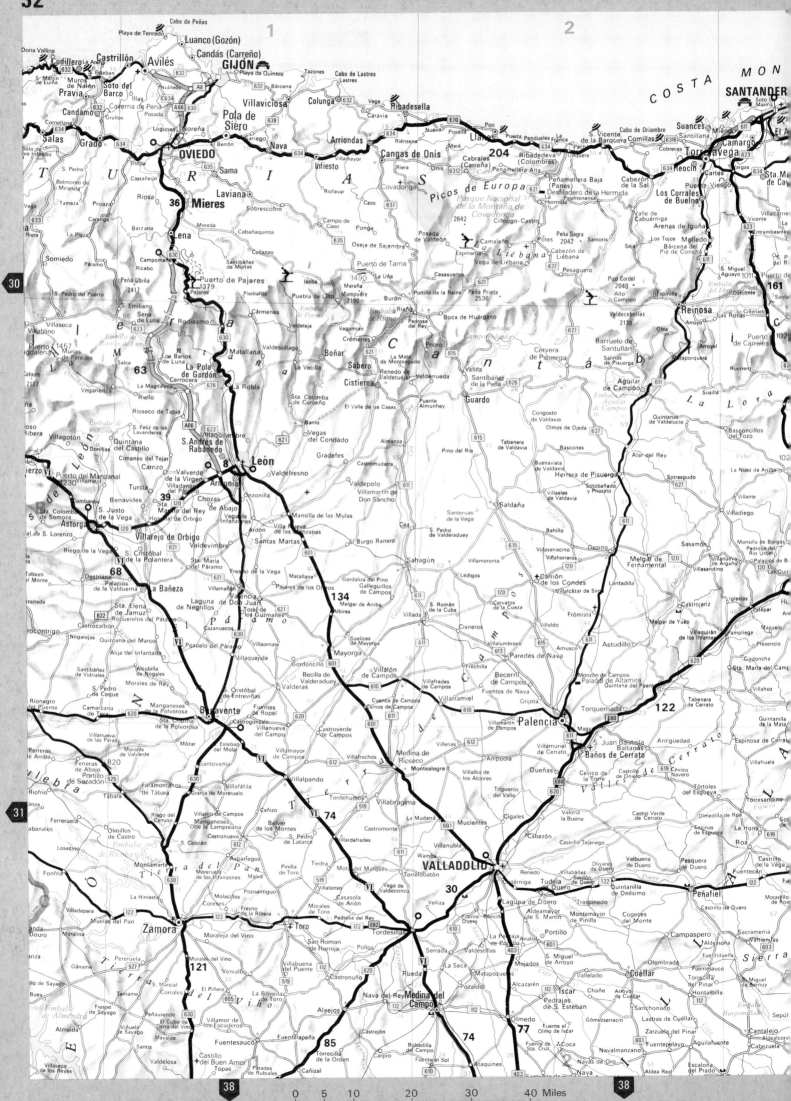

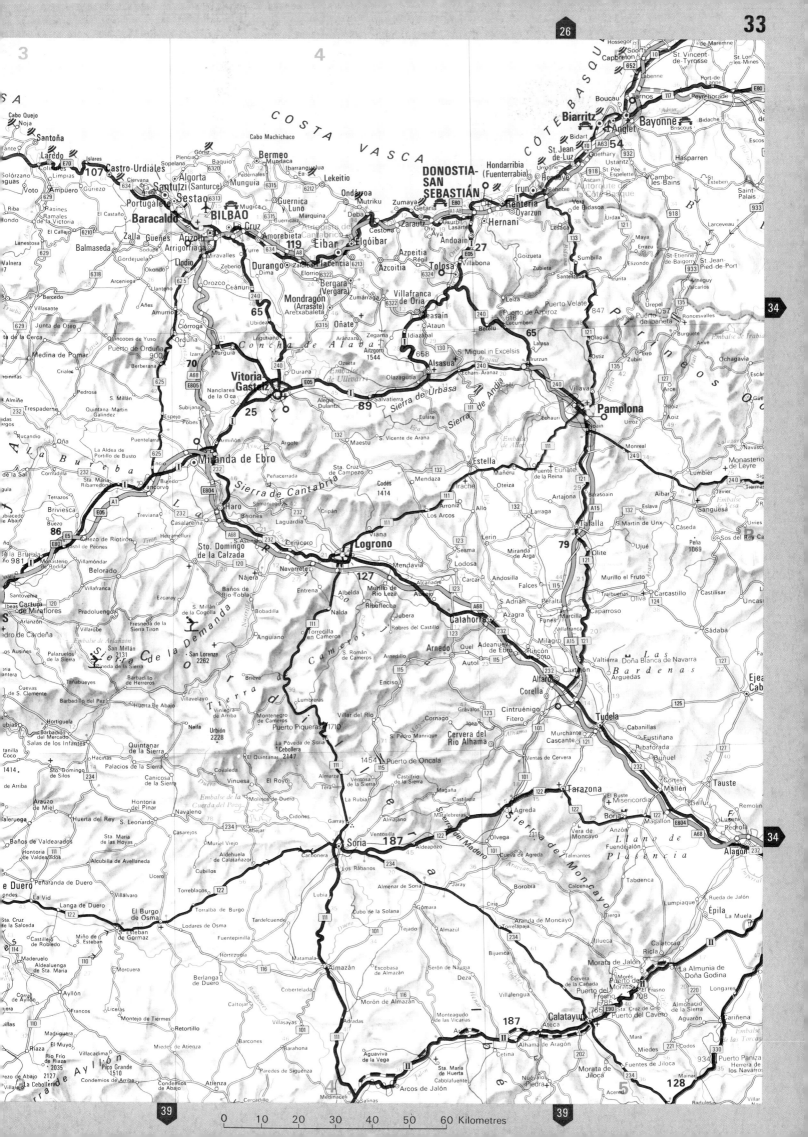

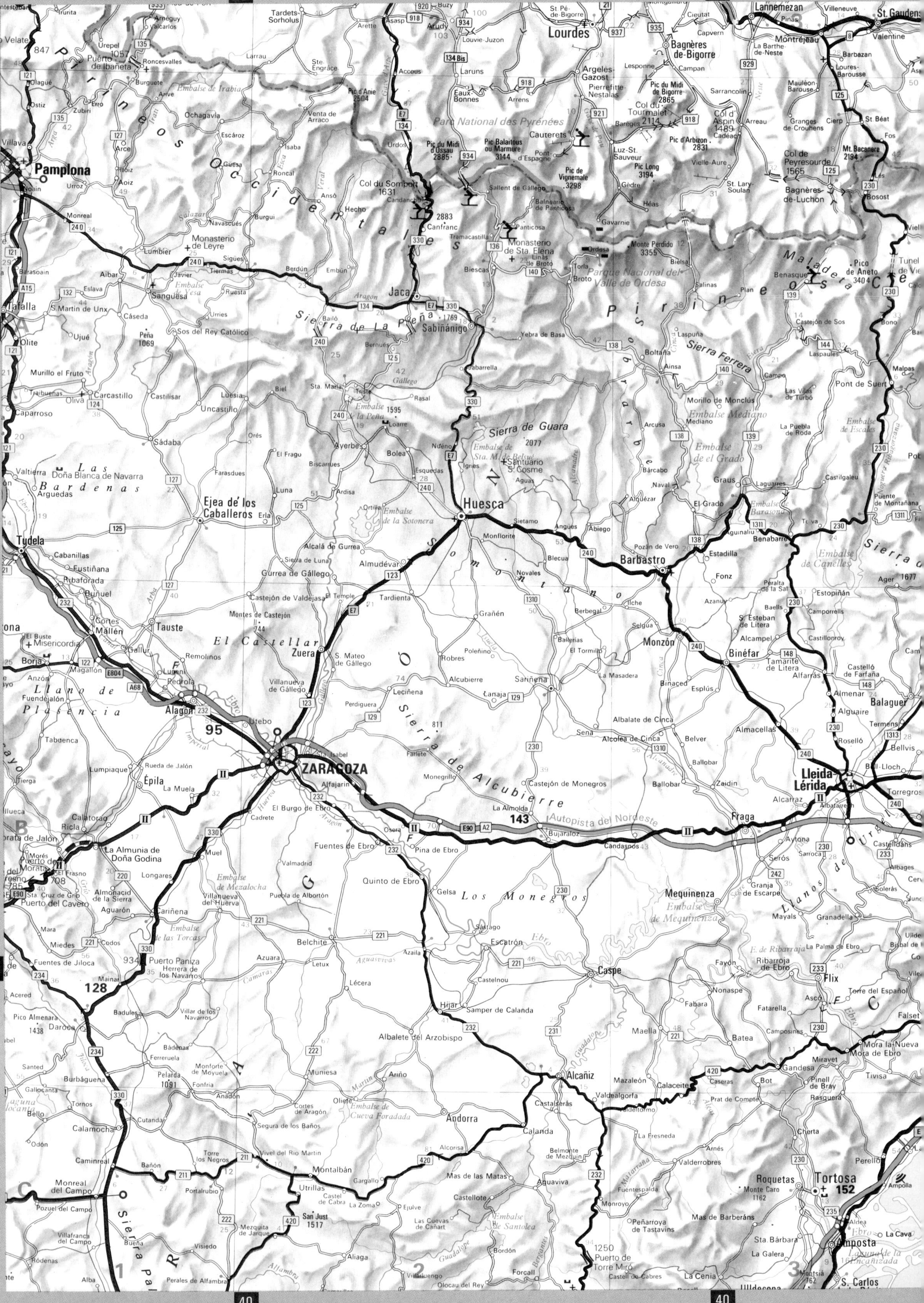

Pamplona
Tafalla
Olite
Tudela
Ejea de los Caballeros
Zaragoza
Huesca
Jaca
Sabiñánigo
Barbastro
Monzón
Binéfar
Lleida / Lérida
Balaguer
Fraga
Caspe
Alcañiz
Tortosa
Calatayud
Daroca
Calamocha
Montalbán
Andorra
Mequinenza

Lourdes
Bagnères-de-Bigorre
Lannemezan
St-Gaudens
Bagnères-de-Luchon
Argelès-Gazost
Cauterets
Gavarnie

Parc National des Pyrénées
Parque Nacional del Valle de Ordesa
Sierra de Guara
Sierra de Alcubierre
Los Monegros
Las Bardenas
Llano de Plasencia

Pic du Midi d'Ossau 2885
Pic Balaïtous ou Marmure 3144
Pic de Vignemale 3298
Vignemale
Monte Perdido 3355
Pic d'Anie 2504
Col du Tourmalet 2114
Pic d'Arbizon 2831
Pic Long 3194
Mt. Bacanère 2194
Pico de Aneto 3404
Col du Somport 1631
Peña 1069

Roncesvalles
Puerto de Ibañeta 1057
Canfranc
Panticosa
Biescas
Boltaña
Ainsa
Graus
Benabarre
Binéfar
Embalse de Mequinenza
Embalse de Ribaroja
Embalse de Canelles
Embalse de el Grado
Embalse de la Sotonera
Embalse de la Peña
Embalse de Yesa
Embalse de Mezalocha
Embalse de las Torcas
Embalse de Cueva Foradada

33
33

95
128
143
152

A2
E90
E804
A68
A15

Autopista del Nordeste

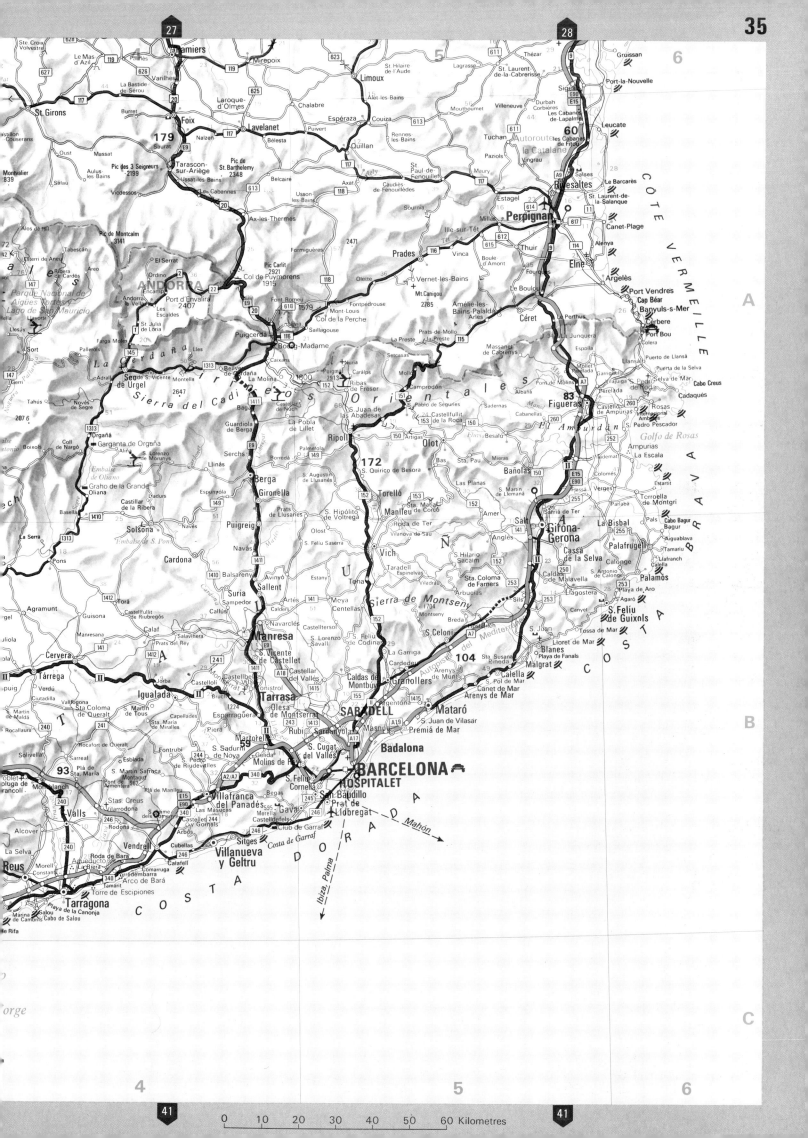

1

Ria de Aveiro · Aveiro · 230

Costa Nova · Ilhavo · Eixo · Lamas · Talhadas · Cambarinho · Penalva do Castelo

Vagos · Oiã · Agueda · 230 · Guardão · Varziela · Parada · Baiuca · Mangualde · Pontos de Algodres

109 · Palhaça · 114 · 1071 · Serra de Caramulo · E801 · Silgueiros · Nelas · Cabra · 232 · Carrapic

Mira · Mamarrosa · Anadia · Tondela · 228 · Carregal do Sal · Oliveira do Conde · Nabais · Folgosinho · Gouveia

234 · Mealhada · Luso · 254 · Mórtagua · Sta. Comba Dão · Lágares · 149 · Manteigas · Poço do Inferno

Palheiros da Tocha · Cantanhede · Buçaco · 235 · Tábua · Candosa · Vide · Unhais da Serra

A

Tocha · Catarruchos · A1 · Pampilhosa · Raiva · Mouronho · Galices · E82 · 1991 · Serra da Estrela · Tortozendo · Covi

109 · Arazede · 234-1 · E01 · Penacova · S. Martinho · Arganil · 342 · Barco · 18

Palheiros de Quiaios · Quiaios · Amieiro · Ançã · Antuzede · 110 · Poiares · 2 · Serra da Guar

Ervedal · Lavaris · Coimbra · Ceira · Semide · Góis · Orvalho · 112 · Foz do Giraldo · Almaceda

Cabo Mondego · Buarcos · Maiorca · Montemor-o-Velho · 111 · Valonga · Portela · Pampilhosa · Tinalhas

Figueira da Foz · Arzila · Condeixa · Vila Seca · 342 · Lousã · Miranda do Corvo · 1223 · Souto · Vale de

Lavos · Outeiro · Soure · Venda Nova · Penela · Espinhal · Alvares · Barragem Sta. Luzia · Silvares · Fundã

Rego de Leirosa · Marinha das Ondas · Louriçal · Alvorge · Castanheira de Pêra · 113 · Pedrógão Grande · Oleiros · Cafede

Guia · Pombal · Ansião · Pontão · Figueiró dos Vinhos · 1080 · Azenha de Cima · Salgueiro

Pedrógão · Barroco · Ramalhais · Santiago da Carpalhosa · Abiul · Alvaiázere · 110 · Barqueiro de Bonjardim · Figueiredo · Isna · 233 · Sarzedas · Caste

Monte Redondo · 109 · Souto da Carpalhosa · Venda Nova · Cabaços · Beco · Sertã · 241 · Proença-a-Nova · Sarnadas

Praia da Vieira · Vieira · Monte Real · Boa Vista · Albergaria dos Doze · Pereiro · 238 · Vila de Rei · Sobreira Formosa · E802

Marinha Grande · 242 · Memória · Aguas Belas · Ferreira do Zêzere · Vila Velha de Ródão · Montalvão

S. Pedro de Muel · Leiria · Caranguejeira · Rio do Couros · Alviobeira · Amendoa · Maxieira · Fratel · 18

Azóia · 113 · Carddosbs · Olival · Vila Nova de Ourém · Chão de Codes · B. de Pracana

Martingança · Maceira · Batalha · Moita · Alvião · Aldeia do Mato · B. de Belver

B

Nazaré · Valado · S. Jorge · 356 · 679 · Fátima · Tomar · Mação · Monte Clara · Nisa · Póvoa de Me

173 · Porto de Mós · 360 · Vargas · Asseiceira · Constância · Sardoal · Amieira · 364 · Barragem

Alcobaça · Aljubarrota · Mendiga · Minde · Assentiz · B. Castelo do Bode · 3 · Gavião · Ataia · Tolosa · 18

S. Martinho do Porto · Murteira · Serra de Aire · Torres Novas · Entroncamento · Barquinha · Sta. Margarida · Tramagal · 118 · 118 · Arez · 246 · Apalhão

Ilhas Farilhões · Alfeizerão · Golegã · 243 · Parceiros · Abrantes · Apalhão · 245 · Portalegr

Praia · Tornada · Turquel · 362 · Chamusca · Monte da Pedra · Vale do Poç

Ilha Berlenga · Foz do Arelho · Caldas da Rainha · Alcanede · Pernes · Golegã · 118 · Pinheiro Grande · 244 · Crato · 119

Ilhas Estrelas · Baleal · Óbidos · 114 · Tremês · Póvoa · Azinhaga · Ulme · Chouto · Bemposta · Torre das Vergens · 119

Cabo Carvoeiro · Peniche · 115 · Rio Maior · S. João da Ribeira · Azambujeira · Alpiarça · Ponte de Sôr · Sêda · Alter do Chão

Consolação · Bombarral · 366 · Cadaval · Cercal · Santarém · Almeirim · Mugen · Domingão · 119 · Galveias · 369 · Cabeço de Vide

S. Bernardino · Moita dos Ferreiros · Vermelha · 22 · Almoster · E01 · Vale de Santarém · Rosquete · 245 · 369

Areia Branca · Lourinha · Campelos · Monte Jupto · Alcoentre · Ereira · Vila Chã de Ourique · Benavila · Fronteira

Vimeiro · Ramalhal · Vilar · 666 · Vila Verde · Cartaxo · Benfica · 3 · Aviz · Ervedal · E802

Santa Cruz · Maxial · 115 · Olhavo · 20 · Valada · Muge · Raposa · Grande

Torres Vedras · Carvoeira · Ota · Azambuja · Reguengo · 114 · B. de Montargil · Sousel · Sto. Amaro · Vieiros

S. Pedro da Cadeira · Runa · Aldeia Gavinha · Tejo · 118 · Gloria · Montargil · B. do Maranhão · 245 · 18 · Orada

Turcifal · Alenquer · Dois Portos · Salvaterra de Magos · Lamarosa · Móra · Pavia · Estremoz

Ericeira · Gradil · Sobral de Monte Agraço · 248 · Cadafais · Benavente · Tapada · Erra · Couço · Brotas · Vimieiro · 4

Mafra · Sapataria · Arruda dos Vinhos · La Franca de Xira · Samora Correia · Coruche · Santana do Mato · Arraiolos · Borba

Carvoeira · Alcainça · Malveira · Póvoa da Galega · Bucelas · Alhandra · 10 · Quinta Grande · 245 · Evoramonte · 254

Foz do Lizandro · Magoito · Lousa · 115 · Alverca · Porto Alto · Sto. Estêvão · S. Geraldo · Arraiolos · E90 · Barragem do Divor · Ossa 698 · Aldeia da Serra · Redondo

Azenhas do Mar · Pero Pinheiro · A1 · Póvoa de Sta. Iria · 118 · Canha · Lavre · Ciborro · Sant'Ana · 18 · S. Miguel · Machede

Praia Grande · Canecas · Loures · 25 · Cortiçadas · Gafanhoeira · 114 · Valeiro · 18

Colares · 247 · Sintra · Odivelas · Sacavem · Alcochete · 45 · 10 · Taipadas · Montemor-o-Novo · 254 · Évora · Sta. Suzana · Santiago Maior

Adraga · Amadora · Moscavide · Alcochete · Montijo · Pegões Velhos · Santiago do Escoural · Montoito

Malveira · Guincho · Oeiras · LISBOA · Alhos Vedros · Pegões-Estação · 4 · Vendas Novas · S. Manços · 256 · Reguengos

Cabo Raso · Cascais · Estoril · Algés · Barreiro · Moita · Rio Frio · Cabrela · Pinhal-Novo · S. Romão · Viana Alentejo · Oriola · S. Marcos de Campo

C

Costa do Sol · Almada · Seixal · Paio Pires · Pinhal-Novo · Poceirão · Maratec · S. Cristóvão · Torre de Coelheiros · Portel

35 · Costa da Caparica · Sto. Antonio da Charneca · Palmela · 65 · Aguas de Moura · Vale de Reis · Alcáçovas · Aguiar · Monte do Trigo

Fernão Ferro · E90 · A2 · Palmela · E01 · Alvito · Vila Ruiva · 406 · Reguengos

Vila Nogueira · Setúbal · Palma · Alcácer do Sal · João de Loura · Vila Nova da Baronia · Serra Mendro · Vera Cruz · Alqueva

Alfarim · Santana · Praia de Tróia · Torrão · Barragem de Vale de Gaio · Barragem de Odivelas

Nossa Senhora do Cabo · Sesimbra · Comporta · Alcáçovas · 2 · Odivelas · Cuba · Vidigueira · E802

Cabo de Espichel · 120 · Porto de Rei · Torrão · Alvito

Baía de Setúbal · Torroal · Casa Branca · 261 · Melides · Grândola · Odivelas

1

0 5 10 20 30 40 Miles

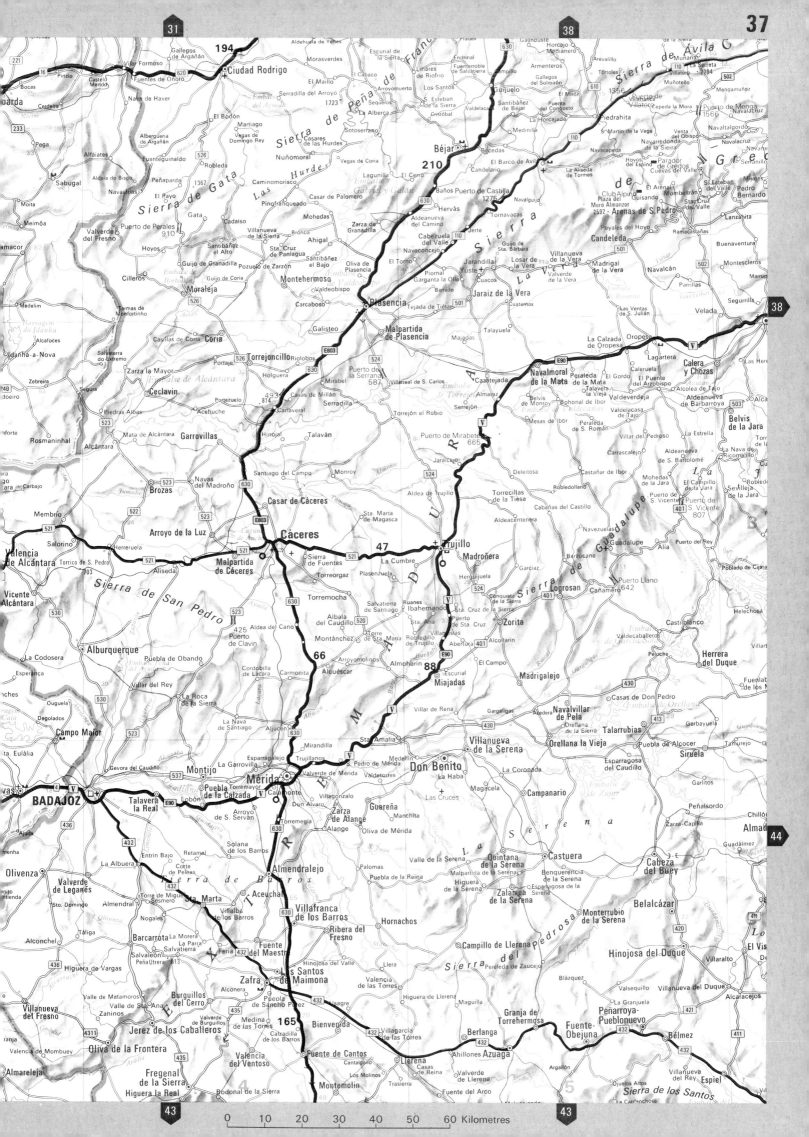

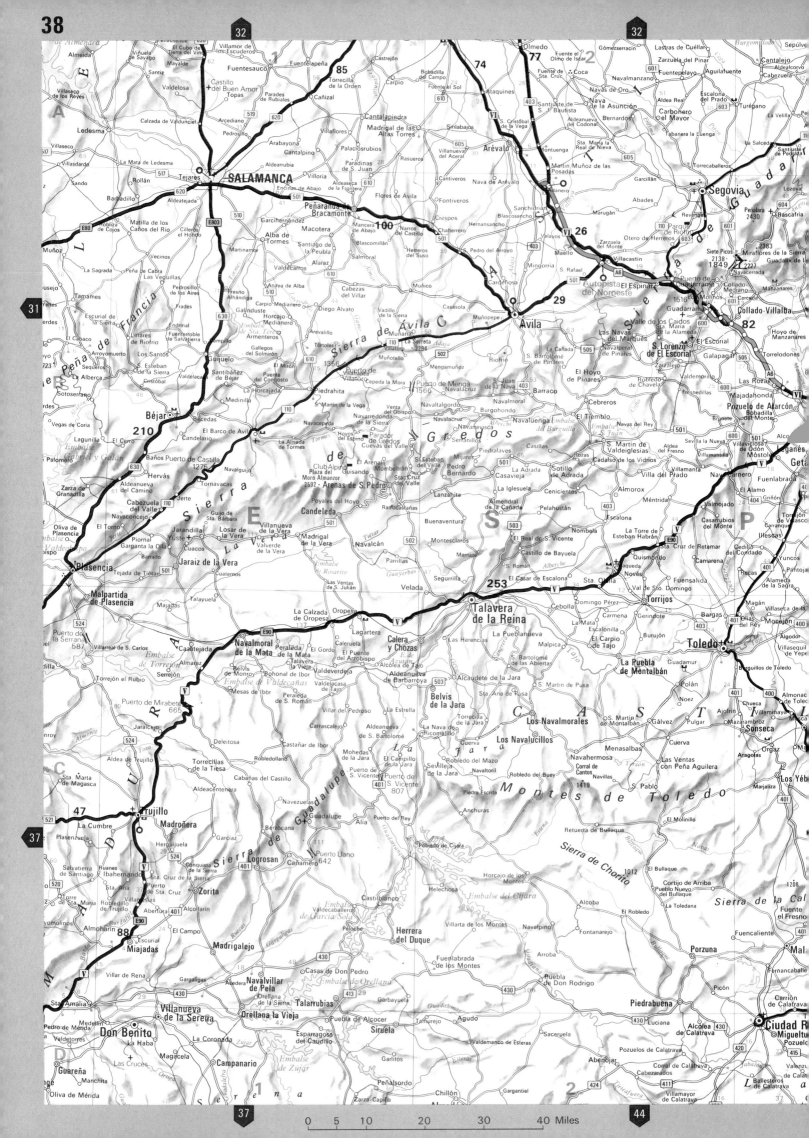

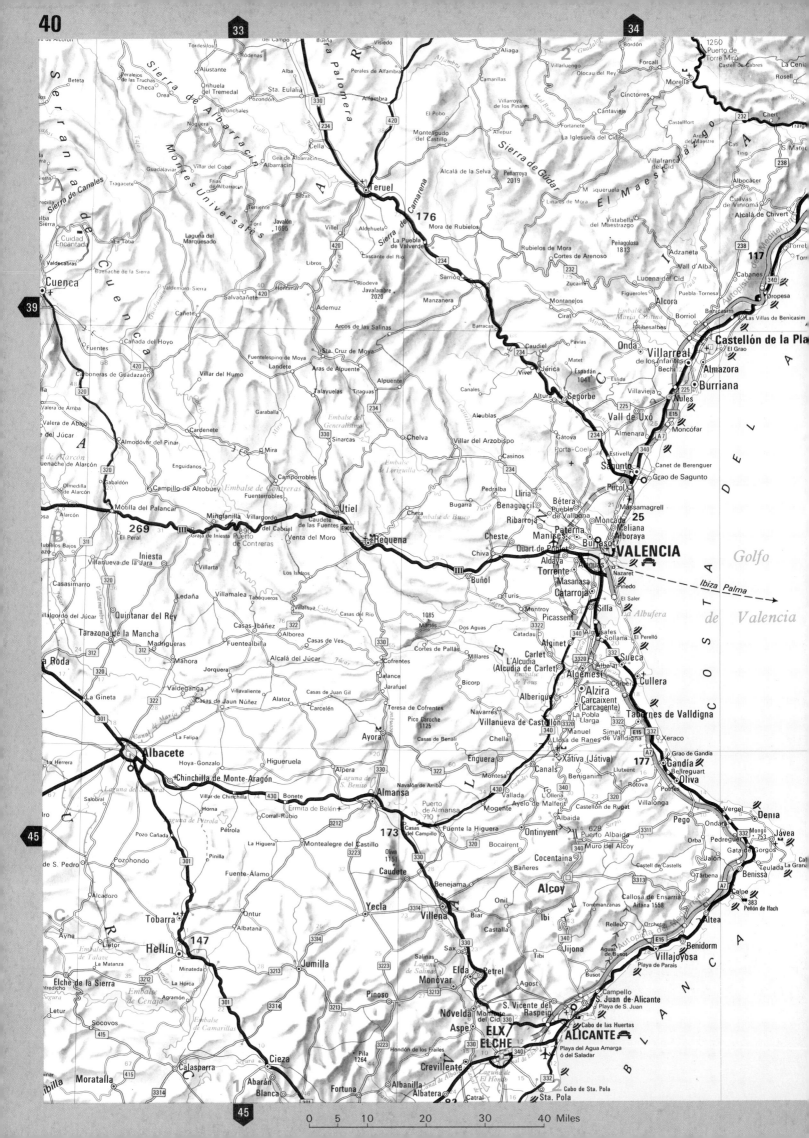

Amposta
Montsià
762
S. Carlos
de la Rápita
340
Punta de la Baña
Alcanar
Vinaros
enicarló
scola

R
A

Islas Columbretes

MENORCA

Cabo de Caballería
Punta Nati
Fornells
Arenal d'en Castell
Barcelona
Ciutadella
de Menorca (Ciudadela)
Cala Forcat
721
723
Mercadal
Toro
358
Sta. Galdana
Ferrerías
Alayor
Sant Cristófol
721
Mahón
Cabo Dartuch
Son Bou
S. Clemente
Villacarlos
S. Luis
Punta Prima
Isla de Aire
Palma

IBIZA

MALLORCA

Cabo de Formentor
Punta Beca
Puerto de Pollensa
Pollença
Cabo del Pinar
710
Alcudia
Puerto de Alcudia
Puerto de Sóller
Sa Pobla
Bahía da Alcudia
La Puebla
C'an Picafort
Cabo Farruch
Fornalutx
Selva
Deyá
Sóller
Muro
712
Morey
560
Cabo del Freu
Alaró
Lloseta
Cala Ratjada
Valldemosa
Inca
Sta. Margarita
Artá
Bañalbufar
713
Buñola
Capdepera
Estellenchs
Esporlas
Binisalem
Cabo des Piná
711
Sta. Maria
715
Son Severa
Puigpuñent
Establiments
Sineu
Petra
Cala Millor
Isla Dragonera
Galatzó
Sancellas
S. Lorenzo
Punta de Amer
1025
Montuiri
de Descardazar
Andraitx
Calviá
Manacor
S. Telmo
Algaida
715
Porto Cristo
Puerto de Andraitx
719
Monasterio
714
Cuevas del Drach
Paguera
Palma
de Cora
Porreres
Santa Ponsa
Nova
Calas de Mallorca
Magallur
PALMA
El Arenal
Felanitx
Cabo de Cala Figuera
Barcelona
Lluchmayor
San Salvador
Calas de Mallorca
Cabo Enderrocat
717
(Monasterio)
Porto Colom
Valencia
Campos del Puerto
Cala d'or
Bahía de Palma
Porto Petro
Ibiza
Ses Salines
Santany
Cabo Blanco
Colonia St. Jordi
Mahón
Cabo de Salinas

Punta d'en Serra
Punta Grosa
S. Juan Bautista
S. Miguel
Sta. Inés
409
Isla de
S. Carlos
Tagomago
a Cunillera
733
Es Caná
Sant Antoni
San Rafael
Cala Llonga
Sta. Eulalia del Rió
Port d'es Torrent
731
Cabo de Llibrell
475
Isla
Eivissa
edrá
S. José
(Ibiza)
Barcelona
Playa d'en Bossa
S. Francisco
Palma
Cabo
Llentrisca
Punta Portás
Valencia
Isla Espalmador
Isla Espardell

Formentera

La Sabina
Es Pujols
S. Fernando
S. Francisco Javier
Ntra. Sra. del Pilar
Isla Conejera
Cabo Berberia
Puerto Cabrera

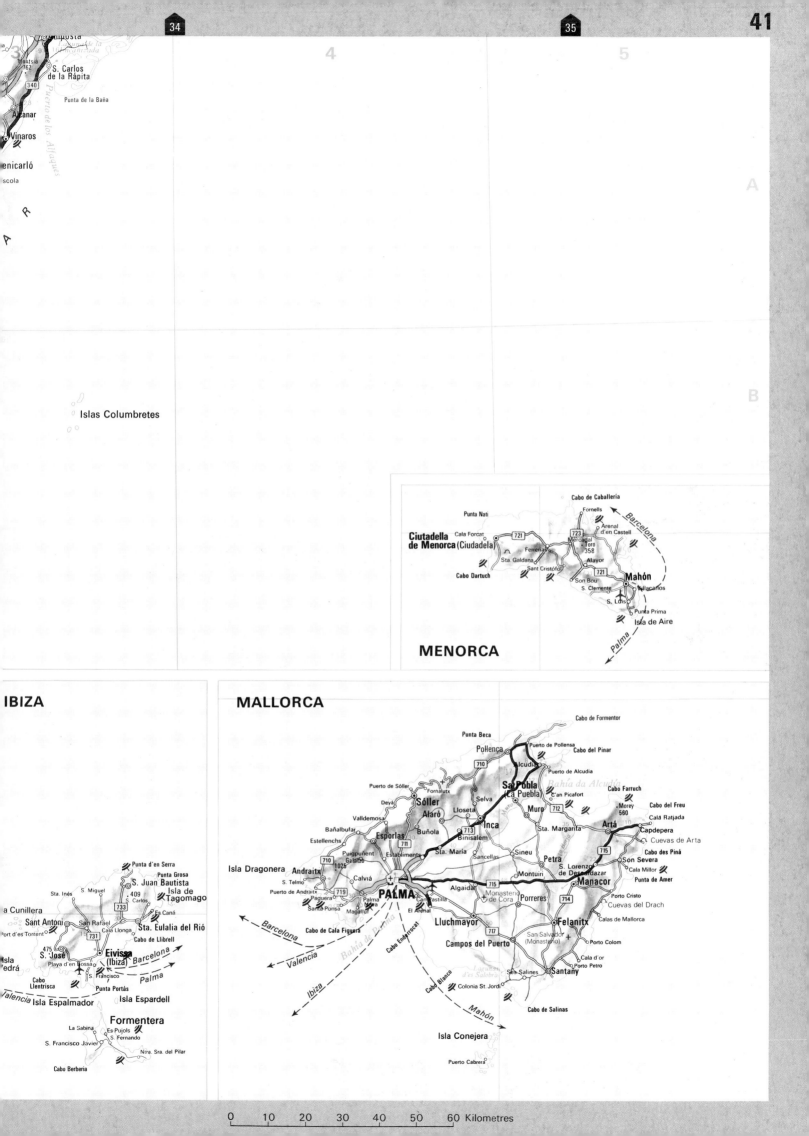

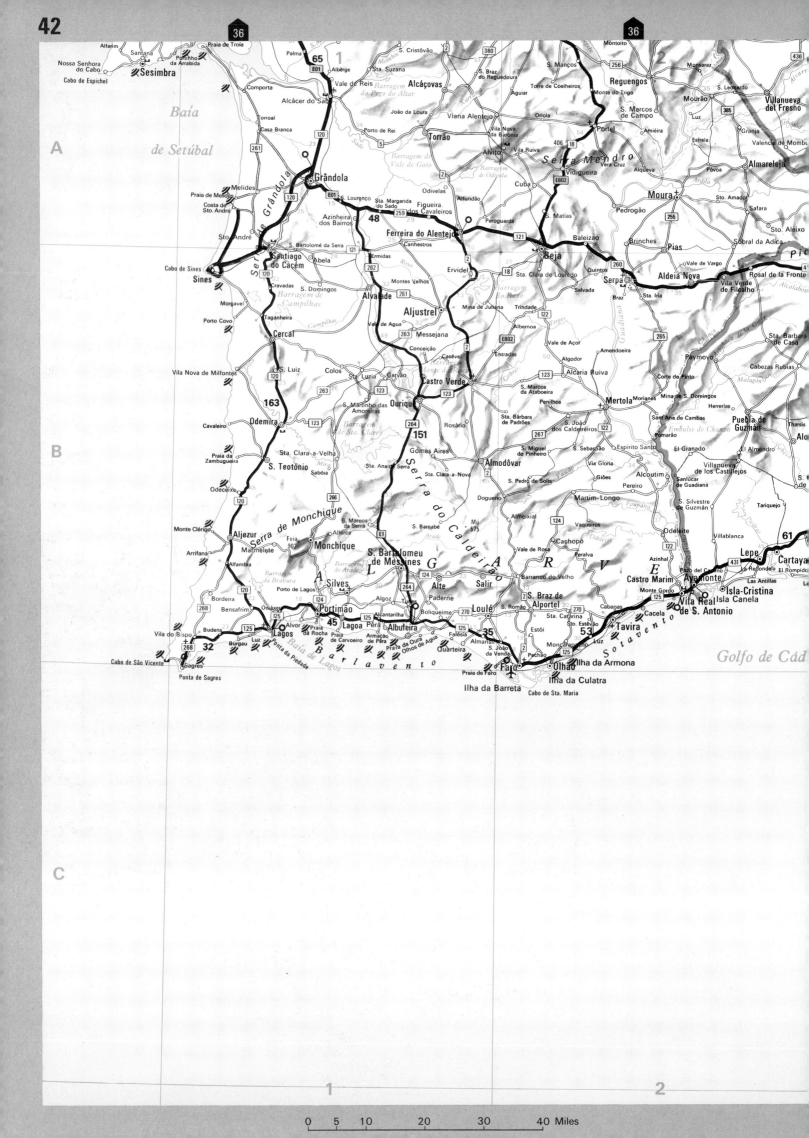

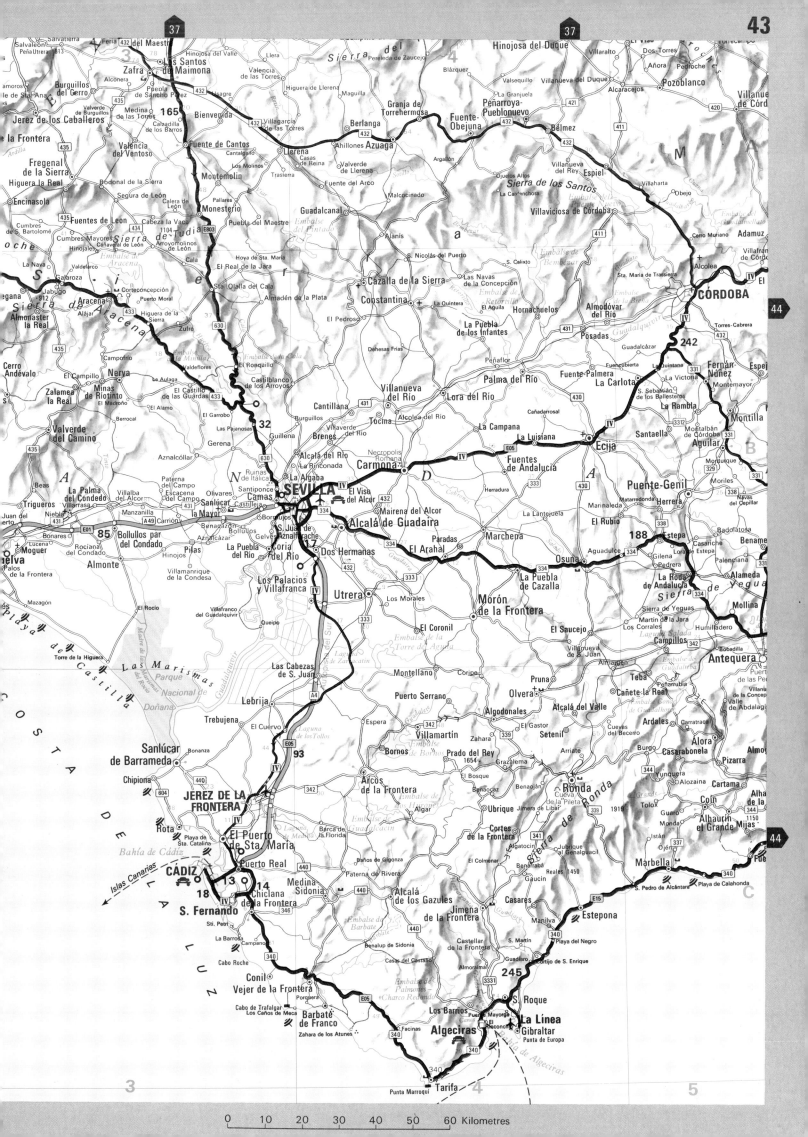

Siruela
Tarragosa
Caudillo
Garlitos
Peñalsordo
Zarza-Capilla
Almadén
Chillón
Guadálmez
Almadenejos
Alamillo
Cabeza del Buey
Belalcázar
Sta. Eufemia
Los Pedroches
El Viso
Dos-Torres
Torrecampo
Guijo
S. Benito
Valdemanco de Esteras
Sacerueia
Luciana
Alcolea de Calatrava
Ciudad Real
Miguelturra
Pozuelo de Calatrava
Almagro
La Solana
Alhambra
S. Carlos del Valle
Abenójar
Corral de Calatrava
Cabezarados
Villamayor de Calatrava
Argamasilla de Calatrava
Aldea del Rey
Calzada de Calatrava
Bolaños de Calatrava
Motel El Hidalgo
Moral de Calatrava
Granátula de Calatrava
Villaralto
Villanueva del Duque
Añora
Pedroche
Pozoblanco
Alcaracejos
Villanueva de Córdoba
Cardeña
Puertollano
Brazatortas
Cabezarrubias del Puerto
Hinojosas de Calatrava
Villanueva de S. Carlos
La Alameda
Mestanza
Solana del Pino
S. Lorenzo de Calatrava
El Hoyo
El Viso del Marqués
Valdepeñas
Sta. Cruz de Mudela
Torrenueva
Torre de Juan Abad
Castellar
Almuradiel
Las Correderas
Aldeaquemada
Venta de los Santos
Chiclana de Segura
Castellar de Santisteban
Santisteban del Puerto
Sorihuela del Guadalimar
Bélmez
Espiel
Villanueva del Rey
Villaharta
Obejo
Villaviciosa de Córdoba
Adamuz
Montoro
Marmolejo
Andújar
Villanueva de la Reina
Arjonilla
Lopera
Arjona
La Carolina
Baños de la Encina
Carboneros
Isabela
Vilches
Arquillos
Navas de S. Juan
Iznatoraf
Villacarrillo
Bailén
Guarromán
Espeluy
Jabalquinto
Linares
Ibros
Rus
Sabiote
Sto. Tomé
Torreperogil
Chilluévar
Cazorla
Ubeda
Baeza
Peal de Becerro
Quesada
Hornachuelos
Almodóvar del Río
Posadas
Calixto
Sta. María de Trassierra
Cerro Muriano
Villafranca de Córdoba
Alcolea
Pedro Abad
El Carpio
Villa del Río
Bujalance
Cañete de las Torres
Porcuna
Escañuela
Higuera de Arjona
Fuerte del Rey
Villadompardo
Mengíbar
Torreblascopedro
Lupión
Begíjar
Jimena
Bedmar
Albanchez de Ubeda
Jódar
Larva
Huesa
Cabra del Sto. Cristo
Pozo Alcón
Córdoba
Torres-Cabrera
Guadalcázar
Fuencubierta
La Quintana
Fernán-Núñez
Espejo
Castro del Río
Valenzuela
Santiago de Calatrava
Martos
Torredonjimeno
Jamilena
Torre del Campo
Jaén
La Guardia de Jaén
Mancha Real
Pegalajar
Cambil
Huelma
Sierra de Magina
Cabra del Sto. Cristo
Alicún de Ortega
Dehesas de Guadix
Fuente Palmera
La Carlota
La Victoria
Montemayor
Montalbán de Córdoba
La Rambla
S. Sebastián de los Ballesteros
Santaella
Ecija
Luisiana
Aguilar
Nueva-Carteya
Doña Mencia
Baena
Luque
Zuheros
Fuente-Tójar
Alcaudete
Los Villares
Fuensanta de Martos
Valdepeñas de Jaén
Noalejo
Campillo de Arenas
Carchelejo
Arbuniel
Montillana
Frailes
Cambil
Guadahortuna
Torre-Cardela
Domingo Pérez
Piñar
Moreda
Gorafe
Benalúa de Guadix
Puente-Genil
Herrera
Marinaleda
Matarredonda
Moriles
Montilla
Cabra
Lucena
Carcabuey
Zambra
Priego de Córdoba
Alcalá la Real
Almedinilla
Castillo de Locubín
La Rábita
Montefrío
Benalúa de las Villas
Dehesas Viejas
Puerto de Zegrí
Colomera
Bogarre
Iznalloz
Huélago
Fonelas
Darro
Diezma
Guadix
El Rubio
Estepa
Aguadulce
Gilena
Pedrera
Lora de Estepa
Casariche
Badolatosa
Benamejí
Encinas Reales
Algarinejo
Iznájar
Villanueva de Tapia
Fuente del Conde
Cuevas de S. Marcos
Huétor-Tájar
Loja
Villanueva de las Torres
Pinos Puente
Deifontes
Cogollos Vega
Moclín
Illora
Albolote
Maracena
Atarfe
Granada
Osuna
Puebla de Cazalla
El Saucejo
Villanueva de S. Juan
Almargen
Campillos
La Roda de Andalucía
Sierra de Yeguas
Martín de la Jara
Los Corrales
Laguna Salada
Humilladero
Mollina
Alameda
Cuevas Bajas
Rincona
Pedroso
Salar
Moraleda de Zafayona
Chauchina
Santa Fé
Chimeneas
Gabia la Grande
Alhendín
Zubia
Ogíjares
Cájar
Antequera
Bobadilla
Archidona
Villanueva del Trabuco
Villanueva del Rosario
Puerto de los Alazores
Sta. Cruz de Alhama
Ventas de Huelma
Agrón
Cacín
Alhama de Granada
Zafarraya
Arenas del Rey
Jayena
Játar
Fornes
Ventas de Zafarraya
Dúrcal
Padul
Pico Veleta
Mulhacén
Sierra Nevada
Ronda
Teba
Cañete la Real
Alcalá del Valle
Setenil
Arriate
Ardales
Carratraca
Cuevas del Becerro
Peñarrubia
Álora
Casarabonela
Pizarra
Almogía
Cártama
Coín
Alhaurín de la Torre
Alhaurín el Grande
Mijas
Málaga
Rincón de la Victoria
Torre del Mar
Vélez-Málaga
Torrox
Nerja
Almuñécar
Salobreña
Motril
Calahonda
Castell de Ferro
Adra
Albondón
Albuñol
Órgiva
Lanjarón
Pampaneira
Trevélez
Bérchules
Cádiar
Ugijar
Yegen
Válor
Las Alpujarras
Torvizcón
Murtas
Marbella
S. Pedro de Alcántara
Fuengirola
Torremolinos
Benalmádena
Playa de Sta. Amalia
Punta de Calaburras
Playa de Calahonda
Jubrique
Genalguacil
Istán
Ojén
Monda
Guaro
Tolox
Alozaina
Yunquera
Cuevas de la Pileta
Arenas de Ronda
Melilla
COSTA DEL SOL

171
242
139
188
105
109
73

0   5   10   20   30   40 Miles

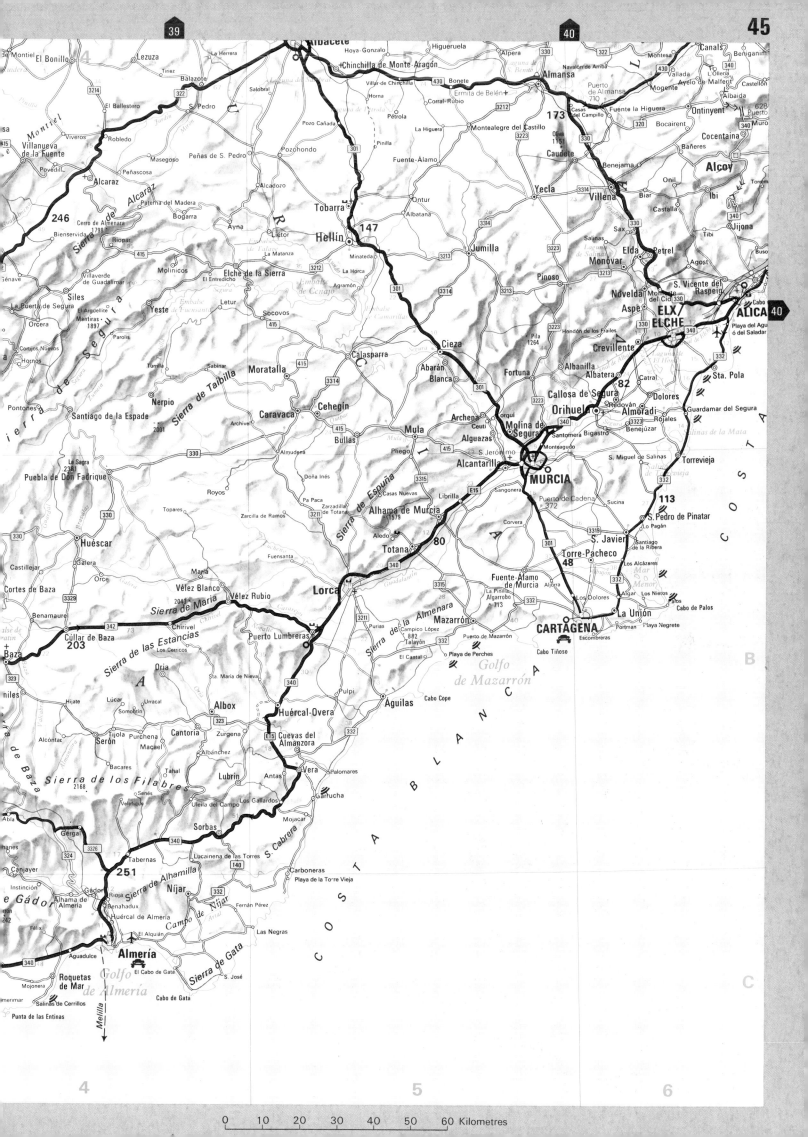

7 8 9 10 11 12 13 14 15 6 Vesterålen

Andøya

A

Nordkapp

B

Honningsvåg

Søröya Hammerfest Sortland F
Kvalsund Porsangen Sigerfjord Hinnöya
Lopphavet Kistrand Ifjord Tananes Risøya
Ringvassöy Alteidet Rustefjelbma Vardö Svolvær
Tromsö Talvik Alta Lakselv Börselv Utsjoki Kiberg F Stamsund Innhavet
Kvalöy Nordreisa Olderdalen Kautokeino Karasjok Kaamanen Nyrud Lofoten Vestfjorden
Lyngseidet Kvænangsbotn Karigasniemi Inari Virtaniemi Röosvik
Senja Skibotn Kaamanen Bodø Fauske
Storfjord Inari Ivalo Lotta Saltfjorden Sulitjelma
Harstad Kilpisjärvi Jitto Nyrud Rognan
Setermoen Kaaresuvanto Hestmona Ölfjellet 494
Gratangen Bjerkvik Kvænangen Enontekiö 1754
Hinnöya Narvik Karesuando 1599
Sigerfjord Ankenes Palojoensuu Svartisen
Bognes Björkåsen Abisko Vuotso Dönna Mo i Rana
Lapland Muonio Portipahdan Lokan Sandnessjöen Overuman
Torneträsk Kiruna tekojärvi tekojärvi Norra Storfjället
Mösjöen Brurskanken Tärna
1443 Rössvatnet
Vega Trofors Svenningdal Gardiken Storuma
Brönnöysund Majavatn Kvigtind Marsfjället
1703 Kultsjön
NORSKEHAVET Leka 396 Limingen Malgomaj
Vikna Rörvik Tunnsjöen Stora Dragan
Foldfjorden Namsos Grong Nordli Gäddede Blåsjön Volgs
Formofoss Mortenslund
Fröya Namdalseid Snåsavatnet Hotagen
Hitra Follafoss Steinkjer Torröjen Strömsund
Smöla Afjord Röra Landösjön Faxälv
Trondheimsleia Rissa Verdalsöra Sandvika Kallsjön Hammerdal
Tustna Trondheim Levanger Duved Åre Jarpen Krokom Lit Ammerån
Kristiansund Örkanger Stjordals 105 Storlien Morsil Nälden 194 Östersund
Averöya Straumsnes Melhus 75 Enafors Hålland Ytterön Frösö Brunflo
Tingvoll Vinje Lökken Stören Nea Helagsfjället Ånnsjön Storsjön Gällö Bispg
Molde Sunndalsöra Trollheimen Ulsberg Gaula Haltdalen 270 1796 Näcken Bräcke
Andalsnes Blåhö Oppdal Kvikne Röros 1762 Funäsdalen Asarna 192 Ange Ljung
Ålesund 1672 Sylene Fjällnäs Hede Alby
Sjöholt Orsta Stranda Valldal Drivaa 200 Glomma Sörvika Tännäs Klövsjö Ostavall Mellansjö
Storfjorden Volda Geiranger Lesjaskog Snöhetta 2302 Sänfjället Råtan Överhogdal
Hellesylt Grotli Dovre- Folldal Femund Sveg Kårböle Ytterhogdal
Nordfjordeid Stryn 69 Fjell Tynset Idre Järvsö
Bremangerlandet Måloy Loen Dovre Dombås Alvdal Engerdal Särna Ramsjö
Nordfjord Sandane Videsetel Lom Rondane Otnes Storsjön Voxna
Eikefjord Olden Böverdal 2453 Vagavatn Otta Koppang Ljusnan
Floro Breim Jostedalsbreen 2079 Glittertind Ringebu Färila Arb
Naustdal Skjolden Galdhöpiggen 2468 162 Innbygda Edsbyn
Forde Jotunheimen Vinstra Harpefoss 559 Rena Rot Alvdalen Voxna Alftä
Sula Vik Marifjöra Bygdin 557 Lomen Stor-Elvdal Ossjön Furudal
Vadheim Höyanger Sogndalsfjöra Bygdin Tretten Åmot Orsa Farnäs Amunger
Sognefjorden Leikanger Kaupanger Tyin Lena Lillehammer Elverum Siljan Rättvik
Lærdalsöyri Borlaug 149 Fagernes Brumunddal Malungsfors Leksand Falun
Gudvangen Hemsedal Gol Dokka Gjövik Hamar Mora Tällberg Borlänge
Stalheim 68 Ål 503 Nesbyen 192 Stange Flisa Malung Vansbro Djurås 291
Bulken Voss Hardangerjökulen Geilo Flå Mjösa Asnes Norra Ny Gräsberg
Bergen Granvin 1876 Haugastöl Brandbu Kongsvinger Ludvika
Arna Ulvik Eidfjord Fla Eidsvoll Torsby Hagfors Filipstad Avesta
Nesttun Norheim- Ustaoset 173 Skarnes Charlottenberg Fagersta
Strandebarm sund 47 Röonefoss Jevnaker Eidsvoll Gunne
Osöyra Lofthus Hardangervidda Kongsberg OSLO Lillström Arvika Filipstad
Stord 58 Tyssedal Mösvatn Tyrifjorden Öyeren Halleforss Karlstad 118
Leirvik Odda Låtefoss Rjukan 200 Drammen Askim Mysen Karlskoga Örebro
Bömlo Seljestad Röldal 1628 Hokksund Oslofjorden Charlottenberg Degerfors
Haugesund Etne Haukeliseter Rauland 1883 Notodden Moss Tönsberg Sarpsborg Årjäng Kristinehamn Saffle
Köpervik Sand Totak Grungedal Bölkesjö Holmestrand Åmål
Skudeneshavn Suldalsvatn Seljord Kongsberg Horten Fredrikstad 241
Stavanger Bykle Dalen Brunkeberg Skien 114 Rakkestad 143 Kristinehamn
Jörpeland Hylestad Valle Ulefoss Larvik Halden

Lerwick Newcastle Hantsholm

0 20 40 60 80 100 120 140 160 Miles

Setermoen
Kilpisjärvi
litto
Kautokeino
Kaaresuvanto
Enontekiö
Karesuando
Palojœnsuu
Ivalo
Vuotso
Abisko
Torneträsk
Lapland
Muonio
Portipahdan tekojärvi
Lokan tekojärvi
Monchegorsk
Apatity
Kiruna
Vittangi
Torneälven
Kittilä
Kiitinen
Kemijoki
Kandalaksha
Kandalakshskiy Zaliv
Svappavaara
Kolari
Sodankylä
Stora Sjöfallets
Stora Lulevatten
Pajala
Kemijärvi
Kelloselka
Salla
Beloye More
Malmberget
Gällivare
Hakkas
Pello
Joutsijärvi
Porjus
Harsprånget
Övertorneå
Rovaniemi
Aavasaksa
Perä-Posio
Posio
Ylikitka
Kuusamo
Jokkmokk
Överkalix
131
Kemijoki
Top-ozero
Kåbdalis
Edefors Harads
Morjärv
Töre
Tornio
Tervola
Ranua
Iinijärvi
Peranka
Murtovaara
Pya-ozero
Arjeplog
Boden
Kalix
Kemi
Simo
Iijoki
Taivalkoski
Pudasjärvi
501
Ukhta
Byske älv
Älvsbyn
Haparanda
27
135
108
Pudasjärvi
267
Kiantajärvi
Suomussalmi
Luleå
269
68
Ojebyn
Piteå
Haukipudas
Kiiminki
Rugozero
Byske
88
Hailuoto
Oulu
Liminka
Puolanka
Hyrynsalmi
Ristijärvi
Luvozero
Perämeri Bottenviken
Kåge
Skellefteå
Skellefteham
Pyhäjoki
Vihanti
Raahe
Rantsila
Paltamo
Leks Ozero
Bureå
Oulainen
Pulkkila
Piippola
Oulujärvi
Kajaani
Sotkamo
Kuhmo
Reboly
Lycksele
Orträsk
141
Norsjö
Bastuträsk
Himanka
Kalajoki
132
94
22
Pyhänta
123
87
18
Gränön
Vindeln
Ylivieska
Nivala
Karsämäki
19
Salahmi
170
Valtimo
Nurmes
Lieksa
Fredrika
Bjurholm
79
Vannäsby
Vännäs
Umeå
326
66
113
Pyhäjärvi
294
Iisalmi
Juuka
Koli
Pielinen
Kottere
Gideälven
122
Nordmaling
76
Jakobstad (Pietarsaari)
Kaustinen
346
Pihtipudas
Viitasaari
Siilinjärvi
Lapinlahti
83
Vuotjärvi
Juurusvesi
Viinijärvi
Outokumpu
Ilomantsi
Husum
Örnsköldvik
293
171
Nyland
Uusikaarlepyy (Nykarleby)
Perho
Keitele
Kuopio
Kallavesi
74
Tuusniemi
123
Vyartsilya
Vaasa (Vasa)
Storjärv
Laihia
Lapua
16
Alajärvi
Kyyjärvi
Könnevesi
Rautalampi
Suonenjoki
Suvasvesi
Tuovjärvi
Joensuu
Pyhäselkä
Ilmajoki
Seinäjoki
Alavus
Aänekoski
Suolahti
80 9
Varkaus
Orivesi
Haukivesi
Koskenkorva
Kurikka
Jalasjärvi
Virrat
239
Jyväskylä
Leppävirta
23
Savonlinna
Sortavala
Närpes (Närpiö)
Kristinestad (Kristiinankaupunki)
79 3
196
Parkano
Ruovesi
Muurame
Mänttä
Jämsä
13
Pieksämäki
Juurikoski
87
Juva
Puruvesi
6
Salmi
Kankaanpää
Nasijärvi
Ikaalinen
Orivesi
Päijänne
Joutsa
Puulavesi
Mikkeli
391
Pihlajavesi
Saimaa
Parikkala
Noormarkku
118
Ylöjärvi
Hämeenkyrö
Tampere
Kuhmoinen
Hartola
Khitola
Priozersk
Ladozhskoye Ozero
Pori
Kokemäenjoki
Nokia
Vammala
80 9
164
Heinola
127
Savitaipale
Imatra
Joutseno
Lauritsala
Lavia
Kankaanpää
Padasjoki
Vesijärvi
Lappeenranta
Rauma
65 2
Kauttua
Toijala
Parola
Lahti
15
Taavetti
87
Vyborg
Selkämeri Bottenhavet
165
187
12
Kuusankoski
6
8 141
Loimaa
236
Forssa
Riihimäki
Hämeenlinna
Mantsala
87
Myllykoski
Hamina
149
Uusikaupunki
Laitila
120
Aura
Somero
Hyvinkää
103
Karhula
Kotka
Primorsk
Zelengorsk
Turku (Abo)
52
167
Salo
Lohja
115
Järvenpää
Kerava
Lovisa (Lovisa)
Borgå (Porvoo)
50
Leningrad
Petrokrepost
Pargas (Parainen)
Pernio
Karis
Karjaa
Helsinki (Helsingfors)
Lomonosov
Åland (Ahvenanmaa)
Mariehamn (Maarianhamina)
Ekenäs (Tammisaari)
Hango (Hanko)
Finskaviken
Narva
Kuressaare (Kingisepp)
Chudovo
Gräsö
Osthammar
Suomenlahti
Gatchina
Tierp
Alvkarleby
Skarplinge
Stockholm Lubeck
Gdańsk
Tallinn
Paldiski
20 11
Rakvere
Kohtla-Järve
Slantsy
Luga
Novgorod
Uppsala
Norrtälje
Kappelskär
Haapsalu
Plyussy
Sundbyberg
Helsinki Tallinn
Chudskoye
HOLM

Pohjanlahti
Bottniska Viken
Selkämeri Bottenhavet
Pohjanlahti

0 20 40 60 80 100 140 180 220 260 Kilometres
53
93

46

46

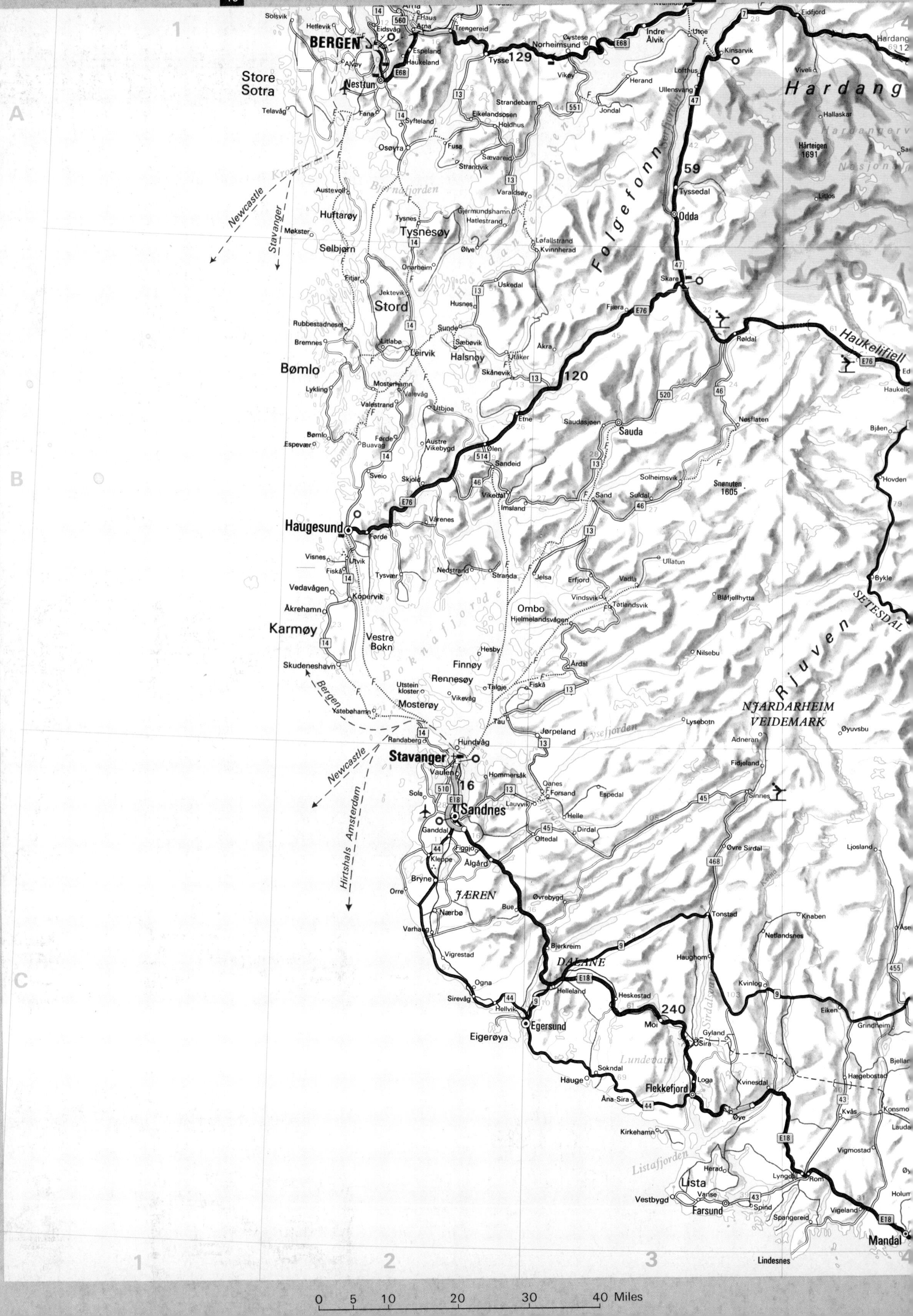

Solsvik
Hellvik
14
Haus
560
Arna
Trengereid
Øystese
Norheimsund
E68
Indre Ålvik
Utøe
Eidfjord
7 28
Hardang
6912

BERGEN
Espeland
Haukeland
Tysse 129
Vikøy
Herand
Ullensvang
Lofthus
Kinsarvik
Viveli

E68
Nesttun
Ålvøy

Store
Sotra
Telavåg
Fana
14
Syfteland
Holdhus
Strandebarm
551
Jondal
47
Hallaskar
Hardang
Hårteigen
1691
Nasjona

Osøyra
Fusa
13
Sævareid
Strandvik

Austevoll
13
Varaldsøy
Løfallstrand
Kvinnherad
Folgefonn
59
Tyssedal
Litlos

Møkster
Huftarøy
Tysnes
Gjermundshamn
Hatlestrand
Ølve
Onarheim
Odda

Selbjørn
Fitjar
14
Tysnesøy
Uskedal
Fjæra
E76
Skare
47

Jektevik
Husnes
Akra
Røldal
Haukelifjell
E76
Ed

Stord
Sunde
Sæbøvik
Skånevik
13
120
Nesflaten
520
46
24
Haukeli

Rubbestadneset
14
Litlabø
Leirvik
Halsnøy
Utåker
Etne
Saudasjøen
Sauda
Bjåen

Bremnes
Bømlo
Mosterhamn
Valevåg
Utbjoa
514
Ølen
Sandeid
13
Solheimsvik
Snønuten
1605
Hovden
79

Lykling
Valestrand
Austre
Vikebygd
13
Sand
Suldal
46
27

Espevær
Bømlo
Førde
Buavåg
14
Skjold
46
Vikedal
Imsland
27
46

Sveio
E76
Varanes
Nedstrand
Stranda
Jelsa
Erfjord
Vadla
Nilsebu
Blåfjellhytta
Bykle
Setesdal

Haugesund
Førde
Tysvær
Ullatun

Visnes
Fiskå
Utvik
14
Tysvær
Ombo
Hjelmelandsvågen
Hesby
Årdal
Vindsvik
Tøtlandsvik

Vedavågen
Køpervik
Finnøy
Talgje
Fiskå
Riuven

Åkrehamn
Karmøy
14
Vestre
Bokn
Rennesøy
Vikevåg
13
Njardarheim
Veidemark
Øyuvsbu

Skudeneshavn
Utstein
kloster
Mosterøy
Tau
Lysebotn
Adneran

Ystebøhamn
14
Randaberg
Hundvåg
Jørpeland
Lysefjorden
Fidjeland

Stavanger
Vaulen
16
Hommersåk
Sola
510
E18
13
Oanes
Forsand
Espedal
45
Sinnes

Sandnes
Lauvvik
Helle
Dirdal
Øvre Sirdal
Ljosland

Ganddal
44
Figgjo
Ålgård
45
Øltedal
468

Kleppe
Orre
Bryne
Jæren
Bue
Øvrebygd
Tonstad
Knaben
Netlandsnes
455

Nærbø
Varhaug
Øvrebygd
Bjerkreim
9
Haughom
Kvinlog
9
Eiken
Grindhei

Vigrestad
Dalane
E18
Helleland
Heskestad
240
Moi
103

Ogna
44
Hellvik
Egersund
9
61
Gyland
Sira

Sirevåg
Eigerøya
Lundevatn
69

Hauge
Sokndal
Flekkefjord
Loga
Kvinesdal
Hægebost
43

Kirkehamn
Åna-Sira
44
Øye
Kvås
Konsmo

Listafjorden
E18
Vigmostad

Lista
Herad
Lyngdal
Rom
Lauda

Vestbygd
Varnes
43
Spind
Vigeland
Holm

Farsund
Spangereid
E18

Mandal

Lindesnes

0 5 10   20   30   40 Miles

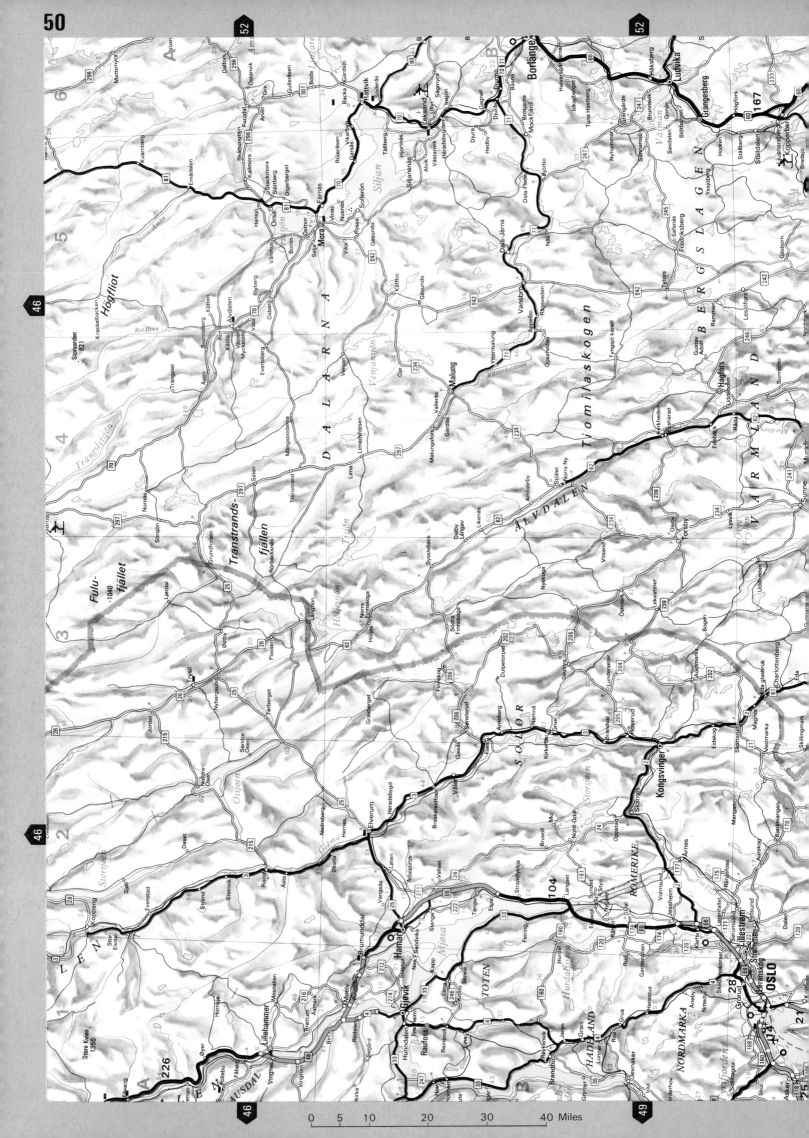

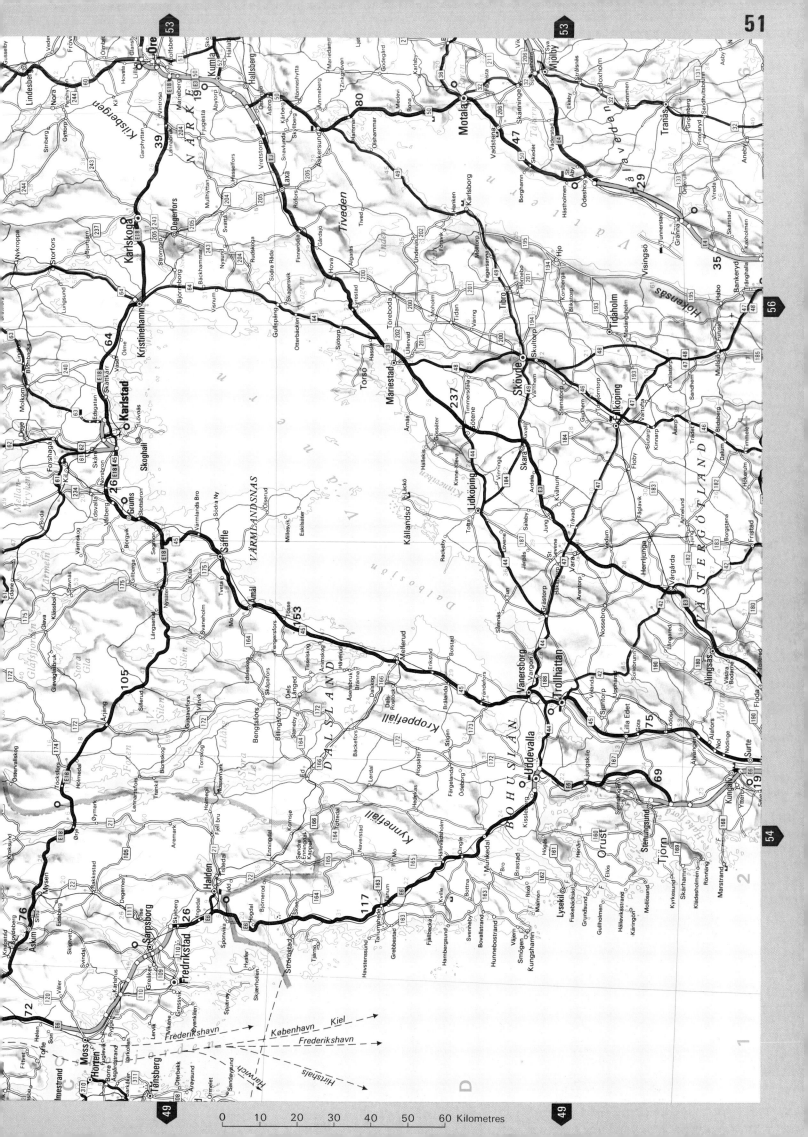

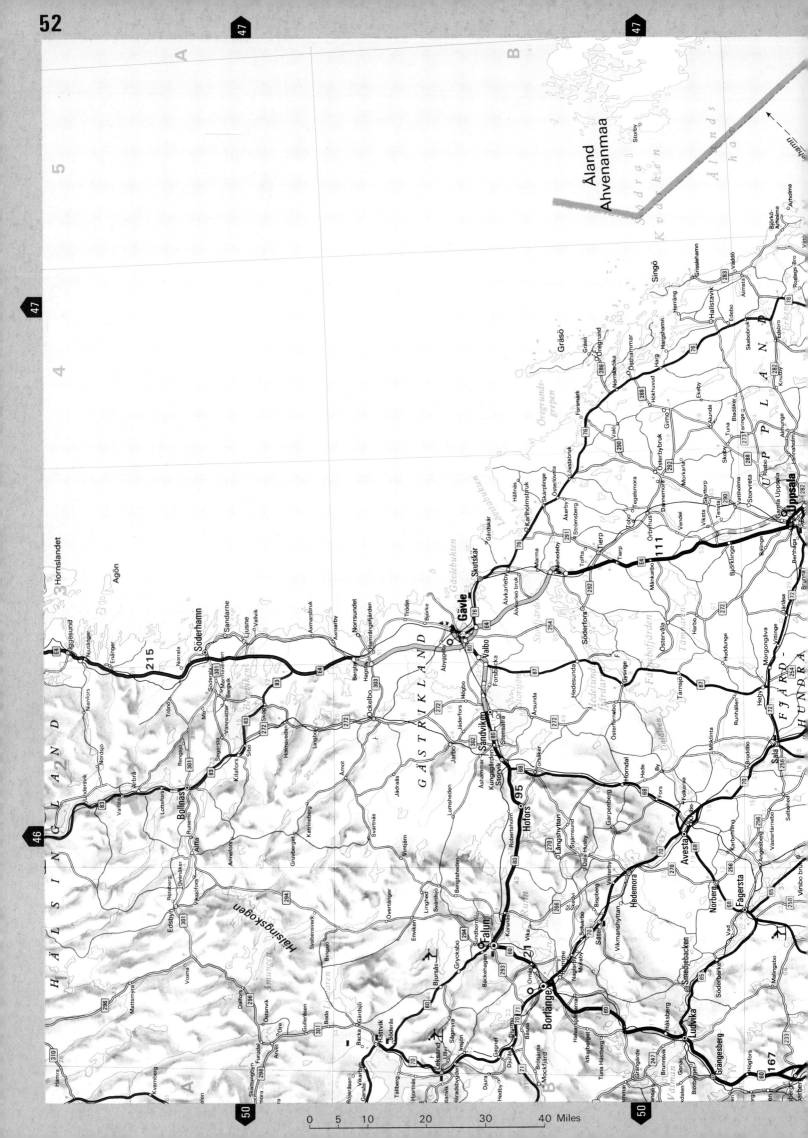

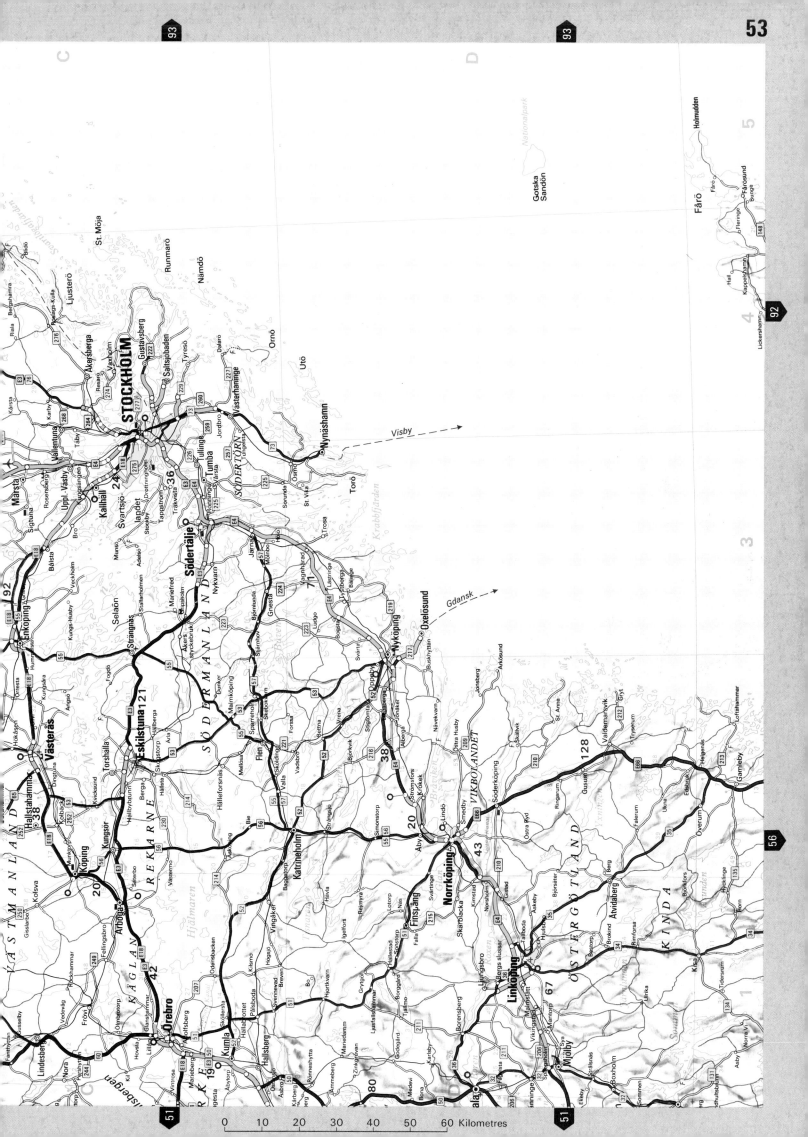

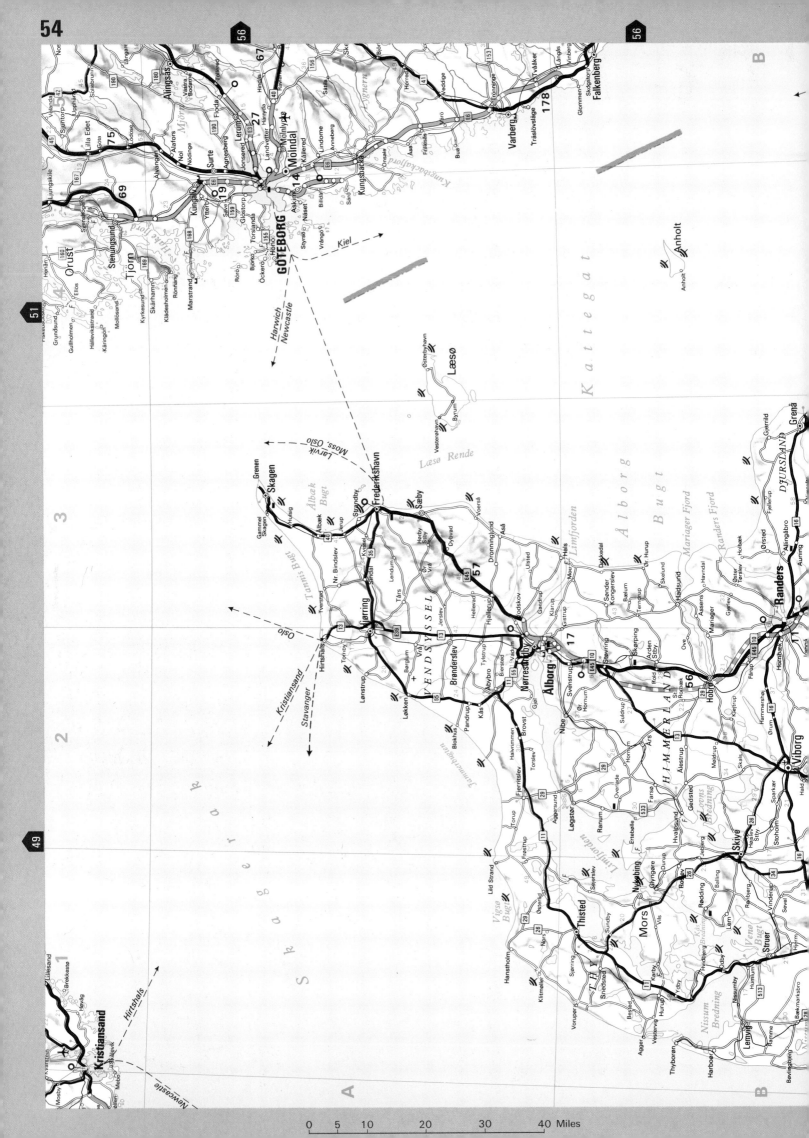

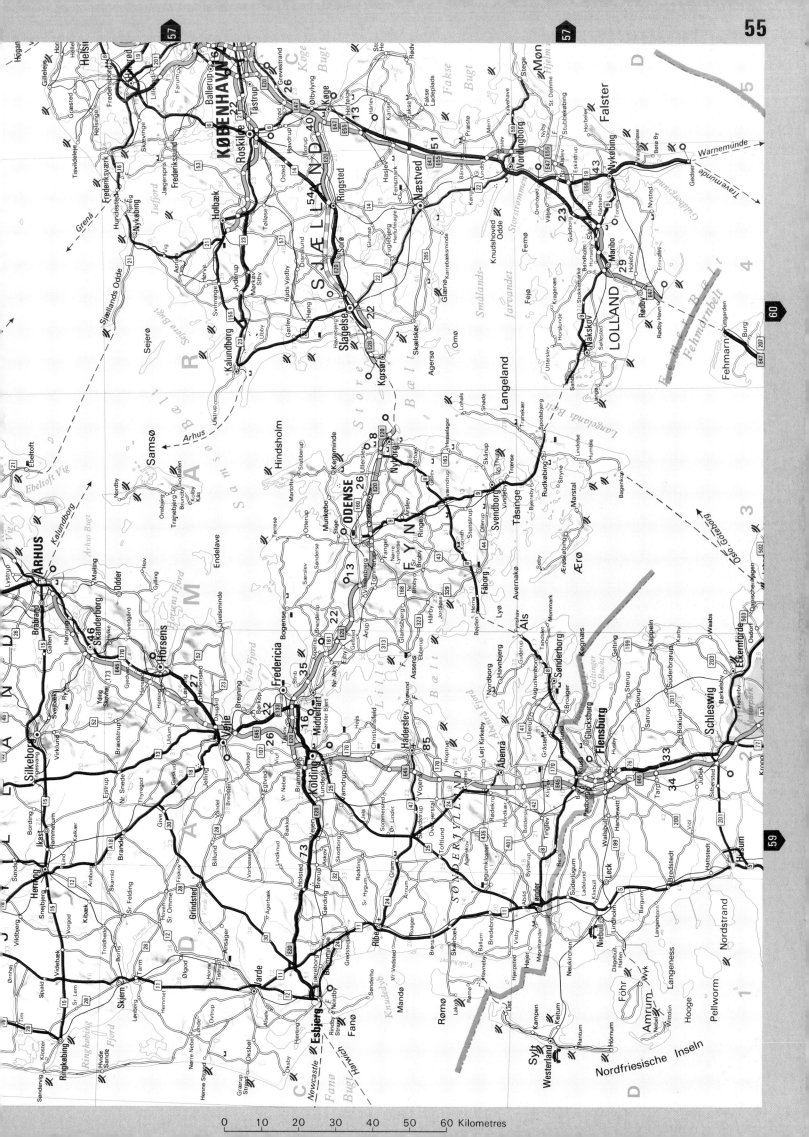

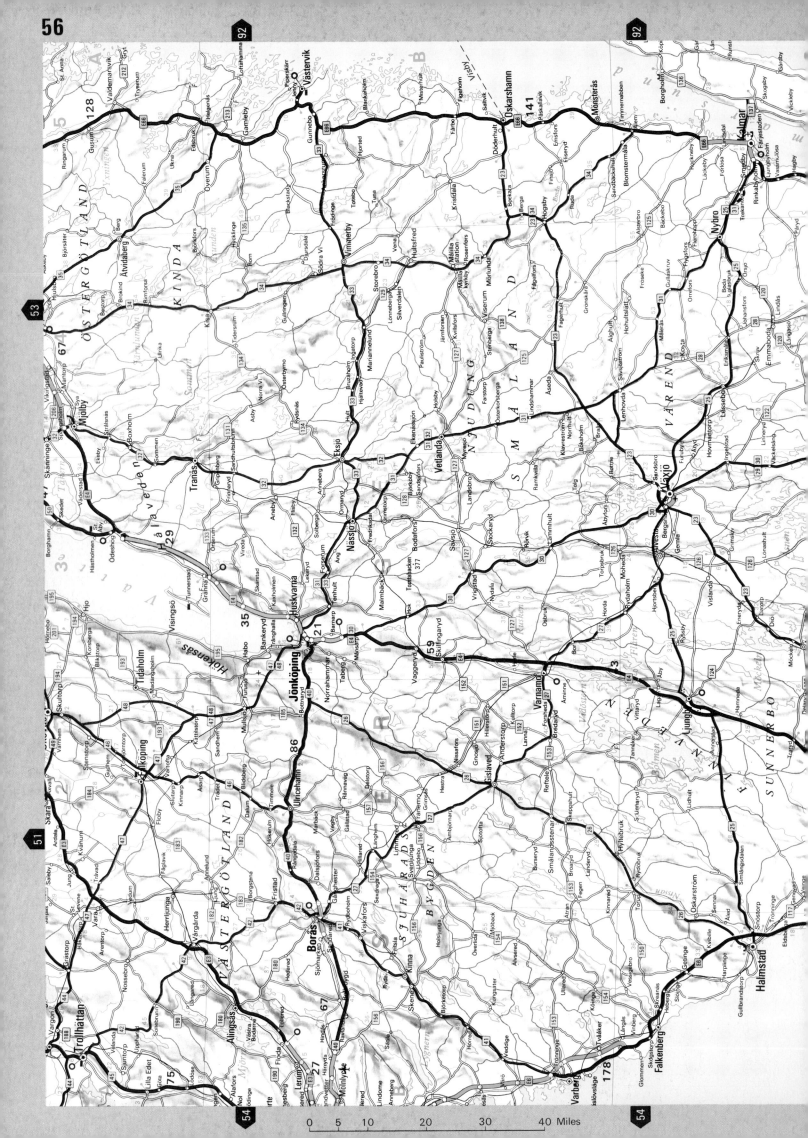

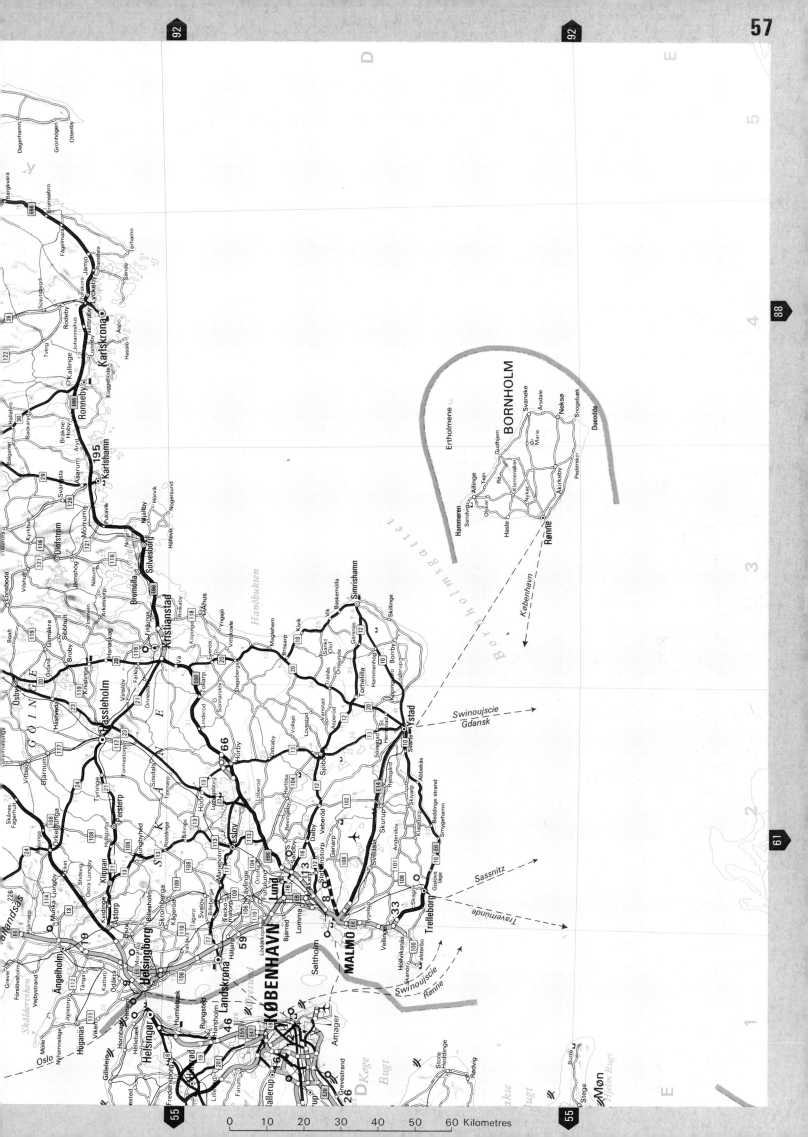

D

E

5

4

88

3

61

2

E

1

BORNHOLM

Ertholmene

Hammeren
Sandvig
Allinge
Tejn
Rø
Gudhjem
Svaneke
Ø.
Marie
Arsdale
Nekso
Snogebæk
Klemensker
Dueodde
Nyker
Åkirkeby
Pedersker
Olsker

Hasle

Rønne

Helsingør

Køge Bugt

Møn

Swinoujscie
Gdansk

Sassnitz

Travemünde

København

Swinoujscie
Rønne

0   10   20   30   40   50   60 Kilometres

1   2   3

A

B

C

Nationalpark Nieder...

Norderney
Juist   Juist   Nessm
Memmert   Norddeich
Borkum   Norddeich   Norden
70

Schiermonnikoog   Eemshaven   Pewsum Loppersum
Ameland   Eemshaven   Uithuizermeeden
Nes   Warffum Uithuizen   Spijk   Emden
Terschelling   Hollum   F   Metslawier   Ulrum Leens   Baflo Usquert   N46   70
Oosterend   Holwerd   Dokkum   Ee Zoutkamp   Middelstum   Delfzijl   Ditzum
West   Ferwerd   Murmerwoude   Noordhorn   Loppersum Bedum   Appingedam   Dollard
Terschelling   Marrum   Veenwouden   Grijpskerk   43   N363 N361   Ten   N362   Nieuwolda
F   St. Annaparochie   Berlikum   Zwaagwesteinde   Buitenpost   N355   Zuidhorn Boer   Siddeburen   N33   Finsterwolde   Nieuwe-
Vlieland   St. Jacobiparochie   Leeuwarden   95   Groningen   Schildwolde   Schans
Oost-   Sexbierum   Dronrijp   Hardegarijp Nd Bergum   Hoogkerk   Haren   Foxhol   Hoogezand   147 Winschoten
Vlieland   Franeker   Winsum   Bergum Garijp   Grootegast Surhuisterveen   38   Leek Paterswolde   Sappemeer   N7   Oude-Pekela
Harlingen   N31   Warga   Opeinde   E22   59   Roden   26   Zuidlaren   Veendam   Nieuwe-Pekela
Texel   N31   Witmarsum   N354 N32   Drachten   A7   Norg   N372   Wildervank   Onstwedde
Makkum   Bolsward   Grouw   Oldeboorn   Beetsterzwaag   Haulerwijk   N28 N34   N33   Vlagtwedde
Den Burg   E22   36 Sneek   Akkrum   Tijnje   Gorredijk   Oosterwolde   Assen   Gieten   42   Stadskanaal
Workum   IJlst   Oppenhuizen   Joure   Heerenveen   Oldeberkoop   Smilde   Borger   N366   Musselkanaal
Den Helder   43   Woudsend   N354   Oudehaske   Noordwolde   Ter Apelkanaal   Walchum   Ter
Hippolytushoef   Koudum   St. Nicolaasga   Wolvega   Vledder   Beilen   Westerbork   Apel
Breezand   N99   Balk   Noordwolde   Djever   N371   E28   N4   Nw-Buinen   N31
N9   N249   Staveren   Oudemirdum   Lemmer   A50   Kuinre   E232   51   Weerdinge
Schagen   A7   IJsselmeer   Rutten   56   Steenwijk   Havelte   Ruinen   Hoogeveen   Emmer-
Nwe Niedorp   E22   Medemblik   A50   Noordoost-   N32   Giethoorn   Compascuum
Nd Scharwoude   N242   Andijk   Polder   Blokzijl   N333 N334   De   Erfscheidenveen
Broek op Langendijk   32   Opmeer Grootebroek   Emmeloord   N331   Marknesse   Wijk Zuidwolde   Emmen   Klazienaveen
Bergen   Berkhout Bovenkarspel   Urk   Nagele   Staphorst   N48 Sleen   N37   Nieuw   Zwartemeer
Alkmaar   57   Enkhuizen   N302   Zwartsluis   N331   Balkbrug   N34   Amsterdam   Schoonebeek
Heiloo   Hoorn   Genemuiden   N50   A28   Dedemsvaart   Coevorden   Nw
Egmond aan Zee   Schermerhorn   Ens   Hasselt   N375   Hardenberg   Schoonebeek
Limmen   N244   Oosthuizen   Kampen   IJsselmuiden   E232   22   Ommen   403
Castricum   A7 N247   32   Purmerend   Edam   A6   Dronten   N309   Zwolle   N34   Vroomshoop
Uitgeest   Volendam   Lelystad   Oostelijk-   Elburg   Hattem   N347 Den   Vriezenveen   Tubbergen
Heemskerk   Flevoland   Oldebroek   N35 N48   Ham   N36   Denekamp
Beverwijk   A9   56   Monnickendam   Biddinghuizen   Doornspijk   Wezep   N349 Almelo   Nordhorn
IJmuiden   Wormerveer   Nederland   Heerde   Wijhe   Hellendoorn   Ootmarsum   403
Haarlem   Zaan Zaandam   Almere   Nunspeet   N305 N302   Raalte   N35   Nijverdal   Wierden   Oldenzaal   N342 N30 E23
Zandvoort   Zwanenburg   Amsterdam   Harderwijk   60   Epe   A50 N337 N48   Rijssen   Borne   Bentheim
Heemstede   N208   Badhoevedorp   Amstelveen   22   Vaassen   35   Deventer
Hillegom   Hoofddorp   Ouderkerk   N27 N301   Ermelo   Bussum   Huizen   Naarden   Weesp

17   62

0   5   10   20   30   40 Miles

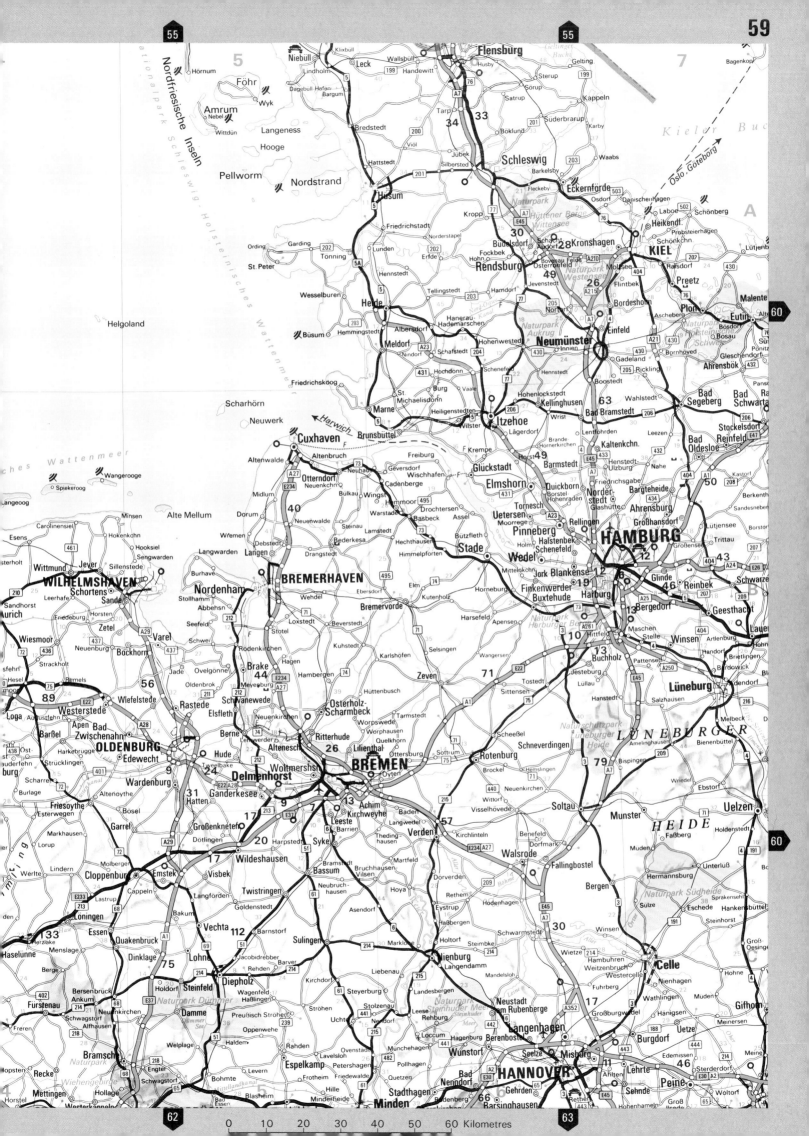

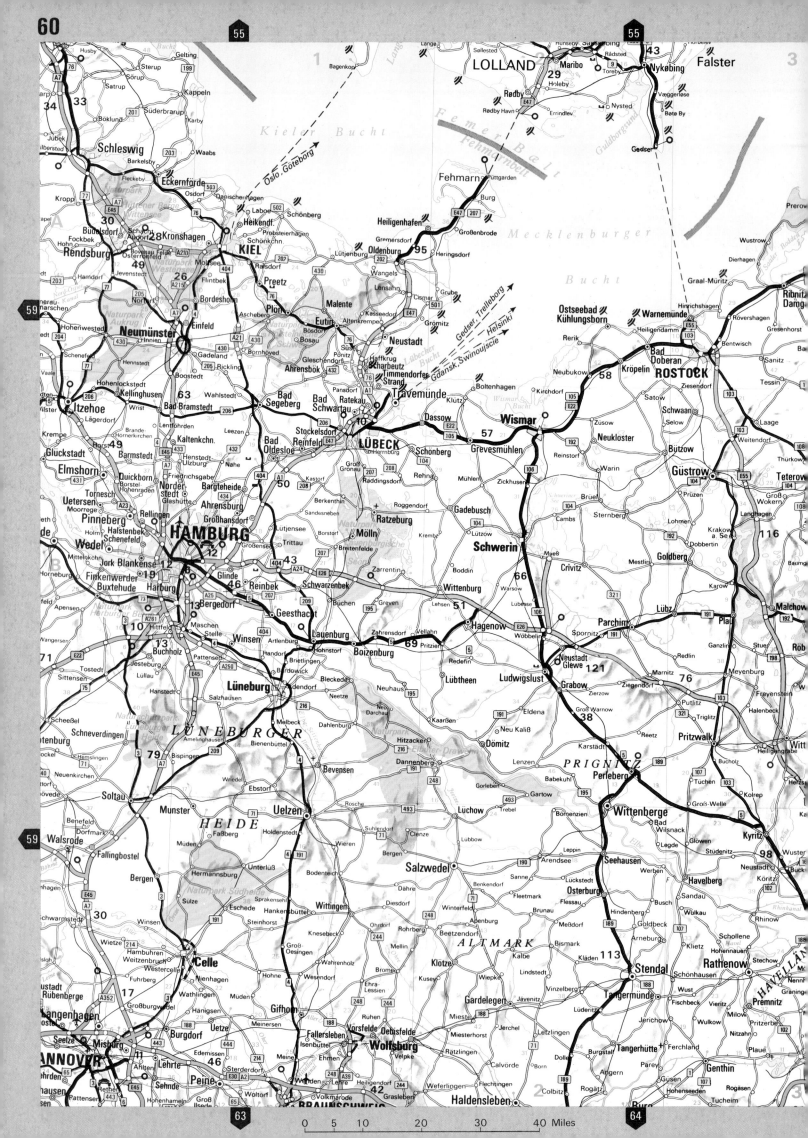

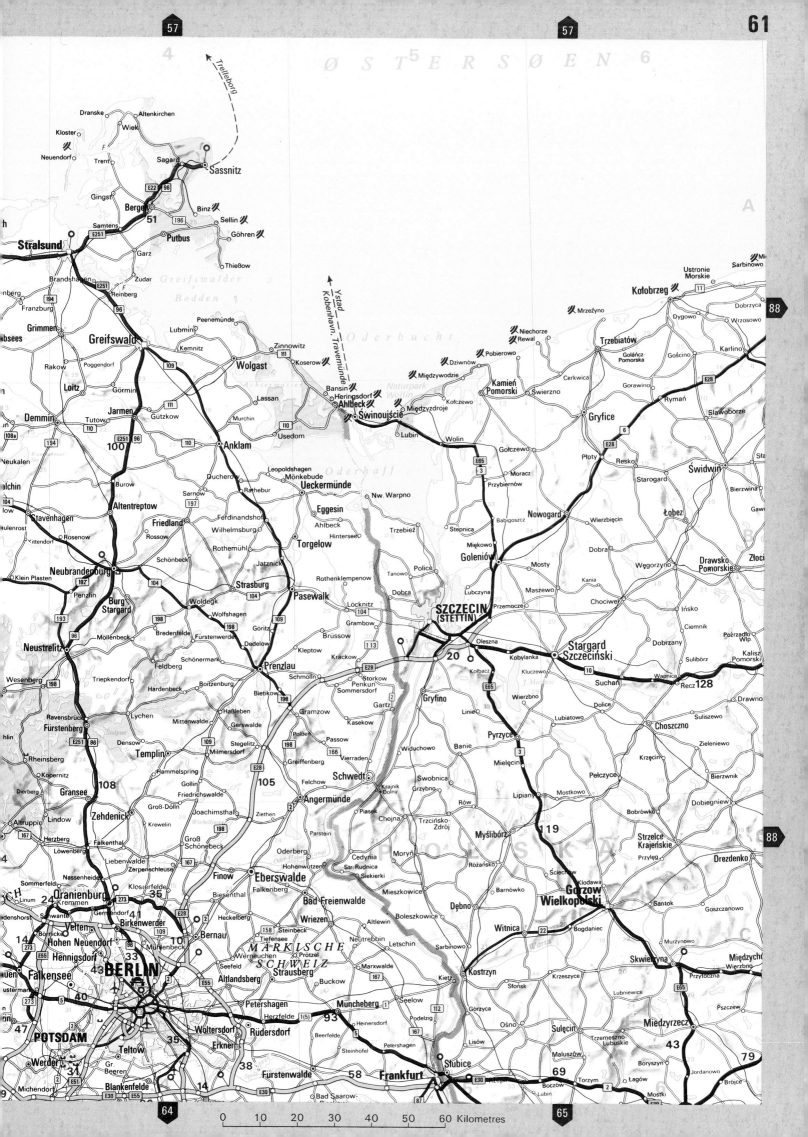

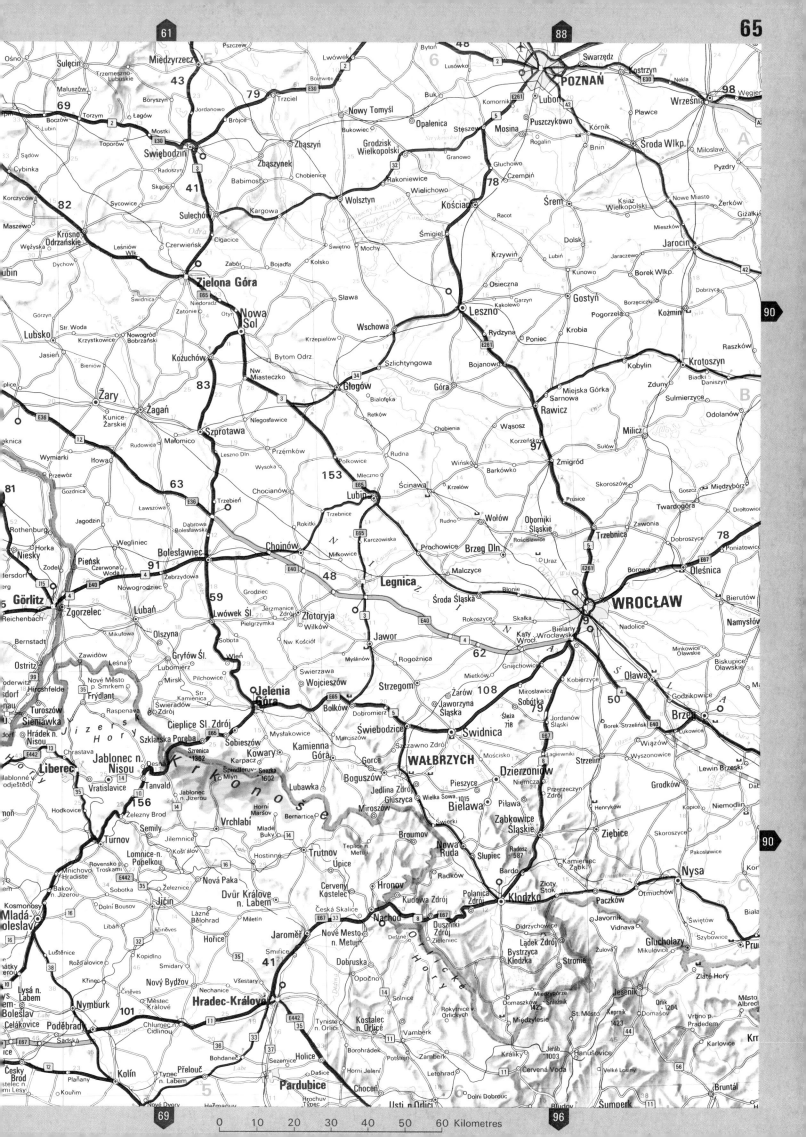

0 5 10 20 30 40 Miles

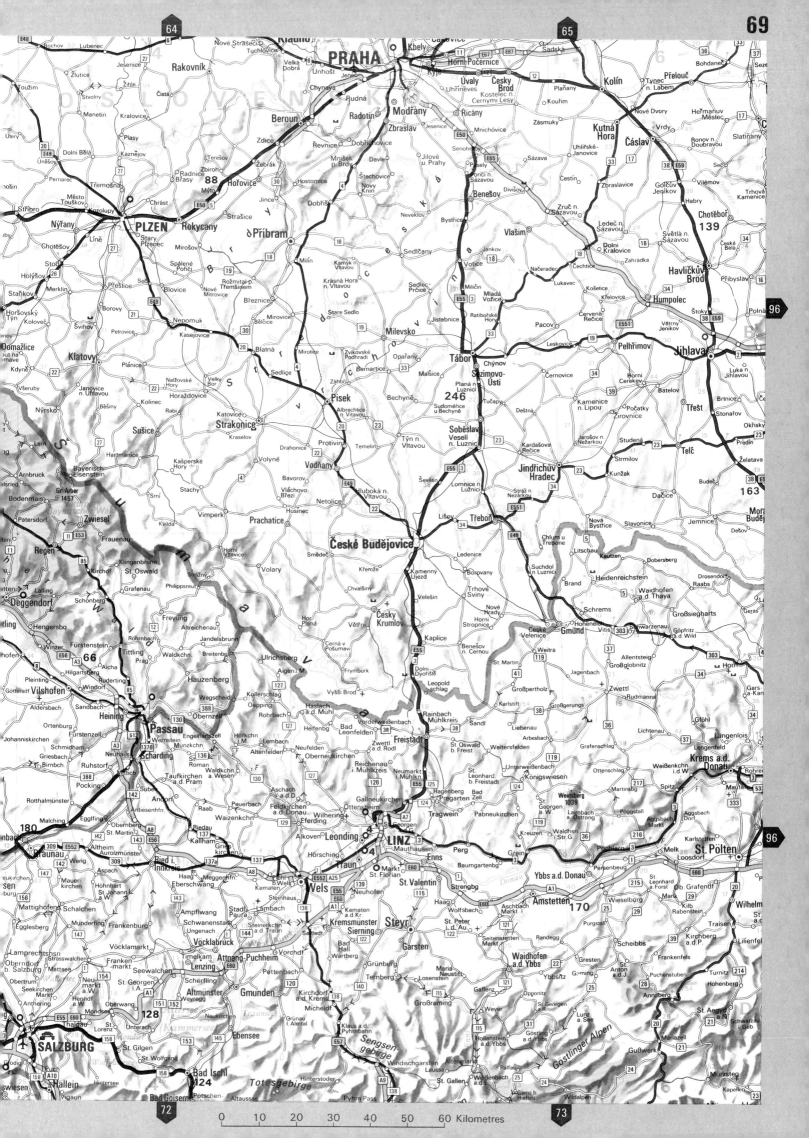

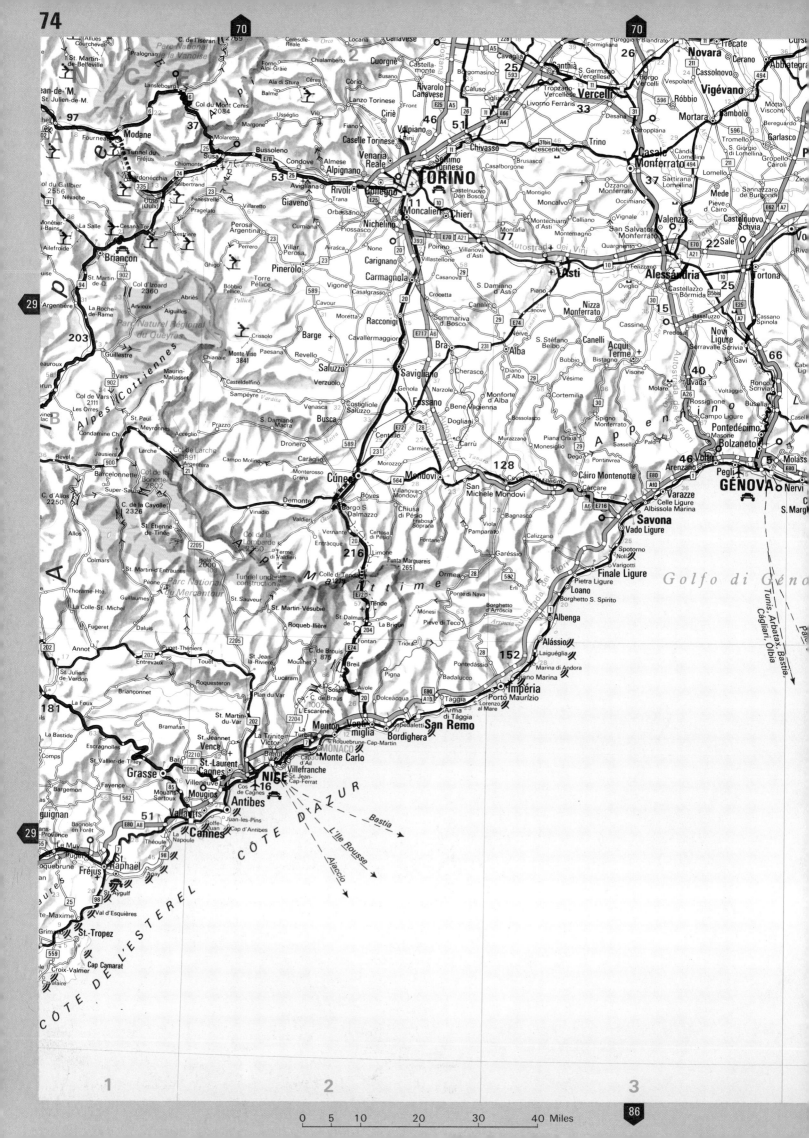

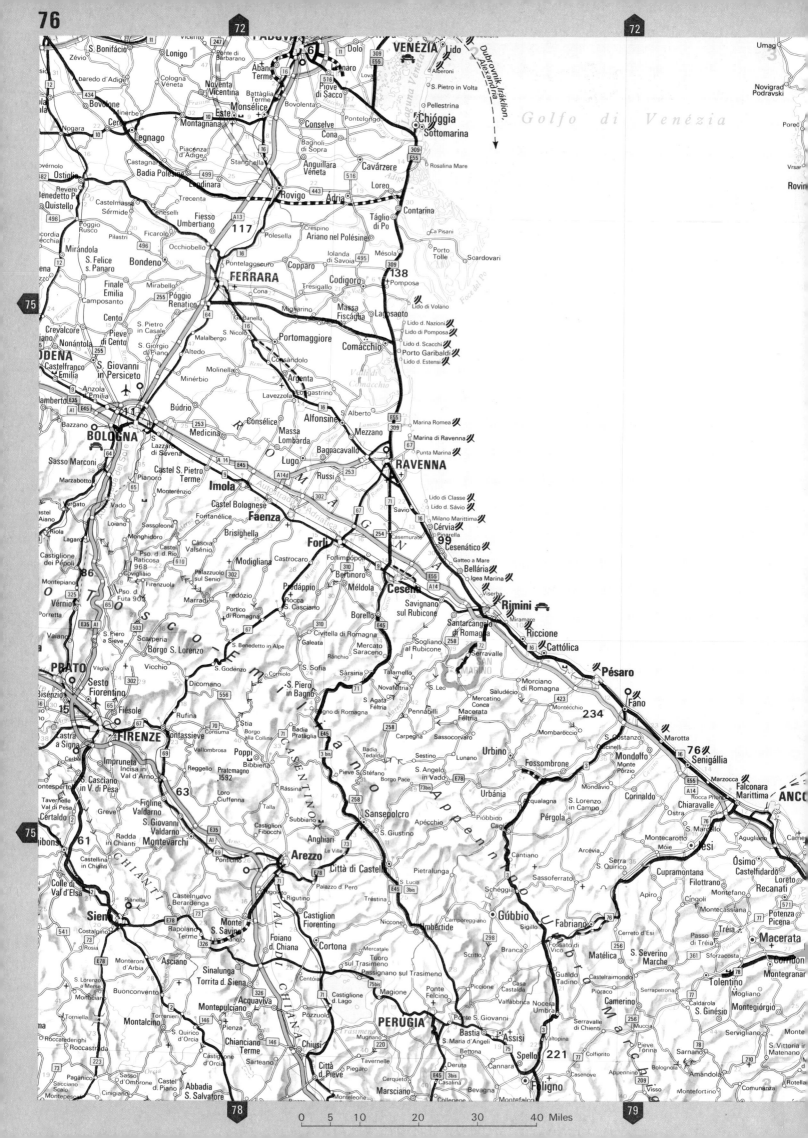

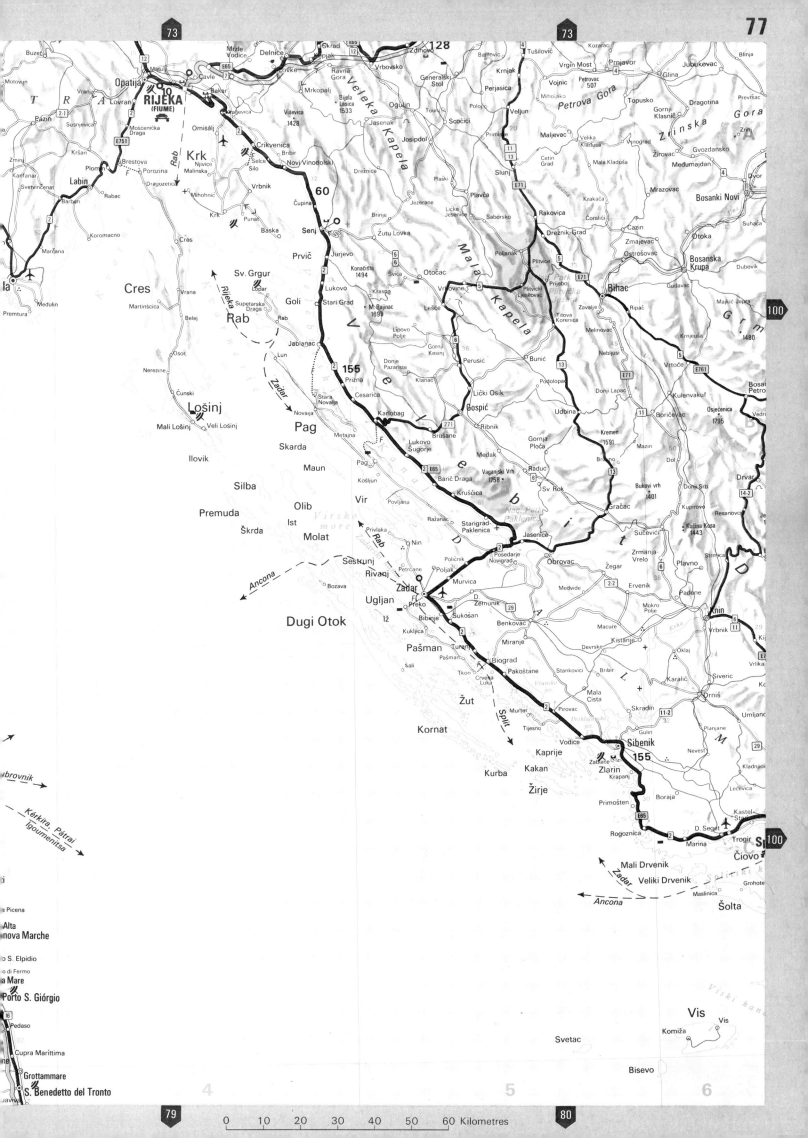

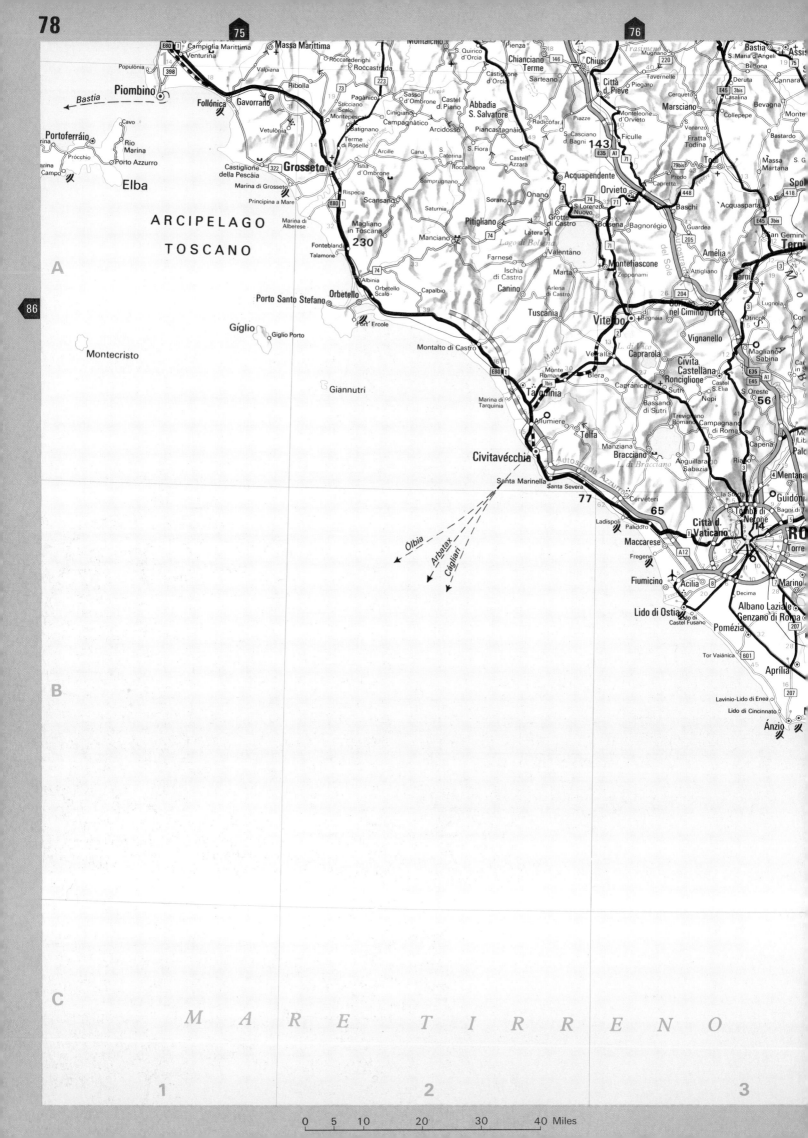

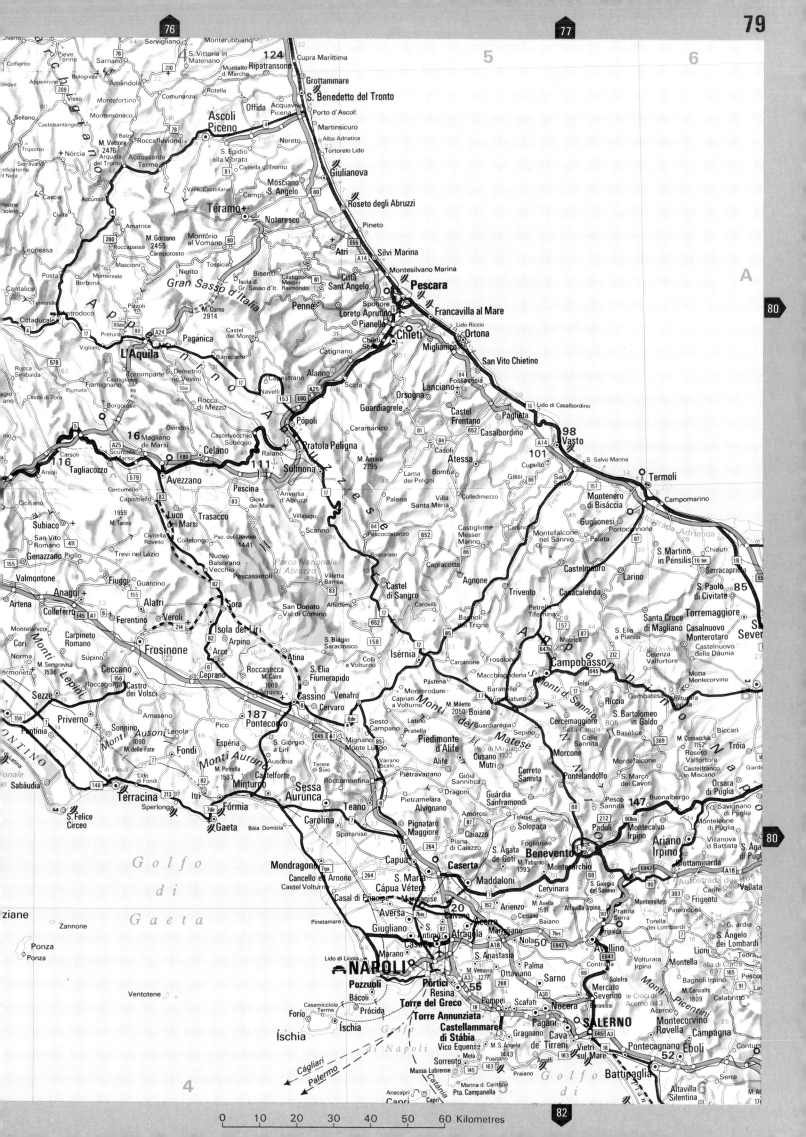

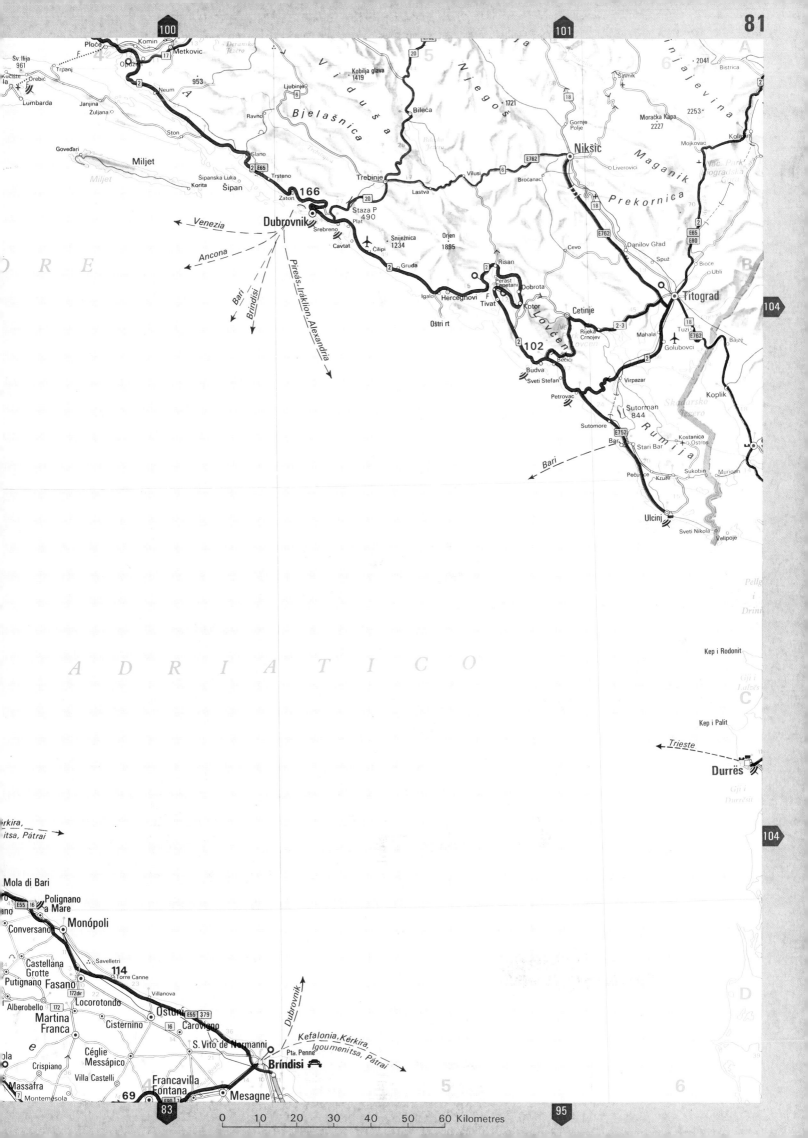

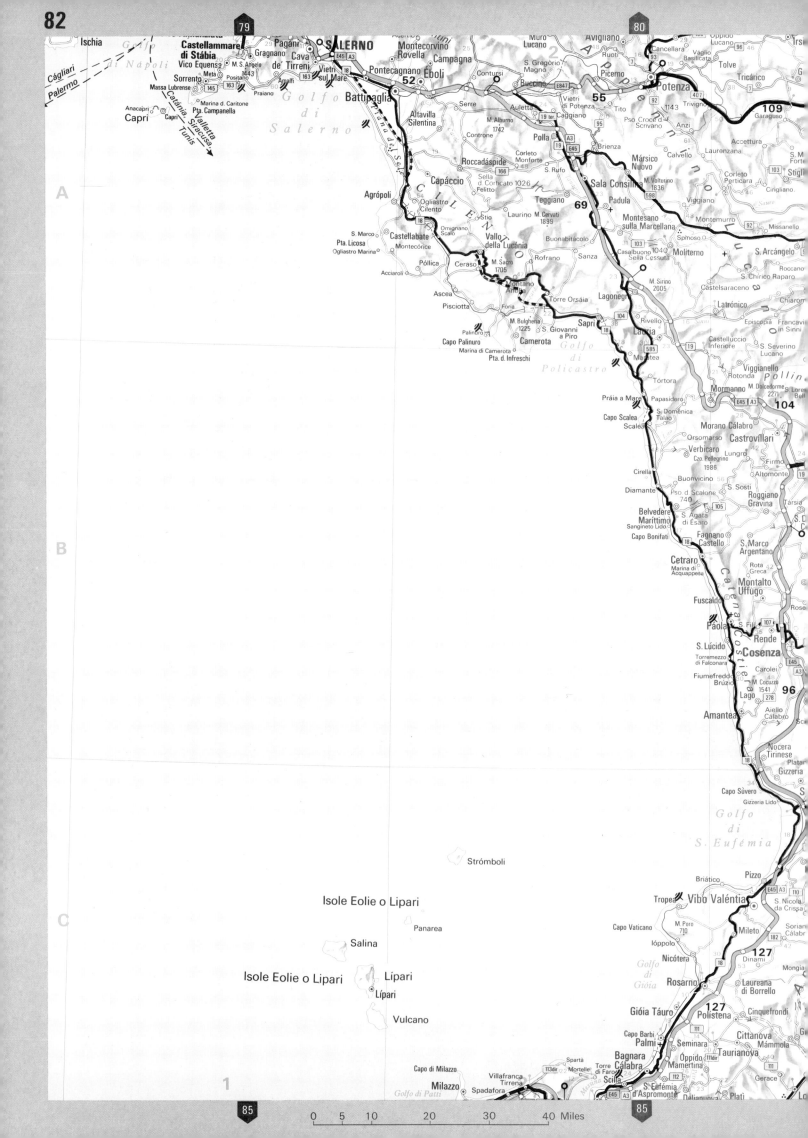

Ischia

Cágliari
Palermo

Golfo di Napoli

Castellammare di Stábia
Vico Equense
M. S. Angelo
Sorrento
Meta 1443
Massa Lubrense
Positano
Amalfi
Praiano
Anacapri
Capri
Capri
Pta. Campanella
Marina d. Caritone
Valletta
Catánia-Siracusa-Tunis

Gragnano
Pagáni
Cava de' Tirreni
Vietri sul Mare
SALERNO
Pontecagnano
Battipaglia

Acerno
Montecorvino
Rovella
Campagna

Muro Lucano
Avigliano
Oppido Lucano
Cancellara
Váglio Basilicata
Tolve

Golfo di Salerno

Piana del Sele

Eboli
Serre
Altavilla Silentina
M. Alburno 1742
Controne
Contursi
Auletta

Capáccio
Roccadáspide
Sella d. Corticato 1026
Felitto
S. Rufo
Polla
Corleto Monforte

Buccino
Vietri di Potenza
Tito
Caggiano

Potenza
Trivigno
Anzi
1143

Agrópoli
Ogliastro Cilento
Teggiano
Sala Consilina
Padula
Montesano sulla Marcellana

Brienza
Mársico Nuovo
Calvello
Laurenzana

CILENTO
Stio
Laurino
M. Cervati 1899
Buonabitácolo
Sanza
Casalbuono 1040
Sella Cessuta
Moliterno

S. Arcángelo

S. Marco
Pta. Licosa
Castellabate
Montecórice
Ogliastro Marina
Póllica
Acciaroli
Vallo della Lucánia
Rofrano
M. Sacro 1705
Montano Antilia
Ceraso

M. Sirino 2005

Latrónico
Episcopia
Francavilla in Sinni

Ascea
Pisciotta
Foria
Torre Orsáia
Lagonegro
Rivello
Latria
Lauria
Castelluccio Inferiore
S. Severino Lucano

Palinuro
Capo Palinuro
Marina di Camerota
Pta. d. Infreschi
M. Bulgheria 1225
S. Giovanni a Piro
Camerota
Sapri
Maratea

Golfo di Policastro

Viggianello
Rotonda
Mormanno
M. Dolcedorme 2271
Póllino

Práia a Mare
Papasidero
S. Doménica Talao
Capo Scalea
Scalea

Tórtora
Morano Cálabro
Castrovíllari
Orsomarso
Verbicaro
Czo. Pellegrino 1986
Lungro
Firmo
Altomonte

Cirella
Diamante
Buonvicino
Pso d. Scalone 740
S. Sosti
Roggiano Gravina
Társia

Belvedere Maríttimo
Sanginéto Lido
Capo Bonifati
S. Agata di Ésaro
Fagnano Castello
S. Marco Argentano

Cetraro
Marina di Acquappesa
Rota Greca
Montalto Uffugo

Fuscaldo
Páola
S. Fili
Rende
Cosenza
S. Lúcido
Torremezzo di Falconara
Carolei
Fiumefreddo Brúzio
M. Cocuzzo 1541
Lago

Amantea
Aiello Cálabro

Nocera Tirinese
Platania
Gizzeria

Capo Súvero
Gizzeria Lido

Golfo di S. Eufémia

Strómboli

Briático
Pizzo

Isole Eolie o Lipari

Panarea
Tropea
Vibo Valéntia
S. Nicola da Crissa

Salina
Capo Vaticano
M. Poro 710
Mileto
Ióppolo

Isole Eolie o Lipari
Lípari
Lípari
Nicótera
Rosarno
Dinami
Laureana di Borrello

Vulcano
Gióia Táuro
Polistena
Cinquefrondi

Capo Barbi
Palmi
Seminara
Cittànova
Mámmola

Capo di Milazzo
Villafranca Tirrena
Spártà
Mortelle
Torre di Faro
Bagnara Cálabra
Óppido Mamertina
Tauriánova

Milazzo
Spadafora
Golfo di Patti
Scilla
S. Eufémia d'Aspromonte
Gerace
Platì

0   5   10   20   30   40 Miles

MARE MEDITERRANEO

0 5 10 20 30 40 Miles

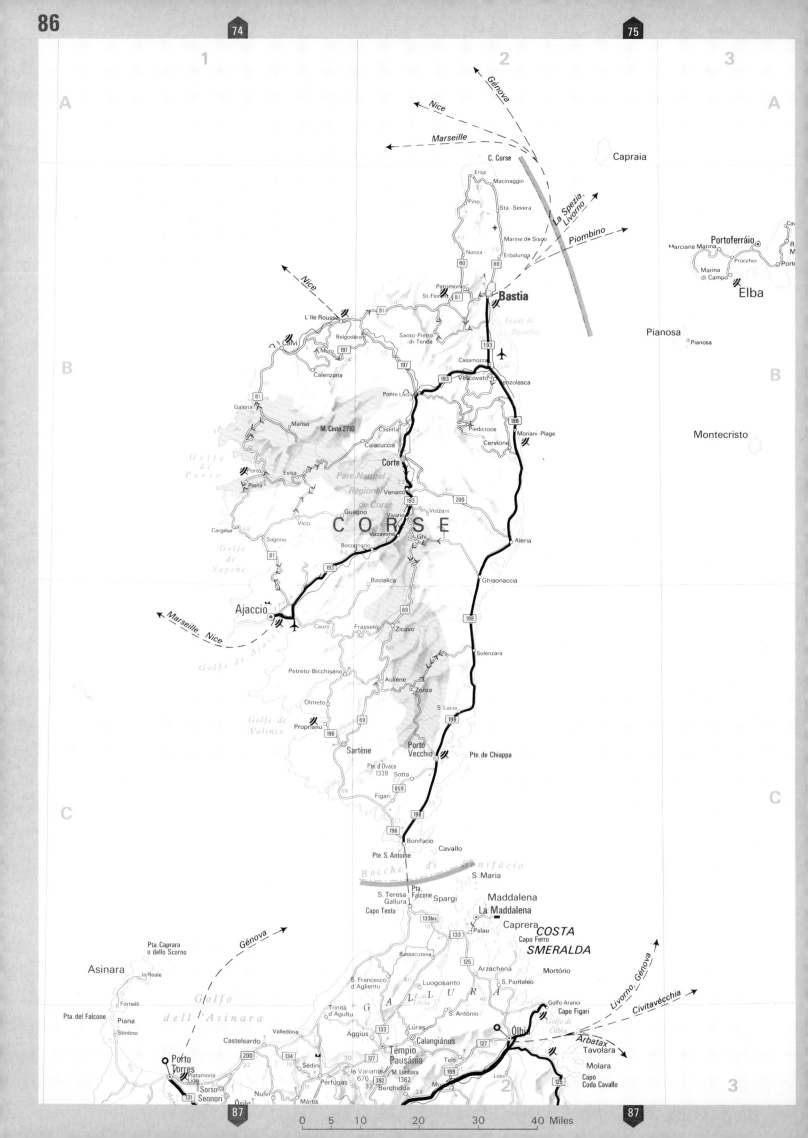

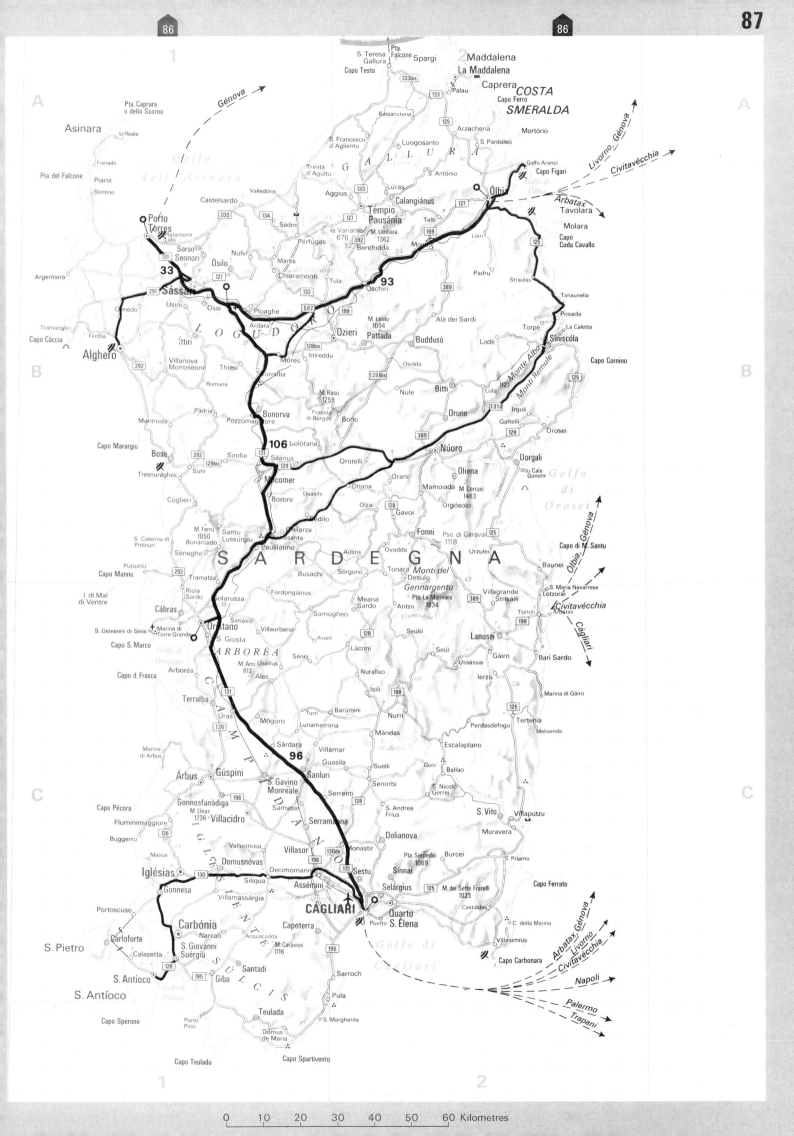

1

2

A

Asinara
Pta. Caprara
o dello Scorno

S. Teresa
Gallura
Pta.
Falcone
Spargi
Maddalena
La Maddalena
Caprera *COSTA*
Capo Ferro
SMERALDA

Génova

la Reale

133bis
Palau

Capo Testa

Livorno, Génova

Pta. del Falcone
Piana
Fornelli
Stintino

Bassacutena

Arzachéna
125

S. Pantaleo
Mortório

Golfo Aranci
Capo Figari
Golfo di
Olbia

Civitavécchia

*Golfo
dell' Asinara*

Valledória
S. Francesco
d'Aglientu
Luogosanto
Olbia
127

Arbatax
Tavolara

Argentiera

Castelsardo
200
134
Sédini
Pérfugas
Trinità
d'Agultu
Aggius

G A L L U R A
Lúras
Calangiánus
Tempio
Pausánia
133
S. António
Telti
127
Molara

Capo
Coda Cavallo

Pta. del Falcone

Porto
Tórres
Platamona
Lido
131
Sorso
Sennori
Osilo
127
Nulvi
Mártis
Chiaramonti
Tula
la Variante
676
M. Limbara
1362
392
Berchidda
199
Mont
125

33
Sássari
291
Úsini
Ossi
Ploaghe
597
199
Oschiri
93
389
Straulas
Tanaunella

Tramariglio
Fertília
Ómedo
127
Ardara
132
M. Lerno
1094
Alà dei Sardi
Posada

Capo Cáccia
L O G U D O R O
Ittiri
Villanova
Monteleone
Móres
128bis
Ozieri
Pattada
Buddusò
Lodè
Torpè
La Caletta
Siniscóla

B
Alghero
292
Thiesi
Ittireddu
Torralba
128 Bis
Osidda
Capo Cornino

Romana
Nule
Bitti

M. Rasu
1259
Bono
Lula
1127

Monti Remule
125

Montresta
Pádria
Bonorva
Foresta
di Burgos
Oruna
Irgoli
Galtelli

Capo Marargiu
Pozzomaggiore
106
389
Núoro
Orosei

Bosa
292
Sindia
Silánus
131
129
Orotelli
129
Dorgali

Tresnurághes
129bis
Suni
Macomer
Orani
Oliena
Cala
Gonone
*Golfo
di*

Cúglieri
Bórore
Dualchi
Olzai
128
Gavoi
Mamoiada
M. Corrasi
1463
Orosei

S. Caterina di
Pittinuri
M. Ferru
1050
Bonárcado
Santu
Lussúrgiu
Sédilo
Orgósolo

Séneghe
Abbasanta
Paulilátino
Fonni
Pso. di Caravà
1118
125
Capo di M. Santu

Putzuldu
Capo Mannu
S A R D E G N A
Busachi
Sórgono
Tonara
*Monti del
Desulo*
Ovodda
Urzulei
Baunei
S. Maria Navarrese
Lotzorai

I. di Mal
di Ventre
292
Tramatza
Fordongiánus
Gennargentu
Meana
Sardo
Pta. La Marmora
1834
389
Villagrande
Strisáili
Civitavécchia
Arbatax

Cábras
Solarussa
Simáxis
Aritzo
Seúlo
Tortolì
198

S. Giovanni di Sinis
Marina di
Torre Grande
Oristano
S. Giusta
Villaurbana
Asuni
Láconi
Seúi
Gáiro
Ussássai
Marina di Gáiro

Capo S. Marco
*Golfo di
Oristano*
ARBORÉA
Sénis
Nurallao
198
Ierzu
Bari Sardo

Capo d. Frasca
Arboréa
M. Arci Uséllus
812
Ales
Ísili
125
Lanusei

Terralba
131
Úras
Turri
Barúmini
Nurri
198

Marina
di Arbus
126
Mógoro
Lunamatrona
Mándas
Escalaplano
Perdasdefogu
Tertenia
Melisenda

Árbus
Gúspini
96
Sárdara
Villamar
Guasila
Suelli
Senorbi
Goni
Ballao

C
Gonnosfanádiga
196
S. Gavino
Monreale
Samassi
Sanluri
Serrenti
128
S. Nicoló
Gerrei
S. Vito
Villaputzu

Capo Pécora
M. Linas
1236
Villacidro
Serramanna
S. Andrea
Frius
Muravera

Fluminimaggiore
126
Vallermosa
Villasor
Dolianova
S. Priamo
Capo Ferrato

Buggerru
Masúa
Domusnóvas
Decimomannu
130dir
196
Monastir
Pta. Serpeddi
1069
Burcei
C. della Marina

Iglésias
130
Siliqua
131
Sestu
Sínnai
125
M. dei Sette Fratelli
1023
Castiádas

Gonnesa
Villamassárgia
Assémini
Selárgius

Portoscuso
CAGLIARI
Quarto
S. Élena
Villasimíus
Capo Carbonara

S. Pietro
Carloforte
Carbónia
Nareao
Capoterra
Poetto

Arbatax, Génova
Livorno

Calasetta
S. Giovanni
Suérgiu
Acquacadda
M. Carávius
1116
195
*Golfo di
Cágliari*
Capo Carbonara

S. Antíoco
126
Santadi
Giba
Sarroch
Napoli

S. Antíoco
195
SÚLCIS
Teulada
Pula
Palermo
Trapani

Capo Sperone
Porto
Pino
S. Margherita

Dómus
de Maria

Capo Teulada
Capo Spartivento

1

2

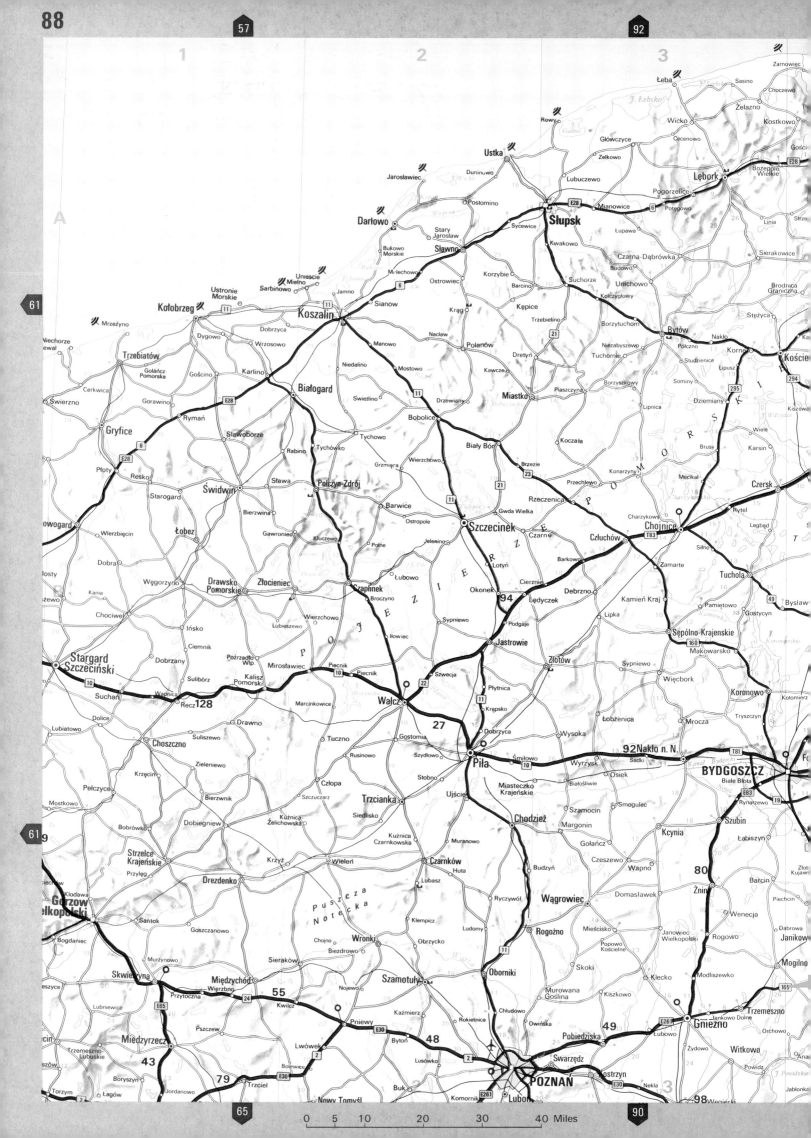

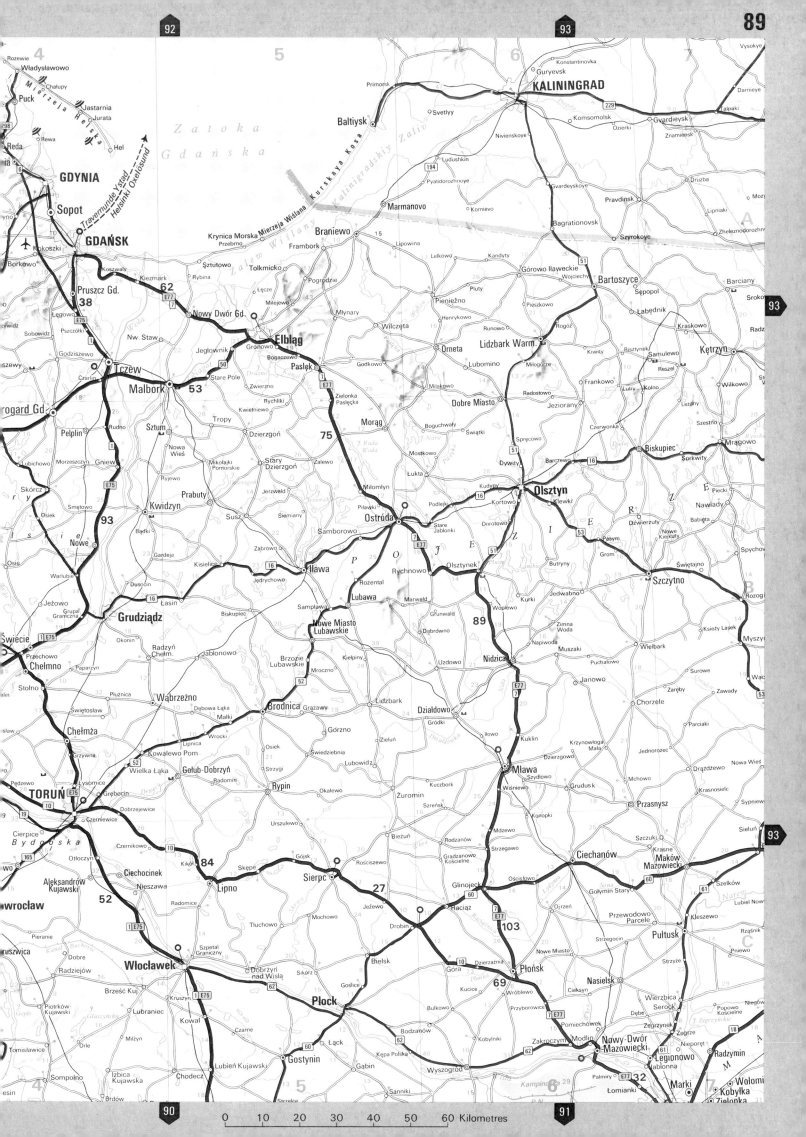

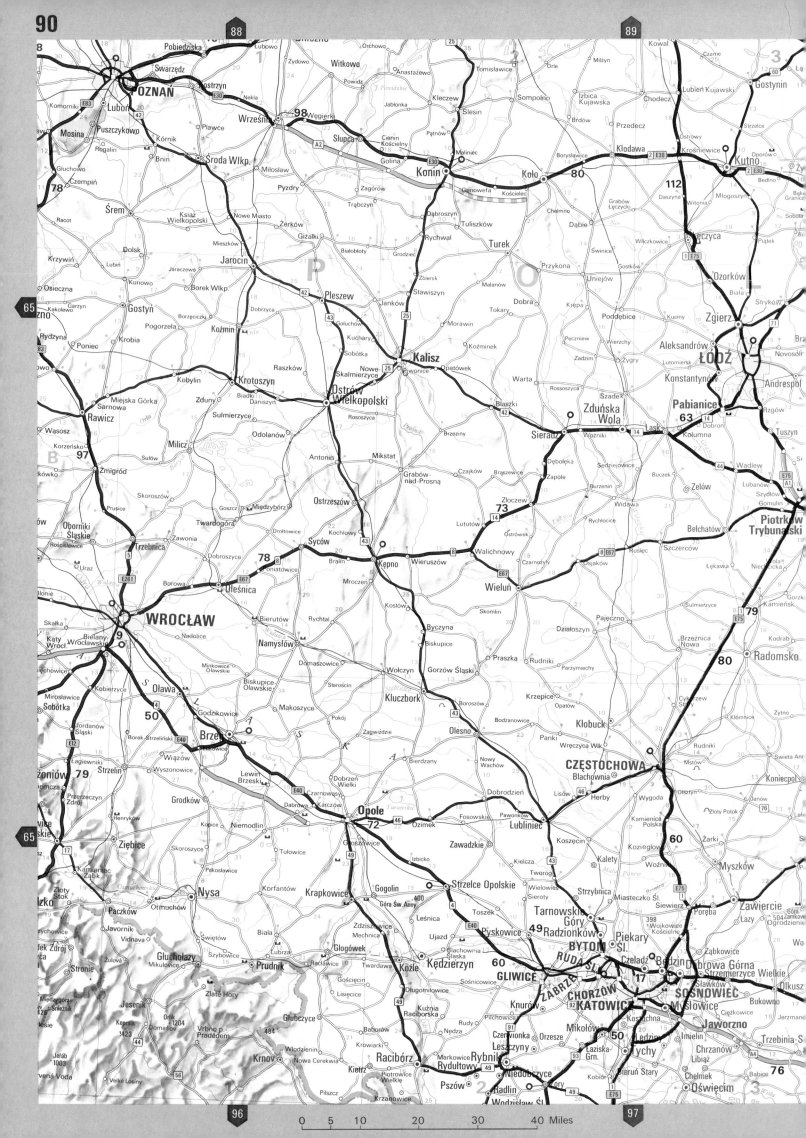

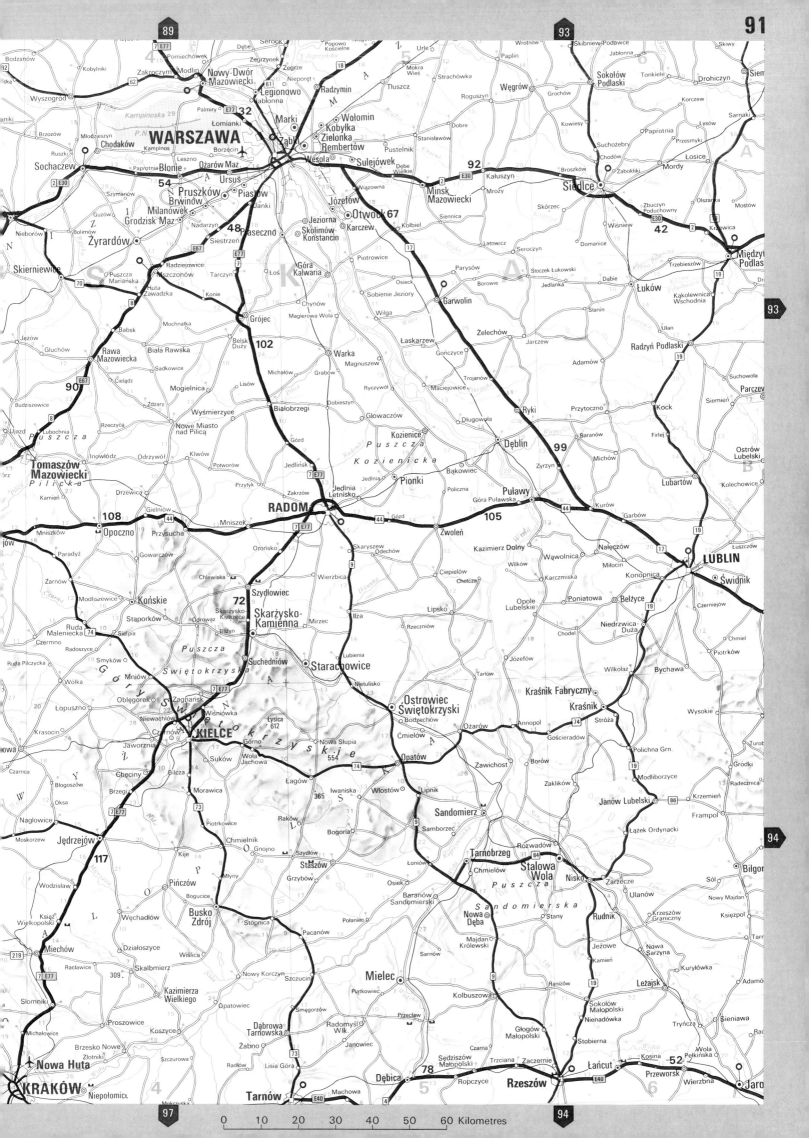

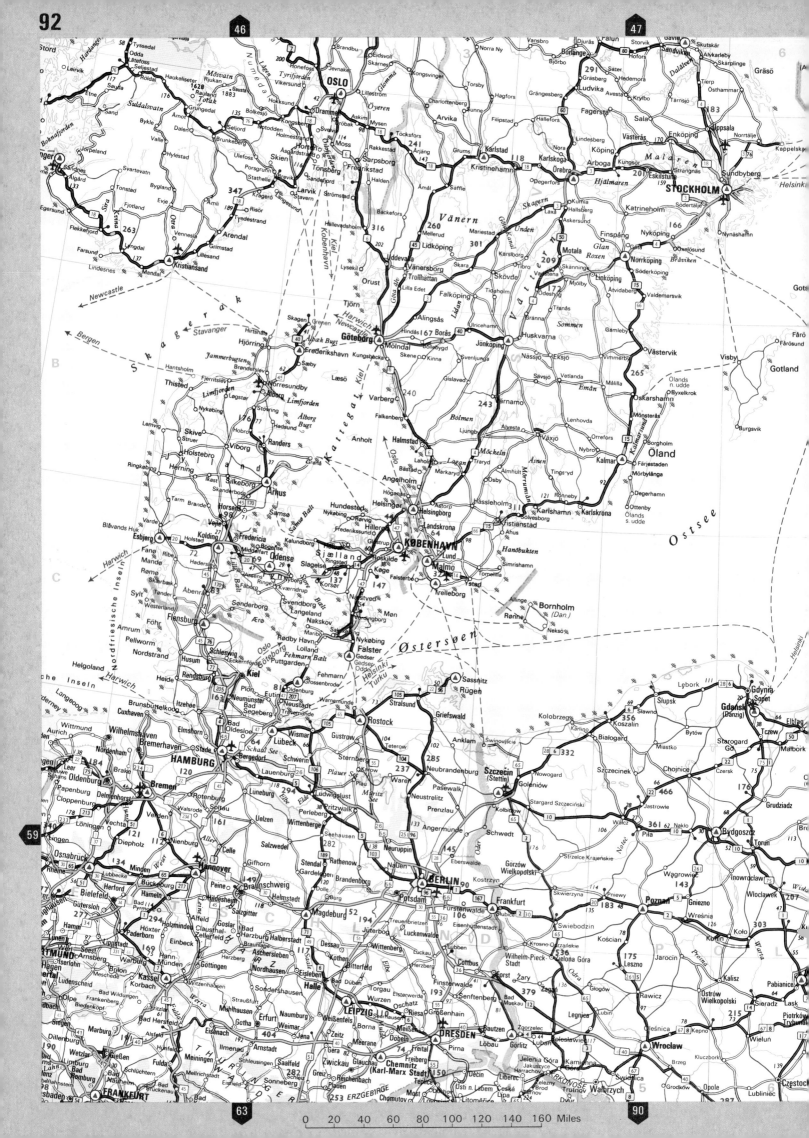

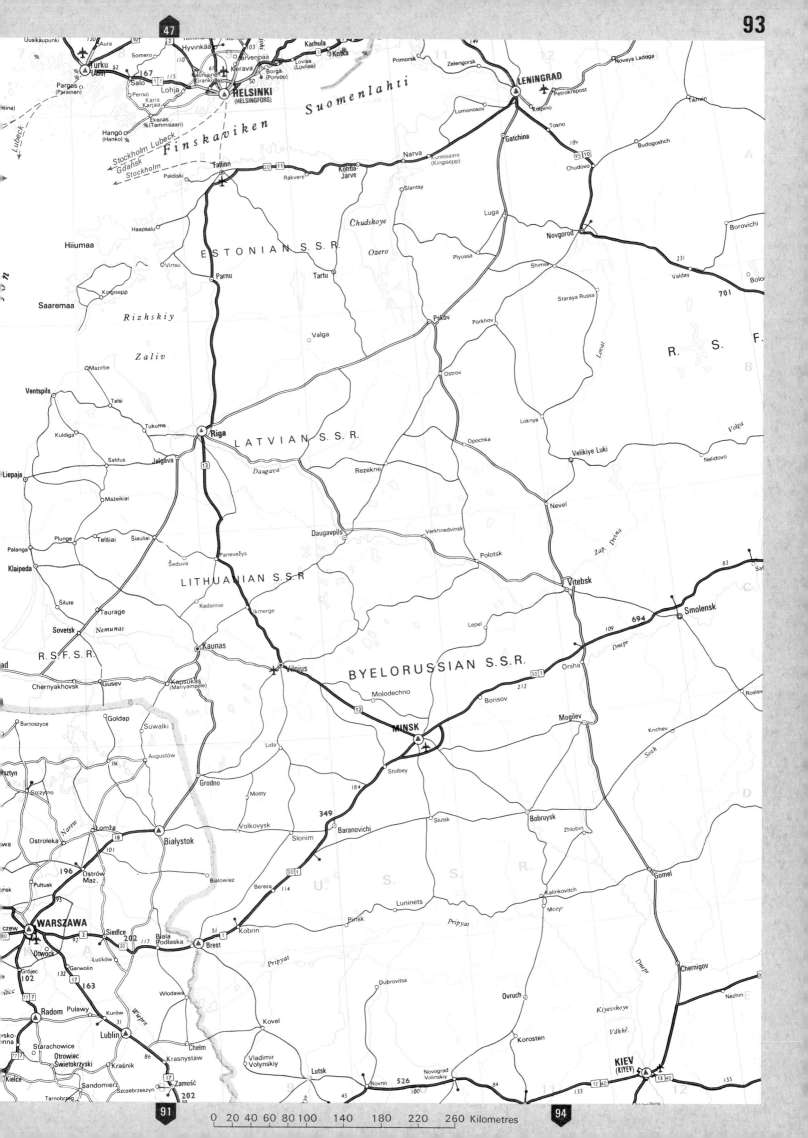

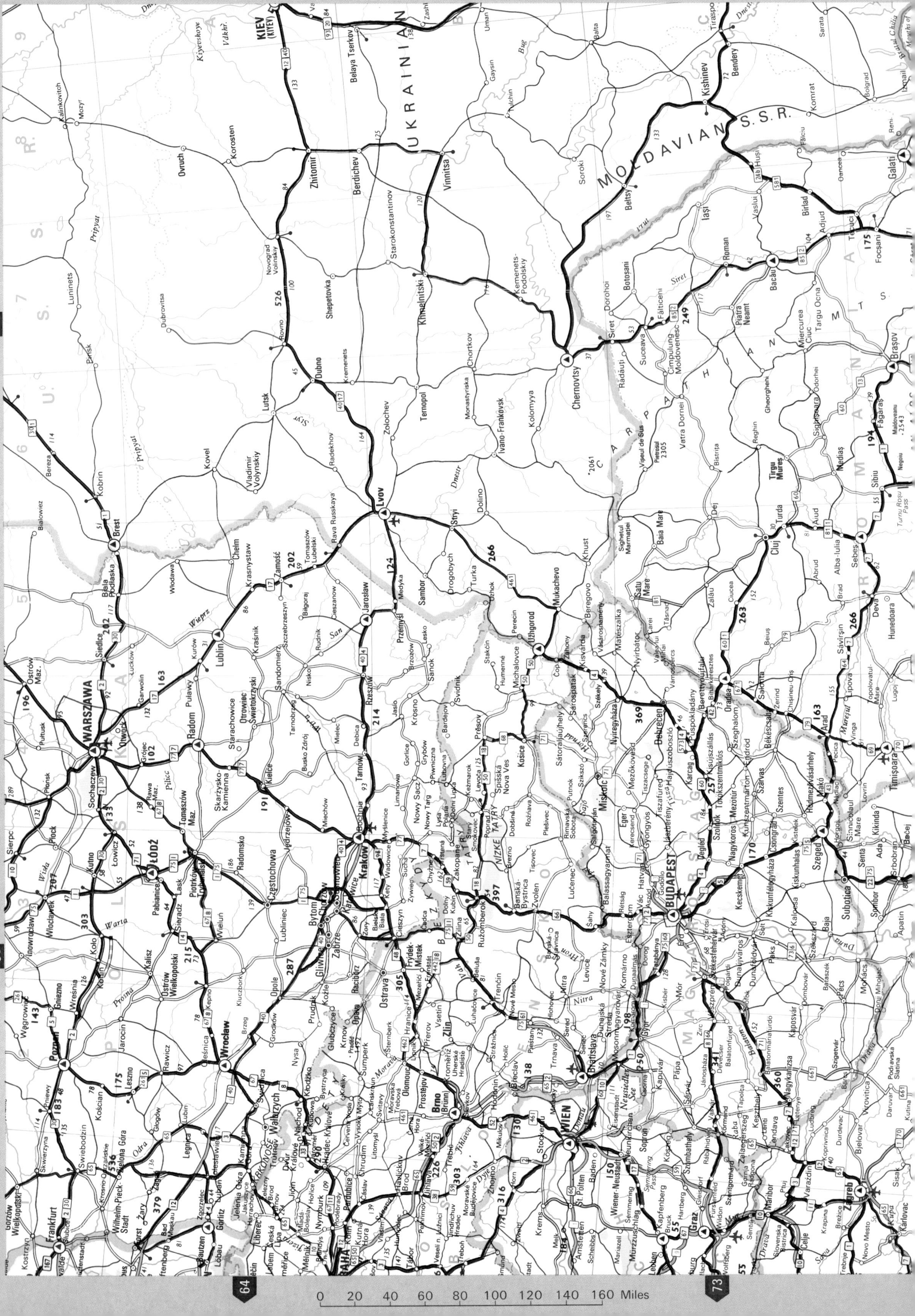

U. S. S. R.

UKRAINIAN S. S. R.

MOLDAVIAN S. S. R.

ROMANIA

POLSKA

WARSZAWA

ŁÓDŹ

Wrocław

Kraków

Poznań

KIEV (KIYEV)

Lvov

Brest

Lublin

Chernovtsy

Kishinev

Iaşi

Galaţi

Braşov

Tirgu Mureş

Cluj

Satu Mare

Oradea

Arad

Timişoara

Zagreb

WIEN

BUDAPEST

MAGYARORSZÁG

Bratislava

Brno Brünn

Ostrava

Košice

Uzhgorod

Mukachevo

0 20 40 60 80 100 120 140 160 Miles

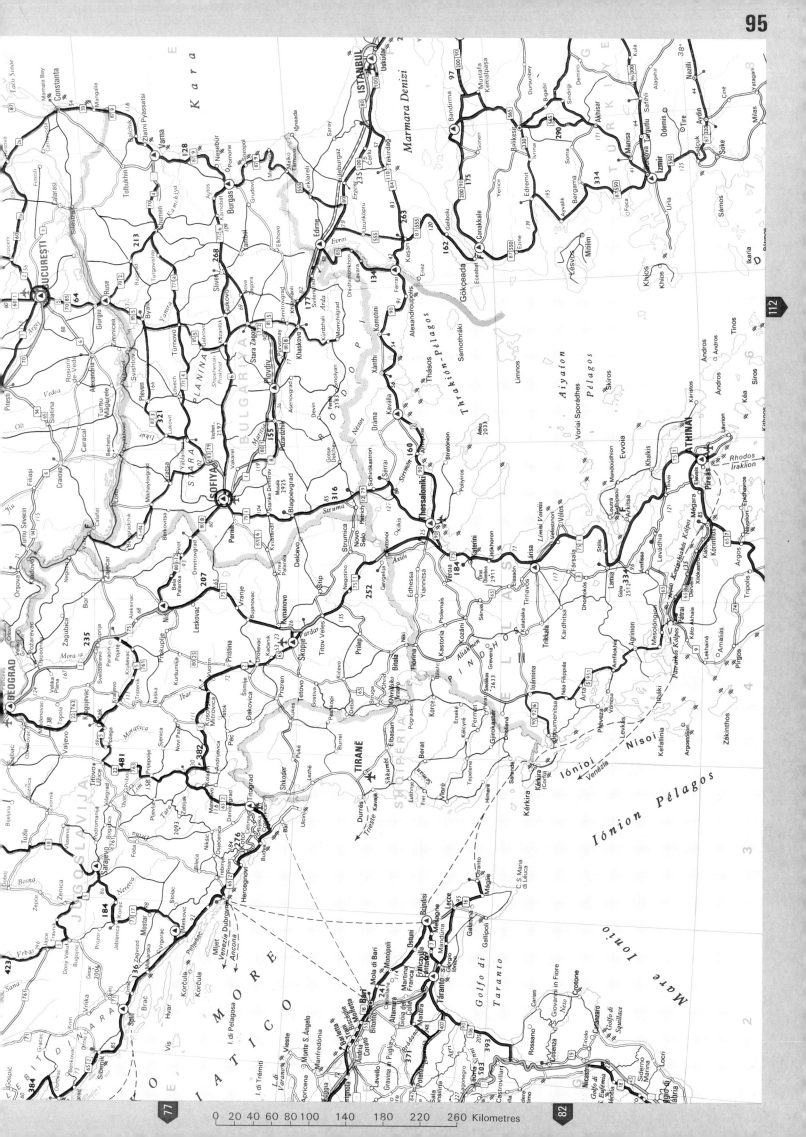

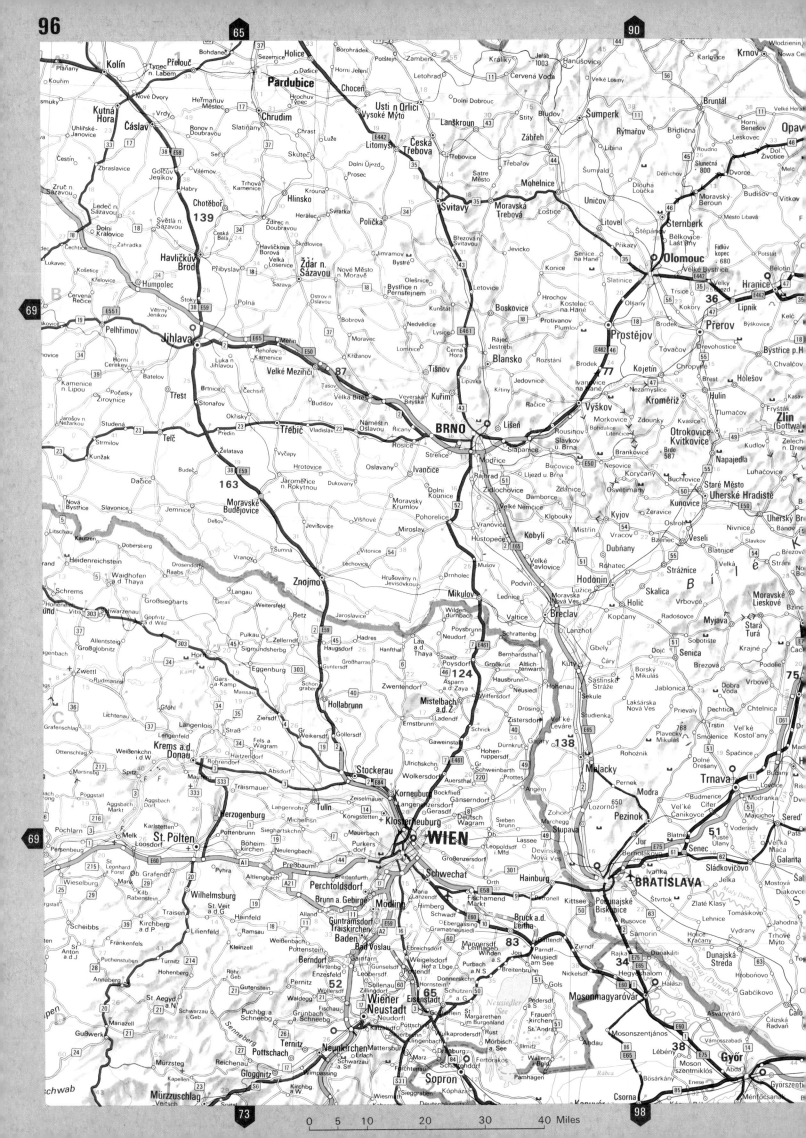

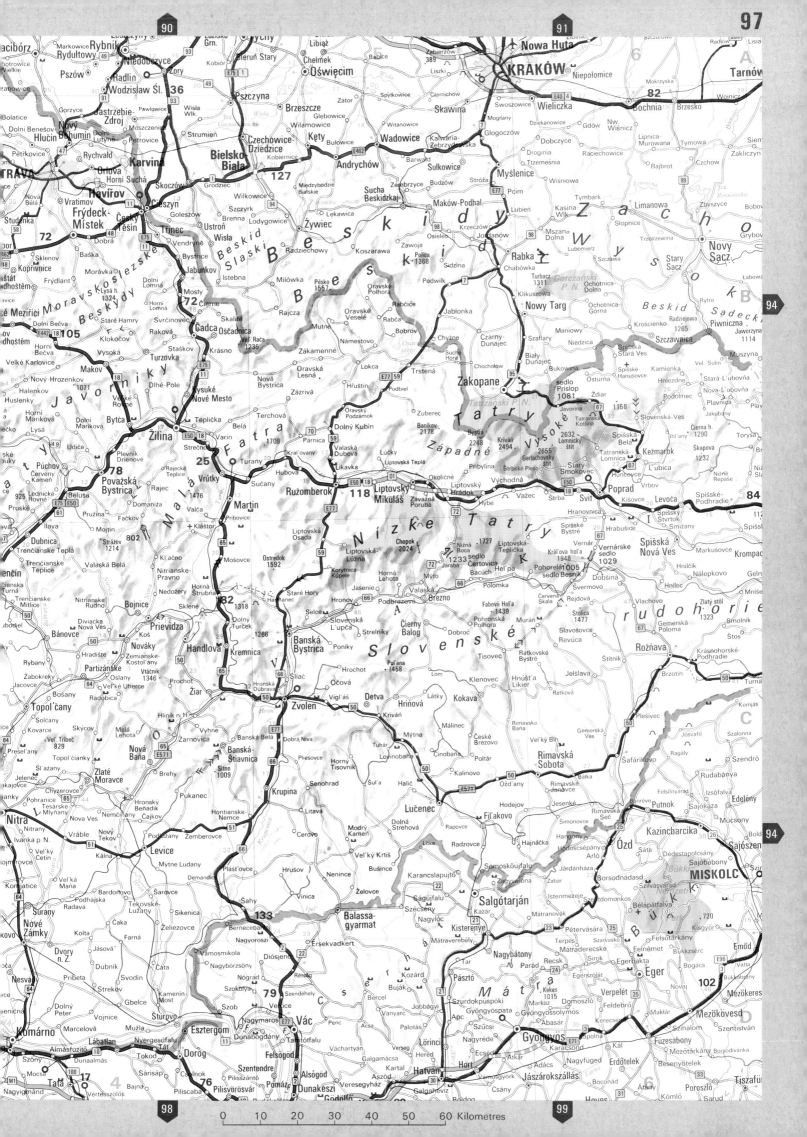

96

96

73

73

Neunkirchen
Gloggnitz
Sopron
Győr
Komárno
Komárom
Tata
Csorna
Kapuvár
Pápa
Szombathely
Sárvár
Celldömölk
Kőszeg
Oberwart
Hartberg
Fürstenfeld
Gleisdorf
Körmend
Szentgotthárd
Veszprém
Várpalota
Székesfehérvár
Ajka
Devecser
Sümeg
Tapolca
Balatonfüred
Siófok
Keszthely
Zalaegerszeg
Nagykanizsa
Marcali
Kaposvár
Dombóvár
Tamási
Komló
PÉCS
Szigetvár
Barcs
Nagyatád
Csurgó
Murska Sobota
Maribor
Ptuj
Čakovec
Varaždin
Koprivnica
Križevci
Bjelovar
Virovitica
Đurđevac
Pitomača
ZAGREB
Velika Gorica
Sisak
Kutina
Daruvar
Podravska Slatina
Našice
Slavonska
Petrinja
M A G Y A
B a k o n y
B a l a t o n
Ivanščica
Kalnik
Medvednica
Moslavačka gora
P a p u k
Drava
Mura
Rába
Sava
0 5 10 20 30 40 Miles

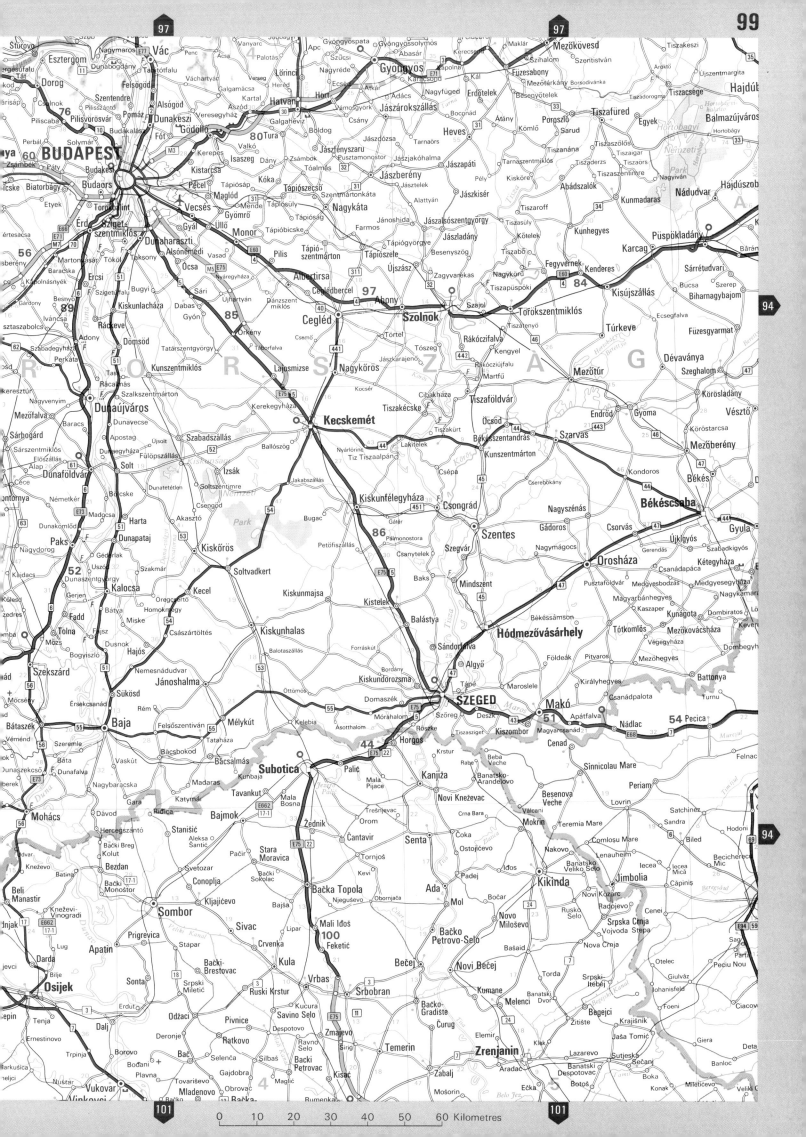

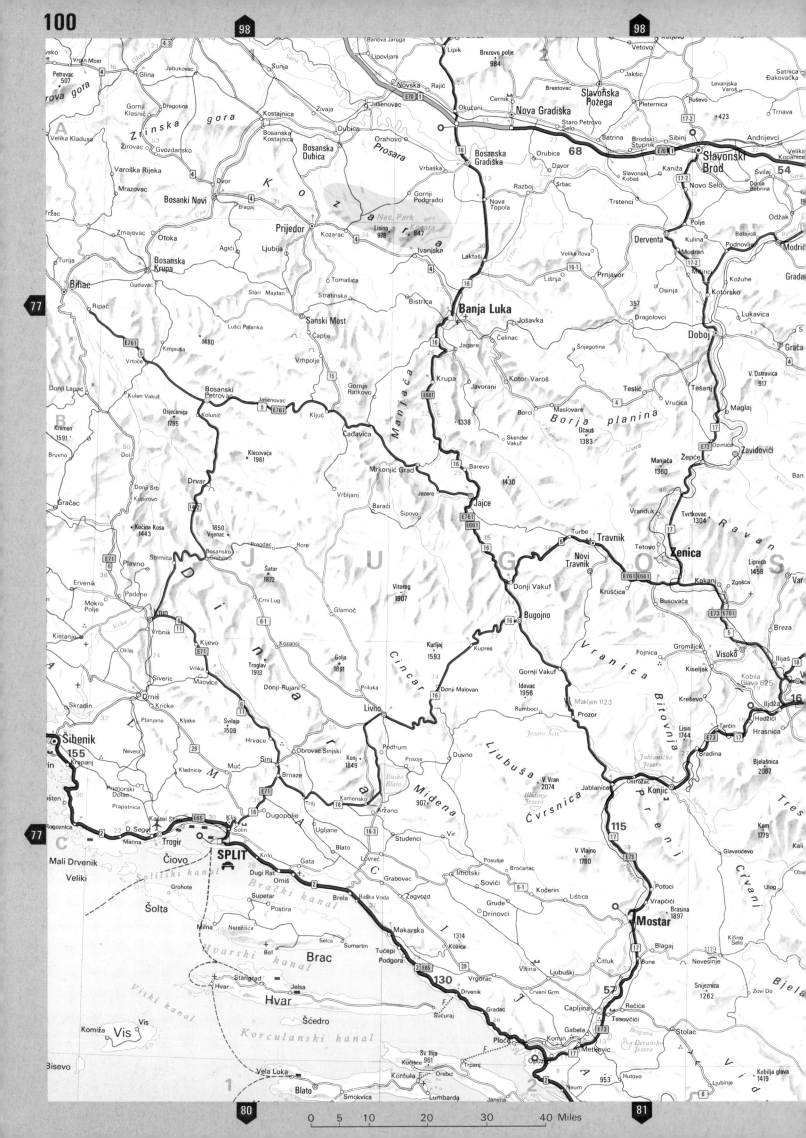

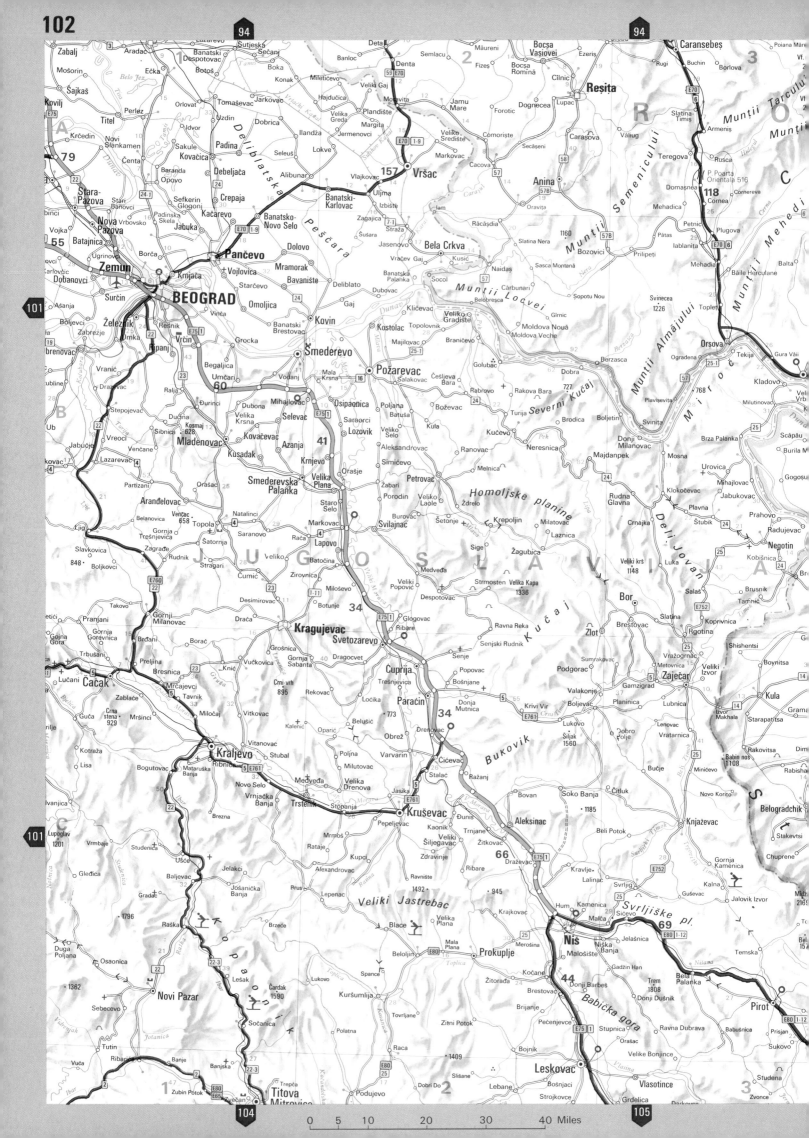

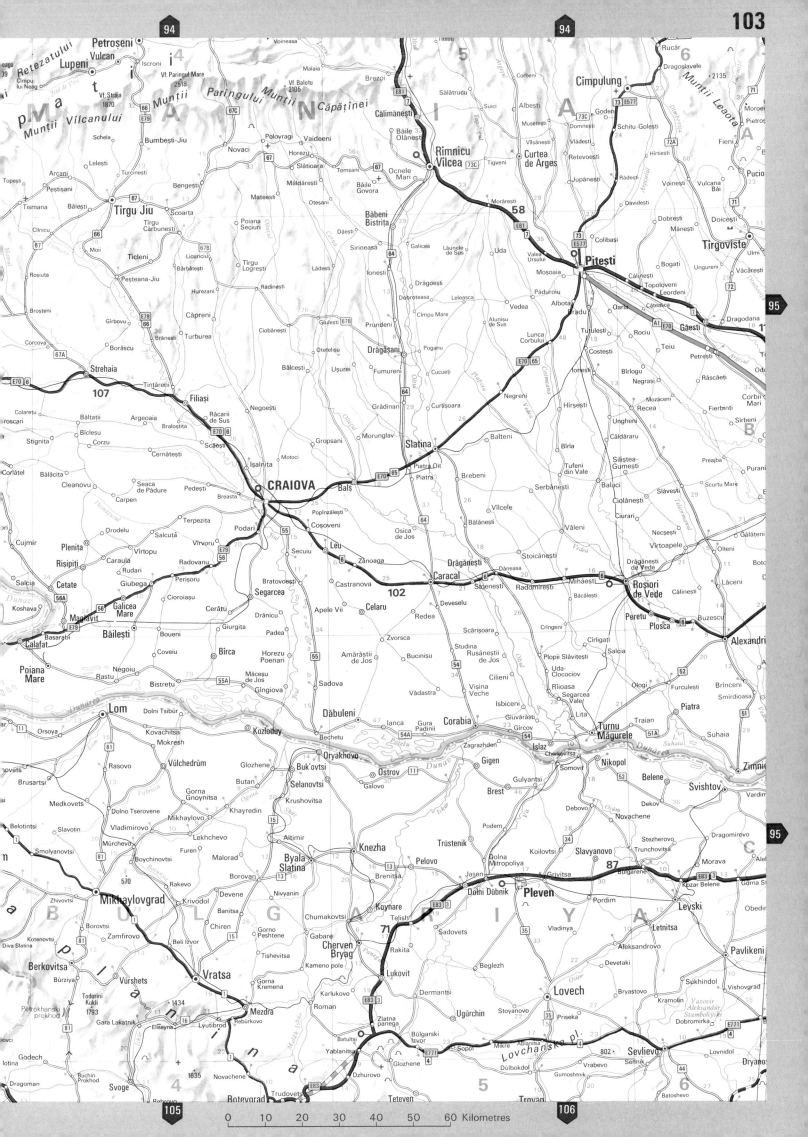

A 1 2

Siniajevina

Pašina Voda
Potrkajci
Bijelo Polje
Sebecevo
Tovrljane
Polatna
Raca

2041
Bistrica
Mojkovac
Poda
Tutin
Vuča
Ribariće
Banje
Banjska
Trepča
Podujevo

Savnik
Biogradsko Nac Park
Crna glava 2137
Trpezi
Kalače
Rožaj
Zubin Potok
Zvečan
Titova Mitrovica
Glavnik
E80

Moračka Kapa 2227
2253
Bjelasica
Ivangrad
Vinicka
Mokra gora
Rudnik
Gornja Klina
Vučitrn
Donje Ljupce
Batlava
Orlane

Niksic
Maganik
Kolašin
Matesevo
Trešnjevik 1598
Andrijevica
Hajla 2400
Istok
Novo Selo
Srbica
Gornja Klina
Obilić
Makovac
Priština

Gornje Polje
Prekornica
Liverovici
Murino
Velika
Kučište
Peć
Vitomirica
Đurakovac
Klina
Iglarevo
Komoran
Novo Brdo

B 81

Cevo
Danilov Grad
Brezojevice
Plav
Marjaš 2530
Stari Raušić
Streoci
Dečani
Orlate
Magura
Lipljan
Janjevo
Paralovo

Cetinje
Titograd
Bioce
Ubli
Gusinje
Prokletije
Junik
Skivjani
Ratkovac
Banja
Crnoljevo
Štimlje
Brasalce

Rijeka Crnojev
Mahala
Spuž
Boge
Jezerce 2694 Theth
Tropoje
Đakovica
Studenčane
Suva Reka
Blace
Uroševac
Požaranje

Golubovci
Bajze
Bajram-Curr
Velika Kruša
Kušnin
Zjum
Pirane
Mašutište
Stari Kačanik

Virpazar
Sutorman 844
Koplik
Nicaj-Shale
Zrze
Doganović
E752
Prizren
Ljuboten 2499
Kačanik

Skadarsko Jezero
Mes
Ur'e Shtrenjtë
Shemeri
Zur
Vrbica
Sredska
Dragaš
Vratnica
Globocnica
Skopje

Sutomore
Rumija
Kostanica
O.Ostros
Shkodër
Pukë
Fushë-Arrez
Kukes
Šar planina
Dobroste
Tearce

Stari Bar
Krute
Murigan
Bushat
Korthpulë
Bicaj
Tetovo
Dorče Petrov
E65

Pečurice
Sukobin
Dajč
Kashnjet
Zelino
Grupčin
Matka
Gorno Nerezi

Ulcinj
Velipoje
Kalmet
Blinisht
Fushe-Lure
Kameniane

Sveti Nikola
Drin
Réshen
Kurbnesh
Suhodoll
Vrapčište
Cegrane
Zdunje
Nova Breznica

Shëngjin
Lezhe
Rubik
Peshkopi
Žirovnica
Mavrovi Hanov
Vrutok
Gostivar
Kodra Taurli 1853
Solunska Glava 2540

Pellg i Drinit
Milot
Rubik
Murrë
Lunar
Maqellare
Mavrovo Nac Park
Rostuša
Galičnik
Zajas
Kičevo
Brod

Kep i Rodonit
Laç
Mamurras
Burrel
Debar
Bistra Pl.
Čelopeci
Debrište
Ropotovo

Gji i Lalzés
Ishm
Klos
Bulqize
Kruševo
Krivogaštani
Sopotnica

C
Krujë
Vore
Ostren i math
Klenjë
Lukovo
Labuništa
Belčište
Botun
Lešani
Murgaševo

Kep i Palit
Shijak
Peshk
Zgozdh
Vevčani
Velešta
Mešeišta
Struga
Kukurecani

Trieste
Durrës
TIRANË
Vaqarr
Petrele
Vrrie
Klenjë
Librazhd
Trebenište
Kosel
Ohrid
Resen

Gji i Durrësit
Ndroq
Mesqetë
Labinot-Mal
Radožda
Kališta
Galičica Nac Park
Carev Dvor

81
Kavajë
Gracen
Prrenjas
Pogradec
Kukurecani
Bitola 2600
Bukovo

Kryevidh
Rrogozhinë
Peqin
Çerrik
Elbasan
Gostimë
Belsh
Radokal i Poshtëm
Peštani
Prespansko Jezero

D
Lushnje
Divjakë
Drizë
Gramsh
Pojan
Maliq
Ljubojno
Medžitli
Flórina

Libofshë
Fier
Stalin
Ure Vajgurore
Sojnik
Moglice
Pustec
Podgori
Áyios Yermanós
2128

Levan
Roskovec
Berat
Uznove
Mali Tomorr
Voskopoje
Bilisht
Kroustallopigí

Patos
Novoselë
Cakran
Ballsh
Vijosë
Korçë
Kató Klinai
Vérnik
E86

0 5 10 20 30 40 Miles

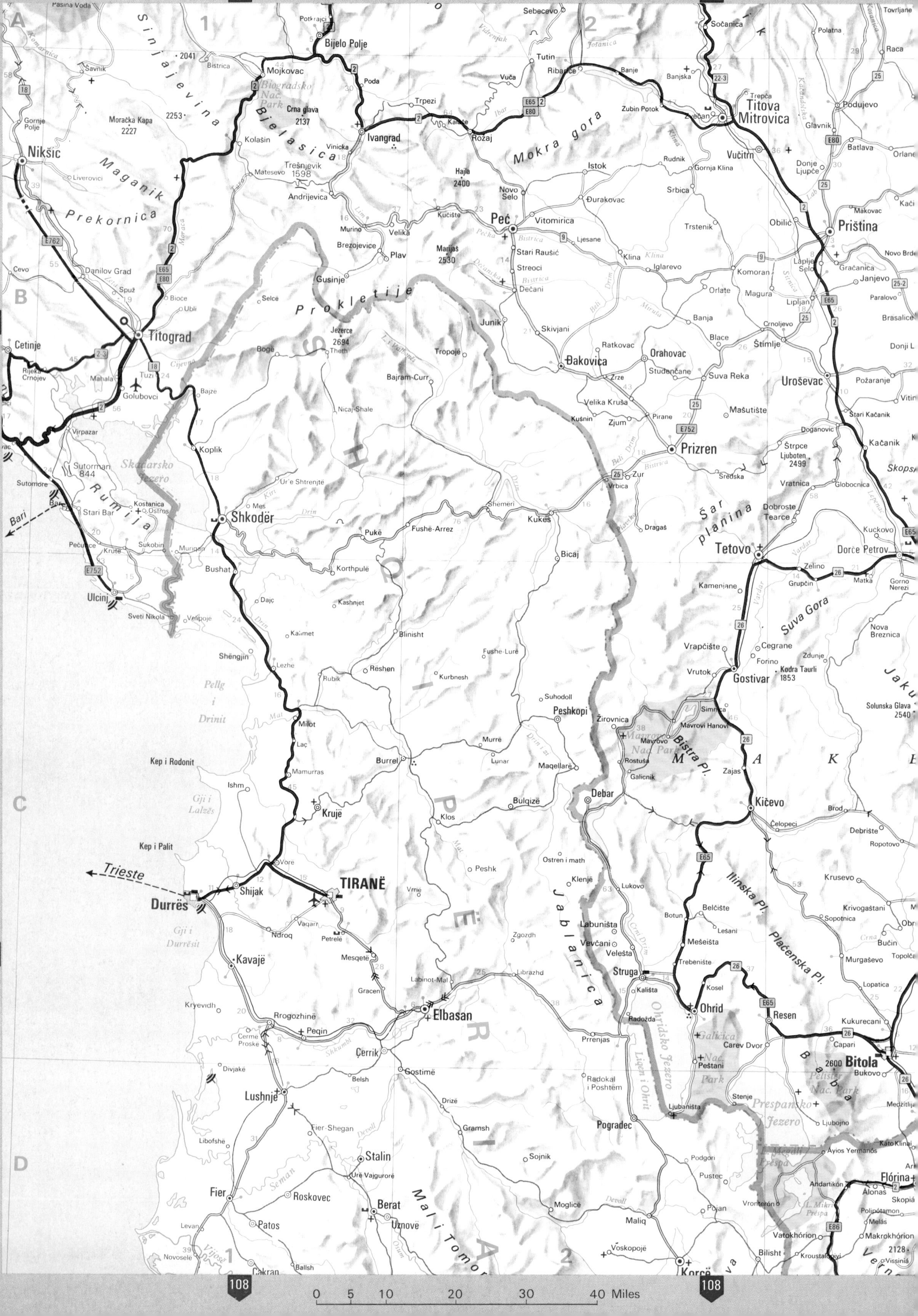

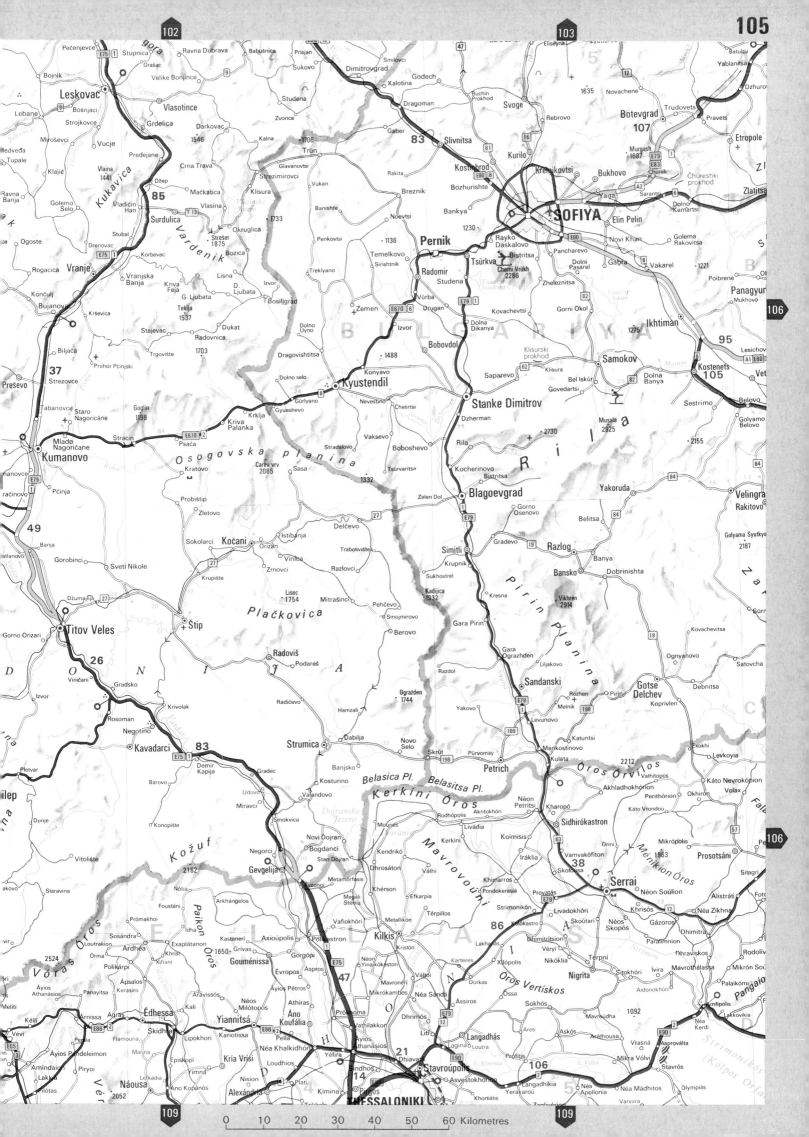

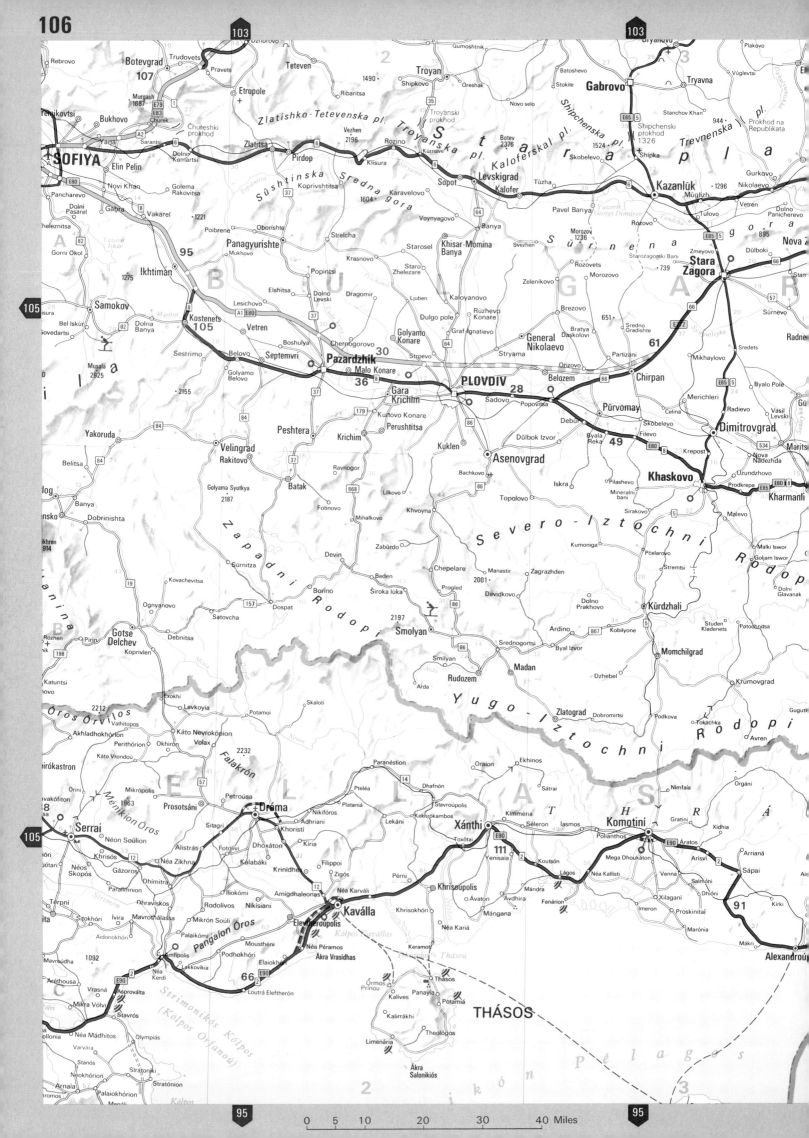

ra Reka
Ticha   Yablanovo   Vŭrbitsa   Rish   133   Veselinovo   Asparuhovo   Georgi Trajkov   Staro Oryakhovo
Kotlenska pl   4   Rishki prokhod   Bilka   Kamchiyska   planina   Rudnik
824   Rishki prokhod   5   planina   E87   Byala
Karnobatska planina   Kamchiya   Lyulyakovo   Prilep   Düskotna   Solnik   Dyulino   Obzor
Kotel   Zheravna   Gradets   Beronovo   Podvis   800   Aytoska planina   Prosenik   Orizare   Emona
Byala   Avramovski prokhod   Sungurlare   Karnobatski prokhod   Lozarevo   Malka Aytoska   Aytoski prokhod   planina   Nos Emene
Slivenska pl.   Avramov   Raklitsa   Müglen   Bryastovets   Kableshkovo   E87   Nesebŭr
Sliven   Gorno Aleksandrovo   108   Venets   6   73   Aytos   Rudnik   9   Pomorie
Karnobat   Stralbha   Bülgarovo   E772   Kameno   Sarafovo   BURGAS
Zhelyu Voyvoda   Ekzarkh Antimovo   Troyanovo   Dolno Ezerovo   Chernomorets
Yambol   Irechekovo   Dobrinovo   Rusokastrovo   34   Sozopol
Konevo   Kermen   Bezmer   Kalchevo   Tamarino   53   Rosen   9
Gülübitsi   Okop   Grudovo   Siredetska   Veselie   Maslen nos
Mlekarevo   Roza   Tenevo   Kamenets   Aleksandrovo   98   Yasna Polyana   Primorsko
Mogili   Inzovo   Krumovo   Vüshilo   Krushevets   Kiten
Novoselets   Skalista   Golyam Manastir   Popovo   Stefan Karadzhovo   Fakiya   Lozenec
vachevo   Elkhovo   Knyazhevo   Bolyarovo   Gorska Polyana   Zvezdets   Gramatikovo   Kondolovo   E87   9   Michurin
Müdrets   78   Topolovgrad   Sharkovo   Izgrev   Varvara   Akhtopol
Glavan   Bülgarska Polyana   Ustrem   Gyurgenbair   556   Brodilovo   Sinemorets
Mladinovo   Studena   Radovets   98   Malko Turnovo   Rezovo
Lyubimets   20   Shtit   Keşirlik   Dereköy   Istranca Dağları   İğneada   İğneada Burnu
Selo   Svilengrad   32   Sarayakpınar   Kirazbayır Tepe 758   Polos   E87   Demirköy
Ormenion   Kapitan Andreevo   E85   Lâlapaşa   Bedre   Mahya Dağ 1030   Serves Burnu
Petrotá   Dhikaia   E80   100   Arnavutköy   Süloğlu   Kırklareli   Üsküp   Yenice   Sergen   Midye
Kómara   45   Edirne   Geçkinli   Haciumur   Karahidir   20   Kızılcıdere   Kaynarca   Evrencik   Pineke
Pendálofos   Kastanéai   Kızılmüsellim   İnece   Kavaklı   Pınarhisar   Cevizköy   Evrenli
Filákion   Rizia   30   Osmanlı   Haskoy   E87   Yancıklar   Çakıllı
Váltos   51   Néa Vissi   Kavili   20   Ahmetbey   Hasbuğa   20   Safaalan
Kkándras   Orestiás   Havsa   55   Küleli   TÜRKİYE   Saray   İstranca   Karacaköy   Ormanlı
Metaxádhes   Máni   Thórion   550   Babaeski   24   Lüleburgaz   Sofular   Büyük Manika   Kapaklı   Danamandıra
Palioúri   Pithion   Prángi   Doğança   Alpullu   E80   100   Evrensekiz   Beyazköy   Çerkezköy   Dağyenice
Mavrokklisi   Dhidhimótikhon   Yeniköy   Tilkıpınar   Velimeşe   Kızılpınar   Beyciler
Mikrón Dhérion   555   Pehlivanköy   Büyük Karıştıran   565   75   Ulaş   Kurfallı
Lávara   Uzunköprü   Lahna   Marmaracık   Fenerköy
Sidhiró   Büyük Doğanca   Çöpköy   Hayrabolu   Dambaslar   Muratlı   Çorlu   E80   567   Çatalca
hérion   Souflion   Kavacik   Türkgücü   95
Likófi   Subaşı   Kurtbey   Susuzmüsellim   Banarlı   E80   Silivri
essáni   Lira   51   Küplü   Balabanköy   Şahin   Bıyıkalı   565   Yeniçiftlik   100   Selimpaşa
Levkimi   Tikherón   İbriktepe   Kozyürük   555   Marmaraereğlisi   Baba Burnu
Péplos   Peşayigit   Yörük   141   Tekirdağ   Mimarsinan
Ardhánion   İpsala   550   48   E90   110   Malkara   E84   110   İnecik   Barbaros
Férrai   Kesan   110   E84   Ballı   Barbaros   MARMARA   DENİZİ
hóriskos   Karpuzlu   Çamlıca   E90   E87   Kura Dağı   Ganos Dağı 945   Hoşköy
Yenice   Sehitler   550   72   Kadıköy   Mürefte   Saraylar
Orhaniye   Celtik   Mecidiye   Kavak   Şarköy   Marmara   MARMARA ADA
Ibrice İskelesi   Bakla Burnu   İnce Burun   İmralı Ada
Koruköy   Avşar Ada   Kapsül Burnu
Karaburgaz   Bolayır   782

Saros Körfezi   4   5   6

0   10   20   30   40   50   60   Kilometres

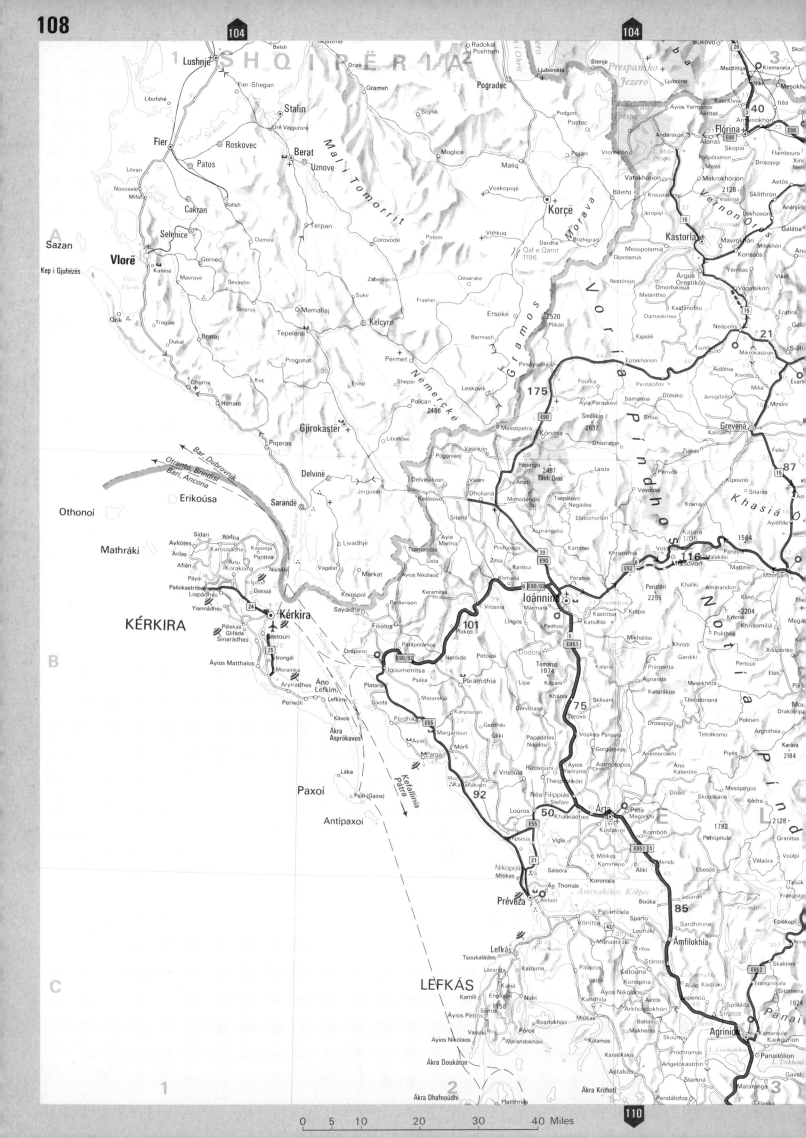

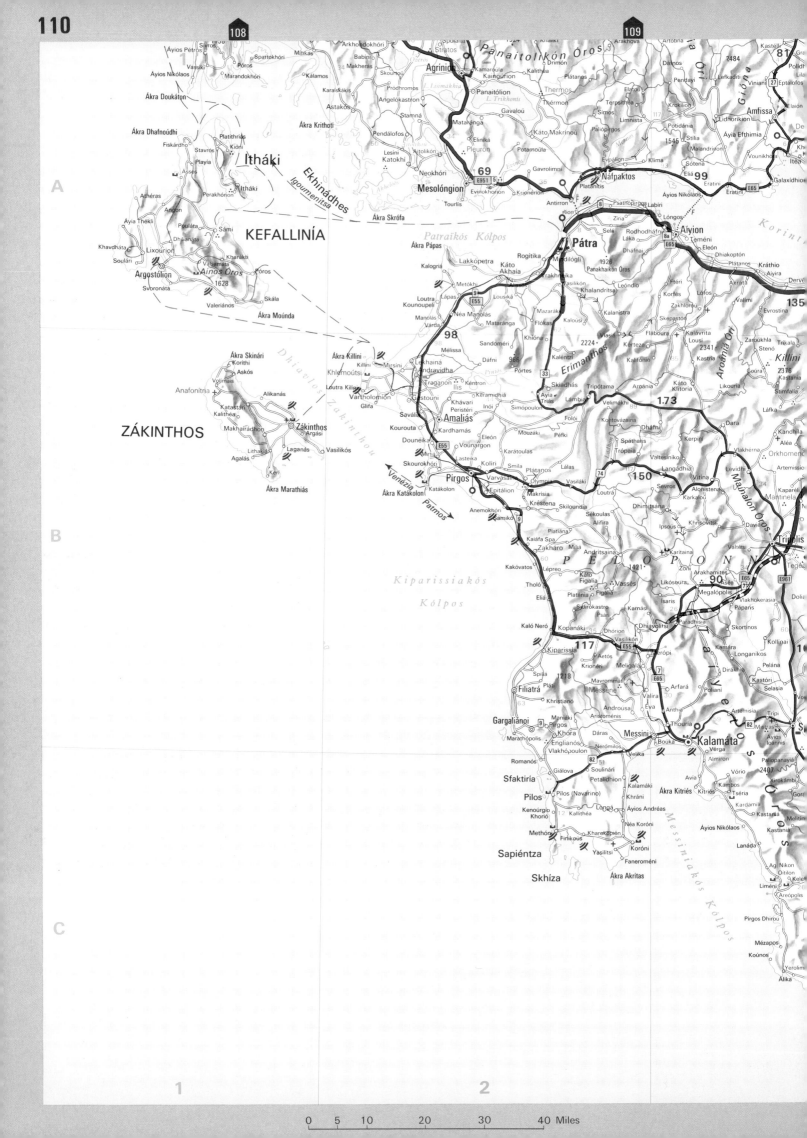

108

109

81

A

Panaitolikón Óros

Agrínion

Ekhinádhes
Igoumenitsa

Ítháki

Ítháki

KEFALLINÍA

Patraïkós Kólpos

Náfpaktos 99

Pátra

Ainos Óros
1628

Argostólion

Lixoúrion

Korinti

Aíyion 135

ZÁKINTHOS

Dhíavlos Zakinthou

98

Ákra Killini

Erimanthos

1.73

Amaliás

Pírgos

Olympia

150

Tripolis

B

Kiparissiakós
Kólpos

P E L O P O N N

90

117

Kiparissia

Messene

Kalamáta

Filiatrá

Messini

Gargaliánoi

Pilos

Koróni

Sapiéntza

Messiniakós Kólpos

Skhíza

Ákra Akrítas

C

1

2

0   5   10   20   30   40 Miles

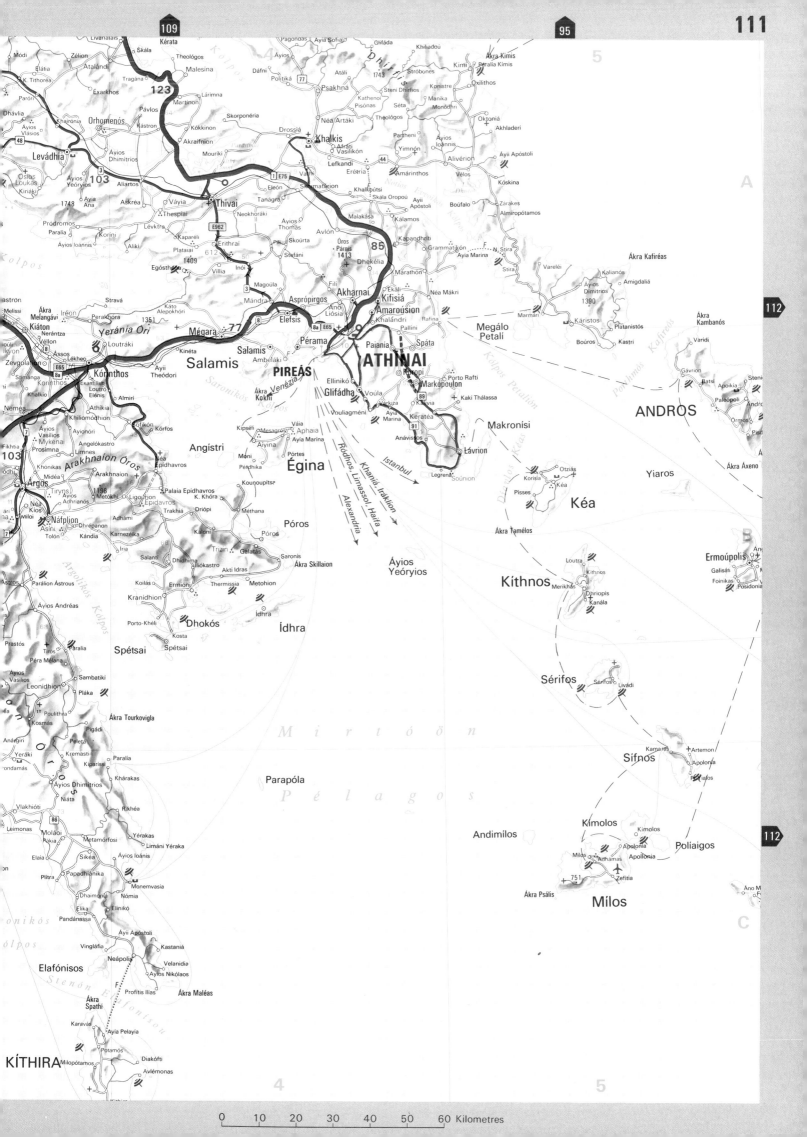

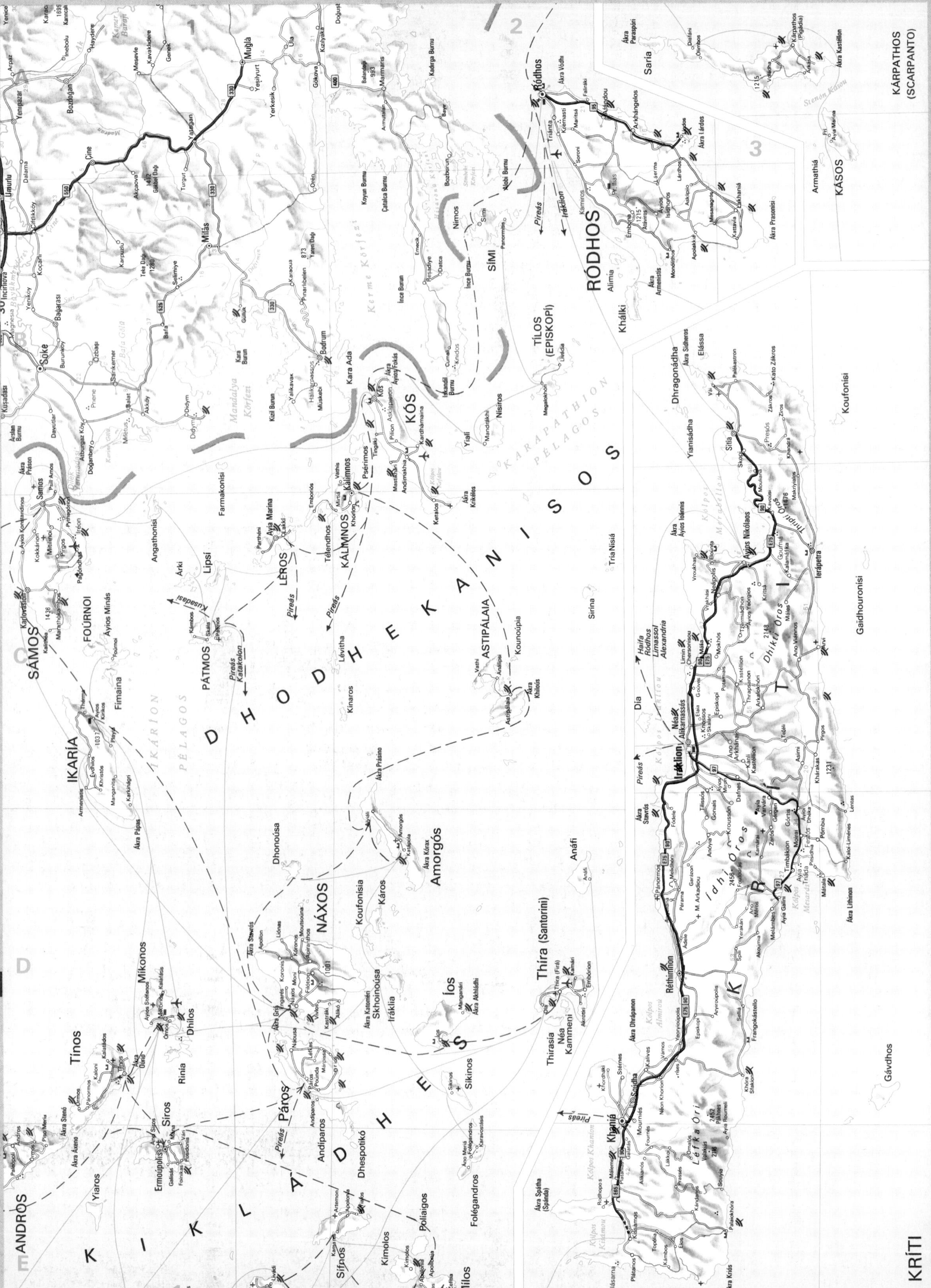

KÁRPATHOS
(SCARPANTO)

KÁSOS

Saría

Ákra Paraspóri
Ákra Kárpathos (Pigádia)

Stenón Kásou

Ákra Sídheros
Eláassa

Dhragonádha

Sítia

Koufonísi

Gaïdhouronísi

KRÍTI

RÓDHOS

Ródhos
Ákra Vódhi

SÍMI

TÍLOS (EPISKOPÍ)

KHÁLKI

Alimiá

Nísiros

KÓS

Psérimos

KÁLIMNOS

Astipálaia
ASTIPÁLAIA

LÉROS

Lipsí
PÁTMOS

Arkí

Angathonísi

Farmakonísi

FOÚRNOI

SÁMOS

Ikaría
IKARÍA

IKÁRION PÉLAGOS

Dhonoúsa

Koufonísia

Káros

AmorgÓs

Anáfi

Thíra (Santoríni)
Néa Kamméni
Thirasía

Íos

Síkinos

Folégandros

Políaigos

Kímolos

Sífnos

Mílos

KIKLÁDHES

NÁXOS

Páros
PÁROS
Andíparos
Dhespotikó

Náxos

Skhoinoúsa
Iráklia

Síros
Ermoúpolis

Míkonos
Dhílos
Rínia

Tínos

ANDROS

Yiáros

Iráklion
Réthimnon
Khaniá
Ayios Nikólaos
Ierápetra

DHODHEKÁNISOS

Mandálya Körfezi

Bodrum

Kara Ada

Kos

Söke

Kuşadasi

Miğla

Milás

Çine

KARAPÁTHION PÉLAGOS

KÓLPOS MESARÁS

LÉFKA ÓRI

ÍDHI ÓROS

DHÍKTI ÓROS

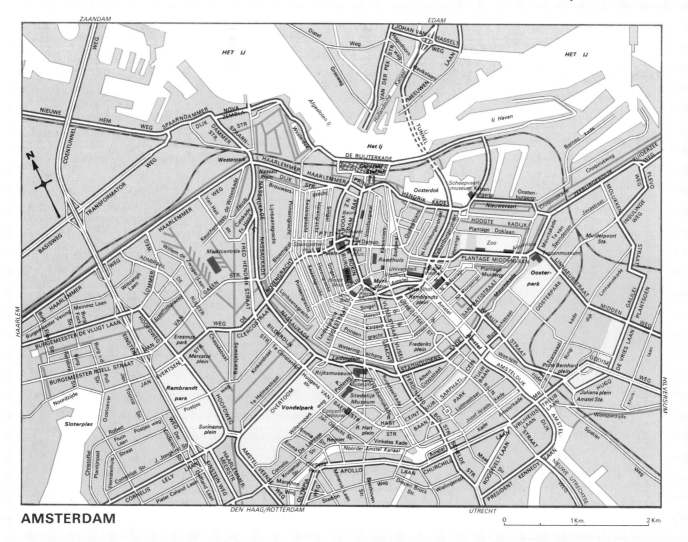

AMSTERDAM

0   1Km.   2 Km.

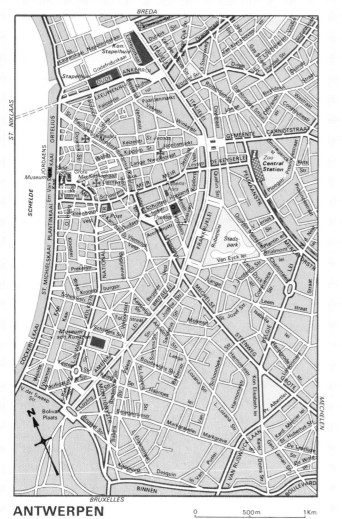

ANTWERPEN

0   500m.   1Km.

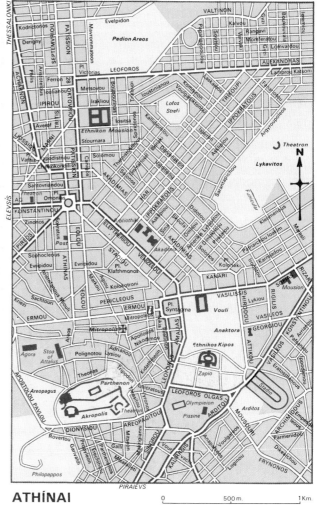

ATHÍNAI

0   500m.   1Km.

BARCELONA   0   500 m.

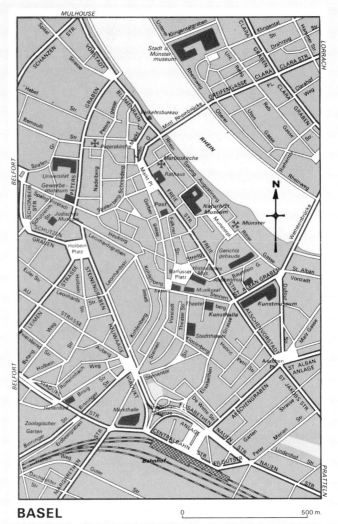

BASEL   0   500 m.

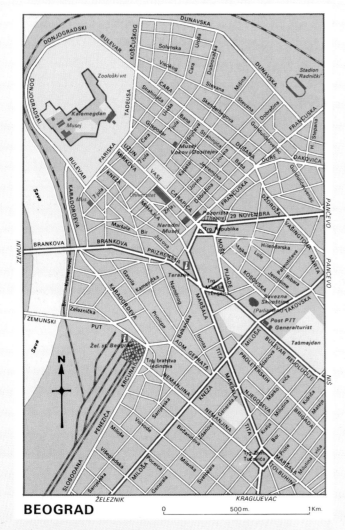

BEOGRAD   0   500 m.   1 Km.

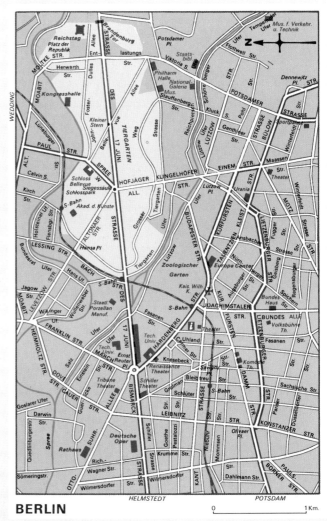

BERLIN   0   1 Km.

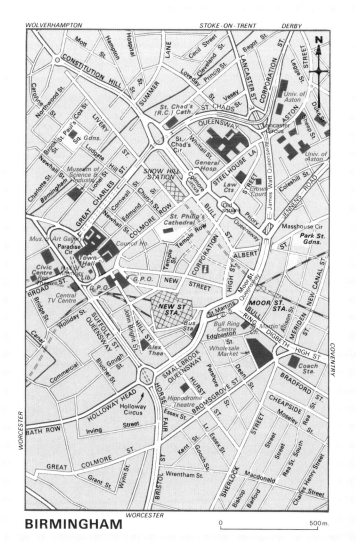

BIRMINGHAM

0 _____ 500 m.

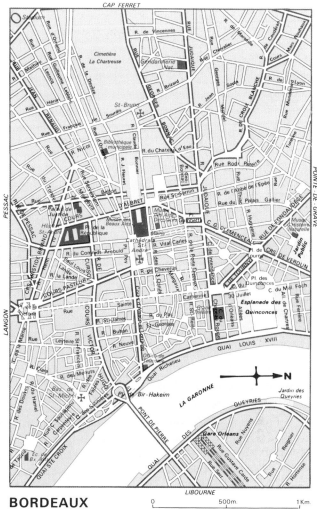

BORDEAUX

0 _____ 500m. _____ 1 Km.

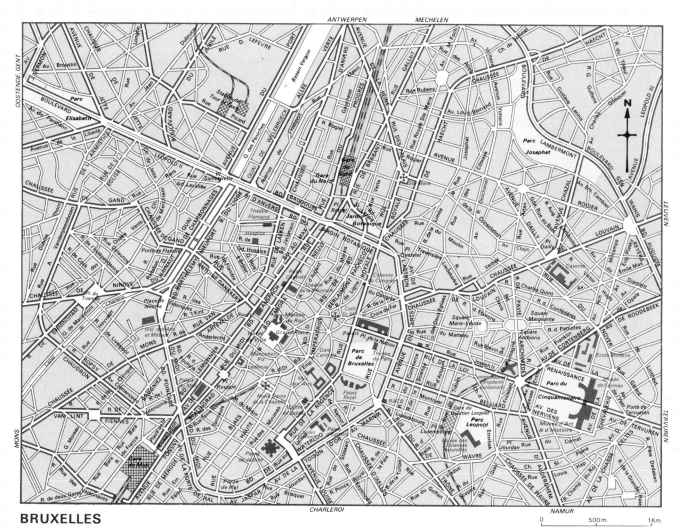

BRUXELLES

0 _____ 500m. _____ 1Km.

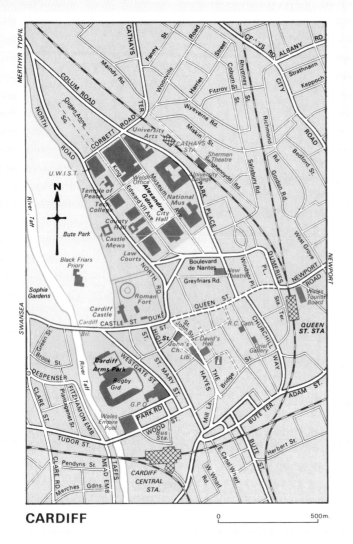

CARDIFF

0   500m.

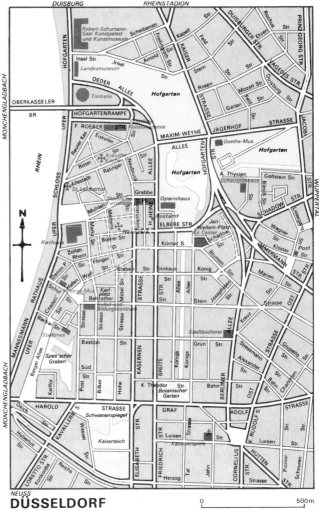

DÜSSELDORF

0   500m.

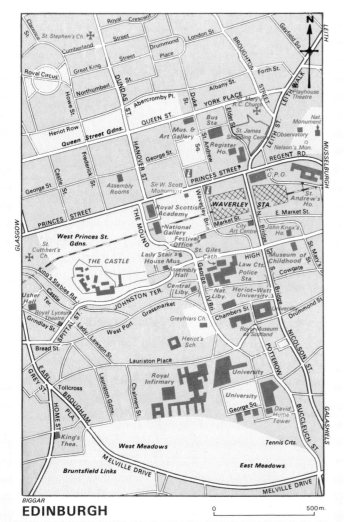

EDINBURGH

0   500m.

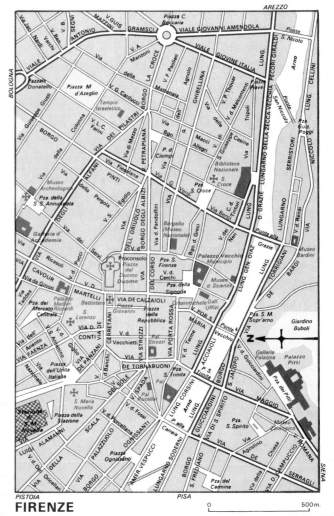

FIRENZE

0   500m.

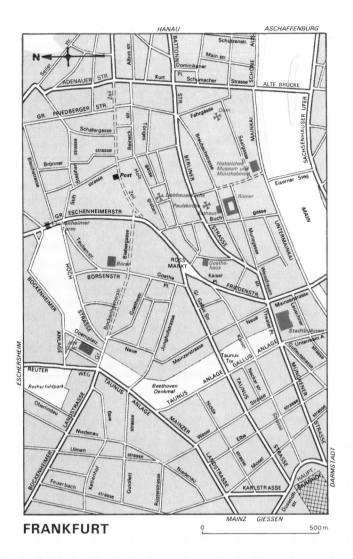

FRANKFURT

0   MAINZ GIESSEN   500 m.

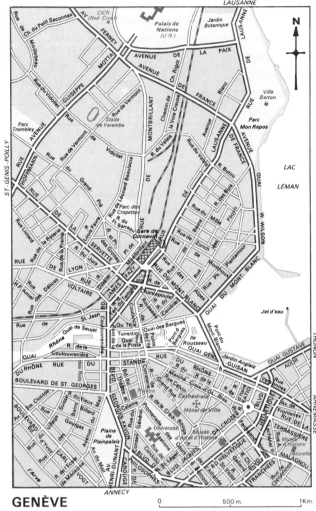

GENÈVE

0   500 m.   1 Km.

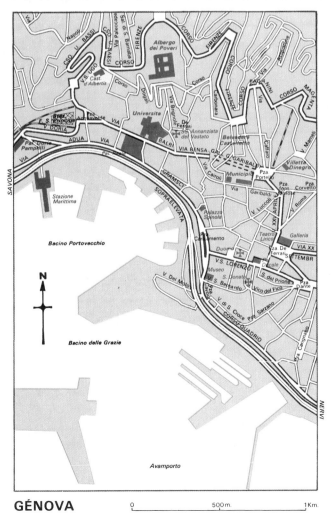

GÉNOVA

0   500 m.   1 Km.

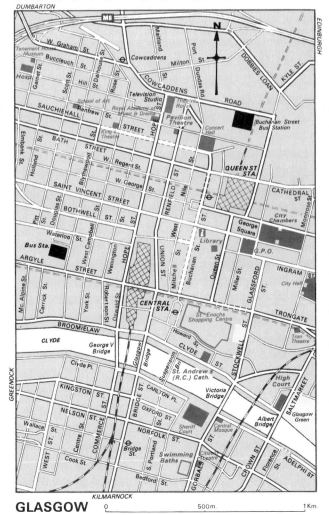

GLASGOW

0   500 m.   1 Km.

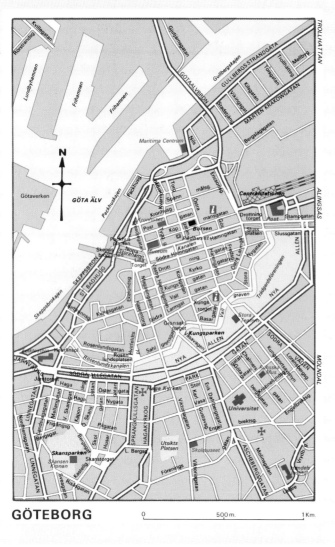

GÖTEBORG

0   500 m.   1 Km.

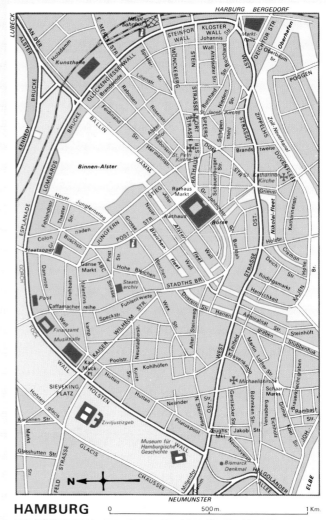

HAMBURG

0   500 m.   1 Km.

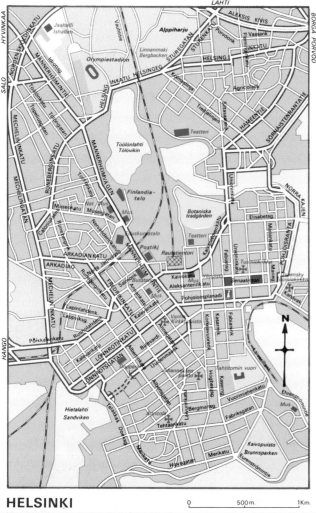

HELSINKI

0   500 m.   1 Km.

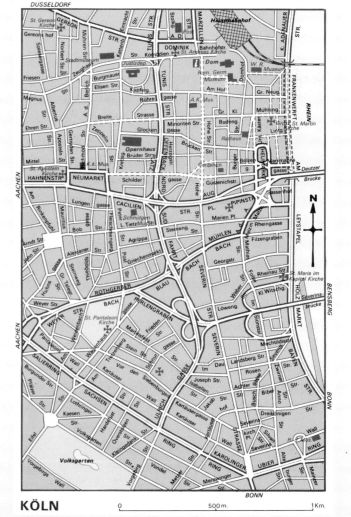

KÖLN

0   500 m.   1 Km.

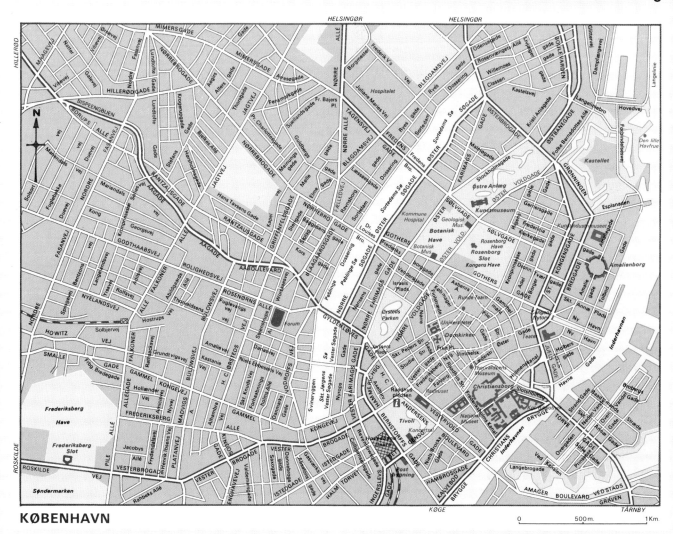

KØBENHAVN

0   500 m.   1 Km.

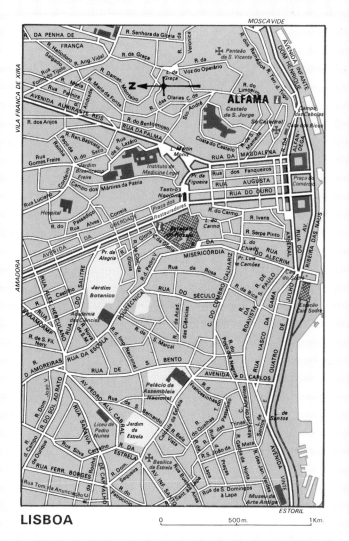

LISBOA

0   500 m.   1 Km.

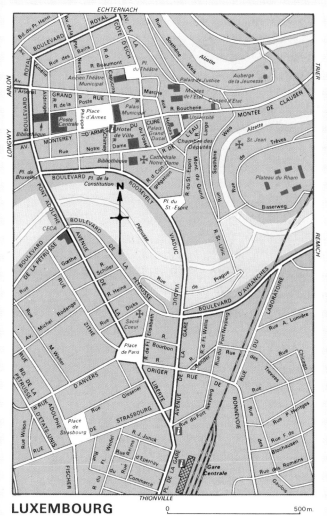

LUXEMBOURG

0   500 m.

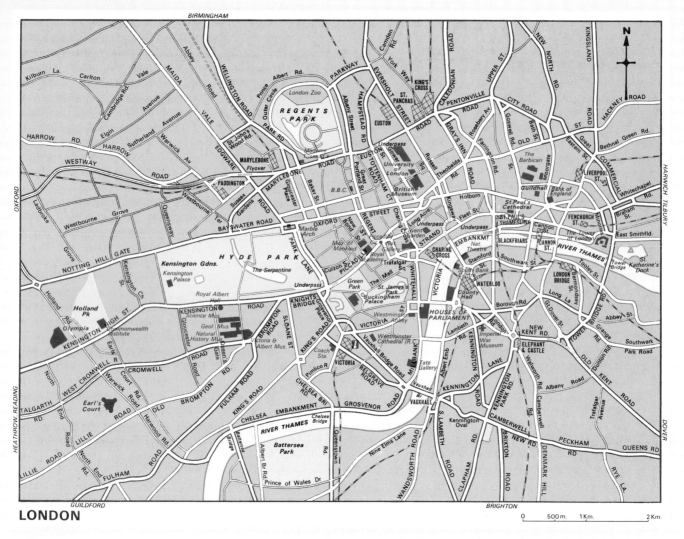

LONDON

0   500 m.   1 Km.   2 Km.

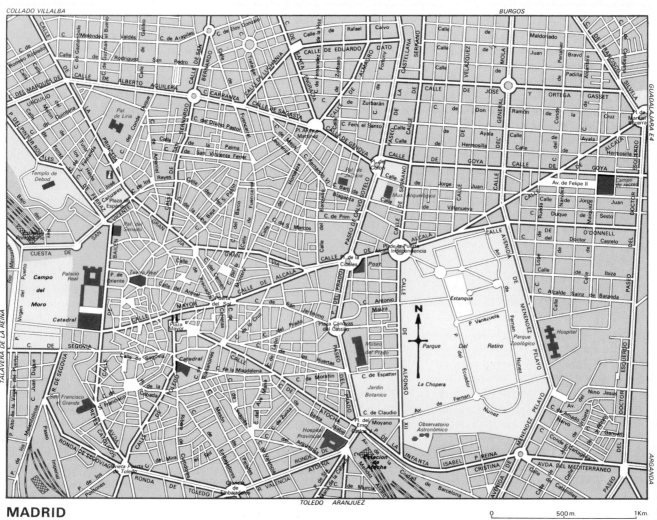

MADRID

0   500 m.   1 Km.

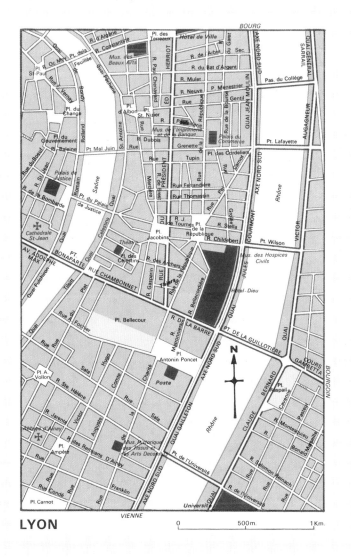

LYON

0   500 m.   1 Km.

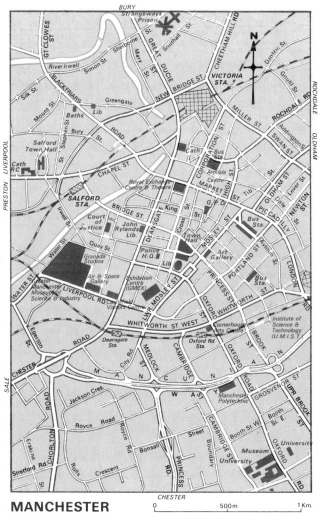

MANCHESTER

0   500 m.   1 Km.

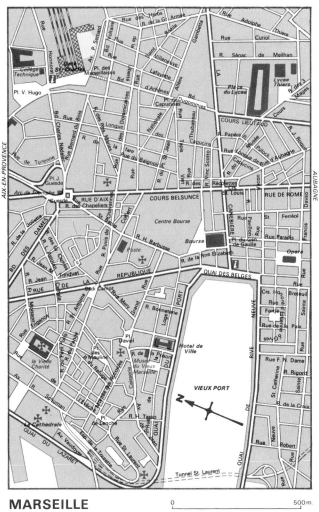

MARSEILLE

0   500 m.

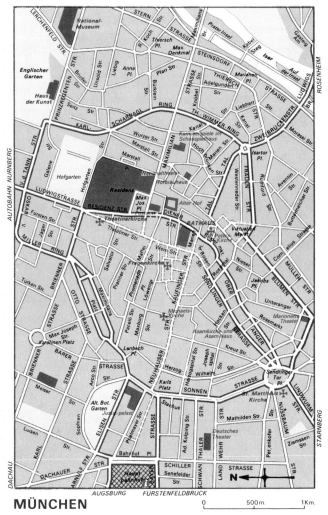

MÜNCHEN

0   500 m.   1 Km.

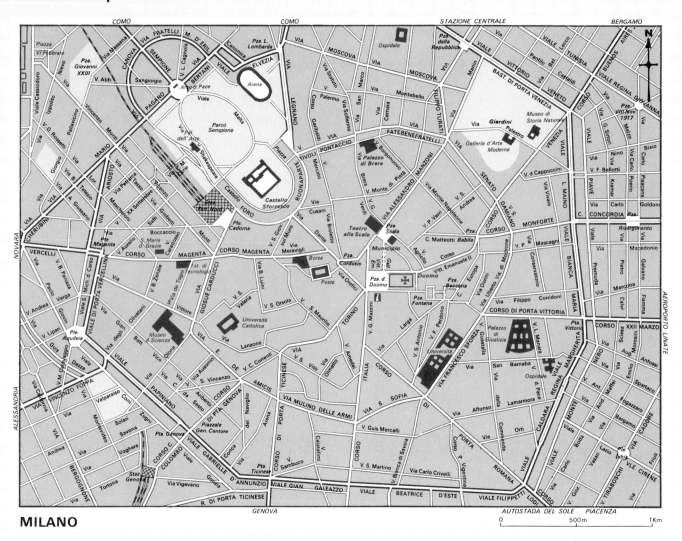

MILANO

AUTOSTADA DEL SOLE   PIACENZA

0   500 m.   1 Km.

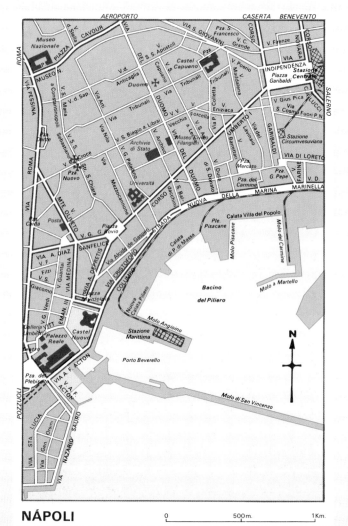

NÁPOLI

0   500 m.   1 Km.

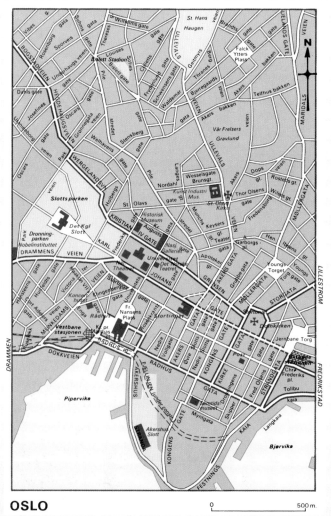

OSLO

0   500 m.

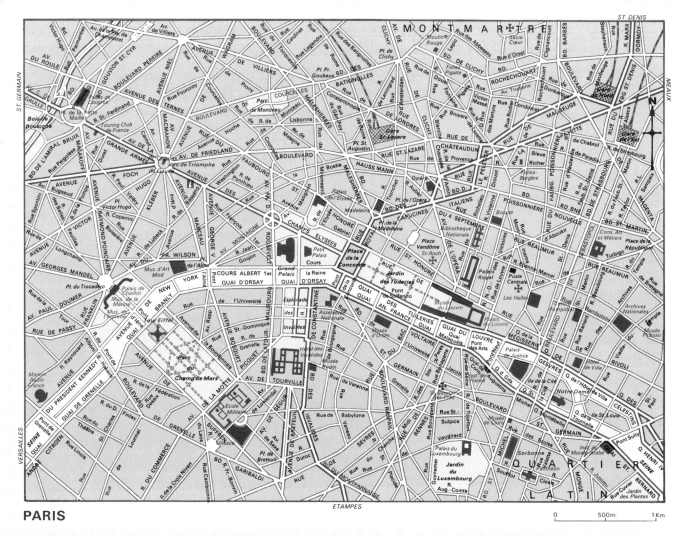

PARIS

0   500m.   1Km.

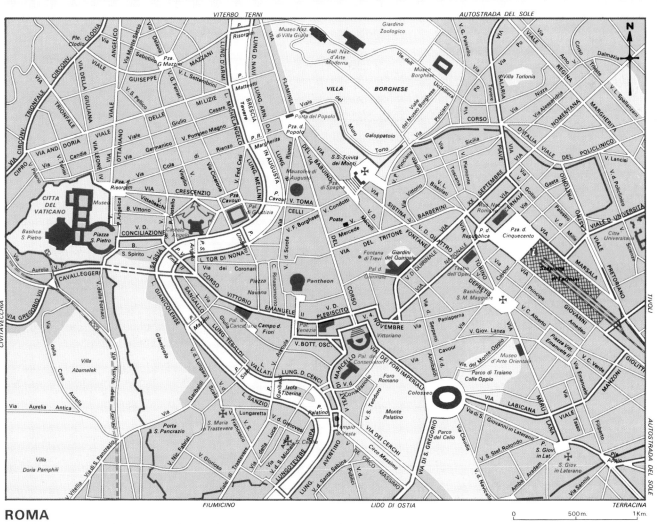

ROMA

0   500m.   1Km.

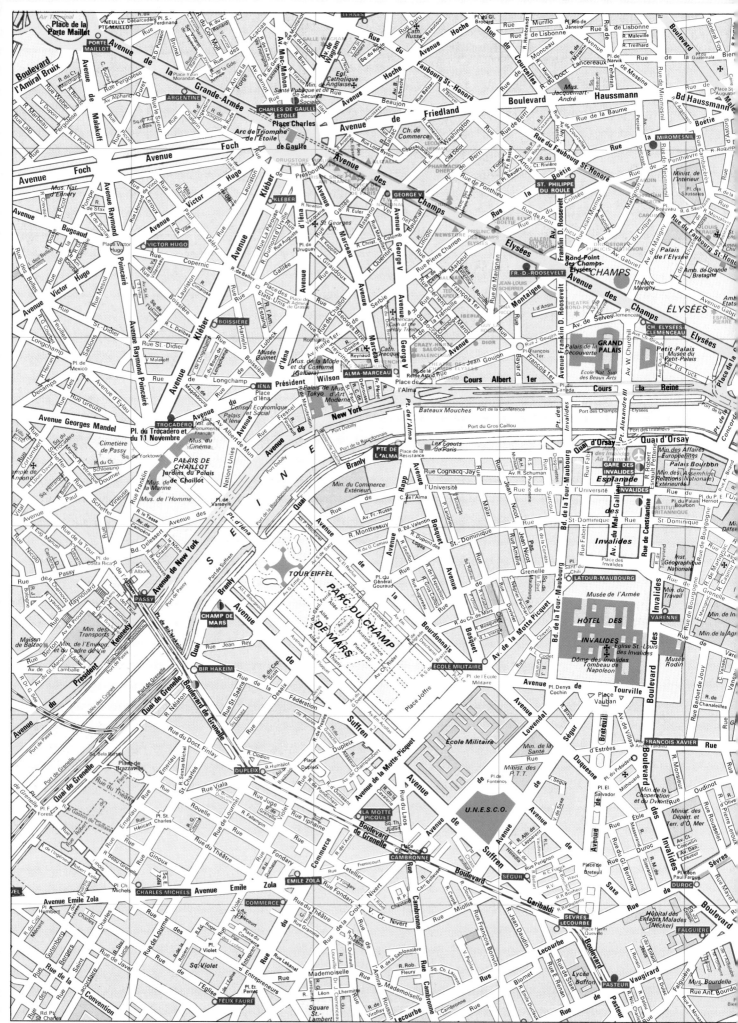

PARIS 1 : 15 000

GARE ST-LAZARE
GARE DE L'EST
JARDIN DES TUILERIES
PALAIS ROYAL
PALAIS DU LOUVRE
LES HALLES
CENTRE POMPIDOU
MARAIS
ÎLE DE LA CITÉ
ÎLE ST-LOUIS
PALAIS DU LUXEMBOURG
JARDIN DU LUXEMBOURG
QUARTIER LATIN
MONTPARNASSE
JARDIN DES PLANTES
Muséum National d'Histoire Naturelle

0   500m.   1Km.

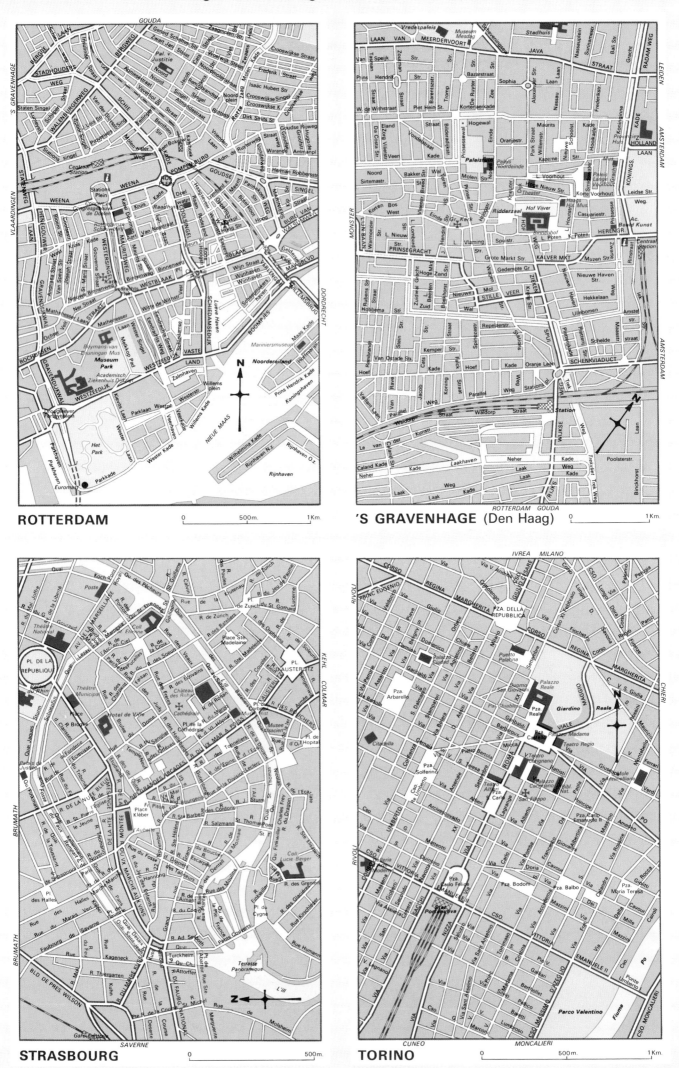

ROTTERDAM 0   500m.   1 Km.

'S GRAVENHAGE (Den Haag) 0   1 Km.

STRASBOURG 0   500m.

TORINO 0   500m.   1 Km.

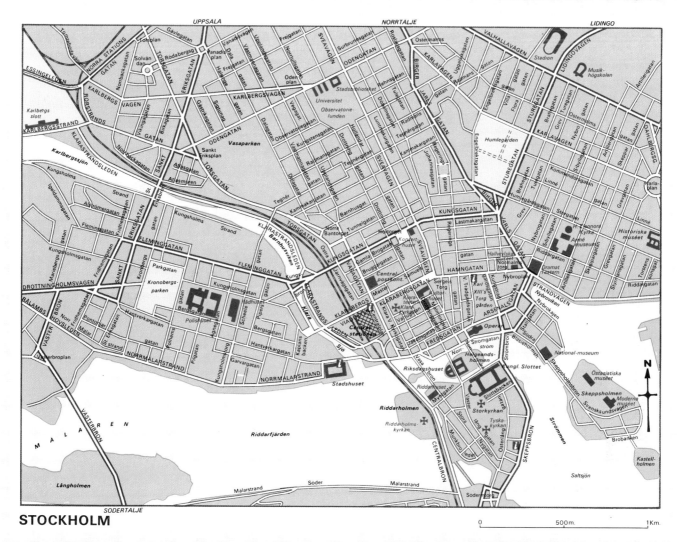

STOCKHOLM

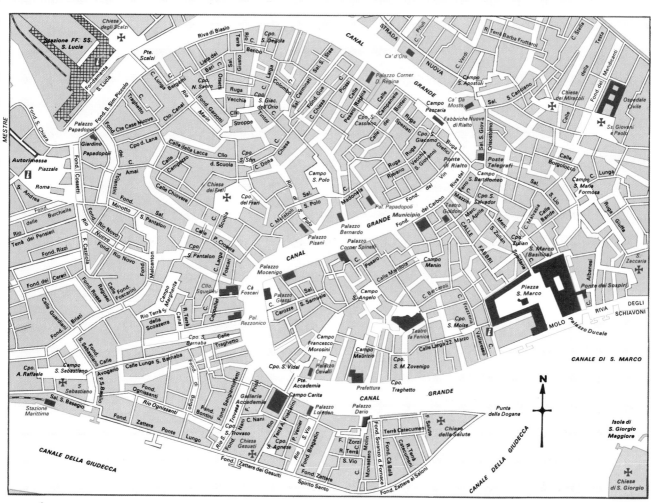

VENÉZIA

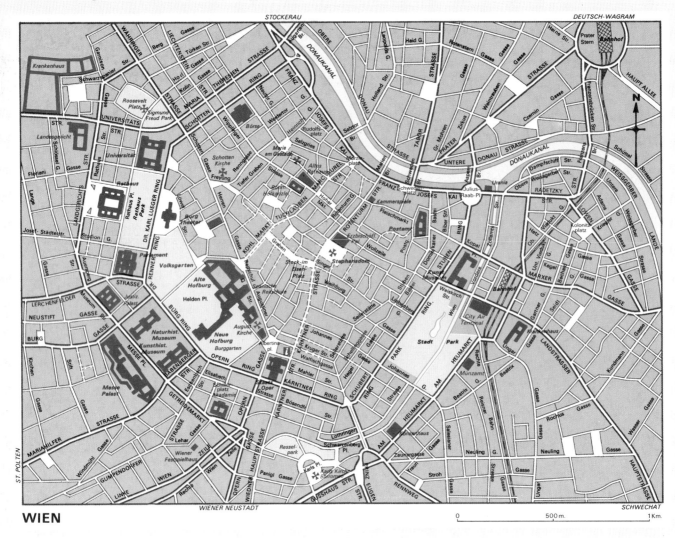

WIEN

0   500 m.   1 Km.

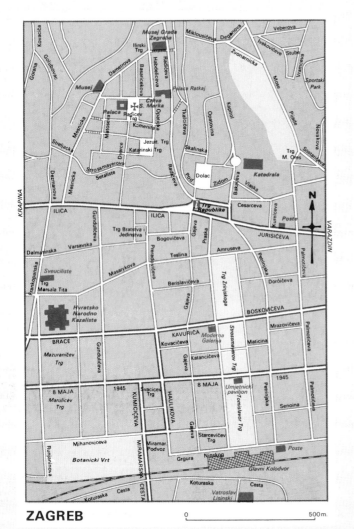

ZAGREB

0   500 m.

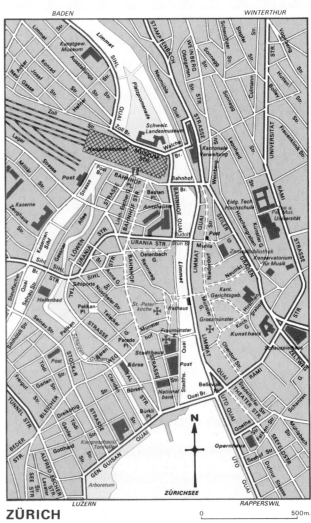

ZÜRICH

0   500 m.

GB	F		D	I	GB	F		D	I
Austria	Autriche	A	Österreich	Austria	Italy	Italie	I	Italien	Italia
Albania	Albanie	AL	Albanien	Albania	Ireland	Irlande	IRL	Irland	Irlanda
Andorra	Andorre	AND	Andorra	Andorra	Liechtenstein	Liechtenstein	FL	Liechtenstein	Liechtenstein
Belgium	Belgique	B	Belgien	Belgio	Luxembourg	Luxembourg	L	Luxemburg	Lussemburgo
Bulgaria	Bulgarie	BG	Bulgarien	Bulgaria	Monaco	Monaco	MC	Monaco	Monaco
Switzerland	Suisse	CH	Schweiz	Svizzera	Norway	Norvège	N	Norwegen	Norvegia
Czechoslovakia	Tchécoslovaquie	CS	Tschechoslowakei	Cecoslovacchia	Netherlands	Pays-Bas	NL	Niederlande	Paesi Bassi
Germany	Allemagne	D	Deutschland	Germania	Portugal	Portugal	P	Portugal	Portogallo
Denmark	Danemark	DK	Dänemark	Danimarca	Poland	Pologne	PL	Polen	Polonia
Spain	Espagne	E	Spanien	Spagna	Rumania	Roumanie	RO	Rumanien	Romania
France	France	F	Frankreich	Francia	San Marino	Saint-Marin	RSM	San Marino	San Marino
United Kingdom	Royaume Uni	GB	Großbritannien und Nordirland	Regno Unito	Sweden	Suède	S	Schweden	Svezia
					Finland	Finlande	SF	Finnland	Finlandia
Gibraltar	Gibraltar	GBZ	Gibraltar	Gibilterra	Soviet Union	Union Soviétique	SU	Sowjetunion	Unione Sovietica
Greece	Grèce	GR	Greichenland	Grecia	Turkey	Turquie	TR	Türkei	Turchia
Hungary	Hongrie	H	Ungarn	Ungheria	Yugoslavia	Yougoslavie	YU	Jugoslawien	Jugoslavia

A

30 A Coruña E A2
30 A Pontenova E A3
31 A-Ver-o-Mar P C2
71 Aach D A4
17 Aachen D C6
67 Aalen D C6
17 Aalsmeer NL A4
17 Aalst B C4
17 Aalst NL B5
62 Aalten NL B1
47 Aanekoski SF E12
70 Aarau CH A3
70 Aarberg CH A2
70 Aarburg CH A2
16 Aardenburg N B3
17 Aarschot B C4
47 Aavasaksa SF C11
99 Aba H A3
39 Abádanes E B4
38 Abades E B2
99 Abádszalók H A5
98 Abaliget H B3
72 Ábano Terme I C1
45 Abarán E A5
97 Abasár H D6
78 Abbadia S. Salvatore I A2
59 Abbehausen D B5
57 Abbekäs S D2
16 Abbeville F C1
4 Abbey IRL A3
9 Abbey Town GB D4
4 Abbeyfeale IRL B2
5 Abbeyleix IRL B4
5 Abbeyside IRL B4
71 Abbiategrasso I C3
11 Abbot's Bromley GB C4
13 Abbotsbury GB C5
98 Abda H A2
33 Abejar E C4
42 Abela P B1
68 Abenberg D B1
38 Abenojar E D2
55 Åbenrå DK C2
68 Abensberg D C2
12 Aberaeron GB A3
13 Abercarn GB B4
7 Aberchirder GB C6
13 Aberdare GB B4
10 Aberdaron GB C1
9 Aberdeen GB A5
9 Aberdour GB B4
10 Aberdovey GB C1
9 Aberfeldy GB B4
10 Aberffraw GB B1
8 Aberfoyle GB B3
13 Abergavenny GB B4
10 Abergele GB B2
13 Aberkenfig GB B4
9 Abernethy GB B4
12 Aberporth GB A3
10 Abersoch GB C1
13 Abertillery GB B4
37 Abertura E B5
10 Aberystwyth GB C1
75 Abetone I B5
72 Abfaltersbach A B2
34 Abiego E A2
55 Abild DK D1
15 Abingdon GB C1
9 Abington GB C4
36 Abiul P B2
45 Abla E B4
103 Ablanitsa BG C5
20 Ablis F C2
47 Abo SF F11
70 Abondance F B1
99 Abony H A5
9 Aboyne GB A5
36 Abrantes P B2
24 Abrest F B3
74 Abriès I B1
94 Abrud RO C5
96 Absdorf A C1
72 Abtenau A A3
67 Abtsgmund D C6
31 Abusejo E D4
56 Åby, *Kronoberg* S C3
53 Åby, *Östergötland* S D2
54 Abybro DK A2
56 Abyfors S B3
52 Åbyggeby S B3
53 Åbytorp S C1
85 Acate I B3
80 Accadia I C2
74 Accéglio I B1
82 Accettura I A3
82 Acciaroli I A2
26 Accons F C3
10 Accrington GB B3
79 Accumoli I A4
37 Acedera E B5
37 Acehuche E B4
39 Acered E A5
80 Acerenza I D2
79 Acerra I C5
37 Aceuchal E C4
7 Achavanich GB B5
17 Achel B B5
72 Achensee A A1
72 Achenthal A A1
67 Achern D C4
20 Acheux en Amienois F A3
6 Achfary GB B4
44 Achidona E B2
2 Achill IRL C2
59 Achim D B6
6 Achnasheen GB C3
6 Achnashellach Lodge GB C3
8 Achosnich GB B1
85 Aci Castello I B4
78 Acilia I B3
85 Acireale I B4
14 Acle GB B4
87 Acquacadda I C1
75 Acquanegra sul Chiese I A5
78 Acquapendente I A2
79 Acquasanta Terme I A4
78 Acquasparta I A3
76 Acquaviva I C1
80 Acquaviva delle Fonti I D3
79 Acquaviva Picena I A4
74 Acqui Terme I B3
20 Acquigny F B2
82 Acri I B3
98 Ács H A3
97 Acsa H D5
21 Acy-en-Multien F B3
99 Ada YU C5
99 Adács H A5
50 Adalsbruk N B2
91 Adamów PL B6
44 Adamuz E A2
98 Ádánd H B3
4 Adare IRL B3
101 Adaševci YU A4
11 Addingham GB B4
33 Adeanueva de Ebro E B5
16 Adegem B B3
70 Adelboden CH B2
112 Adele, *Kriti* GR
63 Adelebsen D B4
80 Adélfia I C3
67 Adelmannsfelden D C6
68 Adelsdorf D B1
67 Adelsheim D B5
53 Adelsö S C3
40 Ademuz E A1
62 Adenau D C1
60 Adendorf D B1
109 Adham GR A5
111 Adhamas GR C5
111 Adhámi GR B4
106 Adhriani GR B2
16 Adinkerke B B2
94 Adjud RO C7
73 Adlešiči YU C5
70 Adliswil CH A3
73 Admont A A4
48 Adneran N B3
53 Adolfsberg S C1
99 Adony H A3
62 Adorf D B3
64 Adorf D C2
44 Adra E C3
33 Adradas E C4
36 Adraga P C1
4 Adrahan IRL A3
85 Adrano I B3
76 Ádria I A2
11 Adwick le Street GB B4
40 Adzaneta E A2
109 Aerinón GR B4
55 Ærøskøbing DK D3
70 Aesch CH A2
108 Aetós, *Aitolía kai Acarnanía* GR C3
108 Aetós, *Florina* GR A3
110 Aetós, *Messinía* GR B2
112 Afándou GR A2
109 Afétai GR B5
63 Afferde D A4
68 Affing D C1
70 Affoltern CH A3
108 Afión GR B1
109 Áfitos GR A5
46 Afjord N E5
79 Afragola I C5
73 Afritz A B3
110 Agalás GR B1
109 Aganderón GR B3
74 Agay F C1
75 Agazzano I B4
28 Agde F C2
27 Agen F B4
34 Ager E A3
55 Agerbæk DK C1
55 Agerskov DK C2
54 Agger DK B1
54 Aggersund DK A2
87 Ággius I B2
96 Aggsbach Dorf A C1
69 Aggsbach Markt A C6
3 Aghalee GB B5
100 Agiči YU B1
109 Agios Ioánis GR B5
85 Agira I B3
108 Ágnanda GR B3
54 Agnesberg S A5
29 Agnières F B4
71 Agno CH B3
79 Agnone I B5
72 Agordo I B2
40 Agost E C2
45 Agramón E A5
35 Agramunt E B4
109 Ágras GR A3
33 Agreda E C5
109 Agriá GR B5
84 Agrigento I B2
109 Agriliá GR B3
108 Agrinion GR C3
44 Agrón E B3
82 Agrópoli I A1
31 Agua Longa P C2
45 Aguadulce, *Almería* E C4
43 Aguadulce, *Sevilla* E B5
30 Agualada E A2
34 Aguarón E B1
34 Aguas E A2
36 Aguas Belas P B2
36 Aguas de Moura P C2
31 Aguas Santas P C2
34 Aguaviva E C2
33 Aguaviva de la Vega E C4
38 Agudo E D2
31 Agueda P D2
28 Aguessac F B2
36 Aguiar P C3
31 Aguiàr da Beira P D3
38 Aguilafuente E A2
44 Aguilar E B2
32 Aguilar de Campóo E B2
45 Águilas E B5
34 Aguinaliu E A3
62 Ahaus D A2
37 Ahigal E A4
31 Ahigal de Villarino E C4
43 Ahillones E A4
61 Ahlbeck D B5
62 Ahlen D B2
63 Ahlten D A4
107 Ahmetbey TR B5
3 Ahogill GB B5
60 Ahrensbök D A1
59 Ahrensburg D B7
62 Ahrweiler D C2
24 Ahun F B2
57 Åhus S D3
70 Aiagna Valsésia I C2
109 Aiani GR A3
33 Aibar E B5
68 Aich D C3
69 Aicha D C4
68 Aichach D C2
37 Aidea de Trujillo E B5
108 Aidénia GR A3
109 Aidhipsós GR C5
85 Aidone I B3
109 Aidonokhóri GR A5
82 Aiello Cálabro I B3
109 Aigáni GR B4
69 Aigen i. M. A C4
70 Aigle CH B1
68 Aiglsbach D C2
26 Aignan F C4
25 Aignay-le-Duc F A4
23 Aigre F C5
22 Aigrefeuille-d'Aunis F B4
22 Aigrefeuille-sur-Maine F A3
35 Aiguablava E B6
25 Aiguebelle F C6
24 Aigueperse F B3
28 Aigues-Mortes F C3
28 Aigues-Vives F C1
74 Aiguilles I B1
27 Aiguillon F B4
24 Aigurande F B1
29 Ailefroide F B5
21 Aillant-sur-Tholon F D4
66 Aillevillers F D2
20 Ailly-sur-Somme F B3
28 Aimargues F C3
70 Aime F C1
72 Ainet A B2
34 Ainsa E A3
74 Airasca I B2
8 Aird GB B2
6 Aird Uig GB B1
9 Airdrie GB C4
26 Aire-sur-l'Adour F C3
16 Aire-sur-la-Lys F C2
74 Airole I C2
70 Airolo CH B3
23 Airvault F B4
25 Aisey-sur-Seine F A4
10 Aisgill GB A3
106 Aisimi GR B3
68 Aislingen D C1
25 Aissey F A6
25 Aisy-sur-Armançon F A4
68 Aiterhofen D C3
7 Aith, *Orkney Is.* GB A6
6 Aith, *Shetland Is.* GB
110 Aitolikon GR A2
94 Aiud RO C5
21 Aix-en-Othe F C4
29 Aix-en-Provence F C4
25 Aix-les-Bains F C5
23 Aixe-sur-Vienne F C6
112 Aiyiáli GR D2
111 Aiyina GR B4
109 Aiyinion GR A4
110 Aiyion GR A3
110 Aiyira GR A3
22 Aizenay F B3
86 Ajaccio F C1
24 Ajain F B2
73 Ajdovšcina YU C3
98 Ajka H A2
105 Ajnovce YU B3
38 Ajofrin E C3
37 Ajuda P C3
57 Åkarp S D2
99 Akasztó H B4
112 Akçaova TR A1
64 Aken D B2
52 Åkerby S B3
48 Åkernes N C4
53 Åkers styckebruk S C3
53 Åkersberga S C4
111 Akharnai GR A4
109 Akhilio GR B4
109 Akhillion GR B4
109 Akhinós GR C4
95 Akhisar TR G7
111 Akhladeri GR A5
111 Akhladhókambos GR B3
107 Akhtobol BG A5
57 Akirkeby DK D3
112 Akkëy TR B1
58 Akkrum NL B2
105 Akladhokhórion GR C5
112 Akoúmia, *Kriti* GR
48 Åkra N B3
111 Akraifnion GR A4
110 Akráta GR A3
48 Åkrehamn N B2
108 Akritas GR A3
105 Akritokhóri GR C5
112 Akrotiri GR D2
111 Akti Idras GR B4
109 Akti Sáni GR A5
108 Aktion GR C2
46 Ål N F4
74 Ala di Stura I A2
87 Alà die Sardi I B2
32 Alaejos E C1
54 Alafors S A5
34 Alagón E B1
40 Alaguas E B2
47 Alajärvi SF E11
38 Alameda de la Sagra E B3
44 Alamedilla E B3
44 Alamillo E A2
39 Alaminos E B4
36 Alandroal P C3
37 Alange E C4
43 Alanis E A4
79 Alanno I A4
99 Alap H B3
32 Alar del Rey E B2
38 Alaraz E B1
39 Alarcón E C4
41 Alaró, *Mallorca* E
95 Alaşehir TR G8
74 Alássio I B3
40 Alatoz E B1
79 Alatri I B4
99 Alattyán H A5
47 Alavus SF E11
41 Alayor, *Menorca* E
40 Alba E A1
74 Alba I B3
79 Alba Adriatica I A4
38 Alba de Tormes E B1
94 Alba-Lulia RO C5
39 Albacete E D5
62 Albachten D B2
54 Albæk DK A3
34 Albafarrech E B3
34 Albages E B3
40 Albaida E C2
27 Albais F B5
37 Albala del Caudillo E B4
45 Albaladejo E A4
40 Albalat E B2
34 Albalate de Cinca E B3
39 Albalete de Zorita E B4
34 Albalete del Arzobispo E B2
28 Alban F C1
35 Albaná E A5
45 Albánchez E B4
44 Albanchez de Ubeda E B3
45 Albanilla E A5
78 Albano Laziale I B3
75 Albaredo d'Adige I A6
40 Albarracin E A1
40 Albatana E C1
45 Albatera E A6
70 Albbruck D A3
44 Albedin E B2
33 Albelda E B4
74 Albenga I B3
25 Albens F C5
53 Alberga S D2
31 Albergaria-a Nova P D2
36 Albergaria dos Doze P B2
36 Alberge P C2
31 Albergeria-a-Velha P D2
31 Albergueria E B3
37 Albergueria de Argañán E A4
40 Alberique E B2
42 Albernoa P B2
72 Alberoni I C2
59 Albersdorf D A6
62 Albersloh D B2
67 Albersweiler D B4
20 Albert F A3
99 Albertirsa H A4
25 Albertville F C6
103 Albesti RO A5
27 Albi F C6
83 Albidona I B3
78 Albinia I A2
71 Albino I C4
32 Albires E B1
74 Albissola Marina I B3
17 Alblasserdam NL B4
40 Albocácer E A3
44 Albolote E B3
44 Albondón E C3
40 Alboraya E B2
40 Alborea E B1
54 Ålborg DK A2
103 Albota RO B5
45 Albox E B4
69 Albrechtice n. Vitavou CS B5
42 Albufeira P B1
107 Albullu TR B5
44 Albuñol E C3
44 Albuñuelas E C3
68 Alburg D C3
37 Alburquerque E B4
46 Alby S E7
36 Alcácer do Sal P C2
36 Alcáçovas P C2
45 Alcadozo E A5
37 Alcafoces P B3
36 Alcainça P C1
36 Alcains P B3
40 Alcalá de Chivert E A3
43 Alcalá de Guadaira E B4
34 Alcalá de Gurrea E A2
39 Alcalá de Henares E B3
40 Alcalá de la Selva E A2
43 Alcalá de los Gazules E C4
40 Alcalá del Júcar E B1
43 Alcala del Rio E B4
43 Alcalá del Valle E C4
44 Alcalá la Real E B3
84 Álcamo I B1
34 Alcampel E B3
33 Alcanadre E B4
41 Alcanar E A3
36 Alcanede P B2
34 Alcañiz E B2
31 Alcañizes E C4
37 Alcántara E B4
42 Alcantarilha P B1
45 Alcantarilla E B5
44 Alcaracejos E A2
45 Alcaraz E A4
42 Alcaria Ruiva P B2
34 Alcarraz E B3
44 Alcaudete E B2
38 Alcaudete de la Jara E C2
39 Alcázar de S. Juan E C3
32 Alcazarén E C2
13 Alcester GB A6
38 Alcoba E C2
36 Alcobaça P B1
39 Alcobendas E B3
40 Alcoceber E A3
39 Alcocer E B4
36 Alcochete P C2
36 Alcoentre P B2
39 Alcohujate E B4
44 Alcolea, *Almería* E C4
44 Alcolea, *Córdoba* E B2
38 Alcolea de Calatrava E D2
34 Alcolea de Cinca E B3
38 Alcolea de Tajo E C1
39 Alcolea del Pinar E A4
43 Alcolea del Rio E B4
37 Alcollarin E B5
14 Alconbury Hill GB B2
37 Alconchel E C3
37 Alconera E C4
45 Alcontar E B4
40 Alcora E A2
34 Alcorisa E C2
38 Alcorón E B3
42 Alcoutim P B2
35 Alcover E B4
40 Alcoy E C2
99 Alcsutdoboz H A3
34 Alcubierre E B2
33 Alcubilla de Avellaneda E C3
32 Alcubilla de Nogales E B1
44 Alcubillas E A3
40 Alcublas E B2
41 Alcudia, *Mallorca* E
44 Alcudia de Guadix E B3
37 Alcuéscar E B4
40 Aldaya E B2
13 Aldbourne GB B6
11 Aldbrough GB B5
34 Aldea E C3
37 Aldea de Cano E B4
38 Aldea del Fresno E B2
44 Aldea del Rey E A3
38 Aldea Real E A2
37 Aldeacentenera E B5
31 Aldeadávila de la Ribera E C4
32 Aldealcorvo E C3
33 Aldealuenga de Sta. Maria E C3
32 Aldeamayor de San Martin E C2
38 Aldeanueva de Barbarroya E C1
38 Aldeanueva de S. Bartolomé E C1
37 Aldeanueva del Camino E A5
38 Aldeanueva del Codonal E A2
33 Aldeapozo E C4
44 Aldeaquemada E A3
38 Aldearrubia E A1
38 Aldeaseca de la Frontera E B1
32 Aldeasoña E C2
38 Aldeatejada E B1
14 Aldeburgh GB B4
40 Aldehuela E A1
33 Aldehuela de Calatañazon E C4
31 Aldehuela de Yeltes E D4
37 Aldeia do Bispo P A4
36 Aldeia do Mato P B2
36 Aldeia Gavinha P B1
42 Aldeia Nova P B2
44 Aldeire E B3
17 Aldekerk D B6
17 Aldenhoven D C6
13 Alderbury GB B6
15 Aldermaston GB C1
69 Aldersbach D C4
15 Aldershot GB C2
104 Aldince YU C3
68 Aldoft D D1
11 Aldridge GB C4
110 Aléa GR B3
56 Aled S C1
45 Aledo E B5
33 Alegia Dulantzi E B4
99 Aleksa Šantić YU C4
102 Aleksandrovac YU B2
103 Aleksandrovo BG C5
107 Aleksandrovo BG A4
90 Aleksandrów PL B3
89 Aleksandrów Kujawski PL C4
102 Aleksinac YU C2
56 Ålem S C5
19 Alençon F B6
36 Alenquer P B1
35 Alenya F A6
86 Aleria F B2
28 Alès F B3
87 Áles I C1
74 Alessándria I B3
84 Alessándria della Rocca I B2
83 Alessano I B5
54 Ålestrup DK B2
46 Ålesund N E3
8 Alexandria GB C3
109 Alexándria GR A4
95 Alexandria RO E6
106 Alexandroúpolis GR C3
102 Alexandrovac YU C2
29 Aleyrac F B3
83 Alézio I A5
44 Alfacar E B3
37 Alfaiates P A4
34 Alfajarin E B2
40 Alfambra E A1
42 Alfambra P B1
31 Alfarela de Jafes P C3
36 Alfarelos P A2
44 Alfarnate E C2
33 Alfaro E B5
34 Alfarras E B3
79 Alfedena I B5
36 Alfeizarão P B1
68 Alfeld, *Bayern* D B2
63 Alfeld, *Niedersachsen* D B4
31 Alfena P C2
31 Alfẽndaga da Fé P C4
42 Alferce P B1
59 Alfhausen D C4
76 Alfonsine I B2
7 Alford, *Grampian* GB C6
11 Alford, *Lincolnshire* GB B6
35 Alforja E B3
11 Alfreton GB B4
52 Alfta S A2
42 Alfundão P A1
41 Algaida, *Mallorca* E
43 Algar, *Cádiz* E C4
45 Algar, *Murcia* E B6
51 Algaräs S D5
48 Algård N C2
44 Algarinejo E B2
44 Algarrobo E C2
43 Algeciras E C4
40 Algemesí E B2
36 Alges P C1
39 Algete E B3
87 Alghero I B1
56 Älghult S B4
40 Alginet E B2
43 Algodonales E C4
38 Algodor E C3
42 Algodor P B2
39 Algora E B4
33 Algorta E A4
42 Algoz P B1
66 Algrange F B2
45 Algu E A5
34 Alguaire E B3
45 Alguazas E A5
99 Algyö H B5
45 Alhama de Almeria E C4
33 Alhama de Aragon E C5
44 Alhama de Granada E C3
45 Alhama de Murcia E B5
39 Alhambra E D3
36 Alhandra P C1
44 Alhaurin de la Torre E C2
44 Alhaurin el Grande E C2
44 Alhendin E B3
39 Alhóndiga E B4
36 Alhos Vedros P C1
85 Ali Terme I B4
38 Alia E C1
84 Ália I B2
34 Aliaga E C2
111 Aliartos GR A4
101 Alibunar YU A5
40 Alicante E C2
44 Alicún de Ortega E B3
79 Alife I B5
110 Alifira GR B2
32 Alija del Infantado E B1
31 Alijo P C3
110 Alika GR C3
111 Alikai GR A4
110 Alikanás GR B1
108 Aliki GR B3
112 Alikianós, *Kriti* GR
112 Alikó GR D2
84 Alimena I B3
35 Aliña E A4
56 Alingsås S B1
25 Alise-Ste. Reine F A4
37 Aliseda E B4
106 Alistráti GR B1
111 Alivérion GR A5
29 Alixan F B4
42 Aljaraque E B2
30 Aljariz E B3
42 Aljezur P B1
45 Aljorra E B5
36 Aljubarrota P B2
37 Aljucen E B4
42 Aljustrel P B1
17 Alken B C5
58 Alkmaar NL C1
69 Alkoven A C5
62 Allagen D B3
20 Allaines F C2
28 Allanche F A1
96 Alland A C2
30 Allande E A4
27 Allasac F A5
29 Allauch F C4
28 Allegre F A2
29 Allemagne-en-Provence F C5
29 Allemont F A5
9 Allendale Town GB D5
62 Allendorf D C3
69 Allentsteig A C6
5 Allenwood IRL A5
40 Allepuz E A2
68 Allersberg D B2
68 Allershausen D C2
29 Allevard F A5
29 Allex F B3
54 Allingåbro DK B3
57 Allinge DK D3
67 Allmendingen D C5
33 Allo E B4
9 Alloa GB B4
24 Allogny F A2
10 Allonby GB A2
20 Allones F C2
26 Allons F B3
29 Allos F B5
63 Allstedt D B6
78 Allumiere I A2
36 Almaceda P B3
34 Almacellas E B3
44 Almachar E C2
36 Almada P C1
44 Almadén E A2
43 Almadén de la Plata E B3
44 Almadenejos E A2
39 Almadrones E B4
38 Almagro E D3
33 Almajano E C4
40 Almansa E C1
42 Almansil P B1
32 Almanza E B1
37 Almaraz E B5
42 Almareleja P A2
43 Almargen E C4
33 Almarza E C4
98 Almásfüzito H A3
33 Almazán E C4
40 Almazora E B2
33 Almazul E C4
62 Alme D B3
44 Almeda E B2
44 Almedinilla E B2
31 Almeida E C4
31 Almeida P D4
36 Almeirim P B2
62 Almelo NL A1
34 Almenar E B3
33 Almenar de Soria E C4
40 Almenara E B2
31 Almendra P D3
37 Almendral E C4
38 Almendral de la Cañada E B2
37 Almendralejo E C4
71 Almenno S. Bart I C4
45 Almeria E C4
45 Almerimar E C4
74 Almese I A2
42 Almexial P B2
56 Älmhult S C3
111 Almiri GR B4
110 Almiron GR C3
111 Almiropótamos GR A5
109 Almirós GR B4
42 Almodôvar P B1
44 Almodovar del Campo E A2
39 Almodovar del Pinar E C5
43 Almodóvar del Rio E B4
31 Almofala P D3
44 Almogia E C2
37 Almoharin E B4
34 Almonacid de la Sierra E B1
38 Almonacid de Toledo E C3
43 Almonaster la Real E B3
13 Almondsbury GB B5
43 Almonte E B3
45 Almoradi E A6
43 Almoraima E C4
38 Almorox E B2
36 Almoster P B2
52 Älmsta S C4
34 Almudévar E A2
45 Almundena E A5
44 Almuñecar E C3
52 Almunge S C4
44 Almuradiel E A3
7 Alness GB C4
9 Alnmouth GB C6
9 Alnwick GB C6
108 Álonas GR A3
109 Alónia GR A4
110 Alonistena GR B3
109 Alónnisos GR B5
35 Alos de Isil E A4
42 Alosno E B2
25 Aloxe-Corton F A4
44 Alozaina E C2
72 Alpbach A A1
39 Alpedrete E B3
17 Alpen D B6
40 Alpera E C1
17 Alphen NL B4
17 Alphen a/d Rijn NL A4
13 Alphinton GB C4
36 Alpiarca P B2
74 Alpignano I A2
67 Alpirsbach D C4
40 Alpuenta E B1
40 Alpuente E B1
42 Alqueva P A2
34 Alquézar E A3
10 Alsager GB B3
33 Alsasua E B4
17 Alsdorf D C6
55 Alselv DK C1
63 Alsfeld D C4
52 Alsike S C3
63 Alsleben D B6
99 Alsógod H A4
99 Alsónémedi H A4
62 Alstätte D A1
56 Alsterbro S C4
9 Alston GB D5
46 Alta N B11
80 Altamura I D3
39 Altarejos E C4
73 Altausse A A3
79 Altavilla Irpina I B5
82 Altavilla Silentina I A2
64 Altdobern D B4
70 Altdorf CH B3
68 Altdorf, *Bayern* D B2
68 Altdorf, *Bayern* D C3
42 Alte P B1
40 Altea E C2
76 Altedo I B1
46 Alteide N A11
62 Altena D B2
63 Altenau D B5
64 Altenberg D C3
62 Altenberge D A2
62 Altenbögge-Bönen D B2
59 Altenbruch D B5
68 Altenbuch D C3
64 Altenburg D C2
59 Altenesch D B5
69 Altenfelden A C4
63 Altengronau D C4
62 Altenhaßlau D C4
67 Altenheim D C3
62 Altenhundem D B3
61 Altenkirchen D A4
62 Altenkirchen D C2
60 Altenkrempe D A1
68 Altenkunstadt D A2
72 Altenmarkt, *Salzburg* A A3
73 Altenmarkt, *Steiermark* A A4
68 Altenmarkt D C3
59 Altenoythe D B4
68 Altenstadt D B3
67 Altensteig D C4
61 Altentreptow D B4
59 Altenwalde D B5
63 Altenweddingen D A6
36 Alter do Chão P B3
62 Alterdünne D A2
68 Alterglofsheim D C3
61 Altewin D C5
68 Altfraunhofen D C3
69 Altheim A C4
67 Altheim, *Baden-Württemberg* D B5
67 Altheim, *Baden-Württemberg* D C6
73 Althofen A B4
103 Altimir BG C4
70 Altkirch F A2
61 Altlandsberg D C4
96 Altlengbach A C1
96 Altlichtenwarth A C2
68 Altmannstein D C2
63 Altmorschen D B4
69 Altmünster A D4
7 Altnaharra GB B4
32 Alto Campoó E A2
84 Altofonte I A2
82 Altomonte I B3
15 Alton GB C2
75 Altopáscio I C5
68 Altötting D C3
67 Altrach D D6
69 Altreichenau D C4
61 Altruppin D C3
67 Altshausen D D5
71 Altstätten CH A4
40 Altura E B2
67 Altusried D D6
52 Alunda S B4
39 Alustante E B5
9 Alva GB B4
36 Alvaiazere P B2
36 Alvalade P B1
54 Älvängen S A5
31 Alvarenga P D2
36 Alvares P A2
46 Alvdal N E5
50 Älvdalen S A5
11 Alvechurch GB C4
36 Alverca P C1
56 Alvesta S C3
13 Alveston GB B5
27 Alvignac F B5
79 Alvignano I B5
46 Ålvik N F3
50 Alvik S B5
20 Alvimare F B1
36 Alviobeira P B2
42 Alvito P A2
52 Älvkarleby S B3
52 Älvkarleö bruk S B3
42 Alvor P B1
36 Alvorge P B2
48 Alvøy N A2
51 Alvsbacka S C4
47 Alvsbyn S D10
9 Alyth GB B4
67 Alzénau D A5
67 Alzey D B4
40 Alzira E B2
27 Alzonne F C6
36 Amadora P C1
21 Amagne F B5
51 Åmål S C3
79 Amalfi I C5
109 Amaliápolis GR B4
110 Amalias GR B2
66 Amance F D2
25 Amancey F A6
76 Amandola I D3
82 Amantea I B3
108 Amárandon GR B3
109 Amárandos GR B3
31 Amarante P C2
103 Amărăstii de Jos RO C5
31 Amares P C2
111 Amarinthos GR A4
111 Amaroúsion GR A4
79 Amaseno I B4
79 Amatrice I A4
23 Ambazac F C6
111 Ambeláki GR B4
109 Ambelákia GR B4
109 Ambélia GR B4
109 Ambelón GR B4
68 Amberg D B2
25 Ambérieu-en-Bugey F C5
25 Amberieux-en-Dombes F C4
66 Amberloup B A1
26 Ambés F A3
50 Ambjörby S B4
56 Ambjörnarp S B2
9 Amble GB C6
10 Ambleside GB A3
16 Ambleteuse F C1
17 Amblève B C6
23 Amboise F A5
24 Ambort F C3

36 Azeiteiros P B3
36 Azenha de Cima P B3
36 Azenhas do Mar P C1
36 Azinhaga P B2
42 Azinhal P B2
42 Azinheira dos Bairros P A1
43 Aznalcázar E B3
43 Aznalcóllar E B3
36 Azóia P B2
33 Azpeitia E A4
43 Azuaga E A4
34 Azuara E B2
39 Azuqueca de Henares E B3
26 Azur F C2

B

71 Baad A A5
30 Baamonde E A3
70 Baar CH A3
17 Baarn NL A5
95 Babadag RO D8
107 Babaeski TR B5
60 Babekuhl D B2
68 Babenhausen D C1
103 Băbeni Bistriţa RO B5
67 Babennen D B4
97 Babice PL A5
89 Babieta PL B7
61 Babigoszcz PL B5
65 Babimost PL A5
101 Babina Greda YU A3
108 Babini GR C3
98 Babócsa H B2
98 Bábolna H A3
90 Baborów PL C2
91 Babsk PL B4
102 Babušnica YU C3
99 Bač YU C4
103 Băcăleşti RO B5
45 Bacares E B4
94 Bacău RO C7
66 Baccarat F C2
67 Bacharach D A3
106 Bachkovo BG B2
6 Back GB B2
52 Backa S B1
101 Bačka Palanka YU A4
99 Bačka Topola YU C4
7 Backaland GB A6
57 Backaryd S C4
56 Backebo S C5
51 Bäckefors S D3
52 Backehagen S B1
51 Bäckhammer S C5
99 Backi Breg YU C3
99 Backi-Breslovac YU C4
99 Bački Monoštor YU C3
99 Backi Petrovac YU C4
99 Bački Sokolac YU C4
67 Backnang D C5
99 Bačko Gradište YU C5
101 Bačko Novo Selo YU A4
99 Bačko Petrovo-Selo YU C5
79 Bácoli I C5
20 Bacqueville F B2
99 Bácsalmás H B4
99 Bácsboked H B4
14 Bacton GB B4
97 Bacúch CS C5
11 Bacup GB B3
68 Bad Abbach D C3
68 Bad Aibling D D3
72 Bad Aussee A A3
67 Bad Bergzabern D B3
63 Bad Berka D C6
68 Bad Berneck D A2
63 Bad Bibra D B6
63 Bad Blankenburg D C6
59 Bad Bramstedt D B6
63 Bad Brückenau D C4
60 Bad Doberan D A2
62 Bad Driburg D B4
64 Bad Düben D B2
67 Bad Dürkheim D B4
64 Bad Dürrenberg D B2
67 Bad Dürrheim D C4
64 Bad Elster D C2
62 Bad Ems D C2
63 Bad Frankenhausen D B6
61 Bad Freiewalde D C5
67 Bad Friedrichshall D B5
63 Bad Gandersheim D B5
73 Bad Gleichenberg A B5
62 Bad Godesberg D C2
72 Bad Goisern A A3
64 Bad Gotteuba D C3
63 Bad Grund D B5
69 Bad Hall A C5
63 Bad Harzburg D B5
63 Bad Hersfeld D C4
72 Bad Hofgastein A A3
62 Bad Homburg D C3
62 Bad Honnef D C2
62 Bad Hönningen D C2
71 Bad Inner-Laterns A A4
72 Bad Ischll A A3
70 Bad Kemmeriboden CH B2
63 Bad Kissingen D C5
71 Bad Kohlgrub D A6
67 Bad König D B5
63 Bad Kösen D B6
64 Bad Köstritz D C2
67 Bad-Kreuznach D B3
66 Bad Krozingen D D3
63 Bad Langensalza D B5
64 Bad Lauchstaßdt D B1
64 Bad Lausick D B2
63 Bad Lauterberg D B5
69 Bad Leonfelden A C5
64 Bad Liebenwerda D B3
67 Bad Liebenzeil D C4
62 Bad Lippspringe D B3
62 Bad Meinberg D B4
67 Bad Mergentheim D B5
73 Bad Mitterndorf A A3
63 Bad Münder D A4
65 Bad Muskau D B4
62 Bad Nauheim D C3
63 Bad Nenndorf D A4
62 Bad Neuenahr D C2
63 Bad Neustadt D C5
62 Bad Oeynhausen D A3
60 Bad Oldesloe D B1
63 Bad Orb D C4
67 Bad Peterstal D C4
63 Bad Pyrmont D B4
71 Bad Ragaz CH B4
67 Bad Rappenau D B5
69 Bad Reichenhall D D3
64 Bad Saarow Pieskow D A4
63 Bad Sachsa D B5
63 Bad Salzdetfurth D A4
62 Bad Salzig D C2
63 Bad Salzschlirf D C4
63 Bad Salzungen D C5
62 Bad Sassendorf D B3
64 Bad Schandau D C4
64 Bad Schmiedeberg D B2
67 Bad Schönborn D B4
62 Bad Schwalbach D C3
60 Bad Schwartau D B1
60 Bad Segeberg D B1
67 Bad Soden D A4
63 Bad Soden-Salmünster D C4
63 Bad Sooden-Allendorf D B4
73 Bad St. eonhard A B4
63 Bad Steben D C6
63 Bad Sulza D B6
60 Bad Sülze D A3
63 Bad Tennstedt D B5
68 Bad Tölz D D2
62 Bad Vilbel D C3
96 Bad Vöslau A D2
67 Bad Waldsee D D5
72 Bad Wiessee D A1
62 Bad Wildungen D B4
60 Bad Wilsnack D C2
67 Bad Wimpfen D B5
68 Bad Windsheim D B1
68 Bad Wörishafen D C1
67 Bad Wurzach D D5
59 Bad Zwischenahn D B4
98 Badacsonytomaj H B2
37 Badajoz E C4
35 Badalona E B5
74 Badalucco I C2
7 Badanloch GB B4
96 Baden A C2
70 Baden CH A3
59 Baden D C6
67 Baden Baden D C4
34 Bádenas E B1
63 Badenhausen D B5
66 Badenweiler D D3
77 Baderna YU A3
63 Badersleben D B5
72 Badgastein A A3
17 Badhoevedorp NL A4
72 Badia (Abtei) I B1
71 Badia Calavena I C6
75 Badia Polésine I A6
76 Badia Pratáglia I C1
76 Badia Tedalda I C2
98 Badjevina YU C2
89 Bądki PL B4
83 Badolato I C3
44 Badolatosa E B2
66 Badonviller F C2
101 Badovinci YU B4
55 Bække DK C2
54 Bækmarksbro DK B1
34 Baells E B3
54 Bælum DK B3
44 Baena E B2
17 Baesweiler D C6
44 Baeza E B3
112 Bafa TR B1
36 Bafede P B3
58 Baflo NL B3
85 Bagaladi I A4
112 Bagarasi TR B1
5 Bagenalstown (Muine Bheag) IRL B5
53 Baggetorp S C2
84 Bagheria I A2
76 Bagnacavallo I B1
78 Bagnaia I A3
85 Bagnara Cálabro I A4
74 Bagnasco I B3
27 Bagnères-de-Bigorre F C4
34 Bagnères-de-Luchon F A3
71 Bagni del Másino I B4
75 Bagni di Lucca I B5
71 Bagni di Rabbi I B5
78 Bagni di Tivoli I B3
76 Bagno di Romagna I C1
19 Bagnoles de l'Orne F B5
79 Bagnoli dei Trigno I B5
76 Bagnoli di Sopra I A1
80 Bagnoli Irpino I D2
71 Bagnolo Mella I C5
29 Bagnols-en-Forêt F C5
29 Bagnols-sur-Cèze F B3
78 Bagnorégio I A3
71 Bagolino I C5
89 Bagrationovsk SU A6
15 Bagshot GB C2
35 Bagur E B6
32 Bahillo E B2
103 Baia de Arama RO B3
79 Báia Domizia I B4
94 Baia Mare RO C5
79 Baiano I C5
31 Baião P C2
67 Baienfurt D D5
67 Baiersbronn D C4
68 Baiersdorf D B2
25 Baigneux-les-Juifs F A4
5 Baile Atha Cliath (Dublin) IRL A5
103 Băile Govora RO A5
102 Băile Herculane RO B3
103 Băile Olăneşti RO A5
44 Bailén E A3
103 Băileşti RO B4
21 Baileux B A5
3 Bailieborough IRL C5
16 Bailleul F C2
34 Bailó E A2
28 Bains F A2
66 Bains-les-Bains F C2
19 Bais F B5
75 Baiso I B5
31 Baiuca P D3
99 Baja H B3
98 Bajánsenye H B1
101 Bajina Bašta YU C4
99 Bajmok YU C4
99 Bajna H A3
104 Bajram-Curr AL B2
99 Bajša YU C4
104 Bajzë AL B1
98 Bak H B1
77 Bakar YU A4
11 Bakewell GB B4
107 Bakla Burnu TR C4
98 Bakonybél H A2
98 Bakonycsernye H A3
98 Bakonyjákó H A2
98 Bakonyszentkirály H A2
98 Bakonyszentlászló H A2
98 Bakonyszombathely H A2
65 Bakov n. Jizerou CS C4
90 Baków Graniczny PL A3
91 Bąkowiec PL B5
99 Baks H B5
98 Baksa H C3
59 Bakum D C5
10 Bala GB C2
107 Balabanköy TR B4
103 Balaci RO B5
103 Balăcita RO B4
30 Balagonga E A3
34 Balaguer E B3
6 Balallan GB B2
103 Bălăneşti RO B5
97 Balassa-gyarmat H C5
99 Balástya H B5
112 Balat TR B1
98 Balatonakali H B2
98 Balatonalmádi H A3
98 Balatonboglár H B2
98 Balatonbozsok H B3
98 Balatonederics H B2
98 Balatonendréd H B2
98 Balatonfenyves H B2
98 Balatonfőkajar H A3
98 Balatonföldvár H B2
98 Balatonfüred H B2
98 Balatonfűzfő H A3
98 Balatonkenese H A3
98 Balatonkiliti H B3
98 Balatonlelle H B2
98 Balatonmariafürdö H B2
98 Balatonszemes H B2
39 Balazote E D4
9 Balbeggie GB B4
25 Balbigny F C4
30 Balboa E B4
3 Balbriggan IRL C5
103 Bălceşti RO B4
11 Balderton GB B5
15 Baldock GB C2
10 Baldrine GB A1
77 Bale YU A3
42 Baleizao P A2
17 Balen B B5
44 Balerma E C4
103 Bälesti RO A4
7 Balfour GB A6
8 Balfron GB B3
57 Bälganet S C4
95 Balikesir TR G7
53 Bälinge, Södermanland S D3
52 Bälinge, Uppsala S C3
67 Balingen D C4
52 Balingsta S C3
7 Balintore GB C5
101 Baljevac YU C5
58 Balk NL C2
58 Balkbrug NL C3
2 Balla IRL C2
8 Ballachulish House GB B2
2 Ballaghaderreen IRL C3
20 Ballancourt F C3
8 Ballantrae GB C2
87 Ballao I C2
10 Ballasalla GB A1
9 Ballater GB A4
10 Ballaugh GB A1
55 Ballen DK C3
63 Ballenstedt D B6
34 Ballerias E B2
19 Balleroy F A5
55 Ballerup DK C5
44 Ballesteros de Calatrava E A3
107 Balli TR C5
5 Ballickmoyler IRL B4
2 Ballina IRL B2
5 Ballinagar IRL A4
5 Ballinakill IRL B4
5 Ballinalea IRL A5
3 Ballinalee IRL C4
3 Ballinamallard GB B4
3 Ballinamore IRL B4
4 Ballinascarthy IRL C3
4 Ballinasloe IRL A3
4 Ballincollig IRL C3
2 Ballindine IRL C3
4 Ballineen IRL C3
54 Balling DK B1
5 Ballingarry IRL A3
5 Ballingary IRL B4
4 Ballingeary IRL C2
4 Ballinhassig IRL C3
2 Ballinlough IRL C3
9 Ballinluig GB B4
71 Ballino I C5
2 Ballinrobe IRL C2
4 Ballinspittle IRL C3
2 Ballintra IRL B3
5 Ballinure IRL B4
5 Ballitore IRL A5
3 Balliver IRL C5
34 Ballobar E B3
20 Ballon F C1
5 Ballon IRL B5
99 Ballószög H B4
108 Ballsh AL A1
55 Ballum DK C1
3 Ballybay IRL B5
3 Ballybofey IRL B4
3 Ballybogey GB A5
3 Ballyboghil IRL C5
4 Ballybunnion IRL B2
5 Ballycanew IRL B5
5 Ballycarney IRL B5
3 Ballycastle GB A5
2 Ballycastle IRL B2
3 Ballyclare GB B5
3 Ballyclare IRL C3
5 Ballyclerahan IRL B4
5 Ballycolla IRL B4
3 Ballyconnell IRL B4
5 Ballycotton IRL C3
2 Ballycroy IRL B2
4 Ballydangan IRL A3
4 Ballydavid IRL A3
4 Ballydehob IRL C2
4 Ballydesmond IRL B2
2 Ballydooley IRL C3
4 Ballyduff IRL B3
4 Ballyforan IRL A3
2 Ballygar IRL C3
3 Ballygawley GB B4
3 Ballygorman IRL A4
3 Ballyhalbert GB B6
2 Ballyhaunis IRL C3
3 Ballyjamesduff IRL C4
4 Ballylanders IRL B3
5 Ballylnar IRL B4
5 Ballylooby IRL B4
3 Ballymagorry GB B4
3 Ballymahon IRL C4
3 Ballymena GB B5
2 Ballymoe IRL C3
3 Ballymoney GB A5
5 Ballymore IRL A4
2 Ballymote IRL B3
2 Ballymurray IRL C3
5 Ballynabola IRL B5
4 Ballynacorra IRL C3
5 Ballynadrumny IRL A7
5 Ballynagore IRL A4
3 Ballynahinch GB B6
5 Ballynahown IRL A4
4 Ballynamona IRL B3
3 Ballynure GB B6
5 Ballyragget IRL B4
3 Ballyroney GB B5
2 Ballysadare IRL B3
2 Ballyshannon IRL B3
4 Ballyvaghan IRL A2
4 Ballyvourney IRL C2
3 Ballyvoy GB A5
3 Ballywalter GB B6
8 Balmaclellan GB C3
6 Balmartin GB C1
33 Balmaseda E A3
74 Balme I A2
7 Balmedie GB C6
70 Balmuccia I C3
34 Balneario de Panticosa E A2
99 Balotaszállás H B4
103 Balş RO B5
35 Balsareny E B4
53 Bålsta S C3
70 Balsthal CH A2
102 Balta RO B3
32 Baltanás E C2
31 Baltar E C3
6 Baltasound, Shetland Is. GB
103 Balţaţii RO B4
103 Balteni RO B5
5 Baltinglass IRL B5
89 Baltiysk SU A5
31 Balugães P C2
62 Balve D B2
28 Balvezet F B2
8 Balvicar GB B2
71 Balzers FL A4
79 Balzo I A4
68 Bamberg D B1
9 Bamburgh GB C6
13 Bampton, Devonshire GB C4
15 Bampton, Oxfordshire GB C1
41 Bañalbufar, Mallorca E
102 Banatska Palanka YU B2
101 Banatske Brestovac YU B5
99 Banatski Despotovac YU C5
99 Banatski Dvor YU C5
102 Banatski-Karlovac YU A2
99 Banatsko-Arandelovo YU B5
101 Banatsko-Novo Selo YU B5
99 Banatsko Veliko Sejo YU C5
3 Banbridge GB B5
15 Banbury GB B1
9 Banchory GB A5
17 Bande B C5
31 Bande E B3
55 Bandholm DK D4
95 Bandirma TR F8
29 Bandol F C4
4 Bandon IRL C3
40 Bañeres E C2
7 Banff GB C6
3 Banger GB B6
22 Bangor F A1
10 Bangor GB B1
2 Bangor IRL B2
61 Banie PL B5
105 Banishte BG B4
103 Banitsa BG C4
104 Banja, A. P. Kosovo YU B2
105 Banja, Makedonija YU C3
101 Banja, Srbija YU C4
101 Banja Koviljača YU B4
73 Banja Loka YU C4
100 Banja Luka YU B2
101 Banjani YU B5
104 Banje YU B2
104 Banjska YU B2
105 Banjsko YU C4
96 Banka CS C3
56 Bankeryd S B3
9 Bankfoot GB B4
7 Bankhead GB C6
105 Bankya BG B5
18 Bannalec F C2
28 Banne F B3
70 Bannio I C3
9 Bannockburn GB B4
31 Bañobárez E D4
35 Bañolas E A5
34 Bañon E C1
29 Banon F B4
37 Baños E A5
32 Baños de Cerrato E C2
43 Baños de Gigonza E C4
44 Baños de la Encina E A3
30 Baños de Molgas E B3
33 Baños de Rio Tobia E B4
35 Baños de S. Vicente E A4
33 Baños de Valdearados E C3
96 Bánov CS C3
98 Banova Jaruga YU C1
97 Bánovce CS C4
100 Banoviči YU B3
100 Banoviči Selo YU B3
97 Bánréve H C6
61 Bansin D B5
97 Banská Belá CS C4
97 Banská Bystrica CS C5
97 Banská-Stiavnica CS C4
105 Bansko BG C5
15 Banstead GB C2
4 Banteer IRL B3
63 Banteln D A4
4 Bantry IRL C2
66 Bantzenheim F D3
13 Banwell GB B5
105 Banya, Blagoevgrad BG C5
106 Banya, Plovdiv BG A2
106 Banya, Sliven BG A3
35 Banyuls-sur-Mer F A6
21 Bapaume F A3
8 Baptiston GB B3
33 Baquio E A4
74 Bar F C1
81 Bar YU B6
66 Bar-le-Duc F C1
21 Bar-sur-Aube F C5
21 Bar-sur-Seine F C5
33 Baracaldo E A3
100 Barači YU B1
99 Baracs H B3
99 Baracska H A3
33 Barahona E C4
39 Barajes de Melo E B4
101 Baranda YU A5
79 Baranello I B5
93 Baranovichi SU D10
91 Baranów PL B6
33 Barasoain E B5
37 Barbacena P C3
30 Barbadás E B3
38 Barbadillo E B1
33 Barbadillo de Herreros E B3
33 Barbadillo del Mercado E B3
33 Barbadillo del Pez E B3
77 Barban YU A4
72 Barbarano Vicento I C1
77 Barbariga YU B3
107 Barbaros TR C5
34 Barbastro E A3
43 Barbate de Franco E C4
103 Bărbăteşti RO B4
39 Barbatona E A4
22 Barbâtre F B2
27 Barbazan F C4
30 Barbeitos E A3
29 Barbentane F C3
21 Barberey F C5
23 Barbezieux F C4
63 Barbis D B5
21 Barbonne Fayel F C4
63 Barby D B6
31 Barca d'Alva P C4
43 Barca de la Florida E C4
34 Bárcabo E A3
37 Barcarrota E C4
85 Barcellona Pozzo di Gotto I A4
35 Barcelona E B5
31 Barcelos P C2
30 Bárcena, Oviedo E A4
32 Bárcena, Oviedo E A1
32 Barcena del Pie de Concha E A2
63 Barchfeld D C5
89 Barciany PL A7
88 Barcin PL C3
88 Barcino PL A2
72 Bárcis I B2
33 Barcones E C4
98 Barcs H C2
26 Barcus F C3
89 Barczewo PL B6
94 Bardejo CS B4
75 Bardi I B4
11 Bardney GB B5
71 Bardolino I C5
29 Bardonécchia I A5
97 Bardonovo CS C4
60 Bardowick D B1
34 Barèges F A3
64 Barenstein D C3
20 Barentin F B1
19 Barenton F B5
100 Barevo YU B2
33 Bareyo E A3
19 Barfleur F A4
75 Barga I B5
38 Bargas E C2
74 Barge I B2
29 Bargemon F C5
71 Barghe I C5
13 Bargoed GB B4
59 Bargteheide D B7
55 Bargum D D1
80 Bari I C3
87 Bari Sardo I C2
77 Barič Draga YU B5
59 Barien D C5
73 Barilovic YU C5
79 Barisciano I A4
28 Barjac F B3
30 Barjacoba E B4
29 Barjols F C5
49 Bårkåker N B7
59 Barkelsby D A6
15 Barking GB C3
65 Barkówko PL B6
88 Barkowo PL B3
63 Barleben D A6
29 Barles F B5
80 Barletta I C3
108 Barmash AL A2
11 Barmby Moor GB B5
10 Barmouth GB C1
59 Barmstedt D B6
4 Barna IRL A2
11 Barnard Castle GB A4
56 Barnarp S B3
68 Bärnau D B3
73 Bärnbach A A5
60 Barnenitz D C3
15 Barnet GB C2
11 Barnetby le Wold GB B5
17 Barneveld NL A5
19 Barneville F A4
19 Barneville Plage F A4
11 Barnoldswick GB B3
91 Barnów Sandomierski PL C5
61 Barnowko PL C5
11 Barnsley GB B4
63 Barnstädt D B6
12 Barnstaple GB B3
59 Barnstorf D C5
62 Barntrup D B4
21 Baron F B3
79 Baronissi I C5
105 Barovo YU C4
36 Barqueiro P B2
36 Barquinha P B2
66 Barr F C3
8 Barr GB C3
31 Barra P D2
40 Barracas E A2
38 Barraco E B2
84 Barrafranca I B3
30 Barral E B2
42 Barranco do Velho P B2
39 Barrax E C4
28 Barre F B2
36 Barreiro P C1
30 Barreiros E A3
29 Barrême F C5
8 Barrhead GB C3
8 Barrhill GB C3
32 Barrio E B1
36 Barroco P B2
10 Barrow in Furness GB A2
11 Barrow upon Humber GB B5
14 Barrow upon Soar GB B1
11 Barrowford GB B3
31 Barruecopardo E C4
32 Barruelo de Santullán E B2
34 Barruera E A3
13 Barry, South Glamorgan GB B4
9 Barry, Tayside GB B5
26 Barsac F B3
55 Bårse DK C4
63 Barsinghausen D A4
59 Barßel D B4
70 Bartenheim F A2
61 Barth D A3
67 Bartholmä D C5
15 Barton in the Clay GB C2
14 Barton Mills GB B3
11 Barton upon Humber GB B5
89 Bartoszyce PL A6
87 Barúmini I C2
64 Baruth D A3
6 Barvas GB B2
17 Barvaux B C5
59 Barver D C5
97 Barwatd PL B5
88 Barwice PL B2
32 Barzana E A1
71 Bárzio I C4
35 Bas E A5
99 Bašaid YU C5
74 Basaluzzo I B3
103 Basarabi RO B4
59 Basbeck D B6
78 Baschi I A3
32 Basconcillos del Tozo E B3
32 Bascones E B2
16 Basécles B C3
70 Basel CH A2
80 Basélice I C1
35 Basella E A4
15 Basildon GB C3
15 Basingstoke GB C1
97 Baška CS B4
77 Baska YU B4
100 Baška Voda YU C1
57 Baskemölla S D3
52 Basna S B1
73 Basovizza I C3
87 Bassacutena I A2
72 Bassano del Grappa I C1
78 Bassano di Sutri I A3
17 Bassilly B C3
21 Bassou F D4
27 Bassoues F C4
59 Bassum D C5
57 Båstad S C1
78 Bastardo I A3
86 Bastelica F B2
86 Bastia F B2
76 Bastia I C2
66 Bastogne B A1
14 Baston GB B2
47 Bastuträsk S D10
99 Bata H B3
101 Batajnica YU B5
106 Batak BG B2
36 Batalha P B2
34 Batea E B3
96 Batelov CS B1
13 Bath GB B5
12 Bath's Plot GB C3
9 Bathgate GB C4
78 Batignang I A2
99 Batina YU C3
104 Batlava YU B3
102 Batočina YU B2
106 Batoshevo BG A3
99 Bátoszék H B3
100 Batrina YU A2
112 Batsi GR E1
76 Battaglia Terme I A1
70 Bätterkinden CH A2
17 Battice B C5
80 Battipaglia I D1
15 Battle GB D3
103 Batultsi BG C5
102 Batuša YU B2
99 Bátya H B3
18 Baud F C2
66 Baudoncourt F D2
16 Baudour B C3
23 Baugé F A4
24 Baugy F A2
20 Baule F D2
71 Bauma CH A3
25 Baume-les-Dames F A6
60 Baumgarten D B3
69 Baumgartenberg A C5
66 Baumholder D B3
87 Baunei I B2
64 Bautzen D B4
101 Bavanište YU B5
16 Bavay F C3
70 Bavilliers F A1
69 Bavorov CS B5
59 Bawinkel D C4
3 Bawnboy IRL B4
11 Bawtry GB B4
9 Baydon GB D6
21 Bayel F C5
19 Bayeux F A5
112 Bayir TR A2
15 Baynards Green GB C1
30 Bayo E A2
66 Bayon F C2
30 Bayona E B2
26 Bayonne F C2
29 Bayons F B5
68 Bayreuth D B2
72 Bayrischzell D A2
45 Baza E B4
21 Bazancourt F B5
26 Bazas F B3
27 Baziege F C5
20 Bazoches-les-Gallerandes F C3
20 Bazoches-sur-Hoene F C1
75 Bazzano I B6
13 Beachley GB B5
15 Beaconsfield GB C2
30 Beade E B2
13 Beaminster GB C5
43 Beas E B3
44 Beas de Segura E A4
33 Beasain E A4
9 Beattock GB C4
25 Beaubery F B4
29 Beaucaire F C3
70 Beaucourt F A1
70 Beaufort F C1
23 Beaufort-en Vallée F A4
20 Beaugency F D2
29 Beaujeu, Alpes-de-Haute-Provence F B5
25 Beaujeu, Rhône F B4
26 Beaulac F B3
74 Beaulieu, Alpes-Maritimes F C2
24 Beaulieu, Loiret F A2
13 Beaulieu GB C6
22 Beaulieu-s/s la Roche F B3
27 Beaulieu-sur-Dordogne F B5
24 Beaulon F B3
7 Beauly GB C4
10 Beaumaris GB B1
20 Beaumesnil F B1
16 Beaumetz-les-Loges F C2
17 Beaumont B C4
27 Beaumont, Dordogne F B4
29 Beaumont, Drôme F B3
24 Beaumont, Puy-de-Dôme F C3
27 Beaumont-de-Lomagne F C4
20 Beaumont-du-Gatinais F C3
21 Beaumont-en-Argonne F B6
19 Beaumont-Hague F A4
23 Beaumont-la-Ronce F A5
20 Beaumont-le-Roger F B1
20 Beaumont-sur-Oise F B3
19 Beaumont-sur-Sarthe F B6
25 Beaune F A4
20 Beaune-la-Rolande F C3
22 Beaupréau F A4
21 Beauraing B A5
16 Beaureins F C2
29 Beaurepaire F A4
25 Beaurepaire-en-Bresse F B5
29 Beaurières F B4
20 Beauvais F B3
20 Beauval F A3
27 Beauville F B4
22 Beauvoir-sur-Mer F B2
23 Beauvoir-sur-Noirt F B4
99 Beba Veche RO B5
63 Bebertal D A6
10 Bebington GB B3
63 Bebra D C4
14 Beccles GB B4
37 Becedas E A5
99 Bečej YU C5
30 Becerreá E B3
32 Becerril de Campos E B2
19 Becherel F B4
103 Bechetu RO C4
68 Bechhofen D B1
40 Bechi E B2
69 Bechyně CS B5
81 Becići YU B5
32 Becilla de Valderaduey E B1
66 Beckerich L B1
9 Beckfoot GB D4
11 Beckingham GB B5
13 Beckington GB B5
62 Beckum D B3
36 Beco P B2
23 Bécon-les-Granits F A4
69 Bečov n Teplou CS A3
98 Becsehely H B1
11 Bedale GB A4
28 Bédarieux F C2
29 Bédarrides F B3
17 Bedburdyck D B6
17 Bedburg D C6
10 Beddgelert GB B1
57 Beddingestrand S D2
19 Bédée F B4
98 Bedegkér H B3
106 Beden BG B2
59 Bederkesa D B5
14 Bedford GB B2
9 Bedlington GB C6
90 Bedlno PL A3
44 Bedmar E B3
29 Bedoin F B4
75 Bedónia I B4
107 Bedre TR B5
70 Bedretto CH B3
58 Bedum NL B3
13 Bedwas GB B4
14 Bedworth GB B1
90 Bedzin PL C3
17 Beek NL C5
17 Beekbergen NL A5
62 Beelen D B3
64 Beelitz D A2
13 Beer GB C4
61 Beerfelde D C5
67 Beerfelden D B4
16 Beernem B B3
64 Beeskow D A4
14 Beeston GB B1
58 Beetsterzwaag NL B3
60 Beetzendorf D C2
70 Beflelay CH A2
35 Bega E A4
101 Begalica YU B5
18 Bégard F B2
35 Begas E B4
99 Begejci YU C5
44 Begijar E B3
17 Begijnendijk B B4
103 Beglezh BG C5
17 Beho B C5
26 Béhobie F C2
63 Behringen D B5
68 Behringersdorf D B2
68 Behringersmühle D B2
58 Beilen NL C3
68 Beilngries D B2
70 Beinwil CH A3
63 Beiseförth D B4
8 Beith GB C3
94 Beius RO C5
42 Beja P A2
37 Béjar E A5
94 Békéscsaba H C4
99 Békéssamson H B5
99 Bekésszentandrás H B5
105 Bel Iskúr BG B5
102 Bela BG C3
97 Bela CS B4
68 Belá n. Radbuzou CS B3
102 Bela Crkva YU B2
65 Bělá p Bezdězem CS C4
102 Bela Palanka YU C3
23 Bélâbre F B6
37 Belalcázar E C5
33 Belanga de Duero E C4
101 Belanovica YU B5
97 Bélapátfalva H C6
35 Belcaire F A4
90 Belchatów PL B3
34 Belchite E B2
69 Bělčice CS B4
104 Belcište YU C2
3 Belcoo GB B4
2 Belderg IRL B2
62 Belecke D B3
98 Beled H A2
77 Belej YU B4
103 Belene BG C6
35 Bélesta F A4
3 Belfast GB B6
9 Belford GB C6
70 Belfort F A1
29 Belgentier F C4
64 Belgern D B3
75 Belgioioso I A4
86 Belgodère F B2
4 Belgooly IRL C3
26 Belhade F B3
103 Beli Izvor BG C4
99 Beli Manastir YU C3
102 Beli Potok YU C3
26 Bèliet F B3
26 Belin F B3
39 Belinchón E B3
98 Belišće YU C3
105 Belitsa BG C5
96 Bělkovice-Lašt'any CS B3
34 Bell-Lloch E B3
80 Bella I D2
23 Bellac F B6
2 Bellacorick IRL B2
71 Bellágio I C4
3 Bellananagh IRL C4
2 Bellangare IRL C3
71 Bellano I B4
76 Bellária I B2
2 Bellavary IRL C2
34 Bellcaire de Urgel E B3
18 Belle-Isle-en-Terre F B2
21 Belleau F B4
2 Belleek GB B3
66 Bellefontaine B B1
25 Bellegarde, Ain F B5
29 Bellegarde, Drôme F B4
28 Bellegarde, Gard F C3
20 Bellegarde, Loiret F D3
25 Bellegarde-en-Forez F C4
20 Bellème F C1
24 Bellenaves F B3
70 Bellentre F C1
24 Bellerive F B3
70 Bellevaux F B1
25 Belleville F B4
22 Belleville-sur-Vie F B3
28 Bellevue-la-Mgne. F A2
25 Belley F C5
67 Bellheim D B4
3 Bellinalack IRL C4
9 Bellingham GB C5
58 Bellingwolde NL B4
70 Bellinzago Novarese I C3
71 Bellinzona CH B4
39 Bello E B5
35 Bellpuig E B4
40 Bellreguart E C2
72 Belluno I B2
35 Bellver de Cerdāna E A4
34 Bellvis E B3
43 Bélmez E A4
44 Belmez de la Moraleda E B3
25 Belmont F B4
6 Belmont, Shetland Is. GB
28 Belmont-sur Rance F C1
39 Belmonte E C4
36 Belmonte P A3
34 Belmonte de Mezquin E C2
30 Belmonte de Miranda E A4
39 Belmonte de Tajo E B3
2 Belmullet IRL B2
102 Belobresca RO B2
16 Belœil B C3
102 Belogradchik BG C3
102 Beloljin YU C2
33 Belorado E B3
101 Belotič YU B4
96 Bělotin CS B3
103 Belotintsi BG C3
106 Belozem BG A3
70 Belp CH B2
85 Belpasso I B3
27 Belpech F C5
11 Belper GB B4
9 Belsay GB C6
104 Belsh AL D1
91 Belsk Duzy PL B4
98 Beltinci YU B1
11 Belton GB B5
2 Beltra, Mayo IRL C2
2 Beltra, Sligo IRL B3
94 Beltsy SU C7
3 Belturbet IRL B4
97 Belusa CS B4
82 Belvedere Marittimo I B2
34 Belver E B3
32 Belver de los Montes E C1
27 Belves F B4
38 Belvis de la Jara E C2
37 Belvis de Monroy E B5
106 Belvovo BG A2
22 Belz F A1
64 Belzig D A2
91 Bełżyce PL B6
30 Bembibre E B4
15 Bembridge GB D1
17 Bemmel NL B5
31 Bemposta, Bragança P C4
36 Bemposta, Santarém P B2
34 Benabarre E A3
43 Benacazón E B3
40 Benaguacil E B2
45 Benahadux E C4
44 Benalmádena E C2
44 Benalúa de Guadix E B3
44 Benalúa de las Villas E B3
43 Benalup de Sidonia E C4
44 Benamargosa E C2
45 Benamaure E B4
44 Benameji E B2
44 Benamocarra E C2
43 Benaocaz E C4
43 Benaoján E C4
107 Benarli TR B5
43 Benarrabá E C4
34 Benasque E A3
65 Benátky Jizerou CS C4
32 Benavante E B1
36 Benavente P C2
36 Benavila P B3
94 Bendery SU C8
62 Bendorf D C2
74 Bene Vagienna I B2
72 Benediktbeuern D A1
59 Benefeld D C6
40 Benejama E C2
45 Benejúzar E A6
69 Benešov CS B5
69 Benešov n. Cernou CS C5
64 Benešov n. Ploučnici CS C4
66 Bénestroff F C2
23 Benet F B4
24 Bénévent-l'Abbaye F B1
79 Benevento I B5
66 Benfeld F C3
36 Benfica P B2
103 Bengeşti RO A4
51 Bengtsfors S C3
52 Bengtsheden S B1

Cambridgeshire GB B2
9 Brampton, *Cumbria* GB D5
14 Brampton, *Suffolk* GB B4
62 Bramsche D A2
59 Bramstedt D C5
69 Branau A C4
76 Branca I C2
85 Brancaleone Marina I B5
14 Brancaster GB B3
69 Brand, *Nieder Österreich* A C6
71 Brand, *Vorarlberg* A A4
64 Brand-Erbisdorf D C3
50 Brandbu N B1
55 Brande DK C2
59 Brande-Hornerkirchen D B6
72 Brandenberg A A1
64 Brandenburg D A2
64 Brandis D B2
62 Brandlecht D A2
30 Brandomil E A2
11 Brandon GB A4
61 Brandshagen D A4
50 Brandval N B3
65 Brandys n. Labem-Słará Boleslav CS C4
103 Brănesti RO B4
102 Braničevo YU B2
89 Braniewo PL A5
96 Brankovice CS B3
101 Brankovina YU B4
96 Branky CS B3
51 Bränna S D3
26 Branne F B3
68 Brannenburg D D3
27 Brantôme F A4
51 Bras S D2
29 Bras d'Asse F C5
104 Brasalice YU B3
50 Braskereidfoss N B2
94 Braşov RO D6
18 Brasparts F B2
28 Brassac F C1
24 Brassac-les-Mines F C3
17 Brasschaat B B4
51 Brastad S D2
69 Břasy CS B4
90 Brąszewice PL B2
108 Brataj AL A1
51 Bräte N C2
73 Bratina YU C5
96 Bratislava CS C3
103 Bratovoeşti RO B4
51 Brattfors S C5
13 Bratton GB B5
101 Bratunac YU B4
106 Bratya Daskolvi BG A3
62 Braubach D C2
62 Braunfels D C3
63 Braunlage D B5
63 Braunschweig D A5
12 Braunton GB B3
21 Braux F B5
71 Bravuogn CH B4
5 Bray IRL A5
16 Bray Dunes F B2
21 Bray-sur-Seine F C4
21 Bray-sur-Somme F B3
42 Braz P B2
44 Brazatortas E A2
25 Brazey F A5
101 Brčko YU B3
101 Brdani YU C5
90 Brdów PL A2
39 Brea de Tajo E B3
103 Breasta RO B4
103 Brebeni RO B5
19 Brécey F B4
9 Brechin GB B5
17 Brecht B B4
62 Breckerfeld D B2
96 Breclav CS C2
13 Brecon GB B4
24 Brécy F A2
35 Breda E B5
17 Breda NL B4
56 Bredaryd S B2
15 Brede GB D3
55 Bredebro DK C1
62 Bredelar D B3
16 Bredene B B2
61 Bredenfelde D B4
62 Bredevoort NL B1
50 Bredsjö S C5
59 Bredstedt D A5
55 Bredsten DK C2
17 Bree B B5
58 Breezand NL C1
72 Breganze I C1
71 Bregenz A A4
102 Bregovo BG B3
19 Brehal F B4
64 Brehna D B2
97 Brehy CS C4
66 Breidenbach F B3
74 Breil F C2
46 Breim N F3
66 Breisach D C3
70 Breitenbach CH A2
63 Breitenbach D C4
69 Breitenberg D C4
96 Breitenbrunn A D2
60 Breitenfelde D B1
96 Breitenfurth A C2
63 Breitenworbis D B5
55 Brejning DK C2
49 Brekkesto N C5
100 Brela YU C1
59 Bremen D B5
59 Bremerhaven D B5
59 Bremervörde D B6
70 Bremgarten CH A3
48 Bremnes N B2
55 Brenderup DK C2
63 Brendlorenzen D C5
43 Brenes E B4
103 Brenitsa BG C5
97 Brenna PL B4
72 Brenner I A1
71 Breno I C5
25 Brénod F B5
67 Brensbach D B4
15 Brent GB C2
15 Brentwood GB C3
75 Brescello I B5
71 Bréscia I C5
16 Breskens N B3
20 Bresles F B3
101 Bresnica YU C5
74 Bressana I A4
72 Bressanone (Brixen) I B1
24 Bressole F B3
23 Bressuire F B4
103 Brest BG C5
96 Brest CS B3
18 Brest F B1
93 Brest SU D8
101 Brestac YU B4
73 Brestanica YU C5
77 Brestova YU A4
100 Brestovac, *Hrvatska* YU A2
102 Brestovac, *Srbija* YU B3
102 Brestovad YU C2
27 Bretenoux F B5
20 Breteuil, *Eure* F C1
20 Breteuil, *Oise* F B3
20 Brétigny-sur-Orge F C3
64 Bretnig D B4
67 Bretten D B4
19 Bretteville-sur-Laize F A5
67 Brettheim D B6
70 Breuil-Cervinia I C2
17 Breukelen NL A5
53 Breven S C1
49 Brevik N B6
100 Breza YU B3
73 Brezice YU C5
29 Bréziers F B5
101 Brezna YU C5
98 Breznica YU B1
98 Breznica Našička YU C3
69 Březnice CS B4
105 Breznik BG B4
97 Brezno CS C5
103 Brezoi RO A5
104 Brezojevice YU B1
20 Brezolles F C2
96 Brezová CS C3
96 Březová n Svitavou CS B2
106 Brezovo BG A3
101 Brezovo Polje YU B3
29 Briançon F B5
29 Brianconnet F C5
24 Briare F A2
27 Briatexte F C5
21 Briaucourt F C6
77 Bribir YU C5
19 Bricquebec F A4
70 Brides-les-Bains F C1
12 Bridestowe GB C3
4 Brideswell IRL A3
15 Bridge GB C4
7 Bridge of Alford GB C6
9 Bridge of Allan GB B4
9 Bridge of Cally GB B4
7 Bridge of Don GB C6
9 Bridge of Earn GB B4
7 Bridge of Forss GB B5
8 Bridge of Orchy GB B3
6 Bridge of Walls, *Shetland Is.* GB
8 Bridge of Weir GB C3
8 Bridgend, *Islay* GB C1
13 Bridgend, *Mid Glamorgan* GB B4
10 Bridgenorth GB C3
11 Bridghouse GB B4
13 Bridgwater GB B5
96 Bridlična CS B3
11 Bridlington GB A5
18 Bridnogan F B1
13 Bridport GB C5
13 Bridstow GB B5
20 Brie-Comte-Robert F C3
18 Briec F B2
60 Brielow D C3
21 Brienne-le-Château F C5
70 Brienz CH B2
82 Brienza I A2
64 Brieskow Finkenheerd D A4
60 Brietlingen D B1
21 Brieulles-sur-Meuse F B6
33 Brieva E B4
66 Briey F B1
11 Brigg GB B5
15 Brighstone GB D1
15 Brightlingsea GB C3
15 Brighton GB D2
29 Brignoles F C5
14 Brigstock GB B2
39 Brihuega E B4
102 Brijanje YU C2
101 Briježde YU B5
62 Brilon D B3
42 Brinches P A2
81 Bríndisi I D4
77 Brinje YU A5
24 Brinon-sur-Beuvron F A3
24 Brinon-sur-Sauldre F A2
7 Brinyan GB A5
30 Brión E B2
33 Briones E B4
20 Brionne F B1
21 Brionon-sur-Armançon F D4
28 Brioude F A2
23 Brioux-sur-Boutonne F B4
19 Briouze F B5
26 Briscous F C2
76 Brisighella I B1
25 Brison F C5
23 Brissac-Quincé F A4
70 Brissago CH B3
13 Bristol GB B5
5 Brittas IRL A5
27 Brive-la-Gaillarde F A5
33 Briviesca E B3
13 Brixham GB C4
72 Brixlegg A A1
14 Brixworth GB B2
101 Brka YU B3
80 Brna YU B3
100 Brnaze YU C1
96 Brno CS B2
51 Bro S D2
13 Broad Clyst GB C4
6 Broadford GB C3
15 Broadstairs GB C4
13 Broadway GB A6
13 Broadwey GB C5
13 Broadwindsor GB C5
55 Broager DK D2
56 Broaryd S B2
57 Broby S C3
100 Bročanac, *Bosna i Hercegovina* YU C2
81 Bročanac, *Crna Gora* YU B5
26 Brocas F B3
62 Brock D A2
59 Brockel D B6
13 Brockenhurst GB C6
13 Brockworth GB B5
88 Broczyno PL B2
104 Brod YU C3
73 Brod na Kupi YU C4
101 Brodarevo YU C4
52 Broddbo S C2
96 Brodek CS B3
62 Brodenbach D C2
102 Brodica YU B2
8 Brodick GB C2
107 Brodilovo BG A5
89 Brodnica PL B5
88 Brodnica Graniczna PL A4
100 Brodski Stupnik YU A2
65 Brody PL B4
58 Broek op Langendijk NL C1
20 Broglie F B1
65 Brójce PL A5
53 Brokind S D1
85 Brolo I A3
60 Brome D C1
15 Bromley GB C2
57 Bromölla S C3
24 Bromont-Lamothe F C2
57 Brömsebro S C4
13 Bromsgrove GB A5
13 Bromyard GB A5
40 Bronchales E A1
37 Bronco E A4
54 Brønderslev DK A2
75 Broni I A4
13 Bronllys GB A4
46 Brönnöysund N D6
55 Brøns DK C1
85 Bronte I B3
72 Bronzolo (Branzoll) I B1
3 Brookeborough GB B4
9 Broomhill GB C6
18 Broons F B3
28 Broquies F B1
7 Brora GB B5
55 Brørup DK C1
103 Broscari RO B3
103 Brosteni RO B3
49 Brøstrud N A5
91 Broszków PL A6
36 Brotas P C2
50 Brötjärna S B6
34 Broto E A2
50 Brøttum N A1
20 Brou F C2
10 Brough, *Cumbria* GB A3
6 Brough, *Shetland Is.* GB
6 Brough Lodge, *Shetland Is.* GB
3 Broughshane GB B5
9 Broughton, *Borders* GB C4
11 Broughton, *Lincolnshire* GB B5
14 Broughton, *Northamptonshire* GB B2
10 Broughton in Furness GB A2
65 Broumov CS C6
21 Broussy le Grand F C4
24 Brout-Vernet F B3
66 Brouvelieures F C2
16 Brouwershaven N B3
54 Brovst DK A2
11 Brownhills GB C4
25 Broye F B4
37 Brozas E B4
71 Brozzo I C5
96 Brtnice CS B1
16 Bruay-en-Artois F C2
35 Bruch E B4
59 Bruchhausen-Vilsen D C5
67 Bruchsal D B4
72 Bruck A A2
64 Bruck D A2
68 Bruck D B3
96 Bruck a.d. Leitha A C2
73 Bruck a.d. Mur A A5
68 Bruckberg D B1
73 Brückl A B4
68 Bruckmühl D D2
29 Brue-Auriac F C4
60 Brüel D B2
24 Bruère-Allichamps F B2
4 Bruff IRL B3
70 Brugg CH A3
16 Brugge B B3
17 Brüggen D B6
24 Brugneas F B3
62 Brühl D C1
17 Bruinisse NL B4
19 Brulon F C5
71 Brumano I C4
66 Brumath F C3
17 Brummen NL A6
50 Brumunddal N B1
60 Brunau D C2
55 Brundby DK C3
21 Brunehamel F B5
62 Brünen D B1
46 Brunflo S E7
72 Brunico (Bruneck) I B1
49 Brunkeberg N B5
96 Brunn a. Gebirge A C2
52 Brunna S C3
70 Brunnen CH B3
50 Brunnsberg S A4
50 Brunnsvik S B6
59 Brunsbüttel D B6
17 Brunssum NL C5
70 Brunstatt F A2
96 Bruntál CS B3
102 Brus YU C2
77 Brušane YU B5
103 Brusartsi BG C4
74 Brusasco I A3
71 Brusio CH B5
102 Brusnik YU B3
28 Brusque F C1
70 Brusson I C2
61 Brüssow D B5
88 Brusy PL B3
13 Bruton GB B5
50 Bruvoll N B2
17 Bruxelles B C4
66 Bruyères F C2
19 Bruz F B4
56 Bruzaholm S B4
91 Brwinow PL A4
107 Bryastovets BG A5
103 Bryastovo BG C5
10 Bryn-Eden GB C2
12 Brynamman GB B4
48 Bryne N C2
13 Brynmawr GB B4
102 Brza Palanka YU B3
102 Brzeč YU C1
90 Brzeg PL C1
65 Brzeg Dolny PL B6
91 Brzegi PL C4
89 Brzesć Kuj PL C4
91 Brzesko Nowe PL C4
97 Brzeszcze PL B5
88 Brzezie PL B2
90 Brzeziny PL B2
90 Brzeziny PL B3
90 Brzežnica Nowa PL B3
97 Brzotin CS C6
89 Brzozie Lubawskie PL B5
91 Brzozów PL A4
94 Brzozów PL B5
54 Bua S A5
36 Buarcos P A2
48 Buaveg N B2
74 Bubbio I B3
73 Bubravica YU C5
18 Bubry F C2
96 Bučany CS C3
85 Buccheri I B3
80 Buccino I D2
36 Bucelas P C1
67 Buch, *Bayern* D C6
68 Buch, *Bayern* D C3
67 Buchau D C5
68 Buchbach D C3
71 Buchboden A A4
67 Buchen, *Baden-Württemberg* D B5
60 Büchen, *Schleswig-Holstein* D B1
71 Buchenberg D A5
21 Buchères F C5
59 Buchholz D B6
63 Buchholz D B5
103 Buchin Prokhod BG D4
68 Buchloe D C1
96 Buchlovice CS B3
8 Buchlyvie GB B3
60 Bucholz D B3
71 Buchs CH A4
20 Buchy F B2
104 Bučin YU C3
103 Bucinişu RO C5
102 Bučje YU C3
14 Buckden GB B2
62 Bückeburg D A4
12 Buckfastleigh GB C4
9 Buckhaven GB B4
7 Buckie GB C6
15 Buckingham GB C1
10 Buckley GB B2
61 Buckow D C5
9 Bucksburn GB A5
60 Buckwitz D C3
96 Bučovice CS B2
95 Bucureşti RO D7
21 Bucy F B4
21 Bucy-lés-Pierreport F B4
90 Buczek PL B3
99 Budakesi H A3
99 Budaörs H A3
99 Budapest H A3
87 Buddusó I B2
12 Bude GB C3
96 Budec CS B1
17 Budel NL B5
59 Büdelsdorf D A6
42 Budens P B1
62 Büderich D B1
39 Budia E B4
62 Büdingen D C4
98 Budinšćina YU B1
96 Budišov, *Jihomoravský* CS B2
96 Budišov, *Severomoravsky* CS B3
13 Budleigh Salterton GB C4
96 Budmerice CS C3
93 Budogoshch SU A13
88 Budowo PL A3
76 Búdrio I B1
81 Budva YU B5
64 Budyně n. Ohří CS C4
91 Budziszewice PL B3
97 Budzów PL B5
88 Budzyń PL C3
48 Bue N C2
34 Bueña E C1
39 Buenache de Alarcón E C4
39 Buenache de la Sierra E B5
38 Buenaventura E B2
32 Buenavista de Valdavia E B2
39 Buendia E B4
62 Buer D A3
30 Bueu E B2
33 Buezo E B3
99 Bugac H B4
24 Bugeat F C1
87 Buggerru I C1
12 Bugle GB C3
100 Bugojno YU B2
99 Bugyi H A4
67 Bühl, *Baden-Württemberg* D C4
71 Bühl, *Bayern* D A5
67 Bühlertal D C4
67 Bühlertann D B5
72 Buia I B3
13 Builth Wells GB A4
29 Buis-les-Baronnies F B4
58 Buitenpost NL B3
39 Buitrago E B3
97 Buják H D5
44 Bujalance E B2
105 Bujanovac YU B3
34 Bujaraloz E B2
72 Buje YU C3
33 Bujedo E B3
98 Bük H A1
65 Buk PL A6
105 Bukhovo BG B5
98 Bükkösd H B2
73 Bukovici YU B5
104 Bukovo YU C3
103 Buk'ovtsi BG C4
65 Bukowiec PL A6
97 Bukowina PL B6
90 Bukowno PL C3
88 Bukowo Morskie PL A2
70 Bülach CH A3
62 Buldern D B2
7 Buldoo GB B5
103 Bulgarene BG C6
107 Bulgarovo BG A5
107 Búlgarska Polyana BG A4
103 Búlgarski Izvor BG C5
59 Bülkau D B5
46 Bulken N F3
89 Bulkowo PL C6
17 Bullange B C6
45 Bullas E A5
70 Bulle CH B2
15 Bullington Cross Inn GB C1
97 Bulowice PL B5
104 Bulqizë AL C2
103 Bumbeşti-jiu RO A4
2 Bunbeg IRL A3
5 Bunclody IRL B5
3 Buncrana IRL A4
58 Bunde, *Niedersachsen* D B4
62 Bunde, *Nordrhein-Westfalen* D A3
63 Bundheim D B5
2 Bundoran IRL B3
8 Bunessan GB B1
14 Bungay GB B4
77 Bunič YU B5
5 Bunmahon IRL B4
30 Buño E A2
40 Buñol E B2
41 Buñola, *Mallorca* E
17 Bunsbeek B C4
15 Buntingford GB C2
33 Buñuel E C5
82 Buonabitácolo I A2
80 Buonalbergo I C1
75 Buonconvento I C6
82 Buonvicino I B2
72 Burano I C2
62 Burbach D C3
13 Burbage GB B6
87 Burcei I C2
47 Bureå S D10
30 Burella de Cabo E A3
62 Büren D B3
70 Büren an der Aare CH A2
13 Burford GB B6
59 Burg D B6
64 Burg, *Cottbus* D B4
63 Burg, *Magdeburg* D A6
61 Burg Stargard D B4
107 Burgas BG A5
73 Burgau A A6
68 Burgau D C1
42 Burgau P B1
67 Burgberheim D B6
70 Burgdorf CH A2
59 Burgdorf D C7
68 Burgebrach D B1
63 Bürgel D C6
15 Burgess Hill GB D2
11 Burgh le Marsh GB B6
68 Burghaslach D B1
63 Burghaum D C4
69 Burghausen D C3
7 Burghead GB C5
84 Búrgio I B2
63 Burgkunstadt D C6
68 Burglengenfeld D B3
43 Burgo E C5
31 Burgo P D2
68 Burgoberbach D B1
38 Burgohondo E B2
33 Burgos E B3
67 Burgsinn D A5
64 Burgstädt D C2
63 Burgstall D A6
62 Burgsteinfurt D A2
92 Burgsvik S B6
34 Burguete E A1
34 Burgui E A2
43 Burguillos E B4
38 Burguillos de Toledo E C3
37 Burguillos del Cerro E C4
59 Burhave D B5
23 Burie F C4
102 Burila Mare RO B3
40 Burjaso E B2
68 Burk D B1
64 Burkau D B4
64 Burkhardsdorf D C2
67 Burladingen D C5
59 Burlage D B4
11 Burley in Wharfedale GB B4
7 Burness GB A6
3 Burnfoot IRL A4
14 Burnham Market GB B3
15 Burnham-on-Crouch GB C3
13 Burnham-on-Sea GB B5
11 Burnley GB B3
9 Burnmouth GB C5
9 Burntisland GB B4
32 Burón E A1
70 Buronzo I C3
102 Burovac YU B2
61 Burow D B4
6 Burrafirth, *Shetland Is.* GB
6 Burravoe, *Shetland Is.* GB
104 Burrel AL C2
9 Burrelton GB B4
4 Burren IRL A2
35 Burret F A4
40 Burriana E B2
12 Burry Port GB B3
71 Burs A A4
56 Burseryd S B2
67 Bürstadt D B4
10 Burton GB A3
11 Burton Agnes GB A5
13 Burton Bradstock GB C5
14 Burton Latimer GB B2
11 Burton upon Trent GB C4
2 Burtonport IRL B3
38 Burujón E C2
112 Burunkoy TR B1
98 Bürüs H C2
15 Burwash GB D3
7 Burwick GB B6
10 Bury GB B3
14 Bury St. Edmunds GB B3
90 Burzenin PL B2
103 Búrziya BG C4
87 Busachi I B1
74 Busalla I B3
75 Busana I B5
74 Busano I A2
74 Busca I B2
60 Busch D C2
104 Bushat AL C1
15 Bushey GB C2
3 Bushmills GB A5
97 Bušince CS C5
53 Buskhyttan S D2
91 Busko Zdrój PL C4
40 Busot E C2
100 Busovača YU B2
44 Busquistar E C3
66 Bussang F D2
75 Busseto I B5
23 Bussière-Poitevine F B5
25 Bussières F C4
71 Bussolengo I C5
74 Bussoleno I A2
17 Bussum NL A5
71 Busto Arsizio I C3
59 Büsum D A5
103 Butan BG C4
84 Butera I B3
17 Butgenbach B C6
89 Butryny PL B6
71 Bütschwil CH A4
68 Buttenwiesen D C1
10 Buttermere GB A2
4 Buttevant IRL B3
63 Buttstädt D B6
62 Butzbach D C3
59 Bützfleth D B6
60 Bützow D B2
24 Buxières F B2
59 Buxtehude D B6
11 Buxton GB B4
25 Buxy F B4
106 Buynovtsi BG A3
107 Büyük Doganca TR B4
107 Büyük Karistiran TR B5
107 Büyük Manika TR B5
23 Buzancais F B6
21 Buzancy F B5
94 Buzău RO D7
73 Buzet YU C3
98 Buzsák H B2
26 Buzy F C3
13 Bwlch GB B4
52 By S B2
106 Byal Izvor BG B3
95 Byala, *Ruse* BG E6
107 Byala, *Sliven* BG A4
106 Byala Reka BG A3
103 Byala Slatina BG C4
106 Byalo Pole BG A3
91 Bychawa PL B6
90 Byczyna PL B2
88 Bydgoszcz PL B3
14 Byfield GB B1
46 Bygdin N F4
49 Bygland N C4
49 Byglandsfjord N C4
48 Bykle N B4
10 Bylchau GB B2
55 Bylderup DK D2
34 Bylie F A3
97 Bylnice CS B4
54 Byrum DK A3
65 Byšice Liblice CS C4
47 Byske S D10
96 Býškovice CS B3
88 Byslaw PL B3
96 Bystré CS B2
97 Bystrice, *Stredočeský* CS B4
69 Bystřice, *Stredočeský* CS B5
96 Bystřice n Pernstejnem CS B2
96 Bystřice p. Hostýnem CS B3
65 Bystrzyca Klodzka PL C6
97 Bytča CS B4
90 Bytom PL C2
65 Bytom Odrz PL B5
88 Byton PL C2
88 Bytów PL A3
92 Byxelkrok S B5
96 Bzenic CS C3
96 Bzince CS C3

C

41 C'an Pastilla, *Mallorca* E
41 C'an Picafort, *Mallorca* E
76 Ca'Pisani I B2
36 Cabacos P B2
26 Cabanac-et-Villagrains F B3
32 Cabañaquinta E A1
30 Cabañas E A2
42 Cabanas P B2
39 Cabañas de Yepes E C3
37 Cabañas del Castillo E B5
35 Cabanellas E A5
40 Cabanes E A3
33 Cabanillas E B5
73 Cabar YU C4
29 Cabasse F C5
31 Cabeceiras de Basto P C2
36 Cabeço de Vide P B3
74 Cabella Ligure I B4
37 Cabeza del Buey E C5
43 Cabeza la Vaca E A3
39 Cabezamesada E C3
38 Cabezarados E D2
44 Cabezarrubias del Puerto E A2
38 Cabezas del Villar E B1
42 Cabezas Rubias E B2
32 Cabezón E C2
32 Cabezón de la Sal E A2
32 Cabezón de Liébana E A2
32 Cabezuela E C3
37 Cabezuela del Valle E A5
39 Cabolfuenta E A4
19 Cabourg F A5
44 Cabra E B2
31 Cabra P D3
44 Cabra del Sto. Cristo E B3
7 Cabrach GB C5
32 Cabrales (Carreña) E A2
87 Cábras I C1
31 Cabreiro P C2
30 Cabreiros E A3
39 Cabrejas E B4
36 Cabrela P C2
28 Cabrières F C2
30 Cacabelos E B4
101 Čačak YU C5
84 Cáccamo I B2
83 Caccuri I B3
42 Cacela P B2
37 Cáceres E B4
30 Cachafeiro E B2
42 Cachopo P B2
96 Cachtice CS C3
44 Cacin E B3
98 Čačinci YU C2
102 Cacova RO A2
36 Cadafais P C1
27 Cadalen F C6
37 Cadalso E A4
5 Cadamstown IRL A4
35 Cadaques E A6
36 Cadaval P B1
30 Cadavedo E A4
100 Čadavica, *Bosna i Hercegovina* YU B1
98 Cadavica, *Hrvatska* YU C2
97 Čadca CS B4
34 Cadéac F A3
75 Cadelbosco di Sopra I B5
71 Cadenazzo CH B3
59 Cadenberge D B6
29 Cadenet F C4
22 Cadeuil F C4
26 Cadillac F B3
43 Cádiz E C3
13 Cadnam GB C6
27 Cadouin F B4
34 Cadrete E B2
19 Caen F A5
11 Caenby Corner GB B5
10 Caergwrle GB B2
10 Caernarfon GB B1
13 Caerphilly GB B4
10 Caersws GB C2
82 Caggiano I A2
76 Cagli I C2
87 Cágliari I C2
80 Cagnano Varano I C2
5 Caher IRL B4
4 Cahercornish IRL B3
4 Cahermore IRL C1
4 Cahersiveen IRL C1
27 Cahors F B5
79 Caiazzo I B5
8 Cairnoch GB B3
8 Cairnryan GB D2
74 Cáiro Montenotte I B3
14 Caister-on-Sea GB B4
11 Caistor GB B5
79 Caivano I C5
35 Caixans E A4
27 Cajarc F B5
101 Cajetina YU C4
97 Čajkov CS C4
101 Čajniče YU C4
97 Čaka CS C4
97 Čakajovce CS C4
107 Çakilli TR B5
98 Čakovec YU B1
64 Čakovice CS C4
108 Cakran AL A1
43 Cala E B3
41 Cala d'Or, *Mallorca* E
41 Cala Foreat, *Menorca* E
87 Cala Gonone I B2
41 Cala Llonga, *Ibiza* E
41 Cala Millor, *Mallorca* E
41 Cala Ratjada, *Mallorca* E
80 Calabritto I D2
34 Calaceite E B3
86 Calacuccia F B2
35 Calaf E B4
103 Calafat RO C3
35 Calafell E B4
44 Calahonda E C3
33 Calahorra E B5
16 Calais F C1
34 Calamocha E C1
37 Calamonte E C4
43 Calañas E B3
34 Calanda E C2
87 Calangiánus I B2
95 Calarasi RO D7
41 Calas de Mallorca, *Mallorca* E
85 Calascibetta I B3
87 Calasetta I C1
45 Calasparra E A5
84 Calatafimi I B1
33 Calatayuo E C5
33 Calatorao E C5
64 Calau D B3
63 Calbe D B6
33 Calcena E C5
71 Calco I C4
103 Căldăraru RO B5
71 Caldaro (Kaltern) I B6
76 Caldarola I C3
36 Caldas da Rainha P B1
34 Caldas de Bohi E A3
35 Caldas de Malavella E B5
35 Caldas de Montbúy E B5
30 Caldas de Reyes E B2
31 Caldas de San Jorge P D2
31 Caldas de Vizela P C2
38 Caldaso de los Vidrios E B2
9 Calder GB C4
10 Calder Bridge GB A2
35 Calders E B4
3 Caledon GB B5
35 Calella, *Barcelona* E B5
35 Calella, *Gerona* E B6
86 Calenzana F B1
43 Calera de León E A3
38 Calera y Chozas E C2
33 Caleruega E C3
38 Caleruela E C1
75 Calestano I B5
8 Calgary GB B1
103 Călimăneşti RO A5
83 Calimera I A5
103 Călineşti RO B6
80 Calitri I D2
74 Calizzano I B3
18 Callac F B2
5 Callan IRL B4
8 Callander GB B3
29 Calles F C5
74 Calliano, *Piemonte* I A3
71 Calliano, *Trentino Alto Adige* I C6
12 Callington GB C3
40 Callosa de Ensarriá E C2
45 Callosa de Segura E A6
2 Callow IRL C2
35 Callús E B4
101 Čalma YU A4
67 Calmbach D C4
13 Calne GB B6
71 Calolziocorte I C4
35 Calonge E B6
96 Čalovec CS D3
96 Čalovo CS D3
40 Calpe E C3
13 Calshot GB C6
84 Caltabellotta I B2
85 Caltagirone I B3
84 Caltanissetta I B3
84 Caltavuturo I B2
33 Caltojar E C4
74 Caluso I A2
31 Calvario E C2
82 Calvello I A2
86 Calvi F B1
41 Calviá, *Mallorca* E
28 Calvisson F C3
63 Calvörde D A6
67 Calw D C4
44 Calzada de Calatrava E A3
38 Calzada de Valdunciel E A1
37 Calzadilla de los Barros E C4
75 Camaiore I C5
34 Camarasa E B3
38 Camarena E B2
28 Camarès F C1
18 Camaret F B1
29 Camaret-sur-Aigues F B3
32 Camargo E A3
40 Camarillas E A2
30 Camariñas E A1
39 Camarma E B3
31 Camarzana de Tera E B4
43 Camas E B3
84 Camastra I B2
6 Camb, *Shetland Is.* GB
30 Cambados E B2
31 Cambarinho P D2
62 Camberg D C3
15 Camberley GB C2
44 Cambil E B3
9 Cambo GB C6
26 Cambo-les-Bains F C2
12 Camborne GB C2
16 Cambrai F C3
30 Cambre E A2
14 Cambridge GB B3
35 Cambrils E B4
60 Cambs D B2
63 Camburg D B6
3 Camdonagh IRL A4
32 Cameleño E A2
12 Camelford GB C3
30 Camello E A1
76 Camerano I C3
76 Camerino I C3
82 Camerota I A2
83 Cami Salentina I A5
83 Camigliatello Silano I B3
31 Caminha P C2
37 Caminomorisco E A4
72 Camisano Vicentino I C1
107 Camlica TR C4
9 Cammachmore GB A5
84 Cammarata I B2
74 Camogli I B4
5 Camolin IRL B5
18 Camors F C3
80 Campagna I D2
78 Campagnano di Roma I A3
78 Campagnático I A2
27 Campan F C4
83 Campana I B3
37 Campanario E C5
44 Campanillas E C2
43 Campano E C3
32 Campaspero E C2
7 Campbelltown GB C4
8 Campbeltown GB C2
40 Campello E C2
36 Campelos P B1
75 Campi Bisénzio I C6
45 Campico López E B5
75 Campiglia Marittima I C5
38 Campillo E B1
39 Campillo de Altobuey E C5
39 Campillo de Aregón E A5
44 Campillo de Arenas E B3
37 Campillo de Llerena E C5
44 Campillos E B2
79 Campli I A4
34 Campo E A3
31 Campo P C2
31 Campo de Bacerros E B3
32 Campo de Caso E A1
39 Campo de Criptana E C3
74 Campo Ligure I B3
37 Campo Maior P B3
74 Campo Molino I B2
39 Campo Real E B3
72 Campo Tures (Taufers) I B1
79 Campobasso I B5
84 Campobello di Licata I B2
84 Campobello di Mazara I B1
72 Campodársego I C1
71 Campodolcino I B4
84 Campofelice di Roccella I B2
84 Campofiorito I B2
72 Campofómide I B3
84 Campofranco I B2
43 Campofrio E B3
75 Campogalliano I B5
72 Campolongo I B2
32 Campomanes E A1
80 Campomarino I C2
84 Camporeale I B2
76 Camporeggiano I C2
34 Camporrells E B3
40 Camporrobles E B1
31 Campos P C3
41 Campos del Puerto, *Mallorca* E
31 Camposa P C2
72 Camposampiero I C1
75 Camposanto I B6
34 Camposines E B3
44 Campotéjar E B3
79 Campotosto I A4
35 Camprodon E A5
27 Campsegret F B4
9 Camptown GB C5
39 Camuñas E C3
78 Cana I A2
39 Cañada del Hoyo E C5
39 Cañadajuncosa E C4
43 Cañadarrosal E B4
95 Canakkale TR F7
74 Canale I B2
72 Canale San Bovo I B1
40 Canales E B2
40 Canals E C2
38 Cañamero E C1
44 Cañar E C3
43 Cañate la Real E C4
37 Cañaveral E B4
43 Cañaveral de León E A3
39 Cañaveras E B4
72 Canazie I B1
19 Cancale F B4
80 Cancellara I D2
79 Cancello ed Arnone I B4
27 Cancon F B4
31 Canda E B4
30 Candamil E A3
30 Candamo E A4
34 Candanchu E A2
32 Candás (Carreñn) E A1
34 Candasnos E B3
22 Candé F A3
80 Candela I C2
37 Candelario E A5
34 Candesnos E B3
72 Candide I B2
30 Candin E B4
36 Candosa P A3
9 Candy GB B5
74 Canelli I B3
44 Canena E A3
40 Canet de Berenguer E B2
35 Canet de Mar E B5
35 Canet-Plage F A6
39 Cañete E B5
44 Cañete de las Torres E B2

Manchester GB B3
11 Cheadle, *Staffordshire* GB C4
68 Cheb CS A3
39 Checa E B5
91 Checiny PL C4
13 Cheddar GB B5
23 Chef-Boutonne F B4
23 Cheffs F A4
37 Cheles E C3
40 Chella E B2
94 Chelm PL A5
97 Chelmek PL A5
89 Chelmno PL B4
90 Chelmno PL A2
15 Chelmondiston GB C4
15 Chelmsford GB C3
89 Chełmża PL B4
13 Cheltenham GB B5
40 Chelva E B2
23 Chémery F A6
23 Chemillé F A4
25 Chemin F B5
64 Chemnitz (Karl-Marx-Stadt) D C2
25 Chénas F B4
24 Chénerailles F B2
23 Chenonceaux F A6
25 Chenove F A4
21 Cheny F D4
106 Chepelare BG B2
13 Chepstow GB B5
40 Chera E B2
33 Cheradi I A4
74 Cherasco I B2
17 Cheratte B C5
19 Cherbourg F A4
82 Cherchiara di Calábria I B3
106 Chernogorovo BG A2
107 Chernomorets BG A5
94 Chernovtsy SU B6
21 Chéroy F B3
40 Chert E A3
34 Cherta E C3
15 Chertsey GB C2
103 Cherven Bryag BG C5
21 Chéry F B4
93 Cheryakhousk SU C7
15 Chesham GB C2
15 Cheshunt GB C2
21 Chessy-lès-Pres F C4
10 Chester GB B3
9 Chester le Street GB D6
11 Chesterfield GB B4
105 Chetirtsi BG B4
24 Chevagnes F B3
26 Chevanceaux F A3
70 Chevenez CH A2
21 Chevillon F C6
20 Chevilly F C2
25 Chevroux F B4
13 Chew Magna GB B5
25 Chézery-Forens F B5
74 Chialamberto I A2
71 Chiampo I C6
74 Chianale I B2
76 Chianciano Terme I C1
85 Chiaramonte Gulfi I B3
87 Chiaramonti I B1
76 Chiaravalle I C3
83 Chiaravalle Centrale I C3
71 Chiaréggio I B4
71 Chiari I C4
82 Chiaromonte I A3
71 Chiasso CH C3
75 Chiavari I B4
71 Chiavenna I B4
23 Chiché F B4
21 Chichée F B4
15 Chichester GB D2
44 Chiciana de Segura E A2
13 Chicklade GB B5
43 Chiclana de la Frontera E C3
15 Chiddingfold GB C2
74 Chieri I A2
71 Chiesa in Valmalenco I B4
79 Chieti I A5
79 Chieti Scalo I A5
80 Chiéuti I C2
16 Chièvres B C3
95 Chiewiska PL B4
39 Chillarón de Cuenca E B4
39 Chillarón del Rey E B4
20 Chilleurs-aux-Bois F C3
44 Chillón E A2
44 Chilluevar E B3
39 Chiloeches E B3
21 Chimay B A5
44 Chimeneas E B3
40 Chinchilla de Monte-Aragón E C1
39 Chinchón E B3
15 Chinnor GB C2
23 Chinon F A5
79 Chióggia I A2
74 Chiomonte I A1
43 Chipiona E C3
13 Chippenham GB B5
13 Chipping Camden GB A6
15 Chipping Norton GB C1
13 Chipping Sodbury GB B5
103 Chiprovski BG C3
28 Chirac F B2
10 Chirbury GB C2
103 Chiren BG C4
25 Chirens F C5
45 Chirivel E B4
10 Chirk GB C2
9 Chirnside GB C5
106 Chirpan BG A3
13 Chiseldon GB B6
94 Chişineu-Criş RO C4
25 Chissey-en-Morvan F A4
72 Chiusa (Klausen) I B1
74 Chiusa di Pésio I B2
84 Chiusa Sclafani I B2
72 Chiusaforte I B3
76 Chiusi I C1
74 Chivasso I A2
88 Chludowo PL C2
69 Chlum u. Trebone CS C5
65 Chlumec n. Cidlinon CS C5
91 Chmielnik PL C4
91 Chmielów PL C5
65 Chobienia PL B6
65 Chobienice PL A5
96 Chocen CS A2
97 Chocholow PL B5
65 Chocianów PL B5
61 Chociwel PL B6
88 Choczewo PL A3
91 Chodaków PL A4
90 Chodecz PL A3
71 Chodel PL B6
64 Chodov CS C2
68 Chodová Planá CS B3
91 Chodów PL A6
88 Chodziez PL C2
61 Chojna PL C5
88 Chojnice PL B3
88 Chojno PL C2
65 Chojnów PL B5
22 Cholet F A4
15 Cholsey GB C1
64 Chomutov CS C3
29 Chorges F B5
10 Chorley GB B3
94 Chortkov SU B6
89 Chorzele PL B6
90 Chorzów PL C2
61 Choszczno PL B6
91 Chotcza PL B5
96 Chotěbor CS B1
69 Chotěšov CS B4
21 Chouilly F B5
23 Chouzy-sur-Cisse F A6
32 Chozas de Abajo E B1
96 Chrast, *Vychodočeský* CS B1
69 Chrást, *Zapadočeský* CS B4
65 Chrastava CS C5
64 Chřibská CS C4
13 Christchurch GB C6
55 Christiansfeld DK C2
96 Chropyne CS B3
96 Chrudim CS B1
90 Chrzanów PL C3
96 Chtelnica CS C3
13 Chudleigh GB C4
93 Chudovo SU A12
38 Chueca E C3
103 Chumakovtsi BG C5
102 Chuprene BG C3
71 Chur CH B4
10 Church Stretton GB C3
105 Čhureshki prokhod BG B5
44 Churriana, *Granada* E B3
44 Churriana, *Málaga* E C2
71 Churwalden CH B4
96 Chvalčov CS B3
69 Chvalšiny CS C5
89 Chwaszczypo PL A4
69 Chynava CS A5
69 Chýnov CS B5
91 Chynów PL B5
97 Chyzerovce CS C4
97 Chyżne PL B5
32 Ciadoncha E B3
84 Cianciana I B2
75 Ciano d'Enza I B5
99 Cibakhaza H B5
36 Ciborro P C2
75 Cicagna I B4
79 Cicciano I C5
102 Cičevac YU C2
75 Cicognolo I A5
31 Cidadelhe P D3
33 Cidones E C4
89 Ciechanów PL C6
89 Ciechocinek PL C4
89 Cieksyn PL C6
91 Cieladz PL B4
88 Ciemnik PL B1
39 Ciempozuelos E B3
73 Cienin Kościelny PL A2
91 Ciepielów PL B5
65 Cieplice Sl. Zdrój PL B5
97 Cierne CS B4
97 Čierny Balog CS C5
34 Cierp F A3
89 Cierpice PL C4
33 Ciervana E A3
88 Cierznie PL B3
94 Cieszanow PL A5
97 Cieszyn PL B4
27 Cieutat F C4
45 Cieza E A5
90 Ciężkowice PL C3
96 Cifer CS C3
112 Ciftlikköy TR B1
39 Cifuentes E B4
65 Cigacice PL A5
32 Cigales E C2
74 Cigliano I A3
103 Cilieni RO C5
81 Čilipi YU B5
96 Cilizská Radvaň CS D3
39 Cillas E B5
37 Cilleros E A4
38 Cilleros el Hondo E B1
32 Cilleruelo E B3
33 Cilleruelo de Arriba E C3
8 Cilmalieu GB B2
102 Cilnic RO A2
103 Cilnicu RO B4
70 Cimalmotto CH B3
32 Cimanes del Tejar E B1
84 Ciminna I B2
72 Cimoláis I B2
95 Cimpina RO D6
103 Cimpu lui Neag RO A4
103 Cimpu Mare RO B5
103 Cimpulung RO A6
94 Cimpulung Moldovenesc RO C6
13 Cinderford GB B5
112 Çine TR A1
65 Činěves CS C5
17 Ciney B C5
31 Cinfães P C2
75 Cinigia de Botti I A5
78 Cinigiano I A2
97 Cinobaňa CS C5
23 Cinq-Mars-la-Pile F A5
82 Cinquefrondi I C3
27 Cintegabelle F C5
40 Cintorres E A2
33 Cintruénigo E B5
103 Ciobăneşti RO B4
103 Ciolănesti RO B6
103 Cioroiaşu RO B4
33 Ciórroga E A4
31 Ciperez E D4
40 Cirat E A2
22 Ciré-d'Aunis F B3
82 Cirella I B2
13 Cirencester GB B6
66 Cirey-sur-Vezouze F C2
33 Ciria E C5
74 Ciriè I A2
82 Cirigliano I B3
103 Cirligati RO C5
83 Ciro I B4
83 Ciro Marina I B4
25 Ciry-le-Noble F B4
60 Cismar D A1
72 Cismon del Grappa I C1
32 Cisneros E B2
26 Cissac-Médoc F A3
69 Čista CS A4
79 Cisterna di Latina I B3
32 Cisterniga E C2
81 Cisternino I D4
32 Cistierna E B1
100 Čitluk, *Bosna i Hercegovina* YU C2
102 Čitluk, *Srbija* YU C3
64 Citov CS C4
78 Città del Vaticano I B3
76 Città della Pieve I D1
76 Città di Castello I C2
79 Citta Sant'Angelo I A5
72 Cittadella I C1
79 Cittaducale I A3
85 Cittanova I A5
94 Ciucea RO C5
38 Ciudad Real E D3
31 Ciudad Rodrigo E D4
103 Ciurari RO B6
41 Ciutadella de Menorca, *Menorca* E
72 Cividale del Friuli I B3
79 Civita I A4
78 Civita Castellana I A3
76 Civitanova Alta I C3
77 Civitanova Marche I C3
78 Civitavécchia I A2
76 Civitella di Romagna I B1
79 Civitella di Tronto I A4
79 Civitella Roveto I B4
23 Civray F B5
18 Clabhach GB B1
6 Clachan, *Skye* GB C2
8 Clachan, *Strathclyde* GB B3
6 Clachan, *Western Isles* GB C1
6 Clachtoll GB B3
9 Clackmannan GB B4
13 Clacton-on-Sea GB C4
8 Cladich GB B2
25 Clairvaux-les-Laes F B5
24 Clamecy F A3
5 Clane IRL A5
8 Claonaig GB C2
5 Clara IRL A4
4 Claracastle IRL B3
15 Clare GB B3
4 Claregalway IRL A3
2 Claremorris IRL C3
4 Clarinbridge IRL A3
7 Clashmore GB C4
5 Clashmore IRL B4
3 Claudy GB B4
10 Claughton GB A3
64 Claußnitz D C2
63 Clausthal-Zellerfeld D B5
72 Cláut I B2
11 Clay Cross GB B4
14 Claydon GB B4
20 Claye-Souilly F C3
4 Cleady IRL C2
103 Cleanovo RO B4
10 Cleator Moor GB A2
18 Cléder F B1
10 Cleedownton GB C3
11 Cleethorpes GB B5
66 Clefmont F C1
18 Cléguérec F B3
60 Clenze D C1
10 Cleobury Mortimer GB C3
29 Cléon-d'Andran F B3
23 Cléré-les-Pins F A5
20 Clères F B2
21 Clérey F C5
20 Clermont F B3
21 Clermont-en-Argonne F B6
24 Clermont-Ferrand F C3
28 Clermont-l'Hérault F C2
70 Clerval F A1
66 Clervaux L A2
20 Cléry F D2
71 Cles I B6
16 Cléty F C2
13 Clevedon GB B5
11 Cleveland Tontine GB A4
14 Cley next the Sea GB B4
4 Clifden IRL A1
15 Cliffe GB C3
2 Cliffony IRL B3
22 Clisson F A3
10 Clitheroe GB B3
5 Cloghan, *Offaly* IRL A4
3 Cloghan, *West Meath* IRL C4
5 Clogheen IRL B4
3 Clogher GB B4
3 Clogherhead IRL C5
5 Cloghjordan IRL B3
5 Cloghran IRL A5
18 Clohars-Carnoët F C2
7 Clola GB C7
4 Clonakilty IRL C3
5 Clonard IRL A4
2 Clonbur IRL C2
5 Clondalkin IRL A5
2 Clonee IRL C5
3 Clones IRL B4
3 Clonmany IRL A4
5 Clonmel IRL B4
3 Clonmellon IRL C4
5 Clonroche IRL B5
2 Clonfad IRL C3
59 Cloppenburg D C5
3 Closeburn GB C4
66 Clouange F B2
3 Clough GB B6
3 Cloughmills GB A5
11 Cloughton GB A5
12 Clovelly GB C3
20 Cloyes F D2
4 Cloyne IRL C3
8 Cluainie Inn GB A2
24 Cluis F B1
94 Cluj RO C5
10 Clun GB C2
8 Clunes GB B3
25 Cluny F B4
70 Cluses F B1
12 Clydach GB B4
8 Clydebank GB C3
91 Ćmielów PL C5
38 Cndeleda E B1
4 Coachford IRL C3
3 Coagh GB B5
3 Coalisland GB B5
14 Coalville GB B1
30 Coaña E A4
9 Coatbridge GB C4
30 Cobas E A2
33 Cobertelade E C4
39 Cobeta E B4
4 Cobh IRL C3
32 Cobreces E A2
63 Coburg D C5
40 Cocentaina E C2
42 Cochem D C6
63 Cochstedt D B6
9 Cock Bridge GB A4
9 Cockburnspath GB C5
10 Cockermouth GB A2
103 Cocorova RO B3
76 Codigoro I B2
75 Codogno I A4
34 Codos E B1
72 Codroipo I C2
10 Coedpoeth GB B2
31 Coelhoso P C4
62 Coesfeld D B2
58 Coevorden NL C3
40 Cofrentes E B1
32 Cogeces del Monte E C3
15 Coggeshall GB C3
23 Cognac F C4
70 Cogne I C2
25 Cognin F C5
29 Cogolin F C5
44 Cogollos de Guadix E B3
44 Cogollos-Vega E B3
39 Cogolludo E B3
6 Coillore GB C2
36 Coimbra P A2
44 Coín E C2
30 Coirós E A2
99 Čoka YU C5
73 Col YU C4
36 Colares P C1
103 Colaretu RO B4
63 Colbitz D A6
15 Colchester GB C3
64 Colditz D B2
9 Coldstream GB C5
13 Coleford GB B5
35 Colera E A6
3 Coleraine GB A5
11 Coleshill GB C4
76 Colfiorito I C3
103 Colibaşi RO B5
71 Colico I B4
33 Colindres E A3
9 Colingham GB C5
35 Coll de Nargó E A4
38 Collado-Mediano E B2
38 Collado-Villalba E B3
75 Collagna I B5
32 Collanzo E A1
75 Collat F A2
75 Colle di Val d'Elsa I C6
72 Colle Isarco (Gossensaß) I B1
79 Colle Sannita I B5
75 Collécchio I B5
79 Colledimezzo I B5
75 Colleferro I B4
74 Collegno I A2
79 Collelongo I B4
83 Collepasso I A5
78 Collepepe I A3
75 Collesalvetti I C5
84 Collesano I B2
28 Collet F B2
79 Colli a Volturno I B5
9 Collin GB C4
78 Collinée F B3
11 Collingham GB B4
59 Collinghorst D B4
71 Cóllio I C5
25 Collobrières F C5
3 Collon IRL C5
2 Collooney IRL B3
66 Colmar F C3
29 Colmars F B5
68 Colmberg D B1
41 Colmenar, *Guadalajara* E A3
44 Colmenar, *Málaga* E C2
39 Colmenar de Oreja E B3
38 Colmenar Viejo E B3
8 Colmonell GB C3
11 Colne GB B3
75 Cologna Véneta I B6
27 Cologne F C4
71 Cologne al Serio I C4
66 Colombey-les-Belles F C1
21 Colombey-les-deux-Eglises F C5
70 Colombier CH B1
30 Colomera E B3
27 Colomiers F C5
41 Colonia St. Jordi, *Mallorca* E
75 Colorno I B5
42 Colos P B1
7 Colpy GB C6
14 Colsterworth GB B2
14 Coltishall GB B4
32 Colunga E A1
9 Colwell GB C5
10 Colwyn Bay GB B2
76 Comácchio I B2
35 Comarruga E B4
30 Combarros E B4
25 Combeaufontaine F A5
3 Comber GB B6
17 Comblain-au-Pont B C5
70 Combloux F C1
19 Combourg F B4
24 Combronde F C3
72 Comeglians I B2
32 Comillas E A2
16 Comines F C3
85 Cómiso I C3
99 Comlosu Mare RO C5
26 Commensacq F B3
24 Commentry F B2
64 Commerau D B4
66 Commercy F C1
71 Como I C4
102 Comoriste RO A2
44 Cómpeta E C3
21 Compiègne F B3
26 Comporta P C2
29 Comps-sur-Artuby F C5
9 Comrie GB B4
79 Comunanza I A4
76 Cona, *Emilia Romagna* I B1
76 Cona, *Veneto* I A2
18 Concarneau F C2
42 Conceição P B1
20 Conches-en-Ouche F C1
72 Concordia Sagittária I C2
75 Concordia sulla Sécchia I B5
27 Concots F B5
29 Condamine Châtelard F B5
28 Condat F A1
21 Condé-en-Brie F B4
16 Condé-sur-l'Escaut F C3
21 Conde-sur-Marne F B5
19 Condé-sur-Noireau F A5
25 Condeissiat F B5
36 Condeixa P A2
39 Condemios de Abajo E A3
39 Condemios de Arriba E A3
71 Condino I C5
27 Condom F C4
74 Condove I A2
66 Condrecourt-le-Château F C1
72 Conegliano I C2
20 Conflans F B3
66 Conflans-en-Jarnisy F B1
66 Conflans-sur-Lanterne F D2
23 Confolens F B5
2 Cong IRL C2
28 Congenies F C3
11 Congleton GB B3
30 Congosto E B4
32 Congosto de Valdavia E B2
39 Congostrina E A3
13 Congresbury GB B5
43 Conil E C3
11 Coningsby GB B5
11 Conisbrough GB B4
10 Coniston GB A2
19 Conlie F B5
25 Conliège F B5
10 Connahs' Quay GB B2
21 Connantre F C4
29 Connaux F B3
8 Connel GB B2
8 Connel Park GB C3
20 Connerre F C1
4 Connonagh IRL C2
99 Conoplja YU C4
28 Conques F B1
28 Conques-sur-Orbiel F C1
44 Conquista E A2
37 Conquista de la Sierra E B5
76 Consándolo I B1
76 Consélice I B1
76 Conselve I A1
9 Consett GB D6
36 Consolação P B1
36 Constancia P B2
95 Constanta RO D8
35 Constanti E B4
43 Constantina E B4
39 Consuegra E C3
76 Consuma I C1
76 Contarina I A2
70 Conthey CH B2
78 Contigliano I A3
26 Contis-Plage F B2
79 Contrada I C5
23 Contres F A6
66 Contrexéville F C1
21 Contrisson F C5
82 Controne I A2
80 Contursi I D2
20 Conty F B3
81 Conversano I D4
3 Convoy IRL B4
10 Conwy GB B2
3 Cookstown GB B5
3 Cootehill IRL B4
94 Čop CS B5
83 Copertino I A4
107 Çöpköy TR B4
76 Copparo I B1
63 Coppenbrugge D A4
25 Coppet CH B6
12 Copplestone GB C4
103 Corabia RO C5
82 Córaci I B3
77 Coralići YU B5
80 Corato I C3
18 Coray F B2
20 Corbeil-Essonne F C3
103 Corbeni RO A5
21 Corbeny F B4
20 Corbie F B3
24 Corbigny F A3
21 Corbion B B6
30 Corbón E B4
9 Corbridge GB D5
14 Corby GB B2
14 Corby Glen GB B2
28 Corconne F C2
32 Corconte E A3
103 Corcova RO B4
30 Corcubjon E B1
79 Corcumello I B4
27 Cordes F B5
44 Córdoba E B2
37 Cordobilla de Lácara E B4
72 Cordovado I C2
33 Corella E B5
32 Coreses E C1
13 Corfe Castle GB C5
31 Corga de Lobão P D2
30 Corgo E B3
79 Cori I B3
37 Coria E B4
43 Coria del Rio E B3
83 Corigliano Calabro I B3
76 Corinaldo I C3
74 Cório I A2
43 Coripe E C4
4 Cork IRL C3
103 Corlätel RO B3
18 Corlay F B3
84 Corleone I B2
82 Corleto Monforte I A2
82 Corleto Perticara I A3
107 Çorlu TR B5
25 Cormatin F B4
20 Cormeilles F B1
23 Cormery F A5
72 Cormons I C3
25 Cormoz F B5
33 Cornago E B4
63 Cornberg D B4
102 Cornea RO A3
35 Cornella E B5
30 Cornellana E A4
102 Cornereva RO A3
75 Corniglio I B5
66 Cornimont F D2
72 Cornuda I C2
34 Cornudella E B3
33 Cornudilla E B3
28 Cornus F C2
66 Corny F B2
108 Corovodë AL A2
8 Corpach GB B2
29 Corps F B4
19 Corps Nuds F C4
39 Corral de Almaguer E C3
33 Corral de Ayllon E C3
38 Corral de Calatrava E D2
40 Corral-Rubio E C1
32 Corrales E C1
8 Corran GB B2
30 Corredoira E A2
75 Corréggio I B5
27 Corrèze F A5
76 Corridonia I C3
8 Corrie GB C2
10 Corris GB C2
30 Corrubedo E B1
6 Corry GB C3
13 Corsham GB B5
71 Córsico I C4
9 Corsock GB C4
86 Corte F B2
37 Corte de Peleas E C4
42 Corte do Pinto P B2
43 Corteconception E B3
31 Cortegaca P D2
30 Cortegada E B2
43 Cortegana E B3
73 Cortemaggiore I A4
74 Cortemilia I B3
33 Cortes E C5
34 Cortes de Aragón E C2
40 Cortes de Arenoso E A2
45 Cortes de Baza E B4
43 Cortes de la Frontera E C4
40 Cortes de Pallás E B2
36 Cortiçadas P C2
31 Cortico P C3
38 Cortijo de Arriba E C2
43 Cortijo de S. Enrique E C4
45 Cortijos Nuevos E A4
72 Cortina d'Ampezzo I B2
76 Cortona I C1
36 Coruche P C2
30 Corullón E B4
72 Corvara in Badia I B1
45 Corvera E B5
10 Corwen GB C2
103 Corzu RO B4
74 Cos de Cagnes F C2
82 Cosenza I B3
39 Coslada E B3
24 Cosne F A2
24 Cosne d'Allier F B2
103 Coşoveni RO B4
70 Cossato I C3
19 Cossé-le-Vivien F C5
70 Cossonay CH B1
36 Costa de Caparica P C1
26 Costa de Santo André P A1
31 Costa Nova P D2
75 Costalpino I C6
4 Costelloe IRL A2
103 Costeşti RO B5
74 Costigliole Saluzzo I B2
28 Costraros F B2
64 Coswig, *Dresden* D B3
64 Coswig, *Halle* D B1
83 Cotronei I B3
64 Cottbus D B4
14 Cottenham GB B3
14 Cottesmore GB B2
11 Cottingham GB B5
25 Coublac F A5
25 Couches F B4
36 Couço P C2
28 Coucouron F B2
21 Coucy-le-Château-Auffrique F B4
24 Coudes F C3
23 Couhe F B5
17 Couillet B C4
21 Couilly F C3
35 Couiza F A5
6 Coulags GB C3
24 Coulanges F B3
24 Coulanges-la-Vineuse F A3
24 Coulanges-sur-Yonne F A3
24 Couleuvre F B2
25 Coulmier-le-Sec F A4
23 Coulognes-sur-l'Autize F B4
21 Coulommiers F C4
8 Coulport GB B3
11 Coundon GB A4
9 Coupar Angus GB B4
21 Coupéville F C5
19 Couptrain F B5
31 Coura P C2
17 Courcelles B C4
66 Courcelles-Chaussy F B2
70 Courchevel F C1
23 Courcheverny F A6
23 Courcôme F C5
23 Courçon F B4
70 Courgenay CH A2
70 Courmayeur I C1
28 Courniou F C1
24 Cournon F C3
28 Cournonterral F C2
24 Courpière F C3
70 Courrendlin CH A2
25 Cours F B4
28 Coursan F C2
19 Courseulles-sur-Mer F A5
24 Courson-les-Carrières F A3
17 Court St. Etienne B C4
20 Courtalain F C2
21 Courtenay F C4
29 Courthezon F B3
20 Courtomer F C1
20 Courville F C2
23 Coussac-Bonneval F C6
19 Coutainville F A4
19 Coutances F A4
19 Couterne F B5
26 Coutras F A3
70 Couvet CH B1
21 Couvin B A5
24 Couzon F B3
33 Covaleda E C4
33 Covarrubias E B3
31 Covas P C2
6 Cove GB C3
103 Coveiu RO C4
14 Coventry GB C1
12 Coverack GB C2
75 Covigliáio I B6
36 Covilhã P A3
13 Cowbridge GB B4
9 Cowdenbeath GB B4
15 Cowes GB D1
15 Cowfold GB D2
27 Cox F C5
8 Coylton GB C3
9 Coylumbridge GB A4
23 Cozes F C4
5 Craanford IRL B5
83 Craco I A3
8 Craggan GB B5
3 Craigavon GB B5
7 Craigellachie GB C5
8 Craighouse GB C2
8 Craignure GB B2
7 Craigtown GB B5
103 Craiova RO B4
21 Cramant F C4
9 Cramlington GB C6
25 Cran Gevrier F C6
13 Cranborne GB C6
15 Cranleigh GB C2
27 Cransac F B6
9 Cranshaws GB C5
19 Craon F C5
21 Craonne F B4
24 Craponne, *Haute-Loire* F A2
25 Craponne, *Rhône* F B4
8 Crarae GB B2
7 Crask Inn GB B4
9 Crathie GB A4
4 Cratloe IRL B3
36 Crato P B3
4 Craughwell IRL A3
42 Cravadas P B1
10 Craven Arms GB C3
9 Crawford GB C4
63 Crawinkel D C5
15 Crawley GB C2
13 Cray GB B4
6 Creagorry GB C1
25 Crèches F B4
30 Creciente E B2
21 Crécy F B4
21 Crécy-en-Brie F C3
16 Crécy-en-Ponthieu F C1
13 Crediton GB C4
8 Creetown GB D3
2 Cregganbaun IRL C2
67 Creglingen D B6
63 Creidlitz D C5
20 Creil F B3
28 Creissels F B2
74 Crema I A4
24 Cremeaux F C3
32 Crémenes E B1
25 Cremieu F C5
63 Cremlingen D A5
75 Cremona I A5
21 Creney F C5
26 Créon F B3
101 Crepaja YU A5
21 Crépy F B4
21 Crépy-en-Valois F B3
77 Cres YU B4
74 Crescentino I A3
106 Creshak BG A2
76 Crespino I B1
38 Crespos E B2
27 Cressensac F A5
74 Cresta CH B4
20 Créten F C3
19 Creully F A5
68 Creußen D B2
66 Creutzwald F B2
63 Creuzburg D B5
75 Crevalcore I B6
24 Crevant-Laveine F C3
20 Crevecoeur le Grand F B3
40 Crevillente E C2
70 Crévola d'Ossola I B3
10 Crewe GB B3
13 Crewkerne GB C5
33 Criales E B3
8 Crianlarich GB B3
10 Criccieth GB C1
11 Crich GB B4
14 Crick GB B1
13 Crickhowell GB B4
13 Cricklade GB B6
9 Crieff GB B4
20 Criel-Plage F A2
20 Criel-sur-Mer F A2
77 Crikvenica YU A4
20 Crillon F B3
64 Crimmitschau D C2
7 Crimond GB C7
8 Crinan GB B2
103 Cringeni RO B5
14 Cringleford GB B4
64 Crinitz D B3
33 Cripàn E B4
20 Criquetot-l'Esneval F B1
83 Crispiano I A4
70 Crissier CH B1
74 Crissolo I B2
38 Cristóbal E B1
60 Crivitz D B2
73 Crna YU B4
99 Crna Bara, *A. P. Vojvodina* YU C5
101 Crna Bara, *Srbija* YU B4
105 Crna Trava YU B3
98 Crnac YU C2
101 Crnča YU B4
100 Crni Lug, *Bosna i Hercegovina* YU B1
73 Crni Lug, *Hrvatska* YU C4
73 Crni Vrh YU C4
104 Crnoljevo YU B3
73 Črnomelj YU C5
74 Crocetta I B2
9 Crocketford GB C4
24 Crocq F C2
70 Crodo I B3
9 Croglin GB D5
29 Crolles F A4
2 Crolly IRL A3
7 Cromarty GB C4
14 Cromer GB B4
11 Cromford GB B4
11 Crook GB A4
7 Crook of Alves GB C5
10 Crooklands GB A3
4 Crookstown IRL C3
4 Croom IRL B3
83 Cropalati I B3
83 Crópani I C3
10 Crosby GB A2
10 Crosby, *Merseyside* GB B2
10 Cross Foxes GB C2
12 Cross Hands GB B3
8 Crossaig GB C2
3 Crossakeel IRL C4
6 Crossbost GB B2
3 Crossdoney IRL C4
3 Crossgar GB B6
13 Crossgates GB A4
4 Crosshaven IRL C3
8 Crosshill GB C3
9 Crosslea GB C4
2 Crossmolina IRL B2
9 Crossroad Inn GB A5
83 Crotone I B4
64 Crottendorf D C2
23 Croutelle F B5
21 Crouy F B4
15 Crowbridge GB C3
14 Crowland GB B2
11 Crowle GB B5
15 Croydon GB C2
18 Crozon F B1
29 Cruas F B3
10 Crudgington GB C3
29 Cruis F B4
3 Crumlin GB B5
25 Cruseilles F B6
4 Crusheen IRL B3
24 Crux-la-Ville F A3
77 Crvena Luka YU C5
100 Crveni Grm YU C2
99 Crvenka YU C4
97 Črveny Kamen CS B4
12 Crymmych GB B3
98 Csabrendek H A2
98 Csákanydoroszló H B1
98 Csákberény H A3
99 Csákvár H A3
99 Csanádpalota H B5
99 Csány H A4
99 Csanytelek H B5
98 Csapod H A1
98 Császár H A3
99 Császártöltés H B4
99 Csemö H A4
99 Csengöd H B4
99 Csépa H B5
98 Csepreg H A1
99 Cserebökány H B5
98 Csetény H A3
98 Csököly H B2
98 Csokonyavisonta H B2
99 Csolnok H A3
99 Csongrád H B5
98 Csopak H B2
98 Csór H A3
98 Csorna H A2
99 Csorvás H B5
98 Csurgó H B2
37 Cuacos E A5
31 Cualedro E C3
32 Cuanca de Campos E B1
37 Cuaternos E A5
42 Cuba P A2
39 Cubel E A5
35 Cubellas E B4
30 Cubide E B2
33 Cubillos E C4
33 Cubo de la Solana E C4
30 Cubullos del Sil E B4
15 Cuckfield GB C2
103 Cucueţi RO B5
29 Cucuron F C4
30 Cudillero E A4
32 Cuéllar E C2
39 Cuenca E B4
29 Cuers F C5
38 Cuerva E C2
33 Cueva de Agreda E C5
44 Cuevas Bajas E B2
44 Cuevas de S. Marcos E B2
33 Cuevas de San Clemente E B3
40 Cuevas de Vinromá E A3
45 Cuevas del Almanzora E B5
43 Cuevas del Becerro E C4
44 Cuevas del Campo E B4
38 Cuevas del Valle E B1
30 Cueya E A4
29 Cuges-les-Pins F C4
87 Cúglieri I B1
27 Cugnaux F C5
17 Cuijk NL B5
25 Cuinzier F B4
25 Cuiseaux F B5
25 Cuisery F B4
35 Cuitadilla E B4
103 Cujmir RO B3
24 Culan F B2
3 Culdaff IRL A4
7 Culdrain GB C6
17 Culemborg NL B5
45 Cúllar de Baza E B4
3 Cullaville GB B5
7 Cullen GB C6
40 Cullera E B2
13 Cullompton GB C4
70 Cully CH B1
25 Culoz F C5
9 Cults GB A5
112 Cumali TR B2
9 Cumbernauld GB C4
43 Cumbres de S. Bartolomé E A3
43 Cumbres Mayores E A3
74 Cumiana I B2
101 Ćumić YU B5
9 Cummertrees GB D4
8 Cumnock GB C3
74 Cúneo I B2
24 Cunlhat F C3
6 Cunningsburgh, *Shetland Is.* GB
77 Čunski YU B4
30 Cuntis E B2
70 Cuorgnè I C2
9 Cupar GB B4
79 Cupello I A5
77 Čupina YU A4
77 Cupra Marittima I C3
76 Cupramontana I C3
102 Ćuprija YU C2
29 Curnier F B4
9 Currie GB C4
13 Curry Rivel GB B5
4 Curryglass IRL C2
103 Curtea de Arges RO A5
30 Curtis E A2
30 Curtis Santa Eulalia E A2
103 Curtişoara RO B5
99 Čurug YU C5
79 Cusano Mutri I B5
3 Cushendall GB A5
3 Cushendun GB A5
5 Cushina IRL A4
24 Cusset F B3
25 Cussy F A4
31 Custóras P C2
34 Cutanda E C1
83 Cutro I B3
83 Cutrofiano I A5
21 Cuts F B4
20 Cuvilly F B3
59 Cuxhaven D B5
65 Cvikov CS C4
98 Čvrstec YU B1
13 Cwmbran GB B4
10 Cwrt GB C2
65 Cybinka PL A4
90 Cykarzew Stary PL C3
12 Cynwyl Elfed GB B3
16 Cysong F C3
90 Czajków PL B2
88 Czaplinek PL B2
89 Czarlin PL A4
88 Czarna-Dąbrówka PL A3
88 Czarna Woda PL B4
91 Czarnca PL C3
88 Czarne PL B2
89 Czarne PL C5
88 Czarnków PL C2
91 Czarnów PL C4
90 Czarnowasy PL C1
89 Czarnowo PL B4
90 Czarnozyly PL B2
97 Czarny-Dunajec PL B5
97 Czechowice-

Dziedzice PL B5
90 Czeladz PL C3
65 Czempiń PL A6
91 Czermno PL B4
97 Czernichow PL B5
89 Czerniewice PL B4
89 Czernikowo PL C4
88 Czersk PL B3
65 Czerwieńsk PL A5
90 Czerwionka PL C2
65 Czerwona Woda PL B5
89 Czerwonka PL B6
90 Częstochowa PL C3
88 Czeszewo PL C3
88 Człopa PL B2
88 Człuchów PL B3

D

62 Daaden D C2
99 Dabas H A4
90 Dabie PL A2
91 Dabie PL B6
105 Dabilja YU C4
66 Dabo F C3
90 Dąbroszyn PL A2
88 Dabrowa PL C3
90 Dąbrowa PL C1
65 Dabrowa Boleslawska PL B5
90 Dabrowa Górna PL C3
91 Dąbrowa Tarnowska PL C4
89 Dabrowno PL B6
103 Dăbuleni RO C5
68 Dachau D C2
96 Dačice CS B1
16 Dadizele B C3
103 Dăeşti RO B5
112 Dafnes, *Kriti* GR
109 Dáfni, *Évia* GR C5
110 Dáfni, *Ilía* GR B2
111 Dáfni, *Korinthía* GR B3
109 Dáfnos GR C4
49 Dagali N A5
55 Dägebüll Hafen D D1
70 Dagmersellen CH A2
64 Dahlen D B3
60 Dahlenburg D B1
64 Dahme D B3
67 Dahn D B3
60 Dähre D C1
8 Dailly GB C3
5 Daingean IRL A4
104 Dajç AL C1
104 Dakovica YU B2
100 Dakovo YU A3
50 Dal, *Akershus* N B2
49 Dal, *Telemark* N B5
50 Dala-Floda S B5
52 Dala-Husby S B1
50 Dala-Järna S B5
71 Dalaas A A5
112 Dalama TR A1
53 Dalarö S C4
9 Dalbeattie GB D4
57 Dalby S D2
50 Dalby Långav S B3
7 Dalcross GB C4
12 Dale GB B2
50 Dalen, *Akershus* N C2
49 Dalen, *Telemark* N B5
52 Dalfors S A1
7 Dalhalvig GB B5
63 Dalhausen D B4
66 Dalheim L B2
45 Dalias E C4
99 Dalj YU C3
9 Dalkeith GB C4
8 Dallachoilish GB B2
67 Dallau D B5
8 Dalmally GB B3
8 Dalmellington GB C3
59 Dalmenhorst D B5
7 Dalmichy GB B4
9 Dalnacardoch Lodge GB B3
8 Dalry, *Strathclyde* GB C3
8 Dalrymple GB C3
51 Dals Långed S D3
51 Dals Rostock S D3
56 Dalsjöfors S B2
51 Dalskog S D3
9 Dalton GB C4
10 Dalton in Furness GB A2
29 Daluis F B5
58 Dalum D C4
56 Dalum S B2
8 Dalwhinnie GB B3
108 Damaskinea GR A3
27 Damazan F B4
107 Dambaslar TR B5
96 Damborce CS B2
108 Damës AL A1
39 Damiel E C3
20 Dammartin-en-Goële F B3
59 Damme D C5
25 Dampierre-sur-Salon F A5
71 Damüls A A4
20 Damville F C2
66 Damvillers F B1
107 Danamandira TR B6
15 Danbury GB C3
103 Däneasa RO B5
23 Dangé F B5
56 Dångebo S C4
20 Dangers F C2
20 Dangeul F C1
81 Danilov Grad YU B6
59 Danischenhagen D A7
90 Daniszyn PL B1
70 Danjoutin F A1
70 Dannemarie F A2
60 Dannenberg D B2
99 Dány H A4
99 Dánzszentmiklós H A4
18 Daoulas F B1
110 Dara GR B3
110 Dáras GR B2
99 Darda YU C3
63 Dardesheim D B5
108 Dardhë AL A2
62 Darfeld D A2
71 Darfo I C5
61 Dargun D B3
105 Darkovac YU B4
11 Darlington GB A4
88 Darlowo PL A2
67 Darmstadt D B4
20 Darnètal F B2
66 Darney F C2
31 Darque P C2
4 Darragh IRL B2
15 Dartford GB C3
13 Dartmouth GB C4
11 Darton GB B4
98 Daruvar YU C2
8 Darvel GB C3
10 Darwen GB B3
96 Dašice CS A1
68 Dasing D C2
109 Dasokhóri GR B3
63 Dassel D B4
108 Dassiá GR B1
60 Dassow D B1
90 Daszyna PL A3
112 Datca TR B2
62 Datteln D B2
62 Dattenfeld D C2
55 Daugard DK C2
93 Daugavpils SU C10
62 Daun D C1
17 Dave B C4
14 Daventry GB B1
110 Davia GR B3
103 Davideşti RO A6
106 Davidkovo BG B2
7 Daviot GB C4
69 Davle CS B5
99 Dávod H C3
100 Davor YU A2
71 Davos CH B4
112 Davutlar TR B1
10 Dawley GB C3
13 Dawlish GB C4
26 Dax F C2
16 De Panne B B2
58 De Wijk NL C3
15 Deal GB C4
19 Deauville F A6
33 Deba E A4
104 Debar YU C2
89 Dębe PL C6
91 Debe Wielkie PL A5
101 Debeljača YU A5
14 Debenham GB B4
91 Dębica PL C5
17 DeBilt NL A5
91 Dęblin PL B5
106 Debnitsa BG B1
61 Dębno PL C5
90 Dębolęka PL B2
103 Debovo BG C5
89 Dębowa Łaka PL B5
94 Debrecen H C4
104 Debrište YU C3
88 Debrzno PL B3
59 Debstedt D B5
106 Debúr BG A3
104 Dečani YU B2
27 Decazeville F B6
96 Dechtice CS C3
16 Dechy F C3
78 Decima I B3
87 Decimomannu I C1
64 Děčín CS C4
24 Decize F B3
67 Deckenpfronn D C4
15 Deddington GB C1
63 Dedeleben D A5
61 Dedelow D B4
58 Dedemsvaart NL C3
14 Deeping St. Nicholas GB B2
30 Degaña E B4
57 Degeberga S D3
51 Degerfors S C5
57 Degerhamn S C5
68 Degerndoft D D3
51 Degernes N C2
69 Deggendorf D C3
67 Deggingen D C5
74 Dego I B3
37 Degolados P B3
44 Dehesas de Guadix E B3
43 Dehesas Frias E B4
44 Deifontes E B3
68 Deining D B2
16 Deinze B C3
67 Deißlingen D C4
75 Deiva Marina I B4
94 Dej RO C5
51 Deje S C4
103 Dekov BG C6
56 Delary S C2
62 Delbrück D B3
105 Delčevo YU C4
62 Delden NL A1
37 Deleitosa E B5
98 Delekovec YU B1
70 Delemont CH A2
17 Delft NL B4
58 Delfzijl NL B3
84 Délia I B2
102 Deliblato YU B2
80 Deliceto I C2
64 Delitzsch D B2
72 Dellach A B3
70 Delle F A2
67 Dellmensingen D C5
66 Delme F C2
73 Delnice YU C4
3 Delvin IRL C4
108 Delvinakion GR B2
108 Delvinë AL B2
97 Demandice CS C4
25 Demigny F B4
105 Demir Kapija YU C4
95 Demirci TR G8
107 Demirköy TR B5
61 Demmin D B4
74 Demonte I B2
58 Den Burg NL B1
58 Den Ham NL C3
58 Den Helder NL C1
16 Denain F C3
10 Denbigh GB B2
17 Dendermonde B B4
17 Denderwindeke B C3
62 Denekamp NL A1
40 Denia E C3
68 Denkendorf D C2
62 Denklingen D C2
9 Denny GB B4
15 Densole GB C4
61 Densow D B4
102 Denta RO A2
14 Denton GB B2
24 Déols F B1
11 Derby GB C4
107 Dereköy TR B5
63 Derenberg D B5
70 Derendingen CH A2
103 Dermantsi BG C5
63 Dermbach D C5
71 Dermulo I B6
99 Deronje YU C4
8 Derryguaig GB B1
3 Derrykeighan GB A5
3 Derrylin GB B4
4 Derryrush IRL A2
14 Dersingham GB B3
76 Deruta I D2
8 Dervaig GB B1
22 Derval F A3
110 Dervéni GR A3
100 Derventa YU B2
108 Dervizianá GR B2
28 Désaignes F B3
74 Desana I A3
14 Desborough GB B2
23 Descartes F B5
71 Desenzano d. Garda I C5
3 Desertmartin GB B5
50 Deset N A2
14 Desford GB B1
101 Desimirovac YU B5
71 Désio I C4
65 Desná CS C5
96 Dešov CS C1
102 Despotovac YU B2
99 Despotovo YU C4
64 Dessau D B2
17 Dessel B B5
16 Destelbergen B B3
69 Deštná CS B5
30 Destriana E B4
87 Desulo I B2
16 Desvres F C1
99 Deszak H B5
62 Detmold D B3
96 Dětřichov CS B3
67 Dettelbach D B6
67 Dettingen D C5
66 Dettwiller F C3
97 Detva CS C5
68 Deuerling D B2
16 Deule F C3
17 Deurne NL B5
73 Deutsch Kaltenbrunn A A6
96 Deutsch Wagram A C2
73 Deutschfeistritz A A5
98 Deutschkreutz A A1
73 Deutschlandsberg A B5
94 Deva RO D5
98 Devecser H A2
103 Devene BG C4
17 Deventer NL A6
103 Deveselu RO B5
103 Devetaki BG C5
10 Devils Bridge GB C2
106 Devin BG B2
96 Devinska Nova Ves CS C2
13 Devizes GB B6
77 Devrske YU C5
11 Dewsbury GB B4
41 Deya, *Mallorca* E
33 Deza E C4
98 Dežanovac YU C2
71 Dezzo di Scalve I C5
110 Dháfnai GR A2
110 Dhafni, *Akhaia* GR B3
110 Dhafni, *Lakonía* GR C3
106 Dhafnón GR B2
111 Dhaimoniá GR C3
109 Dhamási GR B4
111 Dhávlia GR A3
111 Dhekélia GR A4
110 Dhelfoi GR A3
108 Dhèrmi AL A1
110 Dhesfina GR A3
109 Dheskáti GR B3
110 Dhiakoptón GR A3
109 Dhiavate GR A4
110 Dhiavolitsi GR B2
111 Dhidhima GR B4
107 Dhidhimótikhon GR B4
107 Dhikaia GR B4
110 Dhilianáta GR A1
106 Dhimitra GR C1
105 Dhimitritsion GR D5
110 Dhimitsána GR B3
106 Dhióni GR C3
111 Dhistomon GR A3
108 Dhistraton GR A3
108 Dholianá GR B2
109 Dhomenikon GR B4
109 Dhomokós GR B4
10 Dhoon GB A1
110 Dhórion GR B2
109 Dhoxarás GR B4
106 Dhoxáton GR B2
106 Dhraviskos GR C1
111 Dhrépanon GR B3
109 Dhrimós GR A4
111 Dhriopis GR B5
109 Dhriskoli GR B4
105 Dhrosáton GR C4
112 Diafani, *Kárpathos* GR
111 Diakófti GR C4
96 Diakovce CS C3
82 Diamante I B2
55 Dianalund DK C4
74 Diano d'Alba I B3
74 Diano Marina I C3
109 Diáselo GR B4
13 Dibden Purlieu GB C6
76 Dicomano I C1
17 Didam NL B6
15 Didcot GB C1
112 Didym TR B1
29 Die F B4
66 Diebling F B2
67 Dieburg D B4
38 Diego Alvaro E B1
66 Diekirch L B2
19 Dielette F A4
25 Diémoz F C5
72 Dienten A A2
17 Diepenbeck B C5
59 Diepholz D C5
20 Dieppe F B2
61 Dierberg D B3
62 Dierdorf D C2
17 Dieren NL A6
60 Dierhagen D A3
60 Diesdorf D C1
68 Dießen D D2
17 Diest B C5
67 Dietenheim D C6
68 Dietfurt D B2
70 Dietikon CH A3
67 Dietzenbach D A4
66 Dieue F B1
29 Dieulefit F B4
66 Dieulouard F C2
66 Dieuze F C2
58 Diever NL C3
62 Diez D C3
44 Diezma E B3
66 Differdange L B1
50 Digerberget S A5
25 Digion F B4
23 Dignac F C5
72 Dignano I B2
29 Digne F B5
20 Digny F C2
24 Digoin F B3
25 Dijon F A5
16 Diksmuide B B2
62 Dillenburg D C3
68 Dillingen, *Bayern* D C1
66 Dillingen, *Saarland* D B2
13 Dilwyn GB A5
33 Dima E A4
71 Dimaro I B5
106 Dimitrovgrad BG A3
102 Dimitrovgrad YU C3
102 Dimovo BG C3
82 Dinami I C3
19 Dinan F B3
17 Dinant B C4
19 Dinard F B3
62 Dingden D B1
63 Dingelstädt D B5
4 Dingle IRL B1
51 Dingle S D2
68 Dingolfing D C3
53 Dingtuna S C2
7 Dingwall GB C4
67 Dinkelsbühl D B6
68 Dinkelscherben D C1
59 Dinklage D C5
62 Dinslaken D B1
17 Dinteloord NL B4
17 Dinxperlo NL B6
56 Diö S C3
109 Dion GR A4
97 Diósjeno H D5
24 Diou F B3
108 Dipotamiá GR A2
8 Dippen GB C2
63 Dipperz D C4
64 Dippoldiswalde D C3
110 Dirákhio GR B3
48 Dirdal N C3
17 Dirksland NL B4
68 Dirlewang D D1
68 Dischingen D C1
70 Disentis-Muster CH B3
83 Diso I A5
14 Diss GB B4
62 Dissen D A3
10 Distington GB A2
67 Ditzingen D C5
58 Ditzum D B4
103 Diva Slatina BG C3
73 Divaca YU C3
19 Dives F A5
97 Diviacka Nová Ves CS C4
16 Divion F C2
69 Divišov CS B5
104 Divjakë AL D1
25 Divonne les Bains F B6
109 Divri GR C4
21 Dixmont F C4
21 Dizy-le-Gros F B5
50 Djura S B5
52 Djurås S B1
52 Djurmo S B1
56 Djursdale S B4
97 Dlhé-Pole CS B4
96 Dlouhá Loucka CS B3
30 Doada E B3
3 Doagh GB B5
101 Dobanovci YU B5
60 Dobbertin D B3
72 Dobbiaco (Toblach) I B2
97 Dobczyce PL B6
64 Döbeln D B3
64 Doberlug-Kirchhain D B3
64 Dobern D B4
96 Dobersberg A C1
88 Dobiegniew PL C1
91 Dobieszyn PL B5
100 Doboj YU B3
97 Dobrá CS B4
90 Dobra PL B2
61 Dobra, *Szczecin* PL B5
61 Dobra, *Szczecin* PL B6
102 Dobra YU B2
97 Dobrá Niva CS C5
96 Dobra Voda CS C3
105 Dobrčane YU B3
89 Dobre PL C4
91 Dobre PL A5
89 Dobre Miasto PL B6
103 Dobreşti RO B6
104 Dobri Do YU B3
101 Dobrica YU A5
69 Dobřichovice CS B5
105 Dobrinishta BG C5
107 Dobrinovo BG A4
69 Dobříš CS B5
33 Dobro E B3
102 Dobro Polje YU C3
97 Dobroč CS C5
90 Dobrodzien PL C2
98 Döbrököz H B3
65 Dobromierz PL C6
106 Dobromirtsi BG B3
90 Dobron PL B3
104 Dobroste YU B3
90 Dobroszyce PL B1
81 Dobrota YU B5
98 Dobrovnik YU B1
104 Dobruševo YU C3
65 Dobruska CS C6
61 Dobrzany PL B6
89 Dobrzejewice PL B4
90 Dobrzen Wielki PL C1
88 Dobrzyca PL A1
88 Dobrzyca PL B2
90 Dobrzyca PL B1
89 Dobrźyń nad Wistą PL C5
97 Dobšiná CS C6
17 Dochamps B C5
14 Docking GB B3
14 Doddington GB B3
56 Döderhult S B5
17 Dodewaard NL B5
17 Doesburg NL A6
17 Doetinchem NL B6
112 Doğanbey TR B1
107 Dogança TR B4
104 Doganovic YU B3
74 Dogliani I B2
102 Dognecea RO A2
42 Dogueno P B2
36 Dois Portos P B1
96 Dojč CS C3
46 Dokka N F5
58 Dokkum NL B3
100 Dol YU C1
19 Dol-de-Bretage F B4
10 Dolarrog GB B2
10 Dolbenmaen GB C1
74 Dolceácqua I C2
25 Dole F A5
49 Dølemo N C5
21 Dolencourt F C5
73 Dolenja Vas YU C4
73 Dolenji Logatec YU C4
73 Dolenjske Toplice YU C4
10 Dolgellau GB C2
110 Doliana GR B3
87 Dolianova I C2
61 Dolice PL B6
94 Dolino SU B6
72 Döllach A B2
9 Dollar GB B4
63 Dolle D A6
64 Dollegen D A4
21 Dollot F C4
63 Döllstadt D B5
105 Dolna Banya BG B5
105 Dolna Dikanya BG B5
103 Dolna Mitropoliya BG C5
97 Dolná Strehová CS C5
96 Dolné Orešany CS C3
97 Dolni Bečva CS B4
69 Dolni Bělá CS B4
97 Dolni Benešov CS B4
65 Dolni Bousov CS C5
96 Dolni Dobrouc CS B2
103 Dolni Dŭbnik BG C5
69 Dolni Dvořiště CS C5
106 Dolni Glavanak BG B3
96 Dolni Kounice CS B2
69 Dolni Kralovice CS B6
102 Dolni Lom BG C3
97 Dolní Lomná CS B4
97 Dolni Lutyn CS B4
97 Dolni Mariková CS B4
105 Dolni Pasarel BG B5
103 Dolni Tsib-.ur BG C4
96 Dolni Ŭjezd CS B2
68 Dolni Žandor CS A3
107 Dolno Ezerovo BG A5
105 Dolno Kamartsi BG B5
106 Dolno Levski BG A2
106 Dolno Panicherevo BG A3
106 Dolno Prakhovo BG B3
105 Dolno selo BG B4
103 Dolno Tserovene BG C4
105 Dolno Uyno BG B4
97 Dolný Kubin CS B5
97 Dolný Peter CS D4
97 Dolný Turček CS C4
72 Dolo I C2
45 Dolores E A6
101 Dolovo YU B5
9 Dolphinton GB C4
72 Dölsach A B2
65 Dolsk PL B7
10 Dolwyddelan GB B2
101 Domaljevac YU A3
91 Domanice PL A6
90 Domaniewice PL B3
97 Domaniža CS B4
88 Domaslawek PL C3
102 Domasnea RO A3
65 Domašov CS C7
99 Domaszék H B4
65 Domaszków PL C6
90 Domaszowice PL B1
71 Domat-Ems CH B4
69 Domažlice CS B3
46 Dombås N E4
66 Dombasle F C2
98 Dombóvár H B3
16 Domburg N B3
29 Domène F A4
19 Domfront, *Orne* F B5
19 Domfront, *Sarthe* F B6
36 Domingão P B2
44 Domingo Pérez, *Granada* E B3
38 Domingo Pérez, *Toledo* E C2
60 Dömitz D B2
21 Dommartin F C5
21 Dommartin-le-Coq F C5
21 Dommartin-le-Franc F C5
27 Domme F B5
64 Dommitzsch D B2
103 Domnesti RO A5
70 Domodóssola I B3
97 Domoszló H D6
66 Dompaire F C2
25 Dompierre F B5
19 Dompierre-du-Chemin F B4
24 Dompierre-sur-Besbre F B3
22 Dompierre-sur-M. F B3
66 Domrémy-la-Pucelle F C1
99 Dömsöd H A4
25 Domsure F B5
87 Domus de Maria I D1
87 Domusnóvas I C1
73 Domžale YU B4
37 Don Alvaro E C4
37 Don Benito E C5
45 Dona Inés E B5
44 Doña Mencia E B2
30 Donado E B4
3 Donaghadee GB B6
67 Donaueschingen D D4
68 Donauwörth D C1
11 Doncaster GB B4
21 Donchery F B5
23 Doné-la-Fontaine F A4
2 Donegal IRL B3
17 Dongen NL B4
22 Donges F A2
71 Dongo I B4
30 Donillas E B4
14 Donington GB B2
30 Doniños E A2
100 Donja Bebrina YU A3
100 Donja Dobošnica YU B3
100 Donja Dubica YU A3
98 Donja Konjscina YU B1
73 Donja Kupčina YU C5
73 Donja Lommica YU C6
102 Donja Mutnica YU C2
73 Donja Stubica YU C5
101 Donje Crnjelovo YU B4
104 Donje Ljupče YU B3
77 Donje Pazariste YU B5
102 Donji Barbes YU C2
102 Donji Dušnik YU C3
77 Donji Lapac YU B5
104 Donji Livoč YU B3
100 Donji Malovan YU C2
98 Donji Miholjac YU C3
102 Donji Milanovac YU B3
98 Donji Mosti YU B1
100 Donji-Rujani YU C1
100 Donji Srb YU B1
101 Donji Tovarnik YU B4
100 Donji Vakuf YU B2
17 Donk NL B5
85 Donnalucata I C3
21 Donnemarie-Dontilly F C4
73 Donnersbach A A4
73 Donnersbachwald A A4
96 Donnerskirchen A D2
75 Donorático I C5
33 Donostia-San Sebastián E A4
19 Donville-les-Bains F B4
67 Donzdorf D C5
27 Donzenac F A5
29 Donzère F B3
24 Donzy F A3
2 Dooagh IRL C1
4 Doonbeg IRL B2
17 Doorn NL A5
17 Doornspijk NL A5
103 Dooroteasa RO B5
30 Dor E A1
104 Dorce Petrov YU B3
13 Dorchester, *Dorset* GB C5
15 Dorchester, *Oxfordshire* GB C1
17 Dordrecht NL B4
62 Dörenthe D A2
7 Dores GB C4
68 Dorfen D C3
72 Dorfgastein A A3
98 Dorfl. i. Burgenland A A1
59 Dorfmark D C6
87 Dorgali I B2
109 Dorkás GR A5
15 Dorking GB C2
62 Dormagen D B1
21 Dormans F B4
71 Dornbirn A A4
63 Dornburg D C6
63 Dorndorf D C5
24 Dornes F B3
6 Dornie GB C3
7 Dornoch GB C4
67 Dornstadt D C5
99 Dorog H A3
94 Dorohoi RO C7
46 Dorotea S D8
89 Dorotowo PL B6
62 Dorsten D B1
25 Dortan F B5
62 Dortmund D B2
59 Dorum D B5
59 Dörverden D C6
67 Dörzbach D B5
40 Dos Aguas E B2
43 Dos Hermanas E B4
44 Dos-Torres E A2
39 Dosbarrios E C3
108 Dósio GR B3
106 Dospat BG B2
59 Dötlingen D C5
108 Dótsiko GR A3
16 Dottignies B C3
70 Döttingen CH A3
16 Douai F C3
18 Douarnenez F B1
21 Douchy, *Loiret* F D4
16 Douchy, *Nord* F C3
20 Doudeville F B1
10 Douglas, *I. of Man* GB A1
9 Douglas, *Strathclyde* GB C4
66 Doulaincourt F C1
21 Doulevant-le-Château F C5
16 Doullens F C2
7 Dounby GB A5
8 Doune GB B3
110 Dounéika GR B2
16 Dour B C3
20 Dourdan F C3
27 Dourgne F C6
23 Dournazac F C5
31 Douro Calvo P D3
25 Douvaine F B6
21 Douzy F B6
15 Dover GB C4
73 Dovje YU B3
46 Dovre N F4
14 Downham GB B3
14 Downham Market GB B3
3 Downhill GB A5
3 Downpatrick GB B6
24 Doyet F B2
30 Dozón E B2
19 Dozule F A5
101 Drača YU B5
105 Dračevo YU C3
69 Drachselsried D B4
58 Drachten NL B3
103 Drăgăneşti RO B5
103 Drăganeşti de Vede RO B6
104 Dragaš YU B2
103 Drăgăsani RO B5
73 Dragatuš YU C5
101 Draginja YU B4
102 Dragocvet YU C2
103 Drăgoeşti RO B5
100 Dragolovci YU B2
103 Dragoman BG D3
106 Dragomir BG A2
79 Dragoni I B5
100 Dragotina YU A1
105 Dragovishtitsa BG B4
77 Dragozetica YU A4
29 Draguignan F C5
64 Drahnsdorf D B3
69 Drahonice CS B5
96 Drahovce CS C3
108 Drakótripa GR B3
106 Dráma GR B2
49 Drammen N B7
72 Dramsach A A1
49 Drangedal N B6
59 Drangstedt D B5
103 Dränicu RO B4
63 Dransfeld D B4
61 Dranske D A4
3 Draperstown GB B5
96 Draßburg A D2
98 Draßmarkt A A1
98 Drávaszabolcs H C3
73 Dravograd YU B5
88 Drawno PL B1
88 Drawsko Pomorskie PL B1
89 Drązdżewo PL B7
69 Drazenov CS B3
101 Drazevac, *Srbija* YU B5
102 Draževac, *Srbija* YU C2
12 Dre-fach GB B3
64 Drebkau D B4
8 Dreghorn GB C3
67 Dreieich Langen D B4
102 Drenovac, *Srbija* YU C2
105 Drenovac, *Srbija* YU B3
101 Drenovci YU B3
103 Drenovets BG C3
62 Drensteinfurt D B2
109 Drépano, *Kozani* GR A3
108 Drépano, *Thesprotía* GR B2
64 Dresden D B3
88 Dretyń PL A2
20 Dreux F C2
96 Drevohostice CS B3
64 Drewitz D A2
88 Drezdenko PL C1
77 Drežnica YU A5
77 Drežnik-Grad YU B5
17 Driebergen NL A5
39 Driebes E B3
96 Drietoma CS C3
11 Driffield GB A5
109 Driméa GR C4
8 Drimnin GB B2
4 Drimoleague IRL C2
108 Drimón GR C3
109 Drimós GR B4
62 Dringenberg D B4
100 Drinovci YU C2
111 Drióp̈i GR B4
104 Drizë AL D2
101 Drlače YU B4
96 Drnholec CS C2
100 Drniš YU C1
98 Drnje YU B1
71 Dro I C5
49 Drøbak N B7
102 Drobeta-Turnu Severin RO B3
89 Drobin PL C5
59 Drochtersen D B6
3 Drogheda IRL C5
97 Droginia PL B6
94 Drogobych SU B5
5 Droichead Nua IRL A5
13 Droitwich GB A5
3 Dromara GB B5
2 Dromard IRL B3
3 Dromod IRL C4
3 Dromore, *N. Ireland* GB B4
3 Dromore, *N. Ireland* GB B5
2 Dromore West IRL B3
74 Dronero I B2
11 Dronfield GB B4
16 Drongen B B3
54 Dronninglund DK A3
58 Dronrijp NL B2
58 Dronten NL C2
96 Drosendorf A C1
96 Drösing A C2
108 Drosopigi, *Árta* GR B3
108 Drosopigi, *Florina* GR A3
111 Drossiá GR A4
53 Drøttningholm S C3
90 Drottowice PL B1
20 Droué F C2
105 Drugan BG B5
10 Druid GB C2
66 Drulingen F C3
3 Drum IRL B4
6 Drumbeg GB B3
3 Drumcard GB B4
2 Drumcliff IRL B3
8 Drumjohn GB C3
10 Drummore GB A1
7 Drumnadrochit GB C4
3 Drumshanbo IRL B3
3 Drumsna IRL C3
8 Drumvaich GB B3
17 Drunen NL B5
17 Druten NL B5
89 Druzba SU A7
101 Družetići YU B5
100 Drvar YU B1
100 Drvenik YU C2
8 Drymen GB B3
6 Drynoch GB C2
88 Drzewiany PL B2
91 Drzewica PL B4
90 Dtugomilowice PL C2
91 Dtugowola PL B5
87 Dualchi I B1
31 Duas Igrejas P C4
101 Dub YU C4
64 Dubá CS C4
98 Dubar H A2
64 Duben D B3
70 Dübendorf CH A3
64 Dubi CS C3
5 Dublin IRL A5
96 Dubňany CS C3
97 Dubnica CS C4
97 Dubnik CS D4
94 Dubno SU A6
97 Dubodiel CS C4
101 Dubona YU B5
102 Dubovac YU B2
73 Dubranec YU C5
98 Dubrava YU B1
101 Dubrave YU B3
93 Dubrovitsa SU E10
81 Dubrovnik YU B5
19 Ducey F B4
64 Duchcov CS C3
61 Ducherow D B4
101 Ducina YU B5
20 Duclair F B1
14 Duddington GB B2
63 Duderstadt D B5
11 Dudley GB C3
66 Dudweiler D B3
16 Dudzele B B3
32 Dueñas E C2
72 Dueville I C1
17 Duffel B B4
7 Dufftown GB C5
101 Duga Poljana YU C5
73 Duga Resa YU C5
100 Dugi Rat YU C1
66 Dugny-sur-Meuse F B1
98 Dugo Selo YU C1
63 Duingen D A4
72 Duino I C3
62 Duisburg D B1
108 Dukat AL A1
105 Dukat YU B4
96 Dukovany CS B2
106 Dŭlbok Izvor BG A3
103 Dulbokdol BG D5
106 Dŭlboki BG A3
106 Dulgo pole BG A2
17 Dülken D B6
9 Dull GB B4
62 Dülmen D B2
7 Dulnain Bridge GB C5
50 Dulpetorpet N B3
13 Dulverton GB B4
8 Dumbarton GB C3
9 Dumfries GB C4
5 Dun Laoghaire IRL A5
24 Dun-le-Patestel F B1
25 Dun-les-Places F A4
24 Dun-sur-Auron F B2
66 Dun-sur-Meuse F B1
98 Dunaalmás H A3
97 Dunabogdány H D5
99 Dunafalya H B3
99 Dunaföldvár H B3
99 Dunaharaszti H A4
96 Dunajská-Streda CS D3
99 Dunakeszi H A4
96 Dunakiliti H D3
99 Dunakömlöd H B3
3 Dunamanagh GB B4
8 Dunans GB B2
99 Dunapataj H B4
99 Dunaszekcsö H B3
99 Dunaszentgyorgy H B3
99 Dunatetétlen H B4
99 Dunaújváros H B3
99 Dunavecse H B3
9 Dunbar GB B5
7 Dunbeath GB B5
9 Dunblane GB B4
5 Dunboyne IRL A5
7 Duncansby GB B5
14 Dunchurch GB B1
3 Dundalk IRL B5
9 Dundee GB B5
3 Dundonald GB B6
9 Dundrennan GB D4
3 Dundrum GB B6
3 Dunfanaghy IRL A4
9 Dunfermline GB B4
3 Dungannon GB B5
5 Dungarvan IRL B4
8 Dungavel GB C3
3 Dungiven GB B5
2 Dunglow IRL B3
4 Dungourney IRL C3
88 Duninowo PL A2
102 Dunis YU C2
105 Dunje YU C3
9 Dunkeld GB B4
53 Dunker S C2
16 Dunkerque F B2
5 Dunkerrin IRL B4
2 Dunkineely IRL B3
5 Dunleary (Dun Laoghaire) IRL A5
3 Dunleer IRL C5
8 Dunlop GB C3
4 Dunmanway IRL C2
2 Dunmore IRL C3
5 Dunmore East IRL B5
7 Dunnet GB B5
67 Dunningen D C4
8 Dunoon GB C3
9 Duns GB C5
9 Dunscore GB C4
5 Dunshaughlin IRL A5
15 Dunstable GB C2
13 Dunster GB B4
6 Duntulm GB C2
6 Dunvegan GB C2
71 Durach D A5
104 Durakovac YU B2
33 Durana E B4
27 Durance F B4
33 Durango E A4
27 Duras F B4
35 Durban Corbiéres F A5
67 Dürbheim D C4
44 Durcal E C3
98 Durdenovac YU C3
98 Durdevac YU B2
101 Durdevit YU B3
17 Düren D C6
9 Durham GB D6
101 Durinci YU B5
67 Durlach D C4
73 Durmanec YU B5
67 Durmersheim D C4
7 Durness GB B4
96 Dürnkrut A C2
24 Durolle F C3
71 Dürrboden CH B4
70 Dürrenboden CH B3
104 Durrës AL C1
5 Durrow, *Laois* IRL B4
5 Durrow, *Offaly* IRL A4
4 Durrus IRL C2
13 Dursley GB B5
95 Dursunbey TR G8
23 Durtal F A4
54 Durup DK B1
107 Duskotna BG A5
99 Dusnok H B3
89 Dusocin PL B4
62 Dusseldorf D B1
67 Dußlingen D C5
64 Düßnitz D B2
65 Duszniki Zdrój PL C6
73 Dutovlje YU C3
17 Duurstede NL B5
46 Duved S E6
100 Duvno YU C2
100 Dvor YU A1
96 Dvorniky CS C3
97 Dvory n. Z. CS D4
65 Dvur Králove n. Labem CS C5
7 Dyce GB C6
65 Dychow PL B5
88 Dygowo PL A1
9 Dykehead GB B4
9 Dykends GB B4
15 Dymchurch GB C4
13 Dymock GB B5
48 Dyranut N A4
54 Dytvad DK A3
107 Dyulino BG A5
89 Dywity PL B6
105 Džep YU B4
106 Dzhebel BG B3
105 Dzherman BG B5
103 Dzhurovo BG D5
89 Działdowo PL B6
90 Dzialoszyn PL B2
91 Dziatoszyce PL C4
97 Dziekanowice PL B6
88 Dziemiany PL A3
89 Dzierzaźnia PL C6
89 Dzierzgoń PL B5
65 Dzierzoniów PL C6
61 Dziwnów PL A5
105 Džumajlija YU C3
89 Dźwierzuty PL B6

E

33 Ea E A4
9 Eaglesfield GB C4
15 Ealing GB C2
14 Earith GB B3
14 Earl Shilton GB B1
14 Earl Soham GB B4
9 Earlston GB C5
9 Earsdon GB C6
11 Easington GB B6
9 Easington Colliery GB D6
11 Easingwold GB A4
2 Easky IRL B3
15 East Adderbury GB B1
13 East Brent GB B5
14 East Dereham GB B3
15 East Grinstead GB C2
14 East Harling GB B3
15 East Hoathly GB D3
15 East Ilsley GB C1
8 East Kilbride GB C3
9 East Linton GB C5
11 East Markham GB B5
11 East Retford GB B5
14 East Rudham GB B3
9 East Wemyss GB B4
15 Eastbourne GB D3
7 Easter Fearn GB C4
6 Easter Quarff, *Shetland Is.* GB
15 Eastleigh GB D1
13 Easton GB C5
15 Eastry GB C4
11 Eastwood GB B4
14 Eaton Socon GB B2
34 Eaux-Bonnes F A2
26 Eauze F C4
55 Ebberup DK C2
72 Ebbs A A2

13 Ebbw Vale GB B4
63 Ebeleben D B5
55 Ebeltoft DK B3
72 Eben im Pongau A A3
69 Ebensee A D4
68 Ebensfeld D A1
67 Eberbach D B4
96 Ebergassing A C2
63 Ebergötzen D B5
68 Ebern D A1
73 Eberndorf A B4
64 Ebersbach D B4
69 Eberschwang A C4
63 Ebersdorf, *Bayern* D C6
59 Ebersdorf, *Niedersachsen* D B6
73 Eberstein A B4
66 Ebersviller F B2
61 Eberswalde D C4
108 Ebesos GR B3
67 Ebingen D C5
71 Ebnat-Kappel CH A4
80 Éboli I D2
68 Ebrach D B1
96 Ebreichsdorf A D2
24 Ebreuil F B3
60 Ebstorf D B1
17 Ecaussinnes-d'Enghien B C4
9 Ecclefechan GB C4
10 Eccleshall GB C3
33 Eçcobasa de Almazán E C4
95 Eceabat TR F7
70 Echallens CH B1
33 Echarri-Aranaz E B4
33 Echauri E B5
25 Échenoz-la-Méline F A6
23 Echiré F B4
29 Echirolles F A4
27 Echourgnac F A4
9 Echt GB A5
17 Echt NL B5
63 Echte D B5
66 Echternach L B2
43 Ecija E B4
101 Ećka YU A5
63 Eckartsberga D B6
62 Eckelshausen D C3
62 Eckenhagen D C2
59 Eckernförde D A6
11 Eckington GB B4
21 Éclaron F C5
20 Ecommoy F D1
19 Ecouché F B5
20 Ecouen F B3
20 Ecouis F B2
98 Écs H A2
99 Ecséd H A4
23 Ecuellé F A6
51 Ed S D2
50 Eda S C3
50 Eda glasbruk S C3
58 Edam NL C2
51 Edane S C3
64 Edderitz D B1
9 Eddleston GB C4
17 Ede NL A5
50 Edebäck S B4
52 Edebo S B4
47 Edefors Harads S C10
63 Edemissen D A5
3 Eden GB B6
15 Edenbridge GB C3
5 Edenderry IRL A4
67 Edenkoben D B4
3 Ederny GB B4
67 Edesheim D B4
59 Edewecht D B4
17 Edgegem B B4
109 Édhessa GR A4
9 Edinburgh GB C4
107 Edirne TR B4
48 Edland N B4
73 Edlitz A A6
9 Edmondbyers GB D6
71 Édolo I B5
95 Edremit TR G7
56 Edsbruk S A5
52 Edsbyn S A1
51 Edsgatan S C4
51 Edsleskog S C3
51 Edsvalla S C4
9 Edzell GB B5
17 Eefde NL A6
16 Eeklo B B3
17 Eerbeek NL A6
16 Eernegem B B3
17 Eersel NL B5
58 Eexta NL B3
69 Eferding A C5
68 Effeltrich D B2
24 Effiat F B3
105 Efkarpia GR C4
109 Efxinoúpolis GR B4
63 Egeln D B6
97 Eger H D6
97 Egerbakta H D6
55 Egernsund DK D2
48 Egersund N C3
97 Egerszólát H D6
71 Egg A A4
68 Egg D C1
49 Eggedal N A6
96 Eggenburg A C1
68 Eggenfelden D C3
61 Eggesin D B5
69 Egglesberg A C4
69 Egglfing D C4
15 Egham GB C2
17 Eghezée B C4
89 Egiertowo PL A4
24 Egletons F C2
68 Egling, *Bayern* D C1
68 Egling, *Bayern* D D2
3 Eglinton GB A4
70 Eglisau CH A3
28 Égliseneuve-d'Entraigues F A1
71 Eglofs D A4
12 Eglwyswrw GB A3
71 Egna (Neumarkt) I B6
10 Egremont GB A2
55 Egtved DK C2
29 Eguilles F C4
21 Eguilly-sous-Bois F C5
98 Egyházasrádóc H A1
68 Ehekirchen D C2
67 Ehingen D C5
63 Ehmen D A5
60 Ehra-Lessien D C1
66 Ehrang D B2
64 Ehrenfriedersdorf D C2
64 Ehrenhain D C2
62 Ehringshausen D C3
71 Ehrwald A A5
33 Eibar E A4
65 Eibau D C4
67 Eibelstadt D B6
64 Eibenstock D C2
62 Eibergen NL A1
73 Eibiswald A B5
63 Eichenbarleben D A6
69 Eichendorf D C3
68 Eichstatt D C2
62 Eickelborn D B3
46 Eidfjord N F3
51 Eidsberg N C2
49 Eidsfoss N B7
50 Eidskog N B3
48 Eidsvåg N A2
50 Eidsvoll N B2
63 Eienbeck D B4
46 Eikefjord N F2
48 Eikelandsosen N A2
48 Eiken N C4
64 Eilenburg D B2
17 Eilendorf D C6
63 Eilsleben D A6
50 Eina N B1
17 Eindhoven NL B5
16 Eine B C3
59 Einfeld D A7
70 Einsiedeln CH A3
66 Einville F C2
63 Eisenach D C5
64 Eisenberg D C1
67 Eisenberg D B4
73 Eisenerz A A4
64 Eisenhüttenstadt D A4
73 Eisenkappel A B4
96 Eisenstadt A D2
72 Eisentratten A B3
62 Eiserfeld D C2
63 Eisfeld D C5
67 Eisingen D C5
63 Eisleben D B6
67 Eistingen D C5
63 Eiterfeld D C4
62 Eitorf D C2
41 Eivissa, *Ibiza* E
31 Eixo P D2
55 Ejby DK C2
34 Ejea de' los Caballeros E A1
55 Ejstrup DK C2
34 Ejulve E C2
111 Ekáli GR A4
16 Eke B C3
51 Ekeby, *Östergötland* S D6
52 Ekeby, *Uppsala* S B4
47 Ekenas SF G11
56 Ekenässjön S B4
17 Ekeren B B4
57 Eket S C2
106 Ekhinos GR B2
17 Eksel B B5
50 Ekshärad S B4
56 Eksjö S B3
107 Ekzarkh Antimovo BG A4
43 El Aguila E B4
38 El Alamo, *Madrid* E B3
43 El Alamo, *Sevilla* E B3
42 El Almendro E B2
33 El Almiñe E B3
45 El Alquián E C4
43 El Arahal E B4
38 El Arenal, *Avila* E B1
41 El Arenal, *Mallorca* E
45 El Arguellite E A4
32 El Astillero E A3
45 El Ballestero E A4
37 El Barco de Avila E A5
39 El Berrueco E B3
37 El Bodón E A4
30 El Bollo E B3
39 El Bonillo E D4
43 El Bosque E C4
38 El Bullaque E C2
34 El Burgo de Ebro E B2
33 El Burgo de Osma E C3
32 El Burgo Ranero E B1
33 El Buste E C5
31 El Cabaco E D4
45 El Cabo de Gata E C4
33 El Callejo E A3
43 El Campillo E B3
38 El Campillo de la Jara E C1
37 El Campo E B5
39 El Cañavete E C4
45 El Cantal E B5
44 El Carpio E B2
38 El Carpio de Tajo E C2
38 El Casar de Escalona E B2
33 El Castaño E A3
43 El Castillo de las Guardas E B3
44 El Centenillo E A3
37 El Cerro E A5
43 El Cerro de Andévalo E B3
43 El Comenar E C4
43 El Coronil E B4
43 El Cuervo E C3
32 El Cupo de Tierra del Vino E C1
45 El Entredicho E A4
38 El Escorial E B2
38 El Espinar E B2
30 El Ferrol E A2
34 El Frago E A2
30 El Franco E A4
33 El Fransno E C5
43 El Garrobo E B3
43 El Gastor E C4
38 El Gordo E C1
34 El Grado E A3
42 El Granado E B2
40 El Grao E B3
44 El Higuera E B2
38 El Hoya de Pinares E B2
44 El Hoyo E A3
43 El Madroño E B3
31 El Maillo E D4
38 El Mirón E B1
39 El Molar E B3
38 El Molinillo E C2
33 El Muyo E C3
33 El Oimo E C3
38 El Pardo E B3
37 El Payo E A4
39 El Pedernoso E C4
43 El Pedroso E B4
39 El Peral E C5
40 El Perelló E B2
39 El Picazo E C4
32 El Piñero E C1
40 El Pobo E A2
39 El Pobo de Dueñas E B5
39 El Pozo de Guadalajara E B3
39 El Provencio E C4
38 El Puenta del Arzobispo E C1
43 El Puerto de Sta. Maria E C3
33 El Quintanar E C4
43 El Real de la Jara E B3
38 El Real de S. Vincente E B2
38 El Robledo E C2
43 El Rocio E B3
42 El Rompido E B2
43 El Ronquilo E B3
33 El Royo E C4
43 El Rubio E B5
40 El Saler E B2
43 El Saucejo E B4
34 El Temple E B2
38 El Tiemblo E B2
44 El Tocón E B3
34 El Tormillo E B2
32 El Valle de las Casas E B1
39 El Vellón E B3
44 El Viso E A2
43 El Viso del Alcor E B4
44 El Viso del Marqués E A3
109 Elafos GR A4
112 Elaia, *Kriti* GR
111 Elaia, *Lakonía* GR C3
106 Elaiokhóri GR C2
110 Elaión GR A3
109 Elassón GR B4
108 Eláti GR B3
109 Elátia GR C4
108 Elatochorion GR B2
110 Elatou GR A2
104 Elbasan AL C2
20 Elbeuf F B1
63 Elbingerode D B5
89 Elblag PL A5
17 Elburg NL A5
40 Elche E C2
45 Elche de la Sierra E A4
67 Elchingen D C6
40 Elda E C2
63 Eldagsen D A4
60 Eldena D B2
56 Eldsberga S C1
111 Elefsis GR A4
109 Eleftheró GR B4
99 Elemir YU C5
106 Elena BG A3
110 Eleón, *Akhaia* GR A3
110 Eleón, *Ilía* GR B2
111 Eleón, *Voiotía* GR A4
109 Elevtherai GR B4
106 Elevtheroupolis GR C2
63 Elgershausen D B4
7 Elgin GB C5
33 Elgóibar E A4
8 Elgol GB A1
110 Eliá, *Fokís* GR A3
109 Eliá, *Khalkidhikí* GR A5
110 Eliá, *Messinía* GR B2
9 Elie GB B5
111 Elika GR C3
105 Elin Pelin BG B5
110 Eliniká, *Aitolía kai Acarnanía* GR A2
109 Eliniká, *Évia* GR B5
111 Elinikó GR C3
103 Eli-.seyna BG C4
9 Elishaw GB C5
33 Elizondo E A5
107 Elkhovo BG A4
67 Ellenberg D B6
11 Eller Beck Bridge GB A5
10 Ellesmere GB C3
10 Ellesmere Port GB B3
16 Ellezelles B C3
68 Ellingen D B1
9 Ellington GB C6
111 Elliniko GR B4
72 Ellmau A A2
7 Ellon GB C6
51 Ellös S D2
11 Elloughton GB B5
63 Ellrich D B5
67 Ellwangen D C6
71 Elm CH B4
59 Elm D B6
59 Elmshorn D B6
67 Elmstein D B3
35 Elne F A5
33 Elorrio E A4
112 Elos, *Kriti* GR
99 Előszállás H B3
112 Elounta, *Kriti* GR
66 Eloyes F C2
6 Elphin GB B3
17 Elsdorf D C6
67 Elsenfeld D B5
59 Elsfleth D B5
106 Elshitsa BG A2
62 Elspe D B3
17 Elspeet NL A5
17 Elst NL B5
64 Elster D B2
64 Elsterberg D C2
64 Elsterwerda D B3
64 Elstra D B4
68 Eltmann D B1
67 Eltville D A4
37 Elvas P C3
14 Elveden GB B3
18 Elven F C3
16 Elverdinge B C2
50 Elverum N B2
40 Elx E C2
63 Elxleben D B5
14 Ely GB B3
62 Elz D C3
63 Elze D A4
50 Emådelen S A5
9 Embleton GB C6
112 Embona GR B2
112 Embórion GR D2
112 Emborios GR C1
29 Embrun F B5
34 Embún E A2
58 Emden D B4
112 Emecik TR B2
58 Emlichheim D C3
4 Emly IRL B3
56 Emmaboda S C4
57 Emmaljunga S C2
58 Emmeloord NL C2
70 Emmen CH A3
58 Emmen NL C3
67 Emmendinger D C3
58 Emmer-Compascuum NL C4
58 Emmer-Erfscheidenveen NL C4
17 Emmerich D B6
63 Emmern D A4
107 Emona BG A5
75 Empoli I C5
62 Emsbüren D A2
62 Emsdetten D A2
56 Emsfors S B5
68 Emskirchen D B1
59 Emstek D C5
15 Emsworth GB D2
3 Emyvale IRL B5
46 Enafors S E6
35 Encamp AND A4
36 Encarnaçao P C1
38 Encinas de Abajo E B1
32 Encinas de Esgueva E C2
44 Encinas Reales E B2
43 Encinasola E A3
33 Encio E B3
33 Enciso E B4
66 Endingen D C3
68 Endorf D D3
38 Endrinal E B1
99 Endröd H B5
50 Enebakk N C2
56 Eneryda S C3
107 Enez TR C4
15 Enfield GB C2
112 Engarés GR D1
70 Engelberg CH B3
69 Engelhartszell A C4
62 Engelskirchen D C2
67 Engen D D4
62 Enger D A3
46 Engerdal N F5
55 Engesvang DK B2
17 Enghien B C4
69 Engimar D B3
108 Englouvi GR C2
62 Engter D A3
40 Enguera E C2
39 Enguidanos E C5
67 Eningen D C5
67 Enkenbach D B3
58 Enkhuizen NL C2
53 Enköping S C3
49 Enkstrand N B6
85 Enna I B3
62 Ennepetal D B2
24 Ennezat F C3
62 Ennigloh D A3
51 Enningdal N D2
4 Ennis IRL B3
5 Enniscorthy IRL B5
4 Enniskean IRL C3
5 Enniskerry IRL A5
3 Enniskillen GB B4
4 Ennistimon IRL B2
69 Enns A C5
58 Ens NL C2
62 Enschede NL A1
68 Ensdorf D B2
66 Ensisheim F D3
17 Ensival B C5
53 Enstaberga S D2
15 Enstone GB C1
70 Entlebuch CH B3
74 Entrácque I B2
42 Entradas P B1
24 Entrains-sur-Nohain F A3
33 Entrambasaguas E A3
32 Entrambasmestas E A3
28 Entraygues-sur-Truyère F B1
31 Entre-os-Rios P C2
25 Entremont-le-Vieux F C5
29 Entrevaux F C5
37 Entrin Bajo E C4
36 Entroncamento P B2
66 Entzheim F C3
20 Envermeu F B2
52 Enviken S B1
98 Enying H B3
96 Enzesfeld A D2
72 Enzingerboden A A2
67 Enzklösterle D C4
67 Enzweihagen D C4
21 Épagny F B4
23 Epannes F B4
109 Epanomi GR A4
62 Epe D A2
17 Epe NL A5
21 Epehy F A4
21 Épernay F B4
20 Epernon F C2
67 Epfendorf D C4
66 Epfig F C3
25 Epierre F C6
34 Épila E B1
25 Epinac-les-Mines F B4
66 Épinal F C2
82 Episcopia I A3
108 Episkopi, *Evritanía* GR C3
112 Episkopi, *Iráklion, Kriti* GR
109 Episkopi, *Pélla* GR A4
112 Episkopi, *Réthimnon, Kriti* GR
110 Epitálion GR B2
25 Epoisses F A4
17 Eppegem B C4
66 Eppelborn D B2
66 Eppenbrunn D B3
64 Eppendorf D C3
15 Epping GB C3
67 Eppingen D B4
15 Epsom GB C2
108 Eptakhórion GR A3
109 Eptálofos GR C4
11 Epworth GB B5
72 Eraclea I C2
72 Eraclea Mare I C2
110 Eratini GR A3
108 Eratira GR A3
71 Erba I C4
67 Erbach, *Baden-Württemberg* D C5
67 Erbach, *Hessen* D B4
86 Erbalunga F B2
68 Erbendorf D B3
83 Érchie I A4
99 Ercsi H A3
99 Érd H A3
101 Erdevik YU A4
68 Erding D C2
99 Erdötelek H A5
99 Erdut YU C4
111 Erétria, *Évia* GR A4
109 Erétria, *Magnisía* GR B4
59 Erfde D A6
48 Erfjord N B3
62 Erftstadt D C1
63 Erfurt D C5
68 Ergolding D C3
68 Ergoldsbach D C3
58 Erica NL C3
84 Érice I A1
36 Ericeira P C1
56 Eriksmåla S C4
51 Erikstad S D3
108 Erina AL A2
57 Eringsboda S C4
70 Eriswil CH A2
111 Erithrai GR A4
17 Erkelen D B6
61 Erkner D C4
62 Erkralh D B1
34 Erla E A2
96 Erlach A D2
68 Erlangen D B2
74 Erli I B3
72 Erlsbach A B2
109 Ermakiá GR A3
17 Ermelo NL A5
20 Ermenonville F B3
31 Ermezinde P C2
42 Ermidas P B1
111 Ermióni GR B4
112 Ermoúpolis GR E1
63 Ermsleben D B6
62 Erndtebrück D C3
19 Ernèe F B5
99 Ernestinovo YU C3
96 Ernstbrunn A C2
67 Erolzheim D C6
47 Erontekiö SF B11
17 Erquelinnes B C4
18 Erquy F B3
36 Erra P C2
33 Errazu E A5
55 Errindlev DK D4
33 Erro E B5
7 Errogie GB C4
9 Errol GB B4
86 Ersa F B2
99 Érsekcsanád H B3
108 Ersekë AL A2
97 Ersekvadkert H D5
66 Erstein F C3
70 Erstfeld CH B3
54 Ertebølle DK B2
67 Ertingen D C5
36 Ervedal, *Coimbra* P A2
36 Ervedal, *Portalegre* P B3
77 Ervenik YU B5
42 Ervidel P B1
21 Ervy F C4
62 Erwitte D B3
63 Erxleben D A6
41 Es Caná, *Ibiza* E
41 Es Pujols, *Ibiza* E
55 Esbjerg DK C1
21 Esbly F C3
43 Escacena del Campo E B3
30 Escairon E B3
32 Escalada E B3
87 Escalaplano I C2
38 Escalona E B2
38 Escalona del Prado E A2
38 Escalonilla E C2
36 Escalos de Baixo P B3
36 Escalos de Cima P B3
39 Escamilla E B4
44 Escañuela E B2
34 Escároz E A1
34 Escatrón E B2
66 Esch-sur-Alzette L B1
71 Eschach D A4
67 Eschau D B5
60 Eschede D C1
68 Eschenau D B2
68 Eschenbach D B2
71 Eschenz CH A3
63 Escherhausen D B4
63 Eschwege D B5
17 Eschweiler D C6
33 Escobasa de Almazán E C4
16 Escoeuilles F C1
45 Escombreras E B6
26 Escos F C2
26 Escource F B2
29 Escragnolles F C5
37 Escurial E B5
31 Escurial de la Sierra E D5
59 Esens D B4
30 Esgos E B3
15 Esher GB C2
9 Eskaalemuir GB C4
51 Eskilsäter S D4
55 Eskilstrup DK D4
53 Eskilstuna S C2
68 Eslarn D B3
33 Eslava E B5
40 Eslida E B2
62 Eslohe D B3
57 Eslöv S D2
21 Esnes F A4
50 Espa N B2
28 Espalion F B1
28 Espaly-St.-Marcel F A2
37 Esparragalejo E C4
38 Esparragosa del Caudillo E D1
37 Esparragossa de la Serena E C5
35 Esparraguera E B4
29 Esparron F C4
48 Espedal N C3
33 Espejo, *Alava* E B3
44 Espejo, *Córdoba* E B2
48 Espeland N A2
62 Espelkamp D A3
29 Espeluche F B3
44 Espeluy E A3
43 Espera E C4
37 Esperança P B3
35 Espéraza F A5
79 Espéria I B4
43 Espiel E A4
32 Espinama E A2
30 Espiñaredo E A3
35 Espinelvas E B5
36 Espinhal P A2
31 Espinho P C2
32 Espinilla E A2
32 Espinosa de Cerrato E C3
33 Espinosa de los Monteros E A3
42 Espirito Santo P B2
35 Espluga de Francoli E B4
34 Esplús E B3
35 Espolla E A5
41 Esporlas, *Mallorca* E
31 Esposende P C2
35 Espot E A4
35 Espunyola E A4
34 Esquedas E A2
38 Esquivias E B3
17 Essen B B4
59 Essen, *Niedersachsen* D C4
62 Essen, *Nordrhein-Westfalen* D B2
68 Essenbach D C3
20 Essertaux F B3
67 Essingen D C6
67 Esslingen D C5
21 Essoyes F C5
41 Establiments, *Mallorca* E
30 Estacas E B2
34 Estadilla E A3
35 Estagel F A5
16 Estaires F C2
26 Estang F C3
35 Estany E B5
31 Estarreja P D2
35 Estartit E A6
70 Estavayer-le-Lac CH B1
76 Este I A1
30 Esteiro E A2
31 Estela P C2
33 Estella E B4
41 Estellenchs, *Mallorca* E
44 Estepa E B2
32 Estépar E B3
43 Estepona E C4
21 Esternay F C4
35 Esterri de Aneu E A4
59 Esterwegen D C4
21 Estissac F C4
24 Estivareilles F B2
40 Estivella E B2
42 Estói P B2
34 Estopiñan E B3
36 Estoril P C1
29 Estoublon F C5
16 Estrée-Blanche F C2
20 Estrées-St. Denis F B3
42 Estrela P A2
39 Estremera E B3
36 Estremoz P C3
52 Estuna S C4
23 Esyres F A5
97 Esztergom H D4
66 Etain F B1
25 Étalans F A6
66 Etalle B B1
20 Etampes F C3
25 Etang-sur-Arroux F B4
16 Étaples F C1
26 Etauliers F A3
66 Ethe B B1
48 Etne N B2
21 Etoges F C4
21 Etréaupont F B4
20 Étréchy F C3
20 Etrèpagny F B2
20 Etretat F B1
21 Étrœungt F A4
106 Etropole BG A2
70 Étroubles I C2
71 Ettal D A6
66 Ettelbrück L B2
17 Etten NL B4
14 Ettington GB B1
67 Ettlingen D C4
68 Ettringen, *Bayern* D C1
62 Ettringen, *Rheinland-Pfalz* D C2
99 Etyek H A3
68 Etzenricht D B3
20 Eu F A2
33 Eulate E B4
17 Eupen B C6
63 Eurdorf D C5
17 Europoort NL B4
21 Eurville-sur-Marne F C6
62 Euskirchen D C1
60 Eutin D A1
21 Euvy F C5
10 Euxton GB B3
110 Eva GR B2
24 Evaux-les-Bains F B2
112 Évdhiles GR C1
50 Evenstad N A2
13 Evercreech GB B5
16 Evergem B B3
57 Everöd S D3
62 Eversberg D B3
62 Everswinkel D B2
50 Evertsberg S A4
13 Evesham GB A6
70 Evian F B1
110 Evinokhorion GR A2
86 Evisa F B1
49 Evje N C4
70 Evolène CH B2
36 Évora P C3
36 Evoramonte P C3
110 Evpalion GR A2
19 Evran F B4
19 Evrecy F A5
107 Evrencik TR B5
107 Evrenli TR B5
107 Evrensekiz TR B5
20 Evreux F B2
19 Evron F B5
105 Évropos GR D4
110 Evrostina GR A3
20 Évry F C3
105 Evzonoi GR C4
15 Ewell GB C2
62 Ewersbach D C3
15 Ewhurst GB C2
111 Examillia GR B3
105 Exaplátanon GR D4
109 Éxarkhos, *Fthiótis* GR C4
108 Éxarkhos, *Grevená* GR A3
27 Excideuil F A5
13 Exeter GB C4
20 Exmes F C1
13 Exminster GB C4
13 Exmouth GB C4
110 Exo Nimfio GR C3
106 Exokhi GR B1
31 Extremo P C2
49 Eydehamn N C5
14 Eye, *Cambridgeshire* GB B2
14 Eye, *Suffolk* GB B4
9 Eyemouth GB C5
29 Eyguians F B4
29 Eyguières F C3
24 Eygurande F C2
27 Eymet F B4
24 Eymoutiers F C1
15 Eynsham GB C1
59 Eystrup D C6
30 Ezaro E B1
95 Ezine TR G7
31 Ezmoriz P D2

F

34 Fabara E B3
75 Fábbrico I B5
50 Fåberg N A1
30 Fabero E B4
55 Fåborg DK C3
28 Fabrègues F C2
76 Fabriano I C2
82 Fabrizia I C3
31 Facha P C2
43 Facinas E C4
97 Fačkov CS B4
26 Facture F B3
99 Fadd H B3
72 Faédis I B3
76 Faenza I B1
31 Fafe P C2
72 Fagagna I B3
94 Făgăraş RO D6
56 Fågelfors S B4
57 Fågelmara S C4
51 Fågelsta S D6
56 Fagerbult S B4
49 Fagerheim N A4
46 Fagernes N F4
51 Fagersanna S D5
52 Fagersta S B1
56 Fåglavik S A2
82 Fagnano Castello I B3
70 Fahrwangen CH A3
70 Faido CH B3
21 Fains F C6
10 Fairbourne GB C1
13 Fairford GB B6
8 Fairlie GB C3
99 Fajsz H B3
14 Fakenham GB B3
107 Fakiya BG A5
99 Fákozd H A3
55 Fakse DK C5
55 Fakse Ladeplads DK C5
109 Fálaina GR B4
19 Falaise F B5
72 Falcade I B1
2 Falcarragh IRL A3
33 Falces E B5
94 Fălciu RO C8
84 Falconara I B3
76 Falconara Marittima I C3
11 Faldingworth GB B5
53 Falerum S D2
42 Falésia P B1
112 Faliráki GR A2
68 Falkenberg D B3
64 Falkenberg, *Cottbus* D B3
61 Falkenberg, *Frankfurt* D C4
56 Falkenberg S C1
61 Falkensee D C4
64 Falkenstein D C2
68 Falkenstein D B3
61 Falkenthal D C4
9 Falkirk GB C4
9 Falkland GB B4
51 Falköping S D4
72 Fall D A1
53 Falla S D1
63 Fallersleben D A5
59 Fallingbostel D C6
12 Falmouth GB C2
34 Falset E B3
57 Falsterbo S D1
94 Fălticeni RO C7
52 Falun S B1
48 Fana N A2
75 Fanano I B5
109 Fanárion, *Kardhítsa* GR B3
106 Fanárion, *Rodhópi* GR C3
110 Faneroméni GR C2
55 Fangel DK C3
27 Fanjeaux F C5
76 Fano I C3
53 Fantbyttan S C1
78 Fara in Sabina I A3
70 Fara Novarese I C3
32 Faramontanos de Tábara E C1
34 Farasdues E A1
56 Fårbo S B5
15 Fareham GB D1
35 Farga Moles E A4
51 Färgelanda S D2
21 Fargniers F B4
46 Farila S F7
13 Faringdon GB B6
52 Faringe S C4
75 Farini d'Olmo I B4
31 Fariza E C4
56 Farjestaden S C5
109 Farkadón GR B4
34 Farlete E B2
57 Färlöy S C3
99 Farmos H A4
97 Farnă CS C4
52 Färna S C1
50 Färnas S A5
15 Farnborough GB C2
78 Farnese I A2
15 Farnham GB C2
63 Farnoda D C5
63 Farnstädt D B6
42 Faro P B2
92 Farösund S B6
7 Farr GB C4
72 Farra d'Alpago I B2
4 Farranfore IRL B2
109 Fársala GR B4
54 Farsø DK B2
56 Farstorp S B4
48 Farsund N C3
55 Farum DK C5
54 Fařup DK B2
81 Fasano I D4
60 Faßberg D C1
52 Fasterna S C4
34 Fatarella E B3
36 Fatima P B2
66 Faucogney F D2
29 Faucon-du-Caire F B5
27 Fauguerolles F B4
9 Fauldhouse GB C4
61 Faulenrost D B3
66 Faulquemont F B2
16 Fauquembergues F C2
46 Fauske N C7
25 Fauverney F A5
20 Fauville-en-Caux F B1
84 Favaro I B2
25 Faverges F C6
66 Faverney F D2
15 Faversham GB C3
84 Favignana I B1
13 Fawley GB C6
20 Fay-aux-Loges F D3
29 Fayence F C5
66 Fayl-Billot F D1
34 Fayón E B3
7 Fearn GB C5
8 Fearnan GB B3
20 Fécamp F B1
3 Feeny GB B4
56 Fegen S B2
99 Fegyvernek H A5
61 Fehrbellin D C3
73 Fehring A B6
50 Feiring N B2
73 Feistritz i. Rosental A B4
99 Feketić YU C4
41 Felanitx, *Mallorca* E
61 Felchow D B5
73 Feld a. See A B3
73 Feldbach A B5
61 Feldberg D B4
59 Felde D A6
97 Feldebrö H D6
71 Feldkirch A A4
68 Feldkirchen, *Bayern* D C2
68 Feldkirchen, *Bayern* D D2
69 Feldkirchen a.d. Donau A C5
73 Feldkirchen i. Kärnten A B4
31 Felgueiras P C2
108 Felio GR A3
82 Felitto I A2
45 Félix E C4
15 Felixstowe GB C4
74 Felizzano I B3
67 Fellbach D C5
24 Felletin F C2
53 Fellingsbro S C1
97 Felnémet H D6
98 Felpéc H A2
96 Fels a. Wagram A C1
98 Felsöbagod H B1
99 Felsögöd H A4
98 Felsönyék H B3
99 Felsöszentiván H B4
98 Felsöszentmárton H C2
9 Felton GB C6
72 Feltre I B1
14 Feltwell GB B3
3 Fenagh IRL B4
107 Fenerköy TR B6
66 Fénetrange F C3
23 Feneu F A4
51 Fengersfors S D3
70 Fenis I C2
55 Fensmark DK C4
8 Fenwick GB C3
8 Feolin Ferry GB C1
5 Ferbane IRL A4
60 Ferchland D C3
98 Ferdinandovac YU B2
61 Ferdinandshof D B4
21 Fère-Champenoise F C5
21 Fère-en-Tardenois F B4
79 Ferentillo I A3
79 Ferentino I B4
98 Feričanci YU C2
85 Ferla I B3
73 Ferlach A B4
72 Ferleiten A A2
31 Fermil P C2
76 Fermo I C3
31 Fermoselle E C4
4 Fermoy IRL B3
44 Fernán-Núnez E B2
45 Fernán Peréz E C4
38 Fernancabellero E C3
36 Fernão Ferro P C1
25 Fernay-Voltaire F B6
13 Ferndown GB C6
7 Ferness GB C5
6 Fernilea GB C2
5 Ferns IRL B5
70 Ferpécle CH B2
107 Ferrai GR C4
28 Ferrals F C1
83 Ferrandina I A3
76 Ferrara I B1
71 Ferrara di M. Baldo I C5
30 Ferreira E A3
42 Ferreira do Alentejo P A1
36 Ferreira do Zêzere P B2
31 Ferreras de Abajo E C4
31 Ferreras de Arriba E C4
41 Ferrerias, *Menorca* E
34 Ferreruela, *Teruel* E B1
31 Ferreruela, *Zamora* E C4
70 Ferret CH C2
70 Ferrette F A2
75 Ferriere I B4
17 Ferrière-la-Grande F C3
24 Ferrières, *Allier* F B3
21 Ferrières, *Loiret* F C3
20 Ferrières, *Oise* F B3
28 Ferrières-St.-Mary F A2
11 Ferryhill GB A4
98 Fertöszentmiklós H A1
58 Ferwerd NL B2
21 Festieux F B4
95 Fetesti RO D7
5 Fethard IRL B4
50 Fetsund N C2
9 Fettercairn GB B5
68 Feucht D B2
71 Feuchten A A5
68 Feuchtwangen D B1
62 Feudingen D C3
20 Feuquières F B2
25 Feurs F C4
49 Fevik N C5
10 Ffestiniog GB C2
79 Fiamignano I A4
74 Fiano I A2
84 Ficarazzi I A2
75 Ficarolo I B6
71 Fichisau CH A3
68 Fichtelberg D A2
67 Fichtenberg D C5
78 Ficulle I A3
75 Fidenza I B5
48 Fidjeland N C3
72 Fieberbrunn A A2
108 Fier AL A1
104 Fier-Shegan AL D1
72 Fiera di Primiero I B1
70 Fiesch CH B3
75 Fiesole I C6
76 Fiesso Umbertiano I B1
110 Figalia GR B2
86 Figari F C2
27 Figeac F B5
48 Figgjo N C2
75 Figline Valdarno I C6
34 Figols E A3
36 Figueira da Foz P A2
31 Figueira de Gastelo Rodrigo P D4
42 Figueira dos Caveleiros P A1
36 Figueiredo P B3
31 Figueiredo de Alva P D3
36 Figueiró dos Vinhos P B2
35 Figueras E A5
40 Figueroles E A2
31 Figueruela de Arriba E C4
111 Fikhtia GR B3
108 Fiki GR B3
97 Fil'akovo CS C5
82 Filadélfia I C3
109 Filadhón GR B4
109 Filaki GR B4
107 Filákion GR B4
67 Filderstat D C5
106 Filevo BG A3
11 Filey GB A5
103 Filiaşi RO B4
108 Filiátes GR B2
110 Filiatrá GR B2
106 Filippoi GR B2
51 Filipstad S C5
71 Filisur CH B4
109 Filon GR B4
109 Filótas GR A3
112 Filótion GR D1
76 Filottrano I C3

55 Filskov DK C2
49 Filtvet N B7
72 Filzmoos A A3
75 Finale Emilia I B6
4 Finale Ligure I B3
45 Finana E B4
71 Finchingfield GB C3
7 Findhorn GB C5
7 Findochty GB C6
15 Findon GB D2
14 Finedon GB B2
110 Finikoús GR C2
30 Finisterre E B1
72 Finkenberg A A1
59 Finkenwerder D B6
3 Finnea IRL C4
51 Finnerödja S D5
50 Finnskog N B3
61 Finow D C4
56 Finsjö S B5
48 Finsland N C4
53 Finspång S D1
64 Finsterwalde D B3
58 Finsterwolde NL B4
7 Finstown GB A5
3 Fintona GB B4
2 Fintown IRL B3
8 Fintry GB B3
2 Fionnphort GB B3
75 Fiorenzuola d'Arda I B4
4 Firenze I C6
75 Firenzuola I B6
7 Firminy F A3
82 Firmo I B3
7 Fischamend Markt A C2
96 Fischau A D2
56 Fischbach D B3
60 Fischbeck D C3
75 Fishbourne GB D1
71 Fishen D A5
8 Fisherton GB A5
12 Fishguard GB B3
48 Fiskå, *Rogaland* N B4
48 Fiskå, *Rogaland* N B2
110 Fiskardho GR A1
51 Fiskebäckskil S D2
51 Fismes F B4
33 Fitero E B5
7 Fiuggi I B3
82 Fiumefreddo Brúzio I B3
85 Fiumefreddo di Sicília I B4
78 Fiuminico I B5
6 Five Penny Borve GB B2
6 Fivemiletown GB B4
75 Fivizzano I B5
25 Fixin F A4
102 Fizes RO A2
7 Fjaera N B3
57 Fjälkinge S C3
51 Fjällbacka S D2
46 Fjallnäs S E6
7 Fjardhundra S C2
51 Fjell bru N C2
7 Fjellerup DK B3
54 Fjerritslev DK A2
5 Fjugesta S C5
49 Flå N A6
110 Flåboura GR A3
25 Flace F B4
70 Flamatt CH B2
11 Flamborough GB A5
108 Flamouro GR A3
62 Flammersfeld D C2
109 Flamouria GR A4
35 Flassá E A5
7 Flassans F C5
49 Flatdal N B5
8 Flateland N B4
72 Flattach A B3
66 Flavigny F C2
28 Flavin F B1
21 Flavy-le-Martel F A4
71 Flawil CH A4
7 Flayose F C5
59 Fleckeby D A6
7 Fleet GB C2
60 Fleetmark D C2
10 Fleetwood GB B2
67 Flehingen D B4
48 Flekkefjord N C3
53 Flen S C2
51 Flensburg D D2
56 Flerohopp S C4
8 Flers F B5
49 Flesberg N B6
7 Flessau D C2
27 Fleurance F C4
23 Fleuré F B5
25 Fleurie F B4
70 Fleurier F C1
17 Fleurus B C4
7 Fleury, *Côte-d'Or* F A4
28 Fleury, *Hérault* F C1
7 Fleury, *Yonne* F A1
20 Fleury-les-Aubrais F D2
64 Fleury-sur-Andelle F B2
19 Fleury-sur-Orne F A5
7 Fleys F D4
63 Flieden D C4
51 Flimby GB D4
71 Flims CH B4
7 Flines-lès-Raches F C3
10 Flint GB B2
51 Flintbeck D A7
50 Flisa N C3
51 Flisby S B3
56 Fliseryd S B5
71 Flitsch A B5
15 Flitwick GB B2
34 Flix E B3
20 Flixecourt F A3
21 Flize F B5
16 Flobecq B C3
56 Floby S B3
56 Floda S B1
56 Flodden GB B5
21 Flogny F D4
64 Flöha D A3
110 Flókas GR A2
64 Flonheim D B3
28 Florac F C1
17 Floreffe B C4
17 Florennes B C4
27 Florensac F C6
7 Florenville B B3
38 Flores de Avila E B1
7 Floresta I B3
85 Floridia I B4
108 Flórina GR B3
67 Flörsheim D A4
7 Floß D B3
109 Floytá GR A5
73 Flühli CH B3
70 Flumet F C1
84 Fluminimaggiore I C1
71 Flums CH A4
75 Foca TR B8
101 Foča YU C3
7 Fochabers GB C5

59 Fockbek D A6
94 Focșani RO D7
112 Fódele, *Kriti* GR
53 Fogda S C2
80 Fóggia I C2
79 Foglianise I B5
73 Föhrsdorf A A4
76 Foiano della Chiana I C1
112 Foinikas GR E1
35 Foix F A4
100 Fojnica YU C2
99 Földeák H B5
112 Folegandros GR E2
21 Folembray F C6
31 Folgosinho P D3
30 Folgoso de Caurel E B3
30 Folgoso de la Ribera E A4
78 Foligno I A3
52 Folkärna S B2
14 Folkingham GB B1
46 Folkestone GB C4
64 Folldal N E4
50 Follebu N B1
78 Follina I C2
110 Folói GR B2
78 Follónica I A1
30 Foncebadón E B3
25 Foncine-le-Haut F B6
7 Fondi I B6
24 Fondo I A1
44 Fonelas E B3
34 Fonfría, *Teruel* E B1
31 Fonfría, *Zamora* E C4
87 Fonni I B2
30 Fonsagrada E A3
35 Font-Romeu F A5
29 Fontaine F A4
29 Fontaine de Vaucluse F C4
25 Fontaine-Française F A5
24 Fontaine-le-Dun F B1
21 Fontainebleau F C3
24 Fontaines F B4
74 Fontanélice I B1
24 Fontanières F B2
44 Fontanosas E A2
23 Fontenay-le-Comte F B3
21 Fontenay-Trésigny F C3
23 Fontevrault-l'Abbaye F A5
38 Fontiveros E B1
66 Fontoy F A1
35 Fontpédrouse F A5
34 Fontrubí E B4
5 Fontstown IRL B5
99 Fonyód H B2
34 Fonz E A3
71 Fonzaso I B1
74 Fóppolo I B2
67 Forbach D C3
66 Forbach F B3
40 Forcall E B2
29 Forcalquier F C4
30 Forcarey E B2
67 Forchheim, *Baden-Württemberg* D B4
67 Forchheim, *Bayern* D B2
98 Forchtenau A A1
8 Forchtenberg D B5
8 Ford GB B2
48 Førde, *Hordaland* N B2
46 Førde, *Sogn og Fjordane* N F2
13 Förderstedt D C4
14 Fordham GB B3
13 Fordingbridge GB C5
58 Fordon PL B4
87 Fordongiánus I C1
80 Forenza I D2
15 Forest Row GB C4
84 Foresta di Burgos I B1
17 Forêt B B5
73 Forfar GB B5
20 Forges-les-Eaux F A2
82 Foria I B5
104 Forino YU D3
79 Forjães P C2
31 Forlì I C4
76 Forlimpopoli I B2
56 Forlösa S C4
70 Formazza I B2
10 Formerie F B5
79 Fórmia I B5
46 Formigliana I A3
96 Formiguères F A5
46 Formofoss N D6
7 Fornalutx, *Mallorca* E
87 Fornelli I A1
41 Fornells, *Menorca* E
30 Fornelos de Montes E B2
44 Forni Avoltri I B2
72 Forni di Sopra I B2
72 Forni di Sotto I B2
70 Forno I C2
74 Forno Alpi-Gráie I A2
72 Forno di Zoldo I B2
31 Fornos de Algodres P D3
74 Fornovo di Taro I B5
102 Forotic RO A2
99 Forráskút H B4
7 Forres GB C5
52 Forsbacka S B3
51 Forserum S C4
52 Forshaga S D2
7 Forsinain GB B5
8 Forsinard Station GB B5
57 Förslövsholm S C1
52 Forsmark S B4
53 Forssa SF F11
64 Forst D A5
8 Fort Augustus GB C4
16 Fort Mahon Plage F A1
8 Fort William GB B3
75 Forte dei Marmi I C5
72 Fortezza (Franzensfeste) I B1
7 Fortrie GB C6
7 Fortrose GB C4

45 Fortuna E A5
13 Fortuneswell GB C5
17 Forville B C4
34 Fos F A3
75 Fosdinovo I B5
14 Fosdyke GB B2
90 Fosowskie PL C2
79 Fossacesia I A5
74 Fossano I B2
76 Fossato di Vico I C2
17 Fosse B C4
76 Fossombrone I C2
99 Fót H A4
106 Fotina BG B2
106 Fotolivi GR B2
71 Fouchères F C5
18 Fouesnant F C1
112 Foufouras, *Kriti* GR
66 Foug F C2
19 Fougères F B4
66 Fougerolles F D2
10 Foulain F C6
15 Four Marks GB B1
24 Fourchambault F A3
108 Foúrka, *Ioánnina* GR A3
109 Foúrka, *Khalkidhikí* GR A5
21 Fourmies F A5
112 Fournés, *Kriti* GR
112 Foúrnoi GR C1
24 Fournols F A5
35 Fourques F A5
27 Fourquevaux F A5
24 Fours F B3
105 Foustáni GR A4
13 Fovant GB B5
10 Fowey GB C3
10 Foxdale GB A1
2 Foxford IRL C2
11 Foxholes GB A5
4 Foynes IRL B2
30 Foz E A3
36 Foz do Arelho P B1
36 Foz do Douro P C2
36 Foz do Giraldo P B3
72 Foza I C1
74 Frabosa Soprana I B2
12 Fraddon GB C3
38 Frades E B1
34 Fraga E B3
83 Fragagnano I A4
44 Frailes E B3
17 Fraire B C4
66 Fraize F C3
89 Framork PL A5
16 Frameries B C3
11 Framlingham GB B4
67 Frammersbach D A5
49 Frannes N B7
31 França P C4
66 Francaltroff F A5
79 Francavilla al Mare I A5
85 Francavilla di Sicília I B4
83 Francavilla Fontana I A4
82 Francavilla in Sinni I A3
31 Franco P C2
85 Francofonte I B3
33 Francos E B3
51 Franekere S D3
58 Franeker NL B2
108 Frangista GR C3
112 Frangokástello, *Kriti* GR
109 Frangóskala GR C3
25 Frangy F B5
62 Frankenau D C4
62 Frankenberg D C4
64 Frankenberg D A4
69 Frankenburg A D4
96 Frankenfels A D1
69 Frankenmarkt A B4
67 Frankenthal D B4
7 Frankford, see Kilcormac IRL A4
64 Frankfurt D A4
64 Frankfurt D A4
89 Frankowo PL A6
46 Fränsta S E8
73 Frantschach D C3
64 Franzburg D A3
73 Frascati I D3
73 Frasdorf D D3
7 Fraserburgh GB C7
108 Frashër AL A4
25 Frasne F B5
21 Frasnes B A5
27 Frasnes-lez-Buissenal B C3
86 Frasseto F B2
71 Frastanz A A4
36 Fratel P B3
73 Fratta Todina I A3
71 Frauemtal A C5
69 Frauenau D C4
71 Frauenfeld CH A3
96 Frauenkirchen A D2
64 Frauenstein D C3
27 Frayssinet F B4
27 Frayssinet-le-Gélat F B4
27 Frechas P C3
62 Frechen D C2
62 Freckenhorst D B3
62 Fredeburg D B4
62 Fredelsloh D B4
63 Freden D A7
51 Fredensborg DK C5
55 Fredericia DK B2
55 Frederiks DK B2
55 Frederikshavn DK A3
55 Frederikssund DK C5
55 Frederiksværk DK C5
51 Fredheim N B1
51 Fredrika S D9
51 Fredriksberg S C5
55 Fredrikstad N C1
27 Fregenal de la Sierra E A3
19 Fregene I B3
64 Freiberg D C3
67 Freiburg, *Baden-Württemberg* D D3
59 Freiburg, *Niedersachsen* D B6
62 Freienhagen D B4
63 Freienhufen D A5
62 Freienohl D B4
67 Freihung D B3
72 Freilassing D A3
64 Freisach D C4
72 Freising D C2
69 Freistadt A C5
67 Freistett D C4
64 Freital D C3
31 Freixedas P D3
31 Freixo de Espada a Cinta P C4

29 Fréjus F C5
68 Fremdingen D C1
12 Fremington GB B3
2 Frenchpark IRL B3
97 Frenštát p. Radhoštěm CS B4
59 Freren D C4
5 Freshford IRL B3
19 Fresnay-sur-Sarthe F B6
17 Fresne-St.Mamès F A5
39 Fresneda de la Sierra E B4
33 Fresneda de la Sierra Tiron E B3
39 Fresnedillas E B3
66 Fresnes-en-Woevre F B1
32 Fresno Alhándiga E B1
32 Fresno de la Ribera E C1
32 Fresno de la Vega E B5
31 Fresno de Sayago E C5
21 Fresnoy F B2
21 Fresnoy-le-Grand F B4
21 Fressenville F A2
25 Fretigney et Velloreille F A5
7 Freuchie GB B5
64 Freudenberg D C2
67 Freudenstadt D C4
7 Freux B B1
16 Frévent F A2
63 Freyburg D B6
60 Freyenstein D B3
69 Freyung D C4
40 Frias de Abarracin E B1
70 Fribourg CH B2
7 Frick CH A3
57 Fridafors S C3
73 Fridaythorpe GB A5
72 Friedberg, *Bayern* D C1
68 Friedberg, *Hessen* D A4
61 Friedeburg D B4
61 Friedenshorst D B3
62 Friedewalde D A3
61 Friedland D A3
63 Friedland, *Frankfurt* D A4
61 Friedland, *Neubrandenburg* D B3
62 Friedrichroda D C5
62 Friedrichsdof D C3
62 Friedrichsgabe D B6
71 Friedrichshafen D A4
64 Friedrichskoog D A6
64 Friedrichstadt D A6
61 Friedrichswalde D B4
64 Friesack D C2
61 Friesenheim D C3
69 Friesoythe D B7
31 Frigento I C2
40 Frigiliana E C2
15 Frillesås S A5
15 Frinton GB B5
30 Friockheim GB B5
56 Fristad S B1
56 Fritsla S B1
63 Fritzlar D B4
73 Frizington GB A2
10 Frodsham GB B3
29 Fröes F A4
7 Frohburg D B2
62 Frohnhausen D A4
62 Frohnleiten A A5
21 Froissy F B3
13 Frome GB B4
21 Fromentières F C4
32 Frómista E B3
60 Fronhausen D B4
23 Fronteira P B3
74 Front I A2
23 Frontenay-Rohan-Rohan F B3
68 Frontenhausen D C3
20 Frontignan F C2
27 Fronton F C5
79 Frosinone I B3
46 Frosolone I B3
29 Frossay F A4
46 Frosta N E7
61 Frøstrup DK A1
62 Frotheim D A3
66 Frouard F C2
66 Frövi S C2
16 Froyen F A1
16 Fruges F A4
97 Frýdek-Mistek CS B4
97 Frýdlant, *Severočeský* CS B5
97 Frýdlant, *Severomoravsky* CS B4
96 Fryšták CS B3
110 Ftéri GR A3
70 Fucécchio I C5
79 Fuencaliente E A2
32 Fuencemillán E B4
38 Fuendejalón E C1
38 Fuengirola E C2
38 Fuenlabrada E B3
38 Fuenlabrada de los Montes E C2
44 Fuensanta de Martos E B3
45 Fuenta-Alamo de Murcia E A5
32 Fuente al Olmo de Iscar E A2
45 Fuente-Álamo E A5
43 Fuente de Cantos E A4
38 Fuente de San Esteban E B4
38 Fuente de Sta. Cruz E A2
43 Fuente del Arco E A4
37 Fuente del Conde E B?
37 Fuente del Maestre E A4
40 Fuente el Fresno E C3
32 Fuente el Saz E B3
38 Fuente el Sol E A1
43 Fuente Espina E B3
43 Fuente la Higuera E B2
43 Fuente Obejuna E A4
44 Fuente-Palmera E B4
43 Fuente-Tójar E B3
45 Fuente Vaqueros E B3
43 Fuentecén E B3
37 Fuenteguinaldo E D4
32 Fuentealbilla E C5
32 Fuentealamo E C5

33 Fuentelcésped E C3
39 Fuentelespino de Haro E C4
40 Fuentelespino de Moya E B1
32 Fuentenovilla E B1
38 Fuentepelayo E A2
38 Fuenterroble de Salvatierra E B1
39 Fuentes E C4
43 Fuentes de Andalucia E B4
34 Fuentes de Ebro E B2
39 Fuentes de la Alcarria E B4
32 Fuentes de León E A3
32 Fuentes de Nava E B2
31 Fuentes de Oñoro E B1
32 Fuentes de Ropel E B1
32 Fuentesauco, *Segovia* E C2
32 Fuentesauco, *Zamora* E C1
34 Fuentespalda E C3
39 Fuentidueña E C3
39 Fuentidueña de Tajo E B3
33 Fuentipinilla E B3
44 Fuerte del Rey E B3
72 Fügen A A1
44 Fuglebjerg DK C4
49 Fuglevik N B7
59 Fuhrberg D C6
25 Fuissé F B4
63 Fulda D C4
84 Fulgatore I B1
35 Fulioala E E7
70 Fully CH B2
96 Fulnek CS B3
34 Fulpmes A A1
103 Fülöpszállás H B4
21 Fumay F A5
27 Fumel F B4
103 Fumureni RO B5
46 Fünäsdalen S E6
36 Fundão P A3
33 Funes I B1
6 Funzie, *Shetland Is.* GB
31 Furadouro P D2
103 Furculești RO C6
30 Furiolo E B3
9 Fürstenau, *Niedersachsen* D C4
9 Fürstenau, *Nordrhein-Westfalen* D B4
61 Fürstenberg D B4
69 Fürstenstein D C4
73 Fürstenfeld A A5
68 Fürstenfeldbruck D C2
64 Fürstenwalde D A5
69 Fürstenwerder D B4
69 Fürstenzell D C4
68 Fürth, *Bayern* D B1
67 Fürth, *Hessen* D B4
67 Furth i. Wald D B3
67 Furtwangen D C4
52 Furudal S D2
56 Furulund S D2
48 Fusa N A2
82 Fuscaldo I B3
72 Fusch A B3
70 Fusio CH B3
71 Füssen D B5
33 Fustiñana E B5
97 Füzesabony H D6
21 Fyé F B2
55 Fynshav DK D2
49 Fyresdal N B5
7 Fyvie GB C6

G

73 Gaaldorf A A4
39 Gabaldón E C5
103 Gabare BG A3
96 Gabčíkovo CS D3
100 Gabela YU C2
105 Gaber BG A4
44 Gabia la Grande E B3
90 Gabin PL A3
95 Gabra BG A3
28 Gabriac F B1
106 Gabrovo BG A3
20 Gacé F B1
101 Gacko YU C4
46 Gäddede S D7
60 Gadebush D B2
59 Gadeland D A7
70 Gadmen CH B3
45 Gádor E B5
95 Gádoros H B5
103 Gadovets BG C5
102 Gadzin Han YU C3
19 Gael F B3
79 Gaeta I B3
36 Gafanhoeira P C2
29 Gaflenz A D5
67 Gaggenau D C4
79 Gagliano Castelferrato I B3
83 Gagliano del Capo I B5
52 Gagnef S A1
76 Gaibanella I B1
67 Gaildorf D B5
28 Gaillac F C5
28 Gaillac-d'Aveyron F B1
20 Gaillon F B2
91 Gainfarn A D2
11 Gainsborough GB B5
8 Gairloch GB C3
8 Gairlochy GB B3
9 Gairnshiel Lodge GB C5
87 Gáiro I C2
102 Gaj YU B2
95 Gajanejos E B4
96 Gajary CS C2
96 Gajdobra YU A4
28 Galan F C4
96 Galanta CS C3
31 Galápagos E B3
44 Galaroza E B3
8 Galashiels GB C5
111 Galatas, *Argolis* GR B3
110 Galatas, *Korinthia* GR B3
112 Galatas, *Kriti* GR
94 Galați RO D7
108 Galátina GR A4
83 Galátina I A5
108 Galatini GR A3

109 Galátista GR A5
83 Galátone I A5
110 Galaxidhion GR A3
76 Galeata I C1
30 Galende E B4
45 Galera E B4
86 Gáleria F A1
99 Galgaheviz H A4
99 Galgamácsa H A4
10 Galgate GB B3
26 Galgon F A3
103 Galicea RO B5
103 Galicea Mare RO B4
36 Galices P A3
104 Galicnik YU C2
38 Galinduste E B1
112 Galisás GR E1
37 Galisteo E B4
90 Gałków PL B3
20 Gallardon F C2
31 Gallegos de Argañán E D4
38 Gallegos del Solmirón E B1
32 Galleguillos de Campos E B1
70 Galleno I C5
70 Gallneukirchen A C5
99 Gállio I C1
83 Gallipoli I A5
47 Gállivare S C10
73 Gallizien A A3
56 Gällstad S B2
34 Gallur E B2
103 Galovo BG C5
8 Galston GB C3
87 Galtelli I B2
55 Galten DK B2
71 Galtür A B5
36 Galveias P B2
38 Gálvez E C2
4 Galway IRL B2
20 Gamaches F A2
85 Gambárie I A4
75 Gambassi I C5
80 Gambatesa I C1
47 Gammelkarleby SF E11
56 Gamleby S B5
14 Gammlingay GB B2
55 Gammel Lundby DK A4
54 Gammel Skagen DK A3
67 Gammertinger D C5
71 Gams CH A4
73 Gams b. Hieflau A A5
71 Gams o. Frauental A B5
102 Gamzigrad YU C3
69 Ganacker D C3
31 Gánama E C4
71 Ganda di Martello I B5
71 Gandarela I C2
48 Ganddal N C2
59 Ganderkesee D B5
34 Gandesa E B3
40 Gandia E C2
54 Gandrup DK A3
9 Ganges F C2
56 Gånghester S B2
84 Gangi I B3
68 Gangkofen D C3
24 Gannat F B3
96 Gänserndorf A C2
72 Ganzlin D B3
29 Gap F B5
9 Gara H B4
106 Gara Krichim BG B2
103 Gara Lakatnik BG B1
106 Gara Ograzhden BG B3
105 Gara Pirin BG C5
40 Garabella I B3
82 Garaguso I A3
112 Garazon, *Kriti* GR
38 Garbayuela E C1
14 Garboldisham GB B3
91 Garbów PL B6
68 Garching D C3
96 Garcihernández E B1
38 Garcillán E B2
39 Garcinarro E B4
71 Garda I C6
20 Gardanne F C4
55 Gårdby S B3
59 Gardelegen D C2
49 Gardermoen N B7
71 Gardone Riviera I C5
71 Gardone Val Trómpia I C5
99 Gárdony H A3
27 Gardouch F C5
59 Gardelegen D C2
51 Gårdsjö, *Kopparberg* S
51 Gårdsjö, *Skaraborg* S D5
51 Garein F C3
29 Garéoult F C4
96 Gareskiča YU C3
29 Garelochhead GB B3
63 Gareskiča YU D5
98 Gargaliáni GR B2
37 Gargaligas E C1
34 Gargallo E B2
71 Garganta la Olla E A2
71 Gargantiel E A2
24 Gargilesse F B1
32 Gárgoles de Abajo E B4
58 Garijp NL B2
26 Garlin F C3
73 Garlasco I A4
26 Garlin F C3
8 Garlieston GB D4
72 Garmisch-Partenkirchen D A6
69 Garmo N F4
7 Garmouth GB C5
59 Garnat H B4
45 Gánave E B4
71 Garpenberg S B3
52 Garphyttan S C1
59 Garrafe de Torio E B1
30 Garray E A4
59 Garrel D C4
87 Garriguella E A6
34 Garrovillas E A6
45 Garrucha E B5
96 Gars-a-Kamp A C1
96 Garsås S B5
10 Garsdale GB A3

57 Gärsnäs S D3
10 Garstang GB B3
60 Garten A C5
60 Gartow D B2
61 Gartz D B5
7 Garvagh GB B5
7 Garvaghey GB B4
86 Garvão P B1
99 Garwolin PL B6
93 Garwolin PL E7
26 Garynahine GB B2
12 Garz D A3
65 Garzyn PL B6
71 Gaschurn A B5
39 Gascueña E B4
97 Gasny F B2
110 Gastoúni GR B2
110 Gastoúri GR B1
37 Gata E B4
100 Gata de Gorgos E C3
34 Gatarroja E B2
93 Gatchina SU A12
99 Gatehouse of Fleet GB D3
99 Gáter H B3
9 Gateshead GB D6
8 Gátova E B2
67 Gattendorf A C2
76 Gatteo a Mare I B2
70 Gattinara I C3
11 Gattorna I C3
43 Gaucin E C4
36 Gaurain-Ramecroix B C3
68 Gauting D C3
8 Gavaloú GR B2
8 Galston GB C3
87 Galtelli I B2
55 Gavarnie F A3
34 Gavi I B3
74 Gavião P C2
70 Gavirate I C3
52 Gävle S B5
78 Gavorrano I A1
110 Gavrion GR E1
112 Gavron GR A2
67 Gavrolimni GR A2
50 Gåvunda S B5
7 Gaweinstal A C2
88 Gawroniec PL B3
90 Gawrolin PL B4
14 Gayton GB B2
55 Gazoros GR A5
71 Gazzaniga I C4
73 Gbelce CS C3
96 Gbely CS C3
89 Gdańsk PL A4
89 Gdów PL B4
89 Gdynia PL A4
40 Gea de Albarracin E A1
29 Geaune F C3
56 Gebesee D B5
63 Gebra-Hainleite D B5
64 Gebrazhofen D B5
107 Geçkinli TR B4
99 Gederlak H B3
63 Gedern D C4
28 Gedinne B B2
34 Gédre F A3
55 Gedser DK B2
58 Gedsted DK B2
45 Gedved DK B2
56 Geel S B5
58 Geertruidenberg NL B4
62 Geesthacht D B1
17 Geetbets B C5
67 Gefell D C2
67 Gefrees D B6
63 Gegenbach D C4
63 Gehrden D A4
63 Gehren D C6
46 Geilenkirchen D C1
46 Geilo N F4
21 Geiranger N E3
68 Geiselhöring D C3
67 Geiselwind D B1
91 Geisenfeld D C2
63 Geisenheim D A4
64 Geisingen D D4
64 Geisingen, *Baden-Württemberg* D D4
73 Geistthal A A5
46 Geithus N B6
63 Gela I B3
63 Geldermalsen NL B5
46 Geldern D B1
45 Géldo E B2
23 Gençay F B5
68 Gendringen NL B?
17 Gendrinkhagen?
29 Gençlik?
92 Genicsápati H B2
112 Genicsápati?
96 Gendt NL B?
17 Geneiten?
97 Geneulhaut?

96 Gelderkinden CH A2
91 Gelenbach D C2
46 Geilenkirchen D C1
45 Gelida E B4
29 Geisa D C4
55 Geltendorf D C2
103 Gigen BG C1
13 Gigant?
25 Gignac, *Aude* E C4
13 Gignac, *Bouches-du-Rhône* F C4
43 Gijón E A1
7 Gilching D C2
63 Gildehaus D C4
96 Gilena E B4
3 Gilford GB B5
96 Gileppe B C1
25 Gilley, *Doubs* F C4
26 Gilley, *Saône-et-Loire* F
13 Gillingham, *Dorset* GB B5
15 Gillingham, *Kent* GB C3
8 Gilroanie GB D3
7 Gilly F B2
26 Gilocourt F B5
63 Gilserberg D C4
13 Gilwern GB B2
28 Gilze NL C4
96 Gimborn D B2
52 Gimo S B4
29 Gimont F C4
7 Gimont F B4
24 Ginasservis F C4
103 Gi-ngiova RO C4
26 Gingst D A4
7 Ginsheim-

23 Genillé F A6
17 Genk B C5
27 Genkingen D C5
25 Genlis F A5
17 Gennep NL B5
55 Genner DK B2
23 Gennes F A4
74 Genola I B2
7 Genolhac F C2
74 Génova I B3
90 Genowefa PL A2
67 Gensinger D B3
64 Genthin D C2
21 Gentioux F C1
17 Genval B C4
78 Genzano di Lucánia I D3
78 Genzano di Roma I B3
63 Georgenthal D C5
64 Gera D C2
16 Geraardsbergen B C3
85 Gerace I C3
84 Geraci Sículo I B3
109 Gerakini GR A5
96 Gérardmer F C2
96 Geras A C1
96 Gerasdorf A C2
66 Gerbéviller F C2
63 Gerbstedt D B6
48 Gérgal E B4
112 Gérgen, *Kriti* GR
38 Gerindote E C2
64 Geringswalde D B3
99 Gerjen H B3
25 Gerlingen D A5
72 Gerlos A A2
66 Germay F C1
112 Germencik TR B1
61 Germendorf D C4
68 Germering D C2
63 Germersheim D B4
108 Gérnec AL A1
64 Gernrode D B6
67 Gernsbach D C4
69 Gernsheim D B4
63 Geroda D C5
63 Gerola Alta I B4
63 Geroldsgrün D C6
68 Gerolfingen D C1
62 Gerolstein D C1
63 Gerolzhofen D B5
35 Gerona E B5
73 Gerovo YU C4
63 Gersfeld D C4
63 Gerstetten D C5
63 Gerstungen D C1
63 Gerswalde D B4
70 Gerswil CH B2
28 Gerzat F C3
24 Gex F B6
26 Gey D C2
64 Gey D?
96 Gföhl A C1
71 Ghedi I C5
94 Gheorgheni RO C6
86 Ghi F B2
96 Ghigo I B2
87 Ghilarza I B1
110 Ghisonaccia F C?
110 Giáltou GR C3
46 Giardinetto I B?
96 Giardini I B4
71 Giarratana I B3
24 Giat F C6
74 Giaveno I A1
71 Giazza I C6
81 Giba I C1
108 Gibellina I B1
43 Gibraleón E B3
14 Gibraltar GBZ C3
98 Gic H A2
63 Giebelstadt D B5
46 Gieboldehausen D B4
90 Gielniów PL B4
46 Gielow D B3
7 Gien F A2
63 Giengen D C6
29 Giens F C5
96 Gieselwerder D B4
63 Gießen D C4
46 Giethoorn NL C3
11 Gifford GB C5
51 Gilberga S B?
3 Gilford GB B5
96 Gilena E B4
3 Gilford GB B5
26 Gilley, *Doubs* F C4
26 Gilley, *Saône-et-Loire* F C4
13 Gillingham, *Dorset* GB B5
15 Gillingham, *Kent* GB C3
13 Gilroanie GB B2
7 Gilly F B2
26 Gilocourt F B5
63 Gilserberg D C4
13 Gilwern GB B2
28 Gilze NL C4
96 Gimborn D B2
11 Gimdalen S B2
52 Gimo S B4
29 Gimont F C4
24 Ginasservis F C4
103 Gi-ngiova RO C4
26 Gingst D A4
67 Ginsheim-

Gustavsberg D B4
72 Ginzling A A1
42 Giões P B2
79 Gioia dei Marsi I B4
80 Gióia del Colle I D3
79 Gióia Sannitica I B5
82 Gióia Táuro I C2
85 Gioiosa Iónica I A5
85 Gioiosa Marea I A3
80 Giovinazzo I C3
103 Girbovu RO B4
103 Gircov RO C5
102 Girnic RO B2
66 Giromagny F D2
35 Girona see Gerona E B5
66 Gironcourt F C1
35 Gironella E A4
66 Gironville-sous-les-Côtes F C1
8 Girvan GB C3
10 Gisburn GB B3
6 Gisla GB B2
56 Gislaved S B2
55 Gislev DK C3
57 Gislövsläge S D2
20 Gisors F B2
79 Gissi I A5
53 Gisslarbo S C1
53 Gistad S D1
16 Gistel B B2
54 Gistrup DK B3
103 Giubega RO B4
71 Giubiasco CH B4
79 Giugliano I C5
103 Giuleşti RO B4
79 Giulianova I A4
95 Giurgiu RO E6
103 Giuvărăşti RO C5
55 Give DK C2
21 Givet F A5
21 Givonne F B6
25 Givors F C4
25 Givry F B4
55 Givskud DK C2
90 Giżalki PL A1
23 Gizeux F A5
82 Gizzeria I C3
82 Gizzeria Lido I C3
55 Gjedved DK C2
54 Gjerlev DK B3
48 Gjermundshamn N A2
54 Gjerrild DK B3
49 Gjerstad N C6
50 Gjesås N B2
108 Gjirokastër AL A2
54 Gjøl DK A2
49 Gjøvdal N C5
50 Gjøvik N B1
62 Gladbach D C1
62 Gladbeck D B1
62 Gladenbach D C3
109 Glafirá GR B4
109 Gláfki GR B4
9 Glamis GB B5
100 Glamoč YU B1
55 Glamsbjerg DK C3
29 Glandage F B4
62 Glandorf D A2
73 Glanegg A B4
62 Glanerbrug NL A1
53 Glanshammer S C1
71 Glarus CH A4
3 Glasdrummond GB B6
8 Glasgow GB C3
64 Glashütte D C3
72 Glashütte, *Bayern* D A1
59 Glashütte, *Hamburg* D B7
13 Glastonbury GB B5
70 Glattfelden CH A3
64 Glauchau D C2
51 Glava S C3
51 Glavaglasbruk S C3
107 Glavan BG A4
105 Glavanovisi BG B4
100 Glavatičevo YU C3
101 Glavičice YU B4
104 Glavnik YU B3
97 Glebowice PL B5
101 Gledica YU C5
17 Glehn D B6
73 Gleisdorf A A5
14 Glemsford GB B3
2 Glenade IRL B3
2 Glenamoy IRL B2
3 Glenarm GB B6
3 Glenavy GB B5
8 Glenbarr GB C2
4 Glenbeigh IRL B2
8 Glencoe GB B2
2 Glencolumbkille IRL B3
5 Glenealy IRL B5
3 Gleneely IRL A4
6 Glenelg GB C3
3 Glenfarne IRL B4
8 Glenfinnan GB B2
4 Glengarriff IRL C2
9 Glenkerry GB C4
8 Glenluce GB D3
23 Glénouze F B4
9 Glenrothes GB B4
2 Glenties IRL B3
60 Gleschendorf D A1
64 Glesien D B2
70 Gletsch CH B3
109 Glifa, *Fthiótis* GR C4
110 Glifa, *Ilía* GR B2
109 Glifáda, *Évia* GR C5
108 Glifáda, *Kérkira* GR B1
111 Glifádha GR B4
108 Gliki GR B2
57 Glimåkra S C3
4 Glin IRL B2
59 Glinde D B7
89 Glinojeck PL C6
4 Glinsk IRL A2
90 Gliwice PL C2
104 Globocnica YU B3
73 Glödnitz A B4
73 Gloggnitz A A5
97 Glogoczów PL B5
102 Glogovac YU B2
65 Glogów PL B6
91 Glogów Małoposki PL C5
90 Glogówek PL C1
18 Glomel F B2
56 Glommen S C1
47 Glommersträsk S D9
68 Glonn D D2
71 Glorenza (Glurns) I B5
36 Gloria P B2
109 Glośsa GR B5
54 Glöstorp S A4
13 Gloucester GB B5
70 Glovelier CH A2
91 Glowaczów PL B5
88 Glówczyce PL A3
60 Glöwen D C3
90 Glówno PL B3
101 Glożan YU A4
103 Glozhene BG C4
103 Glozhene BG C5
90 Glucholazy PL C1
91 Gluchów PL B4
65 Gluchowo PL A6
55 Glücksburg D D2
59 Glückstadt D B6
55 Glumsø DK C4
101 Glušci YU B4
71 Glusone I C4
65 Gluszyca PL C6
13 Glyn Neath GB B4
54 Glyngøre DK B1
72 Gmünd, *Karnten* A B3
69 Gmünd, *Nieder Östereich* A C5
68 Gmund D D2
69 Gmunden A D4
73 Gnesau A B3
53 Gnesta S C3
65 Gnięchowice PL C6
89 Gniew PL B4
89 Gniewkowo PL C4
88 Gniezno PL C3
104 Gnjilane YU B3
61 Gnoien D B3
91 Gnojno PL C4
11 Gnosall GB C3
56 Gnosjö S B2
10 Gobowen GB C2
17 Goch D B6
68 Gochsheim D A1
15 Godalming GB C2
62 Goddelsheim D B3
103 Godech BG C4
72 Gódega di S. Urbano I C2
53 Godegård S D1
63 Godelheim D B4
103 Goden RO A5
20 Goderville F B1
74 Godiasco I B4
89 Godkowo PL A5
14 Godmanchester GB B2
99 Gödöllo H A4
9 Godon GB C5
98 Gödreszentmárton H B2
15 Godshill GB D1
15 Godstone GB C2
90 Godzikowice PL C1
89 Godziszewo PL A4
16 Goes N B3
66 Goetzenbrück F C3
68 Goggingen D C1
10 Goginan GB C2
70 Góglio I B3
90 Gogolin PL C2
102 Gogoşu RO B3
62 Gohfeld D A3
61 Göhren D A4
17 Goirle NL B5
36 Góis P A2
75 Góito I A5
33 Goizueta E A5
101 Gojna Gora YU C5
89 Gójsk PL C5
46 Gol N F4
30 Golada E B2
88 Golańcz PL C3
61 Golańcz-Pomorska PL A6
66 Golbey F C2
96 Golčuv Jenikov CS B1
61 Golczewo PL B5
71 Goldach CH A4
93 Goldap PL C8
67 Goldbach D A5
60 Goldbeck D C2
60 Goldberg D B3
59 Goldenstedt D C5
11 Goldthorpe GB B4
4 Goleen IRL C2
36 Golega P B2
105 Golema Rakovitsa BG B5
105 Golemo Selo YU B3
61 Goleniów PL B5
101 Goleša YU C4
87 Golfo Aranci I B2
90 Golina PL A2
106 Goljam Iswor BG B3
98 Gölle H B3
96 Göllersdorf A C2
61 Gollin D B4
72 Golling A A3
39 Gollocanta E B5
96 Gols A D2
7 Golspie GB C5
64 Golßen D B3
89 Golub-Dobrzyń PL B5
102 Golubac YU B2
101 Golubinci YU B5
104 Golubovci YU B1
90 Goluchów PL B1
107 Golyam Manastir BG A4
106 Golyamo Belovo BG A2
106 Golyamo Konare BG A2
107 Golyamo Shivachevo BG A4
89 Golynim Stary PL C6
64 Golzow D A2
33 Gómara E C4
67 Gomaringer D C5
109 Gomátion GR A5
93 Gomel SU D12
42 Gomes Aires P B1
32 Gómezserracin E C2
63 Gommern D A6
71 Gomogoi I B5
90 Gomulin PL B3
50 Gonäs S B6
29 Goncelin F A4
91 Gończyce PL B5
30 Gondomar E B2
31 Gondomar P C2
27 Gondrin F C4
95 Gonen TR F7
29 Gonfaron F C5
33 Goñi E B5
87 Goni I C2
112 Goniais, *Kriti* GR
87 Gonnesa I C1
67 Gönningen D C5
109 Gónnoi GR B4
87 Gonnosfanádiga I C1
98 Gönyü H A2
75 Gonzaga I B5
12 Goodwick GB A3
17 Gooik B C4
11 Goole GB B5
17 Goor NL A6
96 Göpfritz a. d. Wild A C1
70 Goppenstein CH B2
67 Göppingen D C5
44 Gor E B4
65 Góra PL B6
89 Góra PL C6
91 Góra Kalwaria PL B5
91 Góra Pulawska PL B5
90 Góra Św. Anny PL C2
90 Gora Zamkowa PL C3
44 Gorafe E B3
110 Goráni GR C3
61 Gorawino PL B6
101 Goražde YU C3
65 Gorce PL C6
66 Gorcy F B1
32 Gordaliza del Pino E B1
33 Gordejuela E A3
55 Gørding DK C1
71 Górdola CH B3
32 Gordoncillo E B1
5 Gorey IRL B5
108 Gorgómilos GR B2
71 Gorgonzola I C4
105 Gorgópi GR D4
98 Gorican YU B1
17 Gorinchem NL B4
15 Goring GB C1
61 Göritz, *Neubrandenburg* D B4
64 Göritz, *Potsdam* D A2
111 Goritzá GR B3
72 Gorízia I C3
60 Gorleben D B2
94 Gorlice PL B4
65 Görlitz D B4
33 Górliz E A4
61 Görmin D B4
103 Gorna Gnoynitsa BG C4
103 Gorna Kremena BG C4
104 Gornaj Klina YU B2
100 Gorni Klasnic YU A1
105 Gorni Okol BG B5
101 Gornja Gorevnica YU C5
102 Gornja Kamenica YU C3
77 Gornja Ploča YU B5
73 Gornja Radgona YU B5
102 Gornja Sabanta YU C2
101 Gornja Trešnjevica YU B5
101 Gornja Tuzla YU B3
81 Gornje Polje YU B5
100 Gornje Ratkovo YU B1
73 Gornji Grad YU B4
77 Gornji Klasnič YU A6
77 Gornji Kosinj YU B5
101 Gornji Milanovac YU B5
100 Gornji Podgradci YU A2
100 Gornji Vakuf YU C2
101 Gornji Žabar YU B3
91 Górno PL C4
107 Gorno Aleksandrovo BG A4
104 Gorno Nerezi YU C3
105 Gorno Orizari YU C3
105 Gorno Osenovo BG C5
103 Gorno Peshtene BG C4
105 Gorobinci YU C3
107 Gorovo BG A5
89 Górowo Iławeckie PL A6
58 Gorredijk NL B3
19 Gorron F B5
12 Gorseinon GB B3
107 Gorska Polyana BG A4
17 Gorssel NL A6
7 Gorstan GB C4
4 Gort IRL A3
3 Gortin GB B4
64 Görzke D A2
90 Gorzkowice PL B3
89 Górzno PL B5
90 Gorzów Sląski PL B2
61 Gorzow Wielkopolski PL C6
61 Górzyca PL C5
97 Gorzyce PL B4
65 Górzyn PL B4
14 Gosberton GB B2
88 Gościcino PL A4
91 Gościeradow PL C6
88 Gościno PL A1
73 Gosdorf A B5
10 Gosforth GB A2
63 Goslar D B5
89 Goslice PL C5
77 Gospić YU B5
15 Gosport GB D1
51 Gössäter S D4
71 Gossau CH A4
17 Gosselies B C4
64 Goßnitz D C2
104 Gostimë AL D2
104 Gostivar YU C2
90 Gostkow PL B3
69 Göstling a.d. Ybbs A D5
88 Gostomia PL B2
88 Gostycyn PL B3
65 Gostyn PL B7
90 Gostynin PL A3
90 Goszcz PL B1
88 Goszczanowo PL C1
51 Göta S D3
54 Göteborg S A4
51 Götene S D4
63 Gotha D C5
55 Gøtlev DK C4
105 Gotse Delchev BG C5
69 Gottersdorf D C3
63 Gottingen D B4
96 Gottwaldov (Zlin) CS B3
71 Götzis A A4
17 Gouda NL A4
15 Goudhurst GB C3
18 Gouesnou F B1
105 Gouménissa GR D4
110 Goúra GR B3
27 Gourdon F B5
9 Gourdon GB B5
18 Gourin F B2
20 Gournay-en-Bray F B2
8 Gourock GB C3
21 Goussancourt F B4
31 Gouveia P D3
112 Gouves, *Kriti* GR
21 Gouzeacourt F A4
24 Gouzon F B2
81 Govedari YU B4
105 Govedartsi BG B5
75 Govérnolo I A5
91 Gowarczów PL B4
12 Gowerton GB B3
64 Goyatz D A4
91 Gózd PL B5
65 Gozdnica PL B5
17 Gozee B C4
60 Graal-Müritz D A3
68 Grabenstätt D D3
100 Grabovac, *Hrvatska* YU C2
101 Grabovac, *Srbija* YU B5
101 Grabovci YU B4
60 Grabow D B2
91 Grabow PL B5
90 Grabów Łęczycki PL A2
90 Grabów-nad-Prosną PL B2
71 Grabs CH A4
77 Gračac YU B5
104 Gračanica, *A. P. Kosovo* YU B3
100 Gračanica, *Bosna i Hercegovina* YU B3
101 Gračanica, *Srbija* YU B4
24 Graçay F A1
104 Gracen AL C1
73 Grad YU B6
101 Gradac, *Crna Gora* YU C4
100 Gradac, *Hrvatska* YU C2
101 Gradac, *Srbija* YU C5
100 Gradačac YU B3
98 Gradec, *Hrvatska* YU C1
105 Gradec, *Makedonija* YU C4
32 Gradefes E B1
73 Grades A B4
107 Gradets BG A4
102 Gradets BG B3
105 Gradevo BG C5
26 Gradignan F B3
36 Gradil P C1
98 Gradina YU C2
103 Grădinaro RO B5
72 Gradisca d'Isonzo I C3
73 Gradišče YU B5
101 Gradište YU A3
30 Grado E A4
72 Grado I C3
105 Gradsko YU C3
89 Gradzanowo Kościelne PL C6
55 Græsted DK B5
106 Graf-Ignatievo BG A2
68 Grafelfing D C2
69 Grafenau D C4
68 Gräfenberg D B2
73 Grafendorf A A5
64 Gräfenhainichen D B2
69 Grafenschlag A C6
73 Grafenstein A B4
63 Gräfenthal D C6
63 Grafentonna D B5
68 Grafenwöhr D B2
68 Grafing D C2
69 Grafling D C3
68 Grafrath D C2
79 Gragnano I C5
73 Grahova YU B3
5 Graigue IRL B5
5 Graiguenamanagh IRL B4
67 Grailsheim D B6
15 Grain GB C3
71 Grainau D A6
11 Grainthorpe GB B6
40 Graja de Iniesta E B1
33 Grajera E C3
55 Gram DK C2
102 Gramada BG C3
71 Gramais A A5
27 Gramat F B5
107 Gramatikovo BG A5
96 Gramatneusiedl A C2
61 Grambow D B5
6 Gramisdale GB C1
52 Gramla Uppsala S C3
111 Grammatikón GR A4
109 Grammeni Oxiá GR C4
85 Grammichele I B3
104 Gramsh AL D2
61 Gramzow D B5
49 Gran N A7
44 Granada E B3
34 Granadella E B3
3 Granard IRL C4
30 Grañas E A3
44 Granátula de Calatrava E A3
25 Grancey-le-Château F A5
18 Grand-Champ F C3
20 Grand Couronne F B2
30 Grandas de Salime E A4
19 Grandcamp-Maisy F A4
70 Grandcour CH B1
42 Grândola P A1
21 Grandpré F B5
17 Grandrieu B C4
28 Grandrieu F B2
70 Grandson CH B1
28 Grandvals F B2
20 Grandvilliers F B2
34 Grañén E B2
50 Grangärde S B5
2 Grange IRL B3
10 Grange over Sands GB A3
9 Grangemouth GB B4
34 Granges-de Crouhens F A3
66 Granges-sur-Vologne F C2
50 Grängesberg S B6
60 Gräningen D C3
84 Granitola I B1
108 Granitsa GR B3
42 Granja P A2
34 Granja de Escarpe E B3
32 Granja de Moreruelo E C1
37 Granja de Torrehermosa E C5
56 Gränna S A3
35 Granollers E B5
47 Granön S D9
65 Granowo PL A6
61 Gransee D B4
49 Gransherad N B6
14 Grantham GB B2
7 Grantown-on-Spey GB C5
19 Granville F B4
46 Granvin N F3
40 Grao de Gandia E C2
40 Grao de Sagunto E B2
63 Grasleben D A6
10 Grasmere GB A2
52 Grasö S B4
80 Grassano I D3
68 Grassau D D3
74 Grasse F C1
11 Grassington GB A4
55 Gråsten DK D2
51 Grästorp S D3
47 Gratangen N B8
106 Gratini GR B3
73 Gratkorn A A5
73 Gratwein A A5
27 Graulhet F C6
34 Graus E A3
50 Gravberget N B3
17 Grave NL B5
71 Gravedona I B4
16 Gravelines F B2
70 Gravellona Toce I C3
16 Gravenpolder N B3
15 Gravesend GB C3
29 Graveson F C3
109 Graviá GR C4
80 Gravina in Púglia I D3
25 Gray F A5
15 Grays GB C3
15 Grayshott GB C2
73 Graz A A5
43 Grazalema E C4
89 Grazawy PL B5
75 Grazzano Visconti I B4
105 Grdelica YU B4
51 Greåker N C1
11 Great Ayton GB A4
15 Great Chesterford GB B3
10 Great Clifton GB A2
15 Great Cornard GB B3
15 Great Dunmow GB C3
10 Great Eccleston GB B3
13 Great Malvern GB A5
15 Great Missenden GB C2
15 Great Shefford GB C1
14 Great Shelford GB B3
12 Great Torrington GB C3
14 Great Yarmouth GB B4
11 Greatham GB A4
51 Grebbested S D2
63 Grebenstein D B4
89 Grębocin PL B4
68 Greding D B2
55 Gredstedbro DK C1
11 Green Hammerton GB B4
9 Greenhead GB D5
3 Greenisland GB B6
9 Greenlaw GB C5
8 Greenock GB C3
3 Greenore IRL B5
12 Greenway GB B3
17 Grefrath D B6
70 Greggio I C3
109 Gregolimano GR C4
72 Greifenburg A B3
61 Greiffenberg D B4
61 Greifswald D A4
69 Grein A C5
49 Greipstad N C4
64 Greiz D C2
60 Gremersdorf D A1
54 Grenå DK B3
27 Grenade F C5
26 Grenade-sur-l'Adour F C3
70 Grenchen CH A2
49 Grendi N C4
54 Grenen DK A3
29 Grenoble F A4
11 Grenside GB B4
29 Gréoux-les-Bains F C4
60 Gresenhorst D A3
6 Gress GB B2
70 Gressoney-la-Trinité I C2
70 Gressoney-St.-Jean I C2
67 Greßthal D A6
51 Gressvik N C1
69 Gresten A D6
9 Gretna GB D4
63 Greußen D B5
75 Greve I C6
60 Greven D B1
62 Greven D A2
108 Grevená GR A3
62 Grevenbroich D B1
62 Grevenbrück D B3
66 Grevenmecher L B2
60 Grevesmühlen D B2
55 Grevestrand DK C5
57 Grevie S C1
10 Greystoke GB A3
5 Greystones IRL A5
17 Grez-Doiceau B C4
19 Grez en Bouère F C5
27 Grèzec F B5
71 Grezzano I C6
101 Grgurevci YU A4
72 Gries A A1
67 Gries D B6
71 Gries in Sellrain A A6
69 Griesbach D C4
67 Griesheim D B4
69 Grieskirchen A C4
73 Griffen A B4
29 Grignan F B3
72 Grignano I C3
72 Grigno I B1
26 Grignols F B3
25 Grignon F C6
25 Grigny F C4
32 Grijota E B2
58 Grijpskerk NL B3
53 Grillby S C3
29 Grimaud F C5
17 Grimbergen B C4
64 Grimma D B2
61 Grimmen D A4
70 Grimmialp CH B2
56 Grimsås S B2
11 Grimsby GB B5
56 Grimslöv S C3
49 Grimstad N C5
56 Grimstorp S B3
70 Grindelwald CH B3
48 Grindheim N C4
55 Grindsted DK C1
38 Griñón E B3
56 Gripenberg S B3
53 Gripsholm S C3
27 Grisolles F C5
52 Grisslehamn S B4
7 Gritley GB B6
105 Grivas GR D4
103 Grivitsa BG C5
109 Grizanon GR B4
10 Grizebeck GB A2
64 Gröbers D B2
73 Gröbming A A3
63 Gröbzig D B6
91 Grochów PL A6
101 Grocka YU B5
64 Gröditz D B3
89 Gródki PL B6
65 Grodków PL C7
93 Grodno SU D8
90 Grodziec PL A2
97 Grodziec, *Bielsko-Biala* PL B4
65 Grodziec, *Legnica* PL B5
91 Grodzisk Maz. PL A4
65 Grodzisk Wielkopolski PL A6
62 Groenlo NL A1
12 Groes-goch GB B2
17 Groesbeek NL B5
100 Grohote YU C1
64 Groitzsch D B2
18 Groix F C2
91 Grójec PL B4
93 Grójec PL E7
89 Grom PL B6
100 Gromiljck YU C3
60 Grömitz D A1
71 Gromo I C4
63 Gronau, *Niedersachsen* D A4
62 Gronau, *Nordrhein-Westfalen* D A2
67 Grönenbach D D6
46 Grong N D6
57 Grönhögen S C5
63 Groningen D B6
67 Gröningen D B6
58 Groningen NL B3
71 Grono Roveredo CH B4
89 Gronowo PL A5
56 Grönskära S B4
58 Grootebroek NL C2
58 Grootegast NL B3
74 Gropello Cairoli I A3
103 Gropsani RO B4
49 Grorud N B7
71 Grósio I B5
101 Grošnica YU C5
64 Groß Beeren D A3
63 Groß Berkel D A4
63 Groß Denkte D A5
61 Groß-Dölln D C4
67 Groß-Gerau D B4
60 Groß Gronau D B1
63 Groß Ilsede D A5
64 Groß Kreutz D A2
63 Groß Lafferde D A5
68 Groß Mehring D C2
60 Groß Oesingen D C1
62 Groß Reken D B2
64 Groß Rosenburg D B1
64 Groß Sarchen D B4
63 Groß Schneen D B4
61 Groß Schönebeck D C4
96 Groß Schweinbarth A C2
67 Groß Umstadt D B4
60 Groß Warnow D B2
96 Groß Weikersdorf A C2
60 Groß-Welle D B3
60 Groß Wokern D B3
63 Großalmerode D B4
72 Großarl A A3
63 Großbodungen D B5
67 Großbotwar D B5
59 Großburgwedel D C6
64 Großchirma D C3
65 Großchönau D C4
60 Großenbrode D A2
63 Großengottern D B5
64 Großenhain D B3
59 Grossenkneten D C5
63 Großenlüder D C4
60 Großensee D B1
96 Großenzersdorf A C2
23 Grossereix F C6
67 Großerlach D B5
78 Grosseto I A2
69 Großgerungs A C5
69 Großglobnitz A C6
68 Großhabersdorf D B1
59 Großhansdorf D B7
96 Großharras A C2
64 Großhartmannsdorf D C3
70 Grosshöchstetten CH B2
96 Großhoflein A D2
96 Großkrut A C2
63 Großörner D B6
69 Großpertholz A C5
98 Großpetersdorf A A1
64 Großpostwitz D B4
69 Großraming A D5
64 Großräschen D B4
67 Grossrinderfeld D B5
64 Großröhrsdorf D B4
96 Großsiegharts A C1
73 Großsölk A A3
98 Großwarasdorf A A1
73 Großwilfersdorf A A6
66 Grostenquin F C2
90 Groszowice PL C1
46 Grotli N E3
83 Grottaglie I A4
80 Grottaminarda I C2
77 Grottammare I C3
78 Grotte di Castro I A2
85 Grotteria I A5
80 Gróttole I D3
58 Grouw NL B2
30 Grove E B2
49 Grua N A7
60 Grube D A2
98 Grubisno Polje YU C2
81 Gruda YU B5
100 Grude YU C2
107 Grudovo BG A5
89 Grudusk PL B6
91 Grudze PL A3
89 Grudziadz PL B4
50 Grue N B3
102 Gruia RO B3
28 Gruissan F C2
30 Grullos E A4
96 Grümbach a. Schneeberg A D1
80 Grumo Appula I C3
51 Grums S C4
69 Grünau i. Almtal A D4
62 Grünberg D C3
69 Grünburg A D5
67 Gründelhardt D B5
50 Grundforsen S A3
73 Grundlsee A A3
51 Grundsund S D2
63 Grünenplan D B4
64 Grunewald D B3
49 Grungedal N B4
64 Grunow D A4
67 Grünsfeld D B5
67 Grünstadt D B4
68 Grunwald D C2
89 Grunwald PL B6
89 Grupa Graniczna PL B4
104 Grupčin YU C3
6 Grutness, *Shetland Is.* GB
52 Gruvberget S A2
70 Gruyères CH B2
94 Grybów PL B4
52 Grycksbo S B1
61 Gryfice PL B6
61 Gryfino PL B5
65 Gryfów Ślaski PL B5
49 Grymyr N A7
53 Grytgol S D1
51 Grythyttan S C5
88 Grzmiaga PL B2
61 Grzybno PL B5
91 Grzybów PL C5
89 Grzywna PL B4
72 Gschnitz A A1
70 Gstaad CH B2
70 Gsteig CH B2
90 Gtubczyce PL C1
44 Guadahortuna E B3
39 Guadalajara E B3
39 Guadalaviar E B5
43 Guadalcanal E A4
43 Guadalcázar E B5
38 Guadalix de la Sierra E B3
44 Guadálmez E A2
38 Guadalupe E C1
38 Guadamur E C2
38 Guadarrama E B2
43 Guadiaro E C4
44 Guadix E B3
83 Guagnano I A4
86 Guagno F B1
44 Guajar-Faraguit E C3
76 Gualdo Tadino I C2
75 Gualtien I B5
79 Guarcino I B4
9 Guard Bridge GB B5
31 Guarda P D3
45 Guardamar del Segura E A6
31 Guardão P D2
83 Guardavalle I C3
78 Guardea I A3
80 Guardia I D2
79 Guárdia Sanframondi I B5
79 Guardiagrele I A5
79 Guardiarégia I B5
45 Guardias Viejas E C4
35 Guardiola de Berga E A4
32 Guardo E B2
37 Guareña E C4
44 Guaro E C2
44 Guarromán E A3
87 Guasila I C2
75 Guastalla I B5
76 Gúbbio I C2
65 Gubin PL B4
101 Guča YU C5
55 Güderup DK D2
57 Gudhjem DK D3
51 Gudhom S D4
66 Güdingen D B3
98 Gudovac YU C1
46 Gudvangen N F3
66 Guebwiller F D3
44 Guéjar-Sierra E B3
22 Guéméné-Penfao F A3
33 Güeñes E A3
19 Guer F C3
22 Guérande F A2
24 Guéret F B1
24 Guérigny F A3
33 Guernica y Luno E A4
33 Guerricaiz E A4
34 Guesa E A1
26 Guèthary F C2
25 Gueugnon F B4
79 Guglionesi I B5
106 Gugutka BG B3
61 Gühlen Glienicke D B3
36 Guia P B2
19 Guichen F C4
75 Guidizzolo I A5
78 Guidónia I B3
75 Guiglia I B5
21 Guignes F C3
44 Guijo E A2
37 Guijo de Coria E A4
37 Guijo de Granadilla E A4
38 Guijuelo E B1
15 Guildford GB C2
29 Guillaumes F B5
43 Guillena E B3
29 Guillestre F B5
18 Guilvinec F C1
31 Guimarães P C2
36 Guincho P C1
16 Guines F C1
18 Guingamp F B2
18 Guipavas F B1
103 Guirgita RO B4
38 Guisando E B1
11 Guisborough GB A4
21 Guiscard F B4
18 Guiscriff F B2
21 Guise F B4
35 Guisona E B4
14 Guist GB B3
30 Guitiriz E A3
26 Guîtres F A3
26 Gujan Mestras F B2
55 Guldborg DK D4
77 Gulin YU C5
56 Gullabo S C4
9 Gullane GB B5
56 Gullaskruv S C4
56 Gullbrandstorp S C1
52 Gulleråsen S A1
49 Gullhaug N B7
51 Gullholmen S D2
56 Gullringen S B4
51 Gullspång S D5
112 Güllük TR B1
49 Gulsvik N A6
107 Gülübitsi BG A4
106 Gülübovo BG A3
103 Gulyantsi BG C5
32 Gumiel de Hizán E C3
62 Gummersbach D B2
103 Gumoshtnik BG D5
106 Gumoshtnik BG A2
102 Gümzovo BG B3
67 Gundel-Fingen D C3
68 Gundelfingen D C1
67 Gundelsheim D B5
66 Gunderschoffen F C3
100 Gundinci YU A3
50 Gunnarskog S C3
56 Gunnebo S B5
96 Gunselsdorf A D2
63 Güntersberge D B5
67 Guntersblum D B4
96 Guntersdorf A C2
30 Guntin de Pallarés E B3
96 Guntramsdorf A C2
21 Guny F B4
68 Günzburg D C1
68 Gunzenhausen D B1
103 Gura Padinii RO C5
102 Gura Väii RO B3
33 Guriezo E A3
73 Gurk A B4
106 Gurkovo BG A3
105 Gŭrlyano BG B4
34 Gurrea de Gállego E A2
89 Guryevsk SU A6
98 Gušće YU C1
64 Güsen D A1
93 Gusev SU C8
102 Guševac YU C3
104 Gusinje YU B1
87 Gúspini I C1
53 Gusselby S C1
98 Güssing A A1
69 Gußwerk A D6
50 Gustav Adolf S B4
53 Gustavsberg S C4
51 Gustavsfors S C3
60 Güstrow D B3
53 Gusum S D2
6 Gutcher, *Shetland Is.* GB
96 Gutenstein A D1
62 Gütersloh D B3
70 Guttannen CH B3
73 Guttaring A B4
64 Guttau D B4
71 Güttingen CH A4
61 Gützkow D B4
14 Guyhirn GB B3
91 Guzów PL A4
89 Gvardeyskoye SU A6
89 Gvardieysk SU A7
100 Gvozdansko YU A1
10 Gwalchmai GB B1
88 Gwda Wielka PL B2
2 Gweedore IRL A3
25 Gy F A5
99 Gyál H A4
98 Gyarmat H A2
21 Gye-sur-Seine F C5
98 Gyékényes H B2
48 Gyland N C3
55 Gylling DK C3
97 Gyögyössolymòs H D5
99 Gyoma H B5
98 Gyömöre H A2
99 Gyömrö H A4
99 Gyón H A4
98 Gyöngyfa H C2
97 Gyöngyös H D5
97 Gyöngyöspata H D5
99 Gyönk H B3
98 Györ H A2
98 Györszemere H A2
98 Györszentivan H A2
98 Györvár H B1
70 Gypsera CH B2
52 Gysinge S B2
51 Gyttorp S C5
105 Gyueshevo BG B4
98 Gyulafirátót H A2
98 Gyulaj H B3

H

17 Haacht B C4
69 Haag, *Nieder Östereich* A C5
69 Haag, *Ober Östereich* A C4
68 Haag D C3
62 Haaksbergen NL A1
62 Haan D B2
93 Haapsalu SU A8
17 Haarlem NL A4
47 Haarpajärvi SF E12
26 Habas F C3
66 Habay-la-Neuve B B1
56 Habo S B3
96 Habry CS B1
62 Hachenburg D C2
33 Hacinas E C3
107 Haciumur TR B4
5 Hacketstown IRL B5
10 Hackthorpe GB A3
62 Hadamar D C2
14 Haddenham GB B3
9 Haddinton GB C5
55 Hadersley DK C2
15 Hadleigh GB B3
15 Hadlow GB C3
63 Hadmersleben D B6
96 Hadres A C2
54 Hadsund DK B3
100 Hadžici YU C3
48 Hægebostad N C4
49 Hægeland N C4
60 Haffkrug D A1
98 Haganj YU C1
56 Hagby S C5
58 Hage D B4
59 Hagen, *Niedersachsen* D B5
62 Hagen, *Nordrhein-Westfalen* D B2
67 Hagenbach D B4
69 Hagenberg A C5
59 Hagenburg D C6
60 Hagenow D B2
26 Hagetmau F C3
50 Hagfors S B4
67 Haguenau F C3
68 Hahnbach D B2
62 Hahnstäten D C3
60 Hahnstorf D B1
98 Hahót H B1
62 Haiger D C3
67 Haigerloch D C4
62 Hailer D C4
15 Hailsham GB D3
53 Hålsta S C2
96 Hainburg A C2
96 Hainfeld A C1
64 Hainichen D C3
96 Haitzendorf A C1
102 Hajdučica YU A2
94 Hajdúszoboszló H C4
98 Hajmásker H A3
97 Hajnáčka CS C5
99 Hajós H B4
51 Håkantorp S D3
47 Hakkas S C10
52 Håksberg S B1
66 Halanzy B B1
96 Halaszi H D3
63 Halberstadt D B6
13 Halberton GB C4
54 Hald DK B2
62 Haldem D A3
51 Halden N C2
63 Haldensleben D A6
17 Haldern D B6
60 Halenbeck D B3
97 Halenkov CS B4
11 Halesowen GB C3
14 Halesworth GB B4
68 Halfing D D3
97 Halič CS C5
11 Halifax GB B4
102 Halinga RO B3
57 Häljaro S D1
7 Halkirk GB B5
57 Hallabro S C4
53 Hällabrottet S C1
46 Hålland S E6
48 Hallaskar N A4
53 Hällberga S C2
17 Halle B C4
62 Halle D A3
64 Halle D B1
50 Hällefors S C5
53 Hälleforsnäs S C2
72 Hallein A A3
51 Hällekis S D4
62 Hallenberg D B3
53 Hällestad S D1
51 Hällevadsholm S D2
57 Hallevik S C3
51 Hälleviksstrand S D2
52 Hållnäs S B3
53 Hallsberg S C1
68 Hallstadt D B1
53 Hallstahammar S C2
72 Hallstatt A A3
52 Hallstavik S B4
56 Halltorp S C5
16 Hallum F C3
12 Hallworthy GB C3
56 Halmstad S C1
54 Hals DK B3
15 Halstead GB C3
59 Halstenbek D B6

Pg	Name	Ctry	Grid
47	Hyvinkää	SF	F12

I

Pg	Name	Ctry	Grid
23	I'lle Bouchard	F	A5
102	Iablanita	RO	B3
103	Ianca	RO	C5
94	Iaşi	RO	C7
106	Iasmos	GR	B3
17	Ibahernando	E	B5
33	Ibarranguelua	E	A4
10	Ibbenburen	D	A2
33	Ibeas	E	B3
40	Ibi	E	C2
41	Ibiza, *Ibiza*	E	
26	Ibos	F	C4
107	Ibrice Iskelesi	TR	B5
107	Ibriktepe	TR	B4
44	Ibros	E	B3
11	Ibstock	GB	C4
62	Iburg	D	A3
67	Ichenhausen	D	C6
13	Ichtegem	B	B3
63	Ichtershausen	D	C5
33	Iciar	E	A4
37	Idanha-a-Nova	P	B3
10	Idar-Oberstein	D	B3
51	Idd	N	C2
105	Idha	GR	C4
111	Idhra	GR	B4
33	Idiazábal	E	A4
52	Idkerberget	S	B1
99	Idos	YU	C5
46	Idre	S	F6
73	Idrija	YU	B4
62	Idstein	D	C3
101	Idvor	YU	A5
79	Ielsi	I	B5
8	Ieper	B	C2
112	Ierápetra, *Kríti*	GR	
109	Ierissós	GR	A5
108	Ieropiyi	GR	A3
87	Ierzu	I	C2
76	Iesi	I	C3
15	Iésolo	I	C2
46	Ifjord	N	A13
98	Igal	H	B2
81	Igalo	YU	B5
33	Igea	E	A4
76	Igea Marina	I	B2
53	Igelfors	S	D1
67	Igersheim	D	B5
9	Iggesund	S	F8
104	Iglarevo	YU	B4
12	Iglesias	E	B3
87	Iglésias	I	C1
29	Igls	A	A1
107	Igneada	TR	B5
108	Igoumenitsa	GR	B2
34	Igries	E	A2
5	Igualada	E	B4
30	Igüeña	E	B4
6	Iguerande	F	B4
98	Iharosberény	H	B2
13	Ihringen	D	C2
68	Ihrlerstein	D	C2
53	Iisalmi	SF	E13
17	Ijmuiden	NL	A4
8	IJsselmuiden	NL	C2
17	IJsselstein	NL	A5
93	IJzendijke	N	B3
47	Ikaalinen	SF	F11
9	Ikast	DK	B2
98	Ikervár	H	A1
105	Ikhtiman	BG	B5
75	Il Castagno	I	C5
101	Ilandza	YU	A5
71	Ilanz	CH	B4
97	Ilava	CS	C4
89	Ilawa	PL	B5
34	Ilche	E	B3
13	Ilchester	GB	B5
63	Ilfeld-Wiegersdorf	D	B5
17	Ilfracombe	GB	B5
31	Ilhavo	P	D2
100	Ilijaš	YU	C3
111	Iliókastro	GR	B4
106	Iliokómi	GR	C4
73	Ilirska Bistrica	YU	C4
100	Ilijca	YU	C3
14	Ilkeston	GB	B1
11	Ilkley	GB	B4
39	Illana	E	B4
30	Illano	E	A4
30	Illas	E	A5
28	Illats	F	B3
35	Ille-sur-Tét	F	A5
67	Illereichen-Altenstadt	D	C6
63	Illertissen	D	C6
38	Illescas	E	B3
11	Ilfurth	F	C3
20	Illiers-Combray	F	C2
10	Illingen	D	B3
66	Ilkich	D	C3
11	Illmersdorf	D	D3
96	Illmitz	A	D2
41	Illora	E	B3
33	Illueca	E	C5
33	Ilminster	GB	C5
101	Ilok	YU	A4
47	Ilomantsi	SF	E15
88	Ilowiec	PL	B6
6	Ilowo	PL	B6
63	Ilsenburg	D	C5
11	Ilshofen	D	C5
73	Ilz	A	A5
11	Iłza	PL	B5
8	Imachar	GB	B2
57	Imatra	SF	F14
106	Imeron	PL	C3
96	Imielin	PL	C3
57	Immeln	S	C3
16	Immendingen	D	C4
63	Immenhausen	D	B4
11	Immenstadt	D	D6
11	Immingham	GB	B5
11	Immingham Dock	GB	B5
76	Imola	I	B1
3	Imon	E	A4
100	Imotski	YU	C2
14	Impéria	I	C3
24	Imphy	F	B3
11	Impruneta	I	C5
48	Imsland	N	B2
7	Imst	A	D5
4	Inagh	IRL	B2
41	Inari	SF	B13
41	Inca, *Mallorca*	E	
10	Inchnadamph	GB	B4
2	Inchture	GB	B4
5	Incisa in Val d'Arno	I	C5
75	Incirliova	TR	C3
101	Indija	YU	A4
48	Indre Alvik	N	A3
107	Inece	TR	B5
107	Inecik	TR	A5
71	Inerthal	CH	A3
31	Infesta	P	C2
32	Infiesto	E	A1
15	Ingatestone	GB	C3
56	Ingatorp	S	B4
51	Ingedal	N	C2
67	Ingelheim	D	B4
16	Ingelmunster	B	C3
56	Ingelstad	S	C3
10	Ingleton	GB	A3
67	Ingolfsland	N	B5
68	Ingolstadt	D	C2
22	Ingrandes, *Maine-et-Loire*	F	A4
23	Ingrandes, *Vienne*	F	B5
66	Ingwiller	F	B3
39	Iniesta	E	C4
4	Inishannon	IRL	C3
2	Inishcrone	IRL	B2
5	Inistioge	IRL	A6
13	Inkberrow	GB	A6
98	Inke	H	B2
46	Innbygda	N	F6
8	Innellan	GB	C4
16	Innerleithen	GB	C4
68	Innermessan	GB	D3
74	Innertkirchen	CH	B3
72	Innervillgraten	A	B2
14	Innhavet	N	C7
59	Innien	D	A6
29	Innsbruck	A	A1
111	Inói, *Attikí*	GR	A4
111	Inói, *Ilía*	GR	B2
91	Inowlódz	PL	B5
70	Inowroclaw	PL	A4
70	Ins	CH	A2
88	Iñsko	PL	B1
70	Instinción	E	A2
70	Interlaken	CH	B2
70	Intra	I	C2
70	Intragna	CH	B3
71	Introbio	I	B2
2	Inver	IRL	B3
7	Inverallochty	GB	C7
7	Inveran	IRL	A2
4	Inveran	IRL	A2
72	Inveraray	GB	A2
17	Inverbervie	GB	B5
13	Invergarry	GB	C4
7	Invergordon	GB	C4
7	Inverie	GB	A2
7	Inverkeilor	GB	B5
16	Inverkeithing	GB	B4
7	Inverlussa	GB	B2
70	Invermoriston	GB	C4
7	Inverness	GB	C4
18	Inversanda	GB	B2
7	Invershiel	GB	C3
70	Inverurie	I	C3
7	Inverurie	GB	C6
107	Inzovo	BG	A4
76	Iolanda di Savoia	I	B1
103	Ioneşti	RO	B5
103	Ioneşti	RO	B5
87	Ióppolo	I	C2
112	Ios	GR	D3
107	Ipáti	GR	C3
107	Ipsala	TR	B1
95	Ipsos	GR	B1
15	Ipswich	GB	C5
15	Iráklia	GR	C5
112	Iráklion, *Kríti*	GR	
73	Irdning	A	A4
98	Irechekovo	BG	A4
87	Iregszemcse	H	B3
87	Irgoli	I	B2
111	Iria	I	B2
101	Irig	YU	B5
10	Iron Bridge	GB	C3
66	Irrel	D	B2
97	Irsina	I	B2
30	Iruela	E	B3
33	Irurita	E	A5
33	Irurzun	E	B5
2	Irvine	GB	C4
2	Irvinestown	GB	B4
25	Is-sur-Tille	F	C4
34	Isaba	E	A2
44	Isabela	E	A2
110	Isaris	GR	B3
87	Isaszeg	H	B4
103	Isbiceni	RO	C5
6	Isbister, *Shetland Is.*	GB	
32	Iscar	E	C2
29	Ischgl	A	C2
78	Ischia	I	A2
78	Ischia di Castro	I	A3
80	Ischitella	I	B3
103	Iscroni	RO	A4
24	Isdes	F	A2
51	Ise	N	B3
70	Iseltwald	CH	B2
68	Iselen	D	C3
63	Isenbüttel	D	A6
71	Iseo	I	C3
75	Isérables	CH	B2
62	Iserlohn	D	B3
79	Isérnia	I	B5
104	Ishm	AL	C1
35	Isigny	F	A4
87	Ísili	I	C2
106	Iskra	BG	B3
42	Isla-Cristina	E	B2
103	Islares	E	A3
103	Islaz	RO	C5
7	Isle of Whithorn	GB	A1
68	Ismaning	D	C2
36	Isna	N	B3
74	Isny	D	B1
74	Isola	I	B2
78	Isola del Gr. Sasso d'Italia	I	A4
79	Isola del Liri	I	B4
84	Isola delle Fémmine	I	A1
75	Isola delle Scala	I	A6
82	Isola di Capo Rizzuto	I	C4
35	Isona	E	B4
28	Ispagnac	F	B2
62	Isselburg	D	B6
27	Issigeac	F	B3
27	Issoire	F	C3
24	Issonne	I	C5
24	Issoire	F	C3
66	Issoncourt	F	C1
27	Issoudun	F	B2
17	Issum	D	B6
24	Issy-l'Evêque	F	B3
44	Istán	E	C2
95	Istanbul	TR	F8
32	Istebna	PL	B4
97	Istenmezeje	H	C6
109	Istiaia	GR	C5
105	Istibanja	YU	A5
78	Istiz d'Ombrone	I	A2
104	Istok	YU	B4
107	Istrance	TR	B6
29	Istres	F	B3
98	Istvándi	H	A5
108	Itéa, *Florina*	GR	A3
110	Itéa, *Fokís*	GR	A3
108	Itéa, *Grevená*	GR	A3
109	Itéa, *Kardhítsa*	GR	B4
110	Itháki	GR	A1
109	Íti	GR	C4
34	Itoize	E	A1
44	Itrabo	E	B3
79	Itri	I	B4
87	Ittireddu	I	B1
87	Íttiri	I	B1
59	Itzehoe	D	B6
47	Ivalo	SF	B13
98	Iván	H	A1
97	Ivančice	CS	B2
3	Ivančsa	H	A3
98	Ivanec	YU	A3
104	Ivangrad	YU	B1
98	Ivanić Grad	YU	C1
73	Ivanjci	YU	A1
101	Ivanjica	YU	C5
100	Ivanjska	YU	B2
97	Ivanka p. N.	CS	C4
101	Ivankovo	YU	C4
94	Ivano-Frankovsk	SU	B6
96	Ivanovice na Hané	CS	B3
98	Ivanska	YU	C1
109	Ívira	GR	A5
70	Ivrea	I	C2
95	Ivrinai	TR	G7
75	Ivry-en-Montagne	F	A3
20	Ivry-la-Bataille	F	C2
12	Ivybridge	GB	C4
91	Iwaniska	PL	C5
16	Iwuy	F	C3
14	Ixworth	GB	A4
33	Izarra	E	B4
90	Izbica Kujawska	PL	A2
102	Izbişté	YU	A2
31	Izeda	P	C4
16	Izegem	B	C3
12	Izernore	F	A5
107	Izgrew	BG	A5
94	Izmail	SU	D9
95	Izmir	TR	G7
44	Iznájar	E	B3
44	Iznalloz	E	B3
44	Iznatoraf	E	A3
72	Izola	YU	C3
99	Izsák	H	B4
105	Izvor	BG	A4
102	Izvor	YU	B2
102	Izvor Makhala	BG	C3
102	Izvor Makhala	BG	C3

J

Pg	Name	Ctry	Grid
44	Jabalquinto	E	A3
34	Jabarrella	E	A2
72	Jablanac	YU	B4
100	Jablanica	YU	C2
96	Jablonec n. Jizerou	CS	C5
96	Jablonec n. Nisou	CS	C5
87	Jablonica	CS	C3
90	Jablonka	PL	A3
97	Jablonka	PL	B5
91	Jablonna	PL	A4
65	Jablonne Podještědí	CS	C4
89	Jablonowo	PL	B5
97	Jablunkov	CS	B4
101	Jabucje	YU	B5
101	Jabuka, *A. P. Vojvodina*	YU	B5
101	Jabuka, *Srbija*	YU	C4
102	Jabukovac	YU	A1
97	Jabukovac	YU	B3
34	Jaca	E	A2
64	Jáchymov	CS	B2
59	Jäckvik	S	C8
59	Jacobidrebber	D	C4
59	Jacovce	CS	C4
59	Jade	D	B2
52	Jäderfors	S	B2
52	Jädraque	E	B3
55	Jægerspris	DK	C4
100	Jagare	E	B3
99	Jagenbach	A	C6
99	Jagodnjak	H	A3
99	Jagstzell	D	B6
96	Jahodna	CS	B3
99	Jajce	YU	B2
98	Ják	H	A1
99	Jakabszálbs	H	B4
44	Jakestad	S	E11
100	Jakšic	YU	A2
32	Jalance	E	B1
40	Jalance	E	B1
44	Jalasjärvi	SF	E11
17	Jalhay	B	A6
35	Jallais	F	A4
25	Jallieu	F	C5
44	Jalón	E	C2
100	Jalovik	E	B4
101	Jalovik Izvor	YU	C3
44	Jambes	B	A5
101	Jamena	YU	B4
44	Jamilena	E	B3
73	Jämjö	S	C4
73	Jamnička Kiselica	YU	C4
91	Jamno	PL	A2
66	Jamoigne	B	B1
90	Jämsä	SF	F12
100	Jämänkoski	SF	F12
102	Jamu Mare	RO	A2
23	Jänickendorf	D	A3
76	Janikowo	PL	A4
55	Janja	YU	B4
98	Janjevo	E	B4
81	Janjina	YU	C3
91	Janki	PL	A5
91	Jankov	CS	B5
88	Jankowo Dolne	PL	A3
99	Jánoshalma	H	B4
98	Jánosháza	H	A2
99	Jánossomorja	H	A3
101	Janovice n.	PL	A5
90	Janów	PL	B2
91	Janów Lubelski	PL	C5
91	Janowiec	PL	B5
88	Janowiec	PL	A3
88	Janów Wielkopolski	PL	C3
89	Janowo	PL	B6
20	Janville	F	C2
19	Janzé	F	C4
97	Jarabá	CS	C5
65	Jaraczewo	PL	B7
40	Jarafuel	E	B1
34	Jaraiz de la Vera	E	C1
101	Jarak	YU	B4
33	Jarandilla	E	A5
33	Jaray	E	C4
52	Jarbo	S	B2
95	Jarcew	PL	B5
22	Jard-sur-Mer	F	B3
91	Járdánháza	H	C6
20	Jargeau	F	D3
101	Jarkovac	YU	A5
53	Järnä	S	C3
24	Jarnac	F	C4
89	Jarocin	PL	B1
65	Jičín	CS	C5
65	Jičíněves	CS	B5
98	Jihlava	CS	B1
96	Jaroměřice n. Rokytnou	CS	B1
96	Jaroslavice	CS	C2
32	Jaroslaw	PL	A5
98	Jaroslawiec	PL	A2
69	Jarošov n. Nežarkou	CS	B6
92	Jarow	GB	D6
51	Järpás	S	D3
39	Järpen	S	E6
47	Järvenpää	SF	F12
47	Järvsö	S	F8
23	Jarzé	F	A4
95	Jaša Tomić	YU	C5
103	Jasen	BG	C5
77	Jasenak	YU	A5
96	Jasenice	YU	B5
65	Jasenice	CS	C5
100	Jasenovac, *Bosna i Hercegovina*	YU	B1
100	Jasenovac, *Hrvatska*	YU	A1
101	Jasenovo	YU	C4
65	Jasenovo	YU	B2
65	Jasien	PL	B5
92	Jasika	YU	C2
77	Jaslo	PL	B4
39	Jásova	CS	D4
26	Jasseron	F	A5
73	Jastarnia	PL	A4
73	Jastrebarsko	YU	C5
88	Jastrzebia-Góra	PL	A4
99	Jastrzebie-Zdroj	PL	B4
99	Jászalsószentgyorgy	H	A5
99	Jászapáti	H	A5
99	Jászarokszállás	H	A4
99	Jászberény	H	A4
99	Jászdózsa	H	A5
99	Jászfényszaru	H	A4
99	Jászjákóhalma	H	A5
99	Jászkarajenő	H	A5
99	Jászkisér	H	A5
99	Jászladány	H	A5
99	Jásztelek	H	A5
44	Játar	E	C3
29	Játiva (Xátive)	E	C2
61	Jatznick	D	B4
21	Jauche	B	C4
21	Jaulgonne	F	B4
2	Jaun	CH	B2
29	Jausiers	F	B5
3	Jävenitz	D	A2
60	Javerlhac	F	C5
100	Javorani	YU	B2
91	Javorina	CS	B6
101	Javornik	E	C7
65	Javron	F	B6
65	Jawor	PL	B6
91	Jaworznia	PL	C4
91	Jaworzno	PL	C4
91	Jaworzyna Śląska	PL	C6
44	Jayena	E	C3
2	Jedburgh	GB	C5
64	Jáchymov	CS	B2
59	Jäckvik	S	C8
91	Jedlicze	PL	B4
91	Jedlina Letnisko	PL	C6
89	Jednorożec	PL	B6
91	Jedrychow	PL	B5
91	Jedwabno	PL	B6
88	Jegłownik	PL	A5
27	Jégun	F	C4
65	Jektevik	N	B2
102	Jelašnica	YU	C1
91	Jelcz	PL	B6
88	Jelenia Góra	PL	B5
88	Jelenino	PL	B2
44	Jelgava	SU	B8
88	Jelka	PL	A4
55	Jelling	DK	C2
40	Jelsa	E	C2
44	Jelsa	SF	E11
17	Jalhay	N	B3
44	Jallais	F	A4
25	Jelsi	F	C5
44	Jelšava	CS	C6
96	Jemnice	CS	B1
18	Jugon	D	B3
71	Jenaz	CH	B4
62	Jeneč	CS	B4
60	Jeneč	B	C4
69	Jenec	CS	C6
17	Jenzal	N	A5
44	Jenzat	F	C1
55	Jerchel	D	A2
3	Julianstown	IRL	C5
60	Jerchel	D	C3
44	Jeres del Marquesado	E	B3
42	Jerez de la Frontera	E	C3
37	Jerez de los Caballeros	E	C4
34	Jergucat	AL	B2
40	Jérica	E	B2
44	Jerichow	D	A3
102	Jermenovci	YU	A2
71	Jenaz	CH	C4
62	Jerte	E	A4
62	Jeneč	CS	B2
60	Jeneč	B	B5
60	Jerxheim	D	A5
90	Jerzmanowice	PL	C3
47	Jesberg	D	C4
92	Jes Praz	GB	B3
65	Jesenice	CS	C7
97	Jesenice	CS	B4

Pg	Name	Ctry	Grid
64	Jeserig	D	A2
64	Jessen	D	B2
66	Jessenice	CS	B5
50	Jessheim	N	B2
64	Jeßnitz	D	B2
64	Jesteburg	D	C3
92	Jesus y Mária	E	C3
17	Jette	B	C1
19	Jettingen	D	C1
19	Jevenstedt	D	A6
59	Jever	D	B4
96	Jevicko	CS	B2
34	Jevier	CS	C2
22	Jevišovice	CS	C2
49	Jevnaker	N	B1
77	Jezerane	YU	A5
100	Jezero	YU	B2
101	Jezersko	YU	C5
89	Jeziorany	PL	A5
91	Jeżów	PL	B4
91	Jeżów	PL	C6
89	Jeżewo	PL	B4
89	Jeżowo	PL	A5
40	Jijona	E	C2
65	Jilemnice	CS	C5
65	Jilové	CS	C5
64	Jílové	RO	C5
44	Jimena	E	B3
43	Jimena de la Frontera	E	C4
96	Jimramov	CS	B2
91	Jince	CS	B4
64	Jindřichovice	CS	B2
69	Jindřichuv Hradec	CS	B5
95	Jirkov	CS	C3
69	Jistebnice	CS	B5
61	Joachimsthal	D	B4
36	João da Loura	P	D2
91	Jobbágyi	H	D5
67	Jochberg	A	A2
67	Jockgrim	D	C3
17	Jodoigne	B	C4
17	Joensuu	SF	E14
66	Jœuf	F	B1
91	Jogodzin	H	D5
64	Johanngeorgenstadt	D	C2
57	Johannishus	S	C4
24	Johanniskirchen	D	C3
56	Johansfors	S	C4
7	John o'Groats	GB	B5
17	Johnshaven	GB	B5
3	Johnstone	GB	C4
2	Johnstown	IRL	B4
2	Johnstown Bridge	IRL	B5
21	Joigny	F	C6
25	Joinville	F	C6
96	Jois	A	D2
47	Jokkmokk	S	C8
62	Jöllenbeck	D	A4
53	Jönåker	S	D2
57	Jonstorp	S	C1
17	Jonzac	F	A5
60	Jordanów	PL	B4
65	Jordanów Śląski	PL	C6
65	Jordanowo	PL	A5
50	Jördenstorf	D	B3
59	Jordøse	DK	C3
64	Jorjaes	P	D3
59	Jork	D	B6
59	Jörlanda	S	A4
48	Jøroinen	SF	E13
48	Jørpeland	N	A2
44	Jorquera	E	C1
101	Jošanička Banja	YU	C4
99	Josipovac	YU	A3
35	Jossefors	S	C3
21	Jouarre	F	C4
22	Joué-les-Tours	F	A5
20	Joué-sur-Erdre	F	A4
58	Joure	NL	B2
53	Joutsa	SF	F13
47	Joutseno	SF	F14
47	Joutsijärvi	SF	C13
20	Joux-la-Ville	F	A3
25	Jouy, *Eure-et-Loir*	F	C3
21	Jouy, *Moselle*	F	B5
21	Jouy-le-Châtel	F	C4
21	Jouy-le-Potier	F	D2
28	Joyeuse	F	B3
3	Joze	F	C3
91	Józefów	PL	B5
91	Józefów	PL	B5
91	Jubek	D	A1
96	Jubera	E	B4
42	Jubrique al Genalguacil	E	C4
61	Jüchsen	D	C6
27	Judenburg	A	A4
60	Juelsminde	DK	C3
18	Jugon	F	B3
31	Jugueros	E	B1
19	Jülich	D	C6
19	Juliénas	F	A4
31	Julianstown	IRL	C5
19	Jullouville	F	B4
19	Jumet	B	A4
96	Jumièges	F	B1
21	Jumilhac-le-Grand	F	C6
44	Jumilla	E	C1
34	Juneda	E	B4
67	Jungingen	D	C5
67	Junglingster	L	B1
104	Junik	YU	B1
31	Junquera de Ambia	E	B3
47	Junsele	S	E7
33	Junta de la Cerca	E	B3
33	Junta de Oteo	E	A3
99	Jupânesti	RO	B3
24	Jur	F	C3
72	Juan-les-Pins	F	C1
91	Jubek	PL	B5
89	Jurata	PL	A4
77	Jurjevo	YU	B4

K

Pg	Name	Ctry	Grid
46	Kaamanen	SF	B13
47	Kaaresuvanto	SF	B11
60	Kaarßen	D	B2
74	Kaatscheuvel	NL	B5
47	Kåbdalis	S	C9
107	Kableshkovo	BG	A5
104	Kačanik	YU	B3
101	Kačarevo	YU	B5
104	Kačikol	YU	B3
64	Kadaň	CS	C3
98	Kadarkút	H	B2
107	Kadıköy	TR	C4
47	Kåge	S	D10
57	Kågeröd	S	D2
63	Kahl	D	A5
63	Kahla	D	C6
110	Kaiáfa Spa	GR	B2
73	Kainach	A	A5
73	Kaindorf	A	A5
73	Kaindorf a.d. Sulm	A	B5
108	Kainourion	GR	C3
62	Kaiserslautern	D	B3
62	Kaisersesch	D	C2
68	Kaisheim	D	C1
66	Kajaani	SF	D13
66	Kájárpéc	H	B2
107	Kajdacs	H	B3
66	Kakanj	YU	B3
111	Kakasd	H	B3
111	Kaki Thálassa	GR	B5
65	Kakolewo	PL	B6
110	Kakóvatos	GR	B2
99	Kál	H	A5
108	Kalabáka	GR	B3
106	Kalábáki	GR	A5
73	Kalace	YU	C4
112	Kalafatis	GR	C2
47	Kalajoki	SF	D11
109	Kalamáfka, *Kríti*	GR	
109	Kalamáki, *Lárisa*	GR	B4
109	Kalamáki, *Magnisía*	GR	B5
110	Kalamáki, *Messinía*	GR	C2
110	Kalamata	GR	B3
111	Kálamos, *Attikí*	GR	A4
108	Kálamos, *Lefkás*	GR	C2
110	Kalamotó	GR	A5
109	Kalandra	GR	A5
110	Kalanistra	GR	A2
112	Kalátádos	GR	D3
110	Kalávrita	GR	A3
60	Kalbe	D	B2
107	Kalchevo	BG	A4
98	Kåld	D	A5
62	Kaldenkirchen	D	B6
62	Kalemouth	GB	C5
102	Kalenic	YU	C1
108	Kalenji	GR	B3
110	Kaléntzi	GR	B3
90	Kalety	PL	C2
10	Kalhovd	N	A5
109	Kali	YU	C4
111	Kalianos	GR	A4
112	Kálimnos	GR	C5
89	Kaliningrad	SU	D11
77	Kalinovac	YU	C6
77	Kalinovik	YU	C3
109	Kalipéfki	GR	B4
104	Kaiirrakhi	GR	C2
73	Kaliska	PL	A4
104	Kalista	GR	C2
73	Kalisz	PL	B4
73	Kalisz Pomorski	PL	B1
109	Kalithéa, *Aitolia kai Acarnanía*	GR	C3
108	Kalithéa, *Khalkidhikí*	GR	
110	Kalithéa, *Lakonía*	GR	C3
110	Kalithéa, *Sámos*	GR	B1
110	Kalithéa, *Zákinthos*	GR	B1
106	Kalithiro	GR	A5
106	Kalives, *Kríti*	GR	
106	Kalives, *Thásos*	GR	C3
109	Kalivia, *Attikí*	GR	B4
109	Kalivia, *Évia*	GR	C5
109	Kalivia, *Lárisa*	GR	A4
109	Kalix	S	D11
109	Kalker	D	A5
56	Kalkar	D	B6
56	Kalmar	S	C4
97	Kálna	CS	C4
105	Kalna, *Srbija*	YU	A4
105	Kalna, *Srbija*	YU	C3
99	Kalocsa	H	B3
106	Kalofer	BG	A3
106	Kalogriá	GR	A2
112	Kaloi-Liménes, *Kríti*	GR	
108	Kalókastro	GR	A5
108	Kaloni, *Argolis*	GR	B3
67	Kaloni, *Tínos*	GR	D2
99	Káloz	H	B3
72	Kals	A	A2
62	Kalsdorf	A	B5
71	Kaltbrunn	CH	A4
63	Kaltenbach	A	A1
59	Kaltenkirchen	D	B6
63	Kaltennordheim	D	C5
55	Kalundborg	DK	C4
91	Kałuszyn	PL	A5
55	Kalvehave	DK	C5
73	Kalwang	A	A4
97	Kalwaria-Zebrzydowska	PL	B5
110	Kamára	GR	C3
112	Kamáres	GR	C2
112	Kamári, *Magnisía*	GR	B5
112	Kamári, *Thíra*	GR	D2
112	Kámbos, *Kríti*	GR	
112	Kámbos, *Pátmos*	GR	C1
62	Kamen	D	B3
101	Kamenets	YU	A4
101	Kamenica, *Srbija*	YU	A4
102	Kamenica, *Srbija*	YU	C1
105	Kamenica, *Srbija*	YU	A4
69	Kamenice n. Lipou	CS	B6
64	Kamenicky Šenov	CS	C4
97	Kamenin	CS	D4
104	Kamenin-Most	YU	D4
104	Kamenny Ujezd	CS	C5
102	Kameno	BG	C5
103	Kamenopole	BG	C5
64	Kamenz	D	B4
88	Kamień	PL	C5
88	Kamień Kraj.	PL	B3
61	Kamień Pomorski	PL	B5
65	Kamienica Polska	PL	C6
70	Kamieniec Zabk.	PL	C6
65	Kamienna Góra	PL	C6
92	Kamiensk	PL	B3
91	Kamionka	PL	A5
108	Kamili	GR	C2
109	Kámmena Voúrla	GR	C4
73	Kammern i. Liesingtal	A	A4
55	Kamp-Lintfort	D	B6
57	Kampen	NL	D1
58	Kampen	NL	C2
91	Kampinos	PL	A5
111	Kanála	GR	C4
69	Kamýk n Vltavou	CS	B5
111	Kanáli	GR	B2
109	Kanália, *Kardhítsa*	GR	B4
109	Kanália, *Magnisía*	GR	B5
47	Kangasniemi	SF	F13
61	Kania	PL	B6
99	Kanjiža	YU	B5
112	Kanli Kastéllion, *Kríti*	GR	
4	Kanturk	IRL	B3
102	Kaonik	YU	C2
56	Kaolinovo	BG	A4
110	Kapandriti	GR	A4
110	Kaparéli	GR	A3
108	Kaparélli	GR	C2
111	Kapellen	D	A5
73	Kapfenberg	A	A5
73	Kapfenstein	A	B5
69	Kaplice	CS	C5
109	Kali	GR	C4
111	Kalianos	GR	A4
111	Kálimnos	GR	C5
112	Kalimnos	GR	C5
89	Kapolnásnyék	H	A3
103	Kapsukas	SU	D8
98	Kaposvár	H	B2
67	Kappel	D	C3
72	Kappeln	D	A1
72	Kappl	A	A1
72	Kaprun	A	A2
72	Kapsáki	GR	A4
98	Kaptol	YU	A2
99	Karacsond	H	A5
104	Karacova	YU	C2
99	Karád	H	B3
104	Karaharid	TR	B4
110	Karamidhká	GR	B3
101	Karan	YU	C4
102	Karanslaputo	YU	C5
112	Karaoua	GR	B12
110	Karátoulas	GR	B3
106	Karavelovo	BG	A3
104	Karavostási	YU	B2
106	Karbenning	S	B2
46	Kårböle	S	F7
54	Karby	DK	B1
94	Karcag	H	A5
91	Karczmiska	PL	A5
90	Karczow	PL	C1
90	Karczowiska	PL	B5
99	Karczów	PL	A4
110	Kariá, *Argolis*	GR	B3
109	Kariá, *Lefkás*	GR	C2
46	Karigasniemi	SF	B12
106	Kalofer	BG	A3
104	Kariès Karja	SF	F11
98	Kalrím	GR	B1
111	Karitaina	GR	B3
112	Karistos	GR	A4
91	Karja	SF	F11
55	Karise	DK	C5
105	Kalotina	GR	B3
94	Karcag	YU	C4
72	Karvak	TR	C4
104	Karvali	AL	C2
108	Kato Akhaia	GR	A2
110	Kato Klitoria	GR	B3
110	Kato Makrinoú	GR	C3
106	Karavelovo	BG	A3
108	Kato Nevrokópion	GR	B1
108	Kato Skholárion	GR	A5
109	Kato Tithoréa	GR	C4
52	Karbenning	YU	C5
46	Kårböle	N	A4
105	Kato Vrondou	GR	C5
54	Karby	H	B1
108	Katoúna, *Aitolía kai Acarnanía*	GR	C3
108	Katoúna, *Lefkás*	GR	C2
110	Katowice	PL	C3
91	Katowice	PL	C3
90	Katowice	PL	C3
91	Katrineberg	S	A5
46	Katrineholm	S	A5
56	Katrineholm	S	D2
110	Katrineholm	GR	A4
91	Katwijk aan Zee	NL	A4
65	Katy Wroclawskie	PL	B6
67	Katymár	H	B4
99	Katzelsdorf	A	D2
67	Kaub	D	A3
46	Kaulsdorf	D	C6
46	Kauniainen	SF	F12
109	Kaunus	SU	D8
98	Kaupanger	SF	F1
110	Kaustinen	SF	E11
110	Kautzen	A	C6
111	Kavadarci	YU	C4
105	Kavadarci	YU	C4
110	Kavajě	AL	C1
72	Kavak	TR	C4
67	Kavakli	TR	B5
106	Kaválla	GR	C2
112	Kavili	GR	A5
2	Kávlinge	S	D2
112	Kavoúsi, *Kríti*	GR	
56	Kaxholmen	S	B3
45	Kaynarca	TR	A2
107	Kaynarca	TR	B5

Col 8

Pg	Name	Ctry	Grid
64	Karlovy Vary	CS	C2
51	Karlsborg	S	D5
53	Karlsby	S	D1
57	Karlshamn	S	C3
11	Karlshöfen	D	B6
49	Karlshus	N	B7
51	Karlskoga	S	C5
51	Karlskrona	S	C5
51	Karlstad	S	B4
51	Karlstadt	D	B5
96	Karlstetten	A	C6
103	Karlukovo	BG	C5
44	Karmacs	H	B2
110	Karnási	GR	B2
111	Karnezéika	GR	B3
107	Karnobat	BG	A4
109	Karoplési	GR	B4
108	Karousadhes	GR	B1
65	Karpacz	PL	C5
112	Karpathóstra, *Kárpathos*	GR	
109	Karpenísi	GR	C3
108	Karperón	GR	A3
109	Karpofóri	GR	C4
112	Karpuzlu, *Aydin*	TR	B1
107	Karpuzlu, *Edirne*	TR	C4
55	Karrebæksminde	DK	C4
47	Karsämäki	SF	E12
88	Karsin	PL	B3
53	Kärsta, *Stockholm*	S	C4
53	Kärsta, *Västmanland*	S	C2
56	Kärstad	H	A4
62	Karstadt	D	B2
99	Kartal	H	A4
109	Kartéres	GR	A5
72	Kartitsch	A	A2
88	Kartuzy	PL	A4
55	Karup	DK	B2
69	Kasejovice	CS	B4
61	Kasekow	D	B5
104	Kašina	AL	C1
98	Kašina	YU	C1
97	Kasina-Wlk.	PL	B6
47	Kaskinen	SF	E10
47	Kasko	SF	E10
69	Kašperské Hory	CS	B4
109	Kassandra	GR	A5
60	Kasseedorf	D	A1
63	Kassel	D	B4
107	Kastanéai	GR	A5
109	Kastaniá, *Imathia*	GR	A4
109	Kastaniá, *Kardhítsa*	GR	B3
110	Kastania, *Korinthía*	GR	A3
110	Kastania, *Lakonía*	GR	C3
110	Kastania, *Messinía*	GR	B3
108	Kastaniá	GR	C3
100	Kaštel Stari	YU	C1
100	Kaštellaun	A	A3
109	Kastelli	GR	
112	Kastéllion, *Kríti*	GR	
17	Kasterlee	B	B4
70	Kastlösa	S	C5
110	Kastóri	GR	B3
108	Kastoria	GR	A3
108	Kastráki, *Aitolía kai Acarnanía*	GR	C3
112	Kastri, *Náxos*	GR	D3
111	Kastri, *Akhaía*	GR	B3
111	Kastri, *Évia*	GR	A5
109	Kastri, *Lárisa*	GR	B4
112	Kastritsa	GR	B3
110	Kastsikás	GR	B3
112	Katapola	GR	D3
112	Kataráktis	GR	D3
109	Katastari	GR	B1
3	Kathenbridge	GB	A2
3	Kathenoi	GR	C5
50	Kathlenburg-Duhm	D	B5
69	Kato Akhaia	GR	A2
110	Kato Klitoria	GR	B3
110	Kato Makrinoú	GR	C3
44	Kato Milia	GR	B1
108	Kato Nevrokópion	GR	B1
108	Kato Skholárion	GR	A5
109	Kato Tithoréa	GR	C4
54	Kato Vermion	GR	A4
105	Kato Vrondou	GR	C5
108	Katoúna, *Aitolía kai Acarnanía*	GR	C3
108	Katoúna, *Lefkás*	GR	C2
90	Katowice	PL	C3
91	Katrineberg	PL	C3
90	Katrineholm	PL	C3
99	Katrineholm	S	A5
11	Katwijk aan Zee	NL	A4
65	Katy Wroclawskie	PL	B6
67	Katymár	H	A3
106	Katzelsdorf	A	A3
67	Kaub	D	C6
63	Kaulsdorf	D	C6
46	Kauniainen	SF	F12
98	Kaunus	SU	F12
55	Kaupanger	SF	E11
110	Kautzen	A	B12
110	Kavadarci	YU	B3
106	Kavajë	AL	C2
105	Kavak	GR	C5
62	Kavakli	TR	A2
106	Kaválla	GR	C2
67	Kavili	GR	B5
69	Kávlinge	S	D2
56	Kaxholmen	PL	A2
107	Kaynarca	TR	B5

66 Kayserberg F C3
106 Kazanlük BG A3
97 Kažár H C5
91 Kazimierz Dolny PL B5
91 Kazimierza Wielkiego PL C4
88 Kaźmierz PL C2
88 Kcynia PL C3
69 Kdyně CS B4
111 Kéa GR B5
3 Keady GB B5
4 Kealkill IRL C2
99 Kecel H B4
99 Kecskemét H B4
93 Kedainiai SU C8
66 Kédange F B2
109 Kédros GR B4
90 Kedzierzyn PL C2
2 Keel IRL C1
17 Keerbergen B B4
111 Kefalári GR B3
110 Kefaléri GR B3
108 Kefalóvrison GR B3
14 Kegworth GB B1
67 Kehl D C3
64 Kehrigk D A3
11 Keighley GB B4
8 Keil GB B2
8 Keillmore GB C2
7 Keiss GB B5
7 Keith GB C6
55 Keitum D D1
106 Kekhrokambos GR B2
62 Kelberg D C1
63 Kelbra D B6
96 Kelč CS B3
72 Kelchsau A A2
108 Këlcyrë AL A2
11 Keld GB A3
99 Kelebia H B4
110 Kelefá GR C3
68 Kelheim D C2
7 Kellas GB C5
109 Kélli GR A3
59 Kellinghusen D B6
47 Kelloselkå SF C14
3 Kells GB B5
9 Kelso GB C5
67 Kelsterbach D A4
15 Kelvedon GB C3
69 Kematen, *Ober Östereich* A C4
71 Kematen, *Tirol* A A6
69 Kematen a.d. kr. A C5
64 Kemberg D B2
70 Kembs F A2
94 Kemenets-Podolskiy SU B7
73 Kemeten A A6
47 Kemi SF D12
47 Kemijärvi SF C13
68 Kemnath D B2
7 Kemnay GB C6
64 Kemnitz, *Frankfurt* D A2
61 Kemnitz, *Rostock* D A4
17 Kempen D B6
13 Kempsey GB A5
14 Kempston GB B2
71 Kempten D A5
70 Kemptthal CH A3
10 Kendal GB A3
99 Kenderes H A5
105 Kendrikó GR C4
99 Kengyel H A5
14 Kenilworth GB B1
4 Kenmare IRL C2
9 Kenmore GB B4
8 Kennacraig GB C2
14 Kenninghall GB B3
110 Kenoúrgio Khorio GR C2
110 Kéntron GR B2
98 Kenyeri H A2
67 Kenzingen D C3
89 Kępa Polska PL C5
88 Kępice PL A2
90 Kępno PL B2
10 Keppel Gate GB A1
109 Keramidi GR B4
108 Keramitsa GR B2
106 Keramot GR C2
109 Kerasiés GR A3
108 Kerasokhori GR C3
108 Kerásovo GR B2
109 Kerasséa GR B4
111 Keratéa GR B4
47 Kerava SF F12
97 Kerecsend H D6
99 Kerekegyháza H B4
99 Kerepes H A4
110 Keri GR B1
18 Kérien F B2
98 Kerkafalva H B1
105 Kerkina GR C5
108 Kérkira GR B1
17 Kerkrade NL C6
17 Kerksken B C3
18 Kerlôuan F B1
107 Kermen BG A4
18 Kernascleden F B2
70 Kerns CH B3
62 Kerpen D C1
110 Kerpini GR B3
6 Kerrysdale GB C3
98 Kerta H A2
55 Kerteminde DK C3
110 Kérteza GR B2
70 Kerzers CH B2
107 Kesan TR C4
3 Kesh GB B4
107 Keşirlik TR B5
66 Keskastel F C3
17 Kessel D B6
62 Kesselbach D C3
72 Kesselfall A A2
14 Kessingland GB B4
10 Keswick GB A2
98 Keszthely H B2
112 Ketalos GR C2
98 Kéthely H B2
89 Ketrzyn PL A7
14 Kettering GB B2
14 Ketton GB B2
97 Kęty PL B5
61 Ketzin D C3
17 Kevelaer D B6
99 Kevi YU C4
11 Keyingham GB B5
15 Keymer GB D2
13 Keynsham GB B5
97 Kežmarok CS B6
111 Khairónia GR A3
111 Khalándri GR A4
110 Khalandritsa GR A2
108 Khaliki, *Evritanía* GR C3
108 Khaliki, *Tríkkala* GR B3
109 Khalki GR B4
108 Khalkiadhes GR B2
111 Khalkio GR B3
111 Khalkis GR A4
111 Khalkoútsi GR A4
112 Khandra, *Kriti* GR
107 Khándras GR B4
108 Khánia, *Ioánnina* GR B2
112 Khaniá, *Kriti* GR
112 Khárakas, *Kriti* GR
111 Khárakas, *Lakonía* GR C4
110 Kharákti GR A1
106 Kharmanli BG B3
110 Kharokopión GR C2
105 Kharopó GR C5
106 Khaskovo BG B3
110 Khávari GR B2
110 Khavdhata GR A1
103 Khayredin BG C4
105 Khérson GR C4
111 Khiliomódhion GR B3
105 Khimarros GR C5
110 Khióna GR B2
95 Khios GR G7
106 Khisar-Momina Banya BG A2
94 Khmelnitski SU B7
111 Khonikas GR B3
110 Khora GR B2
112 Khora Sfakion, *Kriti* GR
112 Khordháki, *Kriti* GR
112 Khorion GR C2
106 Khoristi GR B2
109 Khortiatis GR A5
108 Khouni GR C3
110 Khráni GR C2
110 Khrisafa GR B3
106 Khrisokhóri GR C2
110 Khrisón GR A3
106 Khrisoupolis GR C2
108 Khrisovitsa GR B3
110 Khrisovitsi GR B3
108 Khristi, *Ioánnina* GR B3
105 Khristi, *Pélla* GR D4
110 Khristianó GR B2
112 Khristós GR C1
109 Khrómio GR A3
94 Khust SU B5
106 Khvoyna BG B2
111 Kiáton GR A3
55 Kibæk DK B1
46 Kiberg N A15
14 Kibworth Beachamp GB B1
104 Kičevo YU C2
10 Kidderminster GB C3
15 Kidlington GB C1
11 Kidsgrove GB B3
11 Kidstones GB A3
12 Kidwelly GB B3
72 Kiefersfelden D A2
59 Kiel D A7
91 Kielce PL C4
89 Kiełpino PL A4
89 Kielpiny PL B5
91 Kiernoziz PL A3
62 Kierspe D B2
70 Kiesen CH B2
97 Kietrz PL A4
61 Kietz D C5
93 Kiev SU E12
89 Kiezmark PL A4
100 Kifino Selo YU C3
111 Kifisiá GR A4
47 Kiiminki SF D12
91 Kije PL C4
100 Kijevo YU B1
99 Kikinda YU C5
49 Kil N C6
51 Kil, *Örebro* S C6
51 Kil, *Värmland* S C4
51 Kila S C3
52 Kilafors S A2
109 Kilas GR A3
96 Kilb Rabenstein A C1
5 Kilbeggan IRL A4
4 Kilbeheny IRL B3
8 Kilberry GB C2
8 Kilburnie GB C3
8 Kilchoan GB B1
5 Kilcock IRL A5
4 Kilcoe IRL C2
4 Kilcolgan IRL A3
4 Kilconnell IRL A3
3 Kilcoo GB B5
5 Kilcormac IRL A4
5 Kilcullen IRL A5
3 Kilcurry IRL B5
5 Kildare IRL A5
5 Kildavin IRL B5
7 Kildonan GB B5
4 Kildorrey IRL B3
8 Kildrochat GB D3
49 Kilegrend N C5
49 Kilen N B5
4 Kilgarvan IRL C2
4 Kilkee IRL B2
3 Kilkeel GB B6
5 Kilkenny IRL B4
12 Kilkhampton GB C3
4 Kilkieran IRL A2
4 Kilkinlea IRL B2
105 Kilkis GR D4
4 Kilkishen IRL B3
5 Kill IRL A5
2 Killala IRL B2
4 Killaloe IRL B3
5 Killane IRL A4
5 Killare IRL A4
4 Killarney IRL B2
5 Killeagh IRL C4
8 Killean GB C2
56 Killeberg S C3
5 Killeigh IRL A4
3 Killeshandra IRL B4
4 Killimor IRL A3
8 Killin GB B3
110 Killini GR B2
5 Killinick IRL B5
4 Killorglin IRL B2
3 Killough GB B6
5 Killucan IRL A4
2 Killybegs IRL B3
3 Killyleagh GB B6
8 Kilmacolm GB C3
3 Kilmacrenan IRL A4
5 Kilmacthomas IRL B4
2 Kilmaine IRL C2
4 Kilmallock IRL B3
8 Kilmarnock GB C3
8 Kilmartin GB B2
8 Kilmaurs GB C3
8 Kilmelford GB B2
5 Kilmore IRL B5
5 Kilmore Quay IRL B5
7 Kilmuir GB C4
3 Kilnaleck IRL C4
8 Kilninian GB B1
8 Kilninver GB B2
8 Kiloran GB B1
46 Kilpisjärvi SF B10
3 Kilrea GB B5
4 Kilreekil IRL A3
4 Kilrush IRL B2
5 Kilsheelan IRL B4
53 Kilsmo S C1
8 Kilsyth GB C3
5 Kiltegan IRL B5
5 Kiltoom IRL A3
4 Kiltullagh IRL A3
3 Kilwaughter GB B6
8 Kilwinning GB C3
109 Kimina GR A4
106 Kimméria GR B2
111 Kimolos GR C5
67 Kimratshofen D D6
53 Kimstad S D1
7 Kinbrace GB B5
9 Kincardine GB B4
73 Kindberg A A5
63 Kindelbruck D B6
111 Kinéta GR B4
14 Kineton GB B1
14 King's Lynn GB B3
3 Kingarrow IRL B3
8 Kingarth GB C2
9 Kinghorn GB B4
13 Kinghton GB A4
93 Kingisepp SU A11
93 Kingisepp, *Saaremaa* SU A8
15 Kings Worthy GB C1
9 Kingsbarns GB B5
12 Kingsbridge GB C4
15 Kingsclere GB C1
3 Kingscourt IRL C5
8 Kingshouse Hotel GB B3
13 Kingskerswell GB C4
13 Kingsteighton GB C4
11 Kingston upon Hull GB B5
13 Kingswear GB C4
13 Kingswood GB B5
13 Kington GB A4
9 Kingussie GB A3
7 Kinloch, *Highland* GB B4
6 Kinloch, *Skye* GB C3
8 Kinloch Hotel GB B2
8 Kinloch Hourn GB A2
8 Kinloch Rannoch GB B3
8 Kinlocheil GB B2
6 Kinlochewe GB C3
8 Kinlochleven GB B3
8 Kinlochmoidart GB B2
2 Kinlough IRL B3
56 Kinna S B1
56 Kinnared S B2
56 Kinnarp S A2
51 Kinne-Kleva S D4
5 Kinnegad IRL A4
5 Kinnitty IRL A4
17 Kinrooi B B5
9 Kinross GB B4
4 Kinsale IRL C3
48 Kinsarvik N A3
6 Kintaravay GB B2
7 Kintore GB C6
8 Kintraw GB B2
4 Kinvarra IRL A3
110 Kiono GR A1
111 Kiparissi GR C3
110 Kiparissia GR B2
109 Kipárissos GR B4
68 Kipfenburg D C2
108 Kipourió GR B3
8 Kippen GB B3
67 Kippenheim D C3
111 Kipséli, *Égina* GR B4
109 Kipséli, *Kardhítsa* GR B4
108 Kipséli, *Kastoría* GR A3
110 Kira GR A3
99 Királyhegyes H B5
62 Kirberg D C3
107 Kircasalih TR B4
73 Kirchbach i Steiermark A B5
70 Kirchberg CH A2
67 Kirchberg, *Baden-Württemberg* D B5
66 Kirchberg, *Rheinland-Pfalz* D B3
96 Kirchberg a.d.P. A C1
73 Kirchberg a. Wechsel A A5
72 Kirchberg im Tirol A A2
72 Kirchbichl A A2
72 Kirchdorf A A2
60 Kirchdorf D B2
68 Kirchdorf, *Bayern* D C2
69 Kirchdorf, *Bayern* D C4
59 Kirchdorf, *Niedersachsen* D C5
69 Kirchdorf a.d. Krems A D5
67 Kircheimbolanden D B4
68 Kirchenlaibach D B2
64 Kirchenlamitz D C1
68 Kirchenthumbach D B2
62 Kirchhain D C3
67 Kirchheim, *Baden-Württemberg* D C5
68 Kirchheim, *Bayern* D C1
63 Kirchheim, *Hessen* D C4
62 Kirchhundem D B3
59 Kirchlinteir D C6
98 Kirchschlag A A1
68 Kirchseeon D C2
68 Kirchweidach D C3
59 Kirchweyhe D C5
67 Kirchzarten D D3
67 Kirchzell D B5
3 Kircubbin GB B6
106 Kiria GR B2
111 Kiriaki GR A3
109 Kirinthos GR C5
10 Kirk Michael GB A1
9 Kirkbean GB D4
9 Kirkbride GB D4
10 Kirkby GB B3
10 Kirkby Lonsdale GB A3
11 Kirkby Moorside GB A5
10 Kirkby Stephen GB A3
9 Kirkcaldy GB B4
9 Kirkcambeck GB C5
8 Kirkcolm GB D2
9 Kirkconnel GB C4
8 Kirkcudbright GB D3
48 Kirkehamn N C3
50 Kirkenær N B3
46 Kirkenes N B15
10 Kirkham GB B3
106 Kirki GR C3
8 Kirkintilloch GB C3
107 Kirklareli TR B5
9 Kirkliston GB C4
9 Kirkmichael GB B4
8 Kirkoswald GB C3
9 Kirkstile GB C5
9 Kirkton of Largo GB B5
7 Kirkwall GB B6
66 Kirn D B3
9 Kirriemuir GB B4
14 Kirton GB B2
11 Kirton in Lindsey GB B5
62 Kirtorf D C4
47 Kiruna S C10
56 Kisa S B4
99 Kisač YU C4
98 Kisbárapáti H B2
98 Kisbér H A3
94 Kishinev SU C8
89 Kisielice PL B5
98 Kiskomarom H B2
99 Kisköre H A5
99 Kiskörös H B4
99 Kiskundorozsma H B5
99 Kiskunfélegyháza H B4
99 Kiskunhalas H B4
99 Kiskunlacháza H A4
99 Kiskunmajsa H B4
98 Kisláng H B3
97 Kišovce CS B6
112 Kissamos, *Kriti* GR
51 Kissleberg S D2
67 Kißleg D D5
109 Kissós GR B5
67 Kist D B5
77 Kistanje YU C5
99 Kistarcsa H A4
99 Kistelek H B4
97 Kisterenye H C5
46 Kistrand N A12
99 Kisújszállás H A5
94 Kisvárda H B5
88 Kiszewa Stara PL B4
88 Kiszkowo PL C3
99 Kiszombor H B5
107 Kiten BG A5
111 Kithnos GR B5
110 Kitriés GR C3
109 Kitros GR A4
61 Kittendorf D B3
47 Kittilä SF C12
96 Kittsee A C3
72 Kitzbühel A A2
68 Kitzingen D B1
57 Kivik S D3
108 Kivotós GR A3
89 Kiwity PL A6
107 Kizilamüsellim TR B4
107 Kizilcidere TR B5
107 Kizilpinar TR B5
55 Kjellerup DK B2
49 Kjopmannskjaer N B7
97 Kl'ačno CS C4
101 Kladanj YU B3
60 Kläden D C2
54 Klädesholmen S A4
101 Kladnica YU C5
100 Kladnice YU C1
64 Kladno CS C4
102 Kladovo YU B3
69 Kladruby CS B3
73 Klagenfurt A B4
57 Klagstorp S D2
93 Klaipeda SU C7
64 Klaistow D A2
105 Klajič YU B3
77 Klanac YU B5
73 Klangec YU B5
68 Klardorf D B3
54 Klarup DK A3
51 Klässbol S C3
64 Klášterec n. Ohří CS C3
97 Klášťor CS C4
69 Klatovy CS B4
69 Klaus a.d. Pyrnbahn A D5
56 Klavreström S B4
58 Klazienaveen NL C4
88 Kłecko PL C3
90 Kleczew PL A2
61 Klein Plasten D B3
73 Klein St. Paul A B4
63 Kleinpaschleben D B6
73 Kleinsölk A A3
96 Kleinzell A D1
57 Klemensker DK D3
88 Klempicz PL C2
101 Klenak YU B4
68 Klenci pod Cerchovem CS B3
104 Klenjë AL C2
101 Klenje YU B4
97 Klenovec CS C5
98 Klenovnik YU B1
48 Kleppe N C2
61 Kleptow D B5
89 Kleszewo PL C7
64 Klettwitz D B3
17 Kleve D B6
89 Klewki PL B6
102 Kličevad YU B2
102 Kličevad YU B2
109 Klidi GR A4
73 Kliening A B4
60 Klietz D C3
97 Klikuszowa PL B6
110 Klima GR A2
108 Klimatiá GR B2
97 Klimkovice CS B4
104 Klina YU B2
73 Klinča Selo YU C5
96 Klingenbach A D2
67 Klingenberg D B5
69 Klingenbrunn D C4
64 Klingenthal D C2
108 Klinó GR B3
55 Klipley DK D2
57 Klippan S C2
100 Klis YU C1
105 Klisura BG B5
106 Klisura, *Plovdiv* BG A2
105 Klisura YU B4
54 Klitmøller DK A1
50 Klitten S A5
55 Klixbüll D D1
99 Kljajićevo YU C4
100 Kljake YU C1
100 Ključ YU B1
96 Klobouky CS B2
90 Klobuck PL C2
61 Klodawa PL C6
65 Klodzko PL C6
50 Kløfta N B2
102 Klokočevac YU B3
97 Klokočov CS B4
90 Klomnice PL C3
17 Kloosterzande NL B4
104 Klos AL C2
98 Kloštar YU C2
98 Kloštar Ivanić YU C1
61 Kloster D A4
61 Klosterfelde D C4
71 Klösterie A A5
63 Klostermansfeld D B6
96 Klosterneuburg A C2
71 Klosters CH B4
70 Kloten CH A3
60 Klötze D C2
46 Klövsjo S E7
90 Kluczbork PL C2
88 Kluczewo PL B2
17 Klundert NL B4
62 Kluppelberg D B2
60 Klutz D B2
91 Klwów PL B4
48 Knaben N C4
51 Knapstad N C2
56 Knäred S C2
11 Knaresborough GB A4
15 Knebwart GB C2
98 Kneginec YU B1
60 Knesebeck D C1
16 Knesselare B B3
73 Knežak YU C4
99 Kneževi-Vinogradi YU C3
99 Knezevo YU C3
103 Knezha BG C5
101 Knić YU C5
108 Knidhi GR A3
100 Knin YU B1
57 Knislinge S C3
73 Knittelfeld A A4
53 Knivsta S C3
102 Knjaževac YU C3
10 Knocksharry GB A1
16 Knokke B B3
11 Knowle GB C4
90 Knurów PL C2
52 Knutby S C4
10 Knutsford GB B3
107 Knyazhevo BG A4
72 Kobarid YU B3
55 København DK C5
73 Kobenz A A4
98 Kobersdorf A A1
97 Kobiernice PL B5
106 Kobilyone BG B3
97 Kobiór PL A4
102 Kobišnica YU B3
70 Koblenz CH A3
62 Koblenz D C2
93 Kobrin SU D9
61 Kobylanka PL B5
96 Kobylí CS C2
65 Kobylin PL B7
89 Kobylniki PL C6
91 Kobytka PL A5
102 Kočane YU C2
105 Kočani YU C4
112 Kocarli TR B1
101 Koceljevo YU B4
100 Kočerin YU C2
73 Kočevje YU C4
72 Kochel D A1
105 Kocherinovo BG B5
90 Kochlowy PL B1
91 Kock PL B6
98 Kocs H A3
99 Kocsér H B4
98 Kocsola H B3
88 Koczala PL B3
49 Kodal N B7
65 Kodersdorf D B4
90 Kodrab PL B3
16 Koekelare B B2
66 Koerich L B1
17 Koersel B B5
73 Köflach A A5
55 Køge DK C5
73 Koglhof A A5
68 Kohlberg D B3
17 Kohlscheid D C6
93 Kohtla-Järve SU A10
111 Koilás GR B4
103 Koilovtsi BG C5
105 Koimisis GR C5
56 Köinge S B1
96 Kojetín CS B3
99 Kóka H A4
110 Kokála GR C3
97 Kokava CS C5
112 Kokkárion GR C1
109 Kokkino Nero GR B4
111 Kókkinon GR A4
47 Kokkola SF E11
96 Kokory CS B3
89 Kokoski PL A4
16 Koksijde B B2
50 Köla S C3
104 Kolače YU B2
47 Kolari SF C11
97 Kolárovo CS D3
104 Kolašin YU B1
53 Kolbäck S C2
61 Kolbacz PL B5
91 Kolbiel PL A5
72 Kolbnitz A B3
49 Kolbotn N B7
50 Kolbu N B1
91 Kolbuszowa PL C5
55 Kolby Kås DK C3
61 Kolczewo PL B5
88 Kolczyglowy PL A3
55 Kolding DK C2
99 Kölesd H B3
47 Koli SF E14
69 Kolín CS A6
54 Kolind DK B3
109 Kolindrós GR A4
69 Kolinec CS B4
110 Koliri GR B2
55 Kølkær DK B2
64 Kolkwitz D B4
63 Kölleda D B6
69 Kollerschlag A C4
110 Kollinai GR B3
58 Kollum NL B3
62 Köln D C1
90 Kolo PL A2
61 Kolobrzeg PL A6
64 Kolochau D B3
94 Kolomyya SU B6
69 Koloveč CS B4
93 Kolpino SU A12
60 Kolrep D B3
65 Kolsko PL B6
53 Kolsva S C1
97 Kolta CS C4
90 Kolumna PL B3
100 Kolunič YU B1
91 Koluszki PL B3
99 Kolut YU C3
55 Kølvrå DK B2
109 Kómanos GR A3
107 Kómara GR B4
97 Komárno CS D4
98 Komárom H A3
98 Komárváros H B2
109 Kombotádhes GR C4
108 Kombóti GR B3
100 Komin YU C2
97 Komjatice CS C4
101 Komletinci YU A3
98 Komló, *Barany* H B3
99 Kömlö, *Heves* H A5
109 Kómma GR C4
108 Kommeno GR B3
17 Kommern D C6
73 Komnik YU B4
109 Komniná GR A3
97 Komoča CS D4
104 Komoran YU B2
65 Komornik PL A6
106 Komotiní GR B3
94 Komrat SU C8
89 Komsomolsk SU A6
101 Konak YU A5
88 Konarzyny PL B3
105 Končulj YU B3
107 Kondolovo BG A5
99 Kondoros H B5
107 Konevo BG A4
55 Køng DK C4
56 Konga S C4
49 Kongsberg N B6
49 Kongshamn N C5
50 Kongsvinger N B2
96 Konice CS B2
91 Konie PL B4
90 Koniecpol PL C3
64 Konigs Wusterhausen D A3
63 Königsberg D C5
67 Königsbronn D C6
64 Königsbrück D B3
68 Königsbrunn D C1
68 Konigsdorf D D2
63 Königsee D C6
67 Königshofen, *Baden-Württemberg* D B5
63 Konigshofen, *Bayern* D C5
63 Königslutter D A5
72 Königssee D A2
62 Königstein D C3
96 Königstetten A C2
64 Königswartha D B4
69 Konigswiesen A C5
62 Königswinter D C2
90 Konin PL A2
109 Koniskos GR B3
108 Konispol AL B2
111 Konistre GR A5
108 Kónitsa GR A2
70 Köniz CH B2
100 Konjic YU C2
73 Konjice YU B5
63 Könnern D B6
49 Konnerud N B7
108 Konopina GR C3
105 Konopište YU C4
91 Konopnica PL B6
64 Konradsreuth D C1
91 Końskie PL B4
48 Konsmo N C4
89 Konstantinovka SU A6
90 Konstantynów PL B3
71 Konstanz D A4
109 Kontariotissa GR A4
17 Kontich B B4
110 Kontovázaina GR B2
98 Kóny H A2
105 Konyavo BG B4
66 Konz D B2
17 Koog a/d Zaan NL A4
110 Kopanáki GR B2
96 Kopčany CS C3
72 Koper YU C3
61 Köpernitz D B3
48 Kopervik N B2
98 Kópháza H A1
90 Kopice PL C1
65 Kopidlno CS C5
53 Köping S C2
57 Köpinge S D3
57 Köpingebro S D2
104 Koplik AL B1
46 Koppang N F5
50 Kopparberg S C5
51 Koppem S C3
62 Köppern D C3
105 Koprivlen BG C5
98 Koprivnica, *Hrvatska* YU B1
102 Koprivnica, *Srbija* YU B3
97 Kopřivnice CS B4
106 Koprivshtitsa BG A2
62 Korbach D B3
62 Körbecke D B3
17 Korbeek-Lo B C4
105 Korbevac YU B4
102 Korbovo YU B3
108 Korçë AL A2
81 Korčula YU B4
65 Korczyców PL A4
101 Korenita YU B4
105 Koretin YU B3
90 Korfantów PL C1
110 Korfés GR A3
111 Kórfos GR B4
46 Korgen N C6
111 Korini GR A3
109 Korinos GR A4
55 Korinth DK C3
111 Kórinthos GR B3
111 Korisia GR B5
109 Koriskhádes GR C3
108 Korissós GR A3
110 Korithi GR B1
60 Köritz D C3
98 Körmend H A1
88 Korne PL A3
63 Körner D B5
96 Korneuburg A C2
89 Kornievo SU A6
65 Kórnik PL A7
51 Kørnsjø N D2
67 Kornwestheim D C5
98 Környe H A3
77 Koromacno YU B4
110 Koróni GR C2
112 Koronis GR D1
108 Koronisia GR B2
112 Kóronos GR D1
88 Koronowo PL B3
111 Koropi GR B4
94 Korosten SU A8
51 Korsberga S D5
52 Korsnäs S B1
55 Korsør DK C4
16 Kortemark B B3
106 Korten BG A3
104 Korthpulë AL C1
89 Kortowo PL B6
16 Kortrijk B C3
107 Koruköy TR C4
96 Koryčany CS B3
97 Korytnica-Kúpele CS C5
100 Korzarac YU B1
65 Korzeńsko PL B6
88 Korzybie PL A2
97 Koš CS C4
112 Kós GR B2
101 Kosanica YU C4
68 Kösching D C2
65 Kościan PL A6
90 Kościelec PL A2
88 Kościerzyna PL A3
104 Kosel YU C2
61 Koserow D A5
69 Košetice CS B6
94 Košice CS B4
91 Kosina PL C6
101 Kosjeric YU B4
112 Kösk TR A1
98 Koška YU C3
47 Koskenkorva SF E11
111 Koskina GR A5
109 Koskinás GR B4
77 Kosljun YU B5
111 Kosmás GR B3
65 Kosmonosy CS C4
104 Kosovska Mitrovica YU B2
64 Koßdorf D B3
108 Kossiópi GR B1
65 Košt'álov CS C5
111 Kosta GR B4
56 Kosta S C4
100 Kostajnica YU A1
101 Kostajnik YU B4
108 Kostakioi GR B2
65 Kostalec n. Orlicé CS C6
104 Kostanica YU B1
73 Kostanjevica YU C5
69 Kostelec n Cernymi Lesy CS A5
106 Kostenets BG A1
64 Kostice CS C3
105 Kostinbrod BG B5
101 Kostojeviči YU B4
102 Kostolac YU B2
90 Kostów PL B2
61 Kostrzyn, *Gorzów Wielkopolski* PL C5
65 Kostrzyn, *Posnan* PL A7
90 Kostuchna PL C3
105 Kosturino YU C4
88 Koszalin PL A2
97 Koszarawa PL B5
90 Koszęcin PL C2
98 Köszeg H A1
89 Koszwaly PL A4
91 Koszyce PL C4
107 Kotel BG A4
99 Kötelek H A5
103 Kotenovtsi BG C4
64 Köthen D B1
47 Kotka SF F13
88 Kotomierz PL B4
81 Kotor YU B5
100 Kotor Varoš YU B2
98 Kotoriba YU B1
100 Kotorsko YU B3
101 Kotraža YU C5
110 Kótronas GR C3
72 Kötschach A B3
109 Kotsikiá GR C5
69 Kötzting D B3
58 Koudum NL C2
109 Koufós GR B5
109 Koukounariés GR B5
110 Koúnos GR C3
111 Kounoupitsa GR B4
69 Kouřim CS A5
110 Kourouta GR B2
69 Kout na Sumave CS B4
106 Koutsón GR B3
111 Koutsopódhi GR B3
47 Kouvola SF F13
101 Kovačevac YU B5
106 Kovachevitsa BG B1
107 Kovachevo BG A4
105 Kovachevtsi BG B5
103 Kovachitsa BG C4
101 Kovačica YU A5
98 Kövägoors H B2
97 Kovarce CS C4
94 Kovel SU A6
101 Kovilj YU A5
103 Kovnare BG C5
101 Kovren YU C4
89 Kowal PL C5
89 Kowalewo Pom. PL B4
65 Kowary PL C5
91 Kowiesy PL A6
100 Kozanci YU B1
109 Kozáni GR A3
73 Kozarac YU C5
97 Kozárd H D5
100 Kozica YU C2
90 Kozieglowy PL C3
91 Kozienice PL B5
73 Kozina YU C3
73 Kozje YU B5
90 Koźle PL C2
103 Kozlodoy BG C4
101 Kozluk YU B4
90 Koźmin PL B1
90 Koźminek PL B2
69 Kozolupy CS B4
65 Kożuchów PL B5
100 Kožuhe YU B3
107 Kozyürük TR B4
61 Krackow D B5
88 Krąg PL A2
55 Kragenæs DK D4
49 Kragerø N C6
95 Kragujevac YU B5
68 Kraiburg D C3
99 Krajišnik YU C5
64 Krajková CS C2
102 Krajkovac YU C2
96 Krajné CS C3
61 Krajnik Dolny PL B5
77 Krakaca YU A5
97 Krakow PL A5
60 Krakow a. See D B3
96 Král'or Brod CS C3
97 Kral'ovany CS B5
65 Králiky CS C6
73 Kraljevac YU C5
77 Kraljevica YU A4
101 Kraljevo YU C5
69 Kralovice CS B4
64 Kralupy n. Vltavou CS C4
47 Kramfors S E8
103 Kramolin BG C6
17 Kranenburg D B6
108 Kraniá, *Grevená* GR B3
109 Kraniá, *Lárisa* GR B3
108 Kraniá, *Tríkkala* GR B3
63 Kranichfeld D C6
111 Kranidhion GR B4
73 Kranjska Gora YU B3
9 Krantshouse GB C5
77 Krapanj YU C5
73 Krapina YU B5
90 Krapkowice PL C1
108 Krápsi GR B3
69 Kraselov CS B4
73 Krašic YU C5
89 Kraskowo PL A7
64 Kraslice CS C2
69 Krasná Hora n. Vitavou CS B5
64 Krasna Lipa CS C4
89 Krasne PL C6
91 Kraśnik PL C6
91 Kraśnik Fabryczny PL C6
73 Krašnja YU B4
97 Krásno CS B4
77 Krasno YU B5
89 Krasnosielc PL B7
106 Krasnovo BG A2
94 Krasnystaw PL A5
91 Krasocin PL C4
110 Kráthio GR A3
105 Kratovo YU B4
73 Kraubath a.d. Mur A A4
64 Krausnick D A3
67 Krautheim D B5
64 Kravaře, *Severočeský* CS C4
97 Kraváre, *Severomoravsky* CS B4
98 Kravarsko YU C1
102 Kravlje YU C2
69 Kraznějov CS B4
101 Krčedin YU A5
62 Krefeld D B1
63 Kreiensen D B4
69 Krelovice CS B6
111 Kremasti, *Lakonía* GR C3
112 Kremasti, *Ródhos* GR A2
60 Krembz D B2
94 Kremenets SU A6
104 Kremenica YU C3
105 Kremikovtsi BG B5
61 Kremmen D C4
101 Kremna YU C4
97 Kremnica CS C4
59 Krempe D B6
96 Krems a.d. Donau A C1
72 Kremsbücke A B3
69 Kremsmünster A C5
69 Křemže CS C5
90 Krepa PL B2
102 Krepoljin YU B2
106 Krepost BG A3
88 Krepsko PL B2
100 Kreševo YU C3
105 Kresna BG C5
71 Kreßbronn D A4
110 Kréstena GR B2
17 Kreuaau D C6
72 Kreuth D A1
69 Kreuzen A C5
71 Kreuzlingen CH A4
62 Kreuztal D C3
61 Krewelin D C4
109 Kria Vrisi GR A4
93 Krichev SU D12
106 Krichim BG A2
100 Kričke YU C1
70 Kriens CH A3
109 Krikelo GR C3
100 Krilo YU C1
72 Krimml A A2
17 Krimpen a/d Ijssel NL B4
65 Křinec CS C5
109 Krini GR A5
106 Krinidhes GR B2
108 Krionéri, *Kardhítsa* GR B3
110 Krionéri, *Messinía* GR B2
110 Krionerion GR A2
109 Kriopigi GR A5
56 Kristdala S B5
49 Kristiansand N C5
57 Kristianstad S C3
46 Kristiansund N E3
47 Kristiinankaupunki SF E10
51 Kristinehamn S C5
47 Kristinestad SF E10
105 Kristón GR D4
112 Kritsa, *Kriti* GR
105 Kriva Feja YU B4
105 Kriva Palanka YU B4
97 Kriváň CS C5
102 Krivi Vir YU C2
103 Krivodol BG C4
104 Krivogaštani YU C3
105 Krivolak YU C4
98 Kriź YU C1
96 Křižanov CS B2
98 Križevci, *Hrvatska* YU B1
73 Križevci, *Slovenija* YU B6
77 Krk YU A4
73 Krka YU C4
105 Krklja YU B4
101 Krnjača YU B5
77 Krnjak YU A5
100 Krnjeuša YU B1
102 Krnjevo YU B2
90 Krnov CZ C1
65 Krobia PL B6
49 Krøderen N A6
49 Krødsherad N A6
110 Krokeai GR C3
53 Krokek S D2
110 Krokilon GR A3
46 Krokom S E7
88 Krokowa PL A4
49 Krokstadelva N B6
51 Kroksund N C2
96 Kroměriž CS B3
58 Krommenie NL C1
63 Kronach D C6
59 Kronshagen D A7
60 Kröpelin D A2
59 Kropp D A6
63 Kroppenstedt D B6
64 Kropstädt D B2
97 Krościenko PL B6
90 Krośniewice PL A3
94 Krosno PL B4
65 Krosno Odrańskie PL A5
64 Krostitz D B2
90 Krotoszyn PL B1
73 Krottendorf A B5
96 Krouna CS B2
112 Kroussón, *Kriti* GR
108 Kroustalopiyi GR A3
90 Krowiarki PL C2
77 Kršan YU A4
105 Krševica YU B3
73 Krško YU C5
99 Krstur YU B5
96 Křtiny CS B2
62 Kruft D C2
16 Kruishoutem B C3
104 Krujë AL C1
98 Krumbach A A1
68 Krumbach D C1
106 Krumovgrad BG B3
107 Krumovo BG A4
71 Krun, *Bayern* D A6
72 Krun, *Bayern* D A1
64 Krupá CS C3
100 Krupa YU B2
102 Krupac YU C3
101 Krupanj YU B4
97 Krupina CS C5
105 Krupište YU C4
64 Krupka CS C3
105 Krupnik BG C5
100 Kruščica YU B2
77 Kruščiea YU B5
102 Krũsevac YU C2
104 Krusevo YU C3
107 Krushevets BG A5
103 Krushovitsa BG C4
89 Kruszwica PL C4
89 Kruszyn PL C5
81 Krute YU B6
104 Kryevidh AL C1
89 Krynica Morska PL A5
97 Krzanowice PL A4
97 Krzeczów PL B5
61 Krzęin PL B6
65 Krzelow PL B6
90 Krzepice PL C2

65 Krzepielów PL B6
91 Krzeszów
Graniczny PL C6
90 Krzeszowice PL C3
61 Krzeszyce PL C6
89 Krzynowlaga Mała PL B6
65 Krzystkowice PL B5
65 Krzywin PL B6
88 Krzyź PL C2
91 Ksiaz Wielkopolski PL C4
65 Ksiaź Wielkopolski PL A7
89 Księży Lasek PL B7
90 Ktodawa PL A2
71 Küblis CH B4
108 Kuç AL A1
104 Kučeviste YU B3
102 Kučevo YU B2
90 Kuchary PL B1
67 Kuchen D C5
72 Kuchl A A3
89 Kucice PL C6
90 Kuciny PL B3
104 Kucište YU B2
104 Kuckovo YU B3
99 Kucura YU C4
89 Kuczbork PL B6
96 Kudlov CS B3
65 Kudowa Zdrój PL C6
89 Kudypy PL B6
72 Kufstein A A2
57 Kuggeboda S C4
68 Kühbach D C2
47 Kuhmo SF D14
47 Kuhmoinen SF F12
59 Kuhstedt D B5
58 Kuinre NL C2
104 Kukës AL B2
106 Kuklen BG A2
89 Kuklin PL B6
101 Kukujevci YU A4
104 Kukurecani YU C3
102 Kula BG C3
102 Kula YU B2
99 Kula YU C4
93 Kuldiga SU B7
107 Kuleli TR B4
100 Kulen Vakuf YU B1
105 Kuleta BG C5
100 Kulina YU B3
56 Kulltorp S B2
68 Kulmain D B2
68 Kulmbach D A2
99 Kumane YU C5
105 Kumanovo YU B3
53 Kumla, *Örebro* S C1
52 Kumla,
Västmanland S C2
106 Kumoniga BG B3
99 Kunbaja H B4
72 Kundl A A2
54 Kungälv S A4
53 Kungs-Husby S C3
53 Kungsängen S C3
53 Kungsåra S C2
56 Kungsäter S B1
54 Kungsbacka S A5
52 Kungsgården S B2
51 Kungshamn S D2
53 Kungsör S C2
99 Kunhegyes H A5
65 Kunice Zarskie PL B5
97 Kunin CS B3
101 Kuninovo YU B5
99 Kunmadaras H A5
96 Kunovice CS B3
65 Kunowo PL B7
96 Kunštat CS B2
99 Kunszentmárton H B5
99 Kunszentmiklós H A4
69 Kunžak CS B6
67 Künzelsau D B5
47 Kuopio SF E13
102 Kupci YU C2
67 Kupferzell D B5
100 Kupirovo YU B1
73 Kupjak YU C4
107 Küplü TR B4
67 Kuppenheim D C4
100 Kupres YU B2
63 Küps D C6
98 Kura H B3
104 Kurbnesh AL C2
106 Kŭrdzhali BG B3
47 Kurikka SF E11
105 Kurilo BG B5
96 Kuřim CS B2
89 Kurki PL B6
106 Kŭrnave BG A2
91 Kurów PL B6
90 Kurowice PL B3
102 Kuršumlija YU C2
107 Kurtbey TR B4
62 Kürten D B2
106 Kurtovo Konare BG A2
101 Kusadak YU B5
112 Kusadasi TR B1
66 Kusel D B3
60 Kusey D C2
102 Kusić YU B2
104 Kušnin YU B2
70 Küssnacht CH A3
59 Kutenholz D B6
98 Kutina YU C1
98 Kutjevo YU C2
69 Kutná Hora CS B6
90 Kutno PL A3
70 Küttingen CH A3
96 Kúty CS C3
47 Kuusamo SF D14
101 Kuzmin YU A4
90 Kuźnia Raciborska PL C2
88 Kuźnica
Czarnkowska PL C2
88 Kuźnica
Żelichowska PL C2
46 Kvaenangsbotn N B11
55 Kværndrup DK C3
46 Kvalsund N A12
46 Kvam N D5
46 Kvanndal N F3
51 Kvänum S D4
50 Kvarnberg S A5
49 Kvarstein N C4
48 Kvås N C4
96 Kvasice CS B3
56 Kvibille S C1
53 Kvicksund S C2
57 Kvidinge S C2
46 Kvikne N E5
69 Kvilda CS B4
51 Kville S D2
56 Kvillsfors S B4
48 Kvinesdal N C3
48 Kvinlog N C3
48 Kvinnherad N B3
54 Kvissel DK A3
49 Kviteseid N B5
88 Kwakowo PL A3
89 Kwidzyn PL B4
89 Kwietniewo PL B5
88 Kwilcz PL C2
69 Kyje CS A5
96 Kyjov CS B3
6 Kyle of Lochalsh GB C3
6 Kyleakin GB C3
6 Kylerhea GB C3
6 Kylestrome GB B3
66 Kyllburg D A2
64 Kynšperk-n. Ohří CS C2
60 Kyritz D C3
51 Kyrkesund S D2
50 Kyrkheden S B4
57 Kyrkhult S C3
97 Kysuké Nové
Mesto CS B4
105 Kyustendil BG B4
47 Kyyjärvi SF E12

L

23 L'Absie F B4
20 L'Aigle F C1
22 L'Aiguillon-sur-Mer F B3
40 L'Alcudia E B2
29 L'Alpe-d'Huez F A5
79 L'Aquila I A4
25 l'Arbresle F C4
29 L'Argentière-la-
Bessée F B5
29 L'Epine F B4
74 L'Escarène F C2
23 L'homme F A5
28 L'Hospitalet-du-
Larzac F C2
70 L'Isle CH B1
20 l'Isle-Adam F B3
29 L'Isle-sur-la-
Sorgue F C4
70 L'isle-sur-le Doubs F A1
25 l'Isle-sur-Serein F A4
86 L'Ile Rouse F B1
27 L'Isle-de-noé F C4
27 L'Isle-en-Dodon F C4
27 L'Isle-Jourdain,
Gers F C5
23 L'Isle-Jourdain,
Vienne F B5
40 L'Ollerie E C2
38 La Adrada E B2
44 La Alameda E A3
31 La Alberca E D4
39 La Alberca de
Záncara E C4
37 La Albuera E C4
33 La Aldea de Portillo
de Busto E B3
43 La Algaba E B3
38 La Aliseda de
Tormes E B1
34 La Almolda E B2
34 La Almunia de
Doña Godina E B1
39 La Amarcha E C4
34 La Ametlla de Mar E C3
30 La Arena, *Oviedo* E A4
33 La Arena, *Vizcaya* E A3
43 La Aulaga E B3
25 La Balme-de-
Sillingy F C6
32 La Bañeza E B1
22 La Barre-de-Monts F B2
20 La Barre-en-Ouche F C1
43 La Barrosa E C3
27 La Barthe-de-
Neste F C4
16 la Bassée F C2
29 La Bastide F C5
27 La Bastide-de-
Sèrou F C5
29 La Bastide-des-
Jourdans F C4
28 La Bastide
Puylaurent F B2
70 La Bathie F C1
25 La Batie
Montgascon F C5
22 La Baule F A2
20 La Bazoche-Gouet F C1
22 La Bernerie-en-
Retz F A2
35 La Bisbal E B6
19 La Boissière F A6
30 La Bola E B3
42 La Bota E B2
20 La Boullay Mivoye F C2
24 La Bourboule F C2
32 La Bóveda de Toro E C1
66 la Bresse F C2
25 La Bridoire F C5
74 La Brigue F B2
29 La Brillanne F C4
22 La Bruffière F A3
39 La Bugeda E B4
24 la Bussière F A2
22 La Caillère F B4
87 La Caletta I B2
28 La Calmette F C3
38 La Calzada de
Oropesa E C1
43 La Campena E B4
38 La Cañada E B2
30 La Cañiza E B2
21 la Capelle F B4
29 La Capte F C5
30 La Caridad E A4
43 La Carlota E B5
44 La Carolina E A3
28 la Cavalerie F B2
23 La Celle-St. Avant F A5
40 La Cenia E A3
22 La Chaize-le-
Vicomte F B3
17 La Chalamine B C6
29 la Chambre F A5
24 la Chapelande F B2
20 La Chapelle F D2
24 La Chapelle-
d'Angillon F A2
29 La Chapelle-en-
Valgaudemar F B5
29 La Chapelle-en-
Vercors F B4
22 La Chapelle-Glain F A3
20 la Chapelle la
Reine F C3
28 La Chapelle-
Laurent F A2
22 La Chapelle-sur-
Erdre F A3
29 La Charce F B4
24 la Charité sur-Loire F A3
23 La Chartre-sur-le-
Loir F A5
23 La Châtaigneraie F B4
24 La Châtre F B2
21 la Chaussée-sur-
Marne F C5
70 La Chaux-de-
Fonds CH A1
29 La Chêne F C4
21 la Cheppe F B5
18 La Chèze F B3
29 La Ciotat F C4
25 La Clayette F B4
70 La Clusaz F C1
37 La Codosera E B3
32 La Concha E A3
43 La Contienda E A3
23 La Coquille F C5
37 La Coronada E C5
30 La Coruña E A2
29 La Côte-St. André F A4
22 La Cotinère F C3
23 La Couronne F C5
24 La Courtine le
Trucq F C2
28 La Couvertoirade F C2
29 La Crau F C5
23 La Crèche F B4
23 La Croix F A5
21 La Croix-St. Ouen F B3
29 La Croix Valmer F C5
33 La Cruz E A4
37 La Cumbre E B5
27 La Douze F A4
35 La Escala E A6
30 La Espina E A4
30 La Estrada E B2
38 La Estrella E C1
29 La Farlède F C5
39 La Felipa E C5
21 la Fère F B4
22 La Ferrière F B3
23 La Ferrière-en-
Pathenay F B4
20 la-Ferté-Alais F C3
20 La Ferté-Bernard F C1
21 la Ferté Chevresis F B4
20 La Ferte Fresnal F C1
21 la Ferte Gaucher F C4
24 La Ferté-Imbault F A1
19 La Fertè-Mace F B5
21 la Ferté-Milon F B4
21 la Ferte-sous-
Jouarre F C4
24 La Ferté-St.Aubin F A1
24 La Ferté-St.Cyr F A1
20 La Ferté Vidame F C1
20 La Ferté Villeneuil F D2
20 La Feuillie F B2
23 La Flèche F A4
22 La Flotte F B3
27 La Fouillade F B6
29 La Foux F C5
32 La Franca E A2
31 La Fregeneda E D4
34 La Fresneda E C3
19 La Gacilly F C3
34 La Galera E C3
29 La Garde-Freinet F C5
30 La Garita E A3
22 La Garnache F B3
35 La Garriga E B5
37 La Garrovilla E C4
22 La Gaubretière F B3
39 La Gineta E C5
40 La Granadella E C3
28 La Grand-Combe F B3
25 La Grande-Croix F C4
28 La Grande motte F C3
37 La Granjuela E C5
19 La Gravelle F B4
31 La Guardia,
Pontevedra E C2
39 La Guardia, *Toledo* E C3
44 La Guardia de
Jaén E B3
31 La Gudiña E B3
19 La Guerche-de-
Bretagne F C4
24 la Guerche sur
l'Aubois F B2
22 La Guérinière F B2
37 La Haba E C5
19 La Haye-du-Puits F A4
19 La Haye-Pesnel F B4
16 la Herlière F C2
32 La Hermida E A2
39 La Herrera E D4
40 La Higuera E C1
32 La Hiniesta E C1
45 La Hórca E A5
38 La Horcajada E B1
32 La Horra E C3
17 La Hulpe B C4
19 La Hutte F B6
40 La Iglesuela del
Cid E A2
44 La Iruela E B4
29 La Javie F B5
23 La Jonchère-St.
Maurice F B6
35 La Junquera E A5
43 La Lantejuela E B4
38 La Iglesuela E B2
43 La Linea E C4
29 La Londe F C5
20 La Loupe F C2
17 La Louviere B C4
43 La Luisiana E B4
24 la Machine F B3
87 La Maddalena I A2
32 La Magdalena E B1
20 La Mailleraye F B1
21 La Maison Bleue F B4
28 La Malène F B2
44 La Mamola E C3
34 La Masadera E B2
38 La Mata E C2
38 La Mata de
Ledesma E A1
32 La Mata de
Monteagudo E B1
45 La Matanza E A5
22 La Meilleraye-de-
Bretagne F A3
23 La Membrolle F A5
23 La Ménitré F A4
30 La Merca E B3
31 La Mezquita E B3
29 La Mole F C5
35 La Molina E A4
24 La Monnerie-le-
Montel F C3
37 La Morera E C4
22 La Mothe-Achard F B3
23 La Mothe-St. Héray F B4
29 La-Motte, *Alpes-
de-Haute-
Provence* F B5
29 La Motte, *Isère* F B4
25 La Motte-Servolex F C5
32 La Mudarra E C2
34 La Muela E B1
29 La Mure F B4
74 La Napoule F C1
43 La Nava E B3
38 La Nava de
Ricomalille E C2
37 La Nava de
Santiago E B4
20 La Neuve-Lyre F C1
70 La Neuveville CH A2
24 la Nocle-Maulaix F B3
32 La Nuez de Arriba E B3
24 La Pacaudièe F B3
22 La Pallice F B3
34 La Palma de Ebro E B3
43 La Palma del
Condado E B3
28 La Parade F B2
37 La Parra E C4
32 La Pedraja de
Portillo E C2
39 La Peraleja E B4
30 La Peroja E B3
66 la Petit-Pierre F C3
45 La Pinilla E B5
30 La Plaza E A4
35 La Pobla de Lillet E A4
40 La Pobla Llarga E B2
32 La Pola de Gordón E B1
22 La Pommerave F A4
33 La Póveda de
Soria E B4
35 La Preste F A5
41 La Puebla,
Mallorca E
39 La Puebla de
Almoradie E C3
43 La Puebla de
Cazalla E B4
43 La Puebla de los
Infantes E B4
38 La Puebla de
Montalbán E C2
34 La Puebla de Roda E A3
40 La Puebla de
Valverde E A2
43 La Puebla del Rio E B3
38 La Pueblanueva E C2
45 La Puerta de
Segura E A4
71 La Punt CH B4
44 La Quintana E B2
43 La Quintera E B4
44 La Rábita E B2
44 La Rambla E B2
87 La Reale I A1
42 La Redondela E B2
26 La Réole F B3
28 La Ricamarie F A3
35 La Riera E B4
43 La Rinconada E B4
20 La Rivière-
Thibouville F B1
32 La Robia E B1
37 La Roca de la
Sierra E B4
70 La Roche CH B2
29 La Roche F B4
22 La Roche Bernard F A2
26 La Roche-Chalais F A4
29 La Roche-de-Rame F B5
18 La Roche Derrien F B2
17 La Roche-en-
Ardenne B C5
25 la Roche-en-Brénil F A4
20 La Roche-Guyon F B2
23 La Roche-Posay F B5
25 La Roche-s-Foron F B6
22 La Roche-sur-Yon F B3
25 La Roche-Vineuse F B4
23 La
Rochebeaucourt-
et-Argentine F C5
23 La Rochefoncauld F C5
22 La Rochelle F B3
29 La Rochette F B4
39 La Roda, *Albacete* E C4
30 La Roda, *Oviedo* E A4
44 La Roda de
Adalucia E B2
28 La Roque F B2
29 La Roque-
d'Anthéron F C4
27 La Roque Gageac F B5
29 La
Roquebrussanne F C4
33 La Rubia E C4
30 La Rue E B3
41 La Sabina, *Ibiza* E
31 La Sagreda E D4
38 La Salceda E A3
29 La Salle F B5
72 La Salute di
Livenza I C2
27 La Salvetat-
Peyralés F B6
28 La Salvetat-sur-
Agout F C1
70 La Sarraz CH B1
32 La Seca E C2
35 La Selva E B4
35 La Serra E B4
29 La Seyne F C4
39 La Solana E D3
23 La Souterraine F B6
75 La Spezia I B4
78 La Storta I B3
19 La-Suze-sur-Sarthe F C6
26 La Teste F B2
70 La Thuile I C1
39 La Toba E B5
38 La Toledana E C2
38 La Torre de
Esteban Habrán E B2
39 La Torresaviñán E B4
29 La Tour d'Aigues F C4
25 La Tour du-Pin F C5
22 La Tranche-sur-
Mer F B3
22 La Tremblade F C3
22 La Trinité F A1
18 La Trinité-Porhoët F B3
74 La Trinite-Victor F C2
29 La Tronche F A4
22 La Turballe F A2
74 La Turbie F C2
32 La Uña E A1
45 La Unión E B6
29 La Valette F C4
32 La Vecilla E B1
30 La Vega, *Orense* E B4
30 La Vega, *Oviedo* E A4
38 La Velilla E A3
39 La Ventosa E B4
25 La Verpillière F C5
44 La Victoria E B2
33 La Vid E C3
39 La Villa de Don
Fadrique E C3
27 la Ville Dieu-du-
Temple F B5
23 La Villedieu F B4
29 La Voulte-sur-
Rhône F B3
67 la Wantzenau F C3
34 La Zoma E C2
96 Laa a.d. Thaya A C2
60 Laage D B3
62 Laasphe D C3
4 Laban IRL A3
27 Labastide F C5
27 Labastide-Murat F B5
99 Lábatan H A3
89 Łabednik PL A6
28 Labegude F B3
26 Labenne F C2
68 Laberweinting D C3
77 Labin YU A4
104 Labinot-Mal AL C2
110 Labiri GR A2
88 Łabiszyn PL C3
28 Lablachère F B3
98 Lábod H B2
60 Laboe D A1
26 Labouheyre F B3
26 Labrède F B3
26 Labrit F B3
39 Labros E A5
27 Labruguière F C6
31 Labrujo P C2
104 Labuništa YU C2
104 Laç AL C1
44 Lacalahorra E B3
26 Lacanau F B2
26 Lacanau-Océan F A2
25 Lacanche F A4
27 Lacapelle-Marival F B5
101 Laćarak YU A4
28 Lacaune F C1
11 Laceby GB B5
80 Lacedónia I C2
71 Láces (Latsch) I B5
70 Lachen CH A3
89 Ląck PL C5
64 Lackau D B3
56 Läckeby S C5
98 Lackenbach A A1
14 Lackford GB B3
51 Läckö S D4
13 Lacock GB B5
87 Láconi I C2
26 Lacq F C3
28 Lacroix-Barrez F B1
66 Lacroix-sur-Meuse F C1
62 Ladbergen D A2
65 Lądek Zdrój PL C6
55 Ladelund D D1
96 Ladendorf A C2
103 Ladeşti RO B5
107 Ládhi GR B4
23 Ladignac-le-Long F C6
78 Ladispoli I B3
37 Ladoeiro P B3
20 Ladon F D3
9 Ladybandk GB B4
62 Laer D A2
46 Laerdalsöyn N F3
112 Láerma GR B2
21 Laferté-sur-Aube F C5
5 Laffansbridge IRL B4
110 Láfka GR B3
109 Láfkos GR B5
27 Lafrançaise F B5
56 Lagan S C2
85 Laganadi I A4
110 Laganás GR B1
36 Lagares, *Coimbra* P A3
31 Lagares, *Porto* P C2
75 Lagaro I B6
38 Lagartera E C1
62 Lage D B3
59 Lägerdorf D B6
8 Lagg GB C2
7 Laggan, *Grampian* GB C5
8 Laggan, *Highland* GB A3
2 Laghy IRL B3
65 Lagiewniki PL C6
109 Laginá GR A5
71 Láglio I C4
25 Lagnieu F C5
21 Lagny, *Oise* F B3
21 Lagny, *Seine-et-
Marne* F C3
21 Lagny-le-Sec F B3
82 Lago I B3
42 Lagoa P B1
31 Lagoaça P C4
82 Lagonegro I A2
26 Lagor F C3
28 Lagorce F B3
106 Lágos GR B3
42 Lagos P B1
76 Lagosanto I B2
65 Łagów PL A5
91 Łagów PL C5
28 Lagrasse F C1
34 Laguarres E A3
27 Laguépie F B5
33 Laguerdia E B4
28 Laguiole F B1
32 Laguna de Duero E C2
32 Laguna de
Negrillos E B1
39 Laguna del
Marquesado E B5
37 Lagunilla E A4
26 Laharie F B3
21 Laheycourt F C6
107 Lahna TR B5
56 Laholm S C2
67 Lahr D C3
47 Lahti SF F12
67 Laichingen D C5
7 Laid GB B4
21 Laifour F B5
21 Laignes F D5
74 Laiguéglia I C3
47 Laiha SF E11
69 Laimbach a.
Ostrong A C6
68 Laineck D B2
7 Lairg GB B4
28 Laissac F B1
108 Laista GR B2
47 Laitila SF F10
72 Láives (Leifers) I B1
101 Lajkovaci YU B5
98 Lajoskomárom H B3
99 Lajosmizse H A4
110 Láka, *Akhaia* GR A2
108 Láka, *Paxoi* GR B2
14 Lakenheath GB B3
105 Lakhanás GR D5
112 Lakhaniá GR B3
99 Lakitelek H B5
112 Lakki GR C1
109 Lakkia GR A3
112 Lákkoi, *Kriti* GR
110 Lakkópetra GR A2
109 Lakkovikia GR A5
55 Lakolk DK C1
96 Lakšárska Nová
Ves CS C3
46 Lakselv N A12
100 Laktaši YU B2
26 Lalande F B3
107 Lâlapasa TR B4
110 Lálas GR B2
27 Lalbenque F B5
28 Lalevade F B3
30 Lalin E B2
102 Lalinac YU C3
27 Lalinde F B4
69 Lalling D C4
69 Lam D B4
79 Lama dei Peligni I A5
75 Lama Mocogno I B5
27 Lamagistére F B4
66 Lamarche F C1
25 Lamarche-sur-
Saône F A5
36 Lamarosa P B2
26 Lamarque F A3
31 Lamas P D2
31 Lamas de Moaro P B2
29 Lamastre F B3
69 Lambach A C4
18 Lamballe F B3
15 Lamberhurst GB C3
29 Lambesc F C4
110 Lambia GR B2
15 Lambourn GB C1
31 Lamego P C3
109 Lamia GR C4
8 Lamlash GB C2
56 Lammhult S B3
27 Lamothe-Cassel F B5
27 Lamothe-Montravel F B4
24 Lamotte-Beuvron F A2
67 Lampertheim D B4
12 Lampeter GB A3
14 Lamport GB B2
69 Lamprechtshausen A D3
64 Lamsfeld D B4
63 Lamspringe D B5
59 Lamstedt D B6
25 Lamure-sur-
Azergues F B4
71 Lana I B6
110 Lanáda GR C3
28 Lanarce F B3
9 Lanark GB C4
10 Lancaster GB A3
9 Lanchester GB D6
79 Lanciano I A5
19 Lancieux F B3
91 Łańcut PL C6
40 Landate E B1
68 Landau, *Bayern* D C3
62 Landau, *Hessen* D B4
71 Landeck A A5
17 Landen B C5
59 Landen D C4
18 Landerneau F B1
56 Landeryd S B2
59 Landesbergen D C6
18 Landévant F C2
18 Landévennec F B1
18 Landivisiau F B1
19 Landivy F B4
73 Landl, *Steiermark* A A4
72 Landl, *Tirol* A A2
28 Landos F B2
21 Landouzy F B5
71 Landquart CH B4
21 Landrecies F A4
21 Landreville F C5
75 Landriano I A4
64 Landsberg D B2
68 Landsberg D C1
56 Landsbro S B3
66 Landscheid D B2
68 Landshut D C3
57 Landskrona S D1
17 Landsmer NL A4
66 Landstuhl D B3
54 Landvetter S A5
3 Lanesborough IRL C4
18 Lanester F C2
33 Lanestosa E A3
54 Langå DK B2
33 Langa de Duero E C3
109 Langadhás GR A5
110 Langádhia GR B3
109 Langadhikia GR A5
49 Langangen N B6
56 Långared S A1
56 Långås S C1
56 Långasjö S C4
96 Langau A C1
8 Langbank GB C3
28 Langeac F A2
23 Langeais F A5
63 Langeln D B5
63 Langelsheim D B5
59 Langen D B5
67 Langenau D C6
62 Langenberg,
*Nordrhein-
Westfalen* D B2
62 Langenberg,
*Nordrhein-
Westfalen* D B3
67 Langenburg D B5
59 Langendamm D C6
63 Langeneichstädt D B6
96 Langenenzersdorf A C2
71 Längenfeld A A5
62 Langenfeld D B1
59 Langenhagen D C6
55 Langenhorn D D1
67 Langenionsheim D B3
96 Langenlois A C1
64 Langennaudorf D B3
68 Langenneufnach D C1
96 Langenrohr A C2
62 Langenselbold D C4
67 Langensteinbach D C4
70 Langenthal CH A2
73 Langenwang A A5
68 Langenzenn D B1
59 Langeoog D B4
55 Langeskov DK C3
49 Langesund N B6
63 Langewiesen D C5
50 Långflon S A3
59 Langförden D C5
60 Langhagen D B3
56 Länghem S B2
75 Langhirano I B5
9 Langholm GB C5
72 Langkampfen A A2
70 Langnau CH B2
55 Lango DK D4
28 Langogne F B2
26 Langon F B3
13 Langport GB B5
68 Langquaid D C2
66 Langres F D1
19 Langrune-sur-Mer F A5
51 Långserud S C3
50 Langset N B2
52 Långshyttan S B2
7 Langskaill GB A6
18 Languidic F C2
71 Langundo (Algund) I B6
59 Langwarden D B5
59 Langwedel D C6
68 Langweid D C1
71 Langwies CH B4
31 Lanheses P C2
18 Lanildut F B1
44 Lanjarón E C3
62 Lank-Latum D B1
17 Lanklaar B B5
18 Lanmeur F B2
56 Lanna S B2
51 Lannabruk S C5
52 Lännaholm S C3
18 Lannéanou F B2
27 Lannemezan F C4
21 Lanneuville-sur-
Meuse F B6
18 Lannilis F B1
18 Lannion F B2
27 Lanouaille F A5
70 Lansanne CH B1
28 Lansargues F C3
96 Lanškroun CS B2
27 Lanta F C5
32 Lantadilla E B2
26 Lanton F B2
87 Lanusei I C2
78 Lanuvio I B3
18 Lanvollon F B3
99 Lánycsók H B3
30 Lanza E A2
30 Lanzada E B2
38 Lanzahita E B2
96 Lanzhof CS C2
74 Lanzo Torinese I A2
44 Lao Corrales E B2
21 Laon F B4
20 Laons F C2
24 Lapalisse F B3
28 Lapanouse F B2
110 Lápas GR A2
91 Łapczyna Wola PL C3
26 Lapegrade F B3
24 Lapeyrouse F B2
29 Lapeyrouse-
Mornay F A3
47 Lapinlahti SF E13
104 Laplje Selo YU B3
27 Laplume F B4
66 Lapoutroie F C3
102 Lapovo YU B2
47 Lappeenranta SF F14
47 Lapua SF E11
30 Laracha E A2
5 Laragh IRL A5
29 Laragne-Monteglin F B4
9 Larbert GB B4
26 Larceveau F C2
29 Larche, *Alpes-de-
Haute-Provence* F B5
27 Larche, *Corrèze* F A5
49 Lårdal N B5
112 Lardhos GR A2
33 Laredo E A3
17 Laren NL A5
28 Largentière F B3
8 Largs GB C3
111 Larimna GR A4
30 Lariño E B1
80 Larino I C1
109 Lárisa GR B4
9 Larkhall GB B5
49 Larkollen N B7
18 Larmor-Plage F C2
3 Larne GB B6
8 Laroch GB B2
21 Laroche F D4
66 Larochette L B2
27 Laroque F B4
27 Laroquebron F B6
30 Larouco E B3
33 Larraga E B5
26 Larrau F C3
27 Larrazet F C5
26 Laruns F C3
44 Larva E B3
49 Larvik N B7
42 Las Antillas E B2
39 Las Cabezadas E A3
43 Las Cabezas de S.
Juan E C4
44 Las Correderas E A3
34 Las Cuevas de
Cañart E C2
38 Las Herencias E C2
39 Las Labores E C3
33 Las Machorras E A3
35 Las Masucas E B4
39 Las Mesas E C4
44 Las Navas E B2
43 Las Navas de la
Concepción E B4
38 Las Navas del
Marques E B2
45 Las Negras E C5
43 Las Pajanosas E B3
39 Las Pedroñeras E C4
35 Las Planas E A5
32 Las Quintanillas E B3
38 Las Rozas, *Madrid* E B3
32 Las Rozas,
Santander E B3
31 Las Uces E C4
38 Las Veguillas E B1
38 Las Ventas con
Peña Aguilera E C2
38 Las Ventas de S.
Julián E B1
34 Las Vilas de Turbó E A3
40 Las Villas de
Benicasim E A3
33 Lasarte E A4
89 Łasin PL B5
90 Łask PL B3
91 Łaskarzew PL B5
11 Laskill GB A4
73 Laško YU B5
91 Lasocin PL A3
34 Laspaules E A3
34 Laspuña E A3
61 Lassan D B4
19 Lassay F B5
96 Lassee A C2
21 Lassigny F B3
110 Lasteika GR B2
75 Lastra a Signa I C6
32 Lastras de Cuéllar E C2
32 Lastres E A1
53 Lästringe S D3
59 Lastrup D C4
33 Latasa E B5
78 Látera I A2
80 Laterza I D3
58 Lathen D C4
7 Latheron GB B5
83 Latiano I A4
79 Latina I B3
72 Latisana I C3
97 Látky CS C5
91 Latowicz PL A5
82 Latrónico I A3
27 Latronquière F B6
70 Latterbach CH B2
62 Laubach D C3
28 Laubert F B2
64 Laubusch D B4
63 Laucha D B6
64 Lauchhammer D B3
67 Lauda D B5
48 Laudal N C4
9 Lauder GB C5
63 Lauenau D A4
60 Lauenburg D B1
68 Lauf D B2
67 Laufach D A5
70 Läufelfingen CH A2
70 Laufen CH A2
67 Laufen, *Baden-
Württemberg* D C4
69 Laufen, *Bayern* D D3
70 Laufenburg CH A3
67 Lauffen D B5
12 Laugharne GB B3
68 Lauingen D C1
44 Laujar E C4
12 Launceston GB C3
103 Lăunele de Sus RO B5
70 Laupen CH B2
67 Laupheim D C5
4 Lauragh IRL C2
82 Laureana di
Borrello I C3
9 Laurencekirk GB B5
3 Laurencetown GB B5
4 Laurencetown IRL A3
82 Laurenzana I A2
82 Lauria I A2
23 Laurière F B6
9 Laurieston, *Central* GB C4
8 Laurieston,
*Dumfries &
Galloway* GB D3
82 Laurino I A2
47 Lauritsala SF F14
63 Lauscha D C6
73 Laussa A A4
28 Laussonne F B3
63 Lautenthal D B5
71 Lauterach A A4
67 Lauterbach,
*Baden-
Württemberg* D C4
63 Lauterbach,
Hessen D C4
70 Lauterbrunnen CH B2
66 Lauterecken D B3
68 Lauterhofen D B2
67 Lautrach D D6
27 Lautrec F C6
47 Lauttakyla SF F11
48 Lauvvik N C3
16 Lauwe B C3
27 Lauzerte F B5
27 Lauzun F B4
75 Lavagna I B4
21 Laval, *Marne* F B5
19 Laval, *Mayenne* F B5
73 Lavamünd A B4
107 Lavara GR B4
27 Lavardac F B4
36 Lavaris P A2
71 Lavarone I C6
24 Lavau F A2
27 Lavaur F C5
35 Lavelanet F A4
80 Lavello I C2
62 Lavelsloh D A3
14 Lavenham GB B3
70 Laveno I C3
76 Lavezzola I B1
47 Lavia SF F11
32 Laviana E A1
80 Laviano I D2
28 Lavilledieu F B3
78 Lavinio-Lido di
Enea I B3
71 Lavis I B6
27 Lavit F C4
25 Lavoncourt F A5
36 Lavos P A2
36 Lavre P C2
111 Lávrion GR B5
8 Lawers GB B3
65 Lawszowa PL B5
51 Laxå S D5
10 Laxey GB A1
14 Laxfield GB B4
6 Laxford Bridge GB B3
110 Láyia GR C3
31 Laza E B3
108 Lazaráta GR C2
101 Lazarevac YU B5
99 Lazarevo YU C5
91 Łazek Ordynacki PL C6
71 Lazise I C5
90 Łaziska Grn. PL C2
64 Lázně CS C2
65 Lázně Bělohrad CS C5
102 Laznica YU B2
10 Lazonby GB A3
90 Lazy PL C3
85 Lazzaro I B4
35 Le Barcarès F A6
26 Le Barp F B3
28 Le Béage F B3
29 Le Beausset F C4
29 Le Bégude-de-
Mazenc F B3
23 Le Blanc F B6
28 Le Bleymard F B2
23 Le Boulay F A5
35 Le Boulou F A5
27 Le Bourg F B5
29 Le Bourg-d'Oisans F A5
25 Le Bourget-du-Lac F C5
19 Le Bourgneuf-la-
Forêt F B5
28 le Bousquet d'Orb F C2
25 Le Brassus CH B6
24 Le Breuil F B3
20 Le Breuil-en-Auge F B1
29 Le Brusquet F B5
70 Le Bry CH B2
27 Le Bugue F B4
27 Le Buisson F B4
26 Le Caloy F C3
29 Le Cannet-des-
Maures F C5
28 Le Canourgue F B2
28 Le Cap d'Agde F C2
83 le Castella I C4
21 le Cateau F A4
28 Le Caylar F C2
28 Le Cayrol F B1
25 le Celle F A4
70 Le Châble CH B2
28 Le Chambon-
Feugerolles F A3
28 Le Chambon-sur-
Lignon F A3
22 Le Château F C3
25 Le Châtelard F C6
24 Le Châtelet F B2
21 le Chatelet-en-Brie F C3
21 le Chesne F B5
28 Le Cheylard F B3

62 Montabaur D C2
74 Montafia I B3
28 Montagnac F C2
76 Montagnana I A1
25 Montagny F B4
22 Montaigu F B3
27 Montaigu-de-Quercy F B5
24 Montaiguet F B3
27 Montaigut, *Haute-Garonne* F C5
24 Montaigut, *Puy-de-Dôme* F B2
34 Montalbán E C2
44 Montalbán de Córdoba E B2
85 Montalbano Elicona I A4
83 Montalbano Iónico I A3
39 Montalbo E C4
75 Montalcino I C6
75 Montaldo di Cósola I B4
31 Montalegre P C3
25 Montalieu F C5
26 Montalivet-les-Bains F A2
84 Montallegro I B2
76 Montalto d. Marche I D3
78 Montalto di Castro I A2
75 Montalto Pavese I B4
82 Montalto Uffugo I B3
36 Montalvão P B3
32 Montamarta E C1
70 Montana-Vermala CH B2
37 Montánchez E B4
40 Montanejos E A2
82 Montano Antilia I A2
27 Montans F C5
36 Montargil P B2
21 Montargis F D3
27 Montastruc-la-Conseillère F C5
19 Montauban, *Ille-et-Vilaine* F B3
27 Montauban, *Tarn-et-Garonne* F B5
25 Montbard F A4
27 Montbazens F B6
23 Montbazon F A5
70 Montbéliard F A1
9 Montbenger GB C4
24 Montbengny F B3
70 Montbenoit F B1
35 Montblanch E B4
25 Montbozon F A6
25 Montbrison F C4
23 Montbron F C5
25 Montceau-les-Mines F B4
25 Montcenis F B4
25 Montchanin les Mines F B4
21 Montcornet F B5
23 Montcoutant F B4
27 Montcuq F B5
28 Montdardier F C2
20 Montdidier F B3
74 Monte Carlo MC C2
36 Monte Clara P B3
42 Monte Clérigo P B1
36 Monte-da-Pedra P B3
36 Monte do Trigo P C3
42 Monte Gordo P B2
78 Monte Libretti I A3
76 Monte Porzio I C3
36 Monte Real P B2
36 Monte Redondo P B2
78 Monte Romano I A2
76 Monte San Savino I C1
80 Monte Sant'Angelo I C2
36 Monte Vilar P B1
45 Monteagudo E A5
33 Monteagudo de las Vicarias E C4
40 Monteagudo del Castillo E A2
40 Montealegre del Castillo E C1
85 Montebello Iónico I B4
72 Montebello Vicentino I C1
72 Montebelluna I C2
19 Montebourg F A4
75 Montebruno I B4
80 Montecalvo Irpino I C2
76 Montecarotto I C3
76 Montecassiana I C3
75 Montecatini Terme I C5
76 Montécchio I C2
75 Montécchio Emilia I B5
72 Montécchio Maggiore I C1
27 Montech F C5
82 Montecórice I A1
80 Montecorvino Rovella I D1
30 Montederramo E B3
84 Montedoro I B2
78 Montefalco I A3
80 Montefalcone I C2
79 Montefalcone nel Sánnio I B5
76 Montefano I C3
78 Montefiascone I A3
75 Montefiorino I B5
79 Montefortino I A4
79 Montefranco I A3
44 Montefrio E B3
83 Montegiordano Marina I A3
76 Montegiórgio I C3
76 Montegranaro I C3
37 Montehermoso E A4
44 Montejicar E B3
39 Montejo de la Sierra E A3
33 Montejo de Tiermes E C3
78 Monteleone d'Orvieto I A3
80 Monteleone di Púglia I C2
79 Monteleone di Spoleto I A3
84 Montelepre I A2
29 Montelier F B4
29 Montélimar F B3
35 Montella E A4
80 Montella I D2
43 Montellano E C4
75 Montelungo I B4
75 Montelupo Fiorentino I C6
84 Montemaggiore Belsito I B2
74 Montemagno I B3
44 Montemayor E B2
32 Montemayor de Pinilla E C2
83 Montemésola I A4
80 Montemilleto I C1
80 Montemilone I C2
43 Montemolin E A3
79 Montemónaco I A4
36 Montemor-o-Novo P C2
36 Montemor-o-Velho P A2
82 Montemurro I A2
26 Montendre F A3
33 Montenegro de Cameros E B4
79 Montenero di Bisáccia I B5
19 Monteneuf F C3
83 Monteparano I A4
78 Montepescali I A2
75 Montepiano I B6
76 Montepulciano I C1
79 Montereale I A4
72 Montereale Valcellina I B2
21 Montereau-Faut-Yonne F C3
76 Monterénzio I B1
30 Montero E A2
79 Monteroduni I B5
75 Monteroni d'Arbia I C6
83 Monteroni di Lecce I A5
75 Monterosso al Mare I B4
85 Monterosso Almo I B3
74 Monterosso Grana I B2
75 Monterotondo Marittimo I C5
31 Monterrey E C3
30 Monterroso E B3
37 Monterrubio de la Serena E C5
76 Monterubbiano I C3
42 Montes Velhos P B1
40 Montesa E C2
30 Montesalgueiro E A2
82 Montesano sulla Marcellana I A2
79 Montesarchio I B5
83 Montescaglioso I A3
38 Montesclaros E B2
79 Montesilvano Marina I A5
75 Montesperto I C6
27 Montesquieu-Volvestre F C5
27 Montesquiou F C4
27 Montestruc F C4
76 Montevarchi I C1
21 Montfaucon F B6
28 Montfaucon, *Loire* F A3
22 Montfaucon, *Maine-et-Loire* F A3
25 Montferrat, *Isère* F C5
29 Montferrat, *Var* F C5
17 Montfoort NL A4
19 Montfort F B4
26 Montfort-en-Chalosse F C3
20 Montfort-l'Amaury F C2
20 Montfort-sur-Risle F B1
26 Montgaillard F C4
27 Montgiscard F C5
10 Montgomery GB C2
26 Montguyon F A3
21 Monthermé F B5
21 Monthois F B5
21 Monthyon F B3
75 Monticelli d'Ongina I A4
75 Monticelli-Terme I B5
71 Montichiari I C5
75 Monticiano I C6
45 Montiel E A4
21 Montier-en-Der F C5
75 Montieri I C6
70 Montiers F C1
74 Montiglio I A3
27 Montignac F A5
66 Montigny-le-Roi F C1
21 Montigny-sur-Aube F D5
20 Montihéry F C3
37 Montijo E C4
36 Montijo P C2
44 Montilla E B2
44 Montillana E B3
24 Montilly F B3
19 Montivilliers F A6
28 Montjaux F B1
29 Montjay F B4
22 Montjean-sur-Loire F A4
26 Montlieu-la-Gard F A3
23 Montlouis-sur-Loire F A5
24 Montluçon F B2
25 Montluel F C5
24 Montmarault F B3
21 Montmarq F B3
66 Montmedy F B1
25 Montmélian F C6
25 Montmerle F B4
29 Montmeyan F C5
29 Montmeyran F B3
21 Montmirail, *Marne* F C4
20 Montmirail, *Sarthe* F C1
28 Montmirat F C3
25 Montmirey-le-Château F A5
27 Montmoréau-St. Cybard F A4
20 Montmorency F C3
23 Montmorillon F B5
21 Montmort F C4
22 Montoir F A2
23 Montoire-sur-le-Loir F A5
27 Montolieu F C6
79 Montório al Vomano I A4
44 Montoro E A2
28 Montpellier F C2
27 Montpezat-de-Quarcy F B5
28 Montpezat-sur-Bouzon F B3
27 Montpon-Ménestérol F B4
25 Montpont en Bresse F B5
27 Montreál, *Aude* F C6
27 Montréal, *Gers* F C4
27 Montredon-Labessonnie F C6
27 Montréjeau F C4
23 Montrésor F A6
87 Montresta I B1
25 Montret F B5
16 Montreuil F C1
21 Montreuil-aux-Lions F B4
23 Montreuil-Bellay F A4
70 Montreux CH B1
22 Montrevault F A3
25 Montrevel F B5
23 Montrichard F A6
27 Montricoux F B5
35 Montroig E B3
25 Montrond-les-Bains F C4
9 Montrose GB B5
40 Montroy E B2
23 Monts-sur-Guesnes F B5
28 Montsalvy F B1
35 Montseny E B5
23 Montsoreau F A5
19 Montsurs F B5
38 Montuenga E A2
41 Montuiri, *Mallorca* E
44 Monturque E B2
71 Monza I C4
34 Monzón E B3
32 Monzón de Campos E B2
5 Moone IRL B5
59 Moordorf D B4
17 Moordrecht NL B4
59 Moorrege D B6
16 Moorslede B C3
68 Moosburg D C2
73 Moosburg i. Kärnten A B4
68 Moosinning D C2
98 Mór H A3
38 Mora E C3
36 Móra P C2
50 Mora S A5
34 Mora de Ebro E B3
40 Mora de Rubielos E A2
34 Mora la Nueva E B3
52 Moraby S B1
61 Moracz PL B5
32 Moradillo de Roa E C3
89 Morąg PL B5
99 Mórahalom H B4
31 Morais P C4
108 Moráitika GR B1
44 Moral de Calatrava E A3
44 Moraleda de Zafayona E B3
37 Moraleja E A4
32 Moraleja del Vino E C1
32 Morales de Toro E C1
32 Morales de Vaverde E C1
32 Morales del Vino E C1
31 Moralina E C4
82 Morano Cálabro I B3
103 Morăreşti RO A5
57 Mörarp S C1
31 Morasverdes E D4
33 Morata de Jalón E C5
39 Morata de Jiloca E A5
39 Morata de Tajuña E B3
45 Moratalla E A5
96 Moravec CS B2
102 Moravita RO A2
97 Morávka CS B4
96 Moravska Nová Ves CS C3
96 Moravská Trebova CS B2
96 Moravské Budějovice CS B1
96 Moravské Lieskové CS C3
96 Moravský-Beroun CS B3
96 Moravsky Krumlov CS B2
91 Morawica PL C4
90 Morawin PL B2
66 Morbach D B3
71 Morbegno I B4
25 Morbier F B6
96 Mörbisch a. See A D2
56 Mörbylånga S C5
26 Morcenx F B3
76 Morciano di Romagna I C2
79 Morcone I B5
33 Morcuera E C3
19 Mordelles F B4
91 Mordy PL A6
18 Moréac F C3
9 Morebattle GB C5
10 Morecambe GB A3
44 Moreda, *Granada* E B3
32 Moreda, *Oviedo* E A1
20 Morée F D2
32 Moreles de Rey E B1
35 Morell E B4
40 Morella E A2
35 Morella Castelldefels E B4
32 Moreruela de los Infanzones E C1
33 Morés E C5
87 Móres I B1
25 Morestel F C5
21 Moret F C3
13 Moreton-in-Marsh GB B6
12 Moretonhampstead GB C4
74 Moretta I B2
20 Moreuil F B3
25 Morez F B6
67 Mörfelden D B4
108 Mórfi GR B2
72 Morgano I C2
18 Morgat F B1
42 Morgavel P B1
70 Morges CH B1
70 Morgex I C2
52 Morgong S C2
52 Morgongåva S C2
66 Morhange F C2
66 Morhet B B1
71 Mori I C5
17 Morialmé B C4
42 Morianes P B2
86 Moriani Plage F B2
98 Mórichida H A2
44 Moriles E B2
34 Morillo de Monclús E A3
63 Moringen D B4
64 Moritzburg D B3
47 Morjärv S C11
52 Morkarla S B3
54 Mørke DK B3
55 Mørkøv Stby. DK C4
96 Morkovice CS B3
26 Morlaas F C3
18 Morlaix F B2
56 Mörlunda S B4
82 Mormanno I B3
21 Mormant F C3
25 Mornant F C4
43 Morón de la Frontera E B4
101 Morović YU A4
106 Morozovo BG A3
74 Morozzo I B2
9 Morpeth GB C6
57 Mörrum S C3
54 Mors DK B1
62 Morsbach D C2
67 Mörsch D C4
46 Mörsil S E6
20 Mortagne-au-Perche F C1
23 Mortagne-sur-Gironde F C4
22 Mortagne-sur-Sèvre F A4
36 Mortágua P A2
19 Mortain F B5
74 Mortara I A3
70 Morteau F A1
72 Mortegliano I C3
85 Mortelle I A4
23 Mortemart F B5
46 Mortenslund N D6
19 Mortrée F B6
72 Mörtschach A B2
17 Mortsel B B4
103 Morunglav RO B5
70 Morvillars F A1
61 Moryń PL C5
89 Morzeszczyn PL B4
70 Morzine F B1
67 Mosbach D B5
49 Mosby N C4
31 Mosca P C4
36 Moscavide P C1
77 Moščenicka Draga YU A4
79 Mosciano Sant'Angelo I A4
64 Mosigkau D B2
65 Mosina PL A6
46 Mosjöen N D6
109 Moskhokhorion GR C4
109 Moskhopótamos GR A4
91 Moskorzew PL C3
102 Mosna YU B3
71 Moso (Moos) I B6
103 Moşoaia RO B5
96 Mosonszentjános H D3
98 Mosonszentmiklós H A2
101 Mošorin YU A5
97 Mošovce CS C4
40 Mosquerela E A2
49 Moss N B7
7 Mossat GB C6
67 Mössingen D C5
46 Mossjöen N D6
49 Møsstrand N B5
64 Most CS C3
73 Most na Soci YU B3
100 Mostar YU C2
61 Mostkowo PL C6
38 Mostoles E B3
96 Mostova CS C3
3 Mostrim IRL C4
97 Mosty CS B4
61 Mosty PL B5
93 Mosty SU D9
10 Mostyn GB B2
97 Moszczenica PL B4
39 Mota del Cuervo E C4
32 Mota del Marques E C1
51 Motala S D6
9 Motherwell GB C4
60 Möthlow D C3
39 Motilla del Palancar E C5
103 Motoci RO B4
77 Motovum YU A3
44 Motril E C3
72 Motta I C1
72 Motta di Livenza I C2
80 Motta Montecorvino I C2
85 Motta Sant'Anastásia I B3
74 Motta Visconti I A3
81 Móttola I D4
54 Mou DK B3
74 Mouans-Sartoux F C1
25 Mouchard F B5
70 Moudon CH B1
74 Mougins F C1
23 Mouilleron en-Pareds F B4
112 Mouliana, *Kriti* GR
74 Moulinet F C2
24 Moulins F B3
24 Moulins-Engilbert F B3
20 Moulins-la-Marche F C1
26 Moulis F A3
23 Moulismes F B5
19 Moult F A5
4 Mount Bellew Bridge IRL A3
9 Mount Pleasant GB C5
2 Mount Talbot IRL C3
13 Mountain Ash GB B4
2 Mountcharles IRL B3
3 Mountfield GB B4
5 Mountmellick IRL A4
5 Mountrath IRL A4
14 Mountsorrel GB B1
42 Moura P A2
36 Mourão P C3
30 Mourelle E B3
26 Mourenx Ville-Nouvelle F C3
29 Mouriés F C3
105 Mouriés GR C4
111 Mouriki GR A4
21 Mourmelon-le-Grand F B5
112 Mourniés, *Kriti* GR
36 Mouronho P A2
16 Mouscron B C3
28 Moussac F C3
66 Moussey F C2
18 Mousteru F B2
26 Moustey F B3
106 Mousthéni GR C2
17 Moustier B C4
25 Mouthe F B6
25 Mouthier F A6
35 Mouthoumet F A5
70 Moutier CH A2
22 Moutiers-les-Mauxfaits F B3
112 Moutsoúna GR D1
25 Moux F A4
20 Mouy F B3
110 Mouzáki, *Ilía* GR B2
108 Mouzáki, *Kardhítsa* GR B3
21 Mouzay F B6
21 Mouzon F B6
3 Moville IRL A4
9 Mowtie GB B5
7 Moy, *Highland* GB C4
8 Moy, *Highland* GB B3
3 Moy, *N. Ireland* GB B5
35 Moya E B5
2 Moyard IRL C1
4 Moycullen IRL A2
66 Moyenmoutier F C2
66 Moyenvic F C2
66 Moyeuvre F B2
4 Moylough IRL A3
103 Mozăceni RO B6
32 Mózar E C1
73 Mozirje YU B4
99 Mözs H B3
93 Mozyr SU D11
71 Mozzanica I C4
98 Mraclin YU C1
89 Mragowo PL B7
101 Mramorak YU B5
77 Mrazovac YU A6
101 Mrčajevci YU C5
100 Mrkonjić Grad YU B2
77 Mrkopalj YU A4
102 Mrmoš YU C2
88 Mrocza PL B3
90 Mroczeń PL B1
89 Mroczno PL B5
91 Mrozy PL A5
101 Mršinci YU C5
61 Mrzezyno PL A6
73 Mrzle Vodice YU C4
64 Mšec CS C3
65 Mšeno CS C4
90 Mstów PL C3
97 Mszana Dolna PL B6
91 Mszczonów PL B4
90 Mtogoszyn PL A3
100 Muć YU C1
76 Muccia I C3
13 Much Marcle GB B5
10 Much Wenlock GB C3
63 Mücheln D B6
4 Muchross IRL B2
32 Mucientas E C2
67 Mudau D B5
59 Müden, *Niedersachsen* D C7
60 Müden, *Niedersachsen* D C1
62 Mudersbach D C2
107 Műdrets BG A4
34 Muel E B1
32 Muelas del Pan E C1
3 Muff IRL A4
30 Mugardos E A2
36 Muge P B2
64 Mügeln D B3
72 Múggia I C3
30 Mugia E A1
33 Mugica E A4
107 Muglen BG A5
106 Müglizh BG A3
76 Mugnano I C2
26 Mugron F C3
67 Mühlacker D C4
72 Mühlbach am Hochkönig A A3
64 Mühlberg, *Cottbus* D B3
63 Mühlberg, *Erfurt* D C5
72 Mühldorf, *Karnten* A B3
73 Mühldorf, *Steiermark* A B5
68 Mühldorf D C3
70 Muhleberg CH B2
60 Muhlen D B2
61 Mühlenbeck D C4
63 Mühlhausen D B5
68 Mühlhausen, *Bayern* D B1
68 Mühlhausen, *Bayern* D B2
64 Muhltroff D C1
72 Muhr A A3
17 Muiden NL A5
5 Muine Bheag IRL B5
31 Muiños E C3
7 Muir of Ord GB C4
9 Muirdrum GB B5
9 Muirkirk GB B5
36 Muirteira P B1
94 Mukachevo SU B5
45 Mula E A5
71 Mulegns CH B4
72 Mules (Mauls) I B1
67 Mülheim, *Baden-Württemberg* D C4
67 Mulheim, *Hessen* D A4
62 Mülheim, *Nordrhein-Westfalen* D B1
62 Mülheim, *Rheinland-Pfalz* D C2
70 Mulhouse F A2
2 Mullaranny IRL C2
66 Müllheim D D3
51 Mullhyttan S C5
5 Mullinavat IRL B4
3 Mullingar IRL C4
12 Mullion GB C2
64 Müllrose D A4
56 Mullsjö S B2
38 Munana E B1
30 Muñas E A4
63 Münchberg D C6
61 Müncheberg D C5
62 Munchehagen D A4
68 München D C2
62 Münchhausen D C3
33 Mundaca E A4
69 Munderfing A C4
67 Munderkingen D C5
14 Mundesley GB B4
14 Mundford GB B3
39 Munera E C4
33 Munguia E A4
38 Muñico E B1
34 Muniesa E B2
57 Munka-Ljungy S C1
55 Munkebo DK C3
51 Munkedal S D2
50 Munkfors S C4
53 Munktorp S C2
63 Münnerstadt D C5
38 Muñopepe E B2
38 Muñotello E B1
68 Münsing D D2
70 Münsingen CH B2
67 Münsingen D C5
53 Munsö S C3
70 Münster CH B3
59 Munster, *Niedersachsen* D C7
62 Münster, *Nordrhein-Westfalen* D B2
66 Munster F C3
62 Munstereifel D C1
58 Muntendam NL B3
69 Münzkirchen A C4
47 Muonio SF C11
70 Muotahal CH B3
28 Mur-de-Barrez F B1
18 Mur-de-Bretagne F B3
24 Mur-de-Sologne F A1
98 Murakeresztúr H B1
97 Murán CS C6
72 Murano I C2
88 Muranowo PL C2
30 Muras E A3
28 Murat F A1
28 Murat-sur-Vèbre F C1
107 Muratli TR B5
73 Murau A A4
87 Muravera I C2
74 Murazzano I B3
31 Murça P C3
33 Murchante E B5
103 Mŭrchevo BG C4
61 Murchin D B4
45 Murcia E B5
73 Mureck A B5
107 Murefte TR C5
27 Muret F C5
28 Muret-le-Chateau F B1
71 Murg CH A4
104 Murgaševo YU C3
70 Murgenthal CH A2
33 Murguia E B4
70 Muri CH A3
30 Murias de Paredes E B4
33 Muriel Viejo E C4
33 Murillo de Rio Leza E B4
33 Murillo el Fruto E B5
104 Murino YU B1
104 Muriqan AL B1
8 Murlaggan GB B2
58 Murmerwoude NL B2
41 Muro, *Mallorca* E
86 Muro F B1
40 Muro del Alcoy E C2
80 Muro Lucano I D2
24 Murol F C2
23 Muron F B4
30 Muros E B1
30 Muros de Nalon E A4
88 Murowana Goślina PL C3
104 Murrë AL C2
4 Murreagh IRL B1
70 Mürren CH B2
67 Murrhardt D C5
73 Murska Sobata YU B6
98 Mursko Središce YU B1
44 Murtas E C3
70 Murten CH B2
77 Murter YU C5
9 Murton GB D6
31 Murtosa P D2
47 Murtovaara SF D14
28 Murviel F C2
77 Murvika YU B5
73 Mürzsteg A A5
61 Murzynowo PL C6
73 Mürzzuschlag A A5
26 Musculdy F C3
103 Musetesti RO A5
112 Müskebi TR B1
96 Mušov CS C2
67 Mußbach a.d. Weinstraße D B4
9 Musselburgh GB C4
58 Musselkanaal NL C4
27 Mussidan F A4
84 Mussomeli I B2
21 Mussy-sur-Seine F D5
95 Mustafa Kemalpasa TR F8
89 Muszaki PL B6
73 Muta YU B5
9 Muthill GB B4
97 Mutné CS B5
33 Mutriku E A4
71 Mutterbergalm CH B6
67 Mutterstadt D B4
66 Mutzig F C3
47 Muurame SF E12
22 Muzillac F A2
97 Mužla CS D4
72 Muzzano del Turgnano I C3
7 Mybster GB B5
24 Myennes F A2
96 Myjava CS C3
49 Mykland N C5
64 Mylau D C2
47 Myllykoski SF F13
56 Myresjo S B3
51 Mysen N C2
65 Myslakowice PL C5
97 Myślenice PL B5
61 Myślibórz PL C5
65 Myślinów PL B6
90 Myslowice PL C3
90 Myszków PL C3
89 Myszyniec PL B7
97 Mýtna CS C5
97 Mýtne Ludany CS C4
97 Mýto, *Středoslovensky* CS C5
69 Mýto, *Zapadočeský* CS B4

N

17 Naaldwijk NL B4
17 Naarden NL A5
5 Naas IRL A5
31 Nabais P D3
68 Nabburg D B3
69 Načeradec CS B5
65 Nachod CS C6
62 Nachrodt-Wiblingwerde D B2
88 Naclaw PL A2
91 Nadarzyn PL A4
99 Nădlac RO B5
65 Nadolica PL B7
48 Nærbø N C2
55 Næstved DK C4
71 Näfels CH A4
11 Nafferton GB A5
110 Náfpaktos GR A2
111 Náfplion GR B3
68 Nagel D B2
58 Nagele NL C2
52 Naglarby S B1
91 Naglowice PL C4
67 Nagold D C4
98 Nagyatád H B2
98 Nagybajom H B2
99 Nagybaracska H B3
98 Nagybarát H A2
97 Nagybátony H D5
98 Nagyberény H B3
97 Nagybörzsöny H D4
98 Nagycenk H A1
99 Nagydorog H B3
99 Nagyfüged H A5
98 Nagyhersány H C3
98 Nagyigmánd H A3
98 Nagykanizsa H B2
99 Nagykáta H A4
99 Nagykoiu H A5
99 Nagykörös H A4
97 Nagylóc H C5
99 Nagymágocs H B5
98 Nagymányok H B3
97 Nagymaros H D4
97 Nagyoroszi H C5
97 Nagyréde H D5
99 Nagyszénás H B5
98 Nagyszokoly H B3
98 Nagyvázsony H B2
99 Nagyvenyim H B3
39 Naharros E B4
59 Nahe D B7
102 Naidas RO B2
63 Naila D C6
27 Nailloux F C5
13 Nailsea GB B5
13 Nailsworth GB B5
23 Naintre F B5
7 Nairn GB C5
33 Nájera E B4
49 Nakksjø N B6
88 Naklo PL A3
88 Naklo PL A3
88 Naklo nad Noteçią PL B3
99 Nakovo YU C5
55 Nakskov DK D4
33 Nalda E B4
46 Nalden S E7
22 Nalliers F B3
35 Nalzen F A4
69 Nalžouské Hory CS B4
46 Namdalseid N D5
96 Náměšt n. Oslavou CS B2
97 Námestovo CS B5
50 Namnå N B3
46 Namsos N D5
17 Namur B C4
90 Namystów PL B1
24 Nançay F A2
33 Nanclares de la Oca E B4
66 Nancy F C2
71 Nanders A B5
21 Nangis F C3
28 Nant F B2
20 Nanterre F C3
22 Nantes F A3
21 Nanteuil-le-Haudouin F B3
23 Nantiat F B6
25 Nantua F B5
10 Nantwich GB B3
109 Náousa, *Imathía* GR A4
112 Náousa, *Paros* GR D1
96 Napajedla CS B3
89 Napiwoda PL B6
79 Napoli I C5
30 Naraval E A4
12 Narberth GB B3
28 Narbonne F C2
28 Narbonne-Plage F C2
87 Narcao I C1
83 Nardò I A5
78 Narni I A3
84 Naro I B2
47 Narpes SF E10
47 Närpiö SF E10
38 Narros del Castillo E B1
98 Narta YU C1
93 Narva SU A11
47 Narvik N B8
74 Narzole I B2
50 Nås, *Kopparberg* S B5
53 Näs, *Östergötland* S D1
47 Näsåker S E8
28 Nasbinals F B2
54 Näset S A4
98 Našice YU C3
89 Nasielsk PL C6
85 Naso I A3
62 Nassau D C2
68 Nassenfels D C2
61 Nassenheide D C4
71 Nassereith A A5
56 Nässjö S B3
62 Nastätten D C2
57 Näsum S C3
101 Natalinci YU B5
17 Natoye B C5
69 Natternberg D C3
72 Natters A A1
67 Nattheim D C6
57 Nattraby S C4
71 Naturno (Naturns) I B5
27 Naucelle F B6
61 Nauen D C3
3 Naul IRL C5
63 Naumburg D B6
64 Naundorf D C3
64 Naunhof D B2
46 Naustdal N F2
32 Nava E A1
38 Nava de Arévalo E B2
38 Nava de la Asunción E A2
32 Nava del Rey E C1
38 Navacepeda E B1
38 Navacerrada E B2
37 Navaconcejo E A5
38 Navahermosa E C2
34 Naval E A3
38 Navalacruz E B2
38 Navalcán E B1
38 Navalcarnero E B2
33 Navaleno E C4
37 Navalguijo E A5
38 Navalmanzano E A2
38 Navalmoral E B2
37 Navalmoral de la Mata E B5
40 Navalón de Arriba E C2
38 Navalperal de Pinares E B2
38 Navalpino E C2
38 Navaltalgordo E B2
38 Navaltoril E C2
38 Navaluenga E B2
37 Navalvillar de Pela E B5
3 Navan (An Uaimh) IRL C5
35 Navarclés E B4
38 Navarredonda de la Sierra E B1
26 Navarrenx F C3
40 Navarrés E B2
33 Navarrete E B4
38 Navarrevisca E B2
35 Navás E B4
38 Navas de Oro E A2
44 Navas de S. Juan E A3
44 Navas del Cepillar E B2
37 Navas del Madroño E B4
38 Navas del Rey E B2
34 Navascués E A1
37 Navasfrias E A4
71 Nave I C5
31 Nave de Haver P D4
53 Nävekvarn S D2
79 Navelli I A4
11 Navenby GB B5
51 Naverstad S D2
35 Navés E B4
38 Navezuelas E C1
30 Navia E A4
30 Navia de Suarna E B4
38 Navillas E C2
25 Navilly F B5
89 Nawiady PL B7
112 Náxos GR D1
26 Nay F C3
15 Nayland GB C3
36 Nazaré P B1
40 Nazaret E B2
63 Nazza D B5
104 Ndroq AL C1
109 Néa Agathoúpolis GR A4
112 Néa Alikarnassós, *Kriti* GR
109 Néa Ankhialos GR B4
109 Néa Apollonia GR A5
111 Néa Artáki GR A4
111 Néa Epidhavros GR B4
108 Néa Filippias GR B2
109 Néa Fókaia GR A5
109 Néa Kallikrátia GR A5
106 Neá Kallisti GR B3
106 Néa Kariá GR C2
106 Néa Karváli GR C2
109 Néa Khalkidhón GR A4
111 Néa Kios GR B3
110 Néa Koróni GR C2
109 Néa Mádhitos GR A5
111 Néa Mákri GR A4
110 Néa Manolás GR A2
109 Néa Mikhanióna GR A4
109 Néa Moudhaniá GR A5
106 Néa Péramos GR C2
109 Néa Pláyia GR A5
109 Néa Potidhaia GR A5
109 Nea Radestos GR A5
109 Néa Sánda GR A4
109 Néa Skióni GR B5
109 Néa Triglia GR A5
107 Néa Vissi GR B4
106 Néa Zikhna GR B1
109 Néai Kariai GR B4
108 Neápolis, *Kozani* GR A3
112 Neapolis, *Kriti* GR
111 Neapolis, *Lakonía* GR C4
12 Neath GB B4
55 Nebel D D1
33 Nebieda E C3
77 Nebljusi YU B5
63 Nebra D B6
65 Nechanice CS C5
67 Neckar-Steinach D B4
67 Neckarelz D B5
67 Neckargemünd D B4
67 Neckarsulm D B5
103 Necşeşti RO B6
30 Neda E A2
96 Neded CS C3
98 Nedelišće YU B1
17 Neder Hardinxveld NL B4
16 Nederbrakel B C3
17 Nederweert NL B5
97 Nedožery CS C4
50 Nedreberg N B2
48 Nedstrand N B2
96 Nedvědice CS B2
90 Nędza PL C2
62 Neede NL A1
14 Needham Market GB B4
59 Neermoor D B4
17 Neeroeteren B B5
17 Neerpelt B B5
62 Neesen D A3
60 Neetze D B1
28 Neffies F C2
10 Nefyn GB C1
108 Negádes GR B2
101 Negbina YU C4
63 Negenborn D B4
103 Negoeşti RO B4
103 Negoiu RO C4
105 Negorci YU C4
102 Negotin YU B3
105 Negotino YU C4
71 Negrar I C5
103 Negraşi RO B6
39 Negredo E A4
30 Negreira E B2
103 Negreni RO B5
27 Nègrepelisse F B5
30 Negueira E A4
62 Neheim D B2
66 Neiderbronn-les-Bains F C3
33 Neila E B4
8 Neilston GB C3
74 Néive I B3
64 Nejdek CS C2
90 Nekla PL A1
57 Neksø DK D4
31 Nelas P D3
49 Nelaug N C5
67 Nellingen D C5
11 Nelson GB B3
97 Nemčinany CS C4
111 Neméa GR B3
98 Nemesgörzsöny H A2
98 Nemeskér H A1
99 Nemesnádudvar H B4
98 Nemesszalok H A2
99 Németkér H B3
20 Nemours F C3
97 Nemšova CS C4
4 Nenagh IRL B3
71 Nendeln FL A4
59 Nendorf D C5
97 Nenince CS C5
60 Nennhausen D C3
71 Nenzing A A4
111 Neokhoráki GR A4
110 Neokhóri, *Aitolía kai Acarnanía* GR A2
109 Neokhóri, *Magnisía* GR B5
109 Neokhórion, *Imathia* GR A4
109 Neokhórion, *Khalkidhikí* GR A5
112 Néon Khorion, *Kriti* GR
109 Néon Monastirion GR B4
109 Neon Perivoli GR B4
105 Néon Petritsi GR C5
105 Néon Šoúlion GR C5
105 Néon Yinaikókaston GR D4
109 Néos Marmarós GR A5
109 Néos Milótopos GR A4
105 Néos Skopós GR C5
78 Nepi I A3
69 Nepomuk CS B4
27 Nérac F B4
109 Neráida, *Fthiótis* GR C4
108 Neráida, *Thesprotía* GR B2
111 Nerántza GR B3
64 Neratovice CS C4
21 Nercenay-le-Hayer F C4
23 Néré F C4
68 Neresheim D C1
102 Neresnica YU B2
79 Nereto I A4
77 Nerezine YU B4
100 Nerežišća YU C1
24 Néris-les Bains F B2
79 Nerito I A4
44 Nerja E C3
110 Neromilos GR B2
24 Nérondes F B2
45 Nerpio E A4
43 Nerva E B3
72 Nervesa d. Battáglia I C2
74 Nervi I B4
25 Nervieux F C4
50 Nes N B1
58 Nes NL B2
46 Nesbyen N F4

Q

R

S

69 St. Georgen a.R. A D5
69 St. Georgen a.W. A C5
69 St. Georgen i.A. A D4
73 St. Georgen o. Judenburg A A4
73 St. Georgen o. Murau A A4
17 St. Georges B C5
22 St. Georges F C3
19 St. Georges Buttavent F B5
28 St. Georges-d'Aurac F A2
29 St. Georges-de-Commiers F A4
22 St. Georges-de-Didonne F C4
28 St. Georges-de-Luzençon F B1
25 St. Georges-de-Reneins F B4
24 St. Georges-en-Couzan F C3
23 St. Georges-les Baillargeaux F B5
23 St. Georges-sur-Loire F A4
26 St. Geours-de-Maremne F C2
24 St. Gérand F B3
24 St. Gérand-de-Vaux F B3
17 St. Gérard B C4
70 St. Germain, *Haute-Saône* F A1
20 St. Germain, *Yvelines* F C3
23 St. Germain-de Confolens F B5
25 St. Germain-de-Joux F B5
24 St. Germain-des-Fossés F B2
25 St. Germain du Bois F B5
25 St. Germain-du-Plain F B4
24 St. Germain-du Puy F A2
24 St.-Germain-l'Espinasse F B3
24 St. Germain-l'Herm F C3
24 St. Germain-Laval F C3
24 St. Germain-Lembron F C3
23 St. Germain-les-Belles F C6
70 St. Gervais F C1
24 St. Gervais d'Auvergne F B2
28 St. Gervais-sur-Mare F C2
22 St. Gildas-de-Rhuys F A2
22 St. Gildas-des-Bois F A2
69 St. Gilgen A D4
28 St. Gilles, *Gard* F C3
19 St. Gilles, *Ille-et-Vilaine* F B4
22 St. Gilles-Croix-de-Vie F B3
17 St. Gillis B B4
70 St. Gingolph F B1
26 St. Girons F C2
26 St. Girons-Plage F C2
62 St. Goar D C2
62 St. Goarshausen D C2
21 St. Gobain F B4
18 St. Guénolé F C1
10 St. Helens GB B3
19 St. Helier GB A3
57 St. Herrestad S D2
24 St. Hilaire F B3
27 St. Hilaire-de-l'Aude F C6
22 St. Hilaire-de-Riez F B3
23 St. Hilaire de Villefranche F C4
23 St. Hilaire-des-Lognes F B4
19 St. Hilaire-du-Harcouët F B4
29 St. Hilaire-du-Rosier F A4
28 St. Hippolyte, *Aveyron* F B1
70 St. Hippolyte, *Doubs* F A1
28 St. Hippolyte-du-Fort F C2
24 St. Honoré F B3
28 St. Hostein F A3
66 St. Hubert B A1
66 St. Ingbert D B3
16 St. Inglevert F C1
14 St. Ives, *Cambridgeshire* GB B2
12 St. Ives, *Cornwall* GB C2
73 St. Jacob A B4
58 St. Jacobiparochie NL B2
19 St. Jacques-de-la-Lande F B4
18 St. Jacut F B3
73 St. Jakob i. Walde A A5
72 St. Jakob in Defereggen A B2
19 St. James F B4
18 St. Jean-Brévelay F C3
74 St. Jean-Cap-Ferrat F C2
23 St. Jean-d'Angély F C4
25 St. Jean-d'Ardières F B4
26 St. Jean d'Illac F B3
70 St. Jean-de-Belleville F C1
25 St. Jean-de-Bournay F C5
20 St. Jean de Braye F D3
28 St. Jean-de-Bruel F B2
23 St. Jean-de Côle F C5
19 St. Jean-de-Daye F A4
28 St. Jean-de-Fos F C2
25 St. Jean de Losne F A5
26 St. Jean-de-Luz F C2
29 St. Jean-de-Maurienne F A5
22 St. Jean-de-Monts F B2
29 St. Jean-de-Muzols F A3
28 St. Jean-de-Védas F C2
28 St. Jean-du-Gard F B2
29 St. Jean-en-Royans F A4
74 St. Jean-la-Riviere F C2
20 St. Jean-le-Braye F D2
21 St. Jean les Jumeaux F C4
26 St. Jean Pied de Port F C2
27 St. Jean-Poutge F C4
66 St. Jean-Rohrbach F B2
74 St. Jeannet F C2
70 St. Jeoire F B1
22 St. Joachim F A2
73 St. Johann a Tauern A A4
73 St. Johann i. Saggautal A B5
72 St. Johann im Pongau A A3
72 St. Johann in Tirol A A2
10 St. Johns GB A1
3 St. Johnstown IRL B4
25 St. Joriox F C6
17 St. Joris Winge B C4
27 St. Jory F C5
23 St. Jouin-de-Marnes F B4
27 St. Juéry F C6
35 St. Julia de Loria AND A4
26 St. Julien, *Gironde* F A3
24 St. Julien, *Loire* F C3
28 St. Julien-Chapteuil F A3
22 St. Julien-de-Concelles F A3
22 St. Julien-de-Vouvantes F A3
21 St. Julien-du-Sault F C4
29 St. Julien-du-Verdon F C5
26 St. Julien-en-Born F B2
25 St. Julien-en-Genevois F B6
23 St. Julien-l'Ars F B5
29 St. Julien-Molin-Molette F A3
29 St. Julien-Mont-Denis F A5
25 St. Julien-sur-Reyssouze F B5
23 St. Junien F C5
12 St. Just GB C2
20 St. Just-en-Chaussée F B3
24 St. Just-en-Chevalet F C3
26 St. Justin F C3
73 St. Katharein a.d. Laming A A5
73 St. Katherin a. Hauenstein A A5
73 St. Kathrein a. Offenegg A A5
12 St. Keverne GB C2
16 St. Kruis B B3
23 St. Lambert-des-Levées F A4
73 St. Lambrecht A A4
17 St. Lambrechts-Herk B C5
34 St. Lary-Soulan F A3
19 St. Laurent F A5
74 St. Laurent Cagnes F C2
28 St. Laurent-d'Aigouze F C3
19 St. Laurent-de-Condel F A5
28 St. Laurent-de-la-Cabrerisse F C1
35 St. Laurent-de-la-Salanque F A5
22 St. Laurent des Antels F A3
29 St. Laurent-du-Pont F A4
20 St. Laurent-en-Caux F B1
25 St. Laurent-en-Grandvaux F B5
29 St. Laurent-en-Royans F A4
26 St. Laurent-et-Benon F A3
23 St. Laurent-sur-Gorre F C5
22 St. Laurent-sur-Sèvre F B4
66 St. Leger B B1
25 St. Léger F B4
24 St. Léger-de-Vignes F B3
25 St. Léger-sous-Beuvray F B4
55 St. Lem DK B1
23 St. Léonard-de Noblat F C6
71 St. Leonardo in Passiria (St. Leonhard) I B6
69 St. Leonhard a. Forst A C6
69 St. Leonhard b. Freistadt A C5
71 St. Leonhard i Pitztal A A5
51 St. Levene S D3
16 St. Lô F A4
26 St. Lon-les Mines F C2
69 St. Lorenz A D4
72 St. Lorenzen A B2
73 St. Lorenzen a. Wechsel A A5
24 St. Loup F B3
25 St. Loup-de-la-Salle F B4
66 St. Loup-sur-Semouse F D2
19 St. Lunaire F B3
25 St. Lupicin F B5
27 St. Lys F C5
17 St. Maartensdijk NL B4
26 St. Macaire F B3
20 St. Maclou F B1
23 St. Maixent-l'Ecole F B4
19 St. Malo F B3
28 St. Mamet-la-Salvetat F B1
29 St. Mandrier F C4
71 St. Mang D A5
22 St. Marc F A2
29 St. Marcel, *Ardèche* F A3
29 St. Marcel, *Drôme* F B3
25 St. Marcel, *Saône-et-Loire* F B4
70 St. Marcel, *Savoie* F C1
29 St. Marcel-D'Ardeche F B3
29 St. Marcellin, *Isère* F A4
25 St. Marcellin, *Loire* F C4
27 St. Marcet F C4
66 St. Mard B B1
21 St. Mards-en-Othe F C4
73 St. Marein A A5
73 St. Marein a. Pickelback A A5
15 St. Margaret's at Cliffe GB C4
7 St. Margaret's Hope GB B6
73 St. Margareten i. Rosental A B4
73 St. Margarethen, *Steiermark* A A4
73 St. Margarethen, *Steiermark* A B5
73 St. Margarethen i. Lavattal A B4
96 St. Margarethen im Burgenland A D2
71 St. Margrethen CH A4
73 St. Marien b. Knittelfeld A A4
22 St. Mars-la Jaille F A3
69 St. Martin, *Nieder Österreich* A C5
69 St. Martin, *Ober Österreich* A C4
29 St. Martin F B3
73 St. Martin a. Wöllmißberg A A5
21 St. Martin-d'Ablois F B4
24 St. Martin-d'Auxigny F A2
29 St. Martin-d'Entraunes F B5
24 St. Martin-d'Estreaux F B3
29 St. Martin-d'Hères F A4
29 St. Martin-de-Belleville F A5
21 St. Martin de Bossenay F C4
22 St. Martin-de-Brem F B3
28 St. Martin-de-Londres F C2
29 St. Martin-de-Queyrières F C6
22 St. Martin-de-Ré F B3
28 St. Martin-de-Valamas F B3
28 St.-Martin-de-Valgalgues F B3
19 St. Martin des Besaces F A5
29 St. Martin-du-Crau F C3
25 St. Martin-du-Fresne F B5
74 St. Martin-du-Var F C2
25 St. Martin-en-Bresse F B5
25 St.-Martin-en-Haut F C4
27 St. Martin-la-Méanne F A5
25 St. Martin-Lestra F C4
21 St. Martin-sur-Ouanne F D4
28 St. Martin-Valmeroux F A1
74 St. Martin-Vésubie F B2
27 St. Martory F C4
7 St. Mary's GB B6
23 St. Mathieu F C5
70 St. Maurice CH B1
25 St. Maurice, *Rhône* F C4
25 St. Maurice, *Saône-et-Loire* F B5
66 St. Maurice, *Vosges* F D2
28 St. Maurice-de-Loire F A3
29 St. Maurice-en-Trièves F B4
28 St. Maurice-Navacelles F C2
62 St. Mauritz D B2
12 St. Mawes GB C2
29 St. Maximin-la-Ste. Baume F C4
26 St. Méard de Gurçon F B4
26 St. Médard-de-Guizières F B4
26 St. Médard-en-Jalles F B3
18 St. Méen-le-Grand F B3
13 St. Mellons GB B4
21 St. Memmie F C5
21 St. Menges F B5
65 St. Město CS C6
73 St. Michael, *Karnten* A B4
73 St. Michael, *Steiermark* A A5
98 St. Michael i. Burgenland A A1
72 St. Michael im Lungau A A3
59 St. Michaelisdonn D B6
21 St. Michel, *Aisne* F B5
27 St. Michel, *Gers* F C4
22 St. Michel Chef-Chef F A2
29 St. Michel-de-Maurienne F A5
18 St. Michel-en-Grèvel F B2
22 St. Michel-en-l'Herm F B3
22 St. Michel-Mont-Mercure F B4
29 St. Michel-Peyresq F B5
16 St. Michiels B B3
17 St. Michielsgestel NL B5
66 St. Mihiel F C1
29 St. Mitre F C4
9 St. Monans GB B5
29 St. Montant F B3
71 St. Moritz CH B4
22 St. Nazaire F A2
29 St. Nazaire-en-Royans F A4
29 St. Nazaire-le-Désert F B4
24 St. Nectaire F C2
14 St. Neots GB B2
23 St. Nicholas-de-Bourgueil F A5
58 St. Nicolaasga NL C2
27 St. Nicolas-de-la-Grave F B5
66 St. Nicolas-de-Port F C2
22 St. Nicolas-de-Redon F A2
18 St. Nicolas-du-Pélem F B2
17 St. Niklaas B B4
70 St. Niklaus CH B2
73 St. Nikolai Sölkt A A4
17 St. Oedenrode NL B5
16 St. Omer F C2
29 St. Oswald D C4
69 St. Oswald b. Freist A C5
19 St. Pair-sur-Mer F B4
28 St. Pal-de-Mons F A3
26 Saint-Palais F C2
22 St. Palais-sur-Mer F C3
23 St. Pardoux-la-Rivière F C4
73 St. Paul A B4
29 St. Paul, *Alpes-de-Haute-Provence* F B5
26 St. Paul, *Landes* F C2
27 St. Paul-Cap-de-Joux F C5
35 St. Paul-de-Fenouiller F A5
25 St.-Paul-de-Varax F B5
29 St. Paul-Trois-Châteaux F B3
28 St. Paulien F A2
26 St. Pé-de-Bigorre F C3
26 St. Pée Espelette F C2
20 St. Péravy-la-Colombe F D2
29 St. Péray F B3
22 St. Père en Retz F A2
67 St. Peter, *Baden-Württemberg* D C4
59 St. Peter, *Schleswig-Holstein* D A5
73 St. Peter a. Kammersberg A A4
69 St. Peter i.d. Au A C5
18 St. Peter Port GB A3
22 St. Philbert-de-Grand-Lieu F A3
28 St. Pierre, *Aveyron* F C1
22 St. Pierre, *Charente-Maritime* F C3
25 St. Pierre-d'Albigny F C6
29 St. Pierre-d'Allevard F A5
29 St. Pierre-de-Chartres F A4
27 St. Pierre-de-Chignac F A4
28 St. Pierre-de-la-Fage F C2
19 St. Pierre-Eglise F A4
25 St. Pierre-en-Faucigny F B6
20 St. Pierre-en-Port F B1
24 St. Pierre-le-Moûtier F B3
22 St. Pierre Montlimart F A3
22 St. Pierre Quiberon F A1
19 St. Pierre-sur-Dives F A5
28 St. Pierreville F B3
17 St. Pieters Leeuw B C4
27 St. Plancard F C4
19 St. Poix F C4
18 St. Pol-de-Leon F B2
16 St. Pol-sur-Mer F B2
16 St. Pol-sur-Ternoise F C2
96 St. Pölten A C1
29 St. Poncy F A2
28 St. Pons F C1
23 St. Porchaire F C4
24 St. Pourçain F B3
25 St. Priest, *Ain* F C4
25 St. Priest, *Allier* F B2
27 St. Privat F A6
28 St. Privat-d'Allier F B2
18 St. Quay-Portrieux F B3
21 St. Quentin F B4
28 St. Quentin-la-Poterie F B3
73 St. Radegund A A5
25 St. Rambert F C4
29 St. Rambert d'Albon F A3
25 St. Rambert-en-B F C5
29 St. Raphaël F C5
29 St. Rémy-de-Provence F C3
19 St. Remy-du-Val F B6
21 St. Remy-en-Bouzemont F C5
24 St. Remy-sur Durolle F C3
18 St. Renan F B1
16 St. Riquier F C1
20 St. Romain de Colbosc F B1
69 St. Roman A C4
28 St. Rome-de-Cernon F B1
28 St. Rome-de-Tarn F B1
54 St. Rørbæk DK B2
73 St. Ruprecht a.d. Raab A A5
20 St. Saëns F B2
73 St. Salvator A B4
20 St. Samson-la-Poterie F B2
28 St. Saturnim-de-Lenne F B2
29 St. Saturnin F C4
20 St. Sauflieu F B3
24 St. Saulge F A3
74 St. Sauveur, *Alpes-Maritimes* F B2
18 St. Sauveur, *Finistère* F B2
66 St. Sauveur, *Haute-Saône* F D2
24 St. Sauveur, *Yonne* F A3
28 St. Sauveur de Montagut F B3
28 St. Sauveur-en-Rue F A3
19 St. Sauveur-le-Vicomte F A4
19 St. Sauveur-Lendelin F A4
26 St. Savin, *Gironde* F A3
23 St. Savin, *Vienne* F B5
23 St. Savinien F C4
29 St. Savournin F C4
29 St. Seine-l'Abbaye F A4
28 St. Sernins-sur-Rance F C1
19 St. Serven F B4
26 St. Seurin-de-Cadourne F A3
26 St. Sever F C3
19 St. Sever-Calvados F A4
28 St. Sever-du-Moustier F C1
22 St. Sigismond F A4
29 St. Simeon-de-Bressieux F A4
21 St. Simon F B4
31 St. Skedvi S B1
29 St. Sorlin-d'Arves F A5
21 St. Soupplets F B3
73 St. Stefan A B4
72 St. Stefan a.d. Gail A B3
73 St. Stefan i. Rosental A B5
23 St. Sulpice Laurière F B6
23 St. Sulpice-les-Feuilles F B6
26 St. Symphorien F B3
25 St. Symphorien-d'Ozon F C4
25 St. Symphorien-de-Lay F C4
25 St. Symphorien-sur-Coise F C4
18 St. Thegonnec F B2
17 St. Tönis D B6
25 St. Trivier-de-Courtes F B5
25 St. Trivier sur-Moigans F B4
22 St. Trojan F C3
29 St. Tropez F C5
17 St. Truiden B C5
29 St. Uze F A3
19 St. Vaast-la-Hougue F A4
69 St. Valentin A C5
71 St. Valentino alla Mùta (St. Valentin) I B5
21 St. Valérien F C4
20 St. Valéry-en-Caux F B1
16 St. Valery-sur-Somme F C1
29 St. Vallier F A3
29 St. Vallier-de-Thiey F C5
23 St. Varent F B4
24 St. Vaury F B1
73 St. Veit A B4
96 St. Veit a.d.G. A C1
72 St. Veit in Defereggen A B2
16 St. Venant F C2
29 St. Victor F A3
53 St. Vika S D3
29 St. Vincent F B4
70 St. Vincent I C2
26 St. Vincent-de-Tyrosse F C2
17 St. Vith B C6
22 St. Vivien de Médoc F C3
66 St. Wendel D B3
17 St. Willebrord NL B4
69 St. Wolfgang A D4
68 St. Wolfgang D C3
25 St. Yan F B4
24 St. Yorre F B3
23 St. Yrieix-la-Perche F C6
23 Saintas F C4
19 Ste. Adresse F A6
20 Ste. Anne F C1
18 Ste. Anne d'Auray F C3
29 Ste. Anne-du-Castillet F C4
28 Ste. Chély d'Apcher F B2
21 Ste. Colombe-sur-Seine F D5
70 Ste.-Croix CH B1
27 Ste. Croix-Volvestre F C5
26 Ste. Engrâce F C3
29 Ste. Enimie F B2
28 Ste. Florine F A2
27 Ste. Foy-de-Peyrolières F C5
25 Ste. Foy l'Argentiere F C4
27 Ste. Foy-la-Grande F B4
27 Ste.-Foy-Tarentaise F C1
20 Ste. Gauburge-Ste. Colombe F C1
22 Ste. Gemme la Plaine F B3
20 Ste. Geneviève F B3
25 Ste. Hélène-sur-Isère F C6
22 Ste. Hermine F B3
29 Ste. Jalle F B4
27 Ste. Livrade F B4
66 Ste. Marie-aux-Mines F C3
19 Ste. Marie-du-Mont F A4
23 Ste. Maure-do-Touraine F A5
29 Ste.-Maxime F C5
21 Ste. Menehould F B5
19 Ste. Mère-Eglise F A4
24 Ste. Sévère-sur-Indre F B2
19 Ste. Suzanne F B5
29 Ste. Tulle F C4
19 Sainteny F A4
17 Saintes B C4
3 Saintfield GB B6
27 Saissac F C6
32 Saja E A2
101 Šajkaš YU A5
55 Sakskøbing DK D4
101 Sakule YU A5
96 Šal'a CS C3
52 Sala S C2
75 Sala Baganza I B5
112 Sala Consilina I A2
47 Salahmi SF E13
102 Salakovac YU B2
38 Salamanca E B1
111 Salamis GR B4
82 Salandra I A3
111 Salanti GR B4
108 Salaóra GR B2
84 Salaparuta I B2
44 Salar E B2
34 Salardú E A3
30 Salas E A4
102 Salaš YU B3
33 Salas de los Infantes E B3
103 Sălătrucu RO A5
35 Salau F A4
70 Salavaux CH B2
35 Salavinera E B4
74 Salbertrand I A1
52 Salbohed S C2
24 Salbris F A2
32 Salce E B1
68 Salching D C3
103 Salcia RO B3
103 Salcia RO C5
103 Salcuţă RO B4
32 Saldaña E B2
93 Saldus SU B8
10 Sale GB B3
74 Sale I B3
71 Saleby S D4
71 Salem D A4
84 Salemi I B1
8 Salen GB B2
50 Sålen S A4
29 Salerans F B4
29 Salernes F C5
79 Salerno I C5
28 Salers F A1
28 Salettes F B2
10 Salford GB B3
97 Salgótarján H C5
36 Salgueiro P B3
83 Sàlice Salentino I A4
30 Salientes E B4
26 Salies-de-Béarn F C3
27 Salies-du-Salat F C4
27 Salignac-Eyvignes F B5
24 Saligney-sur-Roudon F B3
40 Salinas, *Alicante* E C2
34 Salinas, *Huesca* E A3
45 Salinas de Cerrillos E C4
32 Salinas de Pisuerga E B2
75 Saline I C5
25 Salins-les-Bains F B5
42 Salir P B1
13 Salisbury GB B6
73 Salla A A4
47 Salla SF C14
70 Sallanches F C1
16 Sallaumines F C2
35 Sallent E B4
34 Sallent de Gállego E A2
29 Salles, *Drôme* F B3
26 Salles, *Gironde* F B3
28 Salles-Curan F B1
27 Salles-sur-l'Hers F C5
64 Sallgast D B3
39 Salmerón E B4
28 Salmiech F B1
38 Salmoral E B1
71 Salò I C5
47 Salo SF F11
45 Salobral E A5
44 Salobreña E C3
29 Salon-de-Provence F C4
109 Salonikiós GR A5
94 Salonta RO C4
37 Salorino E B3
25 Salornay-sur-Guye F B4
71 Salorno (Salurn) I B6
35 Salou E B4
20 Salouël F B3
35 Salses F A5
75 Salsomaggiore Terme I B4
35 Salt E B5
12 Saltash GB C3
11 Saltburn by the Sea GB A5
8 Saltcoats GB C3
11 Saltergate GB A5
11 Saltfleet GB B6
11 Saltfleetby St. Clement GB B6
31 Salto P C3
53 Saltsjöboden S C4
56 Saltvik S B5
76 Saludécio I C2
70 Salussola I C3
74 Saluzzo I B3
40 Salvacañete E A1
42 Salvada P B2
37 Salvaleon E C4
36 Salvaterra de Magos P B2
37 Salvaterra do Extremo P B4
33 Salvatierra, *Avila* E B4
37 Salvatierra, *Badajóz* E C4
37 Salvatierra de Santiago E B4
27 Salviac F B5
62 Salzbergen D A2
69 Salzburg A D4
63 Salzgitter D A5
63 Salzgitter Bad D A5
60 Salzhausen D B1
63 Salzkotten D B3
63 Salzmünde D B6
60 Salzwedel D C2
32 Sama E A1
28 Samadet F C3
33 Samaniego E B4
108 Samarina GR A3
87 Samassi I C1
27 Samatan F C4
111 Sambatiki GR B3
82 Sambiase I C3
74 Sambolò I A3
74 Sambor SU B5
89 Samborowo PL B5
91 Samborzec PL C5
84 Sambuca di Sicilia I B2
71 Samedan CH B4
16 Samer F C1
110 Sámi GR A1
110 Samikó GR B2
80 Sammichele di Bari I B3
71 Samnaun CH B5
73 Samobor YU C5
66 Samogneux F B1
105 Samokov BG B5
36 Samora Correia P C2
96 Šamorin CS C3
30 Samos E B3
112 Samos GR C1
35 Sampedor E B4
34 Samper de Calanda E B2
74 Sampéyre I B2
85 Sampieri I C3
66 Sampigny F C1
89 Samplawa PL B5
10 Sampool Bridge GB A3
78 Samprugnano I A2
108 Sampsoús GR B2
61 Samtens D A4
87 Samugheo I C1
89 Samulewo PL A7
33 San Adrián E B5
30 San Amaro E B2
32 San Andrés de Rabanedo E B1
30 San Antolin E A4
87 San Antonio I B2
41 San Antonio Abad, *Ibiza* E
35 San Antonio de Calonge E B6
33 San Asensio E B4
33 San Augustin de Llusanés E A5
42 San Bartolomé de la Torre E B2
38 San Bartolomé de las Abiertas E C2
38 San Bartolomé de Pinares E B2
80 San Bartolomeo in Galdo I C1
35 San Baudillo E B5
79 San Benedetto del Tronto I A4
76 San Benedetto in Alpe I C1
75 San Benedetto Po I A5
37 San Benito de la Contienda E C3
84 San Biágio Plátani I B2
79 San Biágio Saracinisco I B4
71 San Bonifácio I C6
43 San Calixto E A4
72 San Cándido (Innichen) I B2
70 San Carlo CH B3
84 San Carlo I B2
41 San Carlos, *Ibiza* E
41 San Carlos de la Rápita E A3
39 San Carlos del Valle E D3
78 San Casciano d. Bagni I A2
75 San Casciano in V. di Pesa I C6
83 San Cataldo, *Puglia* I A5
84 San Cataldo, *Sicilia* I B2
32 San Cebrián E C1
35 San Celoni E B5
83 San Cesário di Lecce I A5
82 San Chirico Raparo I A3
84 San Cipirello I B2
30 San Ciprián de Viñas E B3
39 San Clemente, *Cuenca* E C4
30 San Clemente, *León* E B4
41 San Clemente, *Menorca* E
75 San Colombano al Lambro I A4
30 San Cripriano E A3
32 San Crisóbal de Entreviñas E B1
31 San Cristobal E C3
32 San Cristóbal de la Polantera E B1
38 San Cristóbal de la Vega E A2
35 San Cugat de Vallés E B5
74 San Damiano d'Asti I B3
74 San Damiano Macra I B2
72 San Daniele del Friuli I B3
78 San Demétrio Corone I B3
79 San Demetrio ne'Vestini I A4
82 San Donà di Piave I C2
83 San Dónaci I A4
79 San Donato Val Dei Comino I B4
32 San Emilian E B1
30 San Esteban E A4
33 San Esteban de Gormaz E C3
38 San Esteban de la Sierra E B1
34 San Esteban de Litera E B3
30 San Esteban de Valdueza E B4
32 San Esteban del Molar E C1
38 San Esteban del Valle E B2
80 San Fele I D2
79 San Felice Circeo I B4
75 San Felice sul Panaro I B6
32 San Felices E B3
31 San Felices de los Gallégos E D4
35 San Feliu E B5
35 San Feliu de Codinas E B5
35 San Feliu de Guixols E B6
32 San Feliz de las Lavanderas E B1
80 San Ferdinando di Púglia I C3
43 San Fernando, *Cádiz* E C3
39 San Fernando de Henares E B3
41 San Fernando, *Formentera, Ibiza* E
82 San Fili I B3
83 San Foca I A5
72 San Francesco d'Aglientu I A2
41 San Francisco Javier, *Ibiza* E
41 San Fransisco, *Ibiza* E
85 San Fratello I A3
87 San Gavino Monreale I C1
78 San Gemini I A3
74 San Germano Vercellese I A3
78 San Giacomo I A3
72 San Giácomo (St. Jakob) I B1
75 San Gimignano I C6
76 San Ginésio I C3
79 San Giórgio a Liri I B4
72 San Giorgio d. Richinvelda I B2
79 San Giórgio del Sannio I B5
72 San Giórgio di Nogaro I C3
75 San Giorgio di Piano I B6
83 San Giórgio Iónico I A4
75 San Giovani in Croce I A5
82 San Giovanni a Piro I A2
71 San Giovanni Bianco I C4
87 San Giovanni di Sinis I C1
83 San Giovanni in Fiore I B3
75 San Giovanni in Persiceto I B6
79 San Giovanni Reatino I A3
80 San Giovanni Rotondo I C2
87 San Giovanni Suérgiu I C1
76 San Giovanni Valdarno I C1
75 San Giuliano Terme I C5
76 San Giustino I C2
76 San Godenzo I C1
80 San Gregorio Magno I D2
35 San Hilario Sacalm E B5
35 San Hipólito de Voltegá E A5
35 San Jaime dels Domenys E B4
45 San Javier E B6
41 San Jorge E A3
36 San Jorge P B2
45 San José, *Almería* E C4
41 San José, *Ibiza* E
41 San Juan Bautista, *Ibiza* E
35 San Juan de Abadesas E A5
40 San Juan de Alicante E C2
43 San Juan de Aznalfarache E B3
38 San Juan de la Nava E B2
35 San Juan de Vilasar E B5
43 San Juan del Puerto E B3
30 San Justo de la Vega E B4
76 San Lazzaro di Sávena I B1
76 San Leo I C2
33 San Leonardo E C3
75 San Lorenzo a Merse I C6
74 San Lorenzo al Mare I C2
82 San Lorenzo Bellizzi I B3
44 San Lorenzo de Calatrava E A3
41 San Lorenzo de Descardazar, *Mallorca* E
38 San Lorenzo de El Escorial E B2
39 San Lorenzo de la Parilla E C4
35 San Lorenzo de Morunys E A4
72 San Lorenzo di Sebato (St. Lorenzen) I B1
76 San Lorenzo in Campo I C2
78 San Lorenzo Nuovo I A2
35 San Lorenzo Savall E B5
42 San Lourenco P A1
85 San Luca I A5
82 San Lúcido I B3
41 San Luis, *Menorca* E
75 San Marcello Pistoiese I B5
32 San Marcial E C1
82 San Marco I A1
82 San Marco Argentano I B3
80 San Marco dei Cavoti I C1
80 San Marco in Lamis I C2
83 San Marco Squinzano I A5
76 San Marino RSM C2
33 San Martia de Unx E B5
43 San Martin E C4
30 San Martin de Castañeda E B4
38 San Martin de la Vega E B1
30 San Martin de Luiña E A4
35 San Martin de Maldá E B4
38 San Martin de Montalbán E C2
30 San Martin de Oscos E A4
38 San Martin de Pusa E C2
35 San Martin de Tous E B4
38 San Martin de Valdeiglesias E B2
35 San Martin Sarroca E B4
72 San Martino di Campagna I B2
72 San Martino di Castrozzo I B1
80 San Martino in Pénsilis I C2
40 San Mateo E A3
82 San Mâuro Forte I A3
71 San Michele all'Adige I B6
85 San Michele di Ganzaria I B3
74 San Michele Mondovi I B2
41 San Miguel, *Ibiza* E
32 San Miguel Aguayo E A3
32 San Miguel de Arroyo E C2
32 San Miguel de Bernuy E C3
45 San Miguel de Salinas E B6
33 San Millán E B3
33 San Millán de la Cogolla E B4
75 San Miniato I C5
31 San Muñoz E D4
82 San Nicola da Crissa I C3
83 San Nicola del'Alto I B3
43 San Nicolás del Puerto E B4
76 San Nicolò I B1
87 San Nicolò Gerrei I C2
75 San Pablo E C2
35 San Pablo de Seguries E A5
83 San Pancrazio Salentino I A4
87 San Pantaleo I A2
80 San Paolo di Civitate I C2
45 San Pedro, *Albacete* E A4
30 San Pedro, *Oviedo* E A4
36 San Pedro de Cadeira P B1
31 San Pedro de Ceque E B4
32 San Pedro de Latarce E C1
45 San Pedro de Pinatar E B6
35 San Pedro de Riudevitlles E B4
32 San Pedro de Valderaduey E B2
38 San Pedro del Arroyo E B2
30 San Pedro del Puerto E A4
32 San Pedro del Romeral E A3
31 San Pedro do Sul P D2
33 San Pedro Manrique E B4
45 San Pedro Pescador E A6
71 San Pellegrino Terme I C4
75 San Piero a Sieve I C6
76 San Piero in Bagno I C1

78 Spoleto I A3
79 Spoltore I A5
71 Spondigna (Spondinig) I B5
51 Sponvika N C2
60 Spornitz D B2
74 Spotorno I B3
60 Sprakensehl D C1
89 Spręcowo PL B6
64 Spremberg D B4
67 Sprendlingen D B4
72 Spresiano I C2
17 Sprimont B C5
63 Springe D A4
81 Spuž YU B6
89 Spychowo PL B7
51 Spydeberg N C2
97 Spytkowice PL B5
83 Squillace I C3
98 Sračinec YU B1
100 Srbac YU A2
104 Srbica YU B2
99 Srbobran YU C4
26 Sre. Hélène F B3
81 Srebeno YU B5
101 Srebrenica YU B4
101 Srebrnik YU B3
106 Sredets BG A3
98 Središce YU B1
106 Sredno Gradishte BG A3
106 Srednogortsi BG B2
104 Sredska YU B2
65 Śrem PL A7
69 Srní CS B4
100 Srnice YU B3
90 Srock PL B3
65 Środa Śląska PL B6
65 Środa Wielkopolski PL A7
90 Środa Wielkopolski PL A1
99 Srpska Crnja YU C5
99 Srpski Itebej YU C5
99 Srpski Miletić YU C4
71 Sta. Maria CH B5
96 Staatz A C2
17 Stabroek B B4
69 Stachy CS B4
50 Stackmora S A5
5 Stadbally IRL A4
59 Stade D B6
16 Staden B C3
62 Stadhagen D A4
73 Stadl a.d. Mur A A3
69 Stadl-Paura A C4
58 Stadskanaal NL C3
62 Stadt-Allendorf D C4
98 Stadt Schlaining A A1
63 Stadtilm D C6
62 Stadtkyll D C1
63 Stadtlauringen D C5
63 Stadtlengsfeld D C5
62 Stadtlohn D A1
63 Stadtoldendorf D B4
63 Stadtroda D C6
63 Stadtsteinach D C6
70 Stäfa CH A3
57 Staffanstörp S D2
68 Staffelstein D A1
11 Stafford GB C3
76 Staghella I A1
73 Stahovica YU B4
73 Stainach A A4
11 Staindrop GB A4
15 Staines GB C2
66 Stainville F C1
73 Stainz A B5
85 Staiti I A5
105 Stajevac YU B4
94 Stakcin CS B5
102 Stalać YU C2
73 Stalcerji YU C4
70 Stalden CH B2
14 Stalham GB B4
46 Stalheim N F3
108 Stalin AL A1
53 Stallarholmen S C3
50 Ställberg S C5
50 Ställdalen S C5
73 Stallhofen A A5
68 Stallwang D B3
91 Stalowa Woła PL C6
14 Stamford GB B2
11 Stamford Bridge GB B5
67 Stammheim D C4
110 Stamná GR A2
106 Stamovo BG A3
71 Stams A A5
46 Stamsund N B6
106 Stanchov Khan BG A3
10 Standish GB B3
15 Standon GB C3
50 Stange N B2
11 Stànhope GB A3
91 Stanin PL B6
99 Stanišic YU C4
91 Stanislawów PL A5
105 Stanke Dimitrov BG B5
69 Staňkov CS B4
77 Stankovici YU C5
9 Stanley GB D6
9 Stannington GB C6
108 Stános, *Aitolía kai Acarnanía* GR C3
109 Stanós, *Khalkidhikí* GR A5
70 Stans CH B3
15 Stansted Mountfitchet GB C3
14 Stanton GB B3
91 Stany PL C5
73 Stanz i. Murztal A A5
71 Stanzach A A5
99 Stapar YU C4
58 Staphorst NL C3
14 Stapleford GB B1
15 Staplehurst GB C3
91 Staporków PL B4
65 Stara Kamienica PL C5
99 Stara Moravica YU C4
77 Stara Novalja YU B4
101 Stara-Pazova YU A5
107 Stara Reka BG A4
64 Stará Role CS C2
61 Stara Rudnica PL C5
96 Stará Turá CS C3
106 Stara Zagora BG A3
91 Starachowice PL B5
102 Starapatitsa BG C3
105 Staravina YU C3
93 Staraya Russa SU B12
101 Starčevo YU B5
13 Starcross GB C4
97 Staré Hamry CS B4
97 Staré Hory CS C5
89 Stare Jablonki PL B6
96 Staré Město CS B3
89 Stare Pole PL A5
69 Stare Sedio CS B5
61 Stargara Szczeciński PL B6
101 Stari Banovci YU B5
81 Stari Bar YU B6
105 Stari Doiran YU C4
77 Stari Grad YU B4
98 Stari Gradac YU C2
101 Stari Jankovci YU A3
104 Stari Kačanik YU B3
100 Stari Majdan YU B1
101 Stari-Mikanovoi YU A3
104 Stari Raušić YU B2
100 Starigrad YU C1
77 Starigrad-Paklenica YU B5
64 Staritz D B3
68 Starnberg D C2
105 Staro Nagoričane YU B3
100 Staro Petrovo Selo YU A2
102 Staro Selo YU B2
106 Staro Zhelezare BG A2
61 Starogard PL B6
89 Starogard Gd. PL B4
94 Starokonstantinov SU B7
90 Staroścín PL C1
106 Starosel BG A2
106 Starozagorski Bani BG A3
89 Stary Dzierzgoń PL B5
96 Stary Hrozenkov CS C3
88 Stary Jaroslaw PL A2
69 Stary Plzenec CS B4
97 Stary Sącz PL B6
97 Starý Smokovec CS B6
97 Staškov CS B4
63 Staßfurt D B6
91 Staszów PL C5
49 Stathelle N B6
14 Staughton Highway GB B2
13 Staunton GB B5
101 Štavalj YU C5
48 Stavanger N C2
11 Staveley GB B4
17 Stavelot B C5
61 Stavenhagen D B3
17 Stavenisse NL B3
58 Staveren NL C2
51 Stavnäs S C3
109 Stavros, *Imathía* GR A4
110 Stavros, *Itháki* GR A1
109 Stavrós, *Lárisa* GR B4
109 Stavrós, *Thessaloníki* GR A5
109 Stavroúpolis, *Thessaloníki* GR A4
106 Stavroúpolis, *Xánthi* GR B2
50 Stavsjo N B1
88 Stawa PL B1
90 Stawiszyn PL B2
49 Steane N B5
70 Stechelberg CH B2
69 Štechovice CS B5
60 Stechow D C3
71 Steckborn CH A3
71 Steeg A A5
17 Steenbergen NL B4
16 Steenvoorde F C2
58 Steenwijk NL C3
107 Stefan Karadzhovo BG A4
109 Stefanavikion GR B4
108 Stefani, *Préveza* GR B2
111 Stefáni, *Voiotía* GR A4
70 Steffisburg CH B2
68 Stegaurach D B1
55 Stege DK D5
61 Stegelitz D B4
98 Stegersbach A A1
59 Steimbke D C6
70 Stein CH A2
6 Stein GB C2
71 Stein an Rhein CH A3
72 Steinach A A1
63 Steinach D C6
67 Steinach, *Baden-Württemberg* D C4
63 Steinach, *Bayern* D C5
63 Steinau, *Bayern* D C4
59 Steinau, *Niedersachsen* D B5
63 Steinbach-Hallenberg D C5
61 Steinbeck D C4
72 Steinberg am Rofan A A1
73 Steindorf A B3
70 Steinen D A2
69 Steinerkirchen a.d. Traun A C4
72 Steinfeld A B3
59 Steinfeld D C5
66 Steinfort L B1
71 Steingaden D A5
62 Steinhagen D A3
69 Steinhaus A C5
63 Steinheid D C6
67 Steinheim D C6
62 Steinhein D B4
61 Steinhöfel D C5
60 Steinhorst D C1
64 Steinigtwolmsdorf D B4
46 Steinkjer N E5
58 Steins NL B2
64 Steinsdor D A4
49 Steinsholt N B6
50 Steinvik N A2
17 Stekene B B4
59 Stelle D B7
17 Stellendam NL B4
56 Stenåsa S C5
21 Stenay F B6
56 Stenberga S B4
60 Stendal D C2
16 Stene B B2
51 Steneby S D3
111 Steni Dhirfios GR A4
112 Steniés GR E1
104 Stenje YU D2
6 Stenness, *Shetland Is.* GB
110 Steno GR B3
110 Stenón GR B3
47 Stensele S D8
51 Stenstorp S D4
55 Stenstrup DK C3
51 Stenungsund S D2
96 Štěpánov CS B3
68 Stephanskirchen D D3
61 Stepnica PL B5
101 Stepojevac YU B5
63 Sterbfritz D C4
63 Sterderdorf D A5
60 Sternberg D B2
96 Šternberk CS B3
112 Sternes, *Kriti* GR
55 Sterup D D2
62 Sterzhausen D C3
28 Stes. Maries-de-la-Mer F C3
65 Stęszew PL A6
64 Štěti CS C4
67 Stetten am Kalten Markt D C5
61 Stettin (Szczecin) PL B5
15 Stevenage GB C2
8 Stevenston GB C3
8 Stewarton GB C3
3 Stewartstown GB B5
15 Stewkley GB C2
59 Steyerburg D C6
15 Steyning GB D2
69 Steyr A C5
103 Stezherovo BG C6
88 Stężyca PL A3
88 Stężyca PL A3
71 Stezzano I C4
76 Stia I C1
78 Sticciano Scalo I A2
57 Stidsvig S C2
55 Stige DK C3
51 Stigen S D3
82 Stigliano I A3
103 Stigniţa RO B4
53 Stigtomta S D2
110 Stilia GR A3
109 Stilis GR C4
11 Stillington GB A4
83 Stilo I C3
111 Stimánga GR B3
110 Stimfalia GR B3
104 Štimlje YU B3
87 Stintino I B1
105 Štip YU C4
111 Stira GR A5
9 Stirling GB B4
97 Štitnik CS C6
96 Stity CS B2
53 Stjärnhov S C3
52 Stjärnsund S B2
46 Stjördals N E5
91 Stobierna PL C6
88 Stobno PL B2
67 Stockach D D5
70 Stöckalp CH B3
56 Stockaryd S B3
13 Stockbridge GB B6
53 Stockby S C3
60 Stockelsdorf D B1
96 Stockerau A C2
53 Stockholm S C4
11 Stockport GB B3
11 Stocksbridge GB B4
11 Stockton on Tees GB A4
91 Stoczek Łukowski PL B5
69 Stod CS B4
46 Stode S E8
54 Stoholm DK B2
103 Stoicăneşti RO B5
14 Stoke Ferry GB B3
11 Stoke-on-Trent GB B3
13 Stokenham GB C4
11 Stokesley GB A4
106 Stokite BG A3
49 Stokke N B7
55 Stokkemarke DK D4
49 Stokken N C5
96 Štoky CS B1
100 Stolac YU C2
17 Stolberg D C6
63 Stolberg D B5
93 Stolbey SU D10
64 Stollberg D C2
59 Stollhamm D B5
89 Stolno PL B4
64 Stolpen D B4
59 Stolzenau D C6
109 Stómion GR B4
62 Stommeln D B1
81 Ston YU B4
96 Stonařov CS B1
15 Stone, *Buckinghamshire* GB C2
11 Stone, *Staffordshire* GB C3
14 Stone Street GB B4
9 Stonehaven GB B5
8 Stonehouse GB C3
15 Stony Stratford GB B2
98 Stoob A A1
102 Stopanja YU C2
91 Stopnica PL C4
46 Stor-Elvdal N F5
53 Storå S C1
56 Storebro S B4
46 Stören N E5
46 Storfjord N B9
51 Storfors S C5
61 Storkow D B5
64 Storkow, *Frankfurt* D A3
46 Storlien S E6
80 Stornara I C2
6 Stornoway GB B2
71 Storo I C5
15 Storrington GB D2
47 Storuman S D8
52 Storvik S B2
52 Storvreta S C3
63 Stößen D B6
59 Stotel D B5
15 Stotfold GB B2
71 Stötten D A5
63 Stotternheim D B6
11 Stourbridge GB C3
13 Stourport on Severn GB A5
54 Støvring DK B2
9 Stow GB C5
13 Stow-on-the-Wold GB B6
14 Stowmarket GB B3
103 Stoyanovo BG C5
64 Straach D B2
3 Strabane GB B4
9 Strachan GB A5
8 Strachur GB B2
105 Stracin YU B4
59 Strackholt D B4
105 Stradalovo BG B4
14 Stradbroke GB B4
75 Stradella I A4
3 Stradone IRL C4
17 Straelen D B6
14 Strafford-upon-Avon GB B1
101 Stragari YU B5
53 Stråisnäs S D1
69 Strakonice CS B4
107 Straldzha BG A4
73 Strallegg A A5
61 Stralsund D A4
17 Stramproij NL B5
50 Strand N A2
46 Stranda, *Møre og Romsdal* N E3
48 Stranda, *Rogaland* N B2
54 Strandby DK A3
48 Strandebarm N A2
50 Strandlykkja N B2
48 Strandvik N A2
3 Strangford GB B6
53 Strängnäs S C3
53 Strångsjö S D2
96 Stráni CS C3
73 Stranice YU B5
3 Stranorlar IRL B4
8 Stranraer GB D2
84 Strasatti I B1
66 Strasbourg F C3
61 Strasburg D B4
69 Strašice CS B4
96 Straß A C1
73 Straß i. Steiermark A B5
52 Stråssa S C1
73 Straßburg A B4
69 Strasswalchen A D4
8 Strathaven GB C3
6 Strathkanaird GB C3
9 Strathmiglo GB B4
7 Strathpeffer GB C4
8 Strathyre GB B3
100 Stratinska YU B1
109 Stratoniki GR A5
109 Stratónion GR A5
12 Stratton GB C3
13 Stratton on the Fosse GB B5
68 Straubing D C3
87 Straulas I B2
46 Straumsness N E3
64 Straupitz D B4
61 Strausberg D C4
63 Straußfurt D B5
111 Stravá GR A3
69 Straž n. Nezárkou CS B5
102 Straža YU B2
96 Strážnice CS C3
69 Stražný CS C4
97 Štrba CS B6
97 Štrbské Pleso CS B6
15 Streatley GB C1
97 Strečno CS B4
17 Strée B C4
13 Street GB B5
103 Strehaia RO B4
64 Strehla D B3
97 Strekov CS D4
106 Strelcha BG A2
96 Strelice CS B2
97 Strelniky CS C5
98 Strem A A1
101 Stremska Mitrovica YU B4
101 Stremska-Rača YU B4
101 Stremski Karlovci YU A4
106 Stremtsi BG B3
69 Strengberg A C5
11 Strensall GB A4
104 Streoci YU B2
70 Stresa I C3
63 Streuldorf D C5
105 Strezimirovci BG B4
105 Strezovce YU B3
55 Strib DK C2
51 Striberg S C5
69 Stříbro CS B4
7 Strichen GB C6
72 Strigno I B1
98 Strigova YU B1
105 Strimonikón GR C5
100 Strizivonjna YU A3
100 Strmica YU B1
69 Strmilov CS B6
106 Stroevo BG A2
109 Strofiliá GR C5
59 Ströhen D C5
105 Strojkovce YU B3
2 Strokestown IRL C3
50 Ströllet S B4
62 Stromberg, *Nordrhein-Westfalen* D B3
67 Stromberg, *Rheinland-Pfalz* D B3
6 Stromeferry GB C3
6 Stromemore GB C3
49 Strommen N B7
7 Stromness GB B5
102 Stromosten YU B2
52 Strömsberg S B3
56 Strömsnäsbruk S C2
51 Strömstad S D2
53 Strömstors S D2
46 Strömsund S E7
51 Strömtorp S C5
8 Stronachlachar GB B3
8 Strone, *Strathclyde* GB B3
8 Strone, *Strathclyde* GB C3
108 Strongili GR B1
83 Stróngoli I B4
65 Stronie PL C6
8 Strontian GB B2
74 Stroppiana I A3
13 Stroud GB B5
91 Stróża PL C6
97 Stróża PL B5
104 Štrpce YU B3
59 Strücklingen D B4
104 Struga YU C2
68 Strullendorf D B1
105 Strumica YU C4
97 Strumien PL B4
106 Stryama BG A2
94 Stryi SU B5
90 Stryków PL B3
46 Stryn N F3
55 Strynø DK D3
89 Strzegawo PL C6
89 Strzegocin PL C6
65 Strzegom PL C6
90 Strzelce PL A3
61 Strzelce-Krajeńskie PL C6
90 Strzelce Opolskie PL C2
65 Strzelin PL C7
88 Strzelno PL C4
90 Strzemierzyce Wielkie PL C3
88 Strzépcz PL A4
90 Strzybnica PL C2
89 Strzygi PL B5
89 Strzyże PL C7
101 Stubal, *Srbija* YU C5
105 Stubal, *Srbija* YU B4
55 Stubbekøbing DK D5
55 Stubberup DK C3
71 Stuben A A5
73 Stubenberg A A5
73 Stubičke Toplice YU C5
102 Štubik YU B3
101 Stubline YU B5
106 Studen Kladenets BG B3
107 Studena BG B4
105 Studena, *Pernik* BG B5
69 Studená CS B6
104 Studenčane YU B2
100 Studenci YU C2
101 Studencia YU C5
60 Stüdenitz D C3
97 Studénka CS B4
73 Studenzen A A5
96 Studienka CS C3
103 Studina RO C5
13 Studland GB C6
13 Studley GB A6
88 Studzienice PL A3
60 Stuer D B3
62 Stukenbrock D B3
68 Stulln D B3
64 Stülpe D A3
96 Stupava CS C3
90 Stupca PL A1
102 Stupnica YU C3
73 Stupnik YU C5
88 Stupsk PL A3
13 Sturminster Newton GB C5
97 Štúrovo CS D4
15 Sturry GB C4
67 Stuttgart D C5
63 Stützerbach D C5
69 Stvolny CS A4
96 Stvrtok CS C3
50 Styri N B2
54 Styrso S A4
32 Suances E A2
107 Subaşi TR B4
76 Subbiano I C1
69 Suben A C4
79 Subiaco I B4
33 Subijana E B4
24 Subligny F A2
99 Subotica YU B4
97 Sučany CS B5
94 Suceava RO C7
77 Sučevići YU B6
97 Sucha Beskidzkaj PL B5
61 Suchań PL B6
69 Suchdol n. Luznici CS C5
91 Suchedniów PL B4
88 Suchorze PL A3
91 Suchozebry PL A6
17 Suchteln D B6
45 Sucina E B6
100 Sućuraj YU C2
11 Sudbury, *Derbyshire* GB C4
15 Sudbury, *Suffolk* GB B3
59 Süderbarup D A6
69 Sudoměřice u. Bechyně CS B5
40 Sueca E B2
87 Suelli I C2
68 Sugenheim D B1
24 Sugères F C3
21 Sugny B B5
63 Suhl D C5
60 Suhlendorf D C1
104 Suhodoll AL C2
101 Suhopolje, *Bosna i Hercegovina* YU B4
98 Suhopolje, *Hrvatska* YU C2
103 Suici RO A5
21 Suippes F B5
108 Sukë AL A2
105 Sukhostrel BG C4
104 Sukobin YU B1
77 Sukošan YU B5
99 Süküsd H B4
102 Sukovo YU C3
91 Suków PL C4
97 Šul'a CS C5
10 Sulby GB A1
48 Suldal N B3
54 Suldrup DK B2
65 Sulechów PL A5
61 Sulęcin PL C6
91 Sulejów PL B3
91 Sulejowek PL A5
71 Sulgen CH A4
88 Sulibórz PL B1
59 Sulingen D C5
88 Suliszewo PL B1
46 Sulitjelma N C8
97 Sulkowice PL B5
24 Sully F A2
90 Sulmierzyce PL B1
90 Sulmierzyce PL B3
79 Sulmona I A4
107 Süloğlu TR B4
90 Sułoszowa PL C3
65 Sulów PL B7
67 Sülz D C4
67 Sulzbach D B5
68 Sulzbach Rozenberg D B2
59 Sülze D C7
67 Sulzfeld D B4
100 Sumartin YU C1
33 Sumbulla E A5
98 Sümeg H B2
70 Sumiswald CH A2
11 Summer Bridge GB A4
5 Summerhill IRL A5
96 Šumná CS C1
96 Šumperk CS B3
96 Šumvald CS B3
15 Sunbury GB C2
68 Sunching D C3
52 Sundborn S B1
54 Sundby DK B1
48 Sunde N B2
49 Sundebru N C6
55 Sünderlügum D D1
62 Sundern D B3
50 Sundet N B2
55 Sunds DK B1
49 Sundstøyl N C5
47 Sundsvall S E8
107 Sungurlare BG A4
87 Suni I B1
100 Sunja YU A1
50 Sunnansjö S B5
46 Sunndalsöra N E4
50 Sunne S C4
50 Sunnemo S C4
52 Sunnersta S C3
47 Suolahti SF E12
47 Suomussalmi SF D14
47 Suonejoki SF E13
29 Super Sauze F B5
77 Supetarska Draga YU B4
79 Supino I B4
63 Supplingen D A5
98 Súr H A3
53 Surahammer S C2
97 Surany CS C4
101 Surčin YU B5
105 Surdulica YU B4
23 Surgères F B4
69 Surheim D D3
58 Surhuisterveen NL B3
35 Suria E B4
23 Surin F B5
105 Šurlane YU B3
106 Súrnevo BG A3
106 Sŭrnitza BG B2
89 Surowe PL B7
70 Sursee CH A3
54 Surte S A5
59 Surwold D C4
25 Sury F C4
102 Šusara YU B2
71 Susch CH B5
72 Susegana I C2
60 Süsel D A1
69 Sušice CS B4
32 Susilla E B2
77 Susnjevica YU A4
67 Sußen D C5
70 Susten CH B2
17 Susteren NL B5
107 Susuzmüsellim TR B5
89 Susz PL B5
99 Sutjeska YU C5
81 Sutomore YU B6
78 Sutri I A3
14 Sutterton GB B2
15 Sutton GB C2
14 Sutton Bridghe GB B3
11 Sutton Coldfield GB C4
11 Sutton in Ashfield GB B4
11 Sutton-on-Sea GB B6
15 Sutton Scotney GB C1
104 Suva Reka YU B2
75 Suvereto I C5
93 Suwalki PL C8
29 Suze-Rousse F B3
21 Suzy F B4
75 Suzzara I B5
52 Svabensverk S A1
57 Svalöv S D2
51 Svaneholm S C3
57 Svaneke DK D4
57 Svängsta S C3
47 Svappavaara S C10
52 Svärdsjö S B1
49 Svarstad N B6
51 Svartå S C5
57 Svarte S D2
53 Svärtinge S D2
52 Svartnäs S B2
53 Sväta S D3
97 Svčinovec CS B4
57 Svedala S D2
46 Sveg S E7
48 Sveio N B2
55 Svejbæk DK B2
49 Svelvik N B7
55 Svendborg DK C3
49 Svene N B6
56 Svenljunga S B2
51 Svenneby S D2
53 Svennevad S C1
46 Svenningdal N D6
51 Svenshögen S D2
54 Svenstrup DK B2
64 Švermov CS C4
97 Švermovo CS C6
105 Sveti Nikole YU C3
81 Sveti Stefan YU B5
96 Světla n. Sázavou CS B1
89 Svetlyy SU A6
99 Svetozar YU C4
102 Svetozarevo YU C2
77 Svetvincenat YU A3
106 Svezhen BG A3
77 Švica YU B5
94 Svidnik CS B4
69 Švihov CS B4
100 Svilaj YU A3
102 Svilajnac YU B2
107 Svilengrad BG B4
51 Svindal N C2
102 Svinita RO B3
55 Svinninge DK C4
95 Svishtov BG E6
97 Svit CS B6
96 Svitavy CS B2
97 Svodin CS D4
103 Svoge BG D4
46 Svolvaer N B7
110 Svoronáta GR A1
96 Svratka CS B2
102 Svrljig YU C3
50 Svulrya N B3
11 Swadlincote GB C4
14 Swaffham GB B3
17 Swalmen NL B6
13 Swanage GB C6
3 Swanlinbar GB B4
12 Swansea GB B4
103 Swarta RO A4
65 Swarzędz PL A7
3 Swatragh GB B5
13 Sway GB C6
89 Swiątki PL B6
65 Świdnica, *Walbrzych* PL C6
65 Świdnica, *Zielona Góra* PL B5
88 Swidwin PL B1
65 Świebodzice PL C6
65 Swiebodzin PL A5
89 Świecie PL B4
89 Swiedziebnia PL B5
65 Świeradów Zdrój PL C5
65 Swierzawa PL C5
61 Swierzno PL B5
90 Swieta Anna PL C3
89 Świętajno PL B7
88 Swietlino PL A2
65 Świetno PL A6
89 Świętoslaw PL B4
90 Swiętów PL C1
58 Swifterbant NL C2
13 Swindon GB B6
14 Swineshead GB B2
2 Swinford IRL C3
90 Swinice PL A2
61 Swinoujście PL B5
9 Swinton GB C5
61 Swobnica PL B5
5 Swords IRL A5
97 Swoszowice PL B5
53 Sya S D1
88 Sycewice PL A2
90 Syców PL B1
65 Sycowice PL A5
48 Syfteland N A2
59 Syke D C5
49 Sylling N B7
9 Syminton GB C4
12 Synod Inn GB A3
88 Sypniewo PL B2
88 Sypniewo PL B3
89 Sypniewo PL B7
7 Syre GB B4
50 Sysslebäck S B3
14 Syston GB B1
98 Szabadbattyán H A3
99 Szabadegyháza H A3
99 Szabadszállás H B4
90 Szadek PL B2
97 Szaflary PL B6
98 Szakály H B3
98 Szakcs H B3
99 Szakmár H B4
98 Szalánta H C3
99 Szalkszentmárton H B4
88 Szamocin PL B3
88 Szamotuly PL C2
98 Szany H A2
99 Szarvas H B5
97 Szarvaskö H D6
98 Szászvár H B3
97 Szczawa PL B6
97 Szczawnica PL B6
65 Szczawno Zdrój PL C6
94 Szczebrzeszyn PL A5
61 Szczecin (Stettin) PL B5
88 Szczecinek PL B2
91 Szczekociny PL C3
90 Szczerców PL B3
91 Szczucin PL C5
88 Szczuczarz PL B2
89 Szczuki PL C6
91 Szczurowa PL C4
97 Szczyrk PL B5
89 Szczytno PL B6
97 Szécsény H C5
99 Szedies H B3
99 Szeged H B5
94 Szeghalom H C4
94 Śzeghalom RO C4
99 Szegvár H B5
94 Székely H B4
98 Székesfehérvár H A3
99 Szekszárd H B3
89 Szelków PL C7
89 Szemud PL A4
97 Szendehely H D5
98 Szentantalfa H B2
97 Szentdomonkos H C6
99 Szentendre H A4
99 Szentes H B5
98 Szentgál H A2
98 Szentgotthárd H B1
98 Szentlörinc H B2
99 Szentmártonkáta H A4
98 Szenyér H B2
98 Szepetnek H B1
99 Szeremle H B3
94 Szerencs H B4
89 Szestno PL B7
99 Szigetszentmiklós H A4
99 Szigetujfalu H A3
98 Szigetvár H B2
97 Szihalom H D6
94 Szikszó H B4
98 Szil H A2
97 Szilvásvarad H C6
65 Szklarska Poręba PL C5
65 Szlichtyngowa PL B6
97 Szob H D4
97 Szokolya H D4
99 Szolnok H A5
98 Szombathely H A1
98 Szöny H A3
99 Szöreg H B5
98 Szorosad H B3
89 Szpetal Graniczny PL C5
65 Szprotawa PL B5
89 Szreńsk PL B6
89 Sztum PL B5
89 Sztutowo PL A5
88 Szubin PL B3
97 Szücsi H D5
98 Szulok H B2
97 Szurdokpüspöki H D5
88 Szwecja PL B2
90 Szybowice PL C1
90 Szydlów PL B3
91 Szydłów PL C5
91 Szydlowiec PL B4
88 Szydlowo PL B2
89 Szydlowo PL B6
91 Szymanów PL A4
89 Szyrokove SU A6

T

47 Taavetti SF F13
98 Tab H B3
32 Tabanera de Valdavia E B2
38 Tabanera la Luenga E A2
105 Tabanovce YU B3
32 Tábara E C1
63 Tabarz D C5
32 Tabenera de Cerrato E B2
40 Tabequeros E B1
56 Taberg S B3
45 Tabernas E B4
40 Tabernes de Valldiggna E B2
35 Tabescán E A4
75 Tabiano Terme I B5
30 Taboada E B3
30 Taboadela E B3
69 Tábor CS B5
99 Táborfalva H A4
36 Tábua P A2
31 Tabuaco P C3
33 Tabuenca E C5
30 Tabuyo del Monte E B4
53 Täby S C4
98 Tác H A3
68 Tachov CS B3
11 Tadcaster GB B4
15 Tadley GB C1
33 Tafalla E B5
42 Taganheira P B1
57 Tågarp S D1
74 Tággia I C2
79 Tagliacozzo I A4
76 Táglio di Po I A2
21 Tagnon F B5
45 Tahal E B4
97 Tahitótfalu H D5
35 Tahús E A4
67 Tailfingen D C5
19 Taillis F B4
7 Tain GB C4
29 Tain-l'Hermitage F A3
36 Taipadas P C2
101 Takovo YU B5
99 Taksony H A4
93 Takums SU B8
30 Tal E B2
76 Talamello I C2
78 Talamone I A2
38 Talarrubias E C1
37 Talaván E B4
38 Talavera de la Reina E C2
37 Talavera la Real E C4
38 Talavera la Vieja E C1
37 Talayuela E B5
40 Talayuelas E B1
48 Talgje N B2
31 Talhadas P D2
37 Táliga E C3
28 Talizat F A2
76 Talla I C1
6 Talladale GB C3
5 Tallaght IRL A5
29 Tallard F B5
50 Tallberg S B5
53 Tallboda S D1
93 Tallinn SU A9
5 Tallow IRL B3
5 Tallowbridge IRL B3
33 Talmantes E C5
25 Talmay F A5
22 Talmont, *Charente-Maritime* F C4
22 Talmont, *Vendée* F B3
89 Talpaki SU A7
83 Talsano I A4
93 Talsi SU B8
46 Talvik N A11
10 Talybont GB C2
39 Tamajón E B3
32 Tamame E C1
31 Tamames E D4
107 Tamarino BG A4
35 Tamarit E B4
34 Tamarite de Litera E B3
35 Tamariu E B6
98 Tamási H B3
63 Tambach-Dietharz D C5
30 Tameza E A4
17 Tamines B C4
47 Tammisaari SF G11
102 Tamnič YU B3
47 Tampere SF F11
73 Tamsweg A A3
38 Tamurejo E D2
11 Tamworth GB C4
12 Tan-y-groes GB A3
33 Tañabueyes E B3
111 Tanágra GR A4
98 Tanakajd H A1
46 Tananes N A14
87 Tanaunella I B2
20 Tancarville F B1
3 Tandragee GB B5
55 Tandslet DK D2
3 Tang IRL C4
57 Tånga S C1
50 Tanger N B2
60 Tangerhütte D C2
60 Tangermünde D C2
70 Taninges F B1
63 Tann D C5
63 Tanna D C6
56 Tannaker S C2
46 Tannäs S E6
21 Tannay, *Ardennes* F B5
24 Tannay, *Nièvre* F A3
63 Tanne D B5
64 Tannenbergsthal D C2
68 Tännesberg D B3
71 Tannheim A A5
61 Tanowo PL B5
51 Tanum S D2
51 Tanumshede S D2
65 Tanvala CS C5
85 Taormina I B4
36 Tapada P C2
99 Tápe H B5
68 Tapfheim D C1
30 Tapia de Casariego E A4
99 Tápióbicske H A4
99 Tápiógyörgye H A5
99 Tápióság H A4
99 Tápiósáp H A4
99 Tapiószecsö H A4
99 Tápiószentmárton H A4
98 Tapolca H B2
98 Tapolcafö H A2
53 Tappstrom S C3
97 Tar H D5
35 Taradell E B5
30 Taramundi E A3
39 Tarancon E B4
83 Táranto I A4
98 Tarany H B2
25 Tarare F C4
35 Tarascon-sur-Ariège F A4
33 Tarazona E C5
39 Tarazone de la Mancha E C5
40 Tarbena E C2
8 Tarbert, *Strathclyde* GB C2
6 Tarbert, *Western Isles* GB C2
4 Tarbert IRL B2
26 Tarbes F C4
8 Tarbet GB B3
8 Tarbolton GB C3
72 Tarcento I B3
100 Tarčin YU C3
91 Tarczyn PL B4
33 Tardelcuenda E C4
26 Tardets-Sorholus F C3
34 Tardienta E B2
26 Targon F B3
94 Targu Ocna RO C7
43 Tarifa E C4
42 Tariquejo E B2
99 Tarjan H A3
9 Tarland GB A5
10 Tarleton GB B3
91 Tarlów PL B5
55 Tarm DK C1
59 Tarmstedt D B6
46 Tärna S D7
99 Tarnaörs H A5
99 Tarnaszentmiklós H A5
91 Tarnobrzeg PL C5
26 Tarnos F C2
90 Tarnowskie Gory PL C2
52 Tärnsjö S B2
31 Tarouca P C3
55 Tarp D D2
10 Tarporley GB B3
78 Tarquínia I A2
35 Tarragona E B4
13 Tarrant Hinton GB C5
35 Tárrega E B4
71 Tarrenz A A5
54 Tårs DK A3
82 Tarsia I B3
26 Tartas F C3
93 Tartu SU A10
7 Tarves GB C6
10 Tarvin GB B3
94 Tăsnad RO C5
96 Tasov CS B2
100 Tasovčići YU C2
25 Tassin-la-Demi-Lune F C4
55 Tåstrup DK C5
98 Taszár H B2
99 Tat H A3
98 Tata H A3
99 Tatabánya H A3
99 Tataháza H B4
99 Tatárszentgyörgy H A4
97 Tatranská Kotlina CS B6
97 Tatranská-Lomnica CS B6
48 Tau N B2
67 Tauberbischofsheim D B5
64 Taucha D B2
68 Taufkirchen D C3
69 Taufkirchen a.d. Pram A C4
18 Taule F B2
29 Taulignan F B3
55 Taulov DK C2
13 Taunton GB B4
67 Taunusstein D A4
93 Taurage SU C8
85 Taurianova I A5
83 Taurisano I B5
34 Tauste E B1
24 Tauves F C2
99 Tavankut YU B4
70 Tavannes CH A2
25 Tavaux F A5
83 Taverna I B3
71 Taverne CH B3
76 Tavernelle I C2
71 Tavérnola Bergamasca I C5

Pg	Name	Ctry	Grid
42	Vidigueira	P	A2
103	Vidin	BG	C3
6	Vidlin, *Shetland Is.*	GB	
65	Vidnava	CS	C7
23	Viechtach	D	B3
28	Vieille-Brioude	F	A2
35	Vieira, *Braga*	P	C2
36	Vieira, *Leiria*	P	B2
34	Viella	E	A3
34	Vielle Aure	F	A3
22	Vellevigne	F	B3
27	Vielmur	F	C6
23	Viels Maison	F	C4
17	Vielsalm	B	C5
63	Vienenburg	D	B5
25	Vienne	F	C3
60	Vieritz	D	C3
67	Viernheim	D	B4
61	Vierraden	D	B6
17	Viersen	D	A5
24	Vierzon	F	A2
24	Vieselbach	D	C6
80	Vieste	I	D2
79	Vietri di Potenza	I	D3
79	Vietri sul Mare	I	C5
2	Vieux-Boucan	F	C2
29	Vif	F	C4
5	Vig	DK	C4
81	Viganj	YU	B4
75	Vigásio	I	A3
72	Vigaun	A	A3
48	Vigeland	N	C4
9	Vigeois	F	A5
74	Vigévano	I	A3
82	Viggianello	I	B3
82	Viggiano	I	A2
79	Vigiano	I	A2
97	Vigľáš	CS	C5
108	Vigla	GR	B2
74	Vigmostad	N	C4
71	Vignale	I	A3
78	Vignanello	I	A3
21	Vigneux-Hocquet	F	B4
75	Vignola	I	B6
21	Vignory	F	C6
24	Vignoux-sur-Barangeon	F	A2
30	Vigo	E	B2
72	Vigo di Fassa	I	B1
74	Vigone	I	B2
47	Vigrestad	N	C2
47	Vihanti	SF	D12
23	Vihiers	F	A4
47	Viinijärvi	SF	E14
47	Vik	N	
57	Vik, *Kristianstad*	S	D3
52	Vik, *Uppsala*	S	C3
50	Vika, *Kopparberg*	S	B5
52	Vika, *Kopparberg*	S	B1
51	Vikane	N	C1
51	Vikarbyn	S	B6
48	Vikedal	N	B2
48	Vikeland	N	C4
57	Viken	S	C1
48	Vikersund	N	B6
48	Vikevåg	N	B2
48	Vikey	N	A3
53	Vikingstad	S	D1
52	Vikmanshyttan	S	B1
52	Viksjöfors	S	A1
52	Viksta	S	B3
37	Vila Boim	P	C3
36	Vila Chã de Ourique	P	B2
36	Vila de Rei	P	B2
42	Vila do Bispo	P	B1
42	Vila do Conde	P	C2
31	Vila Flor	P	C3
31	Vila Franca das Navas	P	D3
36	Vila Franca de Xira	P	C1
36	Vila Fresca	P	C1
36	Vila Nogueira	P	C1
36	Vila Nova da Baronia	P	C2
31	Vila Nova de Famalicão	P	C2
31	Vila Nova de Foz Coa	P	C3
31	Vila Nova de Gaia	P	C2
42	Vila Nova de Milfontes	P	B1
36	Vila Nova de Ourem	P	B2
31	Vila Nova de Paiva	P	D3
31	Vila Pouca de Aguiar	P	C3
31	Vila Praja de Ancora	P	C2
31	Vila Real	P	C3
42	Vila Real de S. Antonio	P	B2
42	Vila Ruiva	P	A2
36	Vila Seca	P	A2
36	Vila Velha de Ródão	P	B3
31	Vila Verde, *Braga*	P	C2
36	Vila Verde, *Lisboa*	P	B1
42	Vila Verde de Filcalho	P	B2
36	Vila Vicosa	P	C3
35	Vilademat	E	A6
35	Viladrau	E	B5
35	Vilajuiga	E	A6
31	Vilar Formoso	P	D4
31	Vilarandelo	P	C3
35	Vilarrodona	E	A3
30	Vilasantar	E	A2
103	Vilcele	RO	A3
44	Vilches	E	A3
5	Vildbjerg	DK	B1
34	Vilella Baja	E	B3
66	Vilémov	CS	B1
46	Vilhelmina	S	D8
83	Villa Castelli	I	A4
31	Villa Cova de Lixa	P	C2
34	Vila de la Feira	P	B2
30	Villa de Cruces	E	B2
31	Villa de Peralonso	E	B3
38	Villa del Prado	E	B3
34	Villa del Rio	E	
71	Villa di Chiavenna	I	A2
75	Villa Minozzo	I	B5
32	Villa Nueva de las Manzanas	E	B1
85	Villa San Giovanni	I	A4
79	Villa Santa Maria	I	F3
72	Viella Santina	I	C2
42	Villabáñez	E	C2
42	Villablanca	E	A2
33	Villablino	E	A4
32	Villabragima	E	C1
32	Villabuena del Puenta	E	C1
33	Villacadima	E	C3
44	Villacañas	E	C3
41	Villacarlos, *Menorca*	E	
32	Villacarriedo	E	A3
44	Villacarrillo	E	A3
38	Villacastin	E	B2
73	Villach	A	B3
87	Villacidro	I	C1
39	Villaconejos	E	B3
39	Villaconejos de Trabaque	E	B4
32	Villada	E	B2
32	Villadangos del Páramo	E	B1
31	Villadecanes	E	B1
31	Villadepera	E	C4
32	Villadiego	E	B3
44	Villadompardo	E	B2
70	Villadóssola	I	B3
32	Villaeles de Valdavia	E	B2
39	Villaescusa de Haro	E	C4
33	Villafáfila	E	C1
32	Villaflores	E	A1
32	Villafrades de Campos	E	B2
38	Villafranca, *Avila*	E	B1
38	Villafranca, *Burgos*	E	B3
44	Villafranca, *Navarra*	E	B5
44	Villafranca de Córdoba	E	B2
39	Villafranca de los Barros	E	C4
39	Villafranca de los Caballeros	E	C3
33	Villafranca de Oria	E	A4
30	Villafranca del Bierzo	E	B1
35	Villafranca del Cid	E	A2
44	Villafranca del Panadés	E	B4
71	Villafranca di Verona	I	C5
75	Villafranca in Lunigiana	I	A4
85	Villafranca Tirrena	I	A4
43	Villafranco del Guadalquivir	E	B3
84	Villafrati	I	B2
31	Villafrechós	E	C1
32	Villafruela	E	C3
32	Villagarcia	E	B1
37	Villagarcia de las Torres	E	C4
83	Villaggio Mancuso	I	B3
33	Villagonzalo	E	C4
26	Villagrains	F	B4
44	Villaharta	E	A2
45	Villahermosa	E	A4
32	Villaherreros	E	B2
32	Villahoz	E	B3
19	Villaines-la-Juhel	F	B5
40	Villajoyosa	E	B4
79	Villalago	I	B4
30	Villalba	I	B2
84	Villalba	I	B2
39	Villalba de Calatrava	E	A3
39	Villalba de la Sierra	E	B4
32	Villalba de los Alcores	E	C2
32	Villalba de los Barros	E	C4
43	Villalba del Alcor	E	B3
43	Villalba del Rey	E	B4
72	Villalcázar de Sirga	E	B3
33	Villalengua	E	C5
39	Villalgordo del Júcar	E	C4
39	Villalgordo del Marquesado	E	C4
32	Villalon de Campos	E	B1
32	Villalonga	E	C1
32	Villalpando	E	C1
32	Villalumbroso	E	B2
33	Villalvaro	E	B3
40	Villamalea	E	B1
32	Villamañán	E	B1
32	Villamanrique de la Condesa	E	B3
44	Villamanrique S. Cristóbal	E	A4
32	Villamanta	E	B3
32	Villamantilla	E	B3
87	Villamar	I	C1
32	Villamarin	E	C1
32	Villamartin de Campos	E	B2
38	Villamartin de Don Sancho	E	B1
38	Villamartin de Valdeorras	E	B3
87	Villamassárgia	I	C1
44	Villamayor de Calatrava	E	A2
32	Villamayor de Campos	E	C1
39	Villamayor de Santiago	E	C4
37	Villamesias	E	B5
33	Villaminaya	E	C3
33	Villamor de les Escuderos	E	C1
32	Villamoronta	E	B2
38	Villamuelas	E	C3
32	Villamuriel de Cerrato	E	C2
33	Villandraut	F	D4
81	Villanova	I	D4
80	Villanova d. Battista	I	C2
74	Villanova d'Asti	I	B2
74	Villanova Mondovì	I	B2
87	Villanova Monteleone	I	B1
75	Villantério	I	A4
39	Villanueva de Alcardete	E	C4
32	Villanueva de Alcorón	E	B4
32	Villanueva de Argaño	E	B3
	Villanueva de la Jara	E	C5
44	Villanueva de la Reina	E	A3
44	Villanueva de la Serena	E	C5
44	Villanueva de la Sierra	E	A4
37	Villanueva de la Vera	E	A5
31	Villanueva de las Peras	E	C5
42	Villanueva de los Castillejos	E	B2
44	Villanueva de los Infantes	E	A4
44	Villanueva de Mesia	E	B3
44	Villanueva de S. Carlos	E	A4
44	Villanueva de S. Juan	E	B4
44	Villanueva de Tapia	E	B2
38	Villanueva del Aceral	E	A2
39	Villanueva del Arzobispo	E	A4
32	Villanueva del Campo	E	C1
44	Villanueva del Duque	E	A1
37	Villanueva del Fresno	E	C3
34	Villanueva del Huerva	E	B1
43	Villanueva del Rey	E	A4
43	Villanueva del Rio	E	B4
44	Villanueva del Rosario	E	C2
44	Villanueva del Trabuco	E	B2
35	Villanueva y Geltru	E	B4
98	Villány	H	C3
30	Villaodrid	E	A3
30	Villapedre	E	A2
87	Villaputzu	I	C2
32	Villaquejida	E	B1
32	Villaquilambra	E	B1
32	Villaquiran de los Infantes	E	B2
29	Villar d'Arène	F	A5
32	Villar de Barrio	E	A3
39	Villar de Cañas	E	C4
40	Villar de Chinchilla	E	C1
31	Villar de Ciervo	E	D4
39	Villar de Domingo Garcia	E	B4
34	Villar de los Navarros	E	B1
37	Villar de Rena	E	B5
31	Villar de Santos	E	A3
40	Villar del Arzobispo	E	B2
31	Villar del Buey	E	C4
39	Villar del Cobo	E	B5
40	Villar del Humo	E	B1
38	Villar del Pedroso	E	C1
37	Villar del Rey	E	B4
33	Villar del Rio	E	B4
39	Villar del Saz	E	B4
74	Villar Perosa	I	B2
44	Villaralto	E	A2
29	Villard-Bonnot	F	B4
29	Villard-de-Lans	F	A4
70	Villard-S.D.	F	C1
31	Villardeciervos	E	C4
32	Villardefrades	E	C1
31	Villardevós	E	C3
40	Villareal de los Infantes	E	B2
39	Villarejo	E	B2
39	Villarejo de Fuentes	E	C4
32	Villarejo de Orbigo	E	B1
39	Villarejo de Salvanes	E	B3
39	Villares del Saz	E	C4
74	Villaretto	I	B2
40	Villargordo del Cabrie	E	B2
37	Villarino de Conso	E	B3
40	Villarluengo	E	B2
33	Villarobe	E	A3
84	Villarosa	I	B3
32	Villarramiel	E	B2
43	Villarrasa	E	B3
37	Villarreal de S. Carlos	E	B4
39	Villarrobledo	E	C4
40	Villarroya de los Pinares	E	A2
37	Villarrubia de Santiago	E	C3
39	Villarrubia de los Ojos	E	C3
25	Villarrubio	E	C4
40	Villarta	E	B1
25	Villars-les-Dombes	F	B5
40	Villarta de los Montes	E	A1
39	Villarta de S. Juan	E	A3
33	Villasandino	E	B2
33	Villasarracino	E	B2
31	Villasdardo	E	C4
30	Villaseca de Henares	E	B4
38	Villaseca de la Sagra	E	C3
31	Villaseco	E	C4
31	Villaseco de los Reyes	E	C4
38	Villasequilla de Yepes	E	C3
87	Villasimius	I	C2
87	Villasor	I	C1
74	Villastellone	I	B2
38	Villatobas	E	C3
38	Villatoro	E	B1
53	Villatorp	S	C1
111	Villáfia	GR	D4
33	Villava	E	A5
40	Villavaliente	E	C1
33	Villavelayo	E	B4
45	Villaverde de Guadalimar	E	A4
32	Villaverde del Rio	E	A1
43	Villaviciosa de Córdoba	E	A4
34	Villaviciosa de Odón	E	B3
40	Villavieja, *Castellon*	E	B3
32	Villavieja, *Orense*	E	B3
32	Villavieja de Yeltes	E	C4
30	Villayón	E	A4
66	Villé	F	B2
21	Ville-sous-la-Ferté	F	C5
66	Ville-sur-Illon	F	C2
21	Ville-sur-Tourbe	F	B5
23	Villebois-Lavalette	F	C5
19	Villedieu-les-Poêles	F	B4
28	Villedieu-sur-Indre	F	B6
23	Villefagnan	F	B5
74	Villefranche	F	B2
24	Villefranche, *Allier*	F	A5
21	Villefranche, *Yonne*	F	D4
27	Villefranche-d'Albigeois	F	C6
27	Villefranche-de-Lauragais	F	C5
26	Villefranche-de-Lonchat	F	B4
28	Villefranche-de-Panat	F	B1
27	Villefranche-de-Rouergue	F	B6
27	Villefranche-du-Périgord	F	B5
24	Villefranche-sur-Cher	F	A1
25	Villefranche-sur-Saône	F	C4
40	Villel	E	A2
21	Villemaur-sur-Vanne	F	C4
21	Villemer	F	C3
27	Villemur	F	C3
34	Villena	E	C2
21	Villenauxe-la-Grande	F	C4
26	Villenave-d'Ornon	F	B3
74	Villeneuve, *Alpes-Maritimes*	F	C3
27	Villeneuve, *Aveyron*	F	C4
27	Villeneuve, *Haute-Garonne*	F	C4
28	Villeneuve, *Haute-Loire*	F	A2
21	Villeneuve, *Seine-et-Marne*	F	B3
70	Villeneuve	F	D3
28	Villeneuve-de-Berg	F	B3
26	Villeneuve-de-Marsan	F	C3
21	Villeneuve-l'Archevêque	F	C4
21	Villeneuve-la-Guyard	F	C4
21	Villeneuve-la-Comte	F	C3
29	Villeneuve-les-Avignon	F	C3
20	Villeneuve-St.-Georges	F	C3
24	Villeneuve-sur-Allier	F	B3
27	Villeneuve-sur-Lot	F	C4
21	Villeneuve-sur-Yonne	F	C4
23	Villeréal	F	C4
32	Villerías	E	C2
21	Villeromain	F	C2
19	Villers-Bocage, *Calvados*	F	A5
20	Villers-Bocage, *Somme*	F	B3
21	Villers-Bretonneux	F	B3
93	Villers-Carbonnel	F	B3
78	Villers-Cotterêts	F	B4
25	Villers-Farlay	F	B4
70	Villers-le-Gambon	F	C4
70	Villers-le-Lac	F	A6
19	Villers-sur-Mer	F	A6
21	Villersexel	F	A1
19	Villerville	F	A6
21	Villeseneux	F	C5
79	Villetta Barrea	I	D2
29	Villeveyrac	F	C3
111	Villia	GR	D4
74	Villiers-St. Benoit	F	D4
21	Villiers-St. Georges	F	C4
62	Villmar	D	D4
37	Villoldo	E	B2
38	Villoria	E	B2
84	Vilnius	SU	D9
54	Vils	DK	B1
33	Vilsänesti	RO	A5
68	Vilsbiburg	D	C3
57	Vilshofen	D	C3
57	Vilshult	S	B3
47	Viltasaari	SF	E12
81	Vilusi	YU	B3
31	Vilvestre	E	C4
16	Vilvoorde	B	C4
31	Vilz Nova da Cerverra	P	C2
71	Vimercate	I	C4
30	Vimianzo	E	A1
36	Vimieiro	P	C3
56	Vimmerby	S	B4
55	Vimoutiers	F	A6
71	Vinadi	CH	B5
35	Vinaixa	E	B3
50	Vinäs	S	B1
103	Vinători	RO	B3
29	Vinay	F	A4
54	Vinberg	S	C1
35	Vinça	F	A3
101	Vinča	YU	B5
79	Vinchiaturo	I	D1
75	Vinci	I	C1
55	Vindeby	DK	C3
47	Vinderup	DK	B1
21	Vinets	F	C5
53	Vingåker	S	D1
111	Vingláfia	GR	D4
33	Vingrau	F	A5
48	Vingrom	N	A1
31	Vinhais	P	C3
108	Viniani, *Evritania*	GR	B3
109	Viniani, *Fokís*	GR	B4
32	Villaverde del Rio	E	C5
98	Vinica, *Hrvatska*	YU	B1
43	Vinicio	YU	B1
98	Vinica, *Slovenija*	YU	B1
105	Vinica	YU	C5
105	Viničani	YU	B3
33	Viniegra de Arriba	E	B4
46	Vinje, *Sør Trøndelag*	N	E3
48	Vinje, *Telemark*	N	B4
103	Vinju Mare	RO	B3
79	Vinkovci	YU	A3
101	Vinkovci	YU	A3
94	Vinnitsa	SU	B8
29	Vinon	F	C4
57	Vinslöv	S	C2
46	Vinstra	N	F4
52	Vintjärn	S	B2
51	Vintrosa	S	B2
39	Viñuela de Sayago	E	C1
39	Viñuelas	E	C1
33	Vinuesa	E	B4
59	Viol	D	A6
73	Viola	I	B1
27	Violay	F	C4
69	Vipava	YU	C4
72	Vipiteno (Sterzing)	I	B1
100	Vir	YU	C5
70	Vira	CH	B3
19	Vire	F	B5
56	Vireda	S	B3
21	Vireux	F	A5
44	Virgen de la Cabeza	E	A2
3	Virginia	IRL	C4
25	Viriat	F	B5
25	Virieu-le-Grand	F	A4
98	Virje	YU	B4
81	Virpazar	YU	B6
46	Virtaniemi	SF	B14
103	Virtoapele	RO	B6
66	Virton	B	B1
103	Virtopu	RO	B4
93	Virtsu	SU	A8
103	Virvoru	RO	B4
25	Viry	F	B6
100	Vis	YU	C1
29	Visan	F	C3
108	Visani	GR	B2
59	Visbek	D	C5
55	Visby	DK	D1
92	Visby	S	C4
17	Visé	B	C7
101	Visegrad	YU	C4
56	Viserum	S	B4
94	Vişeul de Sus	RO	C5
34	Visiedo	E	C1
103	Visina Veche	RO	C5
56	Viskafors	S	B2
56	Vislanda	S	C3
73	Višnja Gora	YU	C4
29	Višnové	CS	C2
100	Visoko, *Bosna i Hercegovina*	YU	C3
73	Visoko, *Slovenija*	YU	B4
74	Visone	I	B3
70	Visp	CH	B2
56	Vissefjärda	S	C4
59	Visselhövede	D	C6
55	Vissenbjerg	DK	C3
108	Vissinia	GR	A3
55	Visso	I	A4
40	Vistabella del Maestrazgo	E	A2
84	Vita	I	B1
73	Vitanje	YU	B5
101	Vitanovac	YU	C5
93	Vitebsk	SU	C12
78	Viterbo	I	A3
108	Vithkuq	AL	A2
31	Vitigudino	E	C4
110	Vitina	GR	B3
104	Vitina, *A. P. Kosovo*	YU	B3
98	Vitina, *Bosna i Hercegovina*	YU	C2
69	Vitis	A	C6
96	Vitkov	CS	B3
101	Vitkovac	YU	C5
105	Vitolište	YU	B3
104	Vitomirica	YU	B1
97	Vitonice	CS	C2
19	Vitoria-Gasteiz	E	C4
28	Vitrey	F	D1
21	Vitrolles	F	C4
16	Vitry-en-Artois	F	C3
21	Vitry-le-François	F	C5
50	Vitsand	S	B3
47	Vittangi	S	C10
52	Vittaryd	S	B3
71	Vitteaux	F	A4
55	Vittel	F	C1
85	Vittória	I	C3
72	Vittório Veneto	I	C2
57	Vittsjö	S	B3
57	Vittskövle	S	D3
74	Viu	I	A2
55	Viuf	DK	C2
49	Viul	N	A7
34	Vivel del Rio Martin	E	B2
39	Viveli	N	B3
32	Viver	E	A2
33	Vivero	E	A3
28	Viverols	F	A3
21	Vivier-au-Court	F	B5
29	Viviers	F	B3
31	Viviez	F	B6
112	Vivlos	GR	D1
71	Vivonne	F	B4
74	Vivsta	N	E8
31	Vivy	F	A4
77	Vižiňada	YU	A3
96	Vizovice	CS	C3
112	Vizvár	H	B2
85	Vizzavona	F	—
85	Vizzini	I	B3
55	Vlachovice	NL	B1
109	Vláchovo Brezí	GR	B4
55	Vladivik	NL	B3
105	Vladičin Han	YU	A5
103	Vladimirci	YU	B3
101	Vladimirovo	BG	C5
94	Vladimir Volynskiy	SU	A6
103	Vladimiri	YU	B3
101	Vlagtwedde	NL	B3
32	Vlajkovac	YU	C4
98	Vlaho Castellon	YU	B1
102	Vlaho Slovenija	YU	B3
110	Vlakherna	GR	B3
111	Vlakhióti	GR	C3
108	Vlakhokerasia	GR	B3
111	Vlakhópoulon	GR	C2
109	Vlakhópoulon	GR	C3
16	Vlamertinge	B	C3
109	Vlasenica	YU	C1
101	Vlašim	CS	B5
105	Vlasotince	YU	C4
101	Vlasti	GR	A3
58	Vledder	NL	C3
17	Vlijmen	NL	B5
16	Vlissingen	N	B3
109	Vlokhós	GR	B4
108	Vlorë	AL	A1
62	Vlotho	D	A3
73	Vnanje Gorice	YU	C4
71	Vobarno	I	C5
73	Vocance	F	A3
69	Vochdorf	A	D4
98	Vočin	YU	C2
69	Vöcklabruck	A	C4
69	Vöcklamarkt	A	C4
72	Vipiteno (Sterzing)	I	B1
100	Voderady	CS	C5
96	Voderady	CS	C3
73	Vodice, *Hrvatska*	YU	C4
73	Vodice, *Hrvatska*	YU	B1
73	Vodice, *Slovenija*	YU	B4
55	Vodňany	CS	B5
77	Vodnjan	YU	A3
54	Vodskov	DK	A3
6	Voe, *Shetland Is.*	GB	
63	Voerde	D	B1
54	Voerså	DK	A3
108	Vogatsikón	GR	A3
74	Voghera	I	B4
100	Vogogna	I	B3
100	Vogošća	YU	C3
28	Vogüé	F	B3
69	Vohburg	D	C2
68	Vohenstrauß	D	B3
67	Vöhrenbach	D	C4
66	Vöhringen	D	C6
66	Void	F	C1
103	Voineşti	RO	A6
77	Voinic	YU	A5
20	Voiron	F	A4
66	Voisey	F	D1
25	Voiteur	F	B5
73	Voitsberg	A	B5
101	Vojka	YU	B5
101	Vojlovica	YU	B5
97	Vojnice	CS	D4
73	Vojnik	YU	B5
99	Vojvoda Stepa	YU	C5
69	Volary	CS	C4
106	Volax	GR	B1
99	Volcani	RO	C5
46	Volda	N	E3
58	Volendam	NL	C2
73	Volimais	GR	B1
68	Völkach	D	B1
84	Völkermarkt	A	B4
66	Völklingen	D	A6
93	Volkmarode	D	A5
73	Volkmarsen	D	B4
93	Volkovysk	SU	D9
70	Vollore-Montagne	F	C3
54	Vollsjö	S	C4
56	Volmerdingsen	D	A3
25	Volnay	F	A4
105	Vólos	GR	B4
74	Volpiano	I	A5
75	Volta Mantovana	I	A5
75	Voltággio	I	C5
75	Volterra	I	B1
80	Voltura Irpina	I	D1
80	Voltura Appula	I	C3
29	Volvic	F	C3
29	Volx	F	C4
55	Volyné	CS	B4
108	Vónitsa	GR	C2
98	Vönöck	H	A2
55	Vonsild	DK	C2
77	Voorschoten	NL	A4
58	Voorthuizen	NL	A5
73	Vorau	A	A5
73	Vorbasse	DK	C2
17	Vorden	NL	A6
73	Vordernbg	A	A4
69	Vorderweißenbach	A	C5
69	Vordingborg	DK	C4
104	Vorë	AL	C1
29	Voreppe	F	A4
28	Vorey	F	A2
55	Vorgod	DK	B1
110	Vório	GR	C3
70	Vormsund	N	B2
73	Vorra	D	B2
59	Vorsfelde	D	A5
17	Vorst	D	B2
54	Vorupør	DK	B1
108	Voskopojë	AL	A2
21	Vosne-Romanée	F	A4
46	Voss	N	F3
17	Vosselaar	B	B4
69	Votice	CS	B5
73	Voto	I	B4
108	Votonósi	GR	B3
25	Vougeot	F	A5
71	Vouillé	F	B4
111	Voúla	GR	B4
110	Vouliagméni	GR	B4
110	Voúlista Panayía	GR	B3
110	Voúlpi	GR	B3
73	Voulx	F	C3
110	Voúnargon	GR	C2
110	Vounikhóra	GR	B4
29	Vourey-Voroize	F	A4
110	Vourvouroú	GR	A5
73	Voussac	F	B3
110	Voutianói	GR	C3
29	Vouvray	F	B1
29	Vouvry	F	B1
71	Vouziers	F	B5
21	Voves	F	C3
109	Voxna	S	A1
5	Voy	DK	A7
54	Vrå	DK	A2
103	Vrabevo	RO	A5
102	Vračev Gaj	YU	B3
101	Vračov	YU	B5
97	Vrådal	N	D8
110	Vrakhnéika	GR	B3
77	Vrana	YU	A3
100	Vranduk	YU	B3
101	Vranić	YU	B5
101	Vraničí	YU	B3
73	Vranja	YU	B3
105	Vranje	YU	A4
73	Vransko	YU	B4
104	Vranovac	YU	A4
96	Vranovice	CS	C2
109	Vrasná	GR	A5
108	Vrástama	GR	A5
103	Vrata	RO	B3
102	Vratarnica	YU	C3
97	Vratimov	CS	B4
66	Vratislavice	CS	C5
96	Vratnica	YU	B3
73	Vratnica	YU	B1
73	Vrbnik, *Hrvatska*	YU	C4
90	Vrbno p. Pradedem	CZ	C1
53	Vrena	S	D2
101	Vreoci	YU	B3
100	Vréstena	GR	B3
77	Vrgorac	YU	C5
77	Vrhnika	YU	C4
77	Vrhovine	YU	C5
100	Vrhpolje, *Bosna i Hercegovina*	YU	B1
77	Vrhpolje, *Srbija*	YU	B4
58	Vriezenveen	NL	C3
19	Vrigne-aux-Bois	F	B5
56	Vrigstad	S	B3
25	Vrises, *Kríti*	GR	
108	Vrisoúla	GR	B2
111	Vrondádos	GR	C3
108	Vrondoú	GR	A4
110	Vróntero	GR	A3
58	Vroomshoop	NL	C3
112	Vroukhas, *Kríti*	GR	
104	Vrpolje	YU	A3
96	Vrčín	YU	B3
100	Vrmbaje	YU	C1
101	Vrnjačka Banja	YU	A5
73	Vrnograd	YU	A5
69	Vrončice	CS	C3
112	Vrondou	YU	A3
104	Vrpolje	YU	C5
100	Vrbovsko, *Hrvatska*	YU	C5
101	Vrbovsko, *Srbija*	YU	B5
65	Vrchlabi	CS	C5
101	Vrčin	YU	B3
62	Vreden	D	A1
74	Voghera	I	B4
101	Vreoci	YU	B3
51	Vretstorp	S	C5
101	Vrgin Most	YU	C5
77	Vrhovine	YU	C4
16	Wallers	F	C3
62	Waldeck	D	B4
96	Waldegg	A	D2
67	Waldenbuch	D	C5
64	Waldenburg	D	C2
66	Waldfischbach	D	B3
69	Waldhausen Str. G.	A	C4
64	Waldheim	D	B3
63	Waldkappel	D	B4
67	Waldkirch	D	C3
69	Waldkirchen	D	C4
69	Waldkirchen a. Wesen	A	C4
63	Waldkraiburg	D	C3
66	Waldmohr	D	B3
67	Waldmossingen	D	C4
68	Waldmünchen	D	B3
66	waldrach	D	B2
72	Waldring	A	A2
63	Waldsassen	D	A3
70	Waldshut	D	A3
71	Waldstatt	CH	A4
68	Waldthurn	D	B3
66	Waldwisse	F	B3
71	Walenstadt	CH	A4
90	Walichnowy	PL	B2
21	Walincourt	F	A4
63	Walkenried	D	B4
15	Walkern	GB	C2
60	Walkow	D	C3
10	Wallasey	GB	B2
62	Wallau	D	C3
67	Walldürn	D	B5
63	Wallenfells	D	C6
16	Wallers	F	C3
63	Wallersdorf	D	C2
68	Wallerstein	D	C1
68	Wallhausen	D	B6
15	Wallingford	GB	C1
70	Wallisellen	CH	A3
61	Wallitz	D	B3
6	Walls, *Shetland Is.*	GB	
55	Wallsbüll	D	D2
63	Walschleben	D	B5
17	Walshoutern	B	C5
59	Walstrode	D	C6
62	Waltrop	D	B2
71	Waltenhofen	D	A5
63	Waltershausen	D	C5
15	Waltham Forest	GB	C2
15	Waltham on the Wolds	GB	B2
10	Walton le Dale	GB	B3
15	Walton-on-the-Naze	GB	C4
62	Wamba	E	C2
63	Wamba	E	C2
59	Wangerooge	D	B4
60	Wangels	D	A1
71	Wangen	D	A4
59	Wangerooge	D	B4
71	Wangi	CH	A3
62	Wanne-Fickel	D	B2
14	Wansford	GB	B2
15	Wantage	GB	C1
63	Wanzleben	D	A6
88	Wapno	PL	B6
14	Warboys	GB	B2
28	Warburg	D	B4
3	Ward	IRL	A5
16	Waregem	B	C3
17	Waremme	B	B4
61	Waren	D	B3
62	Warendorf	D	B2
16	Warfftum	NL	B2
60	Warga	S	A1
60	Warin	D	C2
9	Wark	GB	B4
90	Warka	PL	B5
15	Warkworth	GB	C6
15	Warlingham	GB	C2
90	Warlubie	PL	B4
14	Warmeriville	F	B5
13	Warminster	GB	B5
67	Warneck	D	A3
60	Warnemünde	D	A3
17	Warnsveld	NL	A6
10	Warrenpoint	GB	B3
16	Warschoot	B	B3
16	Warsingsfehn	D	B4
11	Warsop	GB	B4
59	Warstade	D	B6
62	Warstein	D	B3
91	Warszawa	PL	A4
90	Warta	PL	B2
73	Wartberg i. Mürztal	A	A5
71	Warth	A	A5
14	Warwick	GB	B1
92	Warza	PL	B5
7	Wasbister	GB	B3
17	Wasmes	B	C3
92	Wasosz	PL	B6
68	Wasselonne	F	C3
17	Wassenaar	NL	A4
71	Wassereuen	CH	A4
63	Wassertrüdingen	D	B1
21	Wassy	F	C5
15	Watchet	GB	B4
7	Watten	GB	B5
21	Watten	F	A3
72	Watten	A	A1
17	Wavre	B	C4
11	Wawolnica	PL	B6
10	Waxham	GB	B4
91	Wechadłow	PL	C6
63	Wedmore	GB	B5
10	Weelde	B	A5
16	Weende	D	A3
58	Weener	D	B4

#	Name	Ctry	Grid
17	Weert	NL	B5
17	Weesp	NL	B5
17	Weeze	D	B6
63	Weferlingen	D	A6
17	Wegberg	D	B6
63	Wegeleben	D	B6
70	Weggis	CH	A3
65	Wegieni	PL	A1
65	Wegliniec	PL	B5
61	Węgorzyno	PL	B6
91	Węgrów	PL	A6
63	Wegscheid	D	C4
59	Wehdel	D	B5
60	Wehr	D	A2
67	Weibersbrunn	D	B5
68	Weichering	D	C2
64	Weida	D	C2
68	Weiden	D	B3
62	Weidenau	D	C3
64	Weidenhain	D	B2
67	Weidenstetten	D	C5
92	Weigelsdorf	A	D2
89	Weiherowo	PL	A4
67	Weikersheim	D	B5
68	Weil	D	C1
67	Weil d. Stadt	D	C4
62	Weilburg	D	C3
67	Weilerswist	D	C1
67	Weilheim, Baden-Württemberg	D	C5
68	Weilheim, Bayern	D	D2
63	Weimar	D	B4
63	Weimar	D	C6
63	Weinberg	D	B1
71	Weinfelden	CH	A4
67	Weingarten, Baden-Württemberg	D	B4
67	Weingarten, Baden-Württemberg	D	D5
67	Weinheim	D	B4
67	Weinstadt	D	C5
64	Weischltz	D	C2
68	Weisendorf	D	B1
68	Weismain	D	A2
72	Weißbriach	A	B3
96	Weissenbach, Nieder Österreich	A	D2
71	Weißenbach, Tirol	A	A5
73	Weißenbach a.d. Enns	A	A4
65	Weißenberg	D	B4
63	Weißenbrunn	D	C6
68	Weißenburg	D	B1
63	Weißenfels	D	B6
67	Weißenhorn	D	C6
96	Weißenkirchen i.d. W.	A	C1
92	Weißenstadt	D	C6
73	Weißkirchen i. Steiermark	A	A4
71	Weisstannen	CH	B4
64	Weißwasser	D	B4
60	Weitendorf	D	B3
63	Weiterode	D	C4
96	Weitersfeld	A	C1
64	Weitersfelden	A	C5
71	Weitnau	D	A5
64	Weitra	A	C5
59	Weitzenbruch	D	C7
73	Weiz	A	A5
9	Weldon Bridge	GB	C6
65	Welkenraedt	B	C5
64	Wellaune	D	B2
68	Wellheim	D	C2
21	Wellin	B	A6
68	Wellingborough	GB	B2
10	Wellington, Shropshire	GB	C3
13	Wellington, Somerset	GB	C4
5	Wellingtonbridge	IRL	B5
62	Wellmünster	D	C3
13	Wells	GB	B5
13	Wells next the Sea	GB	B3
62	Welplage	D	A3
96	Wels	A	C5
70	Welschenrohr	CH	A2
67	Welshpool	GB	C2
63	Welsleben	D	A6
73	Weltenfeld	A	B4
62	Welver	D	B3
62	Welwyn	GB	C2
15	Welwyn Garden City	GB	C3
67	Welzheim	D	C5
64	Welzow	D	B4
68	Wemding	D	C1
68	Wemyss Bay	GB	A3
63	Wenden, Niedersachsen	D	A4
62	Wenden, Nordrhein-Westfalen	D	C2
64	Wendisch Rietz	D	A3
67	Wendlingen	D	C5
15	Wendover	GB	C2
88	Wenecja	PL	C3
69	Weng	A	C4
70	Wengen	CH	B2
73	Wenigzell	A	A5
71	Wennigsen	D	A5
71	Wenns	A	A5
13	Wenvoe	GB	B4
17	Wépion	B	C4
64	Werben, Cottbus	B	C4
60	Werben, Magdeburg	D	B3
62	Werbig	D	B3
67	Werchter	B	C4
64	Werdau	D	C2
62	Werder	D	B3
62	Werdohl	D	B3
72	Werfen	A	B3
59	Werite	D	B3
14	Werkendam	NL	B4
62	Werl	D	B3
64	Wermelskirchen	D	B2
64	Wermsdorf	D	C2
60	Wern	D	A5
68	Wernberg	D	B3
61	Werneuchen	D	A4
92	Wernigerode	D	A5
69	Wernstein	A	C4
71	Wertach	D	A6
67	Wertheim	D	B5
67	Wertingen	D	C1
16	Wervik	B	C3
16	Weseke	D	B1
62	Wesel	D	B1
60	Wesenberg	D	B3
60	Wesendorf	D	A5
91	Wesola	PL	A5
62	Wesola	PL	A5
95	Weßelburen	D	B5
62	Wesseling	D	C1
62	Wessobrunn	D	D2
11	West Auckland	GB	A4
14	West Bridgford	GB	B1
11	West Bromwich	GB	C5
9	West Calder	GB	C4
14	West Haddon	GB	B1
8	West Kilbride	GB	C3
10	West Kirby	GB	B2
13	West Linton	GB	B2
13	West Lulworth	GB	C5
15	West Mersea	GB	C5
58	West Terschelling	NL	B2
58	West Wittering	GB	D2
16	Westapelle	B	B3
16	Westapelle	N	B3
62	Westbevern	D	A3
13	Westbury	GB	B5
13	Westbury on Severn	GB	B5
72	Westendorf	A	C4
58	Westerbork	NL	C3
58	Westerburg	D	C7
58	Westercelle	D	C7
58	Westerhaar	NL	C3
59	Westerholt	D	B4
58	Westerkappeln	D	A2
17	Westerlo	B	B4
59	Westersiede	D	B3
67	Westheim, Baden-Württemberg	D	B5
68	Westheim, Bayern	D	B1
62	Westheim, Nordrhein-Westfalen	D	B3
67	Westhofen	D	B3
62	Wetter, Hessen	D	C3
62	Wetter, Nordrhein-Westfalen	D	B2
63	Wetten	D	B3
63	Wettin	D	B6
70	Wettringen	CH	A3
58	Wettringen	D	A3
62	Wetzikon	CH	A3
62	Wetzlar	D	C3
12	Wevelgem	B	B3
62	Wewer	D	B3
5	Wexford	IRL	B5
69	Weyer	A	D5
67	Weyerbusch	D	C2
67	Weyersheim	F	C3
13	Weymouth	GB	C5
69	Weyregg	A	D4
58	Wezemaal	B	C4
17	Wezep	NL	A6
15	Wezyska	PL	A4
11	Whaley Bridge	GB	B4
10	Whalley	GB	B3
13	Whalton	GB	B3
11	Whauphill	GB	D3
11	Wheatley Hill	GB	B4
11	Wheddon Cross	GB	B4
12	Whiddon Down	GB	B2
11	Whitburn	GB	C4
11	Whitby	GB	A5
15	Whitchurch, Buckinghamshire	GB	C2
13	Whitchurch, Hampshire	GB	C1
15	Whitchurch, Hereford & Worcester	GB	B5
7	Whitebridge	GB	C4
4	Whitegate	IRL	B3
7	Whitehall	IRL	A6
13	Whitehall	IRL	B5
10	Whitehaven	GB	A2
3	Whitehead	GB	B6
9	Whitekirk	GB	B5
10	Whithorn	GB	A1
12	Whitland	GB	B3
11	Whitley Bay	GB	B4
14	Whittlesey	GB	B2
11	Whitwell	GB	B5
65	Wiążow	PL	C7
11	Wiązowna	PL	A5
67	Wichester	GB	B5
7	Wick	GB	B5
15	Wickede	D	B3
15	Wickford	GB	C2
15	Wickham	GB	D1
14	Wickham Market	GB	B4
5	Wicklow	IRL	B5
88	Wicko	PL	A3
90	Widawa	PL	B2
9	Widdrington	GB	C6
11	Widnes	GB	B3
15	Widuchowo	PL	B6
66	Wiebelskirchen	D	A3
11	Więcbork	PL	B3
63	Wiedenbrück	PL	B4
59	Wiefelstede	D	B5
71	Wiehe	D	A6
67	Wiehl	D	C2
88	Wielbark	PL	A6
88	Wieleń	PL	A5
88	Wielen	D	C2
91	Wielichowo	PL	A6
91	Wieliczka	PL	B4
59	Wielka Łąka	PL	B4
91	Wielowieś	PL	A4
96	Wien	A	A2
91	Wiener Neustadt	A	D2
60	Wiepke	D	B2
11	Wieren	D	C1
91	Wierszban	PL	B6
61	Wierzbica	PL	B6
88	Wierzbno	PL	C1
88	Wierzchowo	PL	A4
73	Wies	A	B4
67	Wiesbaden	D	A4
58	Wiesburg	D	C5
71	Wiesen	CH	B4
68	Wiesenfelden	D	B3
68	Wiesensteig	D	C5
68	Wiesent	D	B1
68	Wiesenthied	D	B1
11	Wiesloch	D	A4
98	Wiesmath	A	D2
59	Wiesmoor	D	B4
58	Wietmarschen	D	C3
59	Wietze	D	C6
90	Wigan	GB	B3
70	Wiggen	CH	B2
13	Wigmore	GB	A5
14	Wigston	GB	B1
8	Wigton	GB	D3
8	Wigtown	GB	D3
17	Wijchen	NL	B5
17	Wijk bij Duurstede	NL	B5
17	Wijne	NL	A6
16	Wijnegem	B	B4
71	Wil	CH	A4
17	Wilamowice	PL	B5
89	Wilczeta	PL	A5
90	Wilczkowice	PL	A3
73	Wildalpen	A	B4
67	Wildbad	D	C4
60	Wildberg	D	C3
67	Wildberg	D	C3
63	Wildemann	D	B5
96	Wildendürnbach	A	C2
58	Wildervank	NL	B3
73	Wildon	A	A5
71	Wildpoldsried	D	A5
67	Wilferdingen	D	C4
91	Wilga	PL	B5
91	Wilgartswiesen	D	B3
65	Wilhelm-Pieck-Stadt	D	A4
96	Wilhelmsburg	A	C1
59	Wilhelmshaven	D	B5
59	Wilhelmsdorf	D	B5
67	Wilhermsdorf	D	C5
62	Wilhering	A	C5
58	Wilkau-Haßlau	D	C2
91	Wilkotaz	PL	B6
65	Wilków	PL	B5
65	Wilków	PL	C5
97	Wilkowice	PL	A5
89	Wilkowo	PL	A7
60	Willebadessen	D	B4
17	Willebroek	B	B4
13	Willersley	GB	A4
68	Willhermsdorf	D	B1
2	Williamstown	IRL	C3
62	Willich	D	B2
62	Willingen	D	B3
11	Willington	GB	A4
70	Willisau	CH	A3
13	Williton	GB	B4
10	Wilmslow	GB	B3
16	Wilrijk	B	B4
58	Wilsdruff	D	B3
69	Wilster	D	B6
58	Wilsum	D	C3
66	Wiltz	L	B1
14	Wimblington	GB	B2
13	Wimborne Minster	GB	C6
16	Wimereux	F	C1
16	Wimille	F	C1
16	Wimmenau	F	C3
70	Wimmis	CH	B2
73	Wimpassing	A	B4
21	Wimy	F	B4
12	Wincanton	GB	B5
15	Winchcombe	GB	B6
13	Winchelsea	GB	D3
96	Winden a.s.	A	D2
10	Windermere	GB	A3
59	Windischeschenbach	D	B3
73	Windischgarsten	A	A4
69	Windorf	A	C4
91	Windsbach	D	B1
15	Windsor	GB	C2
15	Wing	GB	C2
13	Wingene	B	B3
59	Wingham	GB	C4
59	Wingst	D	C6
91	Winhöring	D	C3
91	Winklarn	D	C3
72	Winklern	A	B2
67	Winnenden	D	C5
67	Winnigstedt	D	A5
67	Winnweiler	D	B3
58	Winschoten	NL	B4
59	Winsen, Niedersachsen	D	C6
60	Winsen, Niedersachsen	D	B1
14	Winsford	GB	B3
15	Winsham	GB	C5
59	Wińsko	PL	B6
15	Winslade	GB	C1
15	Winslow	GB	C2
58	Winsum, Friesland	NL	B2
58	Winsum, Groningen	NL	B3
14	Winterbach	D	B3
14	Winterberg	D	B3
59	Winterbourne Abbas	GB	C5
60	Winterfeld	D	B2
67	Winterlingen	D	C5
70	Winterswijk	NL	B1
70	Winterthur	CH	A3
11	Winterton	GB	B5
14	Winterton-on-Sea	GB	B4
15	Wintzenheim	F	C3
69	Winzer	A	C4
63	Wipperdorf	D	B5
63	Wipperfürth	D	B2
63	Wippra	D	B6
11	Wirksworth	GB	B4
14	Wisbech	GB	B2
90	Wisborough Green	GB	C2
59	Wischhafen	D	B6
7	Wishaw	GB	B4
60	Wisła Wlk	PL	B4
60	Wismar	D	B2
89	Wiśniew	PL	A6
91	Wiśniowa	PL	B5
91	Wiśniówka	PL	C1
16	Wissant	F	C1
66	Wissembourg	F	C3
67	Wissen	D	B3
62	Wißmar	D	C3
60	Wista	D	B4
15	Witanowice	PL	B5
15	Witham	GB	B2
11	Witheridge	GB	B2
10	Withern Tothill	GB	B6
11	Withernsea	GB	B5
88	Witkowo	PL	C3
58	Witkowo	D	D1
15	Witney	GB	C1
59	Witnica	PL	C5
66	Witry	B	B1
66	Wittdüm	D	B5
66	Wittelsheim	F	C3
62	Witten	D	B2
67	Wittenberg	D	B6
67	Wittenberge	D	B3
62	Wittenburg	D	B5
66	Wittenheim	F	C3
64	Wittichenau	D	B4
60	Wittingen	D	C1
13	Wittislingen	D	C1
66	Wittlich	D	B4
59	Wittmannsdorf	A	B4
59	Wittmund	D	B4
86	Wittstock	D	B6
13	Witzenhausen	D	B5
13	Wivelescombe	GB	B4
13	Wivenhoe	GB	C3
89	Władysławowo	PL	A4
65	Włocławek	PL	C5
93	Włodawa	PL	E8
60	Włostow	PL	C1
91	Włoszczowa	PL	C3
96	Woburn Sands	GB	B2
97	Wodzisław Sl.	PL	C4
91	Wodzisław	PL	C5
73	Wohlen	CH	B5
71	Wildeshausen	CH	C5
70	Wohlen	CH	A3
67	Woippy	F	B2
91	Wojciechów	PL	A5
65	Wojcieszów	PL	B5
90	Wojkowice Kościelne	PL	C3
96	Woking	GB	C2
15	Wokingham	GB	C2
90	Wola Jachowa	PL	E8
15	Wola Niechcicka	PL	B3
90	Wilkau-Haßlau	D	C2
62	Wolborz	D	B3
91	Wolbrom	PL	C3
91	Wolczyn	PL	B4
63	Woldegk	D	B4
73	Wolfach	D	C4
73	Wolfau	A	A6
73	Wolfegg	D	D5
63	Wolfenbüttel	D	A5
63	Wolfern	D	D1
63	Wolfertschwenden	D	D1
62	Wolfhagen	D	D2
67	Wolfratshausen	D	D2
71	Wolfsbach	A	C5
73	Wolfsberg	A	B4
61	Wolfshagen	D	A4
71	Wolfstein	D	A3
71	Wolfurt	A	A4
71	Wolgast	D	A4
70	Wolhusen	CH	A3
91	Wolin	PL	B5
64	Wolka	PL	C2
90	Wolkersdorf	A	C2
64	Wölkisch	D	B3
64	Wölkramshausen	D	B5
13	Wollaston	GB	B2
60	Wöllersdorf	A	D2
91	Wollin	D	B6
91	Wolmirsleben	D	A6
91	Wolmirstedt	D	A6
67	Wolnzach	D	C2
91	Wolomin	PL	A6
65	Wolsztyn	PL	B6
91	Wolów	PL	B6
59	Woltmershausen	D	B5
58	Wolvega	NL	C2
10	Wolverhampton	GB	C3
10	Wolverton	GB	C3
14	Wolvey	GB	B1
11	Wolviston	GB	A4
59	Wommels	NL	B2
14	Woodbridge	IRL	B5
11	Woodhall Spa	GB	B5
15	Woodstock	GB	C1
13	Wool	GB	C5
12	Woolacombe	GB	B3
9	Wooler	GB	C5
13	Wootton Bassett	GB	B6
70	Woploewo	PL	B5
13	Worbis	GB	B5
72	Wörgl	A	A2
14	Workington	GB	A2
10	Worksop	GB	B4
58	Workum	NL	B2
67	Wörlitz	D	B6
58	Wormerveer	NL	C1
67	Wormhoudt	F	C2
67	Worms	D	B4
59	Worphausen	D	B5
59	Worpswede	D	B5
67	Worschach	A	B3
67	Wörth, Bayern	D	C2
67	Wörth, Bayern	D	B3
67	Wörth, Rheinland-Pfalz	D	B4
15	Worthing	GB	D2
15	Wotton-under-Edge	GB	B5
16	Woudsend	NL	C2
16	Woumen	B	B2
11	Woźniki	PL	C5
90	Woźniki	PL	C3
90	Wożyczyn Wlk.	PL	C2
59	Wredenhagen	D	B3
14	Wremen	D	B5
14	Wrentham	GB	B4
11	Wroughton	GB	B6
14	Wroxham	GB	B4
88	Wrzesnia	PL	A3
88	Wrzosowa	PL	A3
11	Wschowa	PL	B6
64	Wulfen	D	B2
67	Wülfershem	D	B4
62	Wülfrath	D	B2
67	Wulkaprodersdorf	A	D2
67	Wünnenberg	D	B4
66	Wunsiede	D	A3
62	Wuppertal	D	B2
63	Wurmannsquick	D	C3
63	Wurmlingen	D	C4
63	Wurzbach	D	C6
63	Würzburg	D	B5
64	Wurzen	D	B2
60	Wust	D	C3
63	Wüstensachsen	D	C5
63	Wüstermark	D	C5
61	Wustermark	D	C3
17	Wuustwezel	B	B4
17	Wydda	D	B4
55	Wyk	D	D1
14	Wymondham	GB	B4
91	Wysmierzyce	PL	B4
88	Wysoka	PL	B3
88	Wysoka	PL	B3
91	Wysoka	PL	C5
65	Wyszogrod	PL	C7
65	Wyszonowice	PL	C7

X

#	Name	Ctry	Grid
17	Xanten	D	B6
106	Xánthi	GR	C2
40	Xàtiva	E	C2
40	Xeraco	E	C2
66	Xertigny	F	C2
53	Xidhia	D	B3
106	Xilagani	GR	C2
111	Xilókastron	GR	A3
108	Xilopáriko	GR	A3
105	Xilópolis	GR	D5
109	Xinias	GR	B4
108	Xinón Nerón	GR	A3
109	Xinoúrisi	GR	B5
31	Xinzo de Limia	E	C3
110	Xirokambi	GR	C3
30	Xove	E	A3
30	Xungueira de Espadañedo	E	B3

Y

#	Name	Ctry	Grid
103	Yablanitsa	BG	C5
95	Yablanitsa	BG	E6
107	Yablanovo	BG	B3
107	Yabulchevo	BG	B1
105	Yakoruda	BG	B5
105	Yakovo	BG	C3
112	Yalikavak	TR	B1
107	Yambol	BG	B5
105	Yana	BG	B5
107	Yanciklar	TR	B5
11	Yarm	GB	A4
15	Yarmouth	GB	D1
110	Yasilitsa	GR	C2
107	Yasna Polyana	BG	A5
112	Yatagan	TR	A1
13	Yate	GB	B5
13	Yatton	GB	B5
15	Yaxley	GB	B1
69	Ybbs a.d. Donau	A	C6
69	Ybbsitz	A	D5
54	Ydby	DK	A1
12	Yealmpton	GB	C4
34	Yebra de Bresa	E	A2
40	Yecla	E	C5
31	Yecla de Yeltes	E	D4
109	Yéfira	GR	B4
109	Yefiri	GR	A4
107	Yelverton	GB	C4
107	Yenice	TR	B5
95	Yenice, Canakkale	TR	G7
107	Yenice, Edirne	GR	B5
107	Yeniçiftlik	TR	B5
112	Yenikoy, Aydin	TR	B1
107	Yenikoy, Edirne	TR	A5
112	Yenipazar	TR	A1
106	Yenisala	GR	C4
25	Yenne	F	C5
112	Yeoryioúpolis, Kriti	GR	
112	Yeovil	GB	C5
39	Yepes	E	B3
112	Yerakári, Kriti	GR	
109	Yerakaroú	GR	A5
111	Yérakas	GR	B5
109	Yeráki	GR	C3
109	Yeránia	GR	A4
112	Yerkesik	TR	A1
108	Yérmas	GR	B4
13	Yerolimin	GR	A3
109	Yeroplátanon	GR	A3
17	Yerseke	NL	B1
16	Yerville	F	B1
112	Yeşilyurt	TR	B1
45	Yeste	E	A4
26	Ygos-St. Saturnin	F	B3
24	Ygrande	F	B4
109	Yialtra	GR	C4
108	Yiannádhes	GR	A2
109	Yiannitsá	GR	A4
109	Yiannitsoú	GR	B4
109	Yimnón	GR	A4
110	Yíthion	GR	C3
67	Ylivieska	SF	D12
58	Ylöjärvi	SF	F11
15	Ymonville	F	C2
57	Yngsjö	S	D3
12	Ynys	GB	B4
107	Yörük	TR	C5
3	Youghal	IRL	C5
11	Youlgreave	GB	B5
14	Yoxford	GB	B4
11	Yport	F	A1
11	Yquem	GB	B4
90	Yssingeaux	F	C4
11	Ystad	S	D2
11	Ystalyfera	GB	B4
11	Ystebøhamn	N	B2
11	Ystrad	GB	B4
11	Ystradgynlais	GB	B4
11	Ytre Flåbygd	N	B2
11	Ytteran	S	E7
11	Ytterby	S	D1
11	Ytterhogdal	S	E7
11	Yuncos	E	B3
11	Yunquera de Heras	E	B3
11	Yurre	GB	B4
11	Yverdon	CH	B1
11	Yvetot	F	B1
11	Yvignac	F	B3
11	Yvoir	B	C4
11	Yvonand	CH	B1
11	Yvré-l'Évêque	F	B5
11	Yxsjöberg	S	D5
11	Yzeure	F	B3

Z

#	Name	Ctry	Grid
17	Zaandam	NL	A4
99	Zabalj	YU	C6
97	Zabar	H	C6
102	Zabari	YU	B2
108	Zaberzan	AL	A2
91	Zabki	PL	A5
90	Ząbkowice	PL	C3
101	Zabkowice Slaskie	PL	C5
90	Zablaće	YU	C5
98	Zabljak	YU	C4
73	Zabno	D	C4
73	Zabok	YU	B5
73	Zabokliki	PL	A6
73	Zabokreky	CS	B4
65	Zabor	PL	B5
65	Zábřeh	CS	B5
91	Zabrzeże	PL	B5
89	Zabrowo	PL	B5
73	Zabrze	PL	C5
106	Zabŭrdo	BG	B2
90	Zaczernie	PL	B1
91	Zadar	YU	B5
90	Zadzim	PL	B2
44	Zafarraya	E	C2
37	Zafra	E	C4
102	Zaga	YU	B3
102	Zagajica	YU	B2
68	Zagań	PL	B5
101	Zaglavak	YU	C5
106	Zaglavérion	GR	A5
81	Zagnansk	PL	C5
73	Zagorá	GR	B5
73	Zagorje	YU	B4
101	Zagrade	PL	A1
106	Zagrazhden	BG	C5
106	Zagrazhden	BG	B3
73	Zagreb	YU	C6
65	Zagrilla	E	B2
102	Zagubica	YU	B2
90	Zagvozd	YU	C2
90	Zagwiździe	PL	C1
102	Zagyvarekas	H	A5
43	Zahara	E	C4
43	Zahara de los Atunes	E	C4
24	Zahinos	E	C4
21	Zahna	D	B2
69	Záhoří	CS	B5
81	Zahrádka	CS	B5
34	Zaidin	E	B3
65	Zainingen	D	C5
102	Zaja	YU	C2
98	Zákamenné	CS	B4
98	Zakany	H	B1
110	Zakháro	GR	B2
110	Zákinthos	GR	B1
91	Zakliczyn	PL	C6
89	Zakopane	PL	B5
89	Zakroczym	PL	C6
112	Zákros, Kriti	GR	
91	Zakrzew	PL	B5
98	Zalaapáti	H	B2
88	Zalabaksa	H	B1
98	Zalaegerszeg	H	B1
98	Zalakoppány	H	B2
98	Zalalövö	H	B1
37	Zalamea de la Serena	E	C5
43	Zalamea la Real	E	B3
98	Zalaszenfiván	H	B1
98	Zalaszentiván	H	B1
98	Zalaszentmihály	H	B1
94	Zalău	RO	C5
98	Zalavár	H	B2
73	Žalec	YU	B5
65	Zalewo	PL	B5
102	Zalijevo	YU	C2
90	Zalno	PL	B3
103	Zánoga	RO	B5
54	Zaorejas	E	B4
90	Zapole	PL	B2
109	Záppion	GR	C2
61	Zaprudy	SU	C9
37	Zaragoza	E	B5
111	Zarakes	GR	A5
109	Zarauz	GR	A5
71	Zams	A	A5
67	Zandhoven	B	B4
64	Žandov	CS	B4
67	Zandvoort	NL	A4
37	Zaninos	E	B4
17	Zanza	D	B5
112	Zaoúkla	YU	B4
108	Záos	GR	B4
15	Zapponeta	I	C2
57	Yngsjö	S	D3
12	Ynys	GB	B4
107	Zaralakés	GR	C3
14	Zarça	GB	C5
90	Żary	PL	B5
37	Zarza de Alange	E	B4
37	Zarza de Tajo	E	B3
37	Zarza la Mayor	E	C6
38	Zarza de Alange	E	B3
37	Zarza Capilla	E	C2
36	Zarzuela del Monte	E	B2
38	Zarzuela del Pinar	E	C2
30	Zas	E	A2
101	Zasavica	YU	B4
69	Zásmuky	CS	B6
81	Zaton	YU	B6
90	Zator	PL	B5
77	Zavala	YU	B5
104	Zavlaka	YU	B3
94	Zawichost	PL	C5
65	Zawidow	PL	B5
65	Zawiercie	PL	C3
65	Zawonia	PL	B6
65	Zázrivá	CS	B5
65	Zbaraż	YU	C5
97	Zbehy	CS	C4
69	Zbiroh	CS	B4
99	Zbrachlin	BG	C6
97	Zbrašlavice	CS	B5
102	Žabari	YU	B2
108	Zbucyzn	BG	B2
91	Zabki	PL	A5
44	Zafferana Etnea	I	B4
37	Zafra	E	C4
98	Zaga	YU	B3
102	Zagajica	YU	B2
102	Zagań	PL	B5
101	Zaglavak	YU	A5
109	Zagorá	GR	B5
73	Zagorje	YU	B5
101	Zagrade	PL	A1
106	Zagrazhden	BG	C5
106	Zagreb	YU	C6
73	Zagreb	YU	C6
65	Zagrilla	E	B2
102	Zagubica	YU	B2
90	Zagvozd	YU	C2
90	Zagwiździe	PL	C1
102	Zagyvarekas	H	A5
43	Zahara	E	C4
43	Zahara de los Atunes	E	C4
24	Zahinos	E	C4
21	Zahna	D	B2
69	Záhoří	CS	B5
81	Zahrádka	CS	B5
17	Zele	B	A4
	Zelechovice n. Drev	CS	B3
91	Zelechów	PL	B5
105	Zelen Dol	BG	B5
69	Zelengorsk	SU	A3
106	Zelenikovo	BG	A3
65	Zeleznica	CS	C5
73	Zeleznik	YU	B4
17	Zelhem	NL	A6
97	Zeliezovce	CS	C4
37	Zelina	YU	C1
90	Zelkowo	PL	A3
17	Zellkowo	PL	A3
109	Zelión	GR	B4
65	Zelkowo	PL	A3
70	Zell		
67	Zell, Baden-Württemberg	D	C4
70	Zell, Baden-Württemberg	A	B5
71	Zell, Bayern	D	B5
66	Zell, Rheinland-Pfalz	D	A3
72	Zell am See	A	A3
72	Zell am Ziller	A	A1
73	Zell b. Zellhof	A	C5
96	Zella-Mehlis	D	C5
96	Zellerndorf	D	B5
97	Želovce	D	B4
73	Zeltweg	A	A4
104	Zélovo	YU	C4
109	Zélion	GR	C4
62	Zelkowo	PL	A3
70	Zell		
67	Zell am See	A	A3
102	Zaltemay	CS	A4
105	Zemen	BG	A6
98	Zemberovce	CS	B4
105	Zembrzyce	PL	B5
17	Zemné	CS	D3
17	Zemst	B	C4
101	Zemun	YU	B5
100	Zenica	YU	B3
73	Žepče	YU	B4
72	Zeponami	I	A3
78	Zeprešić	YU	C1
73	Zeravice	CS	B3
65	Zerbst	D	B1
94	Zerind	RO	A4
70	Zermatt	CH	B2
59	Zerf	D	B2
17	Zevenaar	NL	B6
17	Zevenbergen	NL	B4
111	Zevgolatio	GR	B3
81	Zévio	I	A6
90	Zgierz	PL	A3
101	Zgornji Dolic	YU	B5
65	Zgorzeles	PL	B5
104	Zgozdh	AL	C2
89	Zhelezhnodorozhnyy	SU	A7
107	Zheravna	BG	A3
103	Zhivotsi	BG	C4
103	Zhlobin	SU	D11
108	Ziákas	GR	A3
17	Zichusen	D	B5
102	Zidani Most	YU	B5
17	Ziegendorf	D	B3
60	Ziegenrück	D	C5
96	Zidlochovice	CS	B2
102	Zigós	GR	B2
65	Zielenec	PL	A3
101	Zielona Góra	PL	A5
89	Zielonka Pasleęka	PL	A6
16	Ziersdorf	A	C2
67	Ziesar	D	A3
17	Ziesendorf	D	B2
89	Ziethen	D	B4
66	Zihlschlacht	CH	A3
73	Zillingtal	A	D2
67	Ziltendorf	D	A4
70	Zinal	CH	B2
74	Zinasco	I	A4
61	Zingst	S	D1
53	Zinkgruvan	S	D1
61	Zinnowitz	D	A4
98	Zirc	H	A2
97	Ždiar	CS	C6
69	Zdice	CS	C4
110	Ziria	GR	B4
71	Zirl	A	A5
68	Zirndorf	D	B1
112	Ziros, Kriti	GR	
77	Žirovac	YU	A6
102	Žirovnica	YU	C3
104	Žirovnica	YU	C2
96	Zistersdorf	A	C2
96	Žitište	YU	C5
102	Zitni Potok	YU	C4
102	Žitorača	YU	C3
108	Zitsa	GR	B2
64	Zittau	D	C4
100	Zivaja	YU	C4
73	Zivinice	YU	B4
104	Zjum	YU	C1
102	Žkovac	YU	B1
98	Zlatar	YU	B1
90	Zlate Hory	CZ	C1
96	Zlaté Klasy	CS	A3
97	Zlaté Moravce	CS	A4
106	Zlatitsa	BG	A2
103	Zlatna-panega	BG	C5
106	Zlatograd	BG	B3
105	Zletovo	YU	B4
96	Zlín (Gottwaldov)	CS	B3
65	Złocieniec	PL	B1
65	Złoczew	PL	C4
73	Zlonice	CS	C4
102	Zlot	YU	B2
91	Złotniki	PL	B5
88	Złotniki Kujawskie	PL	B5
65	Złotoryja	PL	B5
65	Złotów	PL	B5
91	Złoty Potok	PL	C3
65	Złoty Stok	PL	C6
69	Zlutice	CS	A4
77	Zmajevac	YU	B6
99	Zmajevo	YU	C4
106	Zmeyovo	BG	A3
91	Żmigród	PL	B1
73	Zmijnj	YU	A3
88	Znamensk	SU	A7
88	Žnin	PL	B3
96	Znojmo	CS	C2
64	Zöblitz	D	C3
75	Zocca	I	B5
17	Zoetermeer	NL	A4
70	Zofingen	CH	A2
71	Zogno	I	C4
17	Zolder	B	B5
73	Zollikofen	CH	B2
95	Zolling	D	C2
94	Zolochev	SU	B6
17	Zomba	H	B3
17	Zonhoven	B	C5
110	Zoni	GR	A5
86	Zonza	F	C2
62	Zörbig	D	B2
97	Zory	PL	A4
64	Zossen	D	A3
16	Zottegem	B	C3
99	Zrenjanin	YU	C5
77	Zrmanja-vrelo	YU	B6
105	Zrnovci	YU	C4
69	Zruč n. Sazavou	CS	B6
16	Zsámbék	H	A3
17	Zsámbok	H	A4
73	Zschopau	D	C3
70	Zschortau	D	C2
97	Zuberec	CS	A5
44	Zubia	E	B3
33	Zubieta	E	A5
104	Zubin Potok	YU	B5
33	Zubiri	E	B5
40	Zucaina	E	A5
34	Zudar	D	A3
43	Zufre	E	B3
70	Zug	CH	A3
44	Zuheros	E	B2
70	Zürich	CH	A3
81	Żuljana	YU	B6
73	Žulová	CS	C7
62	Zulpich	D	C1
33	Zumárrage	E	A4
17	Zundert	NL	B4
101	Zupanja	YU	B3
104	Zur	YU	B2
45	Zurgena	E	B3
70	Zürich	CH	A3
81	Žuljana	YU	B6
107	Zuromin	PL	B3
70	Zurzach	CH	A3
33	Zurbaran	E	A4
34	Zuzara	E	A4
43	Zufre	E	B3
99	Zusmarshausen	D	C1
17	Zutphen	NL	A6
73	Žutu Lovka	YU	C4
73	Žužemberk	YU	C4
62	Zvezdets	BG	A5
102	Zvonce	YU	C4
103	Zvornik	YU	B4
58	Zwaagwesteinde	NL	B3
17	Zwanenburg	NL	A5
73	Zwaring	A	B5
70	Zweibrücken	D	B3
70	Zweisimmen	CH	B2
58	Zwenkau	D	B2
67	Zwesten	D	B4
70	Zwettl an der Rodl	D	C5
96	Zwettl	A	C6
62	Zwevegem	B	C3
70	Zwickau	D	C2
71	Zwiefalten	CH	A2
58	Zwierzno	PL	A5
71	Zwieselstein	A	B5
17	Zwijndrecht	B	B4
70	Zwingen	CH	A2
67	Zwingenberg	D	B4
67	Zwingerberg	D	B4
99	Zwönitz	D	C2
58	Zwolle	NL	A6
91	Zychlin	PL	A3
88	Żydowo	PL	A3
88	Żydowo	PL	B6
91	Żyrardów	PL	A4
91	Żyrzyn	PL	A5
90	Żytno	PL	C3